Psychology
for the IB DIPLOMA

Julia Willerton
Jean-Marc Lawton
Simon Green
John Gammon

HODDER
EDUCATION
AN HACHETTE UK COMPANY

Dedication

To my dad: always the mirror to my future.
Jean-Marc

Orders: please contact Bookpoint Ltd, 130 Milton Park, Abingdon, Oxon
OX14 4SB. Telephone: (44) 01235 827720. Fax: (44) 01235 400454. Lines are
open from 9:00–5:00, Monday to Saturday, with a 24-hour message-answering
service. You can also order through our website www.hoddereducation.co.uk.

British Library Cataloguing in Publication Data
A catalogue record for this title is available from the British Library

ISBN: 9781444181166

First Published 2013

Impression number   10 9 8 7 6 5 4 3 2 1
Year   2016 2015 2014 2013

Hachette UK's policy is to use papers that are natural, renewable and recyclable
products and made from wood grown in sustainable forests. The logging and
manufacturing processes are expected to conform to the environmental regulations
of the country of origin.

Cover photo © Ian Cumming/Axiom Photographic Agency/Getty Images

Typeset by Datapage (India) Pvt. Ltd.
Printed in Italy.

Contents

How to use this book

Learning outcomes are clearly stated throughout the book, and at the end of each section there's a summary of what you should have covered.

Links to the three levels of analysis help show how the options topics are related to the core areas of psychology.

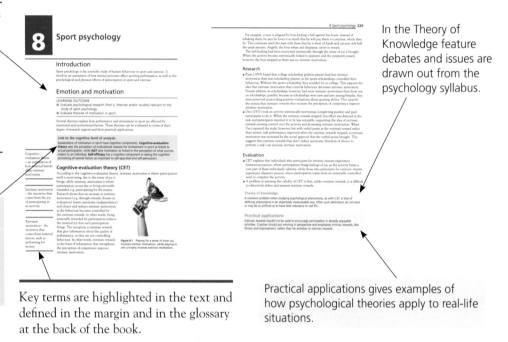

Key terms are highlighted in the text and defined in the margin and in the glossary at the back of the book.

In the Theory of Knowledge feature debates and issues are drawn out from the psychology syllabus.

Practical applications gives examples of how psychological theories apply to real-life situations.

Critical thinking boxes draw out methodological and other issues from the studies discussed to help develop critical analysis skills.

Key study

Some studies are particularly important to understand a topic and are covered in greater depth.

Introduction

Welcome to your study of Psychology within the International Baccalaureate programme. Psychology is the systematic study of behaviour and mental processes (IB 2011). This young human science is the offspring of two rather different parents, with roots in both the natural sciences and in philosophy and the social sciences. As you will see, these different influences have lead to a variety of research methods in modern psychology. Psychologists use methods which you will be familiar with from other forms of science, including experiments in controlled conditions. But, studying people is different from studying forces in physics or the structure of cells in biology. When we study psychology, we are studying our own species and this makes it difficult to be totally objective in the way that natural science requires. In addition, the study of human behaviour poses ethical (moral) challenges for psychologists in relation to what can and should be done. As you progress with your studies, psychology will provide you with a great opportunity to think about the different kinds of knowledge that can be gained and to reflect on the development of your own learning.

The IB core programme begins by introducing three levels of analysis that ask different kinds of questions about human behaviour and experience. Let's look at an example to illustrate this idea. How could you study love at first sight? A biological psychologist would be interested in the physical correlates of such an experience and the role played by hormones such as adrenalin when people experience strong and immediate attraction. The cognitive level of analysis would focus on how we process information, how we recognise faces and the kinds of things we pay attention to in prospective partners. Finally, the socio cultural level would examine how ideas about love are embedded in cultural systems of meaning and how these may differ cross culturally.

In Part 2 (Options) IB Psychology examines how the levels of analysis can help us to understand a range of topics including abnormal psychology, child development, human relationships, health and sports psychology. In these options, an integrative approach is taken by examining how each of these factors influences human behaviour and experience. As you read each section, you should think about the different methods psychologists use to investigate behaviour and experience.

IB Psychology takes a holistic approach that fosters intercultural understanding and respect. Cultural diversity is explored in all of the optional topics and you will be encouraged to increase your understanding of others within and outside your own culture. Understanding how psychological knowledge is generated, developed and applied will enable you to achieve a greater understanding of yourself and to appreciate the diversity of human behaviour.

Part 3 covers the qualitative methods employed by psychologists, and is relevant only to those students taking the Higher Level. Traditional quantitative methods employed in the natural sciences are not always best suited to the study of psychology as they are often unable to take into account emotional or cultural factors. Psychologists have therefore adopted a range of qualitative techniques to help us develop a fuller understanding of human behaviour.

The simple experimental study is covered in Part 4. This is the part of your course where you will be able to apply the skills and knowledge you've developed, by conducting a replication of a simple experiment (or modification for Higher Level candidates) and writing a report.

The last chapter in the book looks at the extended essay component of the IB programme required for Higher Level students. The extended essay is a piece of independent work you will undertake with supervision from your teacher. The chapter outlines how you might tackle planning for, researching and writing your essay.

We hope you are going to enjoy your studies and find your voyage into psychology to be thought-provoking and highly relevant.

Julia Willerton
Jean-Marc Lawton
Simon Green
John Gammon

A note on authorship

This book was written by a team of four authors.

Julia Willerton has written extensively across A Level and HE Psychology. An Associate Lecturer with the Open University she is also an IB examiner. In this book she wrote:

- Sociocultural level of analysis
- Developmental psychology
- Psychology of human relationships

Jean-Marc Lawton is an established writer of psychology textbooks, revision books and guides. He has many years of experience as a teacher and senior examiner and is currently an examiner for the IB. He wrote the following chapters in this book:

- Cognitive level of analysis
- Abnormal psychology
- Sport psychology
- Simple experimental study

Simon Green is a lecturer in Biological Psychology at Birkbeck, University of London. He is an experienced examiner and established author of many successful textbooks for pre-university and undergraduate levels. He wrote the Chapter 1 Biological level of analysis.

John Gammon is a senior examiner for IB and an established author in Psychology. He wrote the following chapters:

- Qualitative methods
- Extended essay

The chapter on Health psychology was written by Julia Willerton, Jean-Marc Lawton and Simon Green.

Acknowledgements

The authors and publishers would like to thank the IB Psychology teachers from around the world who reviewed the book:

- **Bradley Snell**, Braintree Sixth Form, UK
- **Andrea Zara**, Seminole High School, USA
- **Derek Miller**, Bentonville High School, USA
- **Ian Campbell**, Sevenoaks School, UK
- **Jamie Gibson**, St John's School, UK
- **Mary Patrice MacPherson**, Anglo-American School of Moscow, Russia
- **Sheila Thomas**, The Stephen Perse Foundation, UK
- **Zorica Zarkovic**, Sven Eriksonsgymnasiet, Sweden
- **Jacob Mankovsky**, Stony Point High School, USA

Picture credits

The authors and publishers would like to thank the following for the use of photographs in this volume:

Figure 1.1 © Vit Kovalcik – Fotolia; Figure 1.5 © Monkey Business - Fotolia; Figure 1.6 © Jules_Kitano – Fotolia; Figure 1.7 © Papirazzi – Fotolia; Figure 1.8 © davis – Fotolia; Figure 2.7; Figure 2.8 © Sipa Press / Rex Features; Figure 2.10 © The Granger Collection, NYC / TopFoto; Figure 2.17 © DK Limited/Corbis; Figure 2.18 © AP/Press Association Images; Figure 2.21 © Hakan Kızıltan – Fotolia; Figure 2.22 © SUNY, Buffalo State Archives & Special Collections, Courier-Express Collection; Figure 3.2 © Imagestate Media (John Foxx); Figure 3.3 © ALBERT BANDURA, STANFORD CENTER ON ADOLESCENCE, STANFORD UNIVERSITY; Figure 3.4 © Ben Pruchnie/Getty Images; Figure 3.4 © MPI/Getty Images; Figure 3.6 © WARNER BROS TV/BRIGHT/ KAUFFMAN/CRANE PRO / THE KOBAL COLLECTION; Figure 3.7 © Peter Turnley/ Corbis; Figure 3.8 © Jane Elliott; Figure 4.1 © Eamonn and James Clarke/EMPICS Entertainment/PA Photos; Figure 4.2 © Corbis; Figure 4.3 © Joel Sartore/National Geographic/Getty Images; Figure 4.4 © Bettmann/Corbis; Figure 4.5 © Michaela Mueller – Fotolia; Figure 4.7 © RGB Ventures LLC dba SuperStock / Alamy ; Figure 4.8 © BSIP/ UIG Via Getty Images; Figure 4.10 © Artur Golbert – Fotolia; Figure 5.1 © Nina Leen/ Time Life Pictures/Getty Images; Figure 5.2 © Keystone/Getty Images; Figure 5.3 © shiva – Fotolia; Figure 5.4 © nyul – Fotolia; Figure 5.6 © Petro Feketa – Fotolia; Figure 5.7 © Paul Chesley/Getty Images; Figure 6.1 © ehabeljean – Fotolia; Figure 6.2 © Robert Hoetink – Fotolia; Figure 6.4 © Clynt Garnham Medical / Alamy; Figure 6.6 © nyul – Fotolia; Figure 7.1 © Flickr RF/Getty Images; Figure 7.4 © TheFinalMiracle – Fotolia; Figure 7.6 © ROMPER STOMPER/SEON FILMS / THE KOBAL COLLECTION; Figure 8.1 © eAlisa – Fotolia; Figure 8.2 © modestil – Fotolia; Figure 8.3 © Quinn Rooney/Getty Images; Figure 8.4 © Qamar Sibtain/India Today Group/Getty Images; Figure 8.7 © dimasobko – Fotolia; Figure 8.8 © Claudio Villa/Getty Images; Figure 8.9 © AP/Press Association Images; Figure 8.10 © cinexo – Fotolia; Figure 9.1 © Sashkin – Fotolia; Figure 9.2 © Ints Vikmanis – Fotolia; Figure 9.5 © milphoto – Fotolia; Figure 10.2 © http://commons.wikimedia.org/wiki/File:Hans_Pr%C3%BCfung_1907.jpg / from Karl Krall, Denkende Tiere, Leipz. 1912, Tafel 1; Figure 10.4 © Donald Miralle/Getty Images; Figure 10.9 © steheap – Fotolia.

Every effort has been made to trace and acknowledge ownership of copyright. The publishers will be glad to make suitable arrangements with any copyright holders whom it has not been possible to contact.

Biological level of analysis

Introduction

Behaviour can be analysed at many levels. Think of human aggression. This involves other people so it can be analysed at the level of social psychology, for instance through the study of group dynamics (mob violence) or using theories such as social learning theory and deindividuation. Individuals also vary in their degree of aggressive behaviour. This may be due to personality variables or individual differences in early experience. Aggression may also be due to biological factors, however. There is convincing evidence that aggression is influenced by inherited genetic factors as well as by levels of hormones (such as testosterone) and chemicals in the brain (called neurotransmitters, such as serotonin and dopamine).

In order to build a complete picture of aggressive behaviour, it needs to be analysed at all these different levels. In addition, we have to consider interactions between these different levels. For instance, some people may be genetically inclined to be more vulnerable to effects of aggressive imagery that they see in the media or in computer games; exposure to media violence may release or disinhibit aggressive behaviour in these biologically vulnerable individuals.

So while the biological approach studies the role of genetics, hormones, neurotransmitters and brain systems in behaviour, we have to remember all the time that human behaviour is complex. A complete picture will usually require analysis at the biological, cognitive and sociocultural levels.

Technological advances over the last 30 years have transformed the biological approach in psychology. We shall look more closely at some of these technologies later, but in brief, the ability to image the brain, i.e. to look at brain structures and brain activity while participants perform different tasks, has allowed us to map the brain in astonishing detail. This means that there is now a considerable overlap between biological psychology and areas such as cognitive psychology; for instance we can use brain scanning and imaging to support cognitive models of memory and language. In fact, this area of research, linking cognitive and biological psychology, now has its own name – cognitive neuroscience – and for the last ten years this has been the fastest growing area of psychological research.

Cognitive neuroscience is closely followed by behavioural genetics in terms of recent technological advances. We can now analyse (or 'sequence') the human genome (that is, all the genetic material that makes up an individual) and look for genetic variations that are linked, for instance, to particular cognitive abilities or to psychological disorders. This means that questions such as, 'Is this behaviour learnt or inherited, i.e. nature or nurture?' are now seen as old fashioned. We know that most behaviours represent interactions between our genetic inheritance and environmental factors, and we will examine some examples later in this chapter.

The biological level of analysis has therefore developed rapidly over the last two decades. Its basic principles, however, remain the same:

- The first and most important principle behind the biological approach is that all behaviour is reflected in changes in the biology of the body, in particular changes in brain activity. Reading this sentence, tweeting friends, worrying about exams – all produce specific patterns of brain activity that could in theory be measured. They may also produce changes in hormone levels in the body. All behaviour has biological correlates and the aim of the biological approach is to investigate the relationships between behaviour and biology.

- A second principle is that genetics plays a role in many behaviours. Although this area can be controversial, there is evidence for genetic involvement in disorders such as schizophrenia and anorexia nervosa, in gender differences in language, spatial abilities and aggression, and even in aspects of personality.
- A related principle is that some of our behaviours will be influenced by characteristics inherited from our early ancestors millions of years ago.
- A fourth principle is that human and animal biology, in particular that of the nervous system, possess enough similarities for studies with animals to be of value in understanding brain–behaviour relationships in humans.

Critical thinking

The nature–nurture debate

The debate as to whether some behaviours are genetic (innate) or environmentally-determined (acquired) has a long history in psychology. Do you think any behaviour can be neatly divided up in this way? Examples later in this chapter will help you to think about this issue. Remember that simply because a behaviour has biological correlates does not mean that it is automatically 'genetic'; the studies outlined later on brain plasticity show how the environment can directly influence the structure and function of the brain.

How the principles are demonstrated in research

LEARNING OUTCOME
- Outline principles that define the biological level of analysis.
- Explain how principles that define the biological level of analysis may be demonstrated in research (theories and/or studies).

The principle that all behaviour has biological correlates provides the basis for the experimental methods used in the biological level of analysis. A variety of techniques are employed to measure the electrical activity of the brain (electroencephalogram, event-related potentials, single unit recordings). The brain can be systematically lesioned (damaged) in non-human animals and the effects of this on behaviour observed and measured. Over the last 20 years, brain scanning techniques (CAT, MRI, fMRI) have enabled the human brain in living participants to be studied in unprecedented detail; this has drastically reduced the dependence on animal studies. Accidental damage to the human brain allows the cognitive and emotional effects of brain damage to be studied, and, combined with brain scans, localized to particular structures.

The principle that genetics plays a role in many behaviours is more controversial. No-one doubts that genetics can be important, but the extent to which our behaviour is down to nature (genetics) rather than nurture (environment) has always been subject to lively debate. For instance, twin studies (*see page 27*) have shown a genetic contribution to intelligence (IQ), to the eating disorder anorexia nervosa, and to the psychological disorder schizophrenia. In no case is the genetic contribution anything like 100 per cent, however, leaving room for significant non-genetic environmental factors. The issue for the biological level of analysis is unpacking the interaction between genetic and environmental influences.

Evolutionary influences are equally difficult to identify. For instance, males are more aggressive than females. This would have been adaptive for our ancestors living as hunter-gatherers. Competition for females would have meant that the most aggressive males would have had access to more females, leading to a greater chance of their genes surviving into future generations, and thus this trait would have gradually become more dominant in males down the generations. We also know from psychological research, however, that aggression can be learnt from parental and peer group models, and is also influenced by cultural factors. There is likely to be an evolutionary influence, but in itself it is not an adequate explanation of male aggression. We will look in more detail at examples of evolutionary explanations of human behaviour later (*see page 29*).

Research with non-human animals was a major part of the biological level of analysis for most of the twentieth century. Our knowledge of brain structure and function was heavily dependent on studies with rats, cats and primates. Even now there are areas, such as the study of feeding mechanisms, that still rely on animal experimentation. A key issue is the similarity, or not, between the brains of animals and the human brain. The brains of rats, cats and primates are similar to the human brain in that they contain the same structures and are organized in the same way. It is therefore assumed that the brain systems underlying basic behaviours, such as feeding, drinking, aggression and memory, will be roughly comparable, especially between humans and other primates, e.g. chimpanzees and monkeys. Research has generally supported this assumption, but it has also shown that animal studies are of limited value in the study of typically human abilities such as language, high level problem solving, planning ahead, personality and complex social behaviour. This is because these abilities often involve the frontal lobes, cortical areas that have expanded rapidly during human evolution.

Figure 1.1 Research on non-human animals is generalizable when studying basic behaviours, but less useful when studying more complex behaviours, for example language.

Theory of knowledge

Aside from the issue of the degree of similarity between animal and human brains, is the consideration of how ethical it is to experiment upon animals, as such research often causes distress and pain. Some would argue from a cost–benefit perspective that such research is permissable as the benefits, such as discovering cures for disorders, outweigh the costs, such as the pain and suffering of individual animals.

Throughout this chapter there are examples of how these basic principles of the biological level of analysis are reflected in theories and research.

Research methods used in the biological level of analysis

LEARNING OUTCOME
■ Discuss how and why particular research methods are used at the biological level of analysis.

A variety of research methods is used at the biological level of analysis. As a science, the preferred method is experimentation, with manipulation of the independent variable, measurement of dependent variables, and control of extraneous variables. For instance, a study on face recognition might compare patterns of brain activity after viewing faces compared with a control condition of viewing houses. This means that studies are objective; variables are measured, which provides quantitative data, and replication is straightforward.

Case studies – a research method that involves study and testing of an individual person or a small group of people.

Idiographic approach – concentration on the uniqueness of each individual.

Neurotypical – term now used for 'normal' control participants when compared with brain-damaged patients or participants with developmental disorders such as autism.

Nomothetic approach – establishing broad generalizations that apply to large groups of individuals.

Informed consent – prior to taking part in an investigation, researchers should ensure that participants understand what the study involves including how the findings may be used, and provide assurances of anonymity.

Quite often, however, systematic manipulation of the independent variable is impossible for practical or ethical reasons, and the researcher instead relies on natural variation. For instance, Woollett and Maguire (2011) (*see page 18*) used the fact that some trainee taxi drivers completed the training programme and some did not as their independent variable; the Auyeung *et al.*(2009) study (*see page 15*) on testosterone effects used the natural variation in prenatal testosterone levels as the independent variable. As there is no systematic manipulation of the independent variable in these studies, they are not true experiments but are known as 'quasi-experiments'. This also means that cause and effect cannot be convincingly determined, especially with the Auyeung *et al.* study, which used a correlational design.

Case studies or research with brain-damaged participants are idiographic studies (as they study individuals or very small groups). Such studies are necessary as large groups of participants with the same pattern of brain damage and similar behavioural impairments do not occur, and we will see the value of the single case with the case of HM later in the chapter (*see page 20*). Although the performance of brain-damaged participants on various tasks can be compared with groups of neurotypical controls, it is difficult to generalize findings to the wider population (*see the evaluation of Sperry and HM, pages 10, 23*). Studies, such as that of Auyeung *et al.*, that use large groups of participants represent the more common nomothetic approach, where the large sample size allows the use of powerful statistical techniques to produce findings that can be generalized more confidently.

In contrast, research with non-human animals is not limited by availability and usually uses experimental techniques, for example one group of animals (e.g. rats) can be given lesions to the hippocampus and compared with non-lesioned rats on memory tasks. Rosenzweig *et al.*'s (1962) research on the effects of environmental complexity on cortical thickness (*see page 16*) systematically varied the exposure of young rats to either stimulating environments or deprived environments.

Observational studies are not common in the biological level of analysis, but they have been used. Baron-Cohen's group (*see page 15*), for instance, observed children playing and linked the style of play with prenatal levels of testosterone. Some studies with monkeys have observed the effects of lesioning (damaging) the amygdala on social behaviour; they show that amygdala damage causes a monkey to become less dominant and fall to the bottom of the dominance hierarchy.

Ethical considerations

LEARNING OUTCOME
■ Discuss ethical considerations related to research studies at the biological level of analysis.

The main ethical concern in research with human participants is informed consent. With brain scanning studies in intact ('neurotypical') participants this is not a problem. When we consider research with children, brain-damaged participants or those with psychological disorders such as schizophrenia, however, then informed consent becomes a major issue. If the participants cannot themselves give consent, then it is permissible to approach carers, guardians or families to act on their behalf.

Research with non-human animals has long been a feature of the biological level of analysis and raises its own ethical issues. Informed consent is clearly not a problem. The ethical use of the animal is an important aspect, however. In the UK, animal researchers have to be licensed by the Home Office, a government department. This guarantees that they have the research skills and experience to work with animals. Then each research project they are involved in has to have a separate licence; before a licence is issued the project is assessed. The key criteria are the suffering of the animal, and the potential benefit, for example in terms of our understanding of human brain function, or the development of new treatments for brain damage or psychological disorders. If the suffering, stress and pain involved do not justify the potential benefits, a licence will not be issued. Particular care is given to work with primates such as monkeys and chimpanzees. These animals are closely related to humans and possess high level cognitive skills. This makes them desirable as experimental participants, but equally makes them more sensitive to stressful and painful procedures that may be involved. There has been a significant reduction in primate research in psychology over the last 20 years.

Some areas within the biological level of analysis have their own ethical considerations. Genetic studies may suggest that an individual is vulnerable to a particular psychological disorder, or that some ethnic groups are less intelligent than others (*see page 28*). There is no simple answer to these problems, but psychologists do need to be aware of the possible social implications of the research they undertake.

SECTION SUMMARY

- Biological psychology examines the physiological processes that control human behaviour.
- The most important principle of the biological level of analysis is that every behaviour has a biological correlate.
- Experimental research methods are generally preferred by biological psychologists. Traditionally study often used non-human animals, but recent advances in technology have allowed researchers to study the human brain without causing harm to participants.
- There are several ethical considerations to be taken into account in the study of biological psychology, in particular around the issues of informed consent, animal studies and genetics.

Physiology and behaviour
The neuron and how it works

The neuron is the name we give to the cells that make up our brain and the rest of the nervous system. It will help you to understand the material in this chapter if we briefly review the neuron and how it works.

All parts of the body are made up of cells, and each cell has a particular specialization – muscle cells are designed to contract, liver cells to store energy in the form of glycogen, glandular cells to secrete hormones. Neurons are specialized to transmit information in the form of electrical signals.

The neuron (*see Figure 1.2*) has a cell body containing the nucleus, with its set of chromosomes. The axon is an elongated process extending from the cell body; axons come in many forms, but are usually branched. On the other side of the cell body are

Neuron – the basic unit cell of the nervous system. Neurons are specialized to transmit electrical impulses (or 'action potentials') along their length. It is estimated that the brain alone may contain in the order of 100 billion neurons.

Nucleus – all cells, including neurons, contain a nucleus. Within the nucleus we find chromosomes, the genetic material. Besides transmitting genetic information from one generation to the next, chromosomes in the nucleus also control the biochemical activities of the living cell.

Axon – part of the neuron, a long process emerging from the cell body. The axon usually has many branches that end at synapses close to neighbouring neurons.

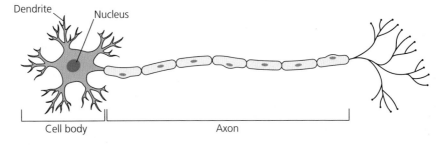

Dendrite   Nucleus

Cell body   Axon

Figure 1.2   The structure of a neuron

Dendrites – a part of the neuron. Dendrites are short processes that usually receive synaptic connections from the axon branches of other neurons; so nerve impulses (action potentials) are usually generated on dendrites.

Cell membrane – the outer covering of all cells, including neurons. With neurons, the cell membrane has a highly complex layered structure that allows it to transmit electrical impulses.

Action potentials – brief bursts of electrical activity. Usually generated at synapses on dendrites, action potentials travel down the neuron and along the axon to axon terminals. At the synapse they may be transmitted to the next neuron, or they may be lost. Action potentials are 'all or none', and always have the same electrical characteristics. All information in the nervous system is carried in the form of patterns of action potentials.

smaller processes called dendrites. The most important part of the neuron is its outer covering, or cell membrane, as this has a complex structure that allows the neuron to fulfil its key role: **electrical transmission**.

The details of how this works are beyond IB level, but the basic principle is relatively simple. Electrical activity in the nervous system is in the form of nerve impulses or action potentials. These are 'blips' of electrical potential produced by complex changes in the cell membrane. These nerve impulses normally start on a dendrite. It is then that we see the key specialization of the neuron. A nerve impulse that starts on a dendrite is automatically transmitted along the cell membrane, down the dendrite, across the cell body, and down the axon. Nerve impulses at any point on the membrane only last for about a millisecond and then move on. A thin wire recording electrode positioned close to an axon can record these nerve impulses as a series of 'blips' of electrical potential as they are transmitted down the cell membrane.

It is impossible to exaggerate the significance of these nerve impulses. All information that the nervous system processes has to be in the form of patterns of nerve impulses. Vision, hearing, pain, memory, conscious awareness, movement, etc., are all **coded** as patterns of nerve impulses in different parts of the brain. Wherever nerve impulses or action potentials are recorded, they all have the same characteristics, i.e. they are identical to each other. This means that they can only code different behaviours by their frequency or patterning (how many there are in given period) and their location in the brain. So patterns of nerve impulses in the visual cortex give rise to the sensation of vision, while nerve impulses in the motor cortex produce movement of our muscles.

We should also note that since the earliest evolution of the neuron, many millions of years ago in sea-dwelling primitive animals, they have worked in this way, through the transmission of nerve impulses. It is remarkable that this apparently simple mechanism can lead to complex human behaviour.

The first principle of neuronal function is electrical transmission, while the second concerns the **communication between neurons**. Estimates vary, but the human brain contains between 50 and 100 *billion* neurons. They are specialized to transmit nerve impulses. If they were physically connected, nerve impulses would simply be conducted randomly throughout the brain; to prevent this there is a tiny gap, visible only under the electron microscope, between neurons. Given the elongated structure of most neurons, this gap, or synapse, is usually between the end of an axon or axonal branch, and the dendrite or cell body of the following neuron.

For the nerve impulse to cross the synapse and be transmitted onwards, the second principle of neuronal function comes into play, that is, **synaptic neurotransmission**. The end of each axon branch is known as the axon terminal. Within this terminal are small packets of chemicals called neurotransmitters. Complex changes occur when nerve impulses reach the region of the axon terminal. These changes result in the packets (known technically as vesicles) releasing their contents into the synapse between the axon terminal and the following dendrite.

The synaptic gap is so small that the molecules of neurotransmitters can diffuse across it and contact the cell membrane of the dendrite on the following neuron. This is known as the post-synaptic membrane. On this membrane are molecular structures known as synaptic receptors; these receptors have structures that match the molecular make-up of the neurotransmitter, and the two combine together like a lock and key. The combination of neurotransmitter and receptor affects the electrical characteristics of the post-synaptic membrane. If sufficient combinations occur in a small space of time, the post-synaptic membrane becomes destabilized and a nerve impulse is generated in the post-synaptic neuron. In this way nerve impulses in the pre-synaptic neuron can jump the synaptic gap and produce nerve impulses in the post-synaptic neuron.

Synapse – the small gap, measured in thousandths of a millimetre, between axon terminals and the dendrites of the following neuron. Release of neurotransmitters, such as dopamine and serotonin, from the axon terminal allows some action potentials to cross the synapse. The synapse is essential to information processing in the nervous system.

Axon terminal – the part of the axon branch just before the synapse between the axon and the following neuron. The axon terminal contains packets (vesicles) of neurotransmitters that are released into the synapse when action potentials arrive at the axon terminal.

Neurotransmitters – neurochemicals such as dopamine, serotonin and acetylcholine that are stored in axon terminals and released into the synapse when action potentials arrive at the axon terminal. They combine with postsynaptic

Synaptic neurotransmission is chemical, and along with electrical conduction along the neuron, makes up the two fundamental principles of neuronal function. Our knowledge of the neuron developed rapidly in the 1960s and 70s and had a number of implications:

- Information in the nervous system is coded as patterns of nerve impulses.
- Each nerve impulse is identical to every other nerve impulse.
- Therefore the information that is coded by nerve impulses depends on their frequency and where in the brain they occur.
- Transmission across the synapse is chemical, using neurotransmitters.
- A single nerve impulse in the pre-synaptic axon terminal will not release sufficient neurotransmitter into the synapse to generate a nerve impulse in the post-synaptic neuron. The information coded by that nerve impulse will therefore not cross the synapse and it will be lost. In this way the synapse acts as an information filter.
- Many pre-synaptic axon terminals may terminate and synapse in the same patch of post-synaptic membrane; the combined activity of all these axon terminals will determine whether a nerve impulse is generated in the post-synaptic neuron. In this way synapses can allow for complex interactions between neurons.

The nervous system is made up of many millions of neurons, organized into various sub-systems and structures. A description of these is beyond the scope of this chapter, but some essential aspects of brain organization will be introduced where appropriate.

Localization of function: Sperry and the split brain

LEARNING OUTCOME
- Explain one study related to localization of function in the brain.

Epilepsy is an uncontrolled electrical discharge in the brain, often caused by 'irritations' to the brain. These can include developing tumours and cysts, or scar tissue from damage to brain tissue. Epileptic discharges interfere with brain function. In some cases the effects are barely noticeable ('petit mal' epilepsy). However the most severe form ('grand mal' epilepsy) can lead to convulsions and temporary unconsciousness, and in the worst cases sufferers can have several attacks each day. This clearly prevents any sort of normal life.

Epilepsy can often be controlled through anticonvulsant drugs, but in some cases these are ineffective. If the epilepsy is severe and disabling, then brain surgery becomes an option. As we shall see later, surgery for epilepsy can be targeted at particular trigger areas (the 'focus') of the brain. Sometimes, however, specific trigger areas for epilepsy cannot be identified and surgery cannot be targeted. In these cases, and as a last resort, a unique operation was devised, the split brain.

Whether or not epilepsy has an identifiable focus, the seizure usually begins in one hemisphere of the brain and is transmitted rapidly to the other hemisphere through the corpus callosum, the large pathway connecting the two hemispheres (*see Figure 1.3*). In this way the epileptic attack involves the whole brain. In the 1930s it was proposed that cutting the corpus callosum would reduce the severity of seizures by confining them to one hemisphere only, preventing transmission to the other hemisphere. Van Wagenen and Herren found exactly this in 1940, reporting that cutting the corpus callosum reduced the severity of epileptic seizures. In addition, follow-up studies by Akelaitis (1944) concluded that the side effects of the surgery were relatively minor and short-lasting.

receptors and this combination allows action potentials to be generated in the postsynaptic neuron.

Vesicles – small storage packets found in the presynaptic axon terminal, which contain neurotransmitters such as dopamine and serotonin. When action potentials arrive at the axon terminal they cause vesicles to travel to the cell membrane, rupture, and release their contents into the synaptic gap.

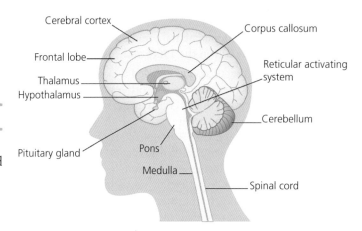

Figure 1.3 The brain

This was surprising given that the corpus callosum is the largest pathway in the brain; cutting it would be expected to result in severe effects on brain function. Note incidentally that while **split brain** has become the popular term for this operation, the technical term is **commissurotomy**.

In the 1950s, Roger Sperry began the work for which he was awarded a Nobel Prize in 1980. Sperry had studied the development of the visual system in reptiles and amphibians, and then moved on to look at hemisphere functions in other non-human animals. He then began a study of split brain patients, intrigued by the fact that the operation helped to reduce epileptic symptoms but did not seem to affect the person's cognitive abilities. Cutting the corpus callosum prevents communication between the hemispheres so that in theory they are operating independently. If methods could be devised to test the separated hemispheres, this would lead to a greater understanding of the differences and similarities between them. The pioneering work of neuropsychologists such as Broca and Wernicke in the nineteenth century had established that, in right-handed people, the centres for the production and understanding of language were in the left hemisphere. As this hemisphere also controls the right hand, it was seen as **dominant**, with the right hemisphere seen as less important.

Although researchers such as Akelaitis had already reviewed the effects of commissurotomy, Sperry's great contribution was to introduce new experimental methods to tease out the effects of the split brain operation more systematically. He used his knowledge of the visual system to design an apparatus known as the divided field.

You will see from Figure 1.4 that *both* eyes project to visual cortical areas in the occipital lobes of *both* hemispheres. The visual receptor cells that respond to light are in the retina at the back of the eye. It turns out that the right side of each retina is connected to the *right* hemisphere, whereas the left side of each retina is connected to the *left* hemisphere. If the eyes point straight ahead, then visual stimuli out to the *right* of the participant (called the right visual field, or RVF) are received by the *left* side of each retina, and so will be transmitted to the **left hemisphere**. Stimuli out to the *left* of the participant (the left visual field, or LVF) will be received by the *right* side of each retina and will be transmitted to the **right hemisphere**.

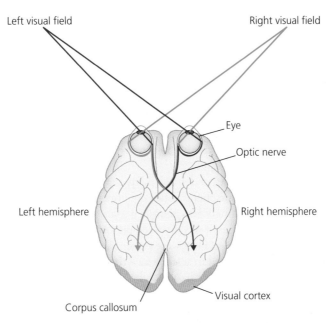

Figure 1.4 How light entering the eyes projects to the brain.

This arrangement was the basis of Sperry's **divided field technique** for testing split brain patients. With the participant's eyes pointing straight ahead, Sperry (1968) presented stimuli either in the RVF or the LVF, for very short periods of time (e.g. 100 milliseconds; if he had presented them for longer the participant would not be able to help moving their eyes towards the stimulus). Sperry asked the patient what they had seen. Importantly, as the corpus callosum (the major pathway connecting the two hemispheres) had been cut, information sent to one hemisphere was not transferred to the other hemisphere. So this gave Sperry a means of testing each hemisphere independently.

An example may make this clearer. If a word, such as 'telephone', is flashed up in the RVF, it is transmitted to the left hemisphere and the participant will report the word 'telephone'. If the word 'ostrich' is flashed up in the LVF, the patient reports nothing, and seems unaware that anything has been presented at all! Why is this? As mentioned earlier, for the majority of us the language centres for reading and writing are in the left hemisphere. The word 'ostrich' has been presented to the LVF and thus the right hemisphere, which has no language centres, and so it cannot be read. If you ask the split brain patient to report the word they saw, the patient has to speak; this must come from the *left* hemisphere language system. The left hemisphere has not seen the word, so the patient reports that they haven't seen anything.

Note that in intact participants this does not work. Although the word 'ostrich' is flashed to the right hemisphere, it is rapidly transferred through the corpus callosum to the left hemisphere, which can then read it and report it.

These divided field studies seemed to confirm that language functions are localized to the left hemisphere. Sperry recognized one key problem, however. If the right hemisphere cannot talk then it has no way of reporting the word even if it can read it. It does control the left hand, however. So Sperry repeated the study, with the left hand positioned behind a screen among an array of objects. When the word 'banana' was flashed to the right hemisphere, the left hand emerged from behind the screen holding a banana! The explanation for this was that the right hemisphere had some capacity to read simple nouns, and it could then instruct the left hand to select the correct object. When asked why they were holding a banana in their left hand the patient was not able to answer; asking them to speak engaged their *left* hemisphere which had not, of course, seen the word as it had been presented to the *right* hemisphere. Thus they could not explain why they had a banana in their left hand.

An even simpler demonstration of these **disconnection** syndromes (so called because they demonstrate a disconnection between the hemispheres) is to blindfold the split brain patient and then put a different object in each hand. When asked to identify them, the one in the right hand is immediately reported, as the right hand is directly connected to the left hemisphere, which has language functions. In contrast, the patient will be unaware that they even have an object in the left hand. Even if the right hemisphere is able to identify the object, it has no language or speech functions with which to report it.

Sperry and his colleagues undertook many similar studies to try and tease out the functions of the two hemispheres. They confirmed the dominance of the left hemisphere for language, but surprisingly also identified some tasks where the right hemisphere showed a superiority. These tasks involved pictorial (or visuospatial) stimuli rather than words. For instance, pairs of faces were presented in both visual fields simultaneously. When the patient was asked to select a face that had been presented from a selection of different faces, they were more likely to choose the one presented in the left visual field and transmitted to the right hemisphere.

Further testing with the right-hemisphere/left-hand system showed that it was better than the left hemisphere at a range of visuospatial tasks involving faces, shapes and patterns. This led Sperry to conclude that the right hemisphere was as specialized for nonverbal visuospatial functions as the left hemisphere was for language. In turn this became the accepted model for hemisphere localization of functions. Even today this division of labour between the hemispheres is seen as a generally accurate picture of hemisphere specializations, and was one of the most importance contributions to our understanding of the brain.

Conclusions of Sperry's research

- Language systems in most people are located in the left hemisphere. A most important additional point is that our self-awareness is heavily dependent on language (e.g. when we ask someone what they are feeling, they use language to think about their feelings and to report them). In Sperry's split brain patients, it was clear than when asked questions about their experience, they could only comment on what had been presented to the left hemisphere.
- The right hemisphere is not a 'poor relation' to the dominant left hemisphere. It has high level specialized functions, with visuospatial abilities localized to the right hemisphere.
- The corpus callosum allows the two hemispheres to communicate with each other. In intact participants this means that the left hemisphere language systems can comment on what is happening in the right hemisphere, and our conscious experience is of an integrated whole brain. The two hemispheres do have different specializations, but the corpus callosum allows them to function together.

Evaluation of Sperry's research

- Sperry's research clearly demonstrated localization of function in the human brain, with language in the left hemisphere and visuospatial functions in the right hemisphere.
- His introduction of the divided field technique for testing lateralized functions of the hemispheres was crucial in the subsequent development of this major area of research in psychology.
- Sperry tested only a few split brain patients, and these differed in important ways – for instance age, gender, age of onset of epilepsy, age of split brain surgery, drug treatment

before and after surgery. This means that his results might have been affected by some of these uncontrolled variables.

■ Later studies with intact ('neurotypical') participants, however, using a modified divided field technique and other experimental methods, has largely confirmed Sperry's pioneering results. Replication of findings is a critical part of the scientific method.

The effects of neurotransmission on human behaviour

LEARNING OUTCOME

▨ Using one or more examples, explain effects of neurotransmission on human behaviour.

Earlier in this chapter we looked at the role of neurotransmitters in synaptic transmission, and therefore why they are so vital to behaviour. The identification of neurotransmitters and their function in the brain also provides us with another approach to studying and explaining behaviour. Although this research area (known as psychopharmacology) has only been around in a systematic form for 50 years or so, it has provided great insights into the brain and behaviour.

One central reason for this is the widespread use of drugs to affect behaviour. This can be legal, as in drug therapy to treat psychological disorders such as schizophrenia, depression and anxiety, or illegal, as with many drugs of abuse. Legal drugs like alcohol and nicotine are regularly used to alter mood. Our knowledge of brain neurotransmitters allows us to explain many of these drug-induced behavioural effects.

Practical applications

Our knowledge of the synapse and how it operates not only allows us to understand the action of drugs on behaviour, it also means that we can develop drugs to target particular brain systems. So once it was discovered that depression was associated with low levels of serotonin in the brain, drugs known as **selective serotonin reuptake inhibitors** could be designed specifically to increase brain serotonin levels.

Schizophrenia

One of the best examples of the use of drugs to affect behaviour comes from the history of drug treatment for the severe psychological disorder schizophrenia. This psychotic disorder, with symptoms of hallucinations and thought disorder, can be disabling and is still responsible for the majority of long-stay patients in psychiatric hospitals. Before the 1950s treatments such as electroconvulsive shock, induced comas and brain surgery were in common use. These were unethical and dangerous, and also largely ineffective. Then in 1952 the first drug, chlorpromazine, was introduced for the treatment of schizophrenia. The effectiveness of chlorpromazine compared with the previous drastic and traumatic therapies led to an explosion in drug treatment and the virtual disappearance of those earlier techniques.

Note that chlorpromazine and other drugs were introduced before anything was known about synaptic neurotransmitters in the brain. They worked, and that was enough. Then in the 1960s and early 70s researchers identified brain neurotransmitters and how they operated at the synapse (*see page 6*). They could then look at the effects drugs had on patients and in some cases explain these effects through actions on specific neurotransmitters.

In the case of **schizophrenia** it turned out that effective drugs acted through the neurotransmitter dopamine. The drugs blocked synapses at which dopamine was the neurotransmitter and so reduced dopamine activity in the brain; these drugs, also known as antipsychotics, were therefore **dopamine antagonists**.

Parkinson's disease

A second strand of the drug story concerns the condition known as **Parkinson's disease**. This is a disease of the brain's motor systems that affects the control of movement. It was first identified and named by James Parkinson in the nineteenth century, and soon after the brain areas responsible were also identified. When nineteenth century pathologists looked at the brains of people who had died with Parkinson's disease, they found that a particular brain pathway had been destroyed; this pathway runs from an area known as the substantia nigra up through the brain to an area known as the striatum. This pathway is therefore called the nigrostriatal pathway. Incidentally, we still do not know what causes this pathway to degenerate and cause the symptoms of Parkinson's disease.

The twentieth century saw a revolution in the production and use of drugs to treat medical and psychological conditions. One new drug was called L-DOPA, and this was found to be effective in treating Parkinson's disease, especially the early stages. As our knowledge of how drugs work accumulated, it turned out that L-DOPA also acted through increasing levels of the brain neurotransmitter dopamine. This knowledge was a breakthrough in the understanding of Parkinson's, as it strongly implied that this disease was caused by a **loss of brain dopamine**. A detailed study of the nigrostriatal pathway then revealed that it was in fact made up of a bundle of axons belonging to neurons that all used dopamine as a neurotransmitter. The neuronal cell bodies (*see Figure 1.2*) were clustered in the substantia nigra and the axons eventually made synaptic contact on neurons in the striatum, and of course released dopamine into these synapses. As the nigrostriatal pathway degenerates in Parkinson's disease (i.e. as the neurons and axons making up the pathway gradually die), so dopamine release in the striatum decreases, causing the symptoms of the disease. L-DOPA works by increasing dopamine production and release in the surviving nigrostriatal neurons. It does not prevent the degeneration of the dopamine neurons, though, and becomes less and less effective as they die off.

The role of dopamine in schizophrenia and Parkinson's disease

One of the features of the drug treatment of schizophrenia is that drugs are taken for long periods, often for the life of the patient. This is because they suppress the symptoms of the disorder but do not 'cure' it. If the drug treatment is stopped, a high proportion of patients relapse into full schizophrenia.

After antipsychotic drugs were first introduced it was noticed, after some months of treatment, that many schizophrenic patients developed a motor disorder with shaking, trembling, and uncontrollable muscle movements. These side effects of treatment looked very much like Parkinson's disease, although they are technically referred to as 'extrapyramidal movement' side effects. Although initially their cause could not be identified, by the early 1970s the observations outlined above could be put together:

- Parkinson's disease is caused by degeneration of the nigrostriatal pathway.
- The nigrostriatal pathway is a dopamine pathway and its loss causes a decrease in brain dopamine activity, which leads to the symptoms of Parkinson's disease.
- L-DOPA can be effective in treating Parkinson's because it increases levels of brain dopamine.
- Schizophrenia is treated with antipsychotic drugs.
- Antipsychotic drugs are dopamine antagonists, reducing brain dopamine activity; this implies that schizophrenia is caused by over-activity in brain dopamine pathways.
- Long-term treatment with antipsychotic drugs leads to a decrease in brain dopamine activity. This helps in reducing the symptoms of schizophrenia, but can also lead to drug-induced Parkinson's disease through the reduction in dopamine activity in the nigrostriatal pathway.

- So schizophrenia and Parkinson's disease therefore represent opposite poles of brain dopamine activity; schizophrenia is associated with over-activity in dopamine pathways, and Parkinson's with a reduction in activity in dopamine pathways.

Once techniques were developed to study the role of neurotransmitters in drug effects on human behaviour, the field expanded rapidly. We now know that antidepressant drugs work by increasing activity in serotonin pathways in the brain. Dopamine, besides its role in schizophrenia and Parkinson's disease, is also the neurotransmitter in 'reward' or 'pleasure' pathways in the brain. These pathways are activated by a variety of events and stimuli that we find rewarding. Examples include drugs of abuse such as cocaine, and natural rewards such as food and sex.

▍Critical thinking

Is depression biological or psychological?

The increase in knowledge of brain neurotransmitters and behaviour has led to an emphasis on the biology of behaviour rather than on its psychology. For instance, depression is seen as a problem with brain serotonin. But think about what depression is. What sorts of events cause it? Is it possible to understand depression without looking at the psychological and sociocultural factors that can cause it?

The role of hormones in human behaviour

Hormones – chemical messengers released from glands. They travel in the bloodstream and affect the activity of other glands and structures in the body. They can also directly affect brain activity.

- Using one or more examples, explain functions of hormones in human behaviour.

Oxytocin

Hormones are chemical messengers secreted by glands in the body, such as the pancreas, pituitary and thyroid glands. They travel in the bloodstream to target cells and organs in the body, and regulate the activity of these target structures. Hormones are therefore vital to the normal physiological functioning of the body. The study of hormones and their effects is known as endocrinology. More recently a related field has developed, known as neuroendocrinology, which investigates interactions between hormones and the brain. This section looks at two examples of why this is such an interesting area.

The pituitary gland lies within the skull cavity, just underneath the hypothalamus, to which it is joined by a stalk, the infundibulum. The pituitary releases a number of hormones into the bloodstream, which in turn have a range of effects on cells and organs in the body. One example of a pituitary hormone is oxytocin.

Oxytocin is manufactured in the hypothalamus and transported down to the pituitary gland for release. Its traditional effects are linked to sexual behaviour, reproduction, and maternal behaviour. Research, mainly in non-human animals, has shown that oxytocin release increases milk production in new mothers, stimulates uterine contractions during birth and plays a major role in copulation and ejaculation in females and males. It has been shown (Campbell, 2007) that oxytocin can induce maternal behaviours in non-pregnant rats, such as nest building, licking and grooming of stranger pups, and retrieval of wandering pups. These findings have led to the suggestion that oxytocin is an 'affiliation' hormone, essential not just to mother–infant bonding but also to adult pair-bonding. In humans oxytocin levels are increased by stroking and massage, and are also associated with lowered levels of anxiety and stress.

Females have higher levels of oxytocin and this has been used to explain why, on average, females are more nurturing, affiliative and sociable than males.

Oxytocin – a hormone released from the pituitary gland, which plays important roles in reproductive and maternal behaviour, e.g. lactation. Recent research has also shown a role for oxytocin in early bonding between mother and child and in adult pair-bonding.

Feldman *et al.* (2007)

Most research in this area has been done on non-human animals. Some studies using humans have tried to confirm the important role of oxytocin in mother–infant bonding, however, Feldman *et al.* (2007) studied 62 pregnant women. Levels of oxytocin were measured at three points: 10 weeks into the pregnancy, 27 weeks into the pregnancy, and 2 weeks after birth. At this last point mother–child interactions were videotaped for 15 minutes, and the mothers were interviewed for 45 minutes. On the basis of the tape each mother was given a maternal-behaviour rating (this included behaviours such as gaze directed at the child, positive emotions towards the child, affectionate touch, and amount of 'babytalk'). From the interview researchers derived ratings for various aspects of maternal behaviour and attitudes, such as checking behaviour (is the baby safe?) and general preoccupation with the child.

Findings from this longitudinal study were firstly that oxytocin levels did not vary significantly across the three testing points. Secondly, levels of oxytocin at the first and last measurement points were significantly positively correlated with maternal behaviour ratings and with checking behaviour.

Figure 1.5 Higher levels of oxytocin are linked to caring behaviours.

This was one of the first studies to show that levels of oxytocin across pregnancy and birth are significantly associated with maternal bonding and mother–infant attachment behaviours in humans. This supports the model of oxytocin as an 'affiliative' hormone, although we should note that this was a correlational study and we cannot conclude a cause–effect relationship. It may be that both oxytocin levels and maternal behaviour are influenced separately by a third variable, such as anxiety. A vast range of research with non-human animals, however, supports the relationship between oxytocin and mother–infant bonding.

There are two further implications from this study. Early attachment experience has been shown to have a major influence on later relationships, even into adulthood. So the effects of maternal oxytocin may effectively be life-long. The evidence also suggests that oxytocin affects quite complex behaviours, and it can only do this by acting on brain systems. It turns out that there are receptors for oxytocin, similar to synaptic receptors for neurotransmitters (*see page 6*), on many structures in the brain. These include the hypothalamus, amygdala, striatum and nucleus accumbens. When oxytocin circulating in the bloodstream reaches the brain, it combines with these receptors and in this way alters the activity of that particular structure.

The action of oxytocin in the brain explains the wide range of effects it has on maternal and bonding behaviour in women. The development of neuroendocrinology as a research area has altered our perception of hormones; these were once seen as only acting on body structures, but now we know that many of them can act in the brain, and function as 'neuromodulators', regulating the activity of neurons in many different brain structures.

Testosterone – a hormone released from the testes in males but also found in females. Important in male sexual characteristics and behaviour, testosterone released early in embryonic development directly affects the brain. Baron-Cohen suggests that this produces the 'male pattern' brain.

Testosterone

Oxytocin, although also found in men in lower quantities, is particularly relevant to women and maternal bonding and affiliative behaviour. Testosterone is to some

Autism – a developmental disorder found mainly in males, with impairments in social communication, language and behavioural flexibility. Baron-Cohen argues that autism may represent an extreme version of the 'male pattern' brain, with an important role for prenatal testosterone.

Developmental disorder – disorders such as autism and dyslexia that can be identified in the developing child, and appear to be subtle problems in the normal development of the brain and brain function.

Asperger's syndrome – a mild form of autism, and one of the 'autism spectrum disorders'.

extent the mirror image to oxytocin. It is a hormone found in both men and women, but in much higher quantities in men. In men, luteinizing hormone is released from the pituitary gland and travels in the bloodstream to the Leydig cells in the testes, where it stimulates the release of testosterone. Testosterone is responsible for the development in boys of external genitalia and secondary sexual characteristics such as facial and pubic hair. Women also have circulating levels of testosterone originating from the adrenal gland, but under normal conditions these levels are much lower than in men.

In non-human animals one area where testosterone is critical is in aggressive behaviour. If aggressive male mice are castrated (thus removing most testosterone from the body), aggressive behaviour disappears. If testosterone injections are then given to these mice, aggressive behaviour reappears. Many other studies have also shown that testosterone plays a vital role in aggressive behaviour in non-human animals. In humans the picture is different, however. Hyper-aggressive criminals do not have consistently higher levels of testosterone, and in general testosterone levels in human males do not correlate with aggressive behaviour.

Interest in testosterone has therefore spread into other areas of behaviour. Autism is a developmental disorder (i.e. observed in young children and persisting into adulthood). The main symptoms divide into three categories – problems with social communication and behaviour; problems with language, where speech, for instance, might be almost completely absent or, if present, is peculiar; and finally a lack of imagination, shown in a narrow range of interests, with repetitive behaviour and perhaps an obsession with detail.

Autism affects around 1 per cent of the population. It varies in severity from person to person, and so is usually referred to as autism spectrum disorder. Asperger's syndrome is a form of mild, high functioning autism at the top end of the spectrum. Interestingly, autism affects more boys than girls, in a ratio of roughly 4:1. Changes in brain structure have been associated with autism, and it also has a significant genetic component. The precise mechanisms and causes of autism have yet to be determined, however. A recent theory has linked autism to the effects of testosterone on the developing brain, with the first clue being the high ratio of boys that develop autism.

Simon Baron-Cohen and his group at Cambridge have for some years been leaders in autism research. They built on the work of Geschwind and Galaburda (1985), who first proposed a detailed model of how testosterone in the developing male might lead to some disorders specifically associated with boys. We know that testosterone levels in the developing embryo are vital in the development of male physical characteristics in the baby, but Baron-Cohen's research suggests that its effects might be more subtle and wide-ranging.

Key study

Auyeung *et al.* (2009)

As part of a long-term (longitudinal) research programme, Auyeung *et al.* (2009) measured levels of testosterone in the amniotic fluid of prenatal babies between 14 and 22 weeks old. Amniotic fluid bathes the developing baby in the uterus, and levels of hormones in this fluid are thought to correlate reasonably well with levels within the foetus itself. These babies were then followed up after birth and regularly assessed on various behavioural and cognitive tasks, e.g. language development, type of preferred play, social behaviour, verbal and spatial IQ, etc. The plan is to follow this group into adulthood.

As an example of what these studies have shown, Auyeung *et al.* (2009) looked at the relationship between amniotic testosterone levels at 14–22 weeks old and autistic symptoms tested when the children were between 6 and 8 years old. There were 235 children in the study, 118 boys and 117 girls (remember that girls also have circulating levels of testosterone). None of these children had been diagnosed with autism; they were a 'normal' sample.

Childhood autistic traits were assessed using a questionnaire, the Child Autistic Spectrum Quotient (ASQ-Child). This is filled in by the parents and is made up of questions relevant to the key areas of autistic symptoms (communication, social skills, attention to detail, imagination). Each of these subscales can be scored and a total ASQ-Child score can also be analysed.

Results showed that, as expected, boys had significantly higher testosterone levels prenatally than girls. They also scored higher on the total ASQ-Child score, and also on each of the individual subscales. This emphasizes the vulnerability of boys to autistic symptoms. More interestingly, testosterone levels were significantly correlated with ASQ-Child total scores, and with scores on each of the subscales. This pattern was found for the combined sample of boys and girls, and for each gender group analysed separately.

The fact that testosterone levels were significantly correlated with ASQ-Child scores in females is very important. It suggests that the relationship between testosterone and autistic symptoms is independent of gender, and the reason more boys than girls develop autism is due to their higher testosterone levels, not just that they are male. It is the hormone that is central.

This was a relatively small study and can only be generalized with caution. In addition, this was a correlational study so cause and effect cannot be assumed. It may be that both testosterone levels and autistic symptoms are influenced in the same way by some third variable. The findings are in line with other research on testosterone and autism, however, which gives the conclusions more credibility.

Amniocentesis carries a slight risk of miscarriage, and is only done when the developing baby needs to be checked, e.g. for Down's syndrome. The mothers tend to be older, and overall are not a typical group. Again, this limits generalization.

Testosterone levels fluctuate during pregnancy. There is a surge during the testing period of 14–22 weeks, but there is another surge shortly before birth. If testosterone is a key factor in vulnerability to autism, it is not known at which point during pregnancy it has its effects.

Testosterone has a vital role in the development of the reproductive system in male children. A few weeks into the pregnancy testosterone plays an equally important role in organizing the nervous system; for instance the hypothalamus (*see page 13*) in the 'male' brain has a clearly different structure to the hypothalamus in the 'female' brain. So testosterone can influence brain development. It seems from the work of Baron-Cohen's group and others that sometimes this hormonal influence can lead to problems with development of the brain and result in the emergence of autistic symptoms.

The effect of the environment on physiology

LEARNING OUTCOME
▨ Discuss two effects of the environment on physiological processes.

Environment and neural plasticity

As early as the 1950s and 60s research showed that the environment can affect the brain. In a series of classic studies, Rosenzweig and his group (Rosenzweig *et al.*, 1962) demonstrated the importance of early stimulation for brain development. Rats reared from birth were raised either in an 'enriched' environment or kept in isolation in basic housing. The enriched environment included cages with other rat pups and toys to play with, daily handling, and practice at learning simple mazes. After some weeks the researchers found that rats raised in the enriched environment had a thicker cortex than rats raised in isolation. There were also significant changes in some neurotransmitters.

▪ Critical thinking

Are findings from studies with rats relevant to human brain function?

No-one would deny that rats are very different from humans. But they are also mammals with complex brains. In fact, all the structures of the human brain can be identified in the rat brain. Obviously the higher level structures such as the cortex are vastly more developed in humans, which is why we have language and other high level cognitive abilities. But rats do have memory and learning, sensation and perception. They also show emotions such as fear and rage. The neurons that make up their brains are the same as the ones that make up human brains. So findings from rats can be cautiously generalized to humans.

Practical applications

The demonstration that early environment can have significant effects on brain growth and development also implies that deprived environments do not allow full brain development. This means that environmental stimulation in infancy is vital for brain development. Projects such as SureStart aim to provide stimulating day care for infants and can be critical in providing children with a positive start in life.

Rosenzweig *et al.* (1962) provided clear evidence that the developing brain is vulnerable to environmental factors, and that normal brain development depends on adequate environmental stimulation and experience. Many subsequent studies have confirmed the importance of environmental factors in brain development, interacting with genetically driven processes. There was an assumption that the fully developed mature brain was far less vulnerable to environmental factors, however.

The introduction of sophisticated scanning techniques has revolutionized the study of the human brain, and one particularly interesting area of research concerns neural plasticity; this is the ability of the nervous system, especially the brain, to alter the number of neurons and/or the connections between them in response to environmental influences. We have seen this in relation to the developing brain, and there can also be reorganization of the brain in response to injury (especially if this occurs early in life). Recent studies, however, have demonstrated a far more subtle and potentially significant type of plasticity in the mature adult brain.

It had been thought that once the brain was fully developed, in the late teens/early 20s, then no new neurons could grow. This was part of the explanation for the often permanent effects of brain damage in adults compared to the plasticity of the developing brain; this plasticity allows the infant brain to compensate remarkably well for the effects of early brain damage. We now know, however, that new neurons can grow in some parts of the adult brain. This process, called neurogenesis, can be found, for instance, in regions of the hippocampus.

The best evidence for neurogenesis in the brain has come from animals, and its significance in the human brain is still uncertain. The introduction of brain scanning has allowed psychologists to study changes in the human brain in response to the environment, however, and some surprising results have emerged. A popular area of study has been the effects of learning on brain structure and function. We know that memories can last for a lifetime and so they must be encoded in brain structure, although it has always been assumed that this would involve microscopic changes in synapses rather than the

Neural plasticity – the ability of the nervous system, especially the brain, to adapt to the environment. Plasticity is most obvious in the infant brain, which can adapt to brain damage and to enriched environments by growing more neurons. Recently, spatial memory in humans has been shown to lead to growth in the hippocampus, another example of neural plasticity.

Neurogenesis – the growth of new neurons. Had been thought to end in humans when the brain matures at about 20 years of age, but recent research suggests neurogenesis is the basis for some forms of memory in adults.

production of new neurons. In real life, however, it can be difficult to find good examples of large numbers of people having to learn substantial amounts of similar material.

One unusual example is London taxi drivers. They have to do what is called 'the Knowledge'; this involves learning all the London streets and routes within six miles of Charing Cross station, and there are around 25,000 streets to be covered. It usually takes between three and four years to complete. If learning does involve neurogenesis then this immense task should certainly result in significant increases in numbers of neurons in particular parts of the brain.

Earlier studies (e.g. Maguire *et al.*, 2006) compared qualified taxi drivers with a control group and found that the taxi drivers had significantly larger amounts of grey matter in parts of their hippocampus. 'Grey matter' in the brain usually refers to neurons. This suggests that learning the Knowledge may have led to increases in the number of neurons in the hippocampus, a structure known to be involved in human memory (*see page 23*). It is possible, however, that the increased hippocampal size is due to other variables, such as natural differences between the two groups. A more powerful technique would be to study the hippocampus before and after learning the Knowledge, i.e. a longitudinal study.

Key study

Woollett and Maguire (2011)

Woollett and Maguire (2011) conducted a longitudinal study following 79 male trainee taxi drivers, along with 31 male controls. They all had MRI brain scans before training started (time T1) and then 3–4 years later after qualification (time T2). At T2 some participants failed to return for testing, but there were still three groups – trainees who qualified successfully (group Q, 39 participants), trainees who failed to qualify (group F, 20 participants), and controls (group C).

Figure 1.6

As well as the brain scans, all participants were given a battery of tests at T1. The groups did not differ on age, handedness, education or IQ, which are all variables that might have affected hippocampal volume. In addition, there were no significant differences on a range of memory tests. Crucially, there were no differences in hippocampal grey matter volume before training began.

The same comparisons at T2 showed that some fascinating differences had emerged. Group Q, the successful trainees, performed far better than the other two groups on memory tests of London landmarks and streets, but worse on general tests of spatial

Key study

memory. Groups F and C did not differ significantly on any of these tests. Crucially, MRI scans at T2 showed that hippocampal grey matter volume had significantly increased between T1 and T2 in the successful trainees. There were no differences in hippocampal volume between T1 and T2 in the other two groups.

Woollett and Maguire concluded that the increase in hippocampal grey matter was linked to the successful learning of the Knowledge, as this was the only major difference between the successful trainees and those who had failed to qualify. This demonstrates that environmental influences, such as learning experiences, can have a direct effect on brain structures, increasing the amount of grey matter. The study confirms the importance of the hippocampus in memory formation.

This study used a longitudinal design that allowed brain changes over time to be correlated with changes in learning over time. Cause and effect cannot be definitely established as this was not an experiment, but the control of many other relevant variables strengthens the conclusion.

MRI scans do not have the resolution (*see page 25*) to identify increases in numbers of neurons, but only increases in grey matter. These may be due to other changes, e.g. increased numbers of synapses. More precise work using non-human animals, however, has shown that successful learning leads to an increase in the number of hippocampal neurons (neurogenesis), and this is the likeliest explanation for the findings of this study.

Other findings are less easy to explain. In group Q, successful learning of the Knowledge appeared to be linked with poorer performance on other tests of spatial ability, as though the successful but highly specific learning was at the cost of other areas of memory.

Maternal diet and childhood obesity

There is a developing crisis of obesity in affluent Western societies. Obesity increases the probability of developing a range of serious illnesses, such as diabetes and heart disease, and these illnesses are placing an increasing burden on NHS resources. Campaigns to improve healthy eating and increase daily exercise have had limited success. Treatments for obesity range from cognitive behavioural therapy to various drugs, and finally surgery to reduce stomach size. Surgery is the most effective treatment for extreme obesity, but it is expensive and carries a significant risk of side effects.

To develop better and cheaper therapies for obesity it is necessary to understand its causes. These are complex, involving the biological control systems that underlie feeding and weight regulation, and environmental factors such as early dietary experience and parental diets. Recent studies have investigated the role of maternal diet during pregnancy, and reveal a fascinating interaction between the environment and the child's genetic make-up.

Key study

Godfrey *et al.* (2011)

Godfrey *et al.* (2011) identified five genes that had been implicated in previous research in the control of fatty tissue in the body. Although genes are inherited intact, the extent to which they express themselves (how active they are in the body) can be affected by a number of processes. One of these processes is **methylation**. And it was this process that Godfrey *et al.* studied.

They used umbilical cord tissue from newborn babies to measure the methylation status of the five candidate genes in each baby. They also recorded the mother's diet during pregnancy, and the child's level of fatty tissue at age nine. The results indicated a significant correlation between the degree of methylation of one particular gene (known as the RXRA gene) and the level of body fatty tissue at age nine. In addition, there was

Key study

a clear and significant correlation between the methylation of RXRA and the amount of carbohydrate in the mother's diet during pregnancy; lower levels of dietary carbohydrate were associated with higher levels of RXRA methylation, and with higher levels of fatty tissue at age nine.

Godfrey *et al.* concluded that a child's fat level at age nine (which is an index of vulnerability to obesity) is powerfully affected by environmental factors operating prenatally. One main factor is the mother's carbohydrate intake during pregnancy. This directly affects the methylation status and activity of the gene RXRA, which in turn biases the body's fat metabolism in the direction of storing more fat.

The argument behind the chain of events they propose is that a poor maternal diet, low in carbohydrate, signals to the developing baby through modification of the gene RXRA, that food is scarce and needs to be stored efficiently. After birth the baby's RXRA gene activity therefore promotes the excessive storage of fats (as an energy reserve) and this can lead to obesity in later years.

Maternal diet is an environmental factor influencing the child's later feeding behaviour and vulnerability to obesity. Now that evidence suggests it operates through modifying the activity of genes in the baby, we have an interaction between genes and environment. In this scenario, obesity in a child of nine or ten is neither purely environmental nor genetic, but an interaction between the two. Note also that it is not 'genetic' in the sense of an inherited tendency; it is the effect of the mother's diet on the baby's gene **expression** that is critical, not simply the genes that the baby inherited from its parents.

Although this was a fairly large study, with over 200 children involved, it only looked at five candidate genes and found effects of only one of these. We know that many more genes are involved in body fat and carbohydrate metabolism. This study is a snapshot only, as the control of fat storage will involve many other genes working together.

Findings were correlations as this was not an experiment, so we cannot be sure of cause and effect. Both maternal diet and RXRA methylation may be affected by a third common factor. The findings support previous animal studies on maternal diet and body weight of offspring, and the importance of gene methylation.

Maternal diet can be a factor in childhood and adult obesity. There are many other factors contributing to the current obesity epidemic, however, and even complex environment–gene interactions will only be one part of a far bigger picture.

Practical applications

The Godfrey *et al.* (2011) study shows that maternal diet can be critical in weight regulation in offspring. How could expectant mothers be encouraged to have an adequate diet?

The interaction of cognition and physiology

LEARNING OUTCOME
- Examine one interaction between cognition and physiology in terms of behaviour. Evaluate two relevant studies.

Anterograde amnesia: the case of Henry Molaison (HM)

Few case studies have made such an impact on psychology as that of the patient known as HM. Henry Molaison (HM) died in 2008 after being studied for over 50 years by psychologists, providing dramatic insights into the organization of memory in the brain.

Born in 1926, HM developed temporal lobe epilepsy when he was about ten (possibly due to a cycling accident a few years earlier). Although many forms of epilepsy can be controlled effectively with drugs, even today some cases are resistant to therapy with these anticonvulsants. In such cases, where the epilepsy is severe and disabling, surgery can be considered, as we saw in the development of the 'splitbrain' operation (*see page 7*). If the source of the epileptic discharges (or 'focus') is clearly identifiable then an alternative to dividing the corpus callosum (the split brain) is to remove the area of the brain containing the focus. The focus for epileptic attacks is often in the temporal lobe of the brain, an area that contains the amygdala and large parts of the hippocampus. In the 1950s an operation was devised – the temporal lobectomy – to remove the part of the temporal lobe containing the epileptic focus and so help to reduce the frequency and severity of epileptic attacks.

This operation proved to be effective in many cases of epilepsy and was therefore considered as a therapy for HM. The vast majority of temporal lobe epileptics have a focus in only one hemisphere (**unilateral**). One key difference between HM and other temporal lobe epileptics, however, was that HM turned out to have a focus in each temporal lobe, i.e. in each hemisphere of the brain (**bilateral**). But as the unilateral operation was known to be beneficial to sufferers and seemed to have few side effects, in 1953 neurosurgeon William Scoville performed a **bilateral** temporal lobectomy on HM, removing the amygdala and large parts of the hippocampus on both sides of the brain.

The operation had the desired effect of significantly reducing the severity and frequency of HM's epileptic attacks, but also had totally unexpected and catastrophic side effects. From the time of the operation onwards, HM had almost complete anterograde amnesia; that is, he was unable to form new memories after the operation. Medical staff looking after him for weeks and months were greeted each day as if they were strangers. HM was unable to register any events in his long-term memory; this was demonstrated systematically by psychologist Brenda Milner when she began testing HM in the late 1950s. When given a list of six words to remember, HM could hold them in memory as long as he could rehearse them by continuously repeating them. The words were forgotten the moment he was distracted, and in fact he could not even remember having had the words presented in the first place.

In terms of models of memory it was rapidly established that HM had a relatively normal short-term or working memory. However his long-term memory for new material was severely impaired. In fact HM, as a case study, provided substantial support for Atkinson and Shiffrin's multistore model of memory (1968), with its separate short- and long-term memory stores.

Link to the cognitive level of analysis

HM provided substantial support for the multistore model of memory, and the existence of different types of memory. This shows how the biological level and the cognitive level of analysis constantly overlap and interact.

Despite his severe and almost complete anterograde amnesia, HM did retain some memory functions. He had patchy retrograde amnesia (amnesia for past events) for some years before the operation, but his memory for distant events was largely intact. He could recognize his family and recall family events from before the operation, and performed well on recognizing public events and celebrities from his earlier years.

Additionally HM could learn new material of a particular type. Think of a triangle with a narrow border around its edge. You have to draw around the triangle within this

---

Temporal lobectomy – operation used for temporal lobe epilepsy where the tip of the lobe is surgically removed. This tip includes the amygdala and part of the hippocampus. The patient HM had a bilateral temporal lobectomy that led to profound anterograde amnesia.

Anterograde amnesia – the inability to learn new facts and information, contrasted with retrograde amnesia, the inability to recall previously learnt material. Classic cases have been caused by temporal lobe damage and by Korsakoff's syndrome (chronic alcoholism).

Multistore model of memory – Atkinson and Shiffrin produced this early model of the stages of memory formation, storage and retrieval. It served to stimulate much research, and was supported in part by some classic case studies, such as HM. It has now been superseded by more complex models that include, for instance, different types of long-term memory.

border. Easy enough, you might think. Now try doing it with your non-preferred hand while looking in a mirror. This motor task is difficult at first but you rapidly improve with practice. HM also improved with practice, i.e. he learnt this task using his long-term memory. But note that each day that he practised the task he denied ever having seen the test before!

This type of motor learning depends on procedural memory – memory for simple motor tasks that does not require conscious recollection. Another example is riding a bicycle; once you have learnt, you do not need to think about it consciously every time you get on the bike. We can compare this with learning the faces and names of strangers, or recalling events from our past. Both the learning and recollection require conscious awareness rather than being largely automatic, as in motor learning. This distinction is shown clearly by HM; he could learn the simple task automatically and successfully, but had no memory for the actual learning experience.

This supports a popular distinction in memory research between episodic and procedural memory. Episodic memory refers to personal events or episodes in our own lives and requires conscious awareness for learning and recall. It is sometimes referred to as autobiographical memory. Procedural memory refers to simple motor learning (and some other simple forms of learning such as classical conditioning) that is automatic and does not require conscious awareness. Patients with anterograde amnesia usually show a pattern of severely impaired episodic memory but intact procedural memory.

A third form of memory is semantic memory. This is our memory for language and for facts about the world. For instance, knowing and understanding the meanings of words and how to use language, and general knowledge such as the fact that Rome is the capital of Italy. Most amnesic patients have preserved semantic memory. Their language and communication skills are intact, and they usually retain their store of general knowledge. But there can be exceptions. The severely amnesic patient Clive Wearing (*see page 23*) lost most of his episodic memory, but retained his procedural memories such as for playing the piano and conducting choirs. He also had some problems with semantic memory, however, failing to recognize pictures of famous people and places, such as the Queen or St Mark's Square in Venice.

The case study of HM came at a crucial time for cognitive and biological psychology. In the 1950s psychology was emerging from years of domination by Skinner's behaviourist approach, and the detailed study of cognitive processes such as memory and attention was beginning. The fact that HM was happy to be tested over and over again for many years (as he did not recall having been tested before…) led to a detailed analysis of his memory problems. In turn these findings helped in the development of major models of the human memory system.

- HM had a relatively normal short-term or working memory, but could not store new material in his long-term memory. This supports a distinction or **dissociation** between short-term and long-term memory stores, as proposed in Atkinson and Shiffrin's (1968) multistore model of memory.
- HM had mild retrograde amnesia for events from before his operation but could recall many early events accurately, especially from his early years. This shows that he could successfully **retrieve** information from long-term store.
- Overall it seems that HM had problems transferring material from short-term into long-term store.
- We can therefore conclude that the parts of the brain damaged in HM's operation are involved in the initial transfer of new material from short-term into long-term memory. They are not the permanent long-term memory store, however, as HM did not have severe retrograde amnesia; his long-term memories were largely intact.

Episodic memory – a category of long-term memory, episodic memory is memory for events in our own lives. These require conscious recollection, and are often dramatically affected in cases of retrograde amnesia.

Procedural memory – category of long-term memory that involves sensory-motor skills such as word-processing, riding a bike, and playing the piano. These skills are not affected even by brain damage that produces severe retrograde amnesia for episodic memories.

Semantic memory – category of long-term memory that deals with facts and information about the world, e.g. the capital of Turkey or the name of the Prime Minister. In general this is less affected by brain damage than episodic memory, although some cases of amnesia clearly show a semantic memory deficit.

■ The bilateral temporal lobectomy removed the amygdala and large parts of the hippocampus on both sides of the brain. Research on other amnesic patients and on non-human animals suggests strongly that it was the damage to the hippocampus that was responsible for the amnesic effects.

Evaluation of HM's contribution to psychology

■ Despite our detailed knowledge of the brain damage that led to HM's dramatic memory loss, there is a limit to how far we can rely on one patient. There will be individual differences in brain organization and in reactions to brain damage. Observations of HM have had to be backed up by research studies on hippocampal function in other brain damaged humans and non-human animals.

■ Findings from HM are still used to support or contradict models of memory. It is worth noting, however, that although he demonstrated a clear dissociation between short-term and long-term stores, there was not such a clear distinction between episodic and semantic memories. Remember that it is a popular view that anterograde amnesia affects episodic memory but leaves semantic memory (memory for language and for facts about the world) intact. But HM found it almost impossible to learn the meanings of new words that came into vogue after his operation, indicating a semantic memory deficit (Parkin, 1996). A cautious conclusion would that episodic and semantic memory are not completely distinct but interact in complex ways.

■ HM was unique in showing an amnesic syndrome that was relatively clear cut and remained stable over 50 years of rigorous testing. He provided data for literally hundreds of research papers, making a major contribution to our knowledge of memory systems and the brain. The tragic outcome of his operation to relieve his epilepsy was a gift to psychology, but we must remember that it totally altered his life. Researchers regularly commented on his calm and placid nature and how happy he was to be tested, but from the day of the operation onwards his normal life ended, and he was left, literally, living in the past, aware only of his preoperative memories.

Amnesia: the case of Clive Wearing

Brain damage can occur in many forms. In the case of HM it was the tragic consequence of a surgical intervention aimed to relieve his epilepsy. Strokes are the most common form of brain damage, where the blood supply to parts of the brain is interrupted.

Infections of the brain are a less common cause. An infection that affects the outer linings of the brain is referred to as meningitis. When the infection involves brain structures, it is called encephalitis. One of the most dramatic examples of such damage caused by herpes encephalitis is the case of Clive Wearing (Campbell & Conway, 1995).

Clive Wearing was a gifted musician who developed a herpes virus infection of the brain. This family of viruses lives inside neurons and is usually harmless. Occasionally they become violently active and cause conditions such as cold sores and genital herpes. Less commonly, herpes viruses in the brain become active and lead to the widespread death of neurons. Incidentally, we do not know what causes such activation of the usually quiescent virus.

Wearing's herpes infection led to damage to the temporal lobes on both sides of the brain and to parts of the frontal lobe.

When he recovered from the initial effects of the infection Wearing was left with a massive and global amnesia (www.youtube.com/watch?v=WmzU47i2xgw). This was both anterograde and retrograde. Anterograde amnesia involves a failure to learn new material *after* the brain trauma (as in the case of HM). Retrograde amnesia involves a failure to retrieve memories from *before* the amnesic event. Most amnesic patients have one or the other or, as in the case of HM, a severe anterograde amnesia with a mild

Retrograde amnesia – the inability to recall previously learnt material, contrasted with anterograde amnesia, the inability to learn new facts and information.

retrograde amnesia. What was unusual in Wearing's case was that he was left with a profound anterograde amnesia and a profound retrograde amnesia.

Think for a moment what this means. There is no recall of previous events in one's life, and no ability to store new memories. Conscious existence is confined to a brief period (about 20 minutes in the case of Wearing), which is constantly being forgotten. The phrase used over and over by Wearing is that he is in a constant state of having just woken up – he remembers nothing from about 20 minutes earlier. This is completely disabling, as he is unable to connect with the past (friends, family, events in his life) or with the future. In fact, the most important contribution of this case is to emphasize how dependent we are on memory.

Besides the personal tragedy involved, there are a number of features of Clive Wearing's case that have implications for models of memory:

- He was a gifted musician, both as a conductor of choirs and as a keyboard player, especially the organ. These skills are still present. He remembers nothing about his life as a musician, but when confronted with a keyboard or a choir, he automatically demonstrates his high level musical skills. These are known as **procedural skills**, and recall that over-learnt procedural skills are usually spared in cases of amnesia (*see page 22*). Clive Wearing supports this conclusion. Procedural memories must be buried deep in the brain so that they are rarely affected by brain damage that is not fatal.
- Also spared are other basic cognitive functions, such as language and thought. One of the most striking of Clive's characteristics is his constant questioning of what has happened to him and why nothing is being done to help him. He understands that something is badly wrong, but of course can never remember the answers to these questions, meaning he constantly repeats them.
- Clive knows that he has children, but does not recognize them or remember having them. Bizarrely he does recognize his wife, Deborah, and is totally reliant on her support. In fact she is his only connection to the outside world. In terms of models of memory this is inexplicable. We can only assume that the close emotional bond developed through their life together means that his memories of her are stored independently of other long-term memories.
- Findings from memory research support the idea that retrograde amnesia usually affects episodic memory, leaving **semantic memories** (facts about the world) unaffected. In Clive's case this does not hold. When tested with pictures of famous people (e.g. the Queen) and places (e.g. Venice), he shows a clear amnesic deficit. This is probably due to the widespread brain damage caused by the herpes infection, but it does mean that we can generalize research findings only with caution. Retrograde amnesia can affect both episodic (memories of events from one's own life, which require conscious recollection) and semantic memory.

Evaluation of Clive Wearing's contribution to psychology

- Case studies have an honourable history within the biological level of analysis. Wernicke and Broca's work in the nineteenth century on patients with language problems is still used in the debate on models of language processing. HM, as discussed earlier, provided clear evidence in support of the influential multistore model of memory. Findings from case studies always have to be backed up by laboratory studies with neurotypical participants (those with no brain damage), however. In addition, there may often be other patients with similar brain damage, and findings can be compared.
- Clive Wearing is unique in surviving extensive brain damage but with the devastating consequences of global retrograde and anterograde amnesia. There are no similar cases with which to compare him. What he does demonstrate is the distributed nature of memories in the brain. It is clear that the radical nature of his memory problems is due

to the widespread nature of his brain damage. This involves both temporal lobes and the frontal lobes. Note that with HM damage was extensive, but confined to the temporal lobes on both sides of the brain. A simple comparison might suggest that Wearing's anterograde amnesia was also due to the temporal lobe damage. The retrograde problems might then be due to the additional damage to the frontal lobes. This is tentative, however – HM also had some retrograde amnesia without frontal lobe damage.

- Clive Wearing supports the preservation of complex over-learnt skills in cases of amnesia and the vulnerability of episodic memory to brain damage. However his problems with semantic memory are a problem for simple models of the amnesic syndrome. Finally, he is the best example we have of how we are absolutely dependent on memory for our sense of self and who we are in the world.

Brain imaging

LEARNING OUTCOME

- Discuss the use of brain imaging technologies in investigating the relationship between biological factors and behaviour.

It is no exaggeration to say that the introduction of brain scanning revolutionized biological psychology. Before the 1980s the biological approach relied heavily on research with non-human animals, predominantly the laboratory rat. Research with humans was largely restricted to case studies with brain damaged patients, such as HM (*see pages 20–3*). Then brain scanning arrived and it was possible to investigate the brains of living human participants. The current methods used are:

- **Computerized axial tomography** (CAT or CT scanner) – this was one of the first scanning techniques introduced. It produces a static 3-D picture of the brain using X-rays, and is most useful for identifying structural changes in the brain – these might include tumours or the extent of brain damage after a stroke or accidental injury. In neuroscience, the CT scan has now been largely replaced by PET and fMRI.

- **Positron emission tomography** (PET) – this is an 'invasive' procedure as it involves the injection of a radioactive substance, usually glucose. This travels to the brain in the bloodstream, where it is used as an energy source by neurons. The glucose emits radioactive particles that are picked up by sensors around the head; after computerization the pattern of radiation can be used to build up a picture of brain activity; this is the PET scan. The more active areas of the brain will use more glucose and this will show up on the scan. PET is a useful procedure as it addresses functional activity of the brain. It is time-consuming, and its spatial (level of detail) and temporal (rapidity of response) resolution are not as good as fMRI, however. It has some specialized uses – for instance, if a radioactive chemical that binds to synaptic receptors is used instead of glucose, it can produce a map of, for example, serotonin receptors in the brain.

- **Magnetic resonance imaging** (MRI) and **functional MRI** (fMRI) – these are highly complex techniques for building brain maps. They use a powerful magnetic field and radio waves to record vibrations from various atomic nuclei within neurons. In particular the signals from haemoglobin in the bloodstream can be recorded. Haemoglobin carries oxygen to the cells that need it, and the MRI technique can discriminate haemoglobin that has given up its oxygen to active neurons from haemoglobin that hasn't. This measure is critically dependent on the blood flow to the region under study, and is known as the blood oxygen-level response, or BOLD. MRI alone produces a static picture of brain activity, while fMRI can record the BOLD response over time, for instance in response to specific stimuli, such as faces. Areas specialized for processing faces will have more active neurons, which use more oxygen. This shows up in the BOLD response recorded by fMRI, giving a picture of the brain in action.

fMRI is now the dominant method used in brain scanning in the biological approach, and hundreds of studies are published every year. The participant lies in the scanner, and stimuli can be presented using small screens. By comparing patterns of brain activation to faces as opposed to pictures of buildings, for instance, we may identify areas specific to face processing. By comparing neutral faces to angry faces we may locate areas dealing with the processing of emotional expressions. fMRI has been used to map out brain regions involved in many behaviours and psychological processes, such as speech and language, emotional reactions to angry and fearful faces, remembering pleasant events, and empathy for others. For the first time it is possible to image the human brain in action.

Evaluation

- Neither PET, MRI nor fMRI directly measure the electrical activity of neurons in the brain. PET uses the rate of glucose uptake, and fMRI depends on blood flow and oxygen uptake as secondary markers of neuronal activity. They require significant changes in glucose uptake or blood flow, and will miss smaller changes that might still be important for brain activity. Additionally, they are slow: the temporal resolution of fMRI is better than that of PET, but still ranges from 2–10 seconds; remember that the brain can respond to stimuli in milliseconds (thousandths of a second), so fMRI can really only be used where longer responses are acceptable, e.g. in face recognition. Spatial resolution is also quite large. Again fMRI is best, but even this technique can only record around 1 mm cubes (which would contain tens of thousands of neurons) from relatively large blocks of brain tissue.
- There is no doubt that techniques will improve, but even so one major problem will remain. As currently used, scanning assumes that functions can be localized to small areas or localized circuits in the brain. Papers have been published claiming to have localized the sites of wisdom, romantic love, perception of beauty, and even religious belief. These are complex behaviours that will involve more than specific areas or even localized circuits, but will use widespread networks involving most of the brain. The challenge for brain scanning is to develop techniques that will match the complexity of the brain.

SECTION SUMMARY

- Sperry's study was highly influential in showing that different functions were carried out in different areas of the brain. Subsequent research has largely supported his findings.
- Neurotransmitters are vital to human behaviour and their importance can be shown in examining the use of drugs to treat disorders such as Parkinson's and schizophrenia.
- Hormones such as oxytocin and testosterone play an important role in human physiology and behaviour.
- The environment can influence physiology, maternal environment can affect foetal development and the environment can even cause the brain to change in adulthood.
- Biological psychology cannot be studied in isolation and its interaction with cognitive processes is crucial in understanding human behaviour.
- The development of new technologies that allow researchers to study the brain in more detail with living participants has helped to advance understanding of how physiology influences behaviour.

Genetics and behaviour

LEARNING OUTCOME
■ With reference to relevant research studies, to what extent does genetic inheritance influence behaviour?

This is an extremely broad question without a simple answer. Many behaviours involve genetic factors, but the extent of genetic influence is extremely variable across different behaviours. To illustrate this we can use some of the many MZ/DZ twin studies that have been done in psychology.

Monozygotic (MZ) twins are also known as identical twins. They have the same genetic make-up; this is why they look so similar, as facial features are heavily determined by genetics rather than the environment. Dizygotic twins come from two eggs fertilized by different sperm at the same time, they are born at the same time, and are also known as non-identical or fraternal twins. They are as genetically similar as brothers or sisters born at different times, so DZ twins can be different genders and/or look very different.

Figure 1.7   Identical (or MZ twins) are important in studying the role of genetics in human behaviour.

If a characteristic is determined entirely by genetic inheritance, then MZ twins should both show it to the same degree. MZ twins also share very similar environments, however, so the fact they demonstrate the same characteristic might be due to this environmental similarity rather than to their identical genetic make-ups. This is why studies also use DZ twins. In theory these also have very similar environments as they are born at the same time, but they do not have identical genetic make-ups. So if MZ twins are more similar for a given characteristic than DZ twins, so the argument goes, then it is because of this key difference – that MZ twins are genetically identical.

'Concordance' refers to the degree of similarity between twins. High concordance means that if one twin has a characteristic, then the other is likely to have it. If MZ twins have higher concordance for, e.g. schizophrenia, than DZ twins, this is used as evidence for the role of a genetic factor in schizophrenia. If schizophrenia was entirely environmentally caused, then concordance rates for MZ and DZ twins should be the same as both kinds of twins share similar environments.

Key study

Holland *et al.* (1984)

Holland *et al.* (1984) were interested in the causes of the eating disorder anorexia nervosa (AN). They identified a series of twin pairs (at that stage they did not know whether they were MZ or DZ) in which one twin had AN. They then determined whether the twins were MZ or DZ, usually by blood group analysis but in a few cases where this was not possible, by a physical resemblance questionnaire.

Then they put the results together. Nine out of 16 (55 per cent) female MZ twin pairs were concordant for AN, while only 1 out of 14 female DZ twin pairs was concordant for AN (7 per cent). The difference in concordance rates was quite striking, and used as strong evidence for a genetic basis to anorexia nervosa.

There are problems with the study, however. The number of twins was quite small (a total of 30), and the classification into MZ and DZ was done by blood group analysis or physical resemblance. These are not completely reliable, and nowadays this would be done by direct genetic analysis. In addition, the concordance rate for MZ twins is only 55 per cent – if AN was entirely determined by genetics, a concordance rate of 100 per cent would be expected, as MZ twins are genetically identical. So even with a genetic factor involved in anorexia nervosa, there are still significant non-genetic environmental influences to be identified.

■ Critical thinking

Although there may be a genetic influence in anorexia nervosa, the increase in the number of cases of eating disorders over the last 20 years suggests that non-genetic factors must also be involved. Consider what some of these factors might be; think about the cognitive and sociocultural levels of analysis.

Another popular area for studying genetic influences on behaviour is intelligence, or more specifically the 'intelligence quotient' or IQ; this refers to scores on intelligence tests. This is an issue that has political and social implications; if IQ is predominantly genetic then efforts to improve the early learning environment, e.g. through the provision of quality nursery care, would be pointless. However, if IQ can also be influenced by environmental factors, then such interventions could have critical effects on the child's IQ. But such interventions are expensive and require political agreement.

A genetic basis for IQ has also been used to explain differences in IQ between ethnic groups. This is an extremely controversial area, as it says that some groups may be genetically less intelligent than others; in addition, if IQ is genetic, there is no point in trying to raise the IQ of such groups by enriched learning programmes. But what is the evidence?

Twin studies have been fundamental to research on IQ. One of the earliest systematic studies was by the British psychologist Cyril Burt, in the 1940s and 50s. He did not use DZ twins as a control, but instead looked at MZ twins reared apart, i.e. in different environments. If their IQs were very different this would suggest environmental influences on IQ; if they were very similar it would support the genetic argument. Burt reported a concordance rate of 0.771 in twins reared apart, a very high value that suggested that IQ was inherited.

However Burt's work was questioned in the 1960s and 70s. His results over the years were suspiciously similar; people he claimed to work with could not be found; he managed to find more twins reared apart (these are not common) than others could believe. It was claimed that his particular views on the inheritance of IQ had biased his findings and led him to fabricate results. His reputation was destroyed.

Although later researchers found evidence that his co-workers did exist, the strongest argument for Burt not making up his results comes from the numerous later twin studies on IQ. Ridley (1999) summarized well over 100 of these; overall the concordance rate for MZ twins reared together was 0.86, for MZ twins reared apart it was 0.76, and for DZ twins reared together it was 0.55. The difference between MZ and DZ twins reared together (0.86 vs 0.55) is strong evidence for a genetic factor influencing IQ scores. The difference between MZ twins reared together and apart (0.86 vs 0.76) is slight evidence for environmental influences on IQ. Note that the 0.76 concordance rate for twins reared apart is close to Burt's earlier results, suggesting that his results may well have been genuine.

Many behaviours, including most psychological disorders, have been studied using the twin methodology. This is often combined with family studies that look at inheritance across generations. But in no case is the genetic influence estimated at 100 per cent. The highest MZ twin concordances are for IQ (*see above*) and conditions such as bipolar disorder (which has a concordance of around 0.7). Usually the genetic influence on behaviours comes out between 0 and 40 per cent, i.e. leaving plenty of room for non-genetic environmental factors.

It can be misleading to think of genetic and environmental factors as independent. It is clear that they interact in complex ways, and in fact one of the most popular models used is this area is 'stress-diathesis'. This model suggests that in many cases a genetically inherited vulnerability needs an environmental trigger – often some form of life stress – for it to be expressed. An example would be depression. Twin studies suggest a moderate genetic influence on depression, but it is also obvious that depression is often a natural reaction to life events such as bereavement, redundancy or serious illness. The stress-diathesis model would say that a genetic predisposition to depression has been triggered by the life event, and the depression will be more severe in people who are more genetically vulnerable.

So it is a mistake to see genetics and the environment as independent factors; they need each other. The Godfrey *et al.* (2011) study on maternal diet and obesity discussed earlier in this chapter (*see pages 19–20*) is an example of how subtle and complex the interactions between the environment and our genes can be.

Evolutionary explanations

Examine one evolutionary explanation of behaviour.

The human line split from other primates about six million years ago. Fossil evidence suggests that by two million years ago homo erectus, almost certainly one of our direct ancestors, was surviving as a hunter-gatherer in many parts of the world. Evolutionary explanations of modern human behaviour look back to this hunter-gatherer time, known as the 'environment of evolutionary adaptation' (EEA). The argument is that the characteristics that helped homo erectus survive then would have become part of our genetic make-up, in which case they can be used to explain some aspects of modern behaviour.

Evolutionary psychologists are particularly interested in basic human behaviours, such as courtship, mate selection, reproduction and child-rearing. They argue that these reflect the demands of the EEA and can be explained through the theory of evolution. Charles Darwin's original theory (1859) proposed that individual variation led to some animals being better adapted to the environment. They would be more likely to survive and reproduce, and their adaptive characteristics would therefore be passed on down the generations. Darwin focused on survival of the individual animal, but Richard Dawkins (1976) later proposed the selfish gene model, and this is now widely accepted. The difference is that for Dawkins the main drive for animals is survival of their genes rather than of any individual animal; animals share their genes with related family members, so it is in their interest to protect living relatives and reproduce so as to spread their genes as widely as possible.

However Trivers (1972) pointed out that males and females may actually have very different aims because they have very different costs associated with reproduction. His parental investment theory is based on the fact that women produce a limited

Figure 1.8   How much of our behaviour can be attributed to our ancient ancestors?

number of eggs in their lifetime, have to carry the baby through pregnancy and then care for it for a minimum of ten or more years after birth. Males can produce a virtually unlimited amount of sperm in their lifetime and need have no involvement in pregnancy or childcare. In terms of ensuring the survival of their genes, women should find healthy partners who can provide resources and support during pregnancy and child-rearing, as well as healthy young; on other hand the most effective strategy for men to ensure survival of their genes is to mate with as many women as possible. They should also look for women who are reproductively fertile.

Psychologists have tried to test these assumptions. For instance, Buss (1989) in an exceptionally wide-ranging study, used questionnaires to assess mate preferences in over 10,000 participants from 37 different cultures. He found a remarkable consistency. Across virtually all cultures, women rated good financial prospects and ambition in a prospective mate more highly than did men. Again across virtually all cultures, men rated good looks in mates as more important than did women, and also expressed a preference for mates on average 2.66 years younger than they were.

Buss interpreted these findings as supporting key assumptions of the parental investment model. Women look for financial resources in prospective mates to provide support during child-bearing and child-rearing. Men look for good looks and younger women as indicators of fertility.

Evaluation

- The cross-cultural consistency of Buss's findings is impressive. It implies that attitudes of men and women to prospective mates are determined more by inherited tendencies than by cultural factors. The whole approach ignores some significant cultural changes, however.
- The most important one is contraception. Pregnancy is no longer a likely consequence of sexual activity, but is far more under the control of couples. Many couples decide not to have children and stay together for a variety of other reasons. In addition, there have been changes in gender roles, especially in technologically advanced societies. Women play a far larger part in the workplace and many are effectively financially independent. Men are increasingly involved in childcare and the pattern of having many children with many different partners is rare.
- There would be few cross-cultural variations in this area if evolutionary pressures were fundamental to relationships. There are significant cultural differences in relationships, however. In some societies, arranged marriages are the norm, while in others marriage for 'love' is traditional. Similarly, there are great differences in attitudes to divorce and having several partners in a lifetime. This indicates that cultural values have major effects on relationships and that relationships cannot be reduced completely to basic evolutionary drives.

Link to the sociocultural level of analysis

To understand cultural variations in relationships we have to use the sociocultural level of analysis. Note that the sociocultural and biological levels are not always completely separate. Parents seeking arranged marriages for their sons and daughters may still look for resources in potential sons-in-law and for reproductive potential in potential daughters-in-law.

That is not to say that the evolutionary drive is irrelevant. A basic aim of long-term heterosexual relationships, however arranged, is to have children and ensure the continuity of one's genes. In 1989 Clark and Hatfield reported a university campus-based study. Attractive collaborators of both sexes approached students of the opposite sex and asked them three questions: *'Would you go on a date with me?'*; *'Would you come back to my flat?'*; *'Would you go to bed with me?'* Roughly 50 per cent of responders, male or female, answered 'yes' to the first question, but while no female responders answered 'yes' to the second or third questions, around 70 per cent of male students were happy to accept the invitation either to go to the woman's apartment or to sleep with her.

Although it can be argued that this is in line with evolutionary theory (males want to spread their genes, females must be more careful in choosing suitable mates), this study illustrates the problems of working in this area. It is almost certain that sex-role stereotypes would play a role in this type of study. It is still far more acceptable for men to 'sleep around' than for women to do so. So in answering the questions in the Clark and Hatfield study, this 'social desirability' bias would inhibit some women from expressing their real attitudes. An additional point emphasized by Clark and Hatfield is that it is far more dangerous for a woman to be alone with a strange man than vice versa, and this also would complicate the findings.

Theory of knowledge

Can the biological perspective alone ever truly inform about the human condition? Any explanation that relies solely on genes, hormones, evolutionary factors etc. can be accused of neglecting other important considerations, such as cognitive, emotional and sociocultural ones. Perhaps a better approach would be one that uses a multitude of different approaches to explain human experience.

Ethical considerations

LEARNING OUTCOME
▪ Discuss ethical considerations in research into genetic influences on behaviour.

As you might guess from the range of studies outlined in the previous sections, there are many ethical issues in genetic research. If studies identify particular genetic profiles that are more vulnerable, for instance to depression or schizophrenia, then it is essential to provide debriefing, accurate clinical advice and professional counselling for the individual concerned.

More traditional methods, such as MZ/DZ twin studies, have similar concerns. If an MZ twin is diagnosed with schizophrenia, bipolar disorder or an eating disorder, for instance, then it is essential that the unaffected twin is given full information on the genetic factors that might underlie these disorders.

The evolutionary approach might seem less ethically complex. It does involve important issues, however. At a social/cultural level it has been used, for instance, to explain, if not justify, male aggression and rape. At the individual level it can be used to justify mate retention strategies (typically where the male uses a variety of techniques, from checking and surveillance to physical violence, to retain their sexual rights over their partner). Note that the problem here is not the approach itself but how we choose to use it.

Studies within evolutionary psychology that investigate sexual and reproductive behaviour must use intrusive interviews and/or questionnaires. So informed consent and full debriefing become essential aspects of the methodology.

SECTION SUMMARY
▪ Genetic inheritance is an important influence on behaviour, but it should not be studied in isolation. Both genetic and environmental factors, and their interaction, need to be considered.
▪ Despite the huge changes in the way we live over thousands of years, evolutionary influences can still be seen in our behaviour, for example, in mate preference.
▪ Genetic research in particular has many ethical issues attached to it.

Cognitive level of analysis

Introduction

The term **cognitive psychology** was first used by Ulric Neisser (1967) to refer to the mental processes with which sensory inputs are dealt within the mind. Cognitive psychology therefore involves the study of mental structures and processes existing in the mind; although as 'mind' is an ambiguous term and difficult to define, cognitive psychologists refer instead to mental processes in terms of **information processing**.

A simple way to understand this is to compare the workings of the mind to that of a computer. Data enters a computer via an input, such as a keyboard, while data enters a human in the form of sensory inputs through specialized sensory organs. In both computers and humans, data is converted to electrical impulses and transported along either circuitry or nerve fibres. In a computer data travels to a central processing unit (CPU) for analysis, a function performed in humans by the brain. After information is processed in this way, a response is initiated, for example a print-out in a computer and behaviour in a human. Information processing in a computer is dependent on which analytical programs the computer is running, while in humans information processing occurs through perception, language, memory, decision-making, problem-solving, attention, etc. – in a sense the programs that our minds are running.

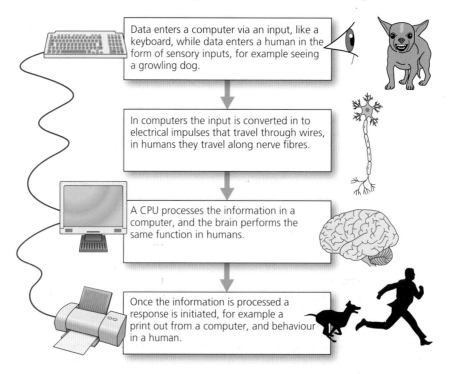

Data enters a computer via an input, like a keyboard, while data enters a human in the form of sensory inputs, for example seeing a growling dog.

In computers the input is converted in to electrical impulses that travel through wires, in humans they travel along nerve fibres.

A CPU processes the information in a computer, and the brain performs the same function in humans.

Once the information is processed a response is initiated, for example a print out from a computer, and behaviour in a human.

Figure 2.1

Until the 1950s, the dominant force within psychology was **behaviourism**, where only observable behaviour was studied; behaviourism seeing no place in the scientific study of psychology for invisible mental processes. Behaviourism replaced the earlier approach of **introspection**, with its emphasis on observing and analysing mental processes. The problem with introspection was that it wasn't possible to directly observe other people's mental processes and one's own mental processes cannot be generalized to others; what is true of how one person's mind works may not be true of how others' minds work.

Behaviourism, especially as applied to humans, had its problems too, in that it could not reveal motivating forces behind behaviour, nor how behaviour was goal-directed. Only by reference to the hidden workings of the mind, the ways in which humans process sensory information, could these shortcomings be addressed, with cognitive psychology presenting an opportunity to do just that, especially as interest in mental processes had been fostered by Jean Piaget with his research into cognitive development in children.

The earlier comparison of a computer with a human mind is fitting, as the development of computer technology went hand-in-hand with that of cognitive psychology. Although computers can be traced back to Charles Babbage's difference engine of 1822, it wasn't until after World War II that computer science really took off, and it wasn't long before psychologists were borrowing from computer science to better understand the mind by perceiving it as an information processing device. In doing so psychology was returning to the earlier tradition of introspection, albeit in a more objective and scientific way. More recent developments within cognitive neuroscience, where the biological basis to cognitive processes is studied, have made it possible to do this in an even more scientifically rigorous manner, especially through scanning, like using magnetic resonance imaging (MRI), which permits the physical workings of mental processes to be directly observed and scrutinized.

Although cognitive psychology exists as a separate psychological discipline in its own right, with many psychologists referring to themselves purely as cognitive psychologists, it also overlaps with other disciplines including computer science, linguistics and artificial intelligence. Indeed, the idea that mental processes can only be understood by reference to biological and sociocultural influences is firmly entrenched within cognitive psychology. Cognitive psychology has made, and continues to make, huge contributions to a fuller understanding of the mind.

Link to the biological level of analysis

The use of biological means of investigation such as cognitive neuroscience techniques, e.g. brain scanning, has allowed cognitive processes to be studied in a more objective, scientific manner.

Practical applications

Cognitive psychology has permitted a greater understanding of how the mind works and develops, leading to important practical applications in education, the treatment of mental disorders, robotics, etc.

Principles that define the cognitive level of analysis

LEARNING OUTCOME
■ Outline principles that define the cognitive level of analysis.

Mental representations – theoretical internal structures of cognitive processes.

The dominating principle behind cognitive psychology is that humans have mental representations of their world and that these mental representations differ between individuals due to different people having different knowledge and experiences of the world, resulting in different world views.

While behaviourists see behaviour in terms of mechanistic, unthinking stimuli and responses, cognitive psychologists focus on the cognitions and mental processing occurring between these stimuli and responses. Such processing is influenced by the mental representations that individuals have of their world, with **schemas** being important examples of such mental representations.

Schemas are cognitive frameworks that assist in the organization and interpretation of information. They are ever-changing and dependent on the experiences and knowledge, whether correct or not, that individuals have of the world. Schemas therefore are structured sets of beliefs about the world that allow information to be perceived in pre-set ways, i.e. in ways that fit an individual's world view. Thus humans never really experience objective reality, but instead experience their own subjective interpretation of information dependent on the mental representations (schemas) of the world that they hold. For example, Turnbull (1961) reported on Kenge, a BaMbuti pygmy who lived in dense rainforest with no experience of wide open spaces. When he was first taken to the vast savannah grasslands, Kenge perceived a herd of buffalo that were miles away, as insects that were but a short distance away. This occurred because Kenge's life experiences had given him little sense of distance perception. His schema was limiting his ability to see what was right in front of him.

mental representations = schemas!

The other main principle behind cognitive psychology, which separates it from introspection, is that mental processes can be scientifically investigated, with support from biological means of investigation, like cognitive neuroscience giving assistance to this process. This means that mental processes – which behaviourism had once deemed invisible and unavailable to scientific scrutiny – could be tested scientifically, through laboratory experiments, where hypotheses are formulated and subjected to rigorous testing.

Overall cognitive psychology is founded on the ideas that:

Principals

- Behaviour is underpinned by mental representations, such as schemas, that enable humans to perceive and understand the world differently due to their differing knowledge and experiences of the world.
- Cognition, the 'hidden' world of mental processing that behaviourism saw as incapable of study, can actually be investigated by accepted forms of scientific scrutiny, thus allowing a more sophisticated view of behaviour than that allowed by behaviourism.
- The cognitive level of analysis permits combination with the biological and sociocultural levels of analysis to give a deeper understanding of human psychology.

How the principles of the cognitive level of analysis are demonstrated in research

LEARNING OUTCOMES
- Explain how principles that define the cognitive level of analysis may be demonstrated in research (theories and/or studies).
- Discuss how and why particular research methods are used at the cognitive level of analysis.

Cognitive psychology uses many research methods that reflect the principles on which the cognitive level of analysis is based. For example, cognitive psychologists use laboratory experiments, as they are an essential part of the scientific method on which cognitive psychology is orientated. Balcetis and Dunning (2006) briefly flashed an ambiguous figure that could be a letter B or a number 13. Participants who were told that a letter would get them a drink, perceived the letter, while those told that a number would earn them the drink, perceived the number. This suggests that perceptual schema influences perception in an indirect fashion, with people seeing what they wish to see.

Although performed under controlled conditions that permit the establishment of causality (cause-and-effect relationships), this method can lack **ecological validity**, due to the artificial nature of laboratory-performed tasks, meaning results cannot be generalized to real-world settings outside the laboratory. Field experiments are similar in that an independent variable manipulated by a researcher is tested, but they take place in a real world setting, which increases ecological validity. For example, Godden and Baddeley (1975) found that divers who learnt word lists underwater recalled them better when underwater again rather than on dry land, which suggests that recall of memory occurs best in the conditions where information was first encoded (learnt). However, as conditions are less controlled than in the laboratory, causality cannot as easily be established.

This is also true of natural experiments, conducted in real world settings, but with naturally occurring independent variables, for example cross-cultural studies examining potential differences in perceptual abilities between people of different cultures, like Segall *et al.*'s (1963) finding that Africans living in open country, where vertical objects were rare and thus important features, were more susceptible to the vertical–horizontal illusion than those living in dense jungle, which suggests that physical environment shapes perception.

■ Critical thinking

Balcetis and Dunning (2006) and Godden and Baddeley (1975) both performed research into cognitive processes, but one using a laboratory experiment and the other a field experiment. What is the difference between these two techniques and what are their relative strengths and weaknesses?

Theory of knowledge

Laboratory experiments allow the methods employed by the natural sciences, like physics, to be directed at human behaviour. This permits the generation of quantitative data that can be submitted to statistical analysis to demonstrate evidence for cause-and-effect relationships, the accepted basis behind scientific truth.

Experiments, whether laboratory, field or natural, form a nomothetic approach, showing generalizations of what humans have in common, in other words the information processing abilities of the average person. Idiographic methods are used too, however, reflecting specific types of processing that different individuals possess, which make them unique. For example, the case study method, where one individual, or a small group of individuals, is studied in detail, like Delvenne *et al.* (2003) who studied a participant with brain damage to find that problems in recognizing faces occurred due to an inability to process objects, like faces, as a whole. The problem is that due to participants' uniqueness it's difficult to generalize findings to everybody.

Neuroimaging – the production of images of the brain by non-invasive scanning methods.

Link to the biological level of analysis

As cognitive processes are located within the physical structures of the brain, **neuroimaging** techniques such as fMRI, PET and CAT scans, which show specific areas of brain activity during different types of information processing, are also used. For example, Hemond *et al.* (2007) used an fMRI scan to find that the fusiform gyrus brain area is activated more during face recognition than object recognition. This informs us about the biological basis to face and object recognition. The use of research activities like these demonstrates the flexibility of cognitive psychology to combine with other levels of analysis, like the biological and sociocultural.

Self-report methods of questionnaires and interviews are also used, as they allow participants to directly report on subjective experiences of mental representations. For example, Christianson and Hubinette (1993) interviewed witnesses to a bank robbery to find that increased arousal led to greater accuracy of memory recall. Although such data is useful, especially when complementing data drawn from more scientific methods, its validity is often dependent on how such self-reports are conducted, for example the degree of bias in data analysis.

Overall cognitive psychology uses several research methods, often in combination with each other, reflecting the ability of the discipline to draw on different sources of investigation and different levels of analysis, like the biological and sociocultural ones, to further the understanding of mental processes.

■ **Critical thinking**

Cognitive psychology uses a variety of research methods, both experimental and non-experimental. No one method is considered best, each having its particular strengths and weaknesses and being best applied in particular circumstances. You may even wish to consider how research methods can be combined to gain the best understanding of mental life.

Ethical considerations related to research studies at the cognitive level of analysis

LEARNING OUTCOME
■ Discuss ethical considerations related to research studies at the cognitive level of analysis.

Ethical considerations – the rules and moral principles that govern the conduct of researchers in investigations.

Cognitive psychologists, like all researchers, must review all **ethical considerations** of research in advance and design and conduct research in ways that meet the ethical guidelines laid down by psychological governing bodies, e.g. the British Psychological Society (BPS). All research methods are subject to similar ethical considerations, but certain ethical considerations are more important in different research settings.

The main consideration with laboratory experiments is informed consent, where participants are not deceived and are given full details of research in advance in order to make a considered decision as to whether they wish to take part. Participants should not be harmed in any way, for example being subjected to stress greater than in everyday life. Informed consent can be difficult to gain with field and natural experiments if participants are unaware of being studied. Such participants should be fully debriefed and offered a chance to withdraw their data.

A major ethical concern with case studies is that researchers may investigate individuals with unusual abilities or brain damage, therefore, aside from ensuring harm doesn't occur in the form of psychological stress, care should also be taken to protect the confidentiality and anonymity of participants.

With neuroimaging techniques, like brain scans, the main consideration is ensuring that participants aren't harmed, as scanning can make many nervous. Therefore participants need to be fully informed of procedures in advance, put at ease at all times and be fully aware of their right to withdraw at any time.

Finally, with self-report methods, ethical issues arise over the sensitivity of material being discussed, so protection from harm is paramount, with interviewers asking questions in a way that does not harm the dignity of those being interviewed, with confidentiality and anonymity again being emphasized. This applies to the questions posed in questionnaires, too.

With all research methods there should be no inducements offered to participate and participants should always be fully debriefed after research is concluded.

Theory of knowledge

Ethical considerations are important in psychological research, as there is a moral obligation to respect the dignity of participants and to protect their well-being. A lack of ethical practices could lead to people being reluctant to participate in research, meaning psychology would not advance its understanding of human behaviour.

SECTION SUMMARY
- Cognitive psychology studies the mental processes by which sensory inputs are dealt with within the mind.
- The dominating principle behind cognitive psychology is that humans have mental representations of their world and these differ between individuals.
- Cognitive psychologists use a combination of methods, both experimental and non-experimental, to further our understanding of mental life.

Cognitive processes

Schema theory

LEARNING OUTCOME
- Evaluate schema theory with reference to research studies.

Schema – a readiness to interpret sensory information in a pre-set manner.

A **schema** is a cognitive framework for structuring information about the physical world and the events and behaviour occurring within it. Knowledge therefore becomes stored within memory in an organized way so that future experiences become perceived in pre-set ways.

Key study

The War of the Ghosts (Bartlett, 1932)

The concept of schemas was devised by Bartlett, who saw them as organizations of past experiences and demonstrated their effect on memory. In his 1932 study, the 'War of the Ghosts,' Bartlett showed that memory isn't accurate as it is distorted by cultural schemas. The War of the Ghosts is a Navajo Indian folk story, which for people of other cultures is written in a culturally unfamiliar way. This distortion of memory occurs because cultural groups have different ways of perceiving and understanding the world and therefore see events in ways that reflects these pre-set cultural viewpoints. The War of the Ghosts concerns a group of Native Americans in a war canoe, but many of the events and references are unfamiliar and alien to people from other cultures. Bartlett assessed the accuracy of readers' memories in two ways:

- **Serial reproduction** – a participant reads the story then writes it down from memory and this version is read by another participant, who writes down what they recall. This version is then read and recalled by a third participant, and so on until six or seven participants have read and written a version of the story.
- **Repeated reproduction** – the same participant reads and writes down the story from memory six or seven times with time gaps of between 15 minutes to several years between readings.

Bartlett found both types of reproduction produced a progressively shorter and more coherent story in terms of a reader's cultural background.

> 'When the Sun rose, he fell down. And he gave a cry, and as he opened his mouth a black thing rushed from it.

> 'When the Sun again rose he suddenly felt faint, and when he would have risen he fell down, and a black thing rushed out of his mouth.

> 'He felt no pain until sunrise the next day, when, on trying to rise, a great black thing flew out of his mouth.

> 'He lived that night, and the next day, but at sunset his soul fled black from his mouth.

> 'He lived through the night and the following day, but at sunset his soul fled black from his mouth.

'He lived during the night and the next day, but died at sunset, and his soul passed out from his mouth.

'Before the boat got clear of the conflict the Indian died, and his spirit fled. Before he could be carried back to the boat, his spirit had left this world. His spirit left the world. ('Nonsense', said one of the others, 'you will not die.') But he did.'

Culturally unfamiliar content, like the inclusion of supernatural elements, was omitted early in reproduction and the story transformed into a simple tale of a fight and a death, bearing little resemblance to the original. Details became increasingly familiar and conventional, for example, references to seal hunting, an activity unfamiliar to non-Native cultures, were changed to references about fishing, a more culturally familiar activity. Sometimes even the order of events within the story changed to become more coherent.

Bartlett's study shows how information was perceived to reflect the organization of previous knowledge in the memory. This knowledge consisted of schemas reflecting the reader's cultural background, a process known as **rationalization**. Ultimately what is thought about something is influenced by what is already known, because events are interpreted in terms of what is thought should happen, based on previous knowledge and experiences. If information is incomplete then the blanks are filled in with information based on schemas. This leads to errors and distortions; indeed sometimes it's possible to perceive situations wrongly because they don't fit what is thought should be perceived.

A simple way to see how situations are perceived wrongly, as they don't fit what is expected, is to present the written statement 'Paris in the the spring' to participants and ask them to state what they can see. Many participants continually read 'Paris in the spring', even though this is wrong, because that's what they think they should see based on previous experiences of language.

Postman and Bruner (1947) illustrated this type of recall error. Participants saw a picture of a black man and a white man arguing, with the white man brandishing a knife. On recall many participants remembered the black man holding the knife, because the idea of black men being oriented to violence and carrying weapons was a cultural stereotype of the time that was reflected in people's schemas.

Figure 2.2 Many people will perceive this as 'Paris in the spring', as that's what they expect to see.

Figure 2.3 A black man and a white man arguing, with the white man brandishing a knife (Postman & Bruner, 1947) – on recall, participants remember the black man holding the knife.

It seems, therefore, that memories are **reconstructed** to fit personal beliefs about the world.

Synder and Uranowitz (1978) also demonstrated the influence of schemas on recall. Participants heard the story of Betty, which contained the information that Betty was a popular girl who had lots of dates, but no steady boyfriend. Participants asked to recall the story after being told that Betty got married, remembered that she was popular and had lots of dates; those told that Betty became a lesbian, recalled her never having a steady boyfriend, a fact not recalled by those told she got married. This illustrates how memories become selective due to whichever schemas are being used.

Schemas even occur as 'scripts', a phenomenon demonstrated by Schank and Abelson (1977) with their restaurant study. The researchers went beyond describing what schemas contain, to showing how schemas were organized and used to allow understanding of recurring social situations involving stereotyped behaviour, like visiting a restaurant. Knowledge of such events was stored as scripts describing sequences of events in a particular order, for example, arriving at the restaurant, hanging up your coat, being seated, ordering your food, etc. Recall and understanding of such social situations is therefore influenced by reference to stored cognitive scripts, as when participants compared written scripts about visiting a restaurant there was general agreement about events that had occurred.

Evaluation of schema theory

- Although Bartlett's 'War of the Ghosts' study supports the existence of schemas as a means by which information and experiences are structured cognitively, especially in relation to memory, it wasn't without criticism, as it was conducted in a non-standardized way, without controlled conditions.
- Replications, like Gauld and Stephenson (1967), however, used more controlled and standardized conditions to produce similar findings to Bartlett, especially in relation to the type of errors and distortions made in recall. This suggests that Bartlett's original findings are valid.
- One question that interested researchers, is where within the information processing procedure do schemas exert their influence? Most interest centred on encoding, which occurs early on in information processing, and retrieval, which occurs later on. Bartlett (1932) believed schemas were influential during retrieval, but Anderson and Pichert (1978) presented a story about two boys spending the day at one of their homes while absent without permission from school. At encoding, participants were given the schema of concentrating on the perspective of a burglar or a prospective house buyer. At recall participants remembered details that fitted their schema, for example those with the burglar's perspective recalled that the house contained valuable items and what these items were, but didn't recall that the house was musty with a leaky roof. Those with the house buyer's perspective did recall this, but not the list of valuable items. Participants then recalled the story from the other perspective, i.e. those presented with the schema of the burglar's perspective had to switch to the prospective house buyer's perspective and vice versa. Participants then recalled details that fitted their new schema, which they hadn't recalled originally. Participants had developed a richer representation of the details in the story than could be explained in terms of the

schema used during encoding; else they wouldn't have retained information relevant from another schematic perspective. 'Irrelevant' information must have been originally encoded for it to be recalled using a later different schema, even though participants claimed that they'd originally recalled everything they could. This suggests that schemas exert an influence at both encoding and retrieval.

- Schema theory has allowed psychologists to develop a unified theory of cognition that shows how all cognitive processes, e.g. thinking, memory, learning, attention, etc., work in conjunction with each other through the influence that schemas collectively exert on these processes. This therefore suggests that cognition is a holistic process consisting of cognitive sub-skills operating together.

- Schemas allow psychologists to comprehend how memory errors occur, but also how prejudices arise through the formation of schemas containing negative stereotypes of people. Such a comprehension is important in devising effective practical applications to reducing such socially harmful prejudices.

- Schemas are activated automatically and effortlessly and so are energy-efficient. They are also resistant to change, ensuring continuity in how information is processed and responded to, though sometimes errors and distortions can occur if events are completely new and unknown, or if inappropriate schemas are referred to.

- A flaw in schema theory is the lack of explanation as to how schemas are acquired and the process by which they work. Schemas are hypothetical ideas as to how the mind works, with no physical presence and so cannot be directly observed.

- Schema theory aids understanding of how the mind works and has withstood rigorous testing to provide an effective explanation of how human learning occurs. Schema theory demonstrates how knowledge is organized within a cognitive framework that influences expectations and interpretations of new events and also how new learning is influenced by previous knowledge.

Link to the biological level of analysis
Schemas can be seen in evolutionary terms, as having an adaptive survival value, as they allows situations/ events to be quickly understood and responded to appropriately.

■ Critical thinking

Gauld and Stephenson's (1967) study is considered superior to Bartlett's (1932) study, as it used more controlled and standardized conditions. But what is meant by controlled and standardized conditions and why does their use make this a superior study?

Models of perception

LEARNING OUTCOME
■ Evaluate two models or theories of one cognitive process, with reference to research studies.

Perception – the interpretation of sensory data.

Perception is a cognitive process concerning how sensory information is understood. This concerns how sensations are received, processed and experienced (as touches, tastes, smells, sights and sounds) as meaningful experiences and create a predictable world of objects, which can be moved about in and interacted with.

Gregory's top-down theory

Top-down (indirect) processing – perception that involves cognitive processing that goes beyond mere sensory input.

Gregory argued that perception is an unconscious, ongoing process of testing hypotheses; an active search for the best interpretation of sensory data based on previous experience. The search is indirect, going beyond data provided by sensory receptors to involve processing information at a higher, '**top-down**' cognitive level.

Gregory sees sensory information as weak, incomplete or ambiguous. For example, the retinal image of a banana cannot display its taste. Perception therefore isn't directly experienced from sensations, but involves a dynamic search for the best interpretation of stimuli, with what is perceived being richer than the information contained within sensory data. The eye for Gregory is not a camera to view the world directly.

Figure 2.4 A duck or a rabbit?

Sensory data is often incomplete or ambiguous, and hypotheses are constructed about its meaning. For example the experience of reversible figures, like being able to see a rabbit's head or a duck's beak in Figure 2.4. Both are perceived, as Gregory believes separate hypotheses are generated and tested out, though usually there would be enough sensory data to decide which interpretation of information is correct. Visual illusions are experienced when confusions occur.

Perceptual set

Perceptual set sees individuals as biased in how they perceive, due to previous experiences, cultural factors and emotional and motivational influences. Thus, people see what they want or expect to see, cutting down the number of possible interpretations that data may suggest, making perception quicker, though increasing opportunities for errors to occur. Perceptual set occurs in several ways:

Expectations

Individuals perceive what they expect to perceive based on previous experience. For example, Brochet and Dubourdieu (2002) gave 54 expert wine tasters a selection of white wines, which they described as 'fresh', 'honeyed', etc. They were then given red wines, some of which were white wine altered to look red by adding a tasteless, odourless substance. No one spotted the frauds, describing them with words relating to red wines, like 'intense' or 'spicy'. As experts have better knowledge of wine they were more influenced by colour, which created an expectation that determined actual perception.

Emotional influences

Emotional factors affect perception by forming a bias to perceive, or not, certain features of sensory data, such as **perceptual defence**, where emotionally harmful stimuli take longer to perceive. For example, Lazarus and McCleary (1951) found that nonsense syllables presented so quickly that they weren't consciously perceived, increased anxiety levels if previously paired with electric shocks. This suggests that emotional factors influence perception unconsciously. (*See also Emotion and perception, page 64.*)

Motivational influences

Perception can be influenced by motivational factors like hunger, with pictures of food seen as more appetizing as people become hungrier. This may have an evolutionary origin, with perception focused on the elements necessary for survival, like finding food. For example, Solley and Haigh (1948) found that children drew a bigger Santa and sack of toys as Christmas approached, but afterwards Santa and his sack shrunk, which implies that motivational factors do influence perception.

Cultural factors

Cultural factors influence individuals to perceive environmental features in set ways. People from different cultural groups may perceive identical sensory data differently, because of different environmental experiences. (*See pages 50–4 for more details.*)

Visual illusions

Gregory believes visual illusions occur because expectations based on previous experience are used to create and test hypotheses from incoming sensory information,

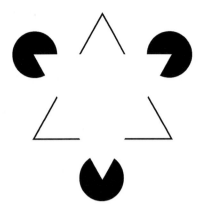

Figure 2.5 The Kanizsa triangle

but that sometimes this is prone to error, with false perceptions occurring. With the Kanizsa illusion, an upright white triangle is perceived over an upside-down white triangle with black edges and three black circles. The upright triangle appears ultra-white, with sharp edges, but is a perceptual invention, as previous experience of what objects look like when superimposed on each other is used to experience the illusion. The third dimension of depth is read into a flat, two-dimensional image, with individuals going beyond the sensory data to perceive something that isn't there.

Evaluation of Gregory's theory

- Gregory's theory increased the understanding of perception, generating interest and research and creating much evidence to support the theory.
- It seems logical that interpretations based on previous experience would occur when viewing conditions are incomplete or ambiguous. For example, if incomplete features indicated an animal could be a duck or a rabbit, the fact it was on water would determine that it was a duck.
- Eysenck and Keane (1990) argue that Gregory's theory is better at explaining the perception of illusions than real objects, because illusions are unreal and easy to misperceive, while real objects provide enough data to be perceived directly. However, Gregory's explanation of visual illusions isn't without criticism; according to him, once it's understood why illusions occur, perception should alter so the illusion isn't experienced anymore. However, they still are, weakening Gregory's explanation.
- Most research supporting Gregory involves laboratory experiments, where fragmented and briefly presented stimuli are used, which are difficult to perceive directly. Gregory thus underestimates how rich and informative sensory data can be in the real world, where it may be possible to perceive directly.
- People's perceptions in general, even those from different cultures, are similar. This wouldn't be true if individual perceptions arose from individual experiences, weakening support for Gregory.
- Gregory's theory suggests that memory is constantly searched to find the best interpretation of incoming sensory data. This would be time-consuming and inefficient, casting doubt on Gregory's explanation.

■ Critical thinking

Instead of evaluating them individually, a more effective way of evaluating Gregory's and Gibson's theories may be to compare the two, highlighting individual weaknesses and strengths. A unification of the theories may even form the best explanation of perception; Gibson's theory working best in ideal viewing conditions and Gregory's working best in less-than-ideal conditions.

Gibson's bottom-up theory

Optical array – the structure of patterned light received by the eyes.

Gibson argued that there was enough information within the **optical array** (the pattern of light reaching the eyes) for perception to occur **directly**, without higher-level cognitive processing. Individuals' movements and those of surrounding objects within an environment aid this process. This involves innate mechanisms that require no learning from experience.

Gibson saw perception as due to the direct detection of **environmental invariances**, unchanging aspects of the visual world. These possess enough sensory data to allow individuals to perceive features of their environment, like depth, distance and the spatial relationships of where objects are in relation to each other.

Gibson believed that texture gradients found in the environment are similar to gradients in the eye, and these corresponding gradients allow the experience of depth perception. This grew into a theory of perception that includes the optical array, textured gradients, optic flow patterns, horizon ratio and affordances.

Gibson believed perception was a '**bottom-up**' process, one constructed directly from sensory data. He saw the perceiver not as the brain but as an individual within their environment. The purpose of perception therefore is to allow people to function in their environment safely and he argued that illusions were two-dimensional, static creations of artificial laboratory experiments.

Bottom-up (direct) processing – perception that arises directly from sensory input without further cognitive processing.

The optical array

The optical array is the composition of patterned light entering the eyes. It is an ever-changing source of sensory information, occurring due to the movements of individuals and objects within their world. It contains different intensities of light shining in different directions, transmitting sensory data about the physical environment. Light itself doesn't allow direct perception, but the structure of the sensory information contained within it does. Movement of the body, the eyes and the angle of gaze, etc., continually update the sensory information being received from the optical array.

The optical array also has **invariant** elements, providing constant sources of information, which contribute to direct perception from sensory information and are not changed by the movements of observers.

Optic flow patterns

Optic flow patterns are unambiguous sources of information concerning height, distance and speed that directly inform perception and provide a rich, ever-changing source of information.

Optic flow patterns – unambiguous sources of information that directly inform perception.

'Optic flow' refers to the visual phenomena continually experienced concerning the apparent visual motion that occurs as individuals move around their environment. Someone sitting on a train looking out of the window sees buildings and trees seemingly moving backwards; it is this apparent motion that forms the optic flow. Information about distance is also conveyed; distant objects like hills appear to move slowly, while close-up objects seem to move quicker. This depth cue is known as **motion parallax**.

As speed increases, the optic flow also increases. The optic flow also varies in relation to the angle between an observer's direction of movement and the direction of an object being viewed. When travelling forwards the optic flow is quickest when the object being regarded is 90 degrees to the observer's side, or when directly above or below. Objects immediately in front have no optic flow and seem motionless. However, the edges of such objects appear to move, as they are not directly in front and thus seem to grow larger.

Mather and West (1993) filmed the movements of black-clad animals with lights on their joints, finding that the

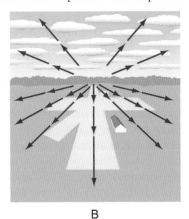

A   B

Figure 2.6   Optic flow patterns as seen by a train driver (A) and a pilot (B)

species of animal was recognizable to observers. This demonstrates the strength of information gained from movement in optic flow patterns, and shows that these can provide enough sensory information for perception to occur directly.

Texture gradient

Texture gradient
– surface patterns that provide sensory information about objects.

Texture gradients are surface patterns providing sensory information about depth, shape, etc. Physical objects have surfaces with different textures that allow direct perception of distance, depth and spatial awareness. Due to constant movement, the 'flow' of texture gradients conveys a rich source of ever-changing sensory information to an observer – for instance, as objects come nearer they appear to expand.

Two depth cues central to the third dimension of depth being directly available to the senses are motion parallax (*see Optic flow patterns, page 43*) and linear perspective. The latter is a cue provided by lines apparently converging as they get further away. These both permit the third dimension of depth to be directly accessible to the senses.

There are several classic texture gradients – for example, frontal surfaces provide a uniform gradient, while longitudinal surfaces, like roads, project gradients that lessen with greater distance from the observer. Frichtel and Lecuyer (2006) presented participants with a film of a car driving through scenery and found that infants as young as four months old could perceive using texture gradient, implying that the ability is innate, supporting to Gibson's idea that perception depends on innate mechanisms.

Horizon ratios

Horizon ratios –
invariant sensory information concerning the position of objects in relation to the horizon.

Horizon ratios are another type of invariant sensory information permitting direct perception. These concern the position of objects in relation to the horizon. Objects of different sizes at equal distances from an observer present different horizon ratios, which can be calculated by dividing the amount of an object above the horizon by the amount below.

Different size objects at equal distances from the observer present different horizon ratios, while objects of equal size standing on level surfaces have the same horizon ratio. When nearing objects, they seem to grow, though the proportion of the object above or below the horizon remains constant and is a perceptual invariant. Creem-Regehr *et al.* (2003) found that restricting participants' viewing conditions did not affect their ability to judge distances using horizon ratio information, suggesting that this form of invariant sensory information is an important means of establishing direct perception.

Affordances

Affordances – the quality of objects that permit actions to be carried out on them.

Affordances involve attaching meaning to sensory information and concern the quality of objects to allow actions to be carried out on them (**action possibilities**). For instance, a cup 'affords' drinking liquids. Affordances are therefore what objects mean to observers and are related to psychological state and physical abilities. For an infant who cannot walk properly, a mountain is not something to be climbed.

Gibson saw affordances as relaying directly perceivable meaning to objects, because evolutionary forces shaped perceptual skills so that learning experiences were not necessary. This rejects Gregory's belief that the meaning of objects is stored in long-term memory from experience and requires cognitive processing to access.

Warren (1984) studied whether participants could judge if staircases portrayed with differently proportioned steps could 'afford' to be climbed. Whether they actually could depended on the length of a participant's leg. It was found that participants were sensitive to the affordance of 'climbability', and according to Gibson, this was achieved by the invariant properties of the light reflected from the staircases. This therefore supports the concept that affordances do not rely on experience.

Evaluation of Gibson's direct theory

- Gibson's theory explains how perception occurs quickly, which Gregory's theory cannot, though Gibson cannot explain why illusions are perceived. He dismissed them as artificial laboratory constructions viewed under restrictive conditions. But some occur naturally under normal viewing conditions.
- The idea that the optical array provides direct information about what objects permit individuals to do (affordances) seems unlikely. Knowledge about objects is affected by cultural influences, experience and emotions. For example, how could an individual directly perceive that a training shoe is for running?
- Gibson's and Gregory's theories are similar in seeing perception as hypothesis-based. Gregory explains this as a process of hypothesis formation and testing, with the flow of information processed from the top down, while Gibson sees it as an unconscious process originating from evolutionary forces, with the flow of information processed from the bottom up. Another similarity is that they both agree that visual perception occurs from light reflected off surfaces and objects and that a specific biological system is required to perceive.
- Gregory's and Gibson's theories involve the nature versus nurture debate. Gregory's indirect theory emphasizes learning experiences and thus the influence of nurture, while Gibson's direct theory sees more of a role for nature.

Link to the biological level of analysis

There may be a biological basis to Gibson's theory. Logothetis and Pauls (1995) identified neurons in the brains of monkeys that seemed to perceive specific objects regardless of their orientation, implying that a biological mechanism allows direct perception. This was supported by Rizzolati and Sinigaglia (2008), who found that the anterior intraparietal brain area is involved in direct perception of object affordances.

Practical applications
Gibson's theory

One practical application of Gibson's theory is putting parallel lines increasingly close together as road junctions approach, giving a false impression of speed to slow drivers down. In this way Gibson's theory can be seen to save countless lives each year.

Figure 2.7 Road markings giving a false impression of speed to slow drivers down.

Another practical application is that of Gaver (1996), who used Gibson's concept of affordances in designing computer displays, which use the material properties of a computer-generated environment to allow people to interact with them.

The influence of biological factors on cognition

LEARNING OUTCOME
■ Explain how biological factors may affect one cognitive process.

Face recognition

Face recognition – the means by which faces are processed and made sense of.

Face recognition is a cognitive process concerning how faces are processed and made sense of. Humans are attracted to faces from birth, as it assists the formation of attachments; this is a skill that has occurred through evolution, because it aids survival. This suggests that biological mechanisms underpin face recognition, and that this has developed via natural selection to be hard-wired into our genetic make-up. Many people even 'see' faces in inanimate objects, like seeing the face of a religious figure in a piece of toast.

Figure 2.8 In 1994 Diana Duyser was preparing to bite into a grilled cheese sandwich when she saw the Virgin Mary staring at her. Having saved the sandwich for ten years, she sold it on eBay. The item received 1.7 million 'hits', eventually selling for $28,000.

Face recognition informs individuals about their level of familiarity with each other, for instance who our friends and enemies are. Face recognition is crucial to conducting safe social interactions and group existence. Reading faces isn't just important in identifying who someone is, but also in establishing an individual's emotional state, level of honesty and whether they are trustworthy.

The major theory of face recognition is Bruce and Young's (1986) model. They used case studies of people with brain damage that limited their ability to process faces, to discover that face recognition involves separate mechanisms for familiar and unfamiliar faces. They also discovered that face recognition is a **holistic** process, where facial features, involving eight independent sub-processes, work together in a sequential fashion, with different processing 'modules' used to comprehend data extracted from faces. (*See Table 2.1.*)

Table 2.1 Face recognition processing modules

TYPE OF PROCESSING MODULE	DESCRIPTION OF MODULE
Structural encoding	Creation of descriptions and representations of faces.
Expression analysis	Analysis of facial characteristics to infer emotional state. For example, smiling indicates happiness.
Facial speech analysis	Analysis of facial movements to aid comprehension of speech.
Directed visual processing	Selective processing of specific facial data, like the colour of eyes.
Facial recognition nodes	Stored structural descriptions of familiar faces.
Person identity nodes	Stored information about familiar people, such as their interests and talents.
Name generation	Separate store for names.
Cognitive storage	Extra information aiding the recognition process, such as what contexts individuals are known in, e.g. a person that you work with.

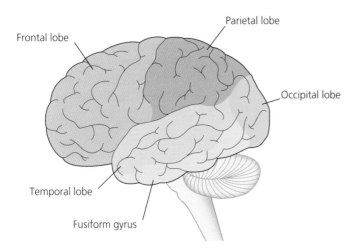

Frontal lobe

Parietal lobe

Occipital lobe

Temporal lobe

Fusiform gyrus

Figure 2.9

Structural encoding, face recognition nodes, person identity nodes and name generation are used to recognize familiar faces, while structural encoding, expression analysis, facial speech analysis and directed visual processing are used to process unfamiliar faces.

Bruce and Young's theory has stood up to rigorous examination, with the main feature that research has revealed being that elements of face recognition are related to specific brain areas, especially areas of the temporal lobe, such as the fusiform gyrus and the occipital temporal pathway.

> **Link to the biological level of analysis**
>
> Case studies of brain damage in prosopagnosics has allowed cognitive psychologists to understand more about how face recognition occurs.

Practical applications
Face recognition software

The police have used identikit drawings of faces since the 1940s, but nowadays several police forces use the **electronic facial identification technique** (E-FIT). This uses a library of computer-stored facial characteristics to produce 3-D colour images of suspects and is based on the idea that humans recognize faces through biological brain mechanisms that reference individual features, like shape of nose. Many criminals have been arrested using this method and E-FIT has also helped reduce the number of wrongful arrests through mistaken identity.

The man who mistook his wife for a hat

Oliver Sacks (1985) tells the story of 'The man who mistook his wife for a hat'. Doctor P, a professional musician, made silly visual mistakes, like confusing parking meters with people. A neurologist found nothing wrong, apart from Dr P's strange way of looking at people. His memory, intellectual functioning and emotional responses seemed fine, indicating no sign of mental abnormality. But as the patient went to leave the neurologist's office, he went to reach for his hat but mistook his wife for the hat stand and reached instead for her head. The clinician realized something was wrong. Subsequent examination revealed that the patient had a vast musical knowledge, but could no longer read music. Visual tests showed that although Dr P could identify abstract patterns and shapes, he could not recognize pictures of familiar faces, even those of his own family. His other sensory abilities were intact, as although he did not recognize a rose by sight, he did when he smelled it. The clinician was amazed to find that Dr P could not play chess with the pieces in front of him, but easily beat his opponent when a game was played mentally.

> **Visual agnosia** – a condition involving an inability to make sense of or use familiar stimuli.

Dr P had a **visual agnosia** caused by brain damage to the fusiform gyrus brain area, whereby he could not relate the parts of anything he saw to a coherent whole. In other words he could not 'see' objects and faces in any meaningful way. However, even though he was unable to make any cognitive visual judgements, Dr P had learnt to use his musical knowledge to create an 'inner sound track', of hummed tunes, to help him to coordinate simple, everyday tasks. His wife assisted by laying out clothes, food, etc., in familiar patterns. Dr P had taught himself to give his fragmented visual world meaning through music, substituting visual with acoustic references. In this manner Dr P was able to continue teaching, living a full life instead of one restricted by his visual in capacities.

Prosopagnosia – a visual agnosia where objects can be described, but not recognized.

Link to the biological level of analysis

Most research into face recognition is conducted on sufferers of **prosopagnosia**, a condition whereby faces can be described, but not recognized. Such people have generally suffered damage to specific brain areas.

The perception of objects and faces was thought to involve processing by the same neural mechanisms, but some studies of prosopagnosia indicate that there may be separate processing systems, with a specific processor for faces.

The occurrence of different types and levels of prosopagnosia suggests a relationship to different modules of face recognition, supporting Bruce and Young's (1986) notion that face recognition occurs as a sequence of stages. The fact there are different types and levels of prosopagnosia indicates each module of the face processing sequence is catered for by a specific brain area and it is damage to these specific areas that causes the different types and levels of the disorder.

Dailey and Cottrell (1999) suggested how a separate face processing mechanism could arise, based on the idea of the biological visual system developing a processing sub-system useful for the recognition of faces. This would occur as a natural response to a child's developmental environment, because children need to identify faces in order to form attachments that are crucial to their survival and development.

Case studies of prosopagnosia, where faces are described, but not recognized, like that of the 'man who mistook his wife for a hat', have aided understanding of the relationship between face recognition and object recognition and whether such phenomenon are processed separately using different neural mechanisms. The use of brain scanning techniques and specially designed visual tests have helped identify specific brain areas involved and highlighted how the cognitive process of face recognition is underpinned by biological mechanisms, illustrating how the cognitive and biological levels of analysis combine to give a better understanding of mental behaviour.

Key study

Delvenne *et al.* (2003)

Delvenne *et al.* (2003) reported on NS, a 40-year-old prosopagnosic patient hit by a car, who was unconscious for 23 days. A **magnetic resonance scan** (MRI) revealed that NS had suffered lesions to the **bilateral occipito-temporal junction** brain area, resulting in various impairments, including a severe visual agnosia for objects and faces. Testing revealed that NS had a full visual field and no weaknesses in visual perception. On object recognition tests he performed well on all perceptual tasks, like length and size match, as well as assessing form, volume and perspective about objects. He easily judged photographs of objects as being the same or different, but found tasks requiring access to stored visual knowledge about objects difficult, for example naming pictures of familiar objects. When shown a salt-shaker he said, 'Is that a little bottle? Hmm… one part is like glass and another contains holes… Fifteen holes… Might it serve to mash fruit, to make orange juice?… Oh, is it a salt-shaker?' NS also could not mime the actions of familiar objects.

With faces NS could successfully classify whether a picture was of a face or not, could find target features, like a nose or a mouth, could find a target face from ten photographs of unfamiliar faces even if the facial expression was changed on the target face. He could even read emotions on unfamiliar faces and determine gender and age. However, he was impaired in face recognition, being unable to judge whether faces were familiar. Further testing revealed that NS had difficulties in integrating individual perceptual features into whole objects, meaning that he was unable to recognize unfamiliar objects and faces. This suggests that prosopagnosia involves a deficit in the perception of high-level perceptual processes necessary to correctly identify individual faces. The results cast doubt on the idea of there being separate brain areas responsible for object and face recognition, as both abilities were equally affected, though possibly several different brain areas were damaged.

Other research

■ Tranel and Damasio (1985) used another form of biological investigation, namely that of measuring electrical skin conductivity through skin conductive response (SCR), to find that conductivity increased when two prosopagnosics were shown photographs of familiar faces, though they claimed the faces were unfamiliar. No such response was recorded with photographs of unfamiliar faces, which suggests that although their ability to retrieve memories associated with familiar faces was destroyed, the memories themselves were intact. This explains why some prosopagnosics recall familiar people from the sound of their voices, by accessing memories using a different sensory modality.

■ Sergent (1992) used positron emission tomography (PET) scans to find that three prominent areas in the occipitotemporal lobe lit up when non-prosopagnosics processed familiar faces and didn't light up when prosopagnosics performed the same task. This suggests that these three areas are biological representations of Bruce and Young's (1986) model of face recognition; one part of the posterior occipital region being involved in the extraction of unique facial features, another area slightly in front of this area being involved in making connections between faces and biographical information, while slightly in front of this area, in the temporal lobe, was an area containing all biographical details of known faces.

■ Takamura (1996) argues that as scans have found clusters of cells involved in face recognition in various brain components along the occipitotemporal pathway, it suggests that rather than there being a specific 'face processing' part of the brain, it's probable that there is a 'face pathway' that is a specific part of the overall visual processing pathway. This implies that several brain areas are involved in face recognition.

■ Kanwisher *et al.* (1997) reported on neurological evidence supporting the idea of face recognition involving a separate processing mechanism. Functional magnetic resonance imaging (fMRI) scans compared brain activity when scrambled faces or hands or houses were presented. The fusiform gyrus was more active in face recognition than object recognition, implying that this brain area is specifically associated with face recognition processing.

■ Brunsdon *et al.* (2006) reported on AL, a boy who could not recognize familiar or unfamiliar faces, suggesting damage to be at the level of structural encoding at the beginning of the face recognition process. This suggests that face recognition is composed of sequential stages, supporting Bruce and Young's (1986) theory.

■ Gauthier *et al.* (2000) cast doubt on the idea of separate processing mechanisms, as he believes faces are complex objects that just take more time to recognize. This is supported by the fusiform gyrus being activated not only during face recognition, but also during object discrimination. Therefore the fusiform gyrus cannot be specifically involved in just face recognition. Some prosopagnosics have problems with complex object recognition too, including faces, suggesting that a specific face processing mechanism may not exist.

■ Humphreys and Riddoch (1987) also cast doubt on there being separate face and object recognition mechanisms. They argued that face recognition is a more complex version of object recognition. If true, then slight damage to a general-purpose recognition system would affect object recognition less than face recognition. This is true, with prosopagnosics tending to have slight damage to object recognition abilities and severe damage to face recognition abilities.

Evaluation

- Biological means of investigation, like brain scanning, contribute to the understanding of how cognitive processes like face recognition work, illustrating how combining cognitive and biological levels of analysis further aids the understanding of the mind and behaviour.
- Case studies of prosopagnosia provide evidence to evaluate Bruce and Young's theory of face recognition, but these may not be representative, especially as they involve studies of abnormal brain conditions. Case studies also sometimes provide contradictory evidence, for instance whether there is a separate face recognition brain area.
- Although research evidence indicates a relationship between biological mechanisms and face recognition, the biological processes underpinning how familiar a given face is are not properly understood.
- There are ethical concerns with case studies of prosopagnosia, as conducting research highlights to sufferers the disabilities they have in processing faces, which could lead to psychological harm. However, from a cost–benefit point of view, if such research leads to effective therapies to counteract the negative effects of prosopagnosia, then the research is justifiable.

The influence of sociocultural factors on cognitive processes

LEARNING OUTCOME
■ Discuss how social or cultural factors affect one cognitive process.

Figure 2.10 In Leeper's ambiguous lady both an old lady and a young woman can be seen. Which is perceived is influenced by the social environment around an individual, i.e. whether they are surrounded by young or old females.

The idea that sociocultural factors influence cognitive processing does not contradict the notion that biological factors also affect cognitive processing. Research indicates that biological factors are involved, but there are indications that factors drawn from social and cultural environments also have an influence. For example, sociocultural factors influence what a person perceives (as well as what they don't perceive). Leeper (1935) demonstrated that participants previously given a picture or verbal description of a young lady, perceive a young lady in an ambiguous picture that could be either that of a young or old woman, while participants previously given a picture or verbal description of an old woman, perceive the old woman in the ambiguous picture. This shows how social environment shapes actual perception and links in with perceptual set, in that people perceive what they expect to perceive based on expectation created through their experience of social environments.

Perception and culture

Cultural factors predispose individuals to perceive environmental features in certain ways. Therefore individuals from different cultural backgrounds perceive identical sensory information in different ways, because they are influenced by different cultural experiences. For instance, the Müller-Lyer **visual illusion** consists of two equally long lines, where one line with out-going fins appears to be longer than another line with in-going fins.

Visual illusions – visually perceived images that differ from objective reality.

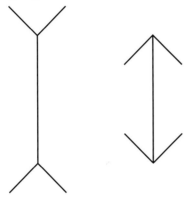

However, the illusion is only experienced by individuals living in cultures dominated by a carpentered world of manufactured straight lines. This occurs in Western cultures, where individuals are surrounded by man-made structures consisting of horizontal and vertical straight lines and angles. The explanation for perceiving the illusion, therefore, is that individuals from a carpentered world culture unconsciously learn from experience to read the third dimension of depth into flat, two-dimensional images. The line with out-going fins is seen as far away, while the line with in-going fins is seen as much nearer. Although our brain sees the lines as the same size, experience teaches us that objects far away appear

Figure 2.11   The Müller-Lyer illusion

smaller than those closer to. Therefore the line with out-going fins must be longer than the one with in-going fins and so that is what is perceived.

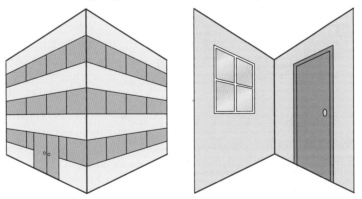

Figure 2.12   The Müller-Lyer illusion – experience tells us that the line on the left must be longer than that on the right.

The Müller-Lyer illusion is experienced by those from a carpentered world culture, as the vertical line in the image on the left seems further away compared to the vertical line in the image on the right. Experience tells us that the line on the left must be longer than that on the right.

However, individuals from non-carpentered world cultures, like those with structures made out of natural materials with few straight lines and angles, do not experience the illusion, as they have not learnt to do so. This demonstrates how cultural factors influence the cognitive process of perception.

Research

- Rivers (1901) reported that Murray Islanders in the Torres Straits between Australia and New Guinea are less prone to the Müller-Lyer illusion than English participants, but are more prone to the vertical–horizontal illusion, especially among younger Murray Islanders. It was concluded at the time that this occurred because the Islanders didn't process the whole of the figures presented to them, or was due to a physiological condition specific to the Islanders.

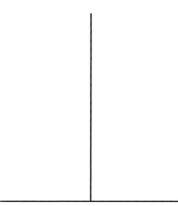

Figure 2.13 In the vertical–horizontal illusion the vertical line appears longer, though in fact both lines are of equal length. However, the illusion is not experienced by some cultures.

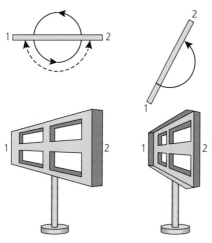

Figure 2.14 The rotating trapezoid is a rectangular window-like stimulus that although revolving in full circles, appears to oscillate back and forth, though not to Zulus unfamiliar with rectangular structures.

- Segall *et al.* (1963) presented various illusions to different non-European samples of participants (mainly Africans, but including some from the Philippines). They found that participants who lived in high, open countryside, like the Batoro and Bayankole peoples, where rare vertical objects, like trees, were regarded as important features, were susceptible to the vertical–horizontal illusion, while Africans who lived in dense jungle, like the Bette people, were less likely to experience the illusion. Americans and white South Africans came in between these two groupings in terms of susceptibility to the illusion. This suggests that physical environments shape cultural influences that in turn affect perception.

- Allport and Pettigrew (1957) found that if an image of a trapezoid was rotated, European participants perceived an illusion of the figure oscillating to and fro, rather than spinning in complete circles, as it does. Zulu participants, however, who weren't familiar with rectangular features, like windows, and who had a cultural tendency towards circular rather than rectangular structures, didn't perceive the illusion. This supports the carpentered world hypothesis that perception is learnt from cultural environmental experiences.

- Stewart (1973) found that Tongan children from rural environments were less likely to experience several visual illusions, including the Müller-Lyer illusion, but the more familiar they became with cultural environments consisting of a carpentered world of straight lines, angles and rectangles, the more likely they were to experience such illusions. This suggests that cultural environmental experiences shape perception.

- Pettigrew *et al.* (1978) found that when presenting a picture of one South African ethnic group to one eye of a participant and another ethnic group to the other eye, white South Africans were not able to distinguish between black and mixed-race peoples. This implies that the cultural influence of their racial prejudice towards other ethnic groupings affected their perception.

■ Critical thinking

Cross-cultural studies allow psychologists to compare people of different cultures to determine whether perceptual abilities are innate or learnt through environmental experience. Cross-cultural studies are not without their weaknesses, however. What criticisms of cross-cultural studies can you think of?

Perceiving depth in pictures

Another apparent cultural difference in perception is that of perceiving the third dimension of depth in two-dimensional flat pictures. This occurs through the use of depth-cues apparent within pictures, for example if one object is partially obscured by another object, then it is deduced that the first object is further away. Research like that by Gibson and Walk (1960) and Campos *et al.* (1972), which attempted to get participants to walk over a vertical cliff (the apparent drop was actually guarded by a non-reflective pane of glass), suggest that the perception of depth is apparent at birth in neonate children and animals. However, some cross-cultural studies suggest there are culturally determined capacities to demonstrating the ability when reading depth into pictures.

Figure 2.15 Hudson found that only those from cultures with experience of pictures developed the ability to read depth into them.

Hudson (1960) showed various cultural groupings a 2-D picture containing depth cues, finding that children from all cultures had difficulty in perceiving depth. Participants who went on to have experience of such types of pictures learnt to interpret the depth cues within them, while those from cultures that didn't have a familiarity with such pictures remained poor in perceiving depth within them.

Deregowski (1972) found that African participants had difficulties in recognizing objects and perceiving depth in pictures, because they were unfamiliar with the Western cultural style drawings used. For instance, problems occurred if shown a view of an elephant, as depicted in a Western cultural style, but not if shown a more culturally familiar 'split-style' drawing.

This suggests that the inability to read depth in pictures relates to the degree of familiarity with how different cultures represent objects in pictures. Interestingly, children of all cultures initially produce split-style drawings, even in cultures where adults regard such drawings as 'wrong', though in these cultures children gradually learn to represent objects in a more culturally acceptable way. This supports the idea that different cultures have different cultural styles of presenting pictorial information and it is this that affects an individual's ability to read depth in non-culturally familiar pictures. In Western cultures architects and engineers use split-style drawings to represent structures and individuals not familiar with these find it difficult to construct models from such diagrams.

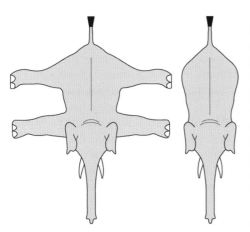

Figure 2.16 African participants had difficulties in recognizing objects in Western style drawings, but not when shown a culturally familiar 'split-style' drawing (Deregowski, 1972).

Evaluation

■ The idea that research from illusions suggests perception is culturally determined was criticized by Pollack and Silva (1967), as they found Europeans more susceptible to the Müller-Lyer illusion, as their retinas permitted them to detect contours better. This suggests a biological reason for cultural differences in perceiving such illusions.

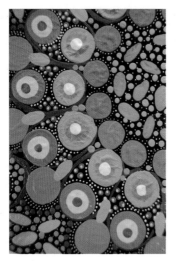

Figure 2.17 Aboriginal art can only be understood if the 'code' behind such drawings is understood.

- Early cross-cultural studies of perception were often anecdotal and not conducted under scientifically controlled conditions. It's also possible that these studies suffered from researcher bias, like a tendency to regard the perceptual abilities of those from non-Western cultures as inferior to those from Western cultures, for example that Western pictorial art represents the world more objectively and correctly and those from cultures who couldn't understand such images were 'deficient'. This casts doubts on the validity of findings. Additionally, researchers tended to use research methods and materials applicable only to certain cultures (e.g. perspective style instead of split-style drawings) and this too may affect the validity of findings.

- With cross-cultural studies it's difficult to obtain identical samples and replicate methodologies exactly, again decreasing the validity of findings.

- The value of using depth-cues in pictures to determine the cultural nature of perception is debatable, as such images don't relate to the real world. For instance, Cox (1992) demonstrated how Aboriginal art is not intelligible to other cultures unless the cultural 'code' behind such drawings is explained. Also, much research in this area uses visual illusions and 2-D drawings, which may not relate to more everyday perceptual abilities.

- Segall *et al.* (1966), after reviewing various cross-cultural studies, concluded that perception is shaped by environmental experiences that allow individuals to function effectively in the environments in which they live. Therefore people learn to perceive in ways in order to maximize survival chances. Therefore it is cultural environments that help to shape perceptual abilities.

- Another cultural influence on perception concerns *magical thinking*, which involves the belief that the mind directly influences the physical world. De Craen *et al.* (1996) found that there were cultural beliefs about the suitability and effectiveness of drugs based on their colours. Many cultures perceive red, orange and yellow as possessing stimulant qualities, with red specifically being seen as having cardiovascular effects due to its perceived link with blood, and orange being perceived as affecting the skin. Blue and green were perceived as possessing sedative qualities. One practical application of this is that tablets should be manufactured in colours fitting their culturally perceived qualities, for example red tablets for heart conditions. This would ensure they were likelier to be taken and may even be successful due to a placebo effect making patients believe that such tablets will work.

- Overall, research – especially cross-cultural studies of perceptual development concerning visual illusions and the perception of depth in pictures – suggests that cognitive processes are affected by sociocultural factors, though biological factors can also have an effect.

Link to the sociocultural level of analysis

Comparison of the perceptual abilities of different cultural groups involves the **nature versus nurture** debate, where perceptual abilities that differ between different cultural groupings are seen as arising through environmental experiences and thus are a product of nurture. Perceptual abilities that are the same within cultural groupings are seen as innate and under genetic control, thus supporting the nature side of the debate.

Reliability of one cognitive process: memory

Reliability (of EWT) – the extent to which EWT produces consistent results.

Memory – the retention of experience.

Eyewitness testimony (EWT) – the recall of observers of events previously experienced.

LEARNING OUTCOME

■ With reference to relevant research studies, to what extent is one cognitive process reliable?

The **reliability** of **memory** has interested psychologists, due to its repercussions within the legal system.

Court cases are especially dependent on the reliability of **eyewitness testimony (EWT)**, which concerns what witnesses to events recall as having occurred, with decisions as to the guilt or innocence of those accused often reliant on such evidence. In 75 per cent of cases where people are found on the basis of DNA to have been wrongly convicted of crimes, the original guilty verdict was formed based on unreliable EWT.

Practical applications

Research into EWT suggests practical applications into how court cases should be conducted and witness testimonies gathered. The Devlin report (1976) recommended that convictions should not occur on the strength of the testimony of a single eyewitness. Barristers are also not allowed to ask leading questions for fear of generating false testimonies.

Bartlett (1932) performed the 'War of the Ghosts' study (*see page 37*), which suggested that memories are not accurate snapshots of events, but instead are reconstructed over time, influenced by active schemas, ready-made expectations based on previous experiences, moods, existing knowledge, contexts, attitudes and stereotypes. Schemas are used to interpret the world and fill in the gaps in knowledge. With EWT, events aren't recalled as they happened, but are **reconstructed** from schemas active at the time of recall. For example, Postman and Bruner (1947) (*see page 38*) found that participants who saw a picture of a black man and a white man arguing, where the white man had a knife and the black man was unarmed, often recalled the black man as brandishing the knife, as participants often held schemas about black people being aggressive and carrying weapons.

Inaccurate EWT can have severe repercussions. In 1984, American college student Jennifer Thompson was raped at knifepoint by a man who burst into her flat. During her ordeal Jennifer concentrated on every detail of her attacker so she could later accurately recall him. She was determined that if she lived, he would be caught and punished. Later that day she worked with police officers to compose an accurate sketch of the assailant. A few days later she identified Ronald Cotton as the rapist and picked him out of an identity parade. On the strength of her EWT Ronald Cotton was imprisoned; Jennifer was so sure of his guilt that she wanted him electrocuted, declaring that she would throw the switch herself. In 1995, after serving 11 years in prison, DNA evidence proved that Ronald Cotton was innocent and that it was another man, Bobby Poole (who was by then already in prison for another rape), who was guilty. Remarkably Jennifer and Ronald became close friends and now campaign against the unreliability of EWT.

There is the serious prospect that innocent people have been executed in the USA on the basis of unreliable EWT. More encouragingly, the 'Innocence Project' in America has helped to overturn the

Figure 2.18 Ronald Cotton and Jennifer Thompson

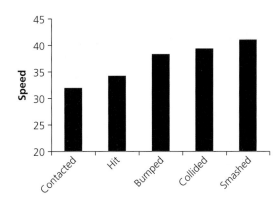

Figure 2.19 Different verbs used in questions about car speeds were found to influence estimates of speed.

Misleading information/ questions – information or questions that suggest a desired answer.

Post-event information – misleading information added to an incident after it has occurred.

wrongful convictions through faulty EWT of 214 men. This is an important area for psychology to investigate as there are such serious implications from unreliable EWT.

Research studies of the reliability of EWT

Elizabeth Loftus, an American psychologist, is famed for her work into the reliability of EWT. In 1974 she and John Palmer performed their classic study, which provided the basis for subsequent interest and research. In this study participants were asked to estimate the speed of cars in a film of traffic accidents. It was found that estimates of speed were influenced by participants being asked how fast the cars were travelling when they 'contacted', 'hit', 'bumped', 'collided' or 'smashed' into each other, which implies that leading questions affected participants' schemas, influencing them to give 'suggested' answers.

The researchers also found that more participants mistakenly remembered a week later seeing non-existent broken glass if they were originally given the verb 'smashed' (32 per cent) rather than 'hit' (14 per cent), which suggests that at recall, **misleading information** is reconstructed along with material from the original memory.

Loftus (1975) found that 17 per cent of participants who watched a film of a car ride and were asked, 'How fast was the car going when it passed the white barn?' when there was no barn, recalled seeing a barn one week later. This supports the idea that **post-event information**, where information is added after an event, affects recall.

Bekerian and Bowers (1983) showed slides of events leading up to a car crash, finding that participants' memories remained intact despite being asked misleading questions, which suggests that post-event information affects the retrieval of memories rather than their storage.

Key study

Loftus and Pickrell (2003)

Loftus and Pickrell (2003) showed how it is possible to create false memories about events in a person's life. They divided 120 participants who had visited Disneyland as children into four groups of 30 and asked them to assess advertising copy, fill out a questionnaire and answer questions about their childhood memories of Disneyland.

- **Group 1** read a fake Disney advert featuring no cartoon characters.
- **Group 2** read the fake advert featuring no cartoon characters, but were exposed to a cardboard figure of Bugs Bunny placed in the interview room.
- **Group 3** read the fake advert featuring Bugs Bunny.
- **Group 4** read the fake advert featuring Bugs Bunny and were exposed to the cardboard figure of Bugs Bunny in the interview room.

Thirty per cent of participants in group 3 and 40 per cent in group 4 remembered meeting Bugs Bunny when visiting Disneyland (impossible, as Bugs Bunny is a Warner Brothers character). A ripple effect also occurred whereby those exposed to misleading information concerning Bugs Bunny were more likely to relate him to other things at Disneyland not suggested in the advert, like seeing Bugs Bunny and Mickey Mouse together. This suggests that false memories can be created through misleading information, showing the vulnerability and malleability of memory.

Evaluation

- Much research into EWT is laboratory-based, where inaccuracies in recall have only minimal consequences, plus witnessing real-life events also has more of an emotional impact. Foster *et al.* (1994) demonstrated that EWT was more accurate for real-life crimes rather than simulations, supporting the notion that laboratory situations may not reflect real-life incidents.
- It's unclear whether recall inaccuracies due to misleading information are due to genuine changes in memory or to demand characteristics. Also participants don't expect researchers to deliberately mislead them, so inaccurate recall is to be expected, as they believe researchers are telling the truth.
- Misleading information only affects unimportant aspects of memory. Memory of important events isn't easily distorted. Also information that is obviously misleading doesn't tend to lead to inaccurate recall.

Other factors affecting the reliability of EWT

Anxiety

Anxiety affects the reliability of EWT, as it directs attention away from important aspects of a situation. Deffenbacher (1983) used the Yerkes-Dodson inverted-U hypothesis to explain how moderate amounts of arousal improve the detail and accuracy of memory up to an optimal point, after which further increases lead to a decline in recall.

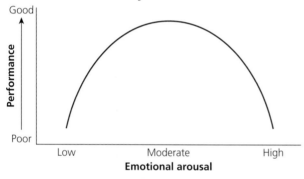

Figure 2.20   The Yerkes-Dodson inverted-U hypothesis

Research

- Loftus *et al.* (1987) found that if a person is carrying a weapon, witnesses focus on the weapon rather than the person's face, negatively affecting their ability to recall facial details, thus supporting the idea that anxiety diverts attention away from important aspects of a situation.
- Ginet and Verkampt (2007) produced moderate arousal in participants by telling them fake electrodes gave electric shocks. These participants' recall of minor details from a film of a traffic accident was superior to that of participants with low arousal produced from believing the electrodes merely monitored physiological reactions. This supports the inverted-U hypothesis that moderate arousal improves recall.
- Further support came from Peters (1988), who tested people attending a health centre where a nurse, who gave an injection, and a researcher were witnessed for equal amounts of time. A week later identification of the researcher from photos proved easier than that of the nurse, suggesting that heightened arousal levels due to the injection impaired memory in line with the inverted-U hypothesis.

Evaluation

- Much research into anxiety effects is laboratory-based and may not reflect real-life scenarios. Yuille and Cutshall (1986) found that witnesses to a fatal shooting with high levels of anxiety recalled fewer details than those with moderate levels, in line with the inverted-U hypothesis, but those with very high anxiety levels had extremely accurate recall, which goes against the hypothesis. However, Fruzzetti *et al.* (1992) argue that those with very high anxiety levels may have recalled more, as they were closer to the event.

- The inverted-U hypothesis provides too simplistic an explanation. Deffenbacher (2004) performed a meta-analysis of 63 studies, finding that EWT accuracy increases gradually up to very high levels of anxiety, after which increases in arousal lead to a sudden, catastrophic drop in recall accuracy.

Age

Another factor impacting on the reliability of memory is age. Children often accept inaccurate information from adults, possibly due to not wanting to contradict authority figures. Younger children are especially vulnerable to being misled by post-event information and leading questions. The elderly can have less accurate or detailed recall than younger and middle-aged people, though research findings on this aren't always consistent, possibly due to methodological flaws.

Research

- Krackow and Lynne (2003) found that children aged 4–6 years who were touched or not on different parts of their body answered truthfully when asked directly, but wrongly half the time when asked indirectly with leading questions, demonstrating the vulnerability of young children to leading questions. Additionally Poole and Lindsay (2001) found that children aged 3–8 years included a wealth of post-event information when recalling details of a science demonstration, suggesting younger children are especially affected by such information to provide inaccurate EWT.
- Roberts and Lamb (1999) found that adults often misinterpreted or distorted children's reports of alleged abuse, but that two-thirds of these inaccuracies weren't challenged by the children, supporting the idea that children accept inaccuracies for fear of contradicting authority figures.
- Brimacombe *et al.* (1997) found that the elderly provide less accurate EWT than younger people of events viewed on video. This was supported by Wright and Holiday's (2007) finding that recall is less complete and contains more inaccuracies as participants age, which suggests reliability of memory decreases with age. Additionally, Cohen and Faulkner (1989) found that elderly participants were more likely to have inaccurate recall when given misleading information, supporting the idea that the elderly are more susceptible to misleading information.

Evaluation

- Elias *et al.* (1990) argues that the superior performances of young adults occurs as they're more used to tests and are motivated to succeed at them. Also, the elderly are often compared to younger participants on stimuli more suited to the young, a notion supported by Anastasi and Rhodes (2006), who found that different age groups performed best when recalling photographs of people from their own age group.
- Studies that find reduced memory ability in the elderly may do so because they use participants from nursing homes, who may be residing in such institutions because they have impaired memory abilities and thus do not form a representative sample.
- Care must be taken not to psychologically harm children when researching memory abilities. There is also an issue of deception through provision of misleading and post-event information.

The use of technology in investigating cognitive processes

LEARNING OUTCOME
■ Discuss the use of technology in investigating cognitive processes.

Originally the only way to study cognitive processes was by inferring them through non-invasive methods, like observations or experiments, etc., or by invasive methods, such as psycho surgery and post-mortems, where actual brain tissue was examined. All these methods had deficiencies in establishing the validity of findings, plus surgical techniques had the added risk of potentially causing harm to live participants.

The establishment of non-invasive methods, like neuroimaging techniques, allows psychologists to study the physical brain structures underpinning cognitive processes in a safer and more ethically desirable manner.

Magnetic resonance imaging (MRI)

Magnetic resonance imaging (MRI) – a form of brain scanning involving magnetic fields and pulses of radio wave energy.

Magnetic resonance imaging (MRI) scanning is a technique used in psychology whereby a participant is placed prone inside a scanning machine while magnetic fields and pulses of radio wave energy are used to create three-dimensional images of structures within the brain. This allows researchers to see, by detecting changes in oxygen consumption, what brain activity and which brain structures are involved in various cognitive processes. Sometimes contrast material, like dyes made from iodine, are introduced into the body before scanning to show relevant brain structures more clearly. (*See Delvenne et al., 2003, page 48.*)

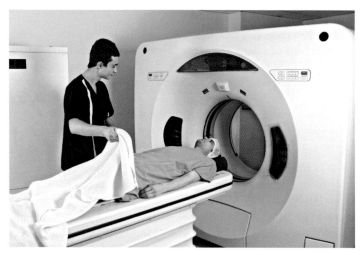

Figure 2.21 A standard MRI scanner

Strengths
■ MRI scans often show evidence of brain activity that other scanning techniques, like X-rays, cannot. It's also regarded as the best scanning technique for soft tissues, like brain structures.
■ Images from MRI scans are digital and can be stored on a computer for further analysis.
■ There are no serious side effects associated with MRI scanning and unlike other forms of scanning, like X-rays, potentially harmful ionizing radiation is not used.

Weaknesses
■ Although there are few side effects from MRI scans, the strong magnetic current can affect pacemakers, artificial limbs and medical devices containing iron. Iron pigments in tattoos can also cause skin irritations. There is an additional slight risk of an allergic reaction if contrast material is used.
■ MRI scans are generally more expensive than other neuroimaging methods and thus are not cost-effective.
■ MRI scanning also requires a trained radiologist to analyse the images produced, again reducing cost-effectiveness.

Functional magnetic resonance imaging (fMRI)

Functional magnetic resonance imaging (fMRI) is a type of MRI scanning that assesses neural activity within the brain by producing images highlighting changes in blood flow. fMRI differs from MRI scanning in that it uses alterations in magnetization between oxygen-poor and oxygen-rich blood flow as its basic measure. (*See Hemond et al., 1997, page 35.*)

Strengths

- Since the 1990s the technique has dominated neuroimaging research, as it doesn't require ingestion of substances or exposure to radiation, and the images produced are of high resolution.
- Brain activity can be presented graphically to enhance understanding, by colour coding the strength of activity in relevant brain structures.
- fMRI scanning can be combined with data from other methods of non-invasive brain scrutiny, like EEG readings and near-infrared spectroscopy (NIRS) to further understanding of biological mechanisms underpinning cognitive processes.
- Lie-detector machines have been devised that use fMRI scanning techniques, though the accuracy of the data produced is not without criticism, as it's liable to produce false positives, where answers deemed as lies are actually true.

Weaknesses

- The procedure is often affected by noise from various sources, entailing the use of complex statistical analysis to decipher images, which complicates the process.
- As with MRI scanning the technique can distress claustrophobics due to the confined nature of the scanner. Loud noises are also produced and some may experience unpleasant nerve-tingling sensations.
- As with MRI scanning the technique is not recommended for those fitted with pacemakers. Also, increases in heat can harm those with fevers, diabetes and circulatory problems.
- The technique is expensive compared to other methods and requires a skilled analyst to interpret the images produced.
- fMRI only examines blood flow and cannot analyse the activity of individual nerve cells, which is vital to an advanced understanding of cognitive processing. As the technique often results in several brain structures 'lighting up', the exact functions of each cannot be deduced.

Positron emission tomography (PET)

Positron emission tomography (PET) is a type of nuclear medicine imaging, where small amounts of radionuclides (radioactive material) are introduced into the body (orally or by injection), which are then detected within brain structures through a scanner to produce three-dimensional images and detailed molecular information generated from blood flow, oxygen use and glucose metabolism. These images are often combined with images from other types of scanning, like MRI scans, in a technique known as image fusion, to produce more informative images. Nowadays most PET scans are performed on a combined PET/CT (computed tomography) scanner to produce images that pinpoint the exact location of metabolic activity within the brain, providing more accurate data than could be gained from two scans produced separately. (*See Sergent, 1992, page 49.*)

Strengths

- Apart from intravenous injections, the procedure is painless and without significant risks or side effects, aside from a cold feeling moving up the arm after the injection is given.

- The small amount of radioactive material used is not harmful and is quickly excreted from the body; a process speeded up by drinking plenty of fluids.
- A small version of the PET scanner exists that permits the brain structures and neural activity of small animals to be additionally studied, so that these may be compared with human functioning to permit a deeper understanding of mental life.

Weaknesses

- The short-lived radionuclides used in the procedure are costly, meaning that the technique is not cost-effective. Also a trained analyst is required to correctly interpret the images produced, adding to the cost of the technique.
- As with other forms of scanning, the technique is not recommended for claustrophobics due to the confined nature of the scanner.
- Considerable re-processing of data generally has to take place for detailed, accurate analysis to occur, making the procedure time-consuming compared to other techniques.
- The images produced are not as clear or detailed as those produced by fMRI scans.

SECTION SUMMARY
- Schemas create a readiness to interpret sensory information in pre-set ways.
- Top-down theories believe perception involves cognitive processing that goes beyond sensory input, while bottom-up theories see perception occurring directly from sensory input.
- Face recognition concerns how faces are processed and understood, with case studies of prosopagnosia forming the main research tool.
- Cultural factors predispose people to perceive environmental features in certain ways.
- Research shows that EWT lacks reliability, due to the reconstructive nature of memory and the influence of schemas.
- Non-invasive forms of scanning are used to study the brain structures underpinning cognitive processes.

Cognition and emotion

LEARNING OUTCOME
- To what extent do cognitive and biological factors interact in emotion?

Emotion – a state of mind determined by one's mood.

One early theory of **emotion** was that of James (1894) and Lange (1885) who independently proposed that emotions don't occur immediately after the perception of an event, but instead occur after the body has responded to an event. This became known as the **James–Lange theory of emotion**, whereby the perception of a stimulus, such as a hissing snake, causes physiological changes, like increased heartbeat and breathing, and the brain identifies these changes in behaviour as an emotion, e.g. fear.

The **Cannon–Bard theory of emotion** challenges this assumption, seeing humans as experiencing physiological changes and emotions simultaneously. Emotions are specifically seen as occurring when the **thalamus**, a lower brain structure forming part of the **limbic system**, relays messages to the cortex of the brain for interpretation of an emotion and simultaneously to the **sympathetic nervous system** for appropriate physiological reactions.

Schachter and Singer's two-factor theory of emotion (1962)

Schachter and Singer's (1962) **two-factor theory of emotion** does not perceive physiological changes and the experience of emotion as being independent of each other, as did Cannon and Bard, but neither do they believe that physiological changes cause the experience of emotion, as did James and Lange. Instead they proposed that an individual decides which emotion they're experiencing and the label attached to the physiological state is dependent on what that physiological state is attributed to. Therefore the first factor is that physiological arousal is necessary for an experience of emotion, though the nature of that arousal isn't important, with the second factor being the interpretation of that arousal.

Key study

Schachter and Singer (1962)

Support for the two-factor theory comes from Schachter and Singer (1962) with their **adrenaline experiment**. Participants were given what they believed was a vitamin injection (actually adrenaline) to examine its effect on vision.

- **Group 1** – participants were given accurate information about the side effects of the injection, e.g. tremors and sweating.
- **Group 2** – participants were given incorrect information about the side effects of the injection, e.g. headache.
- **Group 3** – participants were given no information about side effects.
- **Group 4** – participants were given a saline injection and no information about side effects. (This was the control group.)

Before performing a 'vision' test each participant sat in a waiting room with a pseudo-participant (a fake participant). The pseudo-participant acted in a happy manner for half the participants in each condition and in an angry manner for the other half.

It was found that participants in groups 1 and 4 were less likely to copy the pseudo-participant's behaviour or report feeling happy or sad, while participants in groups 2 and 3 were much more likely to imitate the pseudo-participant's behaviour and to report feeling happy or sad. This supports the researchers' belief that it is the interpretation of physiological arousal, through the label placed on that state of arousal, that determines what particular emotion is experienced.

Evaluation of the two-factor theory

- The theory has research support, like Dutton and Aron (1974), confirming that the autonomic nervous system arousal experienced with all emotions is similar and thus it's the identification/labelling of the arousal that determines the emotion. They found that males who crossed a 'scary' bridge were more likely to subsequently ask a female researcher for a date than those crossing a 'safe' bridge, as those crossing the scary bridge misattributed the arousal they felt from crossing the bridge as sexual attraction towards the female.
- Maslach (1979) criticized the theory. He used hypnosis so that some participants would become aroused at the presentation of a cue (although they wouldn't recall the source of this arousal) and after hypnosis they were subjected to a pseudo-participant behaving in either a happy or a sad manner. They were then subsequently exposed to two more 'happy' pseudo-participants, where for one pseudo-participant they were aware of the source of the arousal, while for the other they weren't (participants were told to expect varying arousal effects). Maslach found that unexplained arousal elicited a negative response, i.e. participants would experience anger or fear even in the presence of a 'happy' pseudo-participant, which suggests that unexplained arousal leads to the experience of negative emotions.

Theory of knowledge

Although psychologists conduct experimental research into the experience of emotion and attempt to identify the associated physiological features and cognitive processes underlying the phenomena, there are many who would argue that emotional experience is beyond the scrutiny of scientific investigation.

Lazarus's cognitive appraisal theory (1982)

Lazarus believed that cognitive factors are most important in determining emotion. He saw emotion as arising from an individual's interpretation and explanation of a particular event, even in the absence of physiological arousal. Lazarus identified two crucial factors in the cognitive aspects of emotion. Firstly, the nature of cognitive appraisals that underlie separate emotional responses, e.g. fear, happiness, etc., and secondly, the determining preceding conditions (those that come before) of those cognitive appraisals. Two types of appraisal methods are perceived as underpinning appraisal: **primary appraisal**, concerning the meaning and significance of an event to an individual, and **secondary appraisal**, concerning an individual's assessment of their ability to cope with the consequences of that event. Primary appraisal assesses the importance of an event, while secondary appraisal assesses coping mechanisms, which Lazarus divided into **direct actions** and **cognitive reappraisal processes**. Overall, Lazarus stresses the importance of cognition (thinking), as when we experience an event thoughts precede physiological arousal and the sensation of emotion (which occur simultaneously). Therefore some cognitive processing must occur before an individual can experience an emotional response to an event.

Research

- Speisman *et al.* (1964) found that when shown a film about Aboriginal circumcision, participants experienced the most physiological arousal when the traumatic element of the film was heightened through manipulation of the sound track, so that emphasis was focused on the jaggedness of the knife, pain of the boys, etc. This suggests that the cognitive appraisal of what people think about a situation affects the level of arousal experienced, giving support to Lazarus's theory.

■ Critical thinking

Speisman *et al.*'s (1964) study can be considered unethical, as it produced psychological distress by exposing participants to traumatic images. Can it be argued from a cost–benefit analysis that this ethical violation was allowable? In other words, do the benefits, in the terms of knowledge gained, outweigh the distress caused?

Evaluation

- Zajonc (1984) argued that although emotion and cognition are independent of each other and that cognition usually precedes emotion and physiological arousal, it is quite possible for emotion to be experienced without cognition occurring. For example, if suddenly confronted by a hissing snake, physiological reactions of increased heart-rate, rapid breathing, etc., would occur before the sensory data concerning the snake was cognitively processed. Zajonc showed that participants had a preference for pictures they'd previously been shown subliminally (too quickly for conscious recognition to occur), even though they didn't recall being shown them, than for pictures never seen before. This supports Zajonc's idea that emotion can occur without cognition.

- Lazarus counter-argues that human liking for stimuli experienced subliminally doesn't mean that such stimuli weren't processed cognitively, as awareness doesn't necessarily equate with conscious thinking.
- Lazarus's theory has been superseded by more recent cognitive neuroscience explanations, which see emotion and cognition as controlled by separate, but interacting, brain systems. Emotional systems are seen as assessing the biological significance of external and internal stimuli, like thoughts and memories, with these assessments occurring before conscious awareness and with only the results of such assessments becoming conscious. Therefore, while all emotional processes have a cognitive component, not all cognition has an emotional component.

Emotion and perception

LEARNING OUTCOME
■ Evaluate one theory of how emotion may affect one cognitive process.

Perceptual defence – the process by which stimuli are not perceived or are distorted due to their threatening or offensive nature.

We have seen how perception can be biased by perceptual set, so that individuals perceive what they wish and expect to perceive based on previous experiences, expectations, cultural factors, etc. Another way in which set affects perception is through emotional factors creating a bias to perceive (or not) certain features of incoming sensory data. An important factor here is **perceptual defence**, where emotionally threatening stimuli take longer to perceive.

Research
- McGinnies (1949) presented participants with 11 emotionally neutral words, like 'apple' and seven emotionally threatening words, like 'rape', with each word presented for increasingly long durations until it was recognized, finding that emotionally threatening words took longer to recognize, which suggests that perceptual defence influences perception through emotional factors.

■ Critical thinking
McGinnies (1949) investigated the effect of emotionally threatening words on perception, but why did he use neutral words, as well as emotionally threatening ones, in his experiment?

- Lazarus and McCleary (1951) found that nonsense syllables presented so rapidly they couldn't consciously be perceived raised anxiety levels if previously paired with electric shocks, which suggests that emotional factors influence perception unconsciously.
- Hardy and Legge (1968) presented participants with an acoustic stimulus that increased in intensity, while emotive or neutral words were flashed subliminally on a screen, to find that the stimulus was detected at a higher intensity with the emotive than the neutral words. This further supports the idea that perceptual defence affects perception.
- Phelps *et al.* (2006) manipulated emotion by briefly showing participants either fearful or neutral faces in various locations on a screen. An image then appeared briefly and participants selected in which direction it tilted. Participants performed best when the figure was paired with fearful faces, especially those in the same orientation as the tilted figure, which implies that emotion facilitates perception early in the processing system. Zeelenberg and Bocanegra (2010) further found that acoustic presentation of negative emotional words enhanced the perception of subsequent visually presented emotionally neutral target words, but impaired performance when they were presented visually. This suggests that emotional stimuli affect perception differently in different sensory modalities, perhaps due to the focusing of attention.

■ Brasel *et al.* (2006) presented a picture, the central image of which was a woman leaping to her death, to assess the perception of 56 participants. An eye-tracker device showed that 88 per cent of participants fixated at least once on the falling woman, with the average fixation time being 25 per cent of exposure time. Only 35 per cent recalled the woman, however, with 30 per cent recalling no central image, though remembering other elements of the image in accurate detail; 35 per cent used schematic processing to transform the image of the falling woman into something safe, like 'the image of an angel'. This again suggests that perceptual defence is used to restrict the perception of emotionally threatening events.

Figure 2.22 The Genesee Hotel suicide picture

Evaluation

■ Findings from early studies of perceptual defence, like McGinnies (1949), may have occurred, as participants were too embarrassed to speak the words aloud. However, when Bitterman and Kniffin (1953) repeated the study, but with participants writing the words down instead of speaking them, no differences in recognition time were found, which suggests that perceptual defence is a valid concept.

■ When using emotionally threatening stimuli, such as the Genesee Hotel suicide picture, to assess perceptual defence, care should be taken not to psychologically harm participants, with fully informed consent being gained prior to participation and full debriefing afterwards.

■ The use of subliminal stimuli, which are presented too quickly for conscious recognition to occur, suggests that perceptual defence is a real phenomenon rather than being a response bias, where participants are embarrassed to recognize such stimuli or are genuinely unfamiliar with them. However, the paradox here is how participants can selectively defend themselves against emotionally threatening stimuli unless they have already consciously recognized them as threatening.

SECTION SUMMARY
■ Cognitive and biological factors interact to create the experience of emotion, with discussion occurring over the relevant contributions of each.
■ Perceptual defence demonstrates how emotional factors influence the perception of threatening and distressing stimuli.

Sociocultural level of analysis

Introduction

The two preceding chapters have shown how human behaviour and experience can be analysed at the biological and cognitive levels of analysis. As you have read these chapters, it may have become clear to you that other important factors also influence much of human behaviour. These factors are commonly grouped together under the umbrella term of 'sociocultural' factors.

Let's look at a simple example using a basic behaviour – eating. Eating is a biologically driven process. We eat when we are hungry, in response to bodily signals, sent via hormones to brain centres when blood sugar levels have dropped. Cognitive factors are involved in deciding when to eat and what to eat. We may be training for a marathon and trying to eat more carbohydrates, or attempting to reduce our caloric intake in order to lose weight. Sociocultural factors also play a role: food availability varies depending on region, and religious background may prohibit certain foods or emphasize how foods should be prepared (e.g. halal or kosher). This example demonstrates that even simple behaviours can be considered at different levels of analysis. Each of the levels – biological, cognitive, sociocultural – reveals a different picture and no single approach can explain a behaviour in its entirety.

The levels of analysis ask different questions and utilize different kinds of data. For example, a biological psychologist might ask questions about eating at the level of genetic inheritance, hormones or the structure of the brain. In contrast, the cognitive level would consider beliefs and thoughts about food. Finally, the sociocultural perspective would consider how social influences and cultural practices – upbringing, family and socialization – influence eating behaviours. Rather than being viewed as competing or conflicting explanations, this combined approach reflects a modern trend in psychology towards integration. All three levels of analysis can help us to understand what, when and why we eat.

The sociocultural level of analysis is the most recent of the three to emerge. It has arisen from the rapid development of psychology and its synthesis with sociology and anthropology. The roots of the perspective lie within 'the fertile grounds of everyday social reality' (Valsiner and Rosa, 2007, p.1) and the realization that the human world is culturally constituted. This chapter begins by examining the three key principles that underlie the sociocultural level of analysis, before moving on to consider the kinds of research methods that are favoured by the sociocultural level of analysis. We will then examine how social and cultural factors influence a range of human behaviours and end by examining some of the important ethical issues relating to this approach.

Principles that define the sociocultural level of analysis

LEARNING OUTCOME
- Outline principles that define the sociocultural level of analysis.

Principle 1: The social and cultural environment influences individual behaviour

Psychology is a relatively young science which began in 1879, when Wilhelm Wundt established the first laboratory devoted to experimental psychology in Germany. In the early days, psychology was concerned with individual processes and there was little consideration of how social or cultural forces influenced behaviour. As the discipline developed, there was an increasing realization that human behaviour could only be fully understood by taking into account the social context in which it occurred. The study of social psychology is thought to have originated with the work of Triplett (1898), who noticed that racing cyclists produced faster lap times when training in pairs than alone. Triplett investigated this in what is thought to be social psychology's earliest experiment, by asking children to complete a simple manual task (winding a fishing reel) alone or in pairs. Triplett found that performance was faster when the children carried out the task in pairs, even though they had not been asked to race with each other. Triplett called this effect 'social facilitation'.

Over the twentieth century, there was growing interest in social influences on many kinds of behaviour. The atrocities of the 1939–45 war led to a strong interest in obedience to authority and conformity to social norms. During the 1950s and 60s, social psychologists examined the influence of groups, crowds and leaders on human behaviour. Today, it is widely accepted that the social environment influences many aspects of individual behaviour and experience.

The sociocultural level of analysis also acknowledges the important role played by cultural factors in human behaviour. Up to the late 1960s, most research was carried out in Western industrialized societies such as North America, northern Europe and Australia. Findings of such research studies were used to devise models of human behaviour that were assumed to apply universally. In the 1960s and 70s, however, many researchers challenged this assumption as a result of emerging evidence demonstrating large cultural variations in behaviours and psychological processes (Hogg & Vaughan, 2005). These findings led to claims that psychology was culture-bound and culture-blind. An interest in cross-cultural psychology grew and flowered in the late 1960s and early 70s with the publication of the first psychological journals devoted to cross-cultural research. Today, culture is seen as an important influence on human behaviour and experience.

Principle 2: We want connectedness with, and a sense of belonging with, others

Human beings are social animals. For most of our evolutionary history, we have lived in relatively small groups of around 150 people. Up to about 10,000 years ago, our ancestors were hunter-gatherers. The tasks that were essential for survival – tracking and hunting animals, finding mates, caring for offspring and defending against predators – were difficult, if not impossible, to accomplish alone and group living was essential for survival. Today, we live in very different environments to those experienced by our distant ancestors. Despite this, most people continue to maintain social relationships with around 150 people (a figure which is known as 'Dunbar's number' after the evolutionary psychologist Robin Dunbar). Traffic data from social networking sites like Facebook shows that, while people may have thousands of Facebook 'friends', most people have an inner circle of around 150 contacts, in a similar way to our ancestors and to social networks in the face-to-face world.

Evolutionary psychologists argue that the human mind was shaped by processes operating during this vital hunter-gatherer period. In evolutionary terms, little real time has passed since then and it is thought that many of the human traits and behaviours seen today date back to that period. Tajfel's social identity theory (SIT) is an influential approach that you will meet later in this chapter. SIT argues that the need to connect with others in social groups is a powerful influence on many aspects of human behaviour. SIT helps us to understand conflict between different groups, along with in-group favouritism and prejudice against people from different groups. These human experiences originate in the powerful need to connect with others and to belong to social groups.

Principle 3: We construct our conceptions of the individual and social self

How would you describe yourself to someone who didn't know you? The way that people view themselves is referred to as the self-concept or simply the 'self'. The self-concept develops in early childhood and continues to be refined throughout adolescence and adulthood. It contains an evaluative component, which is commonly known as self-esteem. Self-esteem develops as children compare themselves with other people and see how others treat them and respond to them.

The third principle of the sociocultural perspective refers to development of the self. This principle is based on an influential approach in social science known as social constructionism. According to social constructionism, the self is complex and multi-faceted (Phoenix, 2007). Most people present different aspects of themselves when at school, work and with friends or family. The self is highly social and the version that is 'constructed' is influenced by the people around and the wider social setting. You may be surprised to find how differently your friends behave at home with their families, to when they are at college.

Western views of the self broadly favour individual achievement, independence and competition. Collectivist societies view people as interdependent and connected to social groups. This illustrates an important principle of the sociocultural level of analysis: the ways in which we understand the world are not 'natural' but are constructions. They are created or constructed between people in everyday interactions using language.

You can read more about the different cultural models of the self in the next section of this chapter (*see page 73*).

Research methods and ethical issues

LEARNING OUTCOMES
■ Discuss how and why particular research methods are used at the sociocultural level of analysis (for example, participant/naturalistic observation, interviews, case studies).
■ Discuss ethical considerations related to research studies at the sociocultural level of analysis.

In this chapter, we will demonstrate how the methods used by sociocultural psychologists have changed and developed over the last 30 years. The previous chapters covering the biological and cognitive levels of analysis have drawn your attention to the use of highly scientific methods in modern psychology and the emphasis on experimentation with manipulation of variables and high levels of control. We have also seen how modern technologies are influencing the study of brain processes in neuropsychology and cognitive science. Many of the classic studies covered in this chapter were carried out in the 1960s and 70s and used the experimental methods that dominated social psychology at the time. These tightly controlled laboratory settings enabled researchers to tease out causal relationships and to see exactly which factors influenced social behaviours such as the pressure to conform to group norms.

The 1980s saw a paradigm shift as many social psychologists pointed to the limitations of laboratory experiments in studying complex social behaviour. Laboratory experiments were criticized for stripping the social world of its richness and complexity and reducing the social and cultural environment to a controlled variable in a laboratory. This led to a turn to more natural methods, in which behaviour was studied in the real environment where possible, using different forms of **observation**. Sociocultural psychologists also borrowed some of the methods used by sociologists and anthropologists such as **ethnography** – a specific type of observation in which researchers immerse themselves in the environment and culture they are studying, often for days or weeks.

Other favoured methods include interviews, focus group discussions and case studies. Unlike experimentation, which produces quantitative data, these methods obtain rich, qualitative data that can be analysed using qualitative techniques such as discourse or thematic analysis, or converted to quantitative data through the use of content analysis.

Some sociocultural psychologists continue to make use of experimentation, but prefer quasi-experimental studies in which the independent variable occurs spontaneously without manipulation. Experiments carried out by Charlton *et al.* (2002) and Becker *et al.* (2002) have investigated changes to behaviour following the introduction of Western television to remote communities. Quasi-experimental studies often involve minimal researcher intervention and are preferred over laboratory experiments, as they are generally higher in validity.

Many of the experiments carried out in the 1960s and 70s involved ethical issues including deception, lack of informed consent and psychological harm to those who took part. Experiments such as those carried out by Bandura *et al.* (1963) would now be seen as unacceptable by the ethical codes and standards that govern psychological research in the twenty-first century. The methods preferred by sociocultural psychologists, however, still involve ethical considerations. In common with experimental research, both the American Psychological Association (APA) and the British Psychological Society (BPS) emphasize the need to gain the fully informed consent of those who take part in research. Consent should be obtained from those who are legally competent (i.e. adults) or their authorized representatives (i.e. parents or legal guardians in the case of children).

The APA guidelines suggest that consent can be dispensed with in anonymous questionnaires, naturalistic observations or archival research when the data collected would not place participants at any form of risk and when their confidentiality is protected (APA, 2002). With respect to observation, the BPS Ethical Principles suggest that this can take place without informed consent, but should be restricted to those places or situations where the people being studied would reasonably expect to be observed by strangers (e.g. shopping centres). In addition, local cultural values and the privacy of individuals should be respected.

The BPS code stresses that researchers should respect individual and cultural differences, especially those relating to 'age, disability, education, ethnicity, gender, language, national origin, race, religion, sexual orientation, marital or family status and socio-economic status' (BPS, 2009). Qualitative researchers are also aware of the importance of a reflexive stance which acknowledges the subjective nature of much qualitative research.

Orientation of this chapter

LEARNING OUTCOME
■ Explain how principles that define the sociocultural level of analysis may be demonstrated in research.

The sociocultural perspective recognizes that social and cultural forces have a strong influence on human behaviour and experience. In this chapter, we will demonstrate these three underlying principles – cultural, social and sociocultural – in theories and research studies. We will begin by examining how culture influences the self along with the impact of cultural forces on behaviour. We will then move on to consider the influences of more direct social forces: how the people around us can influence us by acting as role models or creating group pressures to conform. Finally, we will examine how both cultural and social factors influence the ways in which we process social information – social cognition.

Cultural influences on behaviour

In this section of the chapter, we are going to consider how cultural forces shape human behaviours, values and beliefs. Cultural influences can be subtle and are often taken for granted. For example, personal relationships are organized in different ways in different parts of the world. In many Western societies, young people are free to choose their own partners and can cohabit (live together) or marry. Relationships which are unhappy can be ended by separation or divorce. In many countries, however, partners are chosen by parents in partially or wholly arranged marriages, which may be difficult or impossible to end. In many places, marital relationships are seen as exclusive and marriage to more than one person is an offence punishable by law. Other cultures, however, permit men and/or women to have several marriage partners.

Your view of these different arrangements is likely to depend on the norms of your own culture: it is likely that some of these ways of organizing relationships feel 'normal' whereas others may appear rather 'strange'. It is only when we stand back and compare our expectations with those of someone from a different social group that we begin to see the impact and extent of cultural influences.

Culture and cultural norms

LEARNING OUTCOME
■ Define the terms 'culture' and 'cultural norms'.

Culture – refers to the shared habits of a community.

Although the word **culture** is widely used in daily language and within psychology, it is difficult to define precisely, leading Hogg and Vaughan (2002) to refer to the idea as an important but 'slippery' concept. Triandis (1980) distinguishes between two elements of culture:

■ Objective aspects of culture are physical entities that can be seen. This includes clothing (for example, wearing a veil), foods, music and buildings (e.g. mosque, church or temple).
■ Subjective aspects of culture are non-physical entities that can't be seen. Subjective aspects include beliefs, values and shared ideas, and they exert powerful and subtle influences on behaviour.

Although definitions of culture vary, it is widely agreed that cultural forces exert an important influence on human interactions. Cultural beliefs and practices are passed from generation to generation. Some aspects of cultural transmission are explicit, for example when children are instructed in religious practices. Other cultural practices are learnt implicitly so that children grow up accepting some ways of doing things as 'normal', only to discover that other groups of people have different practices and behave in different ways.

Cultural norms – rules which regulate behaviour within a particular culture.

Cultural norms are rules that regulate behaviour within a particular culture. These norms vary dramatically in different parts of the world. In Arab countries, for example, it is customary for male friends or colleagues to embrace and kiss on both cheeks when they meet. This kind of greeting between men would be unusual in public in the USA or UK and may be interpreted as indicating a sexual relationship between the men. This example demonstrates how a similar behaviour can have different meanings in different places. Some cultural norms are enshrined in laws, for example which side of the road you should drive on, and there are formal sanctions for breaking them. Other norms operate informally and are enforced by people showing disapproval when they are broken. Cultural norms, however, work to promote social control. When people ignore cultural rules, their behaviour stands out and they run the risk of being labelled as deviant.

Figure 3.1 In some cultures it is considered extremely rude to shake hands with your left hand

The importance of cultural norms was noted by the anthropologist Margaret Mead. Mead travelled to Samoa in the Pacific Islands in the 1920s and 30s and observed the behaviours of young people, which appeared very different to those of 1920s America. Mead carried out interviews and observations with a sample of 68 adolescent Samoan girls. From this, she argued that Samoan cultural norms encouraged sexual exploration and casual sexual activity between young women and men (Mead, 1928). In later work, Mead travelled to Papua New Guinea and studied the behaviour of three tribes with very different patterns of behaviour (Mead, 1930). The Mundugomor tribe lived in a harsh physical environment and Mead was surprised by the ways in which young children were treated. Babies were fed rapidly and offered little by way of comfort or cuddling. Young children were expected to fend for themselves by the time they were able to walk. Although Mead's work was later criticized as unscientific, her basic observation that norms vary in different cultures was widely accepted.

Cultural norms have a strong influence on how young children are socialized and the different kinds of qualities which they are encouraged to develop. Cross-cultural studies of attachment have demonstrated differences between mothering style in Japan and Germany that influence the kinds of behaviours demonstrated by young children in response to separation (Van Ijzendoorn & Kroonenberg, 1988). In Germany, babies are encouraged to develop independence and self-reliance, so are less likely to cry when left with a stranger. In contrast, Japanese mothers with young children rarely work outside the house and infants protest loudly at separation. The idea of the Chinese 'Tiger Mother' has been popularized by Amy Chua's 2012 book *Battle Hymn of the Tiger Mother*, which portrays Chinese mothers as using a particularly strict parenting style designed to foster achievement and success in their offspring. Chang and Hynie (2011) have examined the truth of this stereotype, by comparing the parenting styles used by mothers in mainland China with Chinese Canadian and European Canadian mothers. In agreement with the popular stereotype of the Tiger Mother, they found that authoritarian (strict) parenting styles were more notable in both mainland Chinese and Chinese Canadian mothers.

Cultural norms also influence how children are taught to express or emotions such as anger and fear. Novin *et al.*(2011) compared a sample of 141 11-year-old children drawn from the Netherlands and Hong Kong, and examined how they responded to provocation and teasing by other children. Both sets of children preferred to keep angry feelings inside rather than communicating them to the provocateur. The Dutch children, however, were more likely to verbally confront the aggressor if pushed to stand up for themselves, whereas the Chinese children were more likely to react tolerantly and to attempt to appease the aggressor. The results demonstrate the importance of the immediate social environment in perpetuating cultural differences.

'The culture of honour' in the southern USA

Rates of violence and murder are higher in the southern states of America than in the northern states. This has been attributed to the 'culture of honour' that operates in the southern states. According to the culture of honour, men have a right to protect their property and assets using violence. They are particularly sensitive to threats to their honour or insults to their family.

How did this cultural norm originate? According to Todd Shackleford (2005), the southern states of the USA were colonized predominantly by settlers from Scotland and Northern Ireland, who came from herding backgrounds. Herders often resorted to violence to protect wandering animals and assert their ownership. In such environments, rules of law offered little protection so a reputation for violence was one way of ensuring and protecting property. The southern states of the USA were a frontier region, with a low population well into the nineteenth century. According to Nisbett and Cohen (1996), 'a system of order that commonly develops under these circumstances is defined by "the rule of retaliation": *"If you cross me, I will punish you"*.' The culture of honour has its roots in gender socialization. Boys are taught to stand up for themselves and to fight to protect themselves. Cultures of honour have been widely documented elsewhere in the world and are most common in herding societies.

How do cultural dimensions influence behaviour?

LEARNING OUTCOME
■ Examine the role of two cultural dimensions on behaviour (for example, individualism/collectivism, power/distance).

Cultures vary in many ways. In order to simplify this complexity, cross-cultural psychologists have identified key dimensions that can help us to make sense of cultural patterns in values and behaviours. An influential model was put forward by Hofstede (1980), who analysed questionnaires about attitudes and values completed by 117,000 managers working for IBM in 40 countries. Using a statistical technique called factor analysis, Hofstede isolated four key dimensions of cultural variation – individualism/collectivism, masculinity/femininity, power/distance and uncertainty avoidance. In 1991, using a larger sample of 50 countries, Hofstede added a fifth dimension – time perspective, which is also known as 'Confucian dynamism'. Each dimension represents a bipolar scale, with two extreme poles. Table 3.1 outlines Hofstede's four original dimensions and identifies countries that demonstrate the two 'extremes' of each.

Table 3.1 Hofstede's four cultural dimensions (1980)

DIMENSION	EXPLANATION	HIGH-SCORING COUNTRIES	LOW-SCORING COUNTRIES
Individualism/ collectivism	In individualistic cultures, personal identity is viewed as a matter of personal choice. In collectivist cultures, the wider social group (notably the family) has a greater influence and identity is largely defined by roles and relationships.	The UK and USA are strongly individualistic.	Southern American and Asian countries (e.g. Venezuela, Pakistan) are strongly collectivist.
Masculinity/ femininity	Masculine cultures value attributes such as achievement, independence and competition. Feminine cultures value caring and cooperation.	Japan scores highly on masculinity and values personal achievement.	Scandinavian countries (Sweden, Norway and the Netherlands) are highly feminine and value cooperation.
Power/ distance	In 'power' cultures, unequal relationships are tolerated or accepted even by those low down in the social hierarchy. Business organizations and families are strongly hierarchical with people having different status and power. 'Distance' cultures value equality in business and family relationships.	Central and Southern American countries (e.g. Venezuela) value power and are strongly hierarchical.	Denmark and Israel are highly egalitarian and are classed as distance cultures.
Uncertainty avoidance	Uncertainty avoidance cultures are those in which risk-taking is largely disapproved of.	In Greece, Portugal and Japan, risk-taking is generally disapproved of.	In Singapore and Denmark, experimentation is encouraged.

Hofstede's model demonstrates the complexity of cultural variations. For example, Denmark is low on power/distance and uncertainty avoidance but is classed as a highly individualistic culture. Japan is strongly individualistic but risks are avoided and masculine attributes such as personal achievement are highly valued. A simpler version of cultural classification was put forward by Fiske *et al.* (1998) based on two of Hofstede's dimensions, individualism/collectivism and power/distance. Fiske *et al.* suggested that:

- Western European nations (UK, France) tend to be egalitarian (based on equality) and individualistic.
- Eastern European nations (Slovakia, Greece) are hierarchical and individualistic.
- Asian nations are hierarchical and collectivist.

How does individualism/collectivism influence behaviour?

In much psychological research, cultural variations are simplified to comparisons between individualist and collectivist cultures (Hogg & Vaughan, 2002). In collectivist cultures, people are encouraged to be interconnected and individual behaviour is strongly guided by social roles and group membership. In individualistic cultures, people are seen as separate and therefore independent and autonomous. Rather than being driven by social roles and responsibilities, behaviour is seen as arising from personality traits and internal dispositions. For this reason, personal goals are pursued and people compete with each other rather than cooperate.

These differences can be seen in relation to the formation and regulation of romantic relationships. Individualistic cultures place a large emphasis on the pursuit of individual happiness. Relationships are viewed as unions between two people so young people

Figure 3.2 What matters – winning or just taking part?

choose their own partners on the basis of attraction and love. Relationships that are unhappy can be ended by separation or divorce. In collectivist cultures, relationships are largely seen as unions between families; family members play a substantial role in partner choice, often through systems of arranged marriages. Arranged marriages tend to be long-lasting and stable and it may be very difficult to end unhappy relationships through divorce, as this brings shame on both families (Goodwin, 1999). This has led Moghaddam *et al.* (1993) to characterize relationships in individualistic cultures as voluntary, temporary and individualistic whereas those in collectivist cultures are categorized as obligatory, permanent and as alliances between families.

Perhaps the most important difference between individualism and collectivism lies in the self-concept. Cousins (1989) compared 159 Japanese students from Tokyo, with 111 North American students from Michigan. Each student was asked to complete a 'Twenty Statements Test' (TST) by providing 20 answers to the question *'Who am I?'* Japanese students were more likely to refer to social roles (e.g. *'I am a brother'*) and to their membership of social groups (e.g. *'I am in the gymnastics club'*), demonstrating the importance of interconnections and relationships in collectivist cultures. By contrast, American students used personal or psychological attributes (e.g. *'I am intelligent'* or *'I am musical'*), demonstrating how the individualistic self is largely seen as independent. These different models of the self lead to different kinds of behaviours in individualist and collectivist cultures, which are summarized by Triandis (1990, p.42):

'In individualist cultures, most people's social behaviour is largely determined by personal goals ...When a conflict arises between personal and group goals, it is considered acceptable for the individual to place personal goals ahead of collective goals. By contrast, in collectivist cultures,

social behaviour is determined largely by goals shared with some collective, and if there is a conflict between personal and collective goals, it is considered socially desirable to place collective goals ahead of personal goals.'

(Triandis, 1990, p.42, in Bond & Smith, 1996)

These different models of the self also help us to understand other cultural differences, for example conformity to group norms and attributional style, which we will consider in the later sections of this chapter.

How does power/distance influence behaviour?

Another of Hofstede's dimensions is power/distance. This dimension has received less attention than individualism–collectivism but it is important for many aspects of group interaction and performance. In simple terms, power/distance refers to 'the extent to which the less powerful members of institutions and organizations within a country expect and accept that power is distributed unequally' (Hofstede, 2001, p.98). In cultures where power/distance is low, there is a general acceptance that inequalities between people should be minimized and those who are subordinate should be consulted in group decisions. In high power/distance cultures, inequalities are expected and even desired. Subordinates generally expect to be told what to do and leaders are viewed as having undisputed power and authority.

How does power/distance show in daily interactions between individuals? A study by Meeusewen *et al.* (2009) examined the interactions between 307 general practitioners (doctors) and their patients across a range of European countries including Belgium (Western Europe), Romania (Eastern Europe) and Sweden (Northern Europe). Consultations were videotaped and analysed in relation to Hofstede's dimensions. In countries with a higher power/distance score (e.g. Romania) consultations were shorter and patients had less opportunity to ask question or to exchange information. Roles were clearly fixed, with GPs demonstrating considerable power and authority. In countries with a lower PD score (e.g. Sweden) consultations were longer and information was exchanged with opportunities for patients to ask questions.

Power/distance is also influential in relation to attitude change and persuasion. In cultures with a high power/distance score, more respect is generally given to experts and those with higher social status. Pornpitakpan and June (2001) compared 76 Canadian (distance culture) and 185 Thai (power culture) students, varying the source and content of a persuasive message. The social status and expertise of the source figure had a greater impact on the Thai students than on those from Canada. Canadian students were more interested in the quality of the argument presented than where the argument came from.

Practical applications

In an increasingly 'global' world is it important for workers such as medical students and those in multinational companies to appreciate how cultural norms regulate behaviours in different parts of the world. Many companies now offer cross-cultural training and awareness to prepare workers for the global village.

Emic and etic concepts

LEARNING OUTCOME
■ Using one or more examples, explain 'emic' and 'etic' concepts.

As noted in the introduction to this chapter, research must be carried out somewhere – but this does not mean that the results obtained can necessarily be applied to other places and cultures. The assumption that findings from research carried out in one place such as the USA can be applied to others (e.g. Japan) is referred to as ethnocentrism. The most common form of this is eurocentrism – the view that European behaviours are the 'norm' or basis from which to judge others. Many influential psychological theories have reflected eurocentrism in the past.

The distinction between **emic** and **etic analysis** is based on the linguistic distinction between phonemes and phonetics. Phonetics refers to the study of the universal set of sounds which make up all languages, whereas phonemes are the sounds that occur within a specific language. Cross-cultural psychologists have adapted this distinction and refer to two kinds of analysis, 'emic' and 'etic' as shortcuts to talk about the emphasis given to the role of cultural factors:

- **Etic analysis** – rests on the assumption that a particular behaviour is universal and occurs in a similar form across all cultures. This assumption is most likely to be valid in relation to biologically driven behaviours, as these tend to be similar across different cultures. An example of this would be the 90-minute ultradian sleep cycle identified by Dement and Kleitman (1957), which occurs in adults across the world. A consequence of the etic assumption is that findings from a research study (for example, on sleep cycles) could be used to develop a model or theory that could reasonably be applied in other cultures. The etic assumption is less applicable when we consider more complex behaviours, for example broader sleep habits or conforming to group norms. These kinds of behaviours are strongly influenced by context, social and cultural norms, and findings of studies in one culture cannot simply be applied to another. When this misapplication occurs, it is referred to as an **imposed etic**. Look out for examples of this later on in the chapter, when we consider the fundamental attribution error and conformity to social norms – both of which show dramatic cultural variations.

- **Emic analysis** – takes the assumption that a particular behaviour varies in different cultures. Extending the above example, while the 90-minute ultradian sleep cycle appears to be culturally universal, sleep habits show substantial cross-cultural variations and are strongly influenced by social and cultural norms. In Westernized cultures, infants are expected to sleep on their own and only about 5 per cent of young children regularly bed-share with their parents (generally when parents despair of getting them to sleep any other way!). In many Pacific countries such as Vietnam, however, bed-sharing is the norm: over 80 per cent of children sleep in the parents' bed (Mindell *et al.*, 2010) and this behaviour is viewed as entirely normal and desirable. If we take this view, findings from research carried out in one place cannot simply be applied to another place, as they are likely to be invalid. This is the basis of **cultural relativism**, which assumes that all cultures are equally worthy of study. Culture-bound syndromes also demonstrate the importance of an emic assumption. These are psychological problems that occur in some cultures but do not appear universally in all parts of the world. For instance, koro is an intense fear that the penis will shrink and disappear into the body, which is found in male Chinese students; taijin kyofoshu is a chronic social anxiety based on fear of offending or harming other people found in Japan.

Emic analysis – assumes that behaviours are culture-specific and research findings cannot be assumed to apply to other cultures.

Etic analysis – assumes that findings from research in one culture can be applied universally to other cultures.

SECTION SUMMARY
- Culture refers to the shared habits of a community.
- Cultural norms regulate behaviour within a culture.
- Cultural variation is complex. Two key dimensions identified by Hofstede are individualism/collectivism and power/distance.
- Individualistic and collectivist cultures have different concepts of the self.
- Power/distance refers to the acceptance of inequality in a culture.
- Etic analysis assumes that behaviours are universal across cultures. Emic analysis assumes that behaviours are culturally specific.

Social influences on behaviour

In the last section we considered how cultural factors influence behaviour through different cultural conceptions of the self and more obviously through cultural norms. In this section of the chapter, we will consider how people influence each other at a more direct level. Every day, friends, family or workmates may encourage you to act in a particular way and you may experience group pressures to do something – such as laughing at a joke that you don't find particularly funny. We will start by considering how people around us, such as parents, siblings and friends, can influence us to act in particular ways by serving as role models – the basis of social learning theory. We will then consider how social groups can influence us to 'go along with the crowd' and adopt their attitudes or behaviours – the study of conformity. Finally, we will examine the strategies used by those who deliberately set out to persuade us – advertisers, salespeople and health professionals – to buy products or regulate our drinking. As you read this chapter, think about the different ways that people attempt to influence your behaviour on a daily basis.

LEARNING OUTCOME
- ■ Explain social learning theory, making reference to two relevant studies.

A look around any school playground will remind you how young children copy the behaviour of those they see around them, from older siblings to television characters. Albert Bandura, a Canadian psychologist, was interested in the role played by the environment in shaping and guiding social behaviour in young children. In 1963, he worked with two female colleagues, Sheila and Dorothy Ross, to set up an experiment in which he exposed young children to the actions of an adult role model who behaved violently towards a large, inflatable toy, 'Bobo' doll. Bandura varied the conditions of the experiment systematically to establish the important factors influencing observational learning.

Key study

Bandura *et al.* (1963)

Bandura, Ross and Ross used a sample of 96 nursery school children, half boys and half girls, aged on average 52 months. Bandura *et al.* divided the children into four groups, each containing 12 boys and 12 girls. Each child was tested individually.

First the child was taken to a playroom with a variety of toys. After a few minutes, an adult entered the room and proceeded to play aggressively with a large, inflatable 'Bobo' doll – hitting it with a mallet, kicking and punching it. After 10 minutes, each child was taken to a second playroom filled with exciting toys. As they began to explore the room, a researcher told the child that the toys were for some other children to play with, an action designed to create a state of frustration. The researcher finally took the child through to a third playroom containing toys and another Bobo doll. The child's behaviour in room 3 was filmed through hidden mirrors for 20 minutes.

The three-room procedure was repeated for all 96 children, but the condition of the first room was systematically varied to create three further conditions to the one described above:

- ■ **In group 2** – the room contained a TV screen showing a film of the violent adult model acting aggressively towards the Bobo doll.
- ■ **In group 3** – the room contained a TV screen showing a film of the violent adult model dressed as a cartoon cat and acting aggressively towards the Bobo doll.
- ■ **In group 4** – the adult model played quietly with toys and the children were shown no aggressive model. This was the control condition.

At the end of the experiment, Bandura and colleagues divided each 20-minute film of a child's behaviour in room 3 into 5-seconds slots and counted the amount of aggressive behaviours carried out in each slot by each child. They found that:

- Children in groups 1–3 carried out more aggressive acts than children in group 4, the control condition.
- The aggressive acts involved direct copying as well as some novel (new) aggressive behaviours.
- The type of model in conditions 1–3 (live, filmed or cartoon) made little difference to the amount of aggression shown.
- Boys were more aggressive than girls in all groups.

Figure 3.3 Stills from Bandura *et al.* (1963) showing the children playing aggressively with the Bobo doll.

In a second study using the same paradigm, Bandura examined how consequences of behaviour, such as reward or punishment, influenced children's imitation of aggressive behaviour. Three groups of children were exposed to an identical aggressive model but the first group saw the model rewarded for his aggressive behaviour, the second group saw the model punished and the third group saw no consequences. When exposed to the Bobo doll later, the children in groups 1 and 3 carried out more aggressive acts than group 2, who had seen the model receive a punishment for aggression. Using the results of these studies, Bandura argued that 'human nature is characterized as a vast potentiality that can be fashioned by social influences into a variety of forms' (Bandura, 1973, p.113).

Bandura's social learning theory

Social learning theory – claims that behaviours are learnt through observation of role models and imitation of their behaviour.

Social learning theory (Bandura, 1973) was based on three key principles:

- Behaviours could be learnt through the observation and imitation of role models.
- Imitation of behaviour would be more likely if the model received some sort of reward or reinforcement for the behaviour, Bandura called this **vicarious reinforcement**.
- Role models who were similar (for example, in age and sex) were thought to exert a particularly powerful influence on young children.

Evaluation of social learning theory

A limitation of the original version of SLT was the rather obvious point that observation alone is insufficient for the learning of much behaviour. Bandura (1977) and Bandura and Bussey (1984) extended SLT by acknowledging the important role played by cognitive factors in observational learning. In order for imitation to take place, the learner needs to notice the behaviour of the model (attention) and store a representation of it in memory (retention). In order to imitate the behaviour, the learner should also be physically capable of carrying out the action (reproduction), and finally there should be some motivation to carry out the action. Today, SLT is often referred to 'social cognitive theory' and there has been considerable interest in how memories of actions are stored. One

Scripts – complex memories about how to behave in social situations.

suggestion is through the concept of schemas and **scripts**. Schemas are sets of ideas about people or situations that are quickly retrieved. Scripts are plans of how to act in social situations (Huesmann, 1986). Both schemas and scripts are built up from experience and are thought to exert a priming effect on behaviour: when we are in a situation similar to one in which we have witnessed an aggressive act, these memories are triggered rapidly, leading us to be more likely to act aggressively.

Link to the biological and cognitive levels of analysis

These extensions to social learning theory emphasize the important role played by cognitive factors in aggression. Similarly, those children who had been identified as more aggressive before Bandura's experiment were most influenced by the aggressive model, demonstrating the interplay of individual biology with environment.

SLT provides an important explanation of how children and adults learn behaviours from role models. Experimental studies have established that social learning plays an important role in the development of behaviours, not just the aggressive actions identified by Bandura. These include pro-social behaviours such as helping and cooperation. Role models also play an important part in the development of antisocial behaviours, such as addictions to nicotine and alcohol. A piece of research by Bricker *et al.* (2009) found that the most influential factor in the decision to try cigarettes in young people was having friends who smoked.

Children don't just learn behaviours from role models, but also attitudes and schemas. Fagot *et al.* (1992) compared the gender stereotypes shown by children who grew up in egalitarian families, in which childcare was shared between the parents, with those in traditional families in which childcare was carried out by the mothers. Four-year-olds from the egalitarian families had more liberal views about gender roles whereas children who grew up in a traditional family showed stronger gender stereotypes at a young age.

SLT points to the important role played by visual media – TV, internet, films and computer games – in the development of young children. Huesmann argues that the emergence of forms of mass visual media over the last century has led to dramatic changes in child-rearing. Children are now exposed to 'the looks, behaviour and beliefs of a wide variety of others, behaving in a wide variety of manners' (Huesmann, 2010, p.179) through television and the internet. Natural experiments have examined the behaviour of children living in remote communities before and after the introduction of television. One longitudinal study (Charlton *et al.*, 2002) began on the island of St Helena, a remote Atlantic outpost, in 1993. Television (CNN) was introduced to the community in 1995, followed by a range of other TV channels including Cartoon Network and Discovery Channel. Charlton *et al.* found that the overall levels of aggressive and antisocial behaviour on the island did not increase, but that the children who had shown higher levels of antisocial behaviour before television was introduced were more likely to watch larger numbers of cartoons (often the most violent programmes), implying that those with a stronger biological predisposition to aggression may be attracted to more violent television.

Television provides a range of role models and influences many kinds of behaviour in addition to aggression. A study by Becker (2002) indicated that the introduction of television with programmes portraying 'thin' role models appear to have effects on body image, self-esteem and eating behaviours in young women. Becker examined the incidence of eating disorders in Fiji before TV was introduced in 1995 and again in 1998. Each time, a sample of Fijian girls (average age 17) was asked how much TV they watched and about their eating behaviours. Becker found that there was a more than 10 per cent increase in the use of vomiting to control weight between 1995 and 1998 and almost one third (29 per cent) of girls scored highly on the eating disorders scale by 1998.

■ Critical thinking

Bandura's experiments pointed to the important role played by models in the development of behaviour in young children, and many experiments have demonstrated the basic principles of learning though observation. Bandura's experiments have been criticized for their methodology, however. The observation of children's behaviour took place over a very short period of time following exposure to the model, making it difficult to assess if the aggressive behaviour persisted beyond this period. The female researcher behaved unusually in the experiment, showing no response to the aggressive model, which may have puzzled the children. The environment of a university laboratory was strange and unfamiliar and the complex social world was reduced, in this case to the actions of a single role model, with the impact of real-life models – parents, siblings, peers and TV characters – on children's aggressive behaviour ignored. Together, these factors may have led to unusual behaviour by the children in the experiment.

Other criticisms have centred on the ethical issues involved in Bandura's research. The children who took part in the study may have been confused and afraid during the aggressive episode and the possibility of long-term, damaging effects on their behaviour is substantial. While parental consent was sought, it is unlikely that the parents involved fully understood the implications of the research.

Key study

Fleiter *et al.* (2010)

Today, sociocultural psychologists prefer the use of more natural methods to investigate social processes. Observations, interviews and group discussions avoid many of the problems associated with researcher intervention and produce results which are generally higher in validity. Fleiter *et al.* (2010) examined the effects of role models on driving speeds using qualitative methods. Sixty-seven Australian drivers were placed into one of eight categories (e.g. young, mid-age or older, male or female, excessive speeder or rare speeder) and asked to discuss the factors that influenced their driving behaviour.

The conversations were recorded and then transcribed (written out). Thematic analysis identified key themes including speeding to keep up with traffic flow and perceived pressure to drive faster from other drivers. The 'pressure' from others to 'speed up' was expressed in all groups. The analysis revealed that parents were important role models and many young drivers modelled their parents' behaviour in a car, especially when parents drove fast. Passengers were also influential, often producing a slowing effect as drivers responded to feelings of responsibility for the safety of people in the car. This study demonstrates a very different approach to investigating role models to Bandura's experimental methodology. While it does not attempt to establish cause and effect in the same way as experimentation, the data obtained is rich and detailed and relatively free from researcher intervention. It also avoids many of the ethical issues involved in experimentation.

Conformity to group norms

LEARNING OUTCOMES

- ■ Discuss factors influencing conformity (for example, culture, groupthink, risky shift, minority influence).
- ■ Evaluate research on conformity to group norms.

SLT identifies that social influence can take place though observation and imitation of role models. A different kind of social influence was investigated by Solomon Asch (1907–96), who was interested in the ways that groups can exert subtle pressures to conform.

Conformity – changing attitudes or behaviour in response to pressure from a group. Also known as majority influence.

In 1951, Asch began a series of experiments to investigate **conformity** to group pressures; 123 male students were recruited and asked to take part in a 'test of visual perception'. Each student was placed in a group along with six or eight strangers and asked to complete a task in which they were required to judge the length of a set of lines and identify out loud which ones matched. Unbeknown to the real participants, the other group members were 'confederates' who had been instructed to provide identical, incorrect answers on 12 out of the 18 tests (referred to as critical trials). The real participant was placed in the second-to-last position around the table, so Asch was able to see if they would succumb to group pressure and provide an answer that was clearly wrong. As the correct answer was obvious, this would provide a clear behavioural measurement of conformity to group norms (Asch, 1951). Asch found a conformity rate of 37 per cent on the critical trials (indicating that people would go along with the crowd roughly one in every three times). There were wide individual differences in conformity: about one in 20 people were highly influenced by group pressure and conformed on all 12 critical trials. Just over one-quarter remained strongly independent and refused to go along with group pressure at any point.

Asch's findings led to an interest in why people conform. Deutsch and Gerard (1955) identified two reasons for conformity in the dual process dependency model:

■ **Normative social influence** – refers to conformity for acceptance. We go along with the crowd because we want others to like and accept us. People who don't conform risk social embarrassment or ostracism – being left out.
■ **Informational social influence** – refers to conformity due to uncertainty. In unfamiliar social situations, we may be unclear about how to behave so following the behaviour of others is often a safe bet. Even if they are wrong, our behaviour will blend in and we won't appear conspicuous.

Figure 3.4 Conformity of dress at the races

Asch carried out a variety of replications of his experiment that enabled him to tease out some of the situational factors that influenced conformity. Size of the majority was important: when the situation involved a single participant and a single confederate, very few people (3 per cent) would give up their own viewpoint. Conformity increased with a two-to-one majority and reached a maximum level when the group consisted of three against one. Beyond this point, it didn't increase that much.

A different kind of influence takes place where a single dissenting individual or small group 'converts' the dominant group to their alternative viewpoint: this is known as **minority influence**. One of the first investigations into minority influence was carried out by Serge Moscovici, a French psychologist. Using an experimental paradigm similar to Asch's, Moscovici *et al.* (1969) assembled groups of strangers and asked them to take part in a visual task in which they were required to identify the colour of 36 slides of various shades of blue. In order to manipulate minority influence, Moscovici primed two members of each group to call the slides green rather than blue. Moscovici used two experimental conditions:

Minority influence – occurs when an individual or small group 'converts' the larger group to their view.

■ In the consistent condition, the confederates called every slide green.
■ In the inconsistent condition, the confederates called 12 out of 36 slides green.

Using this approach, Moscovici was able to measure how many of the majority group members moved to adopt the minority position. He found that the shift to the minority view was stronger in the consistent condition (around 8 per cent) compared with the inconsistent condition (less than 1 per cent). Moscovici argued that minority influence was more likely to occur when a minority group or individual presented a consistent argument and appeared to know their mind.

■ Critical thinking

The simple perceptual tasks used by Asch and Moscovici were trivial and of little interest to those who participated and the groups consisted of strangers put together for the purpose of the experiment. What effect might this have on the results and why might conformity be different among groups of real friends or co-workers?

Hogg and Turner (1987) carried out a series of conformity experiments using the Asch paradigm but allowing group members to make private rather than public responses, which removed the need to conform for acceptance. They found conformity continued to be high when the groups consisted of 'real' in-groups of friends but almost non-existent when groups of strangers were put together for the purpose of the experiment. Similarly, Prapavessis (1997) investigated conformity to group norms in 13 cricket teams, examining the sacrifices team members were prepared to make for each other and the norms that regulated behaviour in the team. Prapavessis found that norms such as sticking to the training schedule and supporting each other led to strong group cohesiveness in sports teams.

Sociocultural psychologists prefer, where possible, to avoid experimentation and to use methods that closely model social situations. Clark (1998 and 1999) carried out **simulations and role plays** to investigate how minority influence operates in court when jurors are asked to make judgements about guilt or innocence. Clark based his studies on the film *12 Angry Men* (1957), in which Henry Fonda plays a juror who attempts to persuade the 11 other jury members that a young man is innocent of murder. Participants were given a synopsis of the film and told that 11 of the 12 jurors believed the man was guilty. Clark then examined what conditions were required for participants to adopt the minority position. In contrast to Moscovici, Clark found that the quality of counter-evidence was most important in order for students to shift to the minority position. In a second study, he examined the effects of others defecting to the minority position. When four people from the majority group adopted the minority position, the rest would rapidly follow, leading to an overturn of group norms, in which the minority position (not guilty) became the new majority viewpoint.

Theory of knowledge

Both Asch and Moscovici used laboratory experiments to model a social situation and explore conformity. Laboratory experiments allow the methods employed by the natural sciences, like physics, to be directed at human behaviour. This permits the generation of quantitative data that can be submitted to statistical analysis to demonstrate evidence for cause-and-effect relationships, the accepted basis behind scientific truth. However, they have been criticized for lacking validity and for reducing the complexity of the social world to a controlled variable within a laboratory – in this case the number of people in a majority or minority group.

Factors influencing conformity

Culture and time

Asch's 1950s experiments pointed to wide differences in the tendency to conform. A common criticism of Asch's work is that his findings were strongly influenced by the political and cultural climate in which he operated. In the 1950s America was in the era known as McCarthyism; during this time, there was cultural panic about the spread of Communism and many ordinary Americans were accused of being Communist sympathizers or agents. In this climate, conformity to group pressure was unsurprising. Since then, conformity levels have steadily decreased in North America (Bond & Smith, 1996). Perrin and Spencer (1981) found conformity rates of around one in 400 trials in the UK using Asch's paradigm, which implies that conformity is much rarer than in the 1950s. This is not surprising as, 'the extent to which dissent is tolerated in a society will vary at different points in its history' (Bond & Smith, p.111).

Bond and Smith (1996) carried out a meta-analysis of 133 conformity experiments that used Asch's paradigm with a total of almost 5,000 participants. The experiments were carried out in 17 different countries. They found clear cultural differences in conformity, with higher rates in collectivist cultures than individualistic cultures. Why might this be? Markus and Kitayama (1991) argued that cultural differences in conformity reflect the different conceptions of self in individualistic and collectivist cultures. In collectivist cultures, the self is viewed as interdependent and people are strongly motivated to fit in and to belong to the social group. In contrast, the individualistic view of the self is of independence: uniqueness and the pursuit of personal goals are important, providing a strong motive for non-conformity. These examples demonstrate how cultural forces influence social behaviours such as conformity.

Groupthink and the 'risky shift'

Most of our life is spent in groups of different kinds and the study of group decision-making is one area where conformity has been highly relevant. Most groups involve people with different viewpoints. This provides a fertile ground to investigate how conformity operates in everyday situations.

Figure 3.5 Groupthink may have been a factor in the Bay of Pigs invasion

Irving Janis was a social psychologist who worked at Yale University for almost 40 years. Janis was particularly interested in how conscientious and brilliant politicians can sometimes make disastrous political decisions with far-reaching consequences. In an innovative study, Janis (1972) examined historical archives for political records and identified a range of decisions made by American administrations with clear political consequences. Some of these had negative outcomes, for example, the decisions to invade Cuba at the Bay of Pigs (1961) and to escalate the Korean War. Other decisions produced positive outcomes, such as the Cuban missile crisis.

Using a method called content analysis, Janis examined the ways in which the decisions had been reached and identified three important 'antecedents' that seemed to precede poor decisions. These were:

- high group cohesiveness
- insulation from other, expert views about the situation
- situational forces, including a highly stressful environment.

Janis argued that poor decisions arose from a phenomenon he termed '**groupthink**'. Groupthink occurs when:

- each group member conforms to what they believe is the overall group consensus – even when none of the group members personally would have chosen that course of action

Groupthink – the tendency for groups to make poor decisions driven by the need for a united front and conformity.

- group decisions are seen as simple choices between two alternative actions (e.g. invade or don't invade), with other alternatives being overlooked or ignored
- the group is insulated from other people's views and objective experts are not consulted (Phoenix, 2007).

Janis defined groupthink as 'a mode of thinking that people engage in when they are deeply involved in a cohesive in-group, when the members' strivings for unanimity override their motivation to realistically appraise alternative courses of action' (Janis, 1972). A concept related to groupthink is the '**risky shift**'. This occurs when group members have a view in a particular direction but exaggerate this to an extreme position that goes far beyond the beliefs of individual group members.

One major problem for Janis's explanation of 'groupthink' is that tight and cohesive groups sometimes make more cautious decisions rather than risky ones. This demonstrates that group decisions have a tendency become polarized and move to a more extreme position, but this move can sometimes be towards extreme safety. For this reason, the term 'group polarization' is generally preferred over 'risky shift' today.

Since Janis's original analysis, the concept of groupthink has received considerable scrutiny. Many studies using qualitative methodology similar to that employed by Janis have supported his claims. Attempts to generate groupthink experimentally, however, have been largely unsuccessful, leading to claims that the use of qualitative methodology allowed Janis to make claims of cause and effect that are not justified. Hart (1998) reformulated the concept of groupthink as 'collective optimism and collective avoidance', and McCauley (1989) has pointed to the impact of conformity and compliance on groupthink decisions.

Nonetheless Janis made a hugely important contribution to our understanding of conformity within groups. There is no doubt that group polarization exists, but the processes underlying it may be different and more complex than those envisaged by Janis. In order to reduce or minimize the possibility of groupthink, it is suggested that groups should encourage argument and discussion about decisions (employing naysayers rather than yea-sayers) and should bring in outside, objective experts where possible. Similarly, the power of leaders should be reduced and group members should be encouraged to voice their doubts before decisions are taken (Smith & Mackie, 2000).

Risky shift – the tendency for groups to make a decision that is more extreme (riskier) than any of the individual members' views.

Persuasion and compliance: low-balling, foot in the door

LEARNING OUTCOME
- Discuss the use of compliance techniques (for example, low-balling, foot in the door).

Compliance – agreeing to direct requests.

Our last type of social influence refers to the most direct form – attempts made by others to get us to behave in certain ways. The term **compliance** refers to changes in behaviour that are made in response to direct requests. Each day you are likely to receive many different requests – to lend your notes to a college classmate, to give money to a charity collector or to respond to a public appeal for disaster relief. Compliance is different to conformity, where the pressure to change behaviour may be subtle and unspoken. As you can imagine, this area of psychology is highly relevant to health educators who want us to change our behaviours in health-enhancing ways and to commercial companies who wish to sell us products. Here we will look at two techniques that are used to encourage compliance with requests.

Foot in the door (FITD) technique – a compliance technique based on gaining agreement to a small request followed by a large request.

The foot in the door technique (FIDT)

Many compliance techniques rely on the idea of making multiple requests for action. The **foot in the door technique** (Freedman & Fraser, 1966) is based on the idea that compliance is more likely if agreement is gained to a small request that is then followed by a larger request. In simple terms, if you want your friend to lend you $10, you should first get them to agree to lend you a dollar. The FIDT is commonly used by telesales workers who start their negotiations by asking for something small (five minutes of your time to answer a survey) then go on to make a larger request after you have complied with the first.

Many experiments have demonstrated the effectiveness of the FIDT. Freedman and Fraser (1966) demonstrated how participants who had been asked to sign a petition about road safety were more likely to agree to the siting of a large, ugly 'drive carefully' sign in their garden than a group who were asked to site the sign without the prior request. In another experiment, Schwarzwald *et al.*(1983) investigated the effectiveness of the FITD for charity fundraising. Half of the participants were asked to sign a petition two weeks before being asked for a donation to the organization (FITD) and the other half were simply asked to make donation without the FITD. A greater percentage of people made a donation in the experimental condition than the control, demonstrating the basic principle that the likelihood of compliance is increased once the foot is in the door.

Practical applications

The FIDT has also been shown to be an effective way to increase compliance to health screening. Dolin and Booth-Butterfield (1995) allocated women who attended a health fair randomly to a foot in the door (FITD) or control condition in which the target behaviour was making an appointment for health screening. Results indicated that the FITD produced a significant effect with women in the experimental condition, who showed 16 per cent greater compliance with the critical request to go for screening.

Low-ball technique (LBT)

Low-ball – a compliance technique based on getting agreement to an attractive deal, which is then made less attractive.

An alternative method of gaining compliance is the **low-ball technique**. This is also based on multiple requests. Using the LBT, a customer is first asked to agree to an attractive deal, for example, buying a car with lots of extras. When the deal has been agreed, the seller reveals hidden costs – for example, some of the extras cannot be supplied – which makes the deal substantially less attractive. Under these conditions, it is remarkable that many buyers stick with the deal even though it is far less attractive than the one they signed up to.

Why do these simple ideas work so well? One explanation is based on Bem's self-perception theory. If we agree to the first response, this effectively alters our self-perception to that of a helpful person. We then comply with the next request as we do not wish to disconfirm this positive view of ourselves. A slightly different approach is taken by Cialdini *et al.* (2001) who suggest that people are more inclined to agree to the 'target' request because of their desire to remain consistent.

SECTION SUMMARY
- Social learning theory argues that behaviours are learnt via observation and imitation of role models.
- SLT points to the importance of visual media in the development of many behaviours.
- Conformity is the tendency to change attitudes or behaviour in response to group pressure. Conformity is higher in collectivist than individualistic cultures.
- Groupthink takes place when cohesive groups are insulated from outside opinion and in high stress situations. The term 'group polarization' is preferred today.
- FITD and low-balling are compliance techniques based on multiple requests.

Sociocultural cognition

Every day we interact with a range of people. Many of these interactions are with people who are well known to us, such as family members or close friends. Others are acquaintances at work or college, and some interactions are with total strangers. How do we go about making sense of social behaviour in these very different settings? In this section we will examine key processes in **social cognition**. We will consider some of the errors that are made in this process, including the tendency to rely on stereotypes and jump to conclusions. We will consider how membership of social groups can influence our perception of people who are perceived as similar and those who appear different to us. Throughout the section, we will consider how social cognition is influenced by cultural factors, which shape the lens through which we view the world.

Social cognition – making sense of the social environment and other people's behaviour.

Attributions and errors

LEARNING OUTCOMES
■ Describe the role of situational and dispositional factors in explaining behaviour.
■ Discuss two errors in attributions.

The desire to understand others arises from the need to make the complex social environment feel more predictable. Imagine that you have started a new job and are sharing an office with Sam, Roxana and Ivan. On the first day, Roxana and Ivan arrive punctually at 8:30 but Sam is around 20 minutes late. You wonder if Sam is a rather unpunctual person or if something has happened to make him late on this occasion. How would you decide which of these judgements is correct?

Attributions – explanations about the cause of behaviour.

Attributions are explanations of the cause of behaviour. If you decide that Sam is an unpunctual person, this is an internal (or **dispositional**) attribution, as you are assuming Sam's behaviour comes from a consistent personality trait. Alternatively, Sam's lateness could be due to external factors – a road accident that caused traffic problems or a sick child on the way to school. This is a **situational** attribution.

Fritz Heider (1958) argued that laypeople and psychologists face the same task: that of understanding people's behaviour. Heider believed that laypeople act like naïve psychologists, constructing theories to explain why other people act as they do. Several attribution theories have put forward slightly different frameworks of how people make attributions. Jones and Davis (1965) argued that we try to explain others' behaviour in terms of internal causes wherever possible. This is because internal attributions are more useful as they allow us to predict how people might behave in the future. If Sam is generally late and appears to be an unpunctual person, this information can help us decide how to behave towards Sam, for example by scheduling meetings for the afternoon rather than the morning. If the behaviour is a 'one off' and arises from a particular situation, it isn't all that useful to later prediction.

Dispositional attributions – see behaviour as originating from inside the person (i.e. traits).

Situational attributions – see behaviour as originating from situational forces.

An influential attribution theory was put forward by Harold Kelley in 1967 and is known as the covariation model. According to Kelley, people draw on three main sources of information when making attributional judgements. These are:

■ **Consistency** – does X always behave like this in this situation? (Is Sam always late for work?)
■ **Distinctiveness** – does X behave like this in other situations? (Is Sam also late for the pub, gym and cinema?)
■ **Consensus** – do other people also behave in this way? (Are other people in the office also late?)

According to the covariation model, different patterns of answers allow us to make different kinds of attributions. For example, if Sam is consistently late for work and for other appointments but others at work are punctual, this would lead to an internal attribution – Sam is an unpunctual person. In contrast, if everyone at work takes a lax attitude to time-keeping and Sam is on time for other social engagements, this would point to a situational attribution.

Kelley's covariation model was easily tested and many studies in the 1960s and 70s provided strong support for this approach. Researchers made extensive use of vignettes in which different kinds of information about consensus, consistency and distinctiveness were supplied to see how they affected attributions.

■ Critical thinking

While vignette-based research provided a controlled way of testing the covariation model, real-life social situations are often much more complex. The process of making an attribution relies on a significant amount of information to judge distinctiveness, consistency or consensus, and in many social environments, such as a one-off interaction with a call centre worker, this amount of information is simply not available.

Kelley's covariation model implied that people are rational thinkers who pay attention to different kinds of information and engage in lengthy processing before making attributions. Since Kelley's original theory, research studies have demonstrated that the attributional process is filled with errors and biases, implying that people are far from rational. Other studies have indicated that there are wide cultural variations in attributions. Two of the most striking biases are the fundamental attribution error (FAE) and the self-serving bias.

Fundamental attribution error (FAE) – the tendency to attribute other people's behaviour to dispositional causes.

The fundamental attribution error and self-serving bias

The **fundamental attribution error (FAE)** is the tendency to rely on dispositional attributions when explaining other people's behaviour and to overlook the importance of situational forces. Ross (1977, p.183) defined the fundamental attribution error as, 'the tendency for attributors to underestimate the impact of situational factors and to overestimate the role of dispositional factors in controlling behaviour.' The FAE was initially demonstrated in an experiment by Jones and Harris (1967), who gave students a political essay to read that was in favour of Fidel Castro, the Cuban leader of the time. Despite being told that the essay writer had been instructed to write a pro-Castro essay by their lecturer, the students later rated the writer as having a positive attitude towards Castro. Thus, they overlooked the role of situational factors in the behaviour and made an internal, dispositional attribution, showing the FAE in action. Many studies have explored the FAE and considered how and when it operates. Tal-Or and Papirman (2007) examined the FAE in relation to television actors. They found that viewers tended to attribute an actor's behaviour in television dramas to their personality and to overlook the existence of the script in dictating the actor's behaviour.

The FAE is relatively easy to explain. When we observe another person's behaviour, our focus is primarily on the actor (person), which tends to blind us to the external or situational forces that influence them. However, when we consider our own behaviour, we are acutely aware of environmental factors, making us much more

Figure 3.6 Friendly in real life?

likely to refer to situational factors. This explanation is called perceptual salience, which can be summed up as 'the behaviour engulfs the field' (Buchanan *et al.*, 2007, p.77). The actor–observer effect is closely related to the FAE. This effect describes how we explain our own actions in a different way to those of other people, preferring to focus on situational factors for our own behaviour. Thus, my friend Sinita failed the driving test because she is a poor driver (internal attribution) but I failed my test because the examiner was tough or the weather was bad (external attribution).

Self-serving bias – tendency to use internal attributions for our successes but external attributions for our failures.

A second source of bias in the attributional process is the **self-serving bias** (SSB), which relates to attributions of personal success and failure. On balance, people tend to attribute successes to internal factors but failures to external causes. This tendency was demonstrated by Lau and Russell (1980), who examined the attributions for success and failure made by professional sportspeople, both players and managers, for wins and losses. Lau and Russell selected a sample of 107 newspaper reports of games and examined the 594 explanations given within these for the outcome of the game. Each explanation was coded as internal (e.g. '*I played really well on the day*') or external (e.g. '*some of the referee's decisions just went in their favour*') by two independent coders who then compared their judgements for agreement. (Remember that inter-observer reliability is particularly important in observational work.) Lau and Russell's results confirmed that a self-serving bias was at work: winners were significantly more likely to attribute their success to internal factors such as hard work than to situational factors.

Cross-cultural focus: cultural differences in the FAE and SSB

Much of the research on attribution theories was conducted in North America and Northern Europe. Subsequent studies, however, have demonstrated considerable cultural variation in attributional processes. They have also demonstrated that the FAE is not evident in young children but appears in later childhood and adolescence, implying that young Westerners learn to think in this way. Miller (1984) compared the attributions made by a sample of American and Hindu Indian children and adults for their own and others' actions. Adult Americans clearly demonstrated the FAE but the error did not appear in American children until they got older, implying that this way of thinking is learnt through cultural processes. In support of this view, Hindu Indian participants explained other people's behaviour using situational forces and their own behaviour internally, showing a reversed pattern. Later studies (e.g. Cohen *et al.*, 2011) have developed this idea even further, showing that there are religious differences in attributional patterns, with Protestants making internal attributions to a greater extent than Catholics.

Why might this be? The answer could well lie in the different models of the self that develop in individualistic and collectivist cultures. In individualistic cultures, children absorb the values of independence, competition and motivation, which lead them to see behaviour as originating from the individual. In collectivist societies such as India, the social group is viewed as of greater importance than the individual (Markus & Kitayama, 1991). Hence the main explanatory framework is to look at situational factors in explaining others' actions.

■ Critical thinking

Look back at section 1, Cultural influences on behaviour (*see pages 69–75*), and consider how this discussion of cultural differences in error and biases relates to the idea of emic and etic approaches to research. In assuming the FAE is culturally universal, which approach has been taken by researchers in this area? Is there any evidence to suggests that the FAE is an imposed etic?

Are there cultural differences in the SSB? It would be reasonable to predict that there may be, as individualistic cultures prioritize individual achievement and the pursuit of personal goals whereas collectivist cultures are more interested in family or group goals. Mezulis *et al.* (2004) carried out a substantial meta-analysis of 266 studies of the self-serving bias in a wide range of cultures. They found that the strength of the self-serving attributional bias was largest in the USA and other Western cultures but was significantly smaller in Asian cultures. However, there was considerable variation within Asian cultures: the self-serving bias was almost completely absent in Japan and the Pacific Islands, was moderate in India and substantial in China and Korea. Both of these biases point to the importance of etic analysis in relation to social cognition.

Social identity theory

LEARNING OUTCOME
■ Evaluate social identity theory, making reference to relevant studies.

Social identity theory (SIT) was put forward by Henri Tajfel and developed by Turner and Brown (1978). Tajfel was a European Jew who escaped Nazi persecution and fled to work in the UK after the 1939–45 war. Unsurprisingly, Tajfel was particularly interested in identity, group membership and relationships between groups, especially those involving prejudice and discrimination. Settling in Bristol, he carried out pioneering work that demonstrated the powerful effects of group membership.

Key study

Tajfel *et al.* (1971)

In 1971, Tajfel and colleagues carried out an influential series of experiments using 14–15-year-old school boys living in Bristol. Tajfel *et al.* allocated the boys to two groups and provided a trivial reason for group membership – their supposed preference for a painter. However, the allocation was random and the boys were simply put in arbitrary groups. For this reason, the method used by Tajfel *et al.* has come to be known as the 'minimal groups paradigm'.

Tajfel *et al.* then asked the boys to take part in a series of tasks in which they were able to allocate points in different combinations to boys who were members of their own group (the in-group) or to boys in the other group (the out-group). The points were then converted to cash that the group could spend. Tajfel *et al.* found that the boys were likely to favour their own group and allocate them more points. However, what was most interesting was that the boys chose to maximize the difference between their own group and the out-group – even if this meant awarding fewer points in total (and therefore less money) to their own group. In effect, they showed a clear preference for their own group members and discriminated against the out-group even when there was minimal basis for group membership.

These findings demonstrate the strong tendency to favour people with whom we share membership of a social group – however trivial or minimal that membership is. They also show the stark reality of prejudice against those whom we perceive as coming from a different social group.

Principles of SIT

Social identity theory explains how and why people come to identify with particular social groups. According to Tajfel, identity is made up of two aspects: personal identity and social identity. SIT is concerned with social identity – the aspects of identity that are based on membership of social groups, such as gender or ethnicity. SIT claims that:

■ we identify with people who share our social group (the 'in-group') and emphasize the similarities between ourselves and other group members
■ we notice and emphasize differences from people who belong to different social groups (the out-group), effectively dividing ourselves into 'us and them'

- this occurs even when the group is 'minimal' or based on very little real similarity, as in Tajfel *et al.*'s experiments
- we favour members of our own group when given the opportunity and are likely to discriminate against those from different social groups

- the processes of social identity and group membership provide a fertile ground for prejudice and conflict between groups.

Tajfel also noted that social behaviour occurs on a continuum. At one extreme we can act towards someone entirely as a known individual, for example, our next-door neighbour. At the other extreme we can treat them entirely as a group member, for example, as a supporter of AC Milan. In practice, most interactions lie somewhere between these two poles – it is only in extreme conditions that two people might treat each other at the group end of the continuum.

Figure 3.7 Tiananmen Square was an example of group conflict.

Evaluation of social identity theory

There have been many demonstrations of the power of group membership to create in-group favouritism and out-group discrimination in line with Tajfel's predictions. One of the most well-known of these is the 'blue eyes, brown eyes' experiment, which was carried out by Jane Elliott, an elementary schoolteacher in Riceville, Iowa, USA, in 1968 (Phoenix, 2007). Shocked by the casual acceptance of racial segregation in her students, Elliott decided to teach her class of seven-year-old children about racism, using first-hand experience. On the first day of the exercise, Elliott told the brown-eyed children that they were the superior group and had higher intelligence, which was linked to the colour of their eyes. She also told her class that blue-eyed people were stupid and badly behaved. Elliott provided brown fabric collars, which the blue-eyed children were made to wear as a method of identifying them as the minority group. The brown-eyed children were given extra privileges. Elliott observed the students' reaction to the exercise: the blue-eyed children rapidly became sullen, angry and depressed whereas the brown-eyed children taunted them and refused to play with them.

The next day, Jane Elliott reversed the exercise, and told the blue-eyed children that a mistake had been made and they were the group with superior intelligence. Elliott found that the patterns of behaviour were reversed although the blue-eyed children were somewhat less intense in their bullying of the brown-eyed group. Finally all the children were debriefed about the nature of the exercise.

Lonsdale and North (2009) have shown the growing importance of musical taste as a 'badge' of group membership, which contributes to social identity in many young people. Lonsdale and North carried out two experiments to test whether or not people would behave more favourably to those who shared their musical taste than to those who liked a different genre of music. In the first experiment they found that clear, negative stereotypes were applied to fans of a different musical genre. In the second study, Lonsdale and North used Tajfel *et al.*'s **minimal group paradigm** of awarding points to in-group and out-group members. In agreement with Tajfel *et al.*'s original experiment, they found that greater rewards were allocated to in-group members who shared their musical taste than out-group members. These studies demonstrate the continued relevance of social identity theory.

Figure 3.8   Elliott's (1968) blue-eyes/brown-eyes study

Social identity theory has been hugely influential. It has helped to explain many important aspects of inter-group relations behaviour including favouritism of in-group members and prejudice and discrimination against those who are perceived as different. SIT has made an important contribution to our understanding of prejudice and conflict, arguing that prejudice is an inevitable consequence of group membership and will occur even when group membership is minimal. This approach has provided a valuable counterpoint to realistic conflict theory, which views competition for resources as the major cause of group conflict. SIT also helps us to understand many aspects of social cognition including stereotyping of out-group members and conformity to in-group norms.

Stereotypes and behaviour

LEARNING OUTCOME
■ Explain the formation of stereotypes and their effect on behaviour.

The social environment is rich in information and generally provides more information than we can sensibly take in. In order to simplify the complex social world, we rely on stored knowledge or top-down information to shape how we perceive our social environment: 'our knowledge of how things usually happen in the social world' (Buchanan *et al.*, 2007, p.63). Two closely related concepts are schemas and stereotypes.

Schemas are mental structures or packages of knowledge related to an object, situation or social event. We can distinguish between different kinds of schemas:

> **Schemas** – simple ideas built up from experience; mental structures or packages of knowledge.

■ **Role schemas** – the behaviours we expect from someone in a particular social role. For example, a doctor should have medical knowledge.
■ **Event schemas** – schemas relating to common social events, such as going to the cinema. Event schemas are also known as scripts.
■ **Person schemas** – the behaviours we expect from individuals we know well based on our personal knowledge of them.

We develop our schemas from a combination of personal experience (e.g. of going to the cinema or doctor), talking to other people, and from sources such as television and films. Schemas are useful because they enable us to make shortcuts within the social environment and to simplify the social world by giving us ideas about what to expect and how to behave in social situations.

> **Stereotypes** – generalizations about social groups.

Schemas are closely related to stereotypes. Tajfel noted how group membership can lead us to favour people whom we perceive as similar (members of the in-group) while emphasizing differences from those in the out-group. This is the basis of stereotyping. Stereotypes are 'widely shared generalizations about members of a social group' (Hogg & Vaughan, 2005/2002, p.54), which are over-simplified and can be negative or derogatory. The process of stereotyping is based on categorization. We put an individual into a social category, based on their style of dress, social role or ethnic group, then generate ideas of what that group is like. The stereotype is generalizing these ideas from the level of the group to that of the individual and assuming the person is a 'typical' member of that social group.

Stereotypes were clearly shown in an experiment carried out by Darley and Gross in 1983. They showed US students a short film about a young student called Hannah, who was played by an actress. Half of the group saw Hannah living with wealthy parents in an affluent area of town, whereas the other half saw her portrayed as coming from a deprived area.

In the second part of the experiment, all the participants watched the same film, in which Hannah was shown answering quiz questions, getting some correct and others wrong. They were asked to assess her intelligence. Those who had seen Hannah portrayed as coming from an affluent background judged her intellectual ability to be higher than those who had seen the second version of the film. In both cases, the information on socio-economic background had shaped the impression formed.

Cultural stereotypes: alive and well in Europe

Linssen and Hagendorn (1994) investigated the stereotypes held by 16–18-year-olds about different European nationalities and 'north–south differences in Europe'. A sample of just over 250 students selected from Denmark, the Netherlands, England, Belgium, Germany, France and Italy were asked to complete questionnaires in which they rated the occupants of different countries on four different dimensions, including perceived efficiency, emotionality, empathy and dominance. In total, ratings were obtained for 22 personal qualities (e.g. proud, helpful). Linssen and Hagendorn found evidence for clear north–south stereotyping. Southern Europeans were seen as being more emotional and less efficient than northern Europeans

In a second study, Poppe and Linssen (1999) repeated the exercise using a sample of adolescents from six Central and Eastern European countries. In this study, it was found that the national stereotypes were based on perceptions of economic competence and on morality. Western European nationalities were perceived as more competent than the Central and Eastern countries – reflecting the social reality of lower economic status.

SECTION SUMMARY
- Attributions are explanations of the cause of behaviour.
- The FAE is the tendency to attribute other people's behaviour to internal (dispositional) factors.
- The self-serving bias is the tendency to make internal attributions for our successes but external attributions for our failures.
- The FAE and SSB are prevalent in Western, individualistic cultures but much less evident in collectivist cultures. This may be linked to the different models of the self that operate.
- SIT argues that social identity is based on categorization of people into 'in-groups' and 'out-groups'.
- SIT helps us to understand ethnocentric bias and favouritism towards in-group members and prejudice against those from different groups.
- Stereotypes are shared generalizations about groups that are often derogatory. They arise from the categorization of individuals into groups.

Abnormal psychology

Introduction

Psychopathology is a branch of psychology focusing on abnormal psychological conditions, with the aim of gaining an understanding into these conditions in order that effective treatments can be developed. This is important, as one in ten people will spend time in a mental institution at some point in their life and one in three will receive treatment for an abnormal condition. If not you, then someone close to you will be affected.

LEARNING OUTCOME
■ Evaluate psychological research (that is, theories and/or studies) relevant to the study of abnormal behaviour.

Concepts of normality and abnormality

LEARNING OUTCOME
■ Examine the concepts of normality and abnormality.

Abnormality – a psychological or behavioural state leading to impairment of interpersonal functioning and/or distress to others.

Abnormality is difficult to define, as psychologists cannot agree about causes or how abnormality presents itself. Various criteria exist, each having strengths and weaknesses, meaning no one definition is perfect or best. Abnormality is also explained in terms of different psychological approaches that see mental disorders as having biological, cognitive or sociocultural origins. Each of these approaches has strengths and weaknesses and some approaches are more applicable to some disorders than others.

Deviation from social norms

Deviation from social norms – behaviour that violates accepted social rules.

Each society has norms, unwritten rules of acceptable behaviour and beliefs. The deviation from social norms definition therefore sees abnormality as behaviour and/or beliefs that break these rules, with the definition highlighting the distinction between desirable and undesirable behaviours. Individuals exhibiting undesirable behaviours or beliefs are **social deviants**, with society permitting itself the right to intervene and 'cure' such 'deviants'.

Link to the sociocultural level of analysis
This definition gives a social dimension to abnormality, with Szasz (1962) arguing that a prime function of psychiatry is to exclude from society those seen as exhibiting socially unacceptable behaviour or beliefs.

Strengths

■ This definition gives society the right to intervene and 'cure' social deviants, which can be beneficial to those unable to seek help themselves.
■ The definition seeks to protect society from the effects that an individual's abnormal behaviour can have on others.
■ The definition gives a clear differentiation between behaviours or beliefs that are acceptable and those that are unacceptable.

■ The definition is based around what is desirable for the majority of people, in order to protect the values of society.

Weaknesses

■ Social norms aren't real; they are based on the opinions of the elite within a society, rather than majority opinions. These are then used to 'police' those seen as a threat to social order, leading to human rights abuses including the confinement in mental institutions of political dissidents. A true definition of abnormality should be objective and free from such subjective factors.

■ Sometimes it's beneficial to break social norms. The Suffragettes did so by campaigning for women's rights and achieving votes for women. Are such people abnormal?

■ Social norms often relate to moral standards that aren't objective, because they change over time as social attitudes change. For example, homosexuality was removed as a mental disorder from the ICD classification system as late as 1990.

■ The situation or context in which norms are broken is important. Nudity isn't considered abnormal within a naturist setting (indeed, being clothed in such a situation might appear abnormal). Or, filling a nappy (diaper) at age two is quite normal, but maybe not if you're 40.

Failure to function adequately

Failure to function adequately – an inability to cope with day-to-day living.

The failure to function adequately definition believes individuals are abnormal when their behaviour suggests they can't cope with everyday life, with such people often not experiencing the usual range of emotions experienced by others. Behaviour is perceived as abnormal if it causes distress that leads to dysfunction, e.g. disrupting the ability to work and/or conduct satisfying interpersonal relationships. The focus of the definition is on personal suffering, concentrating attention on the individual experiences that are associated with mental disorders.

Rosenhan and Seligman (1989) proposed that personal dysfunction has seven features and the more an individual has, the more they are abnormal:

Table 4.1   Rosenhan and Seligman's (1989) seven features of personal dysfunction

FEATURES OF PERSONAL DYSFUNCTION	DESCRIPTION OF FEATURES
Personal distress	The key feature of abnormality. Includes depression and anxiety disorders.
Maladaptive behaviour	Behaviour that hinders individuals in attaining life goals, both occupational and social.
Unpredictability	Exhibiting unexpected behaviours characterized by loss of control, such as aggressive rages.
Irrationality	Exhibiting behaviour inexplicable in any rational way.
Observer discomfort	Exhibiting behaviour that brings discomfort to others.
Violation of moral standards	Exhibiting behaviour that breaks society's moral expectations.
Unconventionality	Exhibiting unusual or eccentric behaviour.

Strengths

■ Sue *et al.* (1994) found that most individuals seeking clinical help believe they have psychological problems that hinder their ability to function normally; this was supported by Miller and Morley (1986), who found that personal distress was the prime reason for seeking help.

- The definition is humane and non-invasive, as it perceives disorders from the viewpoint of the sufferer, thus allowing more scope to create individually tailored therapies to treat the patient.
- The definition is fairly objective, as categories of behaviour can be created (such as within the Global Assessment of Functioning Scale (GAF)) to assess abnormality, e.g. can the individual get up on time, can they cook food, etc.?
- It is relatively easy for observers to decide if individuals are abnormal, as the focus is on obvious, clearly defined behaviours, such as being able to work, conduct social relationships, etc.

Weaknesses

- Abnormality isn't always accompanied by dysfunction, for example English physician Harold Shipman murdered at least 215 patients over a 23-year period, while maintaining an outward appearance of normality and respectability and not exhibiting any features of dysfunction.
- Dysfunction can be a very subjective experience. Normal behaviour for an eccentric, like wearing bizarre clothes, is abnormal for more introverted individuals. This creates problems in defining and measuring dysfunctional features.
- There are occasions when experiencing distress is normal and psychologically healthy, such as the process of grieving following the death of a loved one.
- Rather than being a negative experience, dysfunctional behaviour can often be rewarding for individuals. For example, exhibiting an eating disorder can bring attention and affection from others.

Figure 4.1 The British doctor Harold Shipman seemed perfectly respectable and normal, but murdered at least 215 of his patients over a 23-year period.

Theory of knowledge

There are various criteria of abnormality, as well as different psychological approaches that try to explain abnormal conditions. All have their criticisms, however, which gives rise to the possibility that the whole concept of abnormality is one beyond the understanding of science.

Deviation from ideal mental health

Deviation from ideal mental health – failure to meet the criteria for perfect psychological well-being.

Jahoda (1958) perceived the concept of **ideal mental health** as being similar to peak physical health, where illness is defined as an absence of well-being. Six criteria were identified that individuals should possess to be characterized as 'normal' (*see Table 4.2*). The more of these criteria an individual fails to meet, and the further they are away from realizing individual criteria, the more abnormal they are perceived to be. Similarly to the **deviation from social norms** and **failure to function adequately** definitions, the focus of the deviation from ideal mental health definition is on behaviours and characteristics seen as desirable, rather than undesirable.

Table 4.2 Jahoda's characteristics of ideal mental health

FEATURES OF PERSONAL DYSFUNCTION	DESCRIPTION OF FEATURES
Positive self-attitude	Having self-respect and a positive self-concept.
Self-actualization	Experiencing personal growth and development. Realizing individual potential.
Autonomy	Being independent, self-reliant and able to make personal decisions.
Resisting stress	Possessing effective coping strategies to deal with stress and being able to deal with everyday anxiety-provoking situations.
Perception of reality	Perceiving the world in an accurate, non-distorted way. Having an objective and realistic view of the world.
Environmental mastery	Being competent in all aspects of life and able to meet the demands of all situations. Possessing the flexibility to adapt to changing life circumstances.

Strengths

- The definition has a much more positive attitude towards mental health, as it emphasizes positive achievements rather than failures and distress.
- The definition identifies specific areas of functioning that need to be addressed when treating abnormality, which allows treatments to be specifically targeted.
- The definition takes a holistic view rather than a reductionist one when considering abnormality. This means that an individual is being considered as a whole person, rather than focusing on individual features of their behaviour.

Weaknesses

- The criteria that form the definition are over-demanding; most individuals would not meet these criteria at any given moment and thus would be perceived as abnormal. For example, most people don't experience constant personal growth. Therefore the criteria may provide ideals to aspire to, rather than describe how individuals actually are.
- Most of the criteria are subjective, as they are vague and difficult to define. Physical health can be measured in objective ways, such as by X-rays and blood tests, but mental health depends on self-reports that may not be reliable.
- Perceptions of reality change over time. For instance, experiencing visions was once seen as a sign of religious purity, but now could be perceived as schizophrenia. Therefore determining accurate perception can be problematic.

Approaches to abnormality

LEARNING OUTCOME
- To what extent do biological, cognitive and sociocultural factors influence abnormal behaviour?

Practical applications

Different psychological approaches suggest not only differing explanations of abnormality, but also varying types of therapies with which to treat mental disorders.

The biological approach

The biological approach (**medical model**) perceives abnormality in a similar way to physical ill-health, as being due to malfunctioning biological processes, especially in the structure and working of the brain. As with physical medicine, mental health practitioners diagnose abnormal conditions from their symptoms, using criteria set out in diagnostic manuals. The two most popular are the *International Classification of Diseases* (ICD) and the *Diagnostic and Statistical Manual of Mental Disorders* (DSM). Each disorder is seen as separate, with its own particular pattern of symptoms, and brain scans are also used to determine diagnosis.

Four types of biological factors cause abnormal conditions, with some overlap between factors.

> **Biological approach** – a model of abnormality that perceives mental disorders as illnesses with physical causes.

Bacterial infections and viruses

Bacterial infections and viruses can damage the brain, causing abnormalities of function. For example, **general paralysis of the insane** is a neuropsychiatric disorder caused by syphilis. The bacterium **treponema palladium** enters the body through sexual activity, initially causing ulcers in the genital area. Later on tumours develop in the brain, impairing memory and intellect, with personality and mood also affected, and delusions and bizarre behaviour commonplace. Eventually patients are bedridden, with death occurring after 3–5 years.

Brain damage

Brain damage leads to abnormality through physical damage or illness within the brain. For example, Alzheimer's disease, caused by destruction of cells within the nervous system, leads to chronic memory impairment.

Biochemistry

Biochemical factors can lead to abnormality by affecting levels of **neurotransmitters**, chemicals that facilitate communication between brain nerve cells, and **hormones**, chemical messengers that regulate the activity of cells and organs. For example, heightened levels of the neurotransmitter acetylcholine are associated with depression.

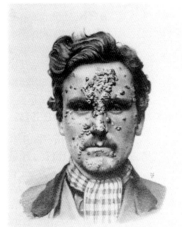

Figure 4.2 Bacterial infections and viruses can cause abnormal conditions, such as the neuropsychiatric disorder general paralysis of the insane, caused by the syphilis bacterium.

Genetic factors

A genetic component is associated with increased risk of developing abnormal conditions. For example, research indicates that obsessive-compulsive disorder is heritable, suggesting a genetic involvement. Several genes combine to give a heightened susceptibility to abnormality, rather than single genes determining mental disorders on their own.

The cognitive approach

> **Cognitive approach** – a model of abnormality that perceives mental disorders as due to negative thoughts and illogical beliefs.

The cognitive approach perceives abnormality as due to dysfunctional thought processes. The model acknowledges the role of maladaptive learning, but sees the mental processes that occur between stimuli and responses – cognitions, appraisals, thoughts, etc. – as more important, because they inform individuals as to how they feel about stimuli. Abnormal conditions are therefore seen as due to distorted and irrational thought processes, such as negative thoughts and illogical beliefs, referred to by Beck (1963), as **cognitive errors**. These exert influence over emotions and behaviour, leading to abnormalities.

The approach sees individuals as making sense of the world through cognitive processes. **Automatic thoughts** are ones that occur unconsciously and are more negative in abnormal conditions. **Attributions** refer to how individuals attempt to make sense of and explain their own and others' behaviour, with those individuals who exhibit abnormal conditions making more inaccurate attributions, like attributing their failed relationships to a lack of social skills. Such attributions can lead to inaccurate expectations, for example expecting relationships to fail, which turn into reality as **self-fulfilling prophecies**. Illogical thoughts don't therefore have to reflect reality, but do affect behaviour.

Overall the cognitive approach sees abnormal conditions as occurring when dysfunctional thought processes lead to maladaptive behaviour. For example, Beck (1963) saw depression as occurring through the **cognitive triad**, three illogical thought processes that result in irrational, negative feelings and lead to actual depression.

- **The self** – where individuals regard themselves as being helpless, worthless and inadequate.
- **The world** – where obstacles are perceived within one's environment that cannot be dealt with.
- **The future** – where personal worthlessness is seen as hindering any improvements.

Examples of these types of thoughts:

- Negative feelings about **themselves** – 'Nobody loves me.' now
- Negative feelings about **the world** – 'I cannot influence events.'
- Negative feelings about **the future** – 'I will always be unlovable.' for eternity

The sociocultural approach

Sociocultural approach – a model of abnormality that perceives mental disorders as determined by social and cultural environments.

The sociocultural approach sees one's social and cultural environment as important factors in determining abnormality. The social and cultural context in which individuals live affects the kind of stressors they're exposed to and thus the types of disorders they're vulnerable to. This is backed up by the fact that different disorders occur in different cultures. For example, **pibloktoq** is a culture-bound syndrome found among Arctic and sub-Arctic Eskimo communities. It is characterized by a brief period of intense excitement during which the sufferer tears off their clothes, breaks furniture, shouts obscenities and eats faeces, followed by seizures and a coma lasting up to 12 hours, after which sufferers have no recollection of the incident.

The fact that certain disorders have different rates of occurrence is explicable by sociocultural factors. For instance, **anorexia nervosa**, where sufferers fail to eat enough to maintain a healthy body weight, is predominately a Western cultural phenomenon, with females the main sufferers. In Western societies there is a cultural obsession, reinforced by the media, of attaining and maintaining a low body weight in order to be attractive. When non-Western cultural groupings are exposed to Western cultural norms, rates of anorexia increase. The sociocultural approach also considers socioeconomic background, which may explain why anorexia nervosa is predominately found among middle-class, white females.

Figure 4.3 Pibloktoq is an example of a culture-bound syndrome found only among Eskimo communities.

The fact that incidence rates of abnormal disorders change in cultural groups who emigrate to become ethnic minorities within other cultural groupings is also explicable through sociocultural means. For example, the incidence of schizophrenia worldwide is 1 per cent, a fact true of people of Caribbean cultures. However, the rate of schizophrenia among people of Caribbean origin living in Great Britain is much higher, which can be explained by the high rate of social stressors, like poor housing, low socioeconomic status, racism, etc., to which they are exposed.

Overall the sociocultural approach sees abnormality as arising from the influence society and culture have on individuals. It considers society's norms, roles within social environments, cultural background, family and the views of others, with its focus centring on cultural rules and ideals, social networks, family structures and religious beliefs. Abnormality is therefore not a disease, but instead is seen as arising from dysfunctional sociocultural systems.

■ Critical thinking

Instead of trying to work out which is the 'correct' explanation of abnormality, students should instead assess criteria of abnormality and different psychological approaches' perceptions of abnormality, in terms of their relative strengths and weaknesses. In this way a balanced consideration of the topic area can be reached.

Diagnosis of mental disorders

Diagnosis – the identification of the nature and cause of a disorder.

As with physical illnesses, mental disorders must first be diagnosed, whereby identification of the nature and cause of a disorder is determined. For this clinicians use **classification systems**, which are based on the idea that certain groups of symptoms can be grouped together as a **syndrome** (an illness or disease), with an identifiable underlying cause, that is separate from all other syndromes.

Link to the biological level of analysis

The concept of diagnosis comes from the medical (biological) model, being based on the notion that, similarly to physical illnesses, causes and types of mental disorders can be diagnosed (identified), treated and cured.

However, many mental disorders have no physical symptoms and clinicians are reliant on the non-physical subjective experiences that sufferers report, along with any observed signs of dysfunctional behaviour. This, coupled with the fact that many dispute whether mental disorders exist as separate, diagnosable conditions, makes diagnosis more unreliable and invalid compared to diagnoses of physical conditions.

DSM-IV

DSM-IV – a diagnostic classification system produced and used in the USA.

The *Diagnostic and Statistical Manual of Mental Disorders, 4th edition* (DSM-IV) is the classification system of the American Psychiatric Association, but is used in many countries worldwide. DSM-IV consists of five **axes** on which disorders are assessed. Assessment involves a clinical interview to obtain information from the patient regarding their disorder, observation of the patient's behaviour, mood states, etc., inspection of medical records and psychometric tests. The first two axes classify patients according to their symptoms. Each disorder is categorized by a set list of symptoms; the more of these a patient has, the more certain the diagnosis is. Axes III–V obtain additional information to assist in diagnosis.

Link to the cognitive level of analysis
With DSM-IV cognitive tests are used to determine cognitive dysfunctions and IQ tests are used to differentiate between mental disorder and mental retardation.

- **Axis I** – Clinical disorders, e.g. psychotic disorders, mood disorders, anxiety disorders, eating disorders.
- **Axis II** – Personality disorders, e.g. anti-social personality disorder, paranoid personality disorder, dependent personality disorder, etc., and mental retardation.
- **Axis III** – General medical conditions connected to mental disorders, such as infectious diseases.
- **Axis IV** – Psychosocial and environmental problems, such as limited social support, poverty, relationship breakdown.
- **Axis V** – Global assessment of functioning, where psychological, social and work-related functions are evaluated on a continuum, between ideal mental health at one end of the continuum and extreme mental disorder at the other end.

The DSM-IV classification system then places disorders into categories, such as anxiety disorders, schizophrenia and other psychotic disorders, mood disorders, etc.

There is an acknowledgement with DSM-IV that each category of mental disorder is an entirely separate disorder with set boundaries dividing it both from other mental disorders and from having no mental disorder (normality).

ICD-10

ICD-10 – a diagnostic classification system produced by the World Health Organization and used in Great Britain.

The *International Classification of Diseases, 10th revision* (ICD-10) is a classification system of illnesses and health complaints, including mental disorders, created by the World Health Organization. Similarly to DSM-IV, signs and symptoms are used to categorize diagnoses and regular revisions occur to reflect changes in clinical knowledge. ICD-10 recognizes 11 general categories of mental disorders, like schizophrenia, mood disorders, stress-related disorders, etc.

Attempts are being made to unify the categories of DSM-IV and ICD-10 to create better reliability. The USA will officially use ICD-10 from 2013.

■ Critical thinking
Although classification systems aren't perfect, they do allow clinicians to share a 'common language', which facilitates communication and the carrying out of research, leading to a better understanding of abnormality and thus the creation of effective treatments and therapies to enrich the lives of the mentally disordered.

Reliability and validity of diagnosis

LEARNING OUTCOME
■ Discuss reliability and validity of diagnosis.

Reliability (of diagnosis) – the consistency of diagnosis.

Reliability of diagnosis refers to the consistency of symptom measurement and affects classification and diagnosis in two ways:

- **Test–retest-reliability** – occurs when a clinician makes the same consistent diagnosis on separate occasions using the same information.
- **Inter-rater reliability** – occurs when several clinicians make identical diagnoses of the same patient, independently of each other.

Evaluation

- Making reliable diagnoses is difficult, as clinicians cannot base decisions on physical signs, but only on what symptoms patients report.
- Due to the wording of DSM-IV, for example comparing patients to 'average people', clinicians have to make subjective decisions regarding diagnosis.
- Classification systems are not objective, as they have an arbitrary number of symptoms that must be evident for diagnosis to occur, for example under DSM-IV, depression requires a depressed mood plus four other symptoms.

Validity of diagnosis refers to how accurate, meaningful and useful a diagnosis is. Validity is assessed in several ways:

> **Validity (of diagnosis)** – the accuracy of diagnosis.

- **Reliability** – a valid diagnosis must first be reliable, though reliability itself doesn't ensure validity.
- **Predictive validity** – if diagnosis leads to successful treatment, the diagnosis is seen as valid.
- **Descriptive validity** – for a diagnosis to be valid, patients diagnosed with different disorders should be different from each other in terms of classification.
- **Etiological validity** – to be valid, patients with the same disorder should have the same cause.

Evaluation

- No matter how much reliability of diagnosis improves, it does not ensure validity.
- Descriptive validity is reduced by **comorbidity**, where patients have two or more simultaneous disorders, which suggests such disorders may not be separate at all.
- Predictive validity is difficult to attain, as therapies are often assigned from clinicians' biased viewpoints as to what constitutes effective treatments.
- Winter (1999) believes that 'diagnostic systems are only aids to understanding, not descriptions of real disease entities'.

Research has assessed the reliability and validity of diagnoses, with initial findings suggesting low levels of reliability and validity for the diagnoses of many disorders. The positive outcome of this is that classification systems were amended and methods used in classification, such as clinical interviews, have greatly changed. For example, specialist inventories are used in the diagnosis of specific disorders, like the **Geriatric Depression Scale** (GDS), used in the diagnosis of depression among the elderly. Recent research suggests that diagnosis of many disorders is now much more reliable and valid.

> **Key study**

On being sane in insane places (Rosenhan, 1973)

In this famous early study of the reliability and validity of psychiatric diagnosis, nine healthy people (including Rosenhan himself) presented themselves at psychiatric hospitals in five American states claiming to hear voices. Eight were admitted (three females and five males), one being refused entry due to falsifying personal details. After admission all eight behaved normally and participated in ward activities, each making notes about their experiences, though such note-taking was often perceived to be part of their abnormal condition. The pseudopatients noted how clinicians ignored them, even when they were speaking directly to them (asking questions like, 'Pardon me doctor, but could you tell me when I will be presented at the staff meeting?'); it was if they were 'invisible' (*see Table 4.3*). It was left to each pseudopatient to secure their release, with the length of hospitalization before release ranging from 7 to 52 days (average stay 19 days). All were released with the diagnosis of 'schizophrenia in remission' after treatment involving being given 2,100 tablets (of which only two were swallowed). Although no pseudopatients were detected by clinicians, many fellow patients had suspicions concerning their authenticity (35 out of 118 patients in the first three hospitalizations). Comments from fellow patients included, 'You're not crazy. You're a journalist or a professor' and 'You're checking up on the hospital'.

On the basis of these results it seems that psychiatric diagnoses had low validity (though reliability was high, as 7 out of 8 were diagnosed as schizophrenic, demonstrating how reliability can be high while validity is low). However, this criticism was somewhat unfair, as clinicians do not expect people to fake abnormal symptoms to attempt admittance to hospital and it is better to admit those who may be ill than to deny admittance, on the basis that the prime function of hospitals is to help people.

To counter this criticism, Rosenhan falsely informed staff at a teaching and research hospital, who were aware of his initial study, that an unspecified number of pseudopatients would attempt to gain admittance during the next three months. Staff rated on a 10-point scale the likelihood of new patients being fake. Out of 193 new patients, 83 aroused suspicions of faking (43 per cent). Rosenhan sent no pseudopatients, however; all were genuine. These results strongly suggested that clinicians couldn't reliably diagnose who was mentally disordered.

Figure 4.4 David Rosenhan

Table 4.3 Responses of clinicians towards pseudopatients

RESPONSE	PERCENTAGE MAKING CONTACT WITH PATIENT	
	PSYCHIATRISTS	NURSES
Moves on with head averted	71	88
Makes eye contact	23	10
Pauses and chats	2	4
Stops and talks	4	0.5

■ Critical thinking

Rosenhan's study is unethical as clinicians were unaware that they were in a study or that the researchers were faking symptoms. The study may be justifiable in terms of a cost–benefit analysis, however, where the costs of the deceit are outweighed by the benefits of highlighting how unreliable diagnosis can be, leading to improvements in diagnostic techniques. Indeed, if the study was repeated now, would similar results be found?

Reliability and validity of the diagnosis of depression

A problem in reliably diagnosing depression is that moods vary over time, though the modern requirement for symptoms to be present for some time aids the diagnostic process.

Another problem is the degree to which people are depressed. Reliability has improved, with use now made of specialist depression inventories, as well as traditional clinical interviews.

- Sato *et al.* (1996) found that the test–retest reliability of the **Inventory to Diagnose Depression, lifetime version** (IDDL) had a concordance rate of 77 per cent, which suggests the use of such inventories has improved the reliability of diagnosis.
- Moca (2007) found that the inter-rater reliability of diagnosis had a concordance rate of 88 per cent and 78 per cent for test–retest reliability, which supports the claim that diagnosis of depression is reliable, though these figures are lower than for the reliability of diagnosis for schizophrenia.
- Van Weel-Baumgarten (2000) assessed the validity of diagnosis among Dutch doctors using DSM-IV criteria, finding 28 of 33 depressive patients were correctly diagnosed, which suggests that validity of diagnosis, though not perfect, is high.
- Sanchez-Villegas *et al.* (2008) assessed the validity of the **Structured Clinical Interview**, finding 74 per cent of those originally diagnosed as depressed had been correctly diagnosed, suggesting the diagnostic method to be valid.

■ Critical thinking

An important type of reliability is **inter-observer reliability**. Explain what is meant by this term and how inter-rater reliability would be established.

Evaluation

- A difficulty in establishing the reliability of diagnosis over time is that patients often improve in condition between assessments.
- Chao-Cheng *et al.* (2002) proposed the use of self-diagnosis of depression by using internet-based self-assessments. The researchers reviewed the test–retest reliability of such a programme, finding a concordance rate of 75 per cent, which implies it is a reliable method of diagnosis. However, Jurges (2008) found that a problem with self-assessment inventories is that improvements in self-ratings are underestimated by patients, reducing the reliability of such a diagnostic method.
- Validation of diagnostic scales is additionally important, as such diagnostic scales can then be used to assess the diagnostic validity of other diagnostic measures. Anderson *et al.* (2003a) used the **Geriatric Depression Scale**, which was proven valid, to assess the value of the **Minimum Data Set Depression Rating Scale**, finding it to be of low validity and thus of little clinical use.

Reliability and validity of the diagnosis of OCD

The development of standardized rating scales, like the Yale–Brown Obsessive Compulsive Scale (Y-BOCS), has improved the reliability and validity of diagnosis, though such scales have their criticisms. There is also a lack of agreement among clinicians as to whether OCD is a separate disorder.

- Di Nardo and Barlow (1987) found an excellent 80 per cent reliability of diagnosis, second only to simple phobias in diagnosis of anxiety and mood disorders. This was supported by Foa *et al.* (1998), who used **Likert scales** to find high correlations among patients', therapists' and independent observers' ratings of OCD features, suggesting good inter-rater reliability.
- Geller *et al.* (2006) assessed the reliability of the **Child Behaviour Checklist**, finding it reliable and possessing psychometric properties that identified children with OCD, which supports the idea that the development of specialist inventories has improved the reliability of diagnosis.

- Leckman and Chittenden (1990), while assessing the validity of diagnosis of OCD, found that 50 per cent of Tourette's syndrome patients also had OCD, which suggests that OCD is not a separate disorder.
- Deacon and Abramovitz (2004) applied the **Yale–Brown Obsessive Compulsive Scale (Y-BOCS)**, the 'gold-standard' measure for OCD, to 100 patients, finding problems with the Y-BOCS sub-scales' ability to accurately measure OCD components, which implies the scales lack validity and need revision.

Evaluation

- The high incidence of OCD in young people, coupled with the secretive nature of the disorder, which leads to its under-recognition, and the lack of specialized child psychiatry services, implies a need for a quick, reliable diagnostic tool to identify cases.
- OCD has easily observable symptoms that assist in clear diagnosis, thus contributing towards high levels of reliability. The American Psychiatric Association (1987) reported that, compared to other anxiety disorders, the diagnostic reliability of OCD is highly favourable.
- Diagnoses of OCD incur long-term negative effects on sufferers, yet such diagnoses are made with little evidence of the disorder actually existing as a separate condition.

Reliability and validity of diagnosis of obesity

Although reaching epidemic proportions in many countries, obesity is not listed as an abnormal disorder under DSM or ICD classification systems, making assessment of the reliability and validity of diagnosis difficult.

> **Link to the biological level of analysis**
>
> The biological measure of body mass index (BMI), a ratio of body weight to height, is currently used as the most accurate and reliable way of measuring obesity.

- Seltzer *et al.* (1970) assessed the reliability of relative body weight (weight relative to height) as an indicator of obesity in US Army veterans, finding low reliability, with only extreme body weights being perceived as obese. This indicated the need for more sophisticated methods of assessment.
- Schneider *et al.* (2010) assessed 11,000 participants for eight years and found that obesity, as measured by BMI, was not a useful indicator of heart attack, stroke or death, with waist-to-height measurement being a better indicator. This suggests that BMI is not a reliable indicator of health-threatening obesity.
- Burkhauser and Cawley (2007) found that compared to using the percentage of body fat as an indicator of obesity, BMI misclassifies many types of individual as obese or non-obese, especially in males, as it does not distinguish between fat and fat-free mass, such as muscle and bone. This suggests that more accurate measurements of fatness are required to increase the validity of diagnosis.
- Romero-Corral *et al.* (2008) tested the correlation between BMI and body fat percentage as indicators of obesity, finding a concordance rate of 71 per cent in women and 44 per cent in men, which suggests that BMI is a reasonably valid measurement of obesity. The diagnostic performance of BMI decreased with age, however, and BMI had a tendency to incorrectly class muscular types as obese. Also very slender people, especially females, with abnormally high levels of fat tended to be incorrectly assessed as non-obese. This implies that BMI is not a valid diagnostic tool for all body types and ages.

Evaluation

- The categorization of obesity as a mental disorder would lead to specific requirements for diagnosis being stated, leading to improved reliability of diagnosis between clinicians.
- The development of specialist inventories to diagnose obesity is desirable, as when introduced with other conditions, reliability of diagnosis has greatly improved.
- Valid diagnoses of obesity are often difficult to achieve due to the presence of comorbid (simultaneous) conditions, such as diabetes.

Cultural considerations in diagnosis

LEARNING OUTCOME
- Discuss cultural and ethical considerations in diagnosis.

Cultural relativism – definitions of what is regarded as normal functioning vary from culture to culture and have equal validity.

Definitions of abnormality suffer from cultural relativism, meaning that no one definition applies to everyone, as normal functioning varies between cultures. This creates problems when clinicians of one culture evaluate and diagnose those from other cultures. Unless clinicians are aware of an individual's cultural background, norms and reference points, they may diagnose the individual's culturally normal behaviour as abnormal from their own cultural viewpoint. In some cultures it's normal to hear the voices of departed loved ones during the grieving process, but in Western cultures this could be an indication of schizophrenia.

Link to the sociocultural level of analysis

Cultural considerations in diagnosis are more widespread in multicultural societies, where several distinctive sub-cultures, each with their own perceptions of what constitutes normality, exist side-by-side, especially in those sub-cultures forming ethnic minorities within a larger society.

Some abnormal conditions are universal, found in all cultures, but others are **culture-bound syndromes**, existing only in certain cultures, like **ghostsickness**, found only in Native American tribes, where failing to observe correct burial procedures is seen as causing a person to become afflicted with weakness and dizziness, attributable to the troubled ghost of the deceased.

With the deviation from social norms definition of abnormality, Western social norms reflect the behaviour of the dominant white population; deviation from these norms by ethnic minorities, who may not subscribe to such norms, means that ethnic minorities become over-represented among those seen as mentally disordered. Cochrane (1977) found that black people of Caribbean origin in Britain were more often diagnosed as schizophrenic than the white population. However, such a high rate of diagnosis is not found in the Caribbean, which suggests that there is a cultural bias among British psychiatrists to over-diagnose black Caribbean people as schizophrenic.

With the failure to function adequately definition of abnormality, what is considered 'normal functioning' varies culturally and so what is perceived as abnormal functioning in one culture shouldn't be used to judge the behaviour of people of other cultures and sub-cultures.

With the ideal mental health definition, the criteria that constitute ideal mental health are specific to one culture and therefore shouldn't be used to judge those from other cultures. One of Jahoda's characteristics of ideal mental health is autonomy (independence), but collectivist cultures regard autonomy as undesirable. Nobles (1976) believes that collectivist cultures have a sense of 'we' rather than the Western cultural sense of 'me', as they favour communal goals, rather than the Western cultural preference for individual attainment.

Ethical considerations in diagnosis

The aim of diagnosis is to correctly identify disorders so that appropriate treatment can be given. However, there are several ethical consequences of diagnosis. Firstly, diagnosis can be used to discriminate against and even punish certain people. For example, diagnostic criteria have been used to classify homosexuality as a mental disorder, thus justifying the forcible 'treatment' of homosexuals to 'cure' their abnormality. Such treatments as aversion therapy, where electric shocks are given if patients become aroused by homosexual images, does not 'cure' homosexuals and turn them into heterosexuals, instead patients often become stressed, depressed and suicidal. Certain regimes have also used diagnostic criteria to classify political and religious dissidents as abnormal and punish them for their beliefs, by incarcerating them in psychiatric institutions to undergo forcibly applied treatments. Xia (2012) reported that China has imprisoned political dissidents in psychiatric institutions and subjected them to forced treatments, such as electro-convulsive therapy (ECT).

Theory of knowledge

The psychological study of abnormality has led to ethical changes in the ways in which mental patients are perceived and treated. Only through research that highlights unethical practices is it possible for radical changes to occur, permitting a more humane treatment of the mentally afflicted.

To be diagnosed as abnormal involves being given a stigmatizing label that is difficult to remove. Rather than being classed as 'people with schizophrenia', sufferers are labelled as 'schizophrenics', as if that is their whole being, and even when symptoms are absent, they are still referred to as 'schizophrenic in remission', a life-long identity that negatively affects employment chances and how others view them. Abelson (1974) showed a video of a young man telling an older man about his work experience. Psychoanalytic clinicians who were told the young man was a job applicant perceived him positively, while those told he was a mental patient viewed him negatively, illustrating the stigmatizing impact of labelling (though there was no difference in judgement among behavioural therapists).

Labelling therefore can sentence those diagnosed as abnormal to a life-time 'career' as mental patients, with frequent periods of hospitalization, treatment and unemployment. Those placed within psychiatric hospital environments may succumb to institutionalization, where they cannot function meaningfully outside the hospital environment. Another aspect of hospitalization is the powerlessness and depersonalization experienced by patients, as reported by Rosenhan's pseudopatients commenting on how they were ignored by clinicians (*see page 100*). An additional danger with labelling people as mentally disordered is that of self-fulfilling prophecy, where people behave in the way that the label suggests they should.

There is also the ethical issue of the use of psychoactive drugs as a 'chemical cosh' to control patients rather than treat them. There is even the viewpoint that drug companies exert an unhealthy influence over doctors and public health figures to promote their wares even though there is evidence that such drugs are often ineffective or even dangerous, with the accusation that the drug companies are suppressing such evidence. It is a lucrative market; sales of anti-psychotic drugs topped £10 billion globally in 2008.

SECTION SUMMARY
■ Several criteria of abnormality exist, each with their strengths and weaknesses.
■ Abnormality can also be defined in terms of psychological approaches.
■ Mental disorders are diagnosed through classification systems, which need to be reliable and valid for disorders to be identified, treated and cured.
■ Diagnosis should also include cultural and ethical considerations.

Psychological disorders

LEARNING OUTCOMES
■ Describe the symptoms and prevalence of one disorder from two of the following groups:
  ■ Anxiety disorders
  ■ Affective disorders
  ■ Eating disorders.
■ Analyse etiologies (in terms of biological, cognitive and/or sociocultural factors) of one disorder from two of the following groups:
  ■ Anxiety disorders
  ■ Affective disorders
  ■ Eating disorders.
■ Discuss cultural and gender variations in the prevalence of disorders.

Depression

Depression – a mood disorder characterized by feelings of despondency and hopelessness.

Major depression (also known as **unipolar depression**) is an affective mood disorder involving prolonged and fundamental disturbance of emotions. The condition can be endogenous, related to internal biochemical and hormonal factors, or exogenous, related to external stressful experiences (though the condition can have elements of endogenous and exogenous depression combined). Depressed people generally experience loss of energy and enthusiasm.

Affective disorders – mood disturbances that affect thoughts, behaviours and emotions.

Twenty per cent of people will suffer from depression at some point in their lifetime, with women twice as vulnerable as men. Depression often occurs in cycles, with symptoms coming and going and generally lasting four to six months. There is a high suicide rate; 10 per cent of severe depressives commit suicide, while 60 per cent of suicides overall are associated with mood disorders. Depression tends to commence from adolescence onwards, with the average age of onset occurring in the late twenties, though age of onset has decreased in the last 50 years, as prevalence rates have increased. With treatment, episodes last two to three months, but can last six months or longer if untreated.

Endogenous depression – depression that is linked to internal biochemical and hormonal influences.

Clinical symptoms

Exogenous depression – depression that is linked to external stressful experiences.

- Constant depressed mood – feelings of sadness reported either by the sufferer or by others.
- Lessened interest – diminished concern with and/or lack of pleasure in daily activities, either reported by the sufferer or observed by others.
- Weight change – significant increase or decrease in weight and/or appetite.
- Sleep pattern disturbance – constant insomnia or oversleeping.
- Fatigue – loss of energy and displacement of energy levels, e.g. becoming lethargic or agitated.
- Reduced concentration – difficulty in paying attention and/or slowed-down thinking, indecisiveness, either reported by the sufferer or observed by others.
- Worthlessness – constant feelings of reduced worth and/or inappropriate guilt.
- Focus on death – constant thought of death and/or suicide.

A distinction is made between **major depression** (clinical depression) and **dysthymic depression** (chronic depression), the difference being in the duration, type and number of symptoms. Patients meeting DSM-IV criteria for dysthymic depression have three or more symptoms, instead of the five required for major depression, including depressed mood, but not suicidal thoughts, and exhibit these symptoms for more than two months.

Gender variations in prevalence of depression

Depression is twice as common among females. There are two possible reasons for this: firstly that females are more **genetically vulnerable**, and secondly that females have more **environmental stressors**, like the discrimination and enhanced social stressors females often face. Females are under pressure to conform to gender stereotypes, have fewer opportunities for social and personal mobility and may experience hostility if perceived as intelligent or ambitious. Females are especially vulnerable to depression in mid- to late adolescence, a time when many will experience body dissatisfaction, sexual abuse, low self-esteem and resistance to achieving.

Link to the biological level of analysis

Another possible reason for the prevalence of female depression is that females are subject to more **biochemical** fluctuations, such as with menstruation, pregnancy and the menopause.

Research

- Zubenko (2002) found that an area of chromosome 2q33-35 containing the gene CREB1, which is linked to depression, is more common in females, supporting the idea that females are more genetically vulnerable.
- Chen *et al.* (2006) suggested a decline in the level of the hormone insulin following childbirth was responsible for post-natal depression. Insulin affects the secretion of serotonin in the brain; therefore decreased insulin may be influencing depression in women. This supports the notion of biochemistry being linked to high depression levels in females.
- Nolen-Hoeksema and Girgus (1994) reported that there are no differences in the prevalence of depression between males and females before the age of 15, but that the increased incidence of depression in females from adolescence on results from the increased stressors that females are subjected to, such as body dissatisfaction and the lesser opportunities for career advancement. This implies that heightened female rates of depression may be due to the discrimination and heightened social stressors that females often face.

Evaluation

- As reduced insulin levels are associated with post-natal depression, it may be possible to prevent the disorder by increasing the amount of carbohydrates eaten, as carbohydrates stimulate the production of insulin.
- An additional factor in the heightened prevalence of female depression is that clinicians may exhibit a **diagnostic bias** in assessing females as depressive, especially as the majority of clinicians are male.

Cultural variations in prevalence of depression

See Etiology: sociocultural factors, page 111.

Etiology – the causes or origins of a disorder.

Etiology: biological factors

Several indicators suggest that biology underpins depression, including genetic factors, the uniformity of symptoms across genders, ages and cultural groupings, the physical aspects of symptoms, such as weight fluctuations and fatigue, and the fact that biological treatments are effective. Although evidence indicates a major role for biology, environmental factors contribute to its etiology, too.

Genetics

Research uses twin, family and adoption studies by examining concordance rates of depression between people with different degrees of genetic relationship, to determine what role genetics play in the causation of the disorder. Findings indicate depression has a genetic component, especially with early onset depression.

Link to the biological level of analysis

Gene mapping is a biological method of comparing genetic material from families with high and low incidences of depression, with results indicating that several genes are involved and that genes make some individuals more vulnerable than others to developing depression.

Caspi *et al.* (2005) used gene mapping to find a relationship between depression and abnormalities in the 5-HTT gene, suggesting a genetic link. The 5-HTT gene is associated with the manufacture of serotonin and therefore implies a link between genetics and biochemical factors.

Gene mapping offers the possibility of developing tests to identify individuals with a high risk of developing depression, though this raises many socially sensitive and ethical concerns.

Key study

Kendler *et al.* (2006)

The researchers aimed to assess whether genetic influences in major depression are more important in women or men and whether the heritability of major depression changes over time.

A meta-analysis of five previous studies was conducted with concordance rates for depression between 15,493 Swedish twin pairs assessed on the DSM-IV classification system. Birth dates ranged from 1900 to 1958.

A moderate level of heritability of 38 per cent was found, with heritability higher in females at 42 per cent than in men at 29 per cent. Levels of depression were constant over time.

It was concluded that although depression seems moderately heritable and constant over time, genetic risk factors are higher for women.

- The high number of participants used from five different studies increases the reliability and validity of the results.
- The study provides support to previous estimates of moderate heritability to depression. The study wasn't able to assess the similarity of environment between male and female MZ twins.
- The findings support those of Bierut *et al.* (1999), who found similar gender differences in Australian twins.

■ Critical thinking

Kendler *et al.* (2006) investigated the heritability of depression by conducting a **meta-analysis** of twin studies. What is a meta-analysis and what is the method's main strength?

Other research

- Taylor *et al.* (1995) reviewed family studies of depression, finding the prevalence of the disorder in the general population was 1 per cent, while in first degree relatives of bipolar depressives it was between 5 and 10 per cent, implying a genetic pathway to bipolar disorder.
- Wender *et al.* (1986) found adopted children who develop depression were more likely to have had a depressive biological parent, even though adopted children are raised in different environments, implying biological factors are more important than environment.

Evaluation

- There's a possibility with twin studies of diagnostic unreliability, i.e. if researchers are aware one twin is depressive, then this clouds their judgement in assessing whether the other twin is also depressive.
- Twin and family studies suggest a genetic factor in the onset of depression, but don't consider the role played by social class and socio-psychological factors between family members. Also, if genes caused depression on their own, the concordance rate between MZ twins would be 100 per cent, which it clearly isn't.
- Findings from studies involving genetics support the **diathesis–stress model**, where individuals inherit different levels of genetic predisposition to developing depression, but ultimately it is environmental triggers that determine if individuals go on to develop depression.

Biochemistry

Biochemical explanations perceive abnormal levels of neurotransmitters and hormones as leading to depression. The focus has been on a group of neurotransmitters called monoamines such as serotonin, noradrenaline and dopamine, low levels of which are found in the brains of depressives. The importance of monoamines is supported by the fact that antidepressant drugs work by increasing the production of monoamines. For instance, **selective serotonin reuptake inhibitors** (SSRIs) raise levels of serotonin, producing an antidepressant effect. Because SSRIs are effective in treating unipolar depressive disorder, a stronger link has been established between low levels of serotonin and depression.

Certain forms of depression, like pre-menstrual syndrome (PMS), seasonal affective disorder (SAD) and post-natal depression are also associated with hormonal changes.

- Mann *et al.* (1996) found the reduction in depressive symptoms achieved by increasing monoamine levels through using antidepressants is reversed when serotonin levels are decreased by dietary manipulation, further supporting the biochemical explanation.
- Klimek *et al.* (1997) performed post-mortems on depressives and non-depressives, finding differences in the structure of the locus coeruleus, a brain area associated with the production of noradrenaline, suggesting abnormal brain structures may affect neurotransmitter levels, which leads to depression.
- Zhou *et al.* (2005) found SSRIs work by increasing dopamine levels in depressives, suggesting a role for the neurotransmitter in the causation of depression.

Evaluation

- The fact that monoamine neurotransmitters are involved in arousal and mood levels indicates them being involved in depression, which itself is a mood disorder.
- Neurotransmitter levels are affected immediately by taking antidepressants, but symptoms often take weeks to improve, weakening support for the biochemical viewpoint.

■ Claridge and Davis (2003) found that when non-depressives are given drugs that reduce levels of serotonin and noradrenaline in the brain, they don't become depressive, weakening support for the explanation.

Etiology: cognitive factors

Beck (1967, 1987) believes individuals become depressed because negative schemas, where the world is perceived destructively, dominate thinking and are triggered whenever situations are encountered resembling those in which negative schemas were learnt.

These negative schemas fuel and are fuelled by cognitive biases, causing individuals to misperceive reality.

Negative schemas

■ **Ineptness schemas** make depressives expect to fail.
■ **Self-blame schemas** make depressives feel responsible for all misfortunes.
■ **Negative self-evaluation schemas** constantly remind depressives of their worthlessness.

Cognitive biases

■ **Arbitrary inference** – conclusions drawn in the absence of sufficient evidence. For example, a man concluding he's worthless because it's raining the day he hosts an outdoor party.
■ **Selective abstraction** – conclusions drawn on the basis of one element of a situation. For example, a worker feeling worthless when a product doesn't work, even though several people made it.
■ **Over-generalization** – sweeping conclusions drawn on the basis of a single event. For example, a student regarding poor performance on a single test as proof of his worthlessness.
■ **Magnification and minimization** – exaggerations in evaluation performance. For example, a man believing he's ruined his car due to a small scratch (maximization), or a woman believing herself worthless despite many praises (minimization).

Negative schemas, together with cognitive biases and/or distortions, maintain the **negative triad**, which regards negative thoughts as being about:

■ **The self** – where individuals regard themselves as being helpless, worthless and inadequate.
■ **The world** – where obstacles are perceived within one's environment that cannot be dealt with.
■ **The future** – where personal worthlessness is seen as hindering any improvements.

Overall, depression is seen as resulting from cognitive vulnerabilities.

Link to the cognitive level of analysis

Abramson *et al.* (1978) proposed another cognitive explanation by revising learned helplessness in terms of **depressed attributional style**, based on three dimensions:

■ **Internal/external locus** – whether individuals perceive the cause of depression as due to themselves or not.
■ **Stable/unstable** – whether the cause is perceived as a permanent feature or temporary.
■ **Global/specific** – whether the cause is perceived as relating to the whole person or just one feature.

Therefore depressives believe failure is due to internal, st

Seligman (1974) reported students who made global, s
depressed for longer after examinations, supporting th
attributional style.

Peterson and Seligman (1984) found people identified
Questionnaire (ASQ) as being prone to depression ex
to internal, global, stable factors and were likelier to
stressors, demonstrating support for the concept of

Research

- Boury *et al.* (2001) monitored students' negative thoughts with the Beck Depress.
  Inventory (BDI), finding depressives misinterpret facts and experiences in a negative
  fashion and feel hopeless about the future, giving support to Beck's cognitive
  explanation.
- Saisto *et al.* (2001) studied expectant mothers, finding those who didn't adjust their
  personal goals to match the specific demands of the transition to motherhood, but
  who indulged instead in negative thinking patterns, increased depressive symptoms,
  supporting Beck's cognitive theory.
- McIntosh and Fischer (2000) tested the negative cognitive triad to see if it contains
  three distinct types of negative thought. They found no clear separation of negative
  thoughts, but instead a single, one-dimensional negative perception of the self,
  suggesting retention of all three areas of the triad as separate dimensions is unnecessary
  for representing the structure of depressive cognition.

Evaluation

- There is a wealth of research evidence supporting the idea of cognitive vulnerability
  being linked to the onset of depression, with depressives selectively attending to
  negative stimuli.
- The cognitive explanation of depression lends itself readily to scientific research,
  allowing refinement of cognitive models that provide greater understanding of the
  disorder.
- The majority of evidence linking negative thinking to depression is correlational and
  doesn't indicate that negative thoughts cause depression. Beck came to believe it was a
  bi-directional relationship, where depressed individuals' thoughts cause depression and
  vice versa.

Link to the cognitive level of analysis

Penland *et al.* (2000) found that depressed university students used more avoidance coping
skills than non-depressed students, which suggests that those with poor coping skills are
more vulnerable to developing depression.

Etiology: sociocultural factors

A prime social factor in depression is **interpersonal relationships**, especially the
emotions expressed between individuals in such relationships as within families,
social environments (where differences in culture and social class come into play) and
interactions between genders and age groups. Cultural factors also impact, with cross-
cultural differences in prevalence rates possibly being due to different perceptions of
culture and different cultural pressures.

Family

Disharmony in family relationships can be a factor in the onset and maintenance of depression. In 30 per cent of cases involving marital relationship problems, one partner will be clinically depressed, with the relationship characterized by hostility and a lack of affection. Pregnancy and the introduction of newborn children also creates stresses in romantic relationships, as well as being stressful in themselves, and can lead to depression. There can be a knock-on effect of the children of depressed parents becoming depressed themselves, with such children experiencing hostility, rejection, self-blame (like in the case of divorce) and low self-esteem. This can become ever-repeating, where the depression of children affects their parents, which in turn affects the children again.

Those experiencing depression in childhood can remain vulnerable into adulthood, where they perform poorly in romantic and family relationships, precipitating depression. Such individuals are also more vulnerable to stressful life events that may trigger depression.

Social environments

Social settings can influence the onset and maintenance of depression, with those in lower social classes and ethnic minorities often experiencing more social stressors, such as poverty, over-crowding, crime, etc., and therefore being more vulnerable to depression. However, those with poor coping strategies to deal with such social stressors are especially vulnerable, as they more easily feel overwhelmed and unworthy.

Research

- Gordon *et al.* (2005) found that in 50 per cent of couples with relationship problems, one partner was clinically depressed. However, this evidence is only correlational and doesn't indicate whether depression is a cause or an effect of relationship discord. Kung (2000), though, reported that marital difficulties are commonly reported prior to the onset of depression, supporting the idea that relationship disharmony leads to depression.
- O'Hara and Phillips (1991) found that the building of interpersonal relationships between mothers and newborn children and the resulting change with romantic partners can cause depression to occur. Goodman (2003) also reported that depression in men after the birth of children is significantly high, illustrating how changes in family structure can lead to depression.
- Lorant *et al.* (2003) carried out a meta-analysis, to find that factors of low socioeconomic status, such as poorer health care, higher levels of social stress and weaker social support, were highly correlated with an increased incidence of depression. This suggests that the onset of depression may occur through social factors.

Figure 4.5 Women often suffer from post-natal depression, but rates of depression are also high among fathers of newborn children.

Cultural factors

Depression may have different rates of incidence between cultures, due to differences in perception of the disorder. For example, in India many conditions characterized by distress are perceived as depression, while in Japan there is a low incidence, because depression is culturally unacceptable with clinicians reluctant to diagnose it. Some cultures, like Japan, are more at ease with reporting physical than mental symptoms of depression, due to the shame associated with mental, but not physical, weakness. People from collectivist cultures are also less prone to depression, as there is less focus on the individual and thus less frustration leading to depression from failing to achieve personal success.

Sub-cultural differences in the prevalence of depression also exist, for instance black women in the USA have lower rates of depression than white women.

Research

- A World Health Organization study (2011) found India to have the highest rate of depression in the world, with 36 per cent experiencing a major depressive incident. This suggests that depression is over-diagnosed compared to other countries, though heightened levels of social stressors, such as poverty, may also play a role.
- Waza *et al.* (1999) reported a low incidence of depression in Japan, due to the tendency of Japanese doctors to categorize depression in physical terms, like headache and neck pain, illustrating the negative cultural perception of depression in Japan.
- Das *et al.* (2006) reported that the lower level of depression among black compared to white American females is in part due to the stigma attached within the black population to being diagnosed with depression, illustrating sub-cultural differences in the prevalence of the disorder.
- Kagitcibasi and Berry (1989) report that people in collectivist cultures receive more and better social support and value cooperation and harmony, while people in individualistic cultures exhibit more alienation and loneliness, which may explain the lower levels of depression in collectivist cultures.

Evaluation

- It is unlikely that one explanation, like the sociocultural one, can explain the onset of depression, or that all types of depression have the same causative factors. More likely is that a mixture of biological, cognitive and sociocultural factors can better explain depression.
- Lower prevalence rates of depression among black Americans may also be due to a reluctance by clinicians to diagnose the disorder and a lack of available health resources for the black population.

Anxiety disorders – abnormal conditions characterized by extreme worry, fear and nervousness.

Obsessive-compulsive disorder – an anxiety disorder characterized by persistent, recurrent unpleasant thoughts and repetitive, ritualistic behaviours.

Obsessive-compulsive disorder (OCD)

All anxiety disorders are characterized by fear and although anxiety can be beneficial in threatening situations, many people experience anxiety levels so high they become maladaptive, negatively affecting day-to-day functioning, with 2 per cent of the population suffering from OCD.

Link to the cognitive level of analysis

OCD has a cognitive component, as it is characterized by persistent, recurrent unpleasant thoughts (as well as repetitive, ritualistic behaviours). Sufferers endure persistent and intrusive thoughts occurring as obsessions or compulsions, or a combination of both.

Obsessions consist of forbidden or inappropriate ideas and visual images leading to feelings of extreme anxiety. Common obsessions include:

- **contamination**, for example by germs
- **losing control**, for example through impulses to hurt others

- **perfectionism**, for example fear of losing important things
- **unwanted sexual thoughts**, for example fear of being homosexual
- **religion**, for example fear of being immoral.

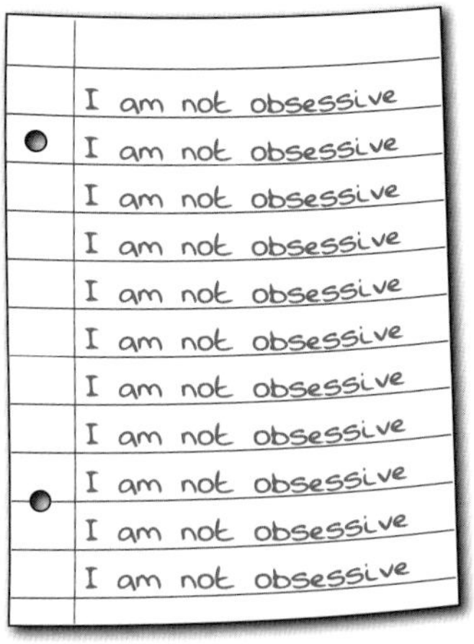

Compulsions consist of intense, uncontrollable urges to repetitively perform tasks and behaviours, like constantly cleaning door handles. Compulsive behaviours serve to counteract, neutralize or make obsessions go away, and although OCD sufferers realize that compulsions are only a temporary solution, they have no other way to cope so rely on their compulsive behaviours as a short-term escape. Compulsions can also include avoiding situations that trigger obsessive ideas or images. Compulsive behaviours are time-consuming and get in the way of meaningful events, such as work and conducting personal relationships. Behaviours are only compulsive in certain contexts, for example arranging and ordering books is not compulsive if the person is a librarian. Common compulsions involve:

Figure 4.6 OCD involves persistent, recurrent, unpleasant thoughts as well as repetitive, ritualistic behaviours.

- **excessive washing and cleaning**, for example teeth-brushing
- **excessive checking**, for example that doors are locked
- **repetition**, for example of body movements
- **mental compulsions**, for example praying in order to prevent harm
- **hoarding**, for example of magazines.

Most OCD sufferers understand their compulsions are inappropriate, but cannot exert conscious control over them, resulting in even greater levels of anxiety.

OCD is an exaggerated version of normal behaviour and is perceived as a mental disorder when an individual's behaviour becomes detrimental to everyday functioning. For instance when a sufferer's obsession with contamination means they cannot perform any meaningful work. Not all repetitive behaviours are compulsions; learning a new skill often involves endless, ritualistic repetition, but this is normal and beneficial.

Symptoms of OCD often overlap with those of other disorders, such as Tourette's syndrome and autism, which suggests that OCD may not actually exist as a truly separate disorder.

Symptoms

Obsessions

- **Recurrent and persistent** – recurrently experiencing unwanted thoughts, impulses and images that are inappropriate and intrusive, leading to high levels of anxiety and distress.
- **Irrelevant to real life** – experiencing thoughts, impulses and images that aren't relevant to real-life situations and are time-consuming so that they hinder an individual's ability to pursue valued activities.
- **Suppressed** – sufferers attempt to suppress thoughts, impulses and images with alternative thoughts or actions.
- **Recognized as self-generated** – sufferers understand their obsessional thoughts, impulses and images are self-invented and not inserted externally.

Compulsions

- **Repetitive** – sufferers feel compelled to repeat behaviours and mental acts in response to obsessional thoughts, impulses and images.
- **Aimed at reducing distress** – behaviours and mental acts are an attempt to reduce distress or prevent feared events, even though there's little chance of doing so.

Other symptoms

- **Recognized as excessive** – sufferer realizes obsessions/compulsions are excessive.
- **Time-consuming** – obsessions/compulsions are time-consuming, cause distress and interfere with the ability to conduct everyday working and social functioning.
- **Not related to substance abuse** – disorder isn't related to substance abuse or other medical condition.

Gender variations in the prevalence of OCD

There is little gender difference in the prevalence of OCD, though there are gender differences in types of OCD. Preoccupations with contamination and cleaning are more apparent in females, while male sufferers focus more on religious and sexual obsessions. OCD is more common among male children than female, as males have an earlier, gradual onset with more severe symptoms, while OCD in females generally has a later, sudden onset with fewer severe symptoms.

Research

- De Mathis *et al.* (2011) found male OCD sufferers were more likely to have early onset of the disorder, to be single, to have greater social impairment and more sexual or religious symptoms, while females generally had later onset and more contamination or cleaning symptoms. This illustrates that there are gender differences in the onset and expression of OCD.

Link to the biological level of analysis

Lomax *et al.* (2009) found that the brains of people with early onset OCD, who tend to be male, have a reduction in size of some brain areas, which isn't apparent in those with later-onset OCD, who tend to be female. This suggests that male OCD may be more biological in nature.

Evaluation

- OCD in females may be more influenced by sociocultural factors, as it tends to have a sudden onset, often in response to stressful life events, like the death of a loved one. OCD in males seems more biological in origin, as it tends to have a gradual, earlier onset with more severe symptoms.
- Not all patients with early-onset OCD are male, nor are those with later-onset OCD all female. This therefore weakens the argument that male OCD is more biological in nature.

Cultural variations in prevalence of OCD

See Etiology: sociocultural factors, page 118.

Etiology: biological factors

Focus centres on hereditary influences through genetic transmission and evolutionary explanations, where OCD is perceived as having an adaptive survival value. Some forms of OCD are linked to breakdowns in immune system functioning, such as through contracting streptococcal infections, Lyme disease and influenza. In such instances, this implies a biological explanation through damage to neural mechanisms.

Genetics

Research uses twin and family studies to assess what role genetics plays in the causation of OCD. Results indicate some genetic influence, though a major problem is separating out environmental influences.

Link to the biological level of analysis

Technology allows gene mapping studies to be undertaken. This involves comparing genetic material from families with high and low incidences of OCD. Results from gene mapping indicate particular genes are involved, making some individuals more vulnerable than others in developing the condition.

Samuels *et al.* (2007) used gene mapping to compare OCD sufferers who exhibited compulsive hoarding behaviour to OCD sufferers who didn't, finding a link to chromosome 14 marker D14S588, implying a genetic influence to compulsive hoarding behaviour, which may also indicate the existence of separate OCD sub-types.

It is unlikely that single genes cause OCD; more likely is that a combination of genes determines an individual's level of vulnerability to the disorder.

Research

- Lenane *et al.* (1990) performed a study into the prevalence of OCD among related family members, finding evidence for the existence of heritable contributions to the onset of the disorder, lending support to the genetic viewpoint.
- Grootheest *et al.* (2005) reviewed 70 years of twin studies into OCD, finding a heritability rate of between 45–65 per cent for OCD in children and between 27–47 per cent in adults, suggesting a genetic contribution.

Evaluation

- Evidence from family and twin studies indicates genetic factors at work in the expression of some forms of OCD, especially obsessions about contamination, aggression and religion, and compulsions involving washing, ordering and arranging.
- The fact that family members often display dissimilar OCD symptoms, for example a child arranging dolls and an adult constantly washing dishes, weakens support for the genetic viewpoint, for if the disorder was inherited then exhibited behaviours would be the same.
- The fact that twin studies like Grootheest *et al.* (2005) find that OCD originating in childhood is more genetic in nature than that originating in adulthood suggests that there may well be different types of OCD, with differing causes.

Evolutionary explanations

The evolutionary explanation argues that if OCD had no useful purpose, natural selection would have selected it out and it would no longer exist. So rather than perceiving OCD in maladaptive terms, evolution views it as fulfilling a beneficial purpose.

OCD involves repetitive behaviours, like washing and grooming, and these would have prevented against infection. Other similar behaviours may have increased vigilance and alertness, again incurring a survival value. Thus behaviours such as continually cleaning door handles can be regarded as exaggerations of prehistoric adaptations.

Research

- Polimeni (2005) reported OCD tendencies, such as counting and checking, carry the potential to benefit society, suggesting an ancient form of behavioural specialization with evolutionary origins.
- Abed and Pauw (1998) believe OCD is an exaggerated form of an evolved ability to foresee situations and predict the outcome of one's own thoughts and behaviour, so that dangerous scenarios can be coped with before they happen, suggesting OCD helps in the avoidance of harm.
- Chepko-Sade *et al.* (1989) found those rhesus monkeys that performed the most grooming of others were retained within a group following group in-fighting, suggesting OCD tendencies have an adaptive value, as continued group membership is crucial to survival.

Evaluation

- Behavioural features of OCD, like precision and hoarding, would be beneficial in hunting and foraging and therefore useful in the Pleistocene era. They remain now due to genome lag, where genes take time to evolve and fit current environments.
- There's a common sense value to OCD having occurred through the process of evolution and thus having a genetic basis, leading to neuroanatomical and biochemical influences.
- Saad (2006) believes OCD may be over-activation of warning systems of evolutionary importance. Therefore gender differences in OCD reflect the evolutionary differences in male/female priorities like mating and parenting.

Etiology: cognitive factors

The cognitive viewpoint sees some as vulnerable to developing OCD because of an attentional bias, where perception is focused on anxiety-generating stimuli. OCD sufferers are seen as having impaired, persistent thought processes, such as believing that the risk of infection in a given environment is much higher than it is in reality. Sufferers cannot dismiss intrusive thoughts, leading to self-blame, depression and heightened anxiety, making it even more difficult to dismiss such thoughts and obsessions as they occur, as sufferers exaggerate the significance of intrusive thoughts. Behaviours that lessen impaired, obsessive thoughts become compulsive because of their anxiety-reducing qualities and therefore become difficult to control.

What separates the normal unwanted intrusive thoughts seen in the general population from those of OCD sufferers is the meanings OCD sufferers attach to these thoughts and their attempts to relieve these thoughts through compulsions and avoidance.

Link to the cognitive level of analysis

Typical cognitive errors:

- Being intolerant of uncertainty due to a need for certainty and control.
- Having a need to be in control of all thoughts and emotions at all times.
- Believing thoughts must be important, as they are being thought about.
- Having unwanted, involuntary thoughts means that an individual is abnormal.
- Having intrusive thoughts and doing what they suggest are the same, morally.
- Thinking about doing harm, and not preventing it is just as bad as committing harm.
- Having unwanted, involuntary thoughts means an individual will act on them.

Even when OCD sufferers feel less anxious as a result of compulsive behaviours, the cognitive doubts quickly return.

Research

- Barrett and Healey (2002) compared children with OCD with anxious children and non-clinic children, finding the OCD children had higher ratings of cognitive appraisals such as probability and severity of events and the fusion of thoughts with actions. This suggests the cognitive conceptualization of OCD occurs in childhood.
- Davison and Neale (1994) found that OCD patients cannot distinguish between fantasy and reality, lending support to the idea of faulty thinking processes being linked to OCD.
- Clark (1992) reported that intrusive thinking is significantly more common in OCD sufferers than in the normal population, again supporting the cognitive argument.

Evaluation

- Cognitive treatments of OCD have proven effective by correcting cognitive bias and helping sufferers to become less vigilant, implying support for the cognitive model.
- The cognitive explanation doesn't really explain the emotional aspect of irrational beliefs, weakening support for the viewpoint.
- The fact that there are different sub-types of OCD, each focusing on different forms of anxiety-arousing, impaired thought processes, such as **emotional contamination**, where fear occurs that by association with people with negative emotions the sufferer will become like them, and **sexual identity**, where sufferers fear being of an opposite sexual orientation, supports the idea of OCD being largely determined by cognitive factors.

Etiology: sociocultural factors

Sociocultural factors are not prime causes of OCD, but increase the chances of its onset in vulnerable individuals by raising anxiety levels, through influences such as major life events and family disharmony. Sociocultural factors, such as family tensions additionally assist in the maintenance of the disorder. There has also been speculation that some childhood experiences, such as contracting streptococcal infections, in association with social factors, such as parental over-protectiveness, predispose individuals to OCD. Sociocultural influences also help shape the expression of the disorder, for example in highly religious environments, obsessions often reflect the particular religious views of that cultural setting. It is also important, if clinicians are to understand the origins of a sufferer's OCD, to consider the specific sociocultural context of an individual, in terms of what is considered shameful or dirty, etc.

Research

- Gothelf *et al.* (2004) reported that anxiety-raising major life events appear to precede the onset of OCD. This suggests such events don't cause OCD, but act as triggers in those biologically or psychologically predisposed to OCD, as not everyone subjected to such life events develops the disorder.
- Fontenelle *et al.* (2004) found that while the exact symptoms of OCD may reflect sociocultural factors, there was no consistent evidence that any particular sociocultural factor has a causal role, which implies that sociocultural factors merely shape the expression of OCD.
- Greenberg and Witztum (1994) found that 13 out of 19 ultra-religious Jews from Jerusalem with OCD exhibited symptoms that reflected religious beliefs relating to prayer, dietary habits, cleanliness and menstrual practices, which suggests that religious rituals do not cause OCD, but help to shape its expression.

Evaluation

- Horwath and Weissman (2000) argue that as studies from different cultures reveal similar prevalence rates and a consistency in the forms of obsessions and compulsions, OCD is likely to be more biological than sociocultural in origin.
- Although OCD appears to be primarily biological in origin, for treatments to work it is important that clinicians understand the origins of each individual sufferer's OCD in terms of their sociocultural background, as only by sensitively targeting the underlying triggers that precipitate the condition can it effectively be addressed.

Obesity

Obesity – an eating disorder whereby excess body fat accumulates to the extent of having a negative effect on health and well-being.

Once seen primarily as a medical illness with metabolic and genetic origins, and thought to be treatable only by medical means, obesity is now recognized as an eating disorder underpinned by a multitude of psychological and biological factors, just like anorexia and bulimia nervosa. As Day *et al.* (2009) argue, there are similarities in phenotype (the observable physical/biochemical properties of an organism, as determined by genetic and environmental influences) between obesity and other eating disorders, like excessive attempts at weight control and binge eating, as well as in risk factors such as low self-esteem, external locus of control, childhood abuse and shared susceptibility genes. One example of shared genetic risk is the brain-derived neurotrophic factor (BDNF) gene in which the valine allele of the Val66Met amino acid polymorphism predisposes to obesity, while the methionine allele predisposes to other eating disorders. Also, similarly to anorexia and bulimia nervosa, obesity is a cultural phenomenon, with differing prevalence rates occurring cross-culturally.

Obesity is influenced by both biological factors (such as genetic vulnerability, hormonal and neurological influences, and evolutionary explanations) and psychological factors (including cognitive and behaviourist influences, as well as psychodynamic ones based on childhood experience). Different obesity sufferers may have different types of causative factors and students should take care to identify and explain these when answering examination questions.

Symptoms

When fat accumulates to an extent that body mass index (BMI) (a calculation of a person's ratio of height to weight) is greater than 30 kg/m², then a person is clinically obese. A high waist-to-hip ratio (for males above 0.9 and for women above 0.8) also indicates obesity and vulnerability to life-threatening conditions. In Britain in 2008, 24 per cent of people were obese, with levels increasing worldwide. Indeed in the USA (with a 35 per cent obesity level), it's the second biggest cause of preventable death, being linked to cardiovascular diseases, diabetes, etc., with 9 per cent of health costs being attributed to the condition.

Symptoms include breathlessness, lethargy, difficulty in performing physical activities, excess fat in breast, abdomen and upper arm regions, often with white or purple blemishes, disproportionate facial features, knock-knees, sore joints and muscles, skin infections under folds of fat, varicose veins.

Obese men tend to have large waists and genitalia that appear disproportionately small. Obese women tend to carry extra weight on their hips and have irregular menstrual periods.

Figure 4.7 Obesity is reaching epidemic proportions, but only by understanding its causes will successful treatments be developed.

Conditions that may accompany obesity include:

- high cholesterol
- diabetes
- high blood pressure
- heart disease
- stroke
- sleep apnoea (persistent pauses in breathing while asleep)
- osteoarthritis
- gallstones.

Gender differences in the prevalence of obesity

There are no gender differences in prevalence of the disorder. However, obesity has increased more among pre-pubescent boys than girls, though female obesity rates are increasing more greatly among adult females than adult males, a phenomenon apparent across cultures where obesity exists.

Research

- The National Health and Nutrition Survey (2010) reported no overall differences in obesity rates in the USA between males and females, but found it more prevalent in boys, at 18.6 per cent (up from 14 per cent in 1999), than girls, at 15 per cent (up from 13.8 per cent in 1999). This suggests boys are more vulnerable to obesity than girls.
- Centers for Disease Control and Prevention (2010) reported that female obesity has increased more greatly than male obesity, with an obesity rate of 35.5 per cent among females over 20 years old, compared to 32.2 per cent of males over 20 years old. As this finding is reflected in other cultures with obesity, it suggests females are more vulnerable to the disorder.
- Hong et al. (2009) fed mice equal amounts of calories and found that male mice were more prone to weight gain than female mice, but that female mice with their ovaries removed (done to establish the role of ovarian hormones) did not gain weight. This suggests that males are more vulnerable to obesity and that ovarian hormones have an influence on female weight gain.

Theory of knowledge

Although experiments permit cause-and-effect relationships to be established, psychological findings are never completely beyond chance factors. This is why findings can only ever 'suggest' a conclusion and not establish an absolute truth.

Evaluation

- More research is needed to understand why there should be age-related gender differences in obesity rates and why obesity appears to be increasing more in females than males, especially if males are more biologically vulnerable to weight gain.
- Understanding metabolic differences between males and females may lead to better preventive strategies and treatments for obesity.
- Results from animal studies, such as Hong et al. (2009), cannot necessarily be generalized to humans, as different species have vastly different metabolisms.

Cultural differences in the prevalence of obesity

From a biological point of view, differences in levels of the **thrifty gene** among different cultures may explain cultural differences in prevalence of obesity (*see Evolutionary explanations, below*). **Sociocultural factors** may also explain such differences (*see Etiology: sociocultural factors, page 123*).

Etiology: biological factors

Although neurological and hormonal factors have some biological influence on obesity, research suggests that the main biological factors emanate from genetic and evolutionary sources.

Genetics

There seems an inherited genetic basis to obesity, with some individuals more genetically predisposed to become obese and those with multiple genes towards obesity having an increased risk of developing the condition. The genetic explanation in combination with the evolutionary explanation explains why only certain people become obese. The genetic explanation can be tested by seeing if obese people share genetic similarity.

Link to the biological level of analysis

Gene mapping involves comparing genetic material from related individuals with high and low incidences of obesity. Results from gene mapping indicate particular genes are involved, making some individuals more vulnerable than others to developing the condition.

Frayling *et al.* (2007) found people with two copies of the fat mass and obesity gene FTO had a 70 per cent increased risk of becoming obese, while people with only one copy had but a 30 per cent increased risk, supporting a genetic explanation.

The discovery of genes related to obesity may lead to effective gene therapies for the treatment of the condition.

Research

- Wardle *et al.* (2008) assessed twins on BMI and body fat deposits, finding a heritability figure of 77 per cent, suggesting genetic factors have a major influence on obesity.
- Sorensen and Stunkard (1994) compared the degree of obesity of adopted participants with their adoptive and biological parents, finding an individual's weight was more correlated with biological relatives, lending support to the genetic explanation.

Evaluation

- Musani *et al.* (2008) suggest obese people may be more fertile, reproduce more and ultimately increase genes favouring obesity in the population.
- Most cases of obesity aren't explained by genetics alone. Genes don't determine obesity, they need an environment in which to be expressed.
- Genes cannot explain the upsurge in obesity. Genes haven't changed, but environmental factors, such as the availability of food, have, suggesting environment plays the larger role.

Evolutionary explanations

Obesity may be an evolutionary hangover. In the Pleistocene era humans existed in a harsh world in which survival depended on expending physical effort to find food, with food not always plentiful or constantly available. Selective pressure favoured those able to store excess energy as fat to see themselves through times of famine. Nowadays many humans live in a world of constant, plentiful, easily available food, but evolution causes bodies to behave as if they were still living in their ancestral past and because the gene pool hasn't substantially altered, genes that once aided survival now favour obesity.

Fatty foods are preferred, as they are energy rich, and humans overeat to lay down fat stores that in ancient times would see them through regular periods of food scarcity. Evolution also sees humans as preferring sedentary (lazy) lifestyles, as in the Pleistocene era conserving energy was essential to survival. Modern humans continue to behave as if food supplies are irregular, resulting in dysfunctional overeating, and humans may also be vulnerable to overeating foods that weren't part of their evolutionary past, such as liquid calories, because they don't trigger the neural mechanisms that control appetite.

Evolution explains why some individuals seem more vulnerable to dramatic weight increases, by reference to the **thrifty gene model**, which believes that in the Pleistocene era there was a selective advantage for people with insulin resistance, as they would have been able to metabolize food more efficiently. This was advantageous in times of food scarcity, but now leads to obesity as food is ever-available.

Research

- Bray *et al.* (2004) believe high fructose corn syrup (HFCS) causes obesity. Used as a drinks sweetener, its consumption in the USA increased by 1,000 per cent between 1970 and 1990, a time of increasing obesity. Not a foodstuff familiar to our evolutionary ancestors, it is seen as not stimulating leptin and insulin production, which normally act to regulate eating, leading to weight gain.
- Friedman (1994) found heightened evidence of the thrifty gene in the Pacific Islanders of Kosrae, where only a small minority remain lean, but possess the same eating habits as those that are seen as not possessing the gene.
- Rowe *et al.* (2007) found Pima Indians have high levels of obesity from a thrifty metabolism that allows them to metabolize food more efficiently. Once an advantage in times of food scarcity, it now leads to obesity, supporting the evolutionary thrifty gene hypothesis.

Evaluation

- The idea that foodstuffs not present in the Pleistocene era cause obesity is critisizable by the fact that obesity levels have also risen in countries where HCFS isn't commonly used.
- The thrifty gene hypothesis is able to explain not just why people tend to overeat to prepare for times of food scarcity, but why only people with the gene would become obese.
- The thrifty gene hypothesis explains why identifiable groups of people who don't have the gene are able to eat lots and not put on weight, such as the people of the Nile Delta where historically there weren't food shortages.

Practical applications

By understanding the adaptive significance of obesity, it may be possible to develop practical applications to successfully treat the condition. Such applications would need to be directed against sedentary lifestyles, which contribute greatly to an increase in bodily fat deposits, as they weren't lifestyles found in the Pleistocene era. Genetic profiling could help identify those most at risk, like those carrying the thrifty gene, so that treatments could be more focused on individuals with greatest need.

Etiology: cognitive factors

Cognitive explanations focus on the faulty thought processes that direct maladaptive behaviours, leading to obesity. For example, *'I need to eat a lot to maintain the energy to work.'* Food is seen as becoming predominant in information processing, with a strong emotional component that leads to an attentional bias, whereby individuals constantly think about food and seek opportunities to eat. Cognitive explanations can be tested by seeing if faulty thought processes are related to overeating and if therapies based on the cognitive approach are successful. Research also suggests that obesity leads to a decline in cognitive functioning.

Link to the cognitive level of analysis

Research has especially focused on childhood obesity, with indications that there is a lack of cognitive control in obese children that gives rise to impulsive eating and thus obesity.

Cserjesi *et al.* (2007) examined cognitive profiles of obese boys, finding them deficient in attention capabilities, suggesting childhood obesity involves cognitive deficits.

Research

- O'Rourke *et al.* (2008) reviewed several methods of treating obesity, finding cognitive behavioural therapy significantly improved weight loss, which suggests cognitive factors may be involved in the development of obesity.
- Singh-Manoux *et al.* (2012) tested 6,401 middle-aged participants over ten years, to find that there was speedier cognitive decline and greater risk of dementia in obese rather than normal weight participants, illustrating the cognitive effects of obesity.

Evaluation

- Attention deficits may be an effect of being obese. Elias *et al.* (2003) found early-onset long-term obesity leads to a decline in cognitive functioning, weakening the cognitive explanation as a cause of obesity.
- The fact that eating isn't a passive response to environmental triggers, but is a motivated behaviour that brings feelings of gratification and pleasure, suggests an information processing element to the onset and maintenance of obesity.
- The cognitive explanation of obesity lends itself readily to scientific research, allowing refinement of cognitive models that lead to greater understanding of the disorder.

Link to the biological level of analysis

The cognitive deficits associated with obesity are thought to originate from high blood sugar levels and elevated blood pressure contributing to changes in blood vessels and the brain, as well as increased fatty tissue leading to hormonal balances that negatively affect brain functioning.

Etiology: sociocultural factors

Although obesity has a genetic basis, the condition is socioculturally distributed, indeed it only exists within certain cultures, with attitudes towards food and its consumption being strongly shaped by social environments. The obesity epidemic in Western cultures has occurred since the 1980s, a time period in which social factors have changed but genetic factors have not. Social factors include what foodstuffs comprise an individual's diet and their level of physical activity. While consumption of high-fat content foods has increased massively, physical activity has decreased with people living increasingly sedentary lifestyles, for instance driving to destinations rather than walking. Advertisers and food producers are also keen to market convenience foods, which are cheap to produce and have a high calorific content. Such foodstuffs are often all that people of lower socioeconomic status can afford, although obesity seems to be spreading through all sections of Western society.

Cultural and sub-cultural groups have different eating practices, with certain groupings favouring high-fat content foods, which when combined with lower levels of physical activity can lead to obesity.

Research

- Noppa and Bengtsson (1980) studied 1,462 middle-aged Swedish women, finding that education, social class and income were negatively correlated with high levels of obesity. This was supported by Kuntz and Lampert (2010) who found that low levels of educational and occupational achievement were correlated with high levels of obesity. This was found especially among women, with those in the lowest income group three times more likely to be obese than those in the highest income group. This illustrates the influence of social factors on the prevalence of obesity and how obesity has been a growing problem in Western cultures since the 1980s.
- Hu (2003) found that increased TV watching was associated with obesity and that men who watched over 40 hours a week of TV had a three-fold chance of developing type 2 diabetes compared with those who watched 1 hour a week. This suggests that health campaigns should promote increased activity levels and a decrease in sedentary activities, such as TV viewing.
- Jeffery *et al.* (2006) found that eating at fast food restaurants was generally practised by families with children and was positively associated with a high-fat diet and obesity, while being negatively correlated with consumption of vegetables and physical activity. This illustrates the link between convenience foods and obesity, especially that of childhood obesity.

Evaluation

- Research suggests support for the **diathesis–stress model**, where genetics determine individual levels of vulnerability to obesity, while sociocultural factors, such as diet and level of physical activity, seem to form the environmental triggers for the condition to actually develop.
- There is an accusation that the 'obesity epidemic' is overstated due to a desire by commercial interests to create guilt about body-weight that will lead to an obsession with expensive forms of dieting, which are doomed to a 95 per cent failure rate and create feelings of guilt and self-loathing. Berman (2004) points out that obesity isn't a 'disease', as it is easily addressed by increasing levels of physical activity.
- People in low socioeconomic groupings may find it harder to avoid obesity, as healthy foods are less available and less affordable, with leisure pursuits involving physical activity, such as gym membership, also not affordable.

Cross-cultural focus

The fact that obesity doesn't exist in many cultures, often ones where malnutrition is more of a problem, such as in many African countries, illustrates that obesity is a cultural construct. Also, many cultures perceive 'fatness' positively, as they associate it with wealth and prosperity through having ample food to survive.

SECTION SUMMARY
- Three major types of mental disorder are depression (affective disorder), OCD (anxiety disorder) and obesity (eating disorder).
- All three disorders can be explained in terms of biological, cognitive and socio-cultural factors.
- All three disorders can also be considered in terms of cultural and ethical variations.

Implementing treatment

LEARNING OUTCOMES
- Discuss the relationship between etiology and therapeutic approach in relation to one disorder.
- Discuss the use of eclectic approaches to treatment.

The relationship between etiology and therapeutic approach

Therapies for mental disorders are based on different etiologies, for instance biomedical therapies are based on the biological model's belief that mental disorders have a biological basis, while cognitive therapies are based on the cognitive viewpoint that mental disorders originate from maladaptive thinking (*see Approaches to abnormality, page* 95). The success rates of specific therapies in treating mental disorders are seen as reflecting how well the psychological approaches on which they are based can explain the origins of those mental disorders. However, the concept of **treatment etiology fallacy** believes it's a mistaken notion that the success of a treatment reveals the cause of a disorder.

Eclectic approaches to treatment

Eclectic treatments
– the use of multiple therapies in the treatment of mental disorders.

Eclectic treatments give a greater flexibility of treatment, as they involve the combination of two or more different therapies, often to suit the particular needs of an individual or group, thus allowing more aspects of a disorder to be treated. Eclectic treatments can be:

- **simultaneous**, where different therapies are applied at the same time
- **sequential**, where therapies are given consecutively to each other
- **stage-orientated**, where one therapy is given during the initial severe phase of a disorder and other therapies are given during the maintenance or recovery stage.

The greatest advantage of eclectic treatments is that the strengths of several therapies can be applied (such as drugs reducing symptoms so that 'talking' therapies can be applied), though the downside is that the collective weaknesses of the therapies being applied are also apparent (such as the addictive nature of some drugs and the overall cost of applying several therapies).

The relationship between etiologies and therapeutic approaches is detailed within the introductions to biomedical, individual and group approaches to treatment. Considerations of the effectiveness of eclectic treatments can be found at the end of this section.

Biomedical approaches

Biomedical
approaches –
physiological
treatments of
abnormality based
on the biological
model.

Drug therapy –
treatment of mental
disorders with
medicines.

ECT – treatment
of mental disorders
by application of
electrical voltage to
the brain.

Psychosurgery
– treatment of
abnormality
by irreversible
destruction of brain
tissue.

The biological/medical approach sees mental disorders as having diagnosable physiological causes and perceives cures as emanating from rectifying the physical problems that originate from such causes. This comes through physical interventions that alter the function of neurological mechanisms, such as the brain and hormonal and neurotransmitter activity. Common treatments include drug therapy, electroconvulsive therapy (ECT) and psychosurgery.

Psychiatric drugs modify the working of the brain, affecting mood and behaviour. Drugs enter the bloodstream to reach the brain and affect the transmission of chemicals in the nervous system known as **neurotransmitters**, such as dopamine, serotonin and acetylcholine, incurring a variety of effects on behaviour. Psychiatric drugs work by increasing or decreasing the availability of neurotransmitters, thus modifying their effects on behaviour. Drugs blocking the effects of neurotransmitters are called **antagonists**, while those mimicking or increasing the effects of neurotransmitters are called **agonists**.

ECT is believed to induce changes in neurotransmitter levels, including sensitivity to serotonin in the hypothalamus and an increase in the release of GABA (gamma-Aminobutyric acid), noradrenaline and dopamine. ECT is used against drug-resistant depression and schizophrenia, with several treatments a week given for a limited period. A general anaesthetic and a muscle relaxant are given to ensure that patients don't feel pain or convulse and incur fractures. Brain stimulation occurs through electrodes placed on the head, with a brief controlled series of electrical pulses. This causes a seizure within the brain, lasting about a minute. After 5–10 minutes, the patient regains consciousness. **Unilateral** ECT occurs when only the non-dominant hemisphere of the brain is stimulated, while **bilateral** ECT involves stimulation to both hemispheres.

Psychosurgery is generally used against depression and anxiety disorders (including OCD) when other treatments have failed, quality of life is reduced and there is enhanced risk of suicide. Psychosurgery involves the irreversible destruction of small amounts of specific pieces of brain tissue, usually in the limbic system, an area associated with emotion, for example **bimedial** and **orbital leucotomies**. There is also **deep-brain stimulation**, a less invasive and less destructive treatment involving electrodes planted in the brain. Gastric surgery is used to treat obesity.

■ Critical thinking

Why may it not be possible for mentally disordered individuals to give informed consent for psychotherapeutic treatments? Who would give consent in such circumstances?

Biomedical treatments of depression

Drugs

The most common treatment is antidepressant drugs, which stimulate the production of monoamine neurotransmitters in the brain, leading to increased physical arousal. Three types of drug are used to treat depression: **monoamine oxidase inhibitors** (MAOIs), **tricyclics** and **selective serotonin reuptake inhibitors** (SSRIs). All of these increase serotonin production, the main difference between them is their side effects rather than effectiveness or speed of action. Most are given once per day and 'kick in' after 10–14 days. They are withdrawn slowly; sudden cessation causes restlessness, insomnia, anxiety and nausea.

First generation antidepressants such as MAOIs stop serotonin, noradrenaline and dopamine being broken down so that levels are increased, while tricyclics stop dopamine and noradrenaline being reabsorbed and some also block the reuptake of serotonin, so that again levels are increased, though some have no known effects on any of these systems.

More modern antidepressants tend to only affect the level of one monoamine, for instance SSRIs such as Prozac prevent serotonin being reabsorbed or broken down, thus making it more available.

Research

- Hirschfield (1999) reported tricyclics are effective in the treatment of mild and severe depression and are the first choice of treatment in the latter; 60–65 per cent of patients taking tricyclics experience improvement in symptoms.
- Kirsch *et al.* (2008) found second generation antidepressants, like SSRIs, work no better than placebos for most patients with mild or even severe depression, and accused drug companies of suppressing research evidence that cast doubt on their effectiveness.
- Furukawa *et al.* (2003) reviewed 35 studies, finding antidepressants superior to placebos, implying antidepressants are an effective treatment.

■ Critical thinking

The purpose of using a placebo in both Kirsch *et al.*'s (2008) and Furukawa *et al.*'s (2003) studies was to act as a **control condition**. Explain what the purpose of a control condition is and how it allows psychologists to establish **causality**.

Evaluation

- MAOIs aren't favoured because side effects, including cerebral haemorrhage, can be triggered by eating certain foodstuffs containing tyramine (like cheese and red wine) or taking other drugs, like decongestants. More recent **reversible selective** MAOIs are designed to avoid these problems.
- Tricyclics have side effects, including toxic effects on the cardiovascular system. They're lethal in overdose, presenting dangers to suicidal patients. Beneficial effects aren't felt for two to three weeks, making it difficult to persuade patients to keep taking them, and medication must continue after improvements in mood are achieved, as 50 per cent relapse if they stop taking them. Modified tricyclics, like **lofepramine**, cause fewer side effects.
- Antidepressant drugs are cost-effective, occur in tablet form, a familiar and trusted form of treatment, and have the added benefit of being self-administered.

ECT

- Sackheim (1989) reviewed studies of ECT, finding real treatments more effective than simulated ones, bilateral treatments more effective than unilateral ones, ECT more effective than medication and the most effective treatment for severe depression, though medication is required post-treatment to prevent relapse.
- Paguin *et al.* (2008) performed a meta-analysis of ECT, comparing studies of ECT, placebos and antidepressant drugs, finding ECT the most effective, suggesting it's a valid therapy for depression, including severe and resistant forms.
- Antunes and Fleck (2009) reviewed studies on the effectiveness of ECT, symptom remission, patients' perceptions, cognitive impairments and quality of life. They found ECT to be more effective than antidepressants, with remission rates between 50 and 80 per cent, quality of life improved and patients having positive perceptions of the treatment, implying ECT is an appropriate treatment, especially since improvements in its procedure were introduced.

Evaluation

- The side effects of ECT are more severe with children, adolescents, the elderly and pregnant women and shouldn't be used as a treatment for these categories of people, unless as a last resort.
- The use of ECT declined in the USA between 1975 and 1986, from 58,667 to 36,558 patients, due to the introduction of new generation antidepressants and negative media reports. However, from 1987 to 1992 the use of ECT rose from 4.2 to 5.1 per 10,000 individuals, suggesting the treatment is seen more favourably and that new generation antidepressants aren't as effective as originally hoped.
- Aside from side effects such as memory loss, ECT also has high relapse rates. Sackeim *et al.* (2001) reported 84 per cent of patients relapsed within six months, implying the treatment isn't effective long-term. Bregin (1997) found the benefits of ECT only lasted four weeks with high relapse rates.

Biomedical treatment of OCD

Drugs

Antidepressants are used to treat OCD, like SSRIs, which elevate levels of serotonin, with anxiolytic drugs also used, due to their anxiety-lowering properties. Anti-psychotic drugs that have a dopamine-lowering effect are also useful in treating OCD, though antidepressants affecting neurotransmitters other than serotonin haven't proved effective.

Beta-blockers also reduce the physical symptoms of OCD. They work by countering the rise in blood pressure and heart rate often associated with anxiety, by lowering adrenaline and noradrenaline production.

Research

- Piccinelli *et al.* (1995) performed a meta-analysis of 36 studies assessing the worth of antidepressants as a treatment for OCD, finding them effective in the short-term, with 61 per cent showing improved symptoms with the tricyclic antidepressant clomipramine and 28 per cent with newer SSRI medications; both treatments proved more beneficial than non-serotonergic drugs.
- Beroqvist (1999) investigated the effect of low doses of the anti-psychotic drug Risperidone in treating OCD, finding treatment effective due to the drug's dopamine-lowering effect.
- Flament *et al.* (1985) tested the ability of the antidepressant drug clomipramine to address the symptoms of childhood OCD in 19 patients, finding the drug superior over a five-week period to placebo treatment, lending support to the use of drug treatments.

Evaluation

- It's not certain if drug treatments that are effective in treating OCD reduce obsessive symptoms, or instead lessen the depressive symptoms that often accompany the condition.
- Drug treatments cannot be regarded as a cure for OCD, as once drug taking stops, symptoms tend to reappear.
- Drug treatments are widely used to treat the symptoms of OCD as they are a cost-effective and user-friendly form of treatment.

Psychosurgery

Psychosurgery destroys brain tissue to disrupt the cortico-striatal circuit by the use of radio-frequency waves. This affects the orbital-frontal cortex, the thalamus and the caudate nucleus brain areas, incurring a reduction in symptoms.

Deep brain stimulation involves the use of magnetic pulses on the supplementary motor area of the brain and is associated with blocking out irrelevant thoughts and obsessions.

Research

■ Liu *et al.* (2008) followed up 35 OCD patients who were non-responsive to medications or psychological and behavioural treatments, who underwent stereotactic bilateral anterior capsulotomy psychosurgery. PET scans and questionnaires were used to find twenty patients (57 per cent) became symptom-free, ten (29 per cent) experienced significant improvements, while five (14 per cent) showed no improvements, suggesting the treatment to be safe and effective in treating OCD.

■ Mallet *et al.* (2008) evaluated deep-brain stimulation of the subthalamic nucleus in 16 individuals with treatment-resistant OCD, comparing it with sham stimulation, and found significant symptom reduction, which suggests the treatment to be effective. This was supported by Greenberg *et al.* (2008) finding symptom reduction and functional improvement in 18 out of 26 OCD patients undergoing stimulation of the ventral internal capsule/ventral striatum brain area.

■ Richter *et al.* (2004) reported that 30 per cent of OCD patients had a 35 per cent or greater reduction in symptoms on the Yale–Brown Obsessive-Compulsive Scale, but there were infrequent complications, such as urinary incontinence and seizures, demonstrating that although psychosurgery can be effective, it is not without its dangers.

Evaluation

■ Psychosurgery should only be used after patients have given fully informed consent. It's debatable whether patients with severe OCD can give fully informed consent, however, suggesting there may be ethical problems in administering the treatment.

■ Whether psychosurgery should be used generally involves a cost–benefit analysis, where the possible costs, such as irreversible side effects, should be compared against the possible benefits, like the lessening of symptoms detrimental to everyday functioning.

 ■ Psychosurgery cannot be considered to be a cure for OCD and patients who undergo neurosurgery will probably continue to need psychiatric support following the procedure, even if it is considered to be a success.

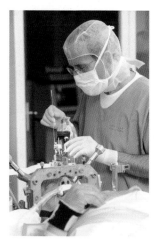

Figure 4.8 Psychosurgery has been used successfully to reduce symptoms of OCD. However, there are risks of serious side effects.

Biomedical treatment of obesity

Drugs

Anti-obesity drugs help regulate weight by altering appetite, metabolism and absorption of food. Orlistat is the main drug treatment; it reduces intestinal fat absorption by inhibiting the production of pancreatic lipase. The undigested fat is then excreted. Rimonabant works as an appetite suppressant by blocking the action of the endocannabinoid system, while Sibutramine is another appetite suppressant, which acts in the brain to inhibit deactivation of neurotransmitters.

Bariatric surgery

Bariatric surgery involves several techniques that reduce the size of the stomach, such as removing part of the stomach, gastroplasty (where surgical staples are used to limit stomach size) and gastric bypass surgery (where the small intestines are re-routed to a small stomach pouch). All techniques reduce the amount of food needed to bring satiety (fullness) and gastroplasty and gastric bypass surgery can additionally prevent the absorption of calories and produce hormonal changes.

Research

- Hauptmann *et al.* (2000) found that obese patients treated with Orlistat and an energy-reduced diet lost significantly more weight than those treated with a placebo and an energy-reduced diet, and 34 per cent of the Orlistat-treated patients sustained their weight loss over a two-year period. This suggests Orlistat is a relatively effective treatment, though side effects of Orlistat include oily loose faeces, excessive flatulence and frequent bowel movements, though these can be reduced by eating a low-fat diet.
- McMahon *et al.* (2002) found Sibutramine to result in 4.1 kg more weight loss over a one-year period compared to a placebo treatment, though there was an increased risk of heightened blood pressure, which lowers the effectiveness of the treatment.
- Christensen *et al.* (2007) found that obese patients treated with Rimonabant lost an average of 4.7 kg of body weight over a one-year period than those treated with a placebo, which suggests the treatment to be effective. There were serious side effects, however, such as depressed mood, anxiety and heightened risk of suicide, which implies the treatment is highly risky.
- Maggard *et al.* (2005) performed a meta-analysis of 147 studies of bariatric surgery, finding that average weight loss was 20–30 kg, maintained for ten years or more and that gastric bypasses incurred more weight loss than gastroplasty. This suggests that surgical treatments are superior to other treatments.

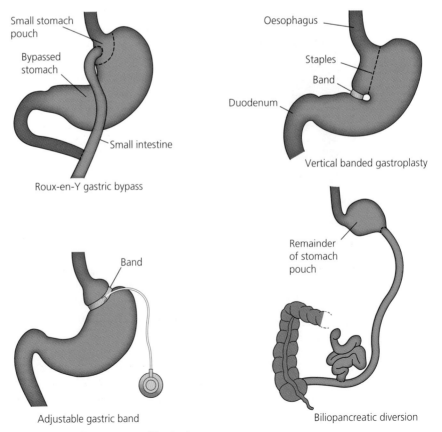

Figure 4.9 Different types of bariatric surgery

Evaluation

- In 20 per cent of cases bariatric surgery incurs adverse effects, such as bloating, pneumonia and a mortality rate of 0.2 per cent. As the procedure is estimated to incur a reduction in mortality risk of up to 40 per cent, the benefits would seem to outweigh the adverse effects.
- In assessing the effectiveness of treatments, potential side effects need to be considered. If the potential benefits appear to outweigh the potential costs, such as health risks, then the treatment can be considered beneficial. No treatment is without its risks, though it should be remembered that non-treatment of obesity also results in potentially high health risks.

Individual approaches to treatment

Individual approaches – forms of psychological therapy in which a client is treated on a one-to-one basis with a therapist.

LEARNING OUTCOMES
- Examine individual approaches to treatment.
- Evaluate the use of individual approaches to the treatment of one disorder.

Two individual approaches to treatment are the behaviourist and cognitive approaches, each of which treats mental disorders based on their viewpoint of what causes abnormal behaviours. Each has strengths and weaknesses, with each more effective in particular instances.

The behaviourist approach sees mental disorders as maladaptive (inappropriate) behaviours learnt through environmental experience. Behavioural treatments replace maladaptive behaviours with adaptive (appropriate) ones, through the use of:

Behavioural therapies – treatments of abnormality that modify maladaptive behaviour by substituting new responses.

- **Classical conditioning**, where learning occurs through association of a neutral stimulus with an involuntary unconditioned stimulus, such as with **systematic desensitization** (SD) and **exposure and response prevention** (ERP), both treatments for OCD.
- **Operant conditioning**, where learning occurs via reinforcement of desirable behaviour, thus increasing the chances of the behaviour occurring again, such as with **behavioural activation therapy** (BAT) and **social skills training** (SST), both treatments for depression.
- **Social learning**, where learning occurs by the observation and imitation of others modelling desirable behaviours.

Cognitive behavioural therapy – treatment of abnormality that modifies thought patterns to alter behavioural and emotional states.

The cognitive approach sees mental disorders as arising from disordered thought processes, with cognitive behavioural therapy (CBT), an umbrella term for several therapies, based on the model. The idea behind CBT is that beliefs, expectations and cognitive assessments of self, the environment and the nature of personal problems affect how individuals perceive themselves and others, how problems are approached and how successful individuals are in coping with and attaining goals. CBT challenges and restructures maladaptive ways of thinking into rational, adaptive ones. Behaviour is seen as being generated from thoughts, therefore maladaptive behaviour is altered by targeting maladaptive thinking. Thoughts are perceived as affecting emotions and behaviour and so are modified to reduce symptoms. Drawings are often employed, illustrating links between thinking, actions and emotions, with understanding where symptoms originate from being useful in reducing symptoms.

Individual treatments of depression

Behavioural therapies

Behavioural therapies perceive depression as acquired through environmental experience and modifiable through conditioning. Reinforcements, in the form of rewards for desirable behaviour, elevate mood and encourage participation in positive behaviours, while social reinforcements, in the form of family members and social networks, provide support for depressed individuals. Social models, who demonstrate desirable behaviours to be imitated, are also used.

Behavioural activation therapy (BAT) perceives depression as an indication of the things in an individual's life that need to change. Exercises are used that help depressives to concentrate on activities delivering feelings of joy and mastery. A schedule of activities is built up that sufferers need to participate in to create normal and satisfying lives. BAT offers quick relief from depression, connecting patients with simple, naturally occurring reinforcements that seek to change how depressives approach day-to-day activities, make life choices and deal with crises.

Social skills training (SST) helps those with difficulties in relating to others, a frequent feature of patients suffering from depression. Individuals lacking social skills have difficulties in building networks of supportive friends and become increasingly socially isolated, increasing the risk of becoming depressive. SST believes that when patients improve social skills, levels of self-esteem increase and others respond more favourably to them. A key goal is to improve the ability to function in everyday social situations. Patients are taught to alter behaviour patterns by practising selected behaviours in individual or group therapy sessions.

Research

- Houghton *et al.* (2008) evaluated the effectiveness of BAT on 42 patients with self-reported depression, finding the treatment effective, tolerable and possessing a low drop-out rate.
- Hersen *et al.* (1984) reported that social skills treatments are equal in effectiveness to traditional psychotherapies in addressing the symptoms of depression.
- La Fromboise and Rowe (1983) found **structured learning therapy**, a treatment based on SST, is more readily employable for different types of patients than traditional psychotherapies, and improves the psychosocial functioning of people of varying ages and ethnic backgrounds, as well as proving useful in treating those who have difficulties with traditional psychotherapy.

Evaluation

- BAT is a useful treatment for depression, as it can be successfully modified for use with different types of patients with very different needs, such as the elderly or adolescents.
- BAT compares favourably with cognitive behavioural therapy, producing a similar success level of 50 per cent immediately after treatment, reducing to 25 per cent after two years. As BAT is a simpler method of treatment, it's arguably more effective than CBT.
- Therapists using SST should progress slowly, so patients aren't overwhelmed by attempting to change too many behaviours at once, which may intensify feelings of social incompetence and hence deepen depression rather than reducing it.
- One problem with SST is the difficulty in generalizing newly learnt social skills to real-life situations. Generalization occurs more readily when SST has a clear focus and patients are highly motivated to reach realistic goals, with skills taught being suitable for specific patients.

Cognitive behavioural therapy (CBT)

CBT therapists and patients work together to verify reality. For instance, if a patient makes the negative statement, '*I'm a poor parent, because my children misbehave*', the therapist gets the patient to assess its truth and examine the idea that someone is a bad parent because their children are sometimes naughty. Patients therefore become more objective, more able to distinguish fact from fiction and don't perceive things in extreme terms.

Treatment entails one or two sessions of CBT every two weeks for around 15 sessions. After an **education phase**, where individuals learn relationships between thoughts, emotions and behaviour, **behavioural activation** and **pleasant event scheduling** are introduced, aimed at increasing physiological activity and engagement in social and other rewarding activities, for instance socializing with others. Cognitive factors are then addressed after patients have experienced improvement in mood or energy, by being taught to identify the faulty thinking responsible for low mood and to challenge these thoughts. Between sessions patients are given goals to boost self-esteem. These involve **hypothesis testing** of negative thoughts through behavioural coping skills, for instance testing the belief they're incapable of being included in conversations, by talking to strangers in social situations. Therapists only set tasks they're confident patients can succeed at; failure reinforces the ineptness patients believe in. To prevent relapse, 'booster' sessions are given in the subsequent year.

Research

- Whitfield and Williams (2003) found CBT had the strongest research base for effectiveness, but recognized the difficulty of health services being able to deliver weekly face-to-face sessions for patients and suggested this could be addressed by introducing self-help versions of the treatment, like the SPIRIT course, which teaches core cognitive behavioural skills using structured self-help materials.
- The Department of Health (2001) reviewed research papers of treatments for depression, including behavioural, cognitive, humanistic and psycho therapeutic ones, finding CBT to be the most effective, but did not endorse the use of CBT alone, as other treatments, such as behavioural therapy, were effective too.
- Flannaghan *et al.* (1997) used a questionnaire to identify stroke victims who had developed clinical depression. Nineteen patients were then given CBT sessions for four months, resulting in reduced symptoms, suggesting CBT to be a suitable treatment for specific groups of depressives.

Evaluation

- CBT is the most effective psychological treatment for moderate and severe depression and one of the most effective treatments where depression is the main problem. It also has few side effects.
- For patients with difficulty concentrating, often problematic with depressives, CBT can be unsuitable, leading to feelings of being overwhelmed and disappointed, which strengthen depressive symptoms rather than reducing them.
- CBT, as with all 'talking therapies', isn't suitable for patients who have difficulties talking about inner feelings, or for those without the verbal skills to do so.

Individual treatments of OCD

Behavioural therapies

With **exposure and response prevention** (ERP), sufferers are introduced to the objects or situations prompting their obsessions, but aren't allowed to make the usual obsessive responses. The idea is because OCD occurred through reinforcement, then if anxiety-creating scenarios are avoided, reinforcement is prevented and relearning can occur. If OCD sufferers are prevented from obsessively sweeping up, they realize the obsession that stimulated feelings of anxiety no longer does so.

Research

- Lindsay *et al.* (1997) randomly assigned 18 OCD patients to either ERP or anxiety-management programmes. After three weeks there was a significant reduction in symptoms for the ERP patients, but not for the control group, implying symptom reduction results from the specific techniques of exposure and response prevention.
- Baer (1991) introduced a self-directed, step-by-step form of ERP that is equally as effective for mild forms of OCD as seeing a therapist and can therefore be considered cost-effective.

Evaluation

- ERP can incur large drop-out rates due to the high levels of anxiety it creates, therefore it's usually combined with drug treatment so anxiety levels are controllable.
- ERP is more effective than drug treatments as relapse rates are lower, suggesting ERP brings long-term, lasting benefits.
- Even patients with long-lasting and severe OCD symptoms benefit from ERP treatment as long as they're suitably motivated to improve. However, the treatment is less effective for patients who don't exhibit overt compulsions and those with moderate-to-severe depression.

Cognitive behaviour therapy (CBT)

CBT is a common treatment for OCD, treatments occurring once every 7 to 14 days for about 15 sessions in total, with CBT orientated at changing obsessional thinking, similar to **habituation training** (HT), where sufferers relive obsessional thoughts repeatedly to reduce the anxiety created. All types of maladaptive thoughts associated with OCD can be successfully addressed with CBT; **intrusive thoughts** are shown to be normal and patients come to understand that thinking about a behaviour isn't the same as actually doing it. Sufferers learn to focus on estimations of potential risks and realistically assess the likelihood of them occurring. Sufferers are encouraged to practise new adaptive beliefs and to disregard their former maladaptive ones.

Research

- Cordioli (2008) reviewed randomized clinical trials and meta-analyses of CBT, finding it effective in reducing OCD symptoms in 70 per cent of patients who complied with treatment, suggesting the therapy to have useful therapeutic value, though reasons for why many sufferers are non-responsive weren't identifiable.
- Vogel and Vogel (1992) investigated the effectiveness of habituation training in treating OCD patients, finding within-session declines in obsessional thinking, but not between sessions, implying the technique is of little value in the real world.
- O'Kearney *et al.* (2006) assessed the ability of CBT to treat children and adolescents under the age of 18 with OCD, finding it effective, but more so when combined with drug treatments.

Evaluation

- The chances of CBT being successful are strongly correlated with the strength of the working relationship created between therapist and client, indicating the pivotal role that the therapist plays in the administering of the treatment.
- Suitably trained nurses have proven as effective as psychiatrists and psychologists in treating clients with OCD, demonstrating the simplicity of the treatment and its cost-effectiveness.

- One problem with CBT, as with all 'talking therapies', is it isn't suitable for patients who have difficulties talking about inner feelings, or for those who don't possess the verbal skills to do so.

Individual treatments of obesity

Behavioural therapies

Behaviour theory views excessive eating leading to obesity as an over-learnt habit, conditioned to internal and external cues. Therefore obesity is addressed by replacing maladaptive eating practices with adaptive ones, as obese people who successfully lose and maintain weight loss seem able to reduce the number of inappropriate stimuli they previously responded to with food intake.

Operant conditioning techniques are used, whereby reinforcements, in the form of praise and heightened self-esteem, are given for meeting energy intake and expenditure goals. For example, **behaviour modification**, as used by Weight Watchers, sets healthy, attainable target weights. The long-term target weight is broken down into achievable short-term goals, with early goals easy to achieve, so that reinforcement for success can be given, leading to increased motivation, confidence and persistence to reach subsequent short-term goals. A maintenance period is also established where food intake is stabilized and weight is neither lost nor gained, with a tangible reinforcement of 'lifetime membership', a status retained free of charge, if members stay within 2lb of their maintenance weight. Weight Watchers also uses social learning through vicarious reinforcement, where role models are provided in the form of successful formerly obese dieters whose eating practices can be observed and imitated.

Many see obese people as lacking willpower, but obesity is often due to exposure to cues that trigger eating, like eating while watching TV. By using behavioural techniques based on classical conditioning, patients learn to break their association of eating in response to such cues and learn new healthy eating practices. **Self-control** is learnt where eating practices are modified, like learning to eat only at set meal times, avoiding high calorie foods and monitoring food intake. One obese person, who ate in junk food restaurants on his way home from work, found a new route home that by-passed such restaurants, eating a healthier meal when reaching home.

Research

- Adachi (2005) found that behaviour therapy permitted the lifestyle modifications necessary for weight loss through dieting and exercise. Patients' self-care was promoted through reinforcement of voluntary behaviour, with patients realizing on average BMI weight loss of -0.9 kg/m^2 through target setting and one month's self-monitoring, followed by six months of regular observations. This illustrates the effectiveness of behaviour therapy in combating obesity.

Figure 4.10 Obesity is often due to exposure to cues that trigger eating, like eating while watching TV.

- Lowe and Timko (2004) found that 72 per cent of Weight Watchers members reaching their target weight maintained it over a five-year period, having initially lost at least 5 per cent of body weight, which emphasizes the importance of operant conditioning and social learning techniques in treating obesity.
- Golan *et al.* (1998) found that significant weight loss occurred in obese children who were reinforced by parents for reducing eating behaviour associated with external food cues, such as eating while standing, watching TV, eating while stressed and between meals. This suggests that breaking associations between eating and negative external food cues is an effective way of treating obesity.

Evaluation

- Evidence of the widespread acceptance of behavioural therapies comes from the fact that most weight-management programmes, for example NutriSystems, have a behaviour-modification component. A recent American government committee also emphasized behaviour change as the first and most important step in the treatment of obesity.
- Recent behavioural techniques have involved non-face-to-face therapies, which utilize self-applied computer-assisted therapies. Such treatments are more cost-effective and can be administered at times and in situations that are convenient to individual patients.
- Although behavioural therapies have a commendable record in producing significant weight loss during treatment, relapse rates back into unhealthy eating habits and weight being regained are high once treatment stops, which suggests that behavioural therapies only treat the symptoms of obesity and not its underlying causes.

Cognitive therapies

Cognitive therapies work on the principle that thinking as well as behaviour needs to change if weight loss is to be maintained. For example, **motivational interviewing** (MI) helps patients to perceive that they have a problem and that by thinking about and creating strategies for change, they can actively pursue change, instead of just being a passive victim of obesity. These realizations motivate the patient to actually pursue change, leading to successful weight loss and increased motivation to pursue and achieve further weight loss.

Research

- West *et al.* (2007) found that MI enhanced both weight loss and glycaemic (metabolic) control among obese women with Type 2 diabetes, even after just two sessions of therapy. These improvements were maintained at a six-month follow up, supporting the idea that thinking as well as behaviour must change for weight loss to be maintained.
- Schwartz *et al.* (2007) found that two sessions of MI led to significant weight loss in obese patients, which was maintained at a six-month follow up, supporting the idea that thinking needs to change for weight loss to be maintained.

Evaluation

- CBT, as with all 'talking therapies', isn't suitable for patients who have difficulties talking about inner feelings, or for those without the verbal skills to do so.
- Although evidence finds CBT effective, there's little research assessing its cost-effectiveness against other treatments.

Group approaches to treatment

LEARNING OUTCOMES
■ Examine group approaches to treatment.
■ Evaluate the use of group approaches to the treatment of one disorder.

In group therapy, a group of clients (patients), generally with similar disorders, meet with one or more therapists and share their experiences and give mutual support to each other. The idea is to construct a confidential, safe environment in which disorders, their causes and possible remedies can be explored.

The idea with **group psychotherapy** is to allow clients to grow emotionally and solve personal issues with group support. Relationships with group members are seen as assisting in problem-solving and developing confidence. Clients learn about themselves, how others view them and the reactions they cause in others, all of which increase self-awareness. Therapists attempt to develop group dynamics to illustrate individual problems. By gaining insight into the origins of their disorders, clients are able to resolve their problems.

In **group cognitive behaviour therapy** (GCBT), clients and therapists work together to challenge maladaptive thought processes and restructure them into adaptive ones. Support is given by group members to practise and develop new adaptive ways of thinking and behaving.

The main aim of **group behavioural therapies** is to assist clients in becoming aware of their maladaptive behaviours and to alter these to adaptive ones. Reinforcement comes from praise and the support of group members and from vicarious reinforcement where group members model behaviours to be observed and imitated.

Group treatments of depression

Group behavioural activation therapy involves groups of about ten patients and one or two facilitators (therapists) meeting once a week for about ten weeks. Group exercises are used to break down the usual maladaptive practices that sustain depression and to practise and reinforce new adaptive behaviours that foster feelings of joy and mastery.

Families/couples psychotherapy is used where an individual's depression involves family dynamics. The focus is on interpersonal relationships, with special emphasis on the roles played by family members in reinforcing depression. The focus is on improving communication, increasing pleasurable interactions and reducing negative ones. Other forms of group psychotherapy concentrate on mutual exploration of problems, with group members providing insight and support to overcome depression.

Research

■ De Jong-Meyer and Hautzinger (1996) assessed **coping with depression**, a course of group therapy treatment based on BAT, finding it achieved comparable acute outcome and better long-term outcome than antidepressant medication, indicating that the therapy provides clinicians with a convenient, cost-effective treatment that can be tailored to the individual needs of patients.

■ Lemmens *et al.* (2009) found that family therapy was effective in treating hospitalized cases of depression, with many patients less likely to be using antidepressant medication at the end of treatment. This suggests the therapy to be a useful means of treating severe cases of depression.

■ McDermut *et al.* (2001) reported that 45 out of 48 studies found group psychotherapy to be effective in reducing depressive symptoms. No difference in effectiveness was found between individual and group psychotherapy and CBT was found to be most effective. This suggests that group psychotherapy is more cost-effective than individual psychotherapy, but less effective than CBT, though CBT is generally a more expensive treatment.

Evaluation

■ Group therapy isn't useful for those who find it difficult to communicate with or trust others. For such patients the intimacy and privacy of a one-to-one relationship with a therapist that individual therapy provides may be preferable.
■ Depression often brings great feelings of shame, which are a barrier to recovery. Therefore the relief found in group therapy in discovering that others share similar feelings and experiences can greatly assist recuperation.
■ Group therapy can assist recovery by improving social skills, such as by providing examples from others of how to react intimately to different types of people. Poor social skills are common among depressives and a barrier to recovery.

Group treatments of OCD

The basic aim of **group CBT** (GCBT), as with individual CBT, is to change obsessional thinking and develop new adaptive beliefs, but interaction with fellow OCD sufferers provides additional support and encouragement and decreases the feelings of isolation that can aggravate OCD symptoms.

GCBT for OCD often incorporates **exposure and response prevention** (ERP), involving **exposure** to a feared obsession (either imagined or for real) until the fear subsides, and **response prevention**, where the usual ritual response is not allowed to occur.

GCBT usually involves 5–12 participants and one or two therapists meeting once or twice a week for up to 12 sessions, with pre, post and follow up measurements.

Family therapy

Family therapy is constructive, as OCD often incurs problems with family relationships and social adjustment; indeed family members sometimes unconsciously help to sustain OCD symptoms, such as by endless reassurance. Family therapy increases comprehension of the disorder within families, which reduces family conflicts and educates family members in how to effectively deal with the disorder and how not to accommodate it and hinder progress to recovery.

Research

■ Jonsson and Hougaard (2009) found that GCBT with ERP was better than drug treatments in reducing OCD symptoms, highlighting the treatment's effectiveness.
■ Freeman *et al.* (2008) found that 69 per cent of child OCD sufferers receiving family CBT demonstrated remission of symptoms after 14 weeks of treatment. Fifty per cent of children not completing the treatment also showed improvements, which suggests the treatment to be a powerful therapeutic tool.
■ Kelly (2011), from a review of studies, reported that family therapy decreased the distress levels of family members and provided an effective treatment through getting family members to act as co-therapists in delivering practice exposure exercises at home.

Evaluation

■ With GCBT the involvement of others helps guard against setbacks and encourages persistence when setbacks do occur. Sufferers can also learn strategies from fellow sufferers in how to cope with their disorder.

- The feelings of isolation that OCD often incurs can be addressed by the social support that group therapies provide and the realization that others have similar problems.
- Group therapies aren't advised for those who have problems with sharing experiences, lack trust in others or who cannot commit to regular attendance. Problems can also occur if one or two individuals dominate proceedings. Group therapy can additionally be difficult to arrange simultaneously for all group members.

Group treatments of obesity

Group behavioural treatment (GBT) occurs where patients develop the skills to achieve a healthier weight through the development of group cohesiveness, with reinforcement occurring via mutual support to establish and meet individual goals. Competition between individuals to lose weight is desirable, because individuals push each other to keep to the group norm; so too is members of the group modelling desirable eating and lifestyle behaviours for others to observe and imitate. Groups typically comprise 10–20 people and one or two therapists, meeting weekly for six months, then monthly for 18 months, with the same group members being retained throughout the treatment programme.

Some forms of obesity have an emotional factor that responds to group psychotherapy, such as **group dialectical behaviour therapy** (GDBT), which seeks to reduce eating psychopathology and achieve weight maintenance. Groups of around five to eight patients receive around twenty 90-minute treatment sessions, comprising cognitive behavioural techniques for emotional self-regulation and assertiveness training and meditation techniques to help achieve new adaptive behaviours. The essential element is that skills are learnt and practised in groups.

Research

- Wing (2002) reported that a GBT programme of six months of weekly meetings and no further contact incurred average weight loss of 4.5 kg, while a similar programme that continued with bi-weekly meetings for another six months incurred 13.6 kg average weight loss, which demonstrates the importance of continued contact.
- Roosen *et al.* (2012) found that obese emotional eaters receiving GDBT achieved significant weight reduction and maintenance, with only one out of 35 patients dropping out of a six-month treatment programme. This suggests that GDBT is an effective treatment of obesity with a high emotional factor.
- Telch and Agras (2000) found that 82 per cent of a group of 11 obese female binge eaters receiving GDBT were no longer binge eating after six months of treatment. Only one patient dropped out and emotion regulation and eating behaviour improvements were maintained post-treatment, illustrating the effectiveness of the therapy.

Evaluation

- The success of GDBT in addressing cases of obesity with a high emotional factor suggests that there may be different types of obesity that respond better to different forms of therapy.
- The fact that group psychotherapy incurs relatively small drop-out levels suggests that although the treatment can seem costly compared to other therapies, it may actually be cost-effective in terms of the number of patients who ultimately benefit.
- It may be that longer treatment sessions are necessary to address underlying eating attitudes and prevent relapse, as Agras (1989) has suggested that cognitive changes may take longer than behavioural changes in establishing healthy eating.

Eclectic treatments of depression

A combination of drugs and psychotherapy has been found to be effective, especially when delivered in a **stage-orientated** manner, with antidepressants beneficial during the acute phase of depression and psychotherapy effective in preventing relapse. **Simultaneous** treatments are also beneficial in ensuring that patients adhere to taking antidepressants.

Research

- Segal *et al.* (2002) reported that 40 per cent of patients do not take prescribed antidepressants, but simultaneous treatment with psychotherapy increases the number adhering to drug treatment, demonstrating a particular benefit of eclectic treatment.
- Peterson (2006) reported that antidepressants are an effective way of treating depression in its acute phase, but after symptom reduction, psychotherapy, either alone or combined with antidepressants, is the best was of preventing relapse. This supports the stage-orientated method of eclectic treatment delivery.

Eclectic treatments of OCD

Combination treatments for OCD are relatively new, which is surprising, as the two main solo treatments have inherent weaknesses; drug therapies incurring a high relapse rate when treatment stops and many patients not tolerating CBT, especially the ERP component because of the anxiety it causes. The idea therefore is that a combination of the two given **sequentially** would cancel out each other's weaknesses; drug treatments, due to their serotonin-raising qualities, would ease anxiety levels, while CBT would decrease relapse rates.

Research

- Neziroglu *et al.* (2000) found that a combined treatment of the drug fluvoxamine and CBT including ERP, given to children with OCD who hadn't previously responded to CBT alone, brought greater improvements than with drug treatment alone and this was retained over a two-year follow-up period. This suggests that combined therapies enhance treatment efficacy.
- Pots (2004) randomly assigned 112 child/adolescent OCD sufferers to receive CBT alone, the drug sertraline alone, the two treatments combined, or a placebo pill. Drug treatment alone and CBT alone did not differ in symptom reduction effects, but a combined treatment proved more effective, which suggests this should be a favoured treatment. Van Balkom (1998) found no difference between success rates for solo and combined treatments with adult patients, however, which suggests combined treatment may only suit younger sufferers.

Eclectic treatments of obesity

A popular eclectic treatment of obesity is combined pharmacotherapy, where two or more drugs are given **simultaneously**. The idea is that the brain utilizes multiple mechanisms working in parallel fashion to regulate appetite and diet, and so drugs are prescribed that affect these different mechanisms. Phentermine and Fenfluramine are two drugs commonly prescribed, but encouraging results have recently been realized through a combination of Phentermine (a stimulant that releases noradrenaline) with the serotonin precursor L-5-Hydroxytryptophan (L-5-HTP) (which stimulates serotonin production) and the peripheral decarboxylase inhibitor, Carbidopa (which has no clinical effect on its own, but increases the effect of L-5-HTP). The overall effect is a reduction in appetite and cravings and a heightening of satiety.

Another **stage-orientated** eclectic treatment is that of initially giving the drug Phentermine to reduce appetite and thus create weight loss, followed by psychotherapy to develop an awareness of anxieties underpinning the disorder and strategies to change eating/exercise habits.

Research

- Rothman (2009) treated 91 obese patients simultaneously with Phentermine, L-5-HTP and Carbidopa and found that significantly more weight was lost than by patients treated with Phentermine alone or a combination of Phentermine and L-5-HTP, and fewer stimulant side effects were experienced than by those treated with Phentermine alone. This suggests that combined pharmacotherapy can be an effective treatment through targeting different brain mechanisms associated with the regulation of eating.
- Roberts (1978) treated 12 patients who had shown only a minimal response to psychotherapy, with a stage-orientated combination of the stimulant Phentermine and psychotherapy. All patients improved, with nine reaching their target weight and weight loss being maintained. Initial weight loss was rapid with patients becoming more amenable to exploring the emotional factors underpinning their overeating and to adopting new lifestyle practices, such as taking regular exercise. This suggests that a combination of biological and psychological techniques can help combat obesity.

SECTION SUMMARY

- ■ Mental disorders can be treated with biomedical, individual and group therapies.
- ■ Different therapies have varying rates of effectiveness against different types of mental disorders.
- ■ Therapies can often be combined to form more effective treatments.
- ■ Therapies can additionally be assessed in terms of the approaches they are based on.

Developmental psychology

Introduction

Developmental psychology is the study of how and why people change over time. While development is most noticeable in the young child, change continues throughout life and this area is often referred to as 'lifespan psychology'. Aspects of development include:

- **social development** – relationships with others
- the development of **cognitive skills** such as perception, memory and problem-solving
- the development of **personal identity**, including gender and cultural identity and self-esteem.

We will look at each of these covering the following learning outcomes:

LEARNING OUTCOMES

- To what extent do biological, cognitive and sociocultural factors influence human development?
- Evaluate psychological research (that is, theories and/or studies) relevant to developmental psychology.

An important principle in developmental psychology is that experiences in infancy and childhood have an effect on subsequent development. Some of these experiences may occur during critical or sensitive periods during early development. These periods are thought of as windows of opportunity during which certain types of experience have a lasting effect on the development of skills or qualities. An important debate in developmental psychology relates to the impact of early experiences on later development and adjustment. Research shows that some children are more resilient than others to adversity and this knowledge has been used to develop programmes to increase resilience. Knowledge about the influence of biological, social and cultural factors in people's lives is helpful not only for families but also in childcare and education to create good opportunities for children and young people all over the world.

Social development

Unlike young animals of other species, human babies are relatively helpless at birth, possessing a few rudimentary reflexes such as crying, suckling and grasping. They are unable to feed or care for themselves until much later in childhood, and babies would simply not survive without the care and protection of a parent figure. Bowlby's attachment theory (1969) argued that the relationship between a child and their parent figure is crucial for the survival of the infant. His more controversial claim was that this attachment sets up expectations for how relationships work that continue to influence our well-being and adjustment throughout adulthood. We will examine Bowlby's theory and consider how early attachment may influence later relationships. The section will end by examining the effects of early adverse experiences and the psychology of resilience.

Attachment in childhood

LEARNING OUTCOME
■ Examine attachment in childhood and its role in the subsequent formation of relationships.

Attachments –
emotional ties
between two people.

Attachments are emotional ties between two people and they are an important characteristic of close relationships between children and their parents, between lovers, and even between owners and their dogs. Maccoby (1980) identified four basic behavioural signs that two people are attached to each other:

■ **Distress on separation** – infants will protest and cry when the parent leaves them temporarily.
■ **Joy at reunion** – infants will welcome the parent back on their return.
■ **Seeking proximity** – infants will crawl or toddle after their parent figure as soon as they are mobile.
■ **Orientation of behaviour towards the other** – infants attempt to engage or attract the interest of the other.

Young animals of many species are able to stand, walk and run within a few hours of birth. In order to survive, they need to stay close to the mother who will protect them from predators. Lorenz (1935) demonstrated how young geese follow the first large moving object they see after hatching out. This type of rapid attachment in young animals is called **imprinting**.

Figure 5.1 Konrad Lorenz

Human babies don't move around until they are 8 or 9 months old and rapid attachment is no longer a matter of life or death. Schaffer and Emerson (1964) studied the development of attachments in a sample of 60 Glasgow babies. Mothers were asked to keep records of their baby's behaviour, for example if they cried at night when put in their cot or when they were left in a push chair outside a shop. The researchers visited the family each month and observed the baby's reaction to them as they made friendly contact. Schaffer and Emerson found a pattern emerging: up to around 6 months, babies became increasingly sociable with a range of people, but didn't prefer anyone in particular. Somewhere around 7 months, two distinct behaviours appeared:

■ **Fear of strangers** – babies would show fear by howling loudly when confronted with the unfamiliar face of the researcher.
■ **Separation anxiety** – babies protested loudly when separated from the parent figure, even briefly.

Schaffer and Emerson argued that these two behaviours marked the development of the first attachment in infants. In most cases, this attachment was to the mother, but in about 30 per cent of the sample first attachments were shown to fathers or both parents jointly. By the age of around 1 year, most babies demonstrated multiple attachments with a range of people such as grandparents and siblings.

Attachment theory (Bowlby, 1969)

An influential theory that emphasized the importance of attachment was put forward by John Bowlby (1969). Bowlby trained as a psychoanalyst and worked with young offenders at a Child Guidance Clinic, before moving to the Tavistock Institute in London. From his work with troubled young people, Bowlby became convinced of the vital importance of attachments in childhood and in later emotional adjustment. He drew on many areas of psychological research to develop his ideas, including the work of ethologist Konrad Lorenz (1935) on imprinting in non-human animals. He also noted the research carried out by Harlow and Harlow (1962), which demonstrated how baby monkeys deprived of a real mother used a surrogate mother to provide comfort and security when they were afraid, an idea he developed into the concept of the 'safe base'. Finally, although Bowlby rejected many of Freud's ideas, he drew on some psychodynamic concepts, notably Melanie Klein's object relations theory, which argued that the relationship between baby and mother creates a 'prototype' for later relationships.

<aside>
Link to the biological level of analysis

Bowlby's theory draws on Darwin's ideas of natural selection and reproductive success – key components of the biological level of analysis.
</aside>

- Bowlby argued that attachment is based on **instincts** that aid the survival of the child. Babies possess instincts such as crying and smiling, which provoke care-giving from the parent figure. Parents, mothers in particular, have instincts to respond to these signals by offering comfort, care and protection. Babies whose instincts were weak in the past would have been less likely to survive and parents who did not protect or care for their infants would be less likely to leave behind surviving offspring.
- One of the most important concepts in Bowlby's theory was the idea of the **internal working model**. Bowlby argued that the first attachment with the mother figure enables babies to build up a model (IWM) of how relationships work. The IWM was believed to provide a template which would shape the child's friendships and later romantic relationships. This idea is known as the **continuity hypothesis** and we will examine it in detail later.
- Bowlby believed that young children use the parent as a **safe base,** returning for security and reassurance when a threat is detected and moving away to explore their environment when the threat disappears.
- Bowlby argued that attachment should take place within a particular window of development – or a **sensitive period**. His view was that children should form an attachment before the age of around 3 years. If they were unable to do this, Bowlby thought that lasting emotional damage would ensue.

Different types of attachment

Mary Ainsworth worked with John Bowlby at the Tavistock Institute in London before moving to Uganda, where she carried out small scale observational studies of mothers and their babies. Ainsworth found that the more responsive mothers appeared to have infants who cried less and appeared more confident. In order to investigate differences in attachment, Ainsworth and Bell (1970) designed a form of controlled observation known as the **Strange Situation** that allowed them to record infants' responses to a variety of situations involving separation from the mother figure and exposure to strangers.

Ainsworth and Bell used a laboratory which was arranged like a normal sitting room within a house. Mothers and babies aged between 12 and 15 months were observed for around 20 minutes. The observation began with mother and baby together in the room and was followed by the entry of a stranger who attempted to interact with the baby. The baby was left briefly with the stranger then rejoined by the mother before being left alone in the playroom. Each episode lasted for 3 minutes and the basic variations were repeated twice. The behaviour of the babies and their mothers was filmed through a hidden camera enabling the team of researchers to observe them in close detail.

■ Critical thinking

Why do you think the episodes were repeated twice in the Strange Situation? What were the advantages of carrying out this study using controlled rather than naturalistic observation?

Ainsworth and Bell found three patterns of behaviour in the infants, which they referred to as attachment types and classified as Type A, B and C. A summary of these is shown in Table 5.1.

Table 5.1 Attachment behaviours in the Strange Situation

	TYPE A (AVOIDANT)	TYPE B (SECURE)	TYPE C (AMBIVALENT)
Separation from the mother	These babies showed little distress when their mother left.	These babies were happy to play and explore when the mother was in the room but became distressed when she left.	Type C babies showed considerable distress when the mother left.
Reunion with the mother	Ignored the mother and did not seek comfort when she returned.	They welcomed the mother back, settling down to play again quickly.	They did not settle when the mother returned. Behaviour alternated between approaching and avoiding/rejecting the mother's attempts at comfort.
Response to the stranger	Treated the mother and stranger in a similar, rather off-hand way.	Wary of the stranger although they did accept some contact and comfort from them when mother was absent.	Rejected the stranger's attempts to comfort them.

Around 70 per cent of the babies in Ainsworth's sample showed Type B (secure) attachments with the remaining 30 per cent being split between the two kinds of insecure attachment. Ainsworth argued that differences in attachment types were related to the sensitivity of the mother in responding to the baby's needs. Mothers who did not respond to their baby's demands would lead to the development of avoidant attachment, as the baby tried to gain attention but effectively gave up, following rejection. Mothers who were responsive to their baby's needs would produce secure infants who expected the mother to respond to their needs and viewed her as a 'safe base' that could be returned to when an environment was stressful. Mothers who were inconsistent, responding to the infant irregularly or erratically would produce ambivalent, anxious infants who were unsure of their parent's affection. Subsequent studies have demonstrated that babies can show different attachment types with mother and father (i.e. secure with one and insecure with the other), supporting Ainsworth's claim that attachment is related to the sensitivity of the parent figure rather than the inbuilt temperament of the infant.

A replication of the Strange Situation by Main and Solomon (1990) identified a group of around 13 per cent of infants who did not 'fit' into the three attachment types clearly. Main and Solomon defined a fourth category as Type D 'disorganized/disoriented' attachments. Subsequent research has indicated that Type D children tend to be very vulnerable in the face of stressful or adverse life events (Main & Hesse, 1990).

Ethical and methodological issues in the Strange Situation

Ainsworth's research has been criticized for ethical and methodological issues. The babies were placed in an unfamiliar environment and were deliberately exposed to a range of stressful situations including separation from their mothers and contact with a stranger. Although this was short-term, it was likely to be an unpleasant experience. However, Ainsworth's research allowed for the situation to be halted at any time by the mother or the researchers if a baby became very distressed.

A second criticism relates to the ecological validity of the Strange Situation, which took place within an environment unfamiliar to the infants. Some critics have argued that this makes it unlike real separations, which generally take place in the familiar surroundings of the child's own home (e.g. babysitting). However, the Strange Situation does reflect some types of real-life separation, for example when a child is left initially with a new childminder. Notwithstanding these criticisms, the Strange Situation has been adapted as the standard way of assessing attachment behaviour, by most people working in the field of infant attachments (Wood *et al.*, 2002).

The role of attachment in later relationships

Bowlby's theory emphasized the crucial importance of the first attachment for later emotional health and adjustment. He argued that attachments lead young children to develop self-worth. Babies whose parents are responsive to their needs are more likely to grow up feeling that they are worthy of love and attention. He also believed that children develop a model of people in general and how much they can be relied on. Children of sensitive and responsive parents are more likely to feel that people can be trusted than those whose parents ignore them or respond inconsistently. Finally, first relationships enable the child to understand how relationships work in general and how people ask for support and comfort from friends and partners. The key claims of attachment theory rest on the assumption that attachment types are relatively consistent from childhood to adulthood.

Consistency of attachment types

The best way to assess if attachment styles persist is to carry out longitudinal studies that examine attachment styles in the same group of people, starting in childhood and following them through to adulthood. Such studies have demonstrated that attachment classifications are generally stable over time, unless important life events take place in the family setting. Hamilton (1994) studied a group of adolescents in California and found a strong link between attachment type in infancy and adult attachment type. However, attachment style changed in a few individuals when major life events, such as loss of a parent, occurred. Similarly, the Bielefeld longitudinal study (Zimmerman *et al.*, 2000) examined the progress of a sample of 44 children in Germany. The children were assessed for attachment type using the Strange Situation at between 12 and 18 months of age and then re-assessed at age 10 and age 16 using Main's Adult Attachment Interview. Zimmerman *et al.* found that child attachment type was not a good predictor of attachment type at 16 when life events such as parental divorce or parental illness had intervened. Other researchers have noted that change may occur in the other direction, from insecure to secure attachment types. Rutter *et al.* (1999) identified a sample of people who had experienced poor relationships with parents but had gone on to achieve secure and happy adult relationships which they termed 'earned security'.

The influence of childhood attachments on adult relationships

Key study

The Love Quiz (Hazan & Shaver, 1987)

Hazan and Shaver set out to test if relationship experiences in adulthood could be mapped on to childhood attachment types. The researchers published a 'Love Quiz' in their local North American newspaper and asked volunteers to read three descriptions (A, B and C below) and place a tick next to the alternative that best described their experiences of romantic relationships. The descriptions were:

A 'I am somewhat uncomfortable being close to others; I find it difficult to trust them completely, difficult to allow myself to depend on them. I am nervous when anyone gets too close, and often others want me to be more intimate than I feel comfortable being.'

B 'I find it relatively easy to get close to others and am comfortable depending on them and having them depend on me. I don't worry about being abandoned or about someone getting too close to me.'

C 'I find that others are reluctant to get as close as I would like. I often worry that my partner doesn't really love me or won't want to stay with me. I want to get very close to my partner and this sometimes scares people away.'

Respondents were also asked to tick items from a checklist of adjectives to describe the relationship they remembered having with their parents (for example, warm, detached, fearful) and to answer questions about how long their adult relationships had lasted. Hazan and Shaver analysed 630 responses chosen randomly from over 1,200 received. The data collection exercise was then repeated with a sample of 108 first year university students.

In agreement with Ainsworth's findings in the Strange Situation, most of the respondents chose statement B, and were classed as securely attached. This group was generally happy and trusting of their partner and expressed a belief in lasting love. Around a quarter chose statement A (avoidant). This group were doubtful about the existence of love and felt that they did not need a close relationship to enjoy their lives. The final group (anxious ambivalent) chose statement C. This group experienced feelings of jealousy and possessiveness; they fell in love easily and often, but rarely found 'true love'.

Over the last ten years, a wealth of research has examined the role played by attachment style in many areas of relationship research. A considerable body of evidence has shown the importance of attachment styles in determining ways of dealing with relationship conflict. Securely attached people are more likely to act constructively by changing their own behaviour, whereas insecurely attached people often deal with conflict in less constructive ways (Levy & Davis, 1988). Attachment types are unsurprisingly linked to relationship breakdown. Feeney and Noller (1992) studied a sample of just under 200 students and found that those with avoidant attachment types were more likely to split up. In agreement, Terling-Watt (2001) found that poor or problematic childhood attachments were a significant factor in later marital breakdown. Parental divorce and a poor relationship with their mother were most significant for women, and for men a poor or problematic relationship with their father was significant.

Commentary on the role of attachments in later relationships

- Much that was controversial in Bowlby's earliest writings is now accepted by pretty much everyone working within developmental psychology (Rutter, 2009). It is clear that early attachments are highly significant in the development of young children as it is within the context of this first relationship that infants learn about intimacy and trust.

- Bowlby's theory was developed in the 1950s and 60s, when most child-rearing was carried out by mothers, so it is unsurprising that he emphasized the importance of the mothering role in the development of young children. Today, it is acknowledged that 'mothering' can be carried out by fathers, grandparents or others who are prepared to form a close attachment with the child.

- The studies considered above show that early attachments are relatively stable when there are no major changes or life events to 'derail' attachment styles. However, rather than being fixed, attachments styles can change in both directions: people who have had adverse childhood experiences can develop 'earned security' later on. Similarly, a problematic adult relationship, perhaps with a jealous or abusive partner, could lead a previously secure person to become wary in subsequent relationships. As Rutter (2009) notes, 'Early experiences are important but they need to be combined with later experiences.' Therefore the link between childhood and adult relationships is better thought of as probable, 'all things being equal', rather than absolute.

The effects of deprivation and trauma on later development

LEARNING OUTCOME
■ Discuss potential effects of deprivation or trauma in childhood on later development.

Some children experience adverse events in childhood. The International Resilience Project (Newman, 2002) collected data from 600 11-year-old children in 30 different countries. The most commonly experienced traumatic events were death of parent, parental divorce or separation and serious family illness. Bowlby (1953) made strong claims for the serious and permanent effects of early adverse experiences and was particularly concerned about the impact of maternal deprivation during the first three years of life.

Early studies of deprivation focused on children who had been separated from their families during the 1939–45 war and brought up in institutions. In many of these institutions, physical care was basic and there was little by way of emotional care, warmth or opportunity for attachment. Unsurprisingly, many studies (e.g. Skeels & Dye, 1939; Skodak & Skeels, 1945/1949) found that institutionally raised children showed permanent intellectual impairment, scoring lower on intelligence tests. However, subsequent studies of institutionalized children indicated that many of the effects were related to the very poor conditions and lack of stimulation in institutions at that time. Tizard and Hodges (1978, 1989) examined a group of children who spent their early childhood in an institution where good physical care was provided and the environment was stimulating. The only area of deprivation experienced by the children was the lack of an ongoing secure attachment with an adult caregiver.

Key study

Tizard and Hodges (1978, 1989)

Tizard and Hodges studied 65 children who were institutionalized from around 4 months of age (i.e. before an attachment had been formed) until the age of 4 years. Institutional policy dissuaded the staff from forming attachments with the children, but the physical care was good and the environment was stimulating. At around the age of 4, 24 of the children were adopted, 15 were returned to their birth parents and the remaining 26 stayed in the institution, making three groups for comparison.

The children were followed up at age 8 and 16. At age 8, 20/21 of the adopted children had formed close and loving attachments with their new families. In the restored group, close attachments were seen in fewer than half of the children (6/13) and these children had poorer relationships with their siblings than the adopted children. All three groups of institution-raised children showed difficulties with peer relationships and friendships, according to their teachers.

Tizard and Hodges demonstrate how lack of early attachment can be largely overcome when the subsequent care provided is of high quality. Even when this occurs, children may struggle with the demands of friendship and peer relationships.

Rutter and colleagues (Rutter *et al.*, 2007) are carrying out an ongoing study of children who spent time in impoverished Romanian orphanages before being adopted by UK families. Conditions in Romanian orphanages during the 1990s were very poor indeed, with children confined to cots and fed through propped-up bottles. They received very little attention from caregivers who often had many babies to attend to, and there were few toys and little intellectual stimulation of any kind. Fifty-eight of the children in Rutter's sample were adopted under the age of 6 months, 59 children between 6 and 24 months and a further group of 48 between the ages of 2 and 4 years (late adoptees). Many of the late adoptees show a behaviour pattern known as **disinhibited attachment**: they demonstrate none of the fear of strangers shown by normally developing children and are often indiscriminately friendly, seeking attention and affection from any adult. Late adoptees also appear vulnerable to a range of behaviour problems and are more likely to receive help from specialist children's services.

■ Critical thinking

Rutter *et al.* (2007) and Tizard and Hodges (1978) make use of natural experimentation where the independent variable occurs without intervention from the researcher. This avoids some ethical problems but still enables comparisons to be made along with conclusions about causal relationships.

Some children experienced lengthy separations from their families due to evacuation in the 1939–45 war. Longitudinal studies following evacuees through adulthood (e.g. the Helsinki Birth Cohort Study of over 13,000 children) have indicated significantly higher levels of psychological problems, with higher rates of illness and mortality in adulthood (Pesonen & Räikkönen, 2012). These studies demonstrate there are lasting effects of early and prolonged separation.

Figure 5.2 Evacuees suffered significantly higher levels of psychological problems in adulthood

Deprivation can occur when parents of young children are unable to provide emotional care due to mental illnesses, such as depression. Hay *et al.* (2010) found that maternal depression before and during pregnancy is associated with a range of problems in offspring, including conduct disorders and violence. This relationship exists even after controlling for family environment; the child's later exposure to maternal depression, the mother's smoking and drinking during pregnancy, and parents' anti-social behaviour. In Hay's study, the offspring of depressed women had a greater chance of becoming violent by age 16.

Some children experience trauma such as the death of a parent or chronic, disabling illness. Jacobs (2009) examined the impact of death of a parent in childhood in relation to later adjustment. Almost 3,500 participants in Baltimore, USA, were identified in 1981 and followed through 1994–95. Jacobs found that the death of a mother did not predict later mental health problems but death of the father during childhood more than doubled the risk for depression in adulthood. Jacobs argues that parental death can lead to serious financial stress (e.g. the need to move house and school), which can continue for years and further complicate adaptation to the loss.

Commentary and conclusion

These studies allow us to draw a number of conclusions about the effects of early adverse experiences.

- When institutionalized children are placed in families, they generally show marked improvements in physical, social and cognitive functioning.
- Children who spend short periods of time in institutions generally experience few long-term negative effects. When the period of institutionalization ends before the age of 6 months, children are likely to show few permanent effects.
- Children who spend longer times in impoverished environments often continue to show persistent behavioural problems and disinhibited attachments (Hodges & Tizard, 1989; Rutter *et al.*, 2007).
- It is difficult, if not impossible, to accurately quantify the type and level of deprivation experienced by children in institutions such as the Romanian orphanages of the 1990s.

■ Children of different temperaments may respond differently to adverse circumstances, making long-term effects difficult to predict. Interest is turning to the potential impact of early adverse experiences on biological processes, notably stress hormones such as cortisol. Some findings imply that specific aspects of brain behavioural circuitry may be particularly vulnerable to early aversive experience and some studies demonstrate a relation between unresponsive or neglectful environments and blunted cortisol responses to stress in young children (Gunnar *et al.*, 2006).

Resilience

LEARNING OUTCOMES
▨ Define resilience.
▨ Discuss strategies to build resilience.

Resilience – the ability to cope positively with negative events and to bounce back.

Resilience is generally thought of as the ability to overcome stress and adverse circumstances. Luthar *et al.* (2003) refer to resilience as 'positive adaptation within the context of significant adversity', and Masten (2001, p.228) defines resilience as 'good outcomes in spite of serious threats to adaptation or development'. Resilience can be shown in different situations, for example by children of drug-using or alcoholic parents who develop coping strategies in situations of chronic stress. It can also be shown by individuals and communities in the face of disasters such as terrorist attacks, earthquakes or the 2004 tsunami.

Building resilience

'Treatment is not just fixing what is broken; it is nurturing what is best'.

(Seligman & Csikszentmihalyi, 2000)

Programmes that aim to build resilience can be targeted at children who have been identified as vulnerable. The foundation of these approaches is building a secure base (attachment) that provides children with the opportunities to develop social skills, along with a sense of control and purpose in their lives. Daniel and Wassell (2002) identify 'domains' of resilience that form the basis of most contemporary interventions with young children. Masten (2001, p. 234) identifies a set of global factors associated with building resilience. There is considerable overlap between these approaches:

Table 5.2

	DANIEL AND WASSELL (2002)	**MASTEN (2001)**
Importance of attachments	A secure base	Connection to competent and caring adults in the family or community
Development of interpersonal skills	Social competencies and skills	Cognitive and self-regulation skills
Development of interests	Talents, interests and education	
Development of personal qualities	Positive values	Positive views of self and motivation to be effective in the environment.

The ARCH project (**A**chieving **R**esilience, **C**hange and **H**ope) has been devised by Barnardo's and aims to increase resilience in vulnerable children. This project has four aims:

■ to build emotional resilience
■ to strengthen protective factors

- to reduce challenging behaviours
- to increase parents' confidence and skills in dealing with vulnerable children.

Children and their families are referred for help and undergo an initial assessment followed by a more detailed analysis. Children and their parents/carers work together with a facilitator to identify a list of goals for improvement and desired outcomes from the intervention. An action plan is constructed using Daniel and Wassell's domains and the family takes part in a series of sessions typically over a 6–12-week period. A second assessment then takes place with questionnaires to parent and child and observations by family workers.

Resilience for high risk professions

Preventative resilience programmes can be targeted at 'high risk' professionals who are likely to confront or experience trauma through the nature of their work. These include front line responders (e.g. fire, police and ambulance crews), workers with victims of child sexual abuse and serving military personnel. Many studies have demonstrated how serving and ex-service personnel are at particularly high risk of later trauma.

The **Comprehensive Soldier Fitness (CSF) programme** has been designed to increase psychological strength and to reduce the incidence of maladaptive responses in the US Army. The programme involves 'Army master resilience trainers', who are taught to instil thinking skills and resilience in service personnel. The programme is structured around an initial assessment of emotional fitness considering social and family relationships, followed by formal resilience training. In contrast to previous approaches, CSF proactively aims to prevent emotional difficulties rather than reactive (responding to those who have negative outcomes after military service). It provides ways of improving resilience for all members of the Army. CSF aims to address the full spectrum of responses to trauma and adversity – ranging from stress-related disorders to ordinary resilience – towards personal growth. This programme may provide a model for implementing similar interventions in other very large institutions.

Figure 5.3 Resilience is important for serving military personnel as they will face difficult situations and trauma on a daily basis.

Developing resilience after trauma

Some programmes are targeted at children who have experienced significant trauma, through conflict or war (Zaghrout-Hodali *et al.*'s 2008 study of EMDR therapy for Israeli children) or through neglect or abuse (Houston's 2010 study of a resilience programme in a residential children's home in Northern Ireland).

A current approach that is generating considerable interest is Eye Movement Desensitization and Reprocessing (EMDR) and variants of this including 'the Butterfly Hug'. EMDR is used to treat children and young people with post-traumatic stress disorder. The approach is based on the idea that disturbing memories of trauma need to be integrated into the memory networks of the individual. When this occurs, Shapiro (2001, 2006) argues that there are associated shifts in symptoms, personal characteristics and the sense of self. The Butterfly Hug was developed by Artigas *et al.* (2000) for use with children but has been extended to work with adults. In the Butterfly Hug, the person is asked to cross his/her arms across the chest and tap alternately with each hand on the contralateral shoulder, upper arm or chest area. An adaptation of the Butterfly Hug has been used successfully with Kosovar Albanian refugee children in Germany (Wilson *et al.*, 2000) and with children who witnessed the Milan air crash in Italy (Fernandez *et al.*, 2004). Zaghrout-Hodali*et al.* (2008) examined the effectiveness of this approach with seven young Palestinian children who had experienced an environment characterized by ongoing violence and trauma. Results indicated that the approach successfully reduced symptoms of post-traumatic stress and is being used to build resilience in a setting of ongoing conflict and trauma. It is unclear, as yet, how and why this unusual approach works and further research is recommended regarding EMDR's effectiveness.

Conclusion and commentary

This section shows how different approaches are needed to develop resilience in vulnerable groups and in those who have already experienced serious trauma. Most interventions with children are underpinned by the theoretical work of John Bowlby along with Mary Ainsworth. These put security in the child's first few years at centre stage. Notably lacking in research on resilience at present is acknowledgement of the possible role played by biology (Luthar, 2000), as early trauma may modify brain structure and functioning.

SECTION SUMMARY
- Attachments are emotional ties between two people.
- Bowlby argued that attachments are instinctive and provide a template for later relationships through internal working models.
- Ainsworth identified three attachment types: secure, insecure–avoidant and insecure–ambivalent. Disorganized attachments were added by Main and Solomon.
- Attachment types are relatively consistent in the absence of serious life events but can change in both directions (e.g. earned security in adulthood).
- Early adverse experiences can have lasting effects when deprivation is severe and prolonged.
- Institutionalized children show few lasting effects when they are adopted at an early age. Children who are late adopted may continue to show problems.
- Resilience is the ability to bounce back from adverse experiences. Most resilience programmes aimed at children are based on providing a secure attachment.
- Resilience training can also be targeted at high risk professions such as military personnel and front line responders.

Cognitive development

Cognitive development is a broad term that refers to the development of thinking skills such as memory, reasoning and problem-solving. Goswami (1998) argues that there are two key questions to address in cognitive development:

- Firstly, what develops (i.e. how do children think at a particular age)?
- Secondly, why development takes place as and when it does. What are the relative roles played by biological factors – such as maturation of brain structures – and experiences, such as the quality of the environment and teaching?

An influential theory of cognitive development was put forward by Swiss biologist Jean Piaget. Piaget emphasized that children think differently to adults, rather than simply knowing less, and his theory was revolutionary at the time as it conceptualized young children as being rather like scientists, constructing their knowledge of the world through discovery. The second theory we will consider was put forward by Russian psychologist Lev Vygotsky at around the same time as Piaget's theory. Vygotsky emphasized the importance of sociocultural factors in cognitive development and effectively saw the child as an apprentice, learning from experienced others. Today, both theories are being integrated with new, biological insights into children's development as the study of children's cognition follows a similar path to that of adult cognition (Goswami, 1998).

Theories of cognitive development

LEARNING OUTCOME
■ Evaluate theories of cognitive development (for example, Piaget, Vygotsky).

Piaget's theory: Genetic epistemology

Jean Piaget (1896–1980) was a Swiss biologist who drew on his biological knowledge of how organisms adapt to their environment to develop his theory of cognitive development. From detailed observations of his own young children, Piaget argued that young children use innate cognitive structures (which he called schemas) to construct their knowledge of the world through active exploration and engagement. Piaget was particularly interested in how children understood the physical world around them – for example the Moon and stars – and the properties of objects in terms of height, length and volume.

Piaget's theory is built on a number of key concepts:

- Knowledge progresses via innate cognitive structures.
- Thinking develops in stages that are loosely linked to age. The child's thinking is qualitatively different at different ages.
- The child constructs their knowledge by acting on the world like a scientist and discovering what happens.

Innate cognitive structures

Organisms adapt to their environment through physical structures, such as the giraffe's long neck. Piaget argued that mental structures – which he called schemas – also help us to adapt to our environments. Schemas are simple ideas about objects or situations built up from experience. The first schemas developed by young infants are based on actions such as grasping or banging objects and putting them in the mouth. A baby around 6 months old will discover that a rattle makes a noise when shaken and will then apply the 'shaking' schema to other toys. Toys that produce the same response are assimilated (taken into) the schema. Toys that do not produce a noise when shaken, however, such as soft dolls, show the schema to be limited or inadequate. When this happens, Piaget believed that the schema is changed or accommodated – or a different schema is used.

This process occurs in a very similar way with adults. You learn to drive in an instructor's car but can make the transition to driving your parents' similar car (assimilation) without too much trouble. However, if you decide to ride a motorbike, some aspects of the driving schema will not apply (for example, accelerating with the hand throttle rather than the accelerator pedal) and the driving schema must be altered to accommodate the new experience.

Stages of development

Piaget argued that development takes place in four main stages. In each of these, the child's thinking is qualitatively different and there is a clear and distinct shift in understanding and beliefs about the world. The stages are loosely linked to age, although some children may move through the stages faster or slower than others. Stages are invariant (i.e. completed in the same order) and cannot be skipped. Crucially, development cannot be speeded up or accelerated by environmental stimuli.

Schemas – simple ideas built up from experience; mental structures or packages of knowledge.

Assimilation – applying a schema to new objects.

Accommodation – altering or updating a schema in the light of experience.

Link to the biological level of analysis

Schemas can be seen in evolutionary terms, as having an adaptive survival value, as they allow situations and events to be quickly understood and responded to appropriately.

Sensory motor stage: 0–2 years

This stage takes place from birth to around 2 years of age and is divided into six sub-stages. Infants start with basic, automatic reflexes such as grasping any object put into their hands. By the age of around 6 weeks, these reflexes are no longer triggered automatically. They become deliberate (purposive) actions by the infant, who begins to reach out for and grasp objects at around 5 months of age.

Figure 5.4 Babies will reach out and grasp for objects at the age of about 5 months.

An important achievement in this stage was thought to be the development of object permanence – the understanding that objects that are out of sight continue to exist. Before the age of around 8 or 9 months, infants will not try to search for a toy when it is hidden under a cloth, but will act as if it no longer exists – effectively, out of sight being out of mind. The stage ends when developing language skills enable the young child to deal with the world by using words as symbols for objects.

Preoperational period: 2–7 years

In this stage, the child's developing language skills enable them to refer to objects and situations that are not present. This allows them to talk about the past and future and to use their imagination – the basis of pretend play. Piaget argued that the child's thinking is characterized by a number of features that disappear at around the age of 7. The main features were as follows:

- **Egocentricism** – preoperational children are unable to appreciate that other people have a different physical viewpoint of the world. An everyday example of this can be seen when a young child closes their eyes in a game of hide and seek and assumes that others can't see them. This is seen in the three mountains task (*see below*).
- **Conservation** – young children are misled by superficial changes in the appearance of objects. For example, when a glass of juice is poured from a short wide glass to a tall thin glass, the preoperational child may claim there is 'more' in the tall glass as the level of juice is higher. This error is made through focusing on only one element of the information (i.e. the height of the juice not the width of the beaker). This is seen in conservation experiments (*see below*).
- **Animism** – preoperational children attribute feelings and intentions to inanimate objects and appear to assume they are alive. So, a teddy bear may be helped up to the window to see the snow or the child may smack a naughty cup when they spill a drink.

Piaget's methods

Piaget used a range of innovative methods to assess young children's beliefs about the world. These included naturalistic observations of his own young children and involvement in children's games such as marbles to gain an insight into how children viewed rules. The extract below is a detailed observation of his daughter Jacqueline, aged 7 months.

'Jacqueline tries to grasp a celluloid duck on top of her quilt. She almost catches it, shakes herself and the duck slides down beside her. It falls very close to her hand but behind a fold in the sheet. Jacqueline's eyes have followed the movement, she has even followed it with her outstretched

hand. But as soon as the duck has disappeared – nothing more! … Everything occurs as though the child believed that the object is alternately made and unmade.'

(Piaget, 1963)

Piaget also devised tasks for young children to complete. In order to investigate egocentricity, Piaget and Inhelder (1967) constructed a papier mâché model of a mountain scene, typical of Switzerland. Young children were seated in front of the model and asked to select a picture to illustrate the view of the mountains which they could see. In the second stage of the task, a doll was placed at a different point around the table, where the view of the mountains would appear different, and Piaget asked the child to select a picture depicting the viewpoint for the doll. Piaget found that young children under the age of around 7 years would typically choose their own viewpoint and seemed unable to appreciate that the viewpoint for the doll would be different.

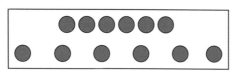

Figure 5.5 When the row was spread out, children under 7 would argue that there were more counters even though none had been added or removed.

Piaget investigated conservation, using a variety of different substances such as plasticine, liquid or counters, which were transformed into a different shape. A typical conservation experiment would involve a set of counters or Smarties laid out in two parallel rows. After the child had agreed that they were 'the same', one row was lengthened by spreading out the counters. Children up to around the age of about 7 would claim that the longer row had 'more', even though nothing had been added or taken away.

The concrete operational stage: 7–11 years

The concrete operational child demonstrates the ability to reason logically but requires real (concrete) objects to help their thinking. The child is able to decentre (appreciate that other people have different viewpoints) in the three mountains task and they can conserve number and volume and understand that superficial changes in appearance do not alter quantity. In relation to the counter and juice tasks, the child may argue that they are the same as:

- one attribute such as height of juice cancels another out, such as width (compensation)
- the action could be reversed (reversibility)
- nothing has been added or taken away.

However, the concrete operational child can only reason logically in the presence of real objects. Seriation tasks, which involve putting things in order (for example, Anish is taller than Jamila but shorter than Kylie), cannot be completed mentally at this age, but require reference to some form of physical object. When concrete operational children are given a scientific problem to solve (for example, the factors that affect the speed at which a pendulum swings), they do this via trial and error rather than approaching the task systematically.

Formal operational stage: 12 years onwards

At the age of around 12, concrete objects are no longer needed for reasoning and the child can carry out seriation tasks mentally without real objects. The child develops the ability to think about things that are not present (abstract thought), opening up the study of science to more abstract topics such as physics and chemistry. Scientific tasks such as the pendulum problem are approached in a systematic manner, by varying one aspect at a time and observing the resultant effects.

Evaluation of Piaget's theory

- Piaget's claim that cognitive development takes place in stages has been widely accepted and most developmental psychologists agree that children can reason at the level of action (doing) before representation or abstract thinking (Goswami, 1998). However, Piaget's claim of a universal fourth stage (formal operations) has met with criticism. Many studies (e.g. Keating, 1979) have shown that around 40 per cent of college students do not reach formal operations and Dasen (1994) argues that only about a third of adults demonstrate the ability of abstract thought.

- Piaget's theory has been extremely influential in the world of education. The educational curriculum is structured around the four stages of development in many parts of the world, with infant schools for children in the preoperational period, junior schools for concrete operations and secondary or high schools aimed at children in the formal operations stage. Piaget's theory has influenced what is taught (i.e. topics in the curriculum) and how it is taught (methods). The primary school classroom includes practical work using real (concrete) objects, and more abstract subjects such as physics and chemistry are not included in the curriculum until children reach the formal operations stage.

Practical applications

The Plowden report into primary education in the UK (HMSO, 1967) argued that young children should learn via discovery. With an emphasis on the practical classroom, Piaget's theory implies that teachers should work individually with each child, providing tasks for them to build their understanding of materials via discovery learning. The teacher should understand which stage of development each child is in and should provide appropriate tasks.

- It is generally agreed that Piaget underestimated the capabilities of young children and that they can often achieve more complex thinking at a younger age than suggested. For example, Bower and Wishart (1972) demonstrated how much young children of 4 months will reach out for a teddy bear that has disappeared into the dark when the light is switched off, showing some sense of object permanence. Piaget argued that this ability did not occur until around 9 months of age.

- One reason why Piaget may have underestimated children's abilities relates to the methods he used to assess children's thinking. Margaret Donaldson's book *Children's Minds* (1978) argued that Piaget's methods and tasks often confused children and did not make sense to them. In conservation tasks the same question ('Are they the same?') is repeated. In many real-life situations, repeating a question to a child implies that the first answer they gave was wrong. When Piaget's tasks were made more child-friendly, children demonstrated the abilities to conserve and decentre at a younger age.

Child-friendly research

Martin Hughes (1975) drew on young children's understanding of the game 'hide and seek' to test egocentricity. Children aged between 3½ and 5 years old were shown a 3-D model of two intersecting walls with a policeman doll placed in a key position. The children were asked to hide a boy doll where the policemen would be unable to see him. Around 90 per cent of the 3½-year-olds were able to do this accurately, implying that even very young children can see the world from another's viewpoint. Many children could even do this when the task was made more complex with two police dolls.

Similarly, Paul Light replicated Piaget's conservation task using pasta shells that were moved from one container to another of different shape. In the classic version of the task, when the transformation took place, around 95 per cent of 6-years-olds failed to conserve. However, when the children were given a reason for the transformation (i.e. the beaker had a chipped edge and could cut someone), an impressive 70 per cent of 6-year-olds were able to conserve and argued that the amount was still the same.

Why are these results so different to Piaget's original experiments? The tasks used here draw on children's existing knowledge – about hide and seek. They also provide clear reasons for the adult's behaviour in the conservation task and the motives and intentions are understandable to the children. However, some critics have argued that the tasks may not be tapping the same level of reasoning skills as Piaget's and may be easier.

Vygotsky's theory of cognitive development

Lev Vygotsky (1896–1934) was a Russian psychologist who presented a holistic theory of development that emphasized the important role played by culture. Vygotsky's ideas were extremely influential in early Soviet psychology and in Eastern Europe but were not widely published in the West until the 1970s when they found favour with many developmental psychologists. Vygotsky died at a young age of tuberculosis and many of the ideas presented here – such as scaffolding – are developments of his writing by others. Vygotsky's theory is built on a number of key concepts:

- Language is crucial to the development of higher mental functions.
- Knowledge develops through social interaction, and culture plays an important role.
- Children can achieve a higher level of reasoning when provided with the support (scaffolding) of a more knowledgeable other. This is referred to as the zone of proximal development (ZPD).

Scaffolding – providing help to a child to achieve a task in their ZPD and gradually removing it as the child becomes competent.

Zone of proximal development (ZPD) – the range of mental abilities that children can achieve with the help of others.

Higher mental functions – complex reasoning skills.

Language and higher mental functions

Vygotsky emphasized the strong and inseparable link between language and thought. He argued that infants are born with **elementary mental functions** such as attention and perception. These basic cognitive skills are transformed into higher mental functions or complex thinking skills, such as reasoning and problem-solving, through the development and use of language.

Vygotsky noticed how young children use speech in a different way to adults, commenting on their own actions aloud as a kind of monologue. This type of speech tends to disappear around the age of 6 or 7 years (although it may resurface in adults who are attempting a complicated mental task). It was referred to as 'egocentric speech' by Piaget and seen as further evidence of the young child's inability to decentre. Vygotsky argued that monologue speech is effectively **internalized** to become inner speech and it is this process that provides the foundation for the development of higher mental abilities. Vygotsky argued that mental abilities, including speech, occur on two planes, firstly socially (with other people), then intellectually or internally. While social speech is used to communicate with others, intellectual or inner speech is used to plan and regulate mental activities. In adults, mature intellectual speech is somewhat unintelligible and does not resemble spoken language, being more fragmented and less coherent.

Knowledge develops through social interaction

Vygotsky argued that the ability to think and reason is the outcome of a fundamentally social process, with social and cultural context playing a key role in the development of the young child. Vygotsky conceptualized young children as apprentices, internalizing the mental tools necessary to thrive in their own culture through social interaction. Learning does not just take place in a formal environment such as school, but occurs within all arenas of the child's life, with friends, siblings and parents. Social interaction enables young children to observe adults and older children and to internalize the problem-solving skills and mental tools they see. There are many examples of this: Brazilian street children with almost no formal schooling show an impressive understanding of mathematical concepts that they have internalized from watching their parents trading (Nunes Carraher, 1991), although they are often unable to show the same grasp of these abilities in the school classroom when knowledge is de-contextualised. Similarly, rice farmers in Liberia are excellent at estimating quantities of rice (Gay & Cole, 1967), and children in Botswana, who are accustomed to story-telling, have an excellent memory for stories.

Link to the sociocultural level of analysis

Vygotsky's theory demonstrates principles of the sociocultural level of analysis. While Piaget saw the young child as a solitary individual working out the world like a scientist, Vygotsky stressed the importance of others and the wider and cultural environments in the development of the child's understanding. Vygotsky's cultural background (Communist Russia) emphasizes principles of collectivism and is strongly apparent here.

Figure 5.6 Vygotsky argued that social interaction was very important in development.

The zone of proximal development (ZPD)

Vygotsky used the term 'zone of proximal development' to refer to the idea that young children can achieve a higher level of ability on a task with the aid of a more knowledgeable other (generally an older sibling, teacher or parent) than they can independently. The ZPD refers to the range of mental abilities that children can achieve with the help of others. This is distinguished from the zone of actual development, which refers to a child's independent ability on a task. Vygotsky (1984) illustrated this with an example of two 8-year-old boys who can complete the same tasks in terms of their actual level of development. However, in collaboration with an adult, one can solve problems at a 9-year-old level, while the other performs at a 12-year-old level. Effectively the boys differ in the breadth of their ZPD.

The process of providing sensitive and appropriate help is generally referred to as 'scaffolding', although Vygotsky did not use this term. Scaffolding could involve showing a child how a problem should be solved or beginning to solve the task and allowing the child to complete it. It could also involve explaining the principles for solving the problem, or asking leading questions (Vygotsky, 1984, p.264).

Key study

Scaffolding in action (Wood & Middleton, 1975)

Wood and Middleton carried out an in-depth observation of 12 mothers with their young children aged 4 years. Each mother was asked to teach her child to assemble a simple wooden jigsaw so they could carry out the task unaided. The interactions were videoed and then analysed and coded by the researchers.

Wood and Middleton identified five different types of help, which varied in degree. These included:

- General suggestions ('*Now you choose a piece*')
- Specific verbal instructions ('*Find one of the corners*')
- Indicating materials ('*Try this piece next*')
- Preparing for assembly ('*You need to turn that one round, then it will fit*')
- Physical demonstrations ('*The square piece fits in this hole*')

The most successful mothers adjusted the type and level of help they offered to their child, accelerating help (moving up a level) when they were struggling and stepping back when they were succeeding.

Commentary on Vygotsky's theory

Vygotsky's emphasis on the importance of sociocultural factors in cognitive development did not fit with the dominant approaches of the time (behaviourism and information processing). His ideas are now thought of as revolutionary as they introduced entirely new principles and challenged previous epistemological assumptions about human development and cognition (Cole & Wertsch, 1996, cited in Damianova & Sullivan, 2011). The important force of multiculturalism in most European and American classrooms has led educators to acknowledge the important role played by culture in learning. Vygotsky challenged the views that prevailed at the time that development should be assessed by looking solely at what children can achieve. Commendably, he realized the need to consider the abilities that are maturing/developing as well as those that are already in place. Hence, 'Vygotsky's theory offers us answers to the questions that only now we are finally ready to ask' (Kozulin, 2004).

Many studies have demonstrated the value of scaffolding with older children and adults as well as infants. Pratt *et al.* (1992) has shown how parents 'scaffold' older children to master mathematical concepts and complete homework. Scaffolding also takes place in the development of many skills. Greenfield and Lave (1982) have shown how young Mexican girls learn the skill of weaving firstly through watching experts, then tackling simple then more complex tasks.

Practical applications

Vygotsky's ideas have been applied to education. His theory emphasizes the importance of providing tasks outside the current ability of the child but within the ZPD. One way in which this has been developed is the idea of peer teaching. This involves pairing an older, more knowledgeable child with a young child in order to master concepts such as seriation. This is now a common practice in many classrooms.

Comparison of Piaget's and Vygotsky's theories

Piaget and Vygotsky were developing their ideas at around the same time and both make use of metaphors to make the rather abstract topic of cognitive development more concrete. However, these theories have very different emphases:

- Piaget was interested primarily in **what** children think and believe at each age, whereas Vygotsky was interested in **how** children develop mental skills through internalization and collaboration.
- Piaget's theory located the cause of development within innate cognitive structures (schemas) that were largely controlled by maturation. However, Vygotsky emphasized the important role played by language and by others (parents, siblings and teachers) in the development of mental abilities.
- In this respect, both theories can be seen to reflect the cultures in which they were created. Piaget's view of the child as scientist, learning through individual discovery, is strongly individualistic. Vygotsky, in contrast, saw young children as apprentices, developing mental skills through contact with more knowledgeable others. This is strongly reflective of the collectivist culture and emphasized the social and cultural nature of cognitive development.
- Today, the study of child cognition largely follows the same approach as the study of adult cognition, with a focus on processes such as attention, memory and perception.

Environmental effects on cognitive development

LEARNING OUTCOME

■ Discuss how social and environmental variables (for example, parenting, diet) may affect cognitive development.

Intelligence test scores are increasing yearly and this effect is found across many different intelligence tests and in different countries (Flynn, 1994). These increases are happening too rapidly to indicate genetic change and they demonstrate the importance of environmental factors in cognitive development. Parents are the first teachers of young children and a wealth of commercial information is available to help them enhance their child's development. Neisser (1996) notes that 'Parents everywhere are now interested in their children's intellectual development and are probably doing more to encourage it than they did in the past.'

What kind of family environment provides a good basis for cognitive development? The Home Observation for Measurement of the Environment (HOME) is an observational scale used by childcare professionals (e.g. health visitors) to measure the quality and quantity of stimulation and support available to a child in their home environment. HOME was developed by Caldwell and her colleagues in a longitudinal study during the 1960s, which examined the relationship between home environments, day care and children's development (Elardo *et al.*, 1975). The overall score of the quality of a child's home environment is based on observation and interview with the primary caregiver in the family home. Important characteristics include the provision of appropriate learning materials, verbal stimulation, responsivity to the child and a warm atmosphere of acceptance. Behavioural checklists for some of these items are shown below.

Table 5.3   The Home scale (adapted from Totsika & Sylva, 2004)

NAME OF SCALE	FOCUS OF OBSERVATION	EXAMPLE
Responsivity of parent	The interactions between the caregiver and the child.	Parent holds child close for 10–15 minutes per day. Parent talks with the child at least twice during visit.
Language stimulation	Verbal communication between child and caregiver that is intended to help language development.	Child is encouraged to learn the alphabet. Child has toys that help teach names of animals.
Availability of learning materials	Toys and activities directed towards the intellectual development of the child.	Child has toys that teach colours, sizes and shapes. Child has three or more puzzles.
Acceptance	The way the caregiver disciplines the child.	No more than one instance of physical punishment occurred during the past week.

Other aspects of the family environment can have negative effects on cognitive development. The ground breaking Rochester Longitudinal Study (Sameroff & Seifer, 1993) followed the development of a group of children in 152 families, from the prenatal period through to adolescence. The children were studied at 4 and 13 years of age and measurement taken of their performance on various cognitive tests.

The Rochester study identified a range of environmental 'risk' factors, which were associated with poorer cognitive development. These included negative life events and ongoing stress in the family home, and each of these factors had the potential to reduce the child's IQ score by up to four points. The factors included:

- absence of father in the family home
- mother's mental health (notably maternal anxiety)
- rigid attitudes and beliefs held by the mother, particularly an orientation towards child conformity (e.g. obedience, good manners and neatness) rather than child self-direction.

■ Critical thinking

Studies in this area cannot be carried out using experimentation, due to ethical consideration, and many researchers make use of correlational analysis. However, a relationship between two variables does not mean that one causes the other.

A second aspect of the family home relates to the provision for the physical child, notably the availability and quality of nutrition provided. Key debates relate to the impact of breast milk and multivitamins on cognitive development. Many studies demonstrate that breast-fed babies go on to perform better on tests of cognitive ability compared to bottle-fed (formula) babies. As an example, Oddy *et al.* (2004) studied a sample of 2,000 children from birth to 8 years old and found that those who had been breast fed for more than 6 months had higher verbal intelligence scores at age 8. However, critics have pointed out that there are difficulties in drawing conclusions about cause and effect from uncontrolled studies of this nature due to the differences between breast- and bottle-feeding mothers. Breast-feeding mothers have higher levels of education and socio-economic status in general and they may also provide a more stimulating environment for their offspring. Therefore, any cognitive superiority of breast-fed babies could arise from a combination of factors.

Der *et al.* (2006) carried out a study in which they controlled for confounding variables (e.g. maternal intelligence) in the link between breast feeding and children's intelligence. A longitudinal study of 5,475 children was carried out with statistical adjustments made to rule out the effects of maternal education and socio-economic class. Before adjustment, breast feeding was associated with an increase of around four points in mental ability. However, when maternal intelligence was taken out of the equation, the effect of breast feeding was statistically insignificant, leading Der *et al.* to conclude that breast feeding has little or no direct effect on intelligence in children. In agreement, Holme *et al.* (2009) examined data from 1,218 children, 61.6 per cent of whom had been breastfed. Before statistical adjustment, breast feeding was significantly associated with higher total, verbal and visual IQ scores in children. However, when mother's socio-economic status was controlled, the effect disappeared, leading the researchers to agree with Der *et al.*'s conclusion. Sloan *et al.* (2010) have attempted to tease out the relative contribution of stimulation at home and the impact of breast milk, however. They carried out an observational study of 137 infants and their mothers, obtaining information on maternal socio-demographic factors and breast-feeding practices through semi-structured interviews. Stimulation in the home was measured using the HOME Inventory. Results indicated that breast-fed infants scored higher than formula-fed infants and this relationship was independent of the main confounding variables, notably stimulation in the home.

A good diet in childhood may produce beneficial effects on cognitive performance. Children who were given a vitamin–mineral supplement to their diet for an eight-month period showed increases in their IQ scores compared to a group of children given a placebo for the same period (Benton & Roberts, 1988). Other studies, however, have found a beneficial effect only in children who have a very poor diet at the start (Schoenthaler *et al.*, 2000). Although most researchers agree that there are negative effects of malnutrition on intelligence, such effects are not easy to establish. This is largely because it is difficult to separate the effects of malnutrition from poor socio-economic conditions (Neisser, 1996).

Commentary

The effects of family environment and of diet are very difficult to study because of the lack of control in the methods available. Studies on breast feeding make use of natural experimentation where the independent variable occurs without manipulation. For this reason, it is difficult to establish cause and effect (e.g. between feeding method and cognitive development) as uncontrolled factors, such as maternal education and socio-economic class, can confound the results. Similarly, studies based on observation (e.g. Sameroff & Seifer 1993; Elardo *et al.* 1975) identify factors associated with better or worse cognitive outcomes, but it is difficult to establish which of these are most important and why.

Clearly, children need a minimum level of care in the family environment and deprivation or neglect can have many negative effects on development. However, beyond a minimum level, the role of the family and indeed diet are unclear. Neisser (1996) argues that differences in lifestyles of families – however important they may be – make little long-term difference to the skills measured by intelligence tests. In contrast, Gottfried and Gottfried (1984) suggest that factors such as parental involvement and daily stimulation are good predictors of IQ levels.

SECTION SUMMARY

- Piaget argued that cognitive development takes place in four stages and is based on innate cognitive structures called schemas.
- Piaget's theory has important applications to education and is the basis of discovery learning.
- Piaget's methods have been criticized for lacking child sense. Subsequent studies have indicated that young children may develop some mental skills earlier than Piaget thought.
- Vygotsky emphasized the importance of social and cultural environment in development.
- Language is internalized and forms the basis of higher mental skills.
- The zone of proximal development refers to tasks the child can achieve with the help of a more knowledgeable other.
- Piaget focused on how children think at a particular age, whereas Vygotsky was interested in why development happens.
- Family environments which are responsive, warm and stimulating are associated with better cognitive development.
- Stressful family environments may be associated with poorer cognitive outcomes.
- It is difficult to separate out the effects of diet from other family variables such as stimulation.

Identity development

Our final area of interest relates to the development of identity. Although the term identity is in common use, the concept is complex as identity involves many different aspects of the self. A good way to establish someone's identity is to ask them to answer the question *'Who am I?'* by writing down a number of statements. Their answers are likely to include reference to aspects such as:

> Identity – a consistent and reliable sense of who we are.

- relationships with others (*'I am a son/sister/boyfriend'*)
- hobbies and interests
- whether they are male or female (gender identity)
- cultural identity (e.g. Afro Caribbean, Hispanic)
- sexual identity (gay, straight, bisexual)
- occupational identity (career or current job)
- personality (*'I am an extrovert'*).

These aspects make up a person's unique identity. We will begin this section by examining the development of gender identity in early childhood before going on to consider development during adolescence. This stage was considered to be extremely influential by Erik Erikson, who argued that the achievement of identity is a major developmental task of adolescence.

The formation and development of gender roles

LEARNING OUTCOME
■ Discuss the formation and development of gender roles.

Sex – the biological state of being male or female.

Gender – behaviours that are appropriate for men and women (i.e. masculine and feminine).

While the terms sex and gender are used interchangeably in everyday life, they have different meanings. Sex refers to the biological state of being male or female and is established informally by examination of a newborn baby's genitals. In about 2 per cent of babies this produces ambiguous results and biological sex is established formally through hormone or chromosome testing. Gender refers to behaviours that are deemed to be appropriate or desirable for males and females: boys are encouraged to develop masculine characteristics while girls are encouraged to behave in a feminine way. For example, crying is often discouraged in boys and fighting in girls.

For many years, it was taken for granted that men were naturally masculine and women feminine. Bem's research contradicted this assumption. Bem (1974) asked a mixed sex sample of 100 students to rate a list of 200 traits (e.g. reliable) in terms of how desirable they were for men and women. She selected 20 items that were consistently seen as desirable for men (e.g. analytical, dominant, competitive) and 20 that were desirable for women (e.g. sympathetic, understanding, soft spoken), along with 20 gender-neutral items. The resulting scale was called Bem's Sex Role Inventory (SRI). Research using the SRI established that gender is a continuum, with extreme masculinity at one pole and extreme femininity at the other. While some people adopt a strongly masculine or feminine gender role, most people fall in between the two extremes with a mixture of masculine and feminine qualities.

There are two key questions to address in relation to the formation and development of gender roles:

■ Firstly, what develops? What behaviours do children show and at what ages do these appear?
■ Secondly, why do gender roles develop? This question focuses on the interplay of biological, cognitive and social factors in the development of gender roles.

What develops?

Boys and girls begin to show differences in behaviour from around 9 months. One of the best documented is differences in aggression. Boys use more aggressive means of communication and by the age of 2 there are significant differences in the use of bodily force, which increase with age. Boys are more likely push, shove or and snatch to get toys from other children or achieve goals (Hay *et al.*, 2011).

By the age of around 2, gender segregation appears in children's relationships, with both girls and boys preferring same sex playmates when they have previously shown little preference. At around the same age, children of both sexes begin to display gender-related preferences for toys and activities. Boys tend to engage in primarily masculine activities (construction, rough and tumble play), while girls engage in feminine activities. Around 10 per cent of boys and 20 per cent of girls deviate from these established gender norms and engage in 'cross sex play'. Older children also demonstrate differences in competitive behaviours (Ensor *et al.*, 2011). Six-year-old boys were less likely to share or interact and more likely to harm their friends than girls of the same age when placed in a competitive situation.

> **Link to the three levels of analysis**
>
> Each of the three levels of analysis asks different questions about sex and gender. Biological psychologists are interested in the action of hormones and brain structures, whereas sociocultural psychologists focus on the influence of the social and cultural environment including reinforcement and the impact of role models. Psychologists working from the cognitive level of analysis are interested in children's beliefs and understanding about gender and how these may shape young children's behaviour.

Biological factors

The sex of a baby is established at conception: each embryo has 23 pairs of chromosomes, made up of one from the sperm and one from the ovum. The 23rd chromosome determines the biological sex:

- If the embryo has an X chromosome from both parents (XX), the baby will be a girl.
- If the embryo has an X chromosome from the mother and a Y chromosome from the father (XY), the baby will be a boy.

There are a couple of genetic exceptions to this rule: around one in 500 men have Klinefelter's Syndrome, which results from an XXY pattern; they tend to be exceptionally tall with enlarged breasts and they are often infertile. XYY males were viewed for a long time as 'super males', who were much more aggressive than other men and more likely to commit violent crimes – although this assumption has been challenged.

The chromosome pattern controls the action of hormones. Around 4 weeks after conception genes switch on the production of male hormones notably testosterone in the male foetus. It is thought that testosterone acts on a part of the brain called the hypothalamus. Swaab and Fliers (1985) scanned the brains of 13 males and 18 females aged between 10 and 93. They identified an area of the hypothalamus called the 'sexually dimorphic nucleus', which was around 2½ times larger on average in males than females. It is thought that prenatal male hormones (testosterone) masculinize the male brain even though sex differences in brain structure cannot be detected until the age of around 6 years old.

Evidence and evaluation of biological factors

- The impact of sex hormones on gender roles is debatable. While studies with rats indicate that high levels of prenatal testosterone may be linked with masculine behaviour patterns, studies with human children have been less supportive.
- Young (1964) exposed pregnant rats to high levels of testosterone and found that their female offspring showed typically male behaviours. They were more aggressive than other females and adopted a dominant male mating position, supporting the claim that masculine behaviour may have a hormonal basis.
- Money and Erhardt (1972) studied the daughters of women who were given anti-miscarriage drugs containing high levels of testosterone. The mothers reported that their daughters played more energetically/boisterously than their non-affected sisters, also supporting the claim that male hormones underpin masculine behaviours. However, critics have cast doubt on the validity of these findings, noting that mothers were asked rather leading questions about their children ('Which of your daughters is the most boyish?'), potentially influencing the validity of the data.
- Case studies of children with congenital adrenal hyperplasia (CAH), a naturally occurring condition in which high levels of male hormones affect the developing foetus, have found little evidence of effects on behaviour (Hines and Kaufman, 1994). Such studies imply that hormone exposure may have relatively little effect on the gender roles adopted by young children.

Theory of knowledge

Animal experiments allow the methods employed by the natural sciences to be directed at human behaviour. An independent variable (in this case hormone exposure) is manipulated and the effect on a dependent variable is measured. This enables a cause-and-effect relationship to be established between two variables.

Cognitive factors

Cognitive theories focus on what young children understand about gender and argue that gender roles are driven by what children believe to be appropriate masculine or feminine behaviour. Kohlberg's cognitive developmental theory (1966) argued that children pass through three stages in which their understanding of gender develops in complexity. According to Kohlberg, it is only when children reach the final stage of gender consistency from about 4½ years of age that they begin to adopt gender roles:

- **Gender identity** – at the age of around 2, children can identify themselves accurately as a boy or a girl and they begin to use this label to refer to themselves and other people. However, a 2-year-old boy might say that he will grow up to become a 'mummy'.
- **Gender stability** – at around 3½, children grasp the idea that gender is stable and that girls grow up into women and boys into men. They are still misled by changes in appearances and may mistake a female soldier with a shaved head and battle dress for a male.
- **Gender consistency** – between 4½ and 7 years, children work out that gender is constant and people remain the same sex despite changes in appearance. A woman who shaves her hair off, like Demi Moore playing GI Jane, is still a woman. This understanding is very similar to Piaget's concept of conservation: the understanding that the essence of something stays the same despite changes in appearance.

Martin and Halverson's gender schema (1981) theory builds on Kohlberg's framework but argues that children adopt basic gender roles at a much earlier age than 4½. Gender schema theory suggests that as soon as young children identify themselves as a boy or girl (i.e. reach the stage of gender identity), they develop a simple gender schema with two groups, male and female. Their own sex group is the 'in-group' and the other sex is the 'out-group'. The child directs their attention to finding out about the in-group and pays minimal attention to anything that is perceived as relating to the out-group. So, girls will dismiss toys, games or TV programmes that they see as 'for boys' and boys will show no interest in anything that they deem girly. Initially gender schemas are rudimentary, incorporating clothes (i.e. trousers for boys and a dress for girls) and toys. They rapidly develop so that games, sports, school subjects and even musical instruments are 'gendered'.

Evaluation of cognitive factors

- While Kohlberg's developmental stages have been verified many times, a substantial amount of research shows that children begin to demonstrate gender roles at a much younger age than Kohlberg's theory would predict. Campbell *et al.* (2000) found that boys as young as 9 months old spent longer looking at boy's toys (e.g. cars and trucks) than girl's toys. Similarly, a longitudinal study of infants showed that more than half of children could label toys as suitable for boys or girls by the age of 3 and by the same age children are beginning to identify activities such as playing football as 'for boys' (Campbell *et al.*, 2004). This demonstrates how simple gender schemas become much more complex as children develop. Poulin-Dubois *et al.* (2002) found that Canadian toddlers aged around 2 years of age could choose a doll of the appropriate gender to carry out gender-related activities such as shaving and vacuuming. These studies provide support for gender schema theory as they demonstrate how children are tuned in to the same sex group and how gender schemas rapidly encompass many different objects and activities.

■ One real strength of cognitive theories is their acknowledgement of social factors. The gender schema developed by a child will relate to their unique social world. Parents with strongly differentiated parental roles will show their children different approaches to gender than more egalitarian parents.

Social factors

An important principle of the sociocultural level of analysis is that behaviour is influenced by the social and cultural environment. Social theories are focused on the impact of the immediate environment in shaping gender roles. From birth – and sometimes even before – the sex of a baby is one of the most important aspects of its identity. In China where a one child policy operates, prenatal screening may be used to select a child of the desired sex – often a boy. Skinner's principles of operant conditioning are highly relevant in the development of gender roles. Parents may shape their child's behaviour by providing positive reinforcements when the children show the desired masculine or feminine characteristics, making the behaviours likely to be repeated. Children may also receive teasing for showing characteristics that are seen as gender-inappropriate by parents, siblings and peers, making these behaviours less likely to be repeated.

Social learning theory (Bandura, 1973) predicts that gender roles are learnt through the observation and imitation of role models. Important sources of gender roles include parents, friends, TV characters and sports people. Imitation of a model's behaviour is more likely when the role model receives some sort of reward or reinforcement for their behaviour (**vicarious reinforcement**).

Evidence and evaluation

Although many parents claim that they treat girls and boys the same, evidence suggests that parents encourage and reinforce gender stereotypical activities for their sons and daughters. Lytton and Romney (1991) carried out a meta-analysis of 175 research studies that had examined parental treatment of children. Most of these had been carried out in the USA. They found no differences in the amount of attention, interaction and warmth given to girls and boys but parents were more likely to encourage girls to engage in activities around the house (e.g. cooking) whereas boys were more likely to be encouraged to take part in outdoor tasks such as sport. In Europe, boys were more likely to be physically punished (smacked) than girls.

Peers are important socializers of young children in nursery and at school. Archer and Lloyd (1982) found that by the age of 3, children will tease or ridicule other children who engage in 'cross sex' play activities. Ewing Lee and Troop-Gordon (2011) investigated the impact of peer victimization/teasing on children's behaviour. They asked 199 children aged between 10 and 11 years to complete two questionnaire-based measures:

■ a peer victimization scale recording how many times their classmates were teased, called names, pushed, etc., by other children
■ a rating scale of how often they engaged in a series of 24 'gender-related' activities (playing house, playing with Lego, etc.).

Researchers found that peer victimization was generally followed by withdrawal from both feminine and masculine behaviours in girls. However, while general victimization predicted lower levels of feminine behaviours in boys, social exclusion (leaving out) tended to increase boys' engagement in feminine activities. These findings show how peer relationships can influence gender non-conformity in both directions. Egan and Perry (2001) suggest that children experience 'felt pressure' from other children to conform to gender norms resulting in gender role behaviour.

Commentary

- As Leman notes, the topic of gender poses a real challenge for psychologists and can be seen as 'a messy inconvenience for researchers who would rather focus on illuminating universal laws of human behaviour' (Leman & Tenenbaum, 2011). It is clear that a range of factors – biological, social and cognitive – influence how and why young children adopt gender roles. Udry (2000) argues that hormone levels set limits on the flexibility of gender by affecting how sensitive the child is to female or male socialization. Thus, girls who have been exposed to high levels of testosterone (i.e. CAH) may be less sensitive to female socialization processes and boys who have not been exposed to normal amounts of testosterone may be less sensitive to male socialization. This approach suggests an interaction between hormonal levels (biology) and sensitivity to socialization processes.
- While theories differ in the importance they attach to cognitive or social factors, peers are seen as significant contributors to children's gender role development (Ewing Lee & Troop-Gordon, 2011) and considerable attention is being paid to the importance of gender-segregated peer groups in the development of gender roles (Leaper).

Cultural variations in gender roles

LEARNING OUTCOME
- Explain cultural variations in gender roles.

Cross-cultural studies of gender roles are interesting as they help us to tease out why gender roles develop and the relative interplay of biological cognitive and social factors.

- If gender roles are fairly consistent across cultures, this may provide evidence that they are underpinned by biological factors – such as sex hormones.
- If gender roles differ substantially across cultures, this implies that social factors may be more influential than biological factors in the development of gender.

In fact, there is evidence for both of these. In most parts of the world, there is some differentiation between men and women's roles, supporting the claim that gender roles are underpinned by biology. The extent of gender differentiation varies, however:

- In traditional cultures there are considerable differences in men and women's roles.
- In egalitarian cultures men and women's roles are largely interchangeable, so women may work out of the home and men are equally likely to be involved in bringing up children. Scandinavian countries, which have high levels of gender equality, score highly on egalitarianism.

Whiting and Edwards (1973) studied the allocation of tasks and socialization of young children in 11 traditional cultures. They found that young girls spent more time in the home with their mothers and were expected to take on domestic and childcare duties. Boys were assigned tasks outside the household, such as caring for animals or herding and they spent less time with adults and more time with peers. Girls showed higher levels of maturity and responsibility than boys. This is unsurprising as they had ample opportunity to observe and imitate these behaviours from their mothers.

In the Six Cultures Study of Socialization, Whiting and Whiting (1988) observed children in their natural environments with parents, sibling and friends. The children were drawn from two relatively affluent countries (the USA and Japan) and four developing countries (Kenya, India, the Philippines and Mexico). The research team found that boys were more likely to behave aggressively and girls showed more nurturing behaviours across all cultures, implying that these differences may have some form of biological underpinning. In India, Mexico and Japan, boys and girls were treated very differently, with girls undertaking domestic tasks and often having caring responsibilities for younger siblings. However, in the USA, Kenya and the Philippines, boys and girls were treated fairly similarly.

Adolescence

LEARNING OUTCOMES
- Describe adolescence.
- Discuss the relationship between physical change and development of identity during adolescence.

Adolescence – the transitional stage between puberty and adulthood (i.e. legal age of majority).

Adolescence refers to the transitional period from the start of puberty to the legal 'age of majority' when the rights and responsibilities of adulthood are achieved. The word is taken from the Latin 'adolesco', which loosely translates as 'to grow up or to become established'. Adolescence is associated with changes in many arenas of life:

- **Social changes** – the family becomes generally less influential and peer relationships increase in salience and intimacy. At 12 to 14, social relationships are organized around close groups of 4–6 same sex friends known as cliques. Cliques join together into mixed sex groups with some individuals pairing off into couples at 15 or 16 (Dunphy, 1963).
- **Cognitive changes** – the adolescent's thinking abilities develop in relation to attention, memory and processing speed. By the time individuals have reached age 15, their thinking skills are generally comparable to those of adults.

Puberty brings about a range of **biological changes**, some obvious and others less so:

- **Growth spurt** – this begins at around the age of 12 in girls and 13½ in boys. Height increases by several inches a year before slowing down. Hands and feet usually grow to their adult-size first, giving some adolescents a clumsy appearance.
- **Levels of body fat** – during adolescence the level of body fat in girls increases from around 21 per cent to 24 per cent of body weight. In boys, body fat drops from 16 to 14 per cent of body weight.
- **Hormones** – instructed by the hypothalamus and pituitary gland, the testes and ovaries instruct the secretion of hormones. Testosterone levels increase 18-fold in boys and estradiol (a type of oestrogen) increases by around eight times in girls. These changes lead to an increase in genital size (boys) and to the development of breasts and menstruation (girls).

The child's sense of identity – which is largely taken for granted – comes unglued at adolescence by the rapid physical growth and sexual changes taking place. Adolescents are faced with a range of bewildering decisions about the future, relating to education, career choices and sexuality as well as wider beliefs and ideologies. It is unsurprising that self-esteem falls during early adolescence then gradually rises.

Physical changes and identity

Faust (1983) argued that young people have an internal model about the 'normal' timing for puberty and children who are ahead or behind this mental timetable tend to think less of themselves. Puberty is associated with increased body fat in girls and these changes conflict with cultural models of beauty and slimness in many Western cultures. This would suggest that early maturing would be particularly problematic for girls. Williams and Currie (2000) examined the relationship between self-esteem and timing of puberty in a sample of more than 1,000 Scottish schoolgirls aged 11–13. Early maturation and lower ratings of body image (body size and perceived appearance) were associated with lower self-esteem in 11-year-olds. At age 13, late maturing along with concerns with body size were associated with lower self-esteem.

Concerns about weight are also characteristic of adolescence with notable differences between males and females. The West of Scotland 11–16 Teenage Health Study (Sweeting & West, 2002) found that boys' concerns about weight fell across early adolescence (30 per cent at 11, 23 per cent at 15), as did the proportion of boys who were actively dieting (8 per cent falling to 5 per cent). This is consistent with physical changes (e.g. the decrease of body fat in males). In contrast, girls' concerns about weight increased rapidly in adolescence (44 per cent at age 11 rising to 70 per cent at 15, with more than one-quarter of 15-year-olds on a diet). Concerns about weight occur regardless of BMI (i.e. actual body size) and there is a strong link between self-esteem and dieting in teenage girls. Barker and Bornstein (2010) examined the changes in self-esteem and appearance satisfaction in a sample of teenagers aged 10 to 14 along with self-reported dieting behaviour at age 14. Girls who had a higher BMI score at age 10 were more likely to diet at 14.

The age at which puberty begins has decreased gradually over the last century. In 1860, puberty took place at around the age of 16 for both boys and girls. By the mid-twentieth century this had dropped to 12/13 years and in many Westernized countries children are now reaching puberty even earlier, at around the age of 10. This may be linked to increasing weight gain and size and has important implications for mental health in adolescents (AAP, 2010 & 2012).

Psychological research into adolescence

LEARNING OUTCOME

■ Examine psychological research into adolescence (for example, Erikson's identity crisis, Marcia).

Figure 5.7 Adolescence is a crucial time in identity formation.

Erik Erikson (1902–1994) and James Marcia saw identity as **psychosocial,** meaning that it was both psychological (personal) and social (involved in relations with others) at the same time. Erikson was a psychoanalyst and he developed his theory from clinical work with ex-servicemen in the period after the 1939–45 war.

Erikson (1968) argued that the development of identity was a lifelong process characterized by eight stages. Erikson conceptualized each stage as centred on a 'crisis' relating to an important developmental task or quality. The first stage in infancy involved the development of trust in other people and was strongly in line with Bowlby's and Ainsworth's ideas of the importance of secure attachment. Erikson argued that a healthy resolution of the crisis involved taking a middle point so that extreme mistrust of others was psychologically unhealthy – but so was being too trusting.

Erikson regarded Stage 5, adolescence, as crucial to the development of 'ego identity' – a secure feeling of who and what we are. The major developmental task of this stage was to make decisions about education, establishing independence from parents and future occupational identity (career) and to commit to these decisions. Erikson conceptualized adolescence as a time of 'psychological moratorium' – a socially approved period in which decisions could be postponed while different identities were tried out. He noted that many young people find it hard to make decisions about the future, effectively falling into a state of role diffusion or identity crisis and drifting without taking active decisions about their future. The social group at this stage may become hugely important as they provide a sense of identity and belonging.

Psychological moratorium – a socially approved postponement of decisions.

Role diffusion – drifting without making a commitment to the future.

Evaluation of psychosocial theory

■ Erikson's theory was developed using clinical evidence and his own experiences as an analyst so it is unsurprising that he emphasized the normative nature of identity crises in young people's lives. While evidence supports the claim of adolescence as a time of moratorium, this period is not a crisis for many young people (Coleman & Hendry, 1990).

■ Erikson's theory was developed in the 1950s when decisions about the future related largely to occupational identity. Social and economic changes of the last 50 years have meant that the concept of a job for life has largely been superseded and most people change career several times in their lives. Similarly, Erikson's theory emphasized the importance of marriage for women's identity. Today, sex equality and involvement in higher education and the workplace have lead to similar identity decisions for both sexes in adolescence.

■ Erikson's psychosocial theory provided an important framework for researchers such as Marcia to consider identity development in adolescence.

The identity status model: James Marcia

Erikson's ideas were developed by Marcia, who extended Erikson's original framework to explore different kinds of identity (or statuses) taken on by adolescents. Marcia used semi-structured interviews with large samples of 18–25-year-olds, to explore their views about education, politics, sexuality and other identity issues (Marcia, 1966, 1980). Drawing on the data obtained from these interviews, Marcia argued that successful identity achievement involves two elements:

■ **Exploration** – this involves making efforts to learn about opportunities and choices, for example in education or career choice.

■ **Commitment** – this involves making a deliberate decision on the basis of the exploration.

Marcia developed a model that identified four different **identity statuses**, which could be adopted in adolescence. These were made up of different combinations of high and low exploration and commitment. Marcia emphasized that these were not stages in the way that Piaget conceptualized cognitive development. A teenager might move through all four in any order, or may experience just one or two of the statuses. However, Marcia believed that diffusion and foreclosure were less developmentally advanced states than moratorium and achievement. A common identity path might involve diffusion at age 14 followed by moratorium, a period of questioning at 16, before decisions and commitments are made and identity is achieved.

Table 5.4 Marcia's identity status model

	LOW COMMITMENT	**HIGH COMMITMENT**
Low exploration	**Identity diffusion** is characterized by low exploration and low commitment. The young person may live a carefree life and be untroubled by the decisions they have to take. If asked about their future plans, the essence of the answer may well be *'I don't know and I don't really care'*. They are also likely to be impressionable and easily influenced.	**Identity foreclosure** is characterized by low exploration and high commitment. The young person commits to a decision – for example about occupation or education – without examining alternatives. They may simply accept the path suggested by their parents.
High exploration	**Moratorium** is characterized by high exploration and low commitment. The young person actively searches for answers to the questions of what and who to be. Moratorium may be uncomfortable for the adolescent and their parents.	**Identity achievement** is characterized by high exploration and high commitment and is the most mature status.

Most research into identity in adolescence is based on Marcia's model, showing how influential this approach has been.

Schwartz (2002) argues that Marcia was the first to create 'an empirically measureable construct' from Erikson's theory and the identity status model has driven subsequent research for over 40 years. An extensive meta-analysis of 124 studies that examined identity status change during adolescence and early adulthood was been carried out by Kroger *et al.*(2010) and indicated that:

- The proportion of adolescents in moratorium rises steadily to around age 19 years and then declines.
- The proportion of adolescents who have achieved identity rises through late adolescence and young adulthood.
- The proportion of adolescents in foreclosure and diffusion declines over the high school years, but fluctuates throughout late adolescence and young adulthood.

Similarly, there is evidence that the identity statuses may occur in patterns that create common developmental trajectories (Meeus *et al.*, 2012) and the idea of moratorium should be extended to refer to two kinds of moratorium: classical and searching.

■ Critical thinking

Studies of adolescent identity can be longitudinal or cross-sectional. Cross-sectional studies enable conclusions to be drawn from larger populations relatively quickly. In contrast, longitudinal studies are time-consuming and tend to have high rates of participant attrition.

SECTION SUMMARY

- Biological, cognitive and social factors play a part in the development of gender roles.
- Animal experiments suggest that male hormones play a role in masculine behaviours such as dominance. However, case studies of CAH children are less supportive.
- Children's understanding of gender develops in stages (Kohlberg).
- Gender schema theory argues that children begin to adopt gender roles from around age 2 when they form a basic gender schema.
- Parents and peers 'police' the development of gender roles through selective reinforcement.
- Hormones may make children more or less susceptible to gender socialization.
- Adolescence is the transitional period between puberty and adulthood.
- The major task of this stage is the development of a secure sense of identity, according to psychosocial theory.
- Marcia identifies four identity statuses with different combinations of exploration and commitment. These may occur in developmental trajectories.

Health psychology

Introduction

LEARNING OUTCOMES
- To what extent do biological, cognitive and sociocultural factors influence health-related behaviour?
- Evaluate psychological research (that is, theories and/or studies) relevant to health psychology.

In this section of the course we are going to consider how psychology can help us to understand stress, obesity and substance abuse. Each of these clearly has biological components, as well as psychological ones. The biomedical model views people largely as 'physical machines' (Banyard, 1996), assuming that illnesses are caused by the malfunctioning of internal physiological mechanisms, such as biochemical imbalances or the invasion of outside forces (such as bacteria or viruses). The biopsychosocial model developed by Engel (1977, 1980), however, argues that a full understanding of these experiences requires all three levels of analysis – biological, psychological (cognitive) and sociocultural. Health psychologists work within this biopsychosocial framework (Ogden, 2007).

Every day we are confronted with stressful situations. Some people cope well with these and appear 'ruffled' by very little, whereas others find stressful events very hard to deal with. In the first section of this chapter we will examine biological responses to stress, before moving on to consider how and why people differ in their abilities to cope with stress.

In the second section of the chapter we will consider what health psychologists have discovered about obesity and substance abuse. Obesity rates are rising rapidly in Western countries and current discourses refer to the obesity epidemic as a 'time bomb'. While substance abuse is often thought of in relation to illegal drugs, such as heroin and cocaine, most damage to health comes from two drugs that are both legal and widely used in many parts of the world: nicotine (found in tobacco) and alcohol. The World Health Organization estimates that there are around 1.3 billion smokers in the world, of which almost 1 billion are men. The vast majority of smokers live in developing countries where there is little help or treatment available for those wishing to quit. As we will see, biological, cognitive and sociocultural factors play an important role both in obesity and in substance use and addiction.

Figure 6.1 Most people think of substance abuse as involving illegal drugs like heroin, but most damage to health involves legal drugs, such as nicotine.

In the final section of the chapter, we will examine health promotion and consider how people can be persuaded to make healthy choices. This strong practical emphasis is evident throughout this chapter. We will examine how insights from health psychology can help us to tackle the problems associated with stress, obesity and addiction.

Stress

What is stress?

Stressor –
something that
requires an
individual to
make some sort of
adjustment.

Most of us would agree that certain situations are stressful. Being confronted by an angry dog, facing a critical examination, the death of a close friend or family member. These situations are known as stressors. Unfortunately, there is a range of situations that some people might find stressful, yet that others will not. For a small number of people, being in a confined space is highly stressful, yet most people would not see getting into a lift as a stressor. Even exams are less stressful for students who know the syllabus well and have done lots of revision.

Definitions of stress are not straightforward, and there have been three different approaches to defining it:

- **Stress as stimulus** – dangerous situations, such as being in a blazing building, are clearly stressors, as is bereavement. But even with the loss of a family member there are likely to be different reactions from different relations. Stimuli such as bereavement are not inevitably stressors.
- **Stress as response** – stress involves clear physiological arousal patterns in the body, so we could define a stressor as anything that produces the stress response. But this runs into similar problems to stress as stimulus. Some people will produce a stress response getting onto a train, but most people would not class trains as stressors.
- **The transactional approach** – what seems clear is that there are individual variables that affect whether or not certain situations and stimuli are found stressful. This has led to the development of the transactional approach; this simply refers to the fact that stressful situations involve an interaction or transaction between the individual and the situation. This idea is easy to understand if we introduce Lazarus's (1982) ideas of primary and secondary appraisal:
  - **Primary appraisal** – this is our initial assessment of the demands of a situation. We can assess an event as threatening and stressful, or as non-threatening and harmless.
  - **Secondary appraisal** – the process of assessing our abilities and resources for coping. If the situation is appraised as stressful, it will require action/resources from us.

The transactional approach states that stress exists where there is a discrepancy or gap between the demands on us and our ability to cope with those demands. So, unrestrained angry dogs are stressors because they may attack ('demand'), and unless you are very strong or can run very fast, there is not much you can do by way of coping. Redundancy is a stressor because loss of income ('demand'), coupled with an economic recession that means jobs are hard to find, produces a large gap between demand and coping ability.

The advantage of the transactional approach is that individual differences are incorporated. 'Appraisal' is a cognitive process involving perception of demands and coping resources. This perception is not always accurate. A student who underestimates the demands of an examination and overestimates their preparation will not perceive much demand and will not be very stressed about it. Another student may do the opposite, overestimating the demand and underestimating their preparation (coping); they will feel very stressed. The two students may do equally well, but have very different experiences. The transactional approach can also explain the person who is phobic about lifts – it is their perception that is maladaptive and means that they are highly stressed by the experience.

Measuring stress

A related problem to defining stressors is how to measure them. This is vital if you want to do research into stress and its effects, but it is not straightforward. For instance, how might you go about measuring the stress in your own life? It could involve a mix of major events, such as examinations, leaving school and going to university perhaps, but also everyday stressors such as commuting to college and dealing with classmates and teachers. Various self-report measures have been devised to measure these types of stressors.

Life events

The full name of this questionnaire is the **Holmes-Rahe Social Readjustment Rating Scale** (SRRS). Working in the 1950s and 60s, Holmes and Rahe noticed that people in hospital with serious conditions such as heart attacks and strokes had often experienced major life events in the previous months. These events included bereavement, separation and divorce, and redundancy. They concluded that life event stress could lead to illness.

Figure 6.2 The SRRS measures the stressful impact of life events, such as the death of a loved one, on health.

They then asked hundreds of participants to rate the impact of 43 life events, from the most stressful to the least. They gave the event rated most stressful – death of a partner – an arbitrary value of 100, and ordered the remaining events in relation to death of a partner (*see Table 6.1 for extracts from the list*). Even 'pleasant' events such as Christmas and holidays were rated as having some stressful impact.

By adding up the scores for all the events that have happened to a person in the previous year, the SRRS provides an overall index of life event stress. Holmes and Rahe further predicted that the higher the score, the greater the chances of developing a stress-related illness. We will look at the evidence for this relationship later in this section.

Table 6.1 Examples of events listed on the Holmes-Rahe Social Readjustment Rating Scale.

LIFE EVENT	LIFE CHANGE UNITS
Death of partner	100
Divorce	73
Death of a close family member	63
Personal injury or illness	53
Dismissal from work	47
Pregnancy	40
Change in financial state	38
Change in responsibilities at work	29
Outstanding personal achievement	28
Change in residence	20
Change in working hours or conditions	20
Holiday	13
Christmas	12

Evaluation

- The Holmes-Rahe scale takes a 'stimulus' view of stressors, assuming that everyone will find the list of events equally stressful. This approach is rather simplistic, as individuals vary greatly in how they might perceive the same event. Reactions to the death of a partner vary depending on the quality of the relationship, and for some people Christmas would be at number 3 in the list rather than at number 42!
- The SRRS is still in use as it provides a crude estimate of the amount of life stress an individual experiences as a result of various events.
- Life events are relatively rare, and everyday hassles are a more common source of stress. Lazarus and his group (1981) argued that the major life events of the Holmes-Rahe scale do not occur often enough to explain the everyday stress that people report. They therefore devised the **Hassles scale** for assessing everyday stressors, such as commuting problems, family arguments, and worries about friends, relationships and appearance. They also introduced an **Uplifts scale** for assessing the positive things that can happen every day, such as making new friends, getting good marks on coursework, being complimented on appearance, etc. They propose that Uplifts can counteract the negative effects of Hassles, but also found evidence that scores on Hassles scales correlated better with illness outcomes than scores on life event scales.

Perceived stress

Cohen *et al.* (1983) used a different approach, arguing that if you want to know how stressed someone is, you should ask them. The **Perceived Stress Scale** is made up of 14 questions about how you have coped with life over the previous month, for example:

- Have you felt irritated, angry or stressed?
- Have you felt that you cannot cope with everything you have to do?

Questions are rated on a 5-point scale from 'not at all' to 'very much so', and by adding up the 14 ratings a perceived stress score is produced. This can be correlated with measures of health or illness.

This seems an intuitive and sensible approach, but there is evidence that some of the physiological reactions to stress (*see the next section*) occur even when the person denies feeling stressed at all; in fact one type of personality is known as a 'repressor', as they show all the signs of high arousal and anxiety, but score very low on questionnaire measures of psychological stress.

Physiological, psychological and social aspects of stress

LEARNING OUTCOME
- Discuss physiological, psychological and social aspects of stress.

Physiological aspects of stress

Working in the 1930s and 40s, Hans Selye was the first researcher to detail the physiological effects of stressors. In a study that was not connected with stress, he noted that rats that were given repeated injections developed gastric ulcers and other signs of stress-related illness. He then systematically identified the stress of the injections as the key factor in the development of these symptoms. Following this up with a number of other studies he proposed that animals, including humans, respond to a range of different stressors with the same pattern of physiological changes. He called this pattern the general adaptation syndrome (GAS). Although some details have been shown to be inaccurate, the GAS still serves as a useful framework for outlining the stress response. It has three stages:

- **Alarm** – a stressor (a danger or threat, for instance) is identified by the processes of appraisal outlined above (*see page 173*). This activates the body's physiological arousal systems, which we will examine in the next section, leading to increases in heart rate and blood pressure, and mobilization of energy reserves for use by the body's muscles. These systems allow us to cope with the stressor.
- **Resistance** – if the stressor persists, our arousal systems maintain a high level of activity.
- **Exhaustion** – eventually our arousal systems are unable to maintain their high levels of activity and become exhausted. It is at this stage that stress-related illnesses are likely to occur.

Selye was the first researcher to identify the potential relationship between stress and illness, and this relationship is now the focus of extensive research. The arousal systems underlying the alarm stage are basic to our understanding of the stress–illness relationship. We now know that there are two key arousal pathways (*see the next section*).

The arousal pathways

The general effect of the two arousal pathways is to set up a state of high physiological arousal in the body. The aim is to prepare the body for physical action in a stressful or dangerous situation; energy reserves are made available, and blood flow increases to provide the oxygen necessary for energy expenditure. Systems that we do not need in dangerous situations, such as the immune system, are damped down.

The hypothalamic-pituitary-adrenal cortex (HPA) pathway

Threatening situations are identified by perceptual and appraisal processes in the higher cortical centres. Messages are sent to the hypothalamus, buried deep in the brain. The pituitary gland lies just below the hypothalamus and is connected to it by a stalk, the infundibulum. The pituitary gland is the most important gland in the body, releasing many hormones into the bloodstream, which in turn control the secretions of many other glands in the body. In stressful situations the hypothalamus stimulates the pituitary to release the hormone ACTH (adrenocorticotrophic hormone) into the bloodstream. ACTH travels to the adrenal gland, which lies just above the kidney.

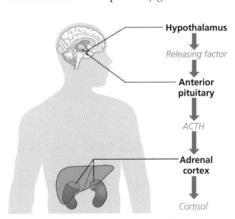

Figure 6.3 The hypothalamic-pituitary-adrenal cortex pathway.

The adrenal gland is a key element in the stress system. It is divided into two distinct components, the adrenal cortex and the adrenal medulla. ACTH stimulates the adrenal cortex to release a range of chemicals or hormones, the most important of which are the corticosteroids. These include cortisone, corticosterone and cortisol. They have a range of effects in stressful situations. Most importantly they mobilize energy reserves, increasing blood levels of sugars and free fatty acids that can be burnt up by muscle activity, i.e. increasing these levels allows for rapid behavioural responses to stressors. Corticosteroids also suppress the immune system.

The sympatho-adrenomedullary system (SAM)

In addition to activating the pituitary gland, in states of stress the hypothalamus also activates autonomic centres in the brainstem (an area at the core of the brain). The autonomic nervous system is part of the nervous system that plays a vital role in regulating our internal organs, such as the heart, circulatory system and digestive system. It is divided into two subsystems, the sympathetic and parasympathetic nervous systems. In a stressful situation the hypothalamus stimulates the sympathetic pathway, which sends neural impulses to the adrenal medulla. These result in the adrenal medulla releasing adrenaline and noradrenaline into the bloodstream.

Adrenaline and noradrenaline have similar effects on the body. You will probably have heard of adrenaline. This chemical (which can also be referred to as a hormone) has arousing effects. It directly increases heart rate and blood pressure, speeding up the flow of oxygen that the muscles need to be fully active over a long period. It also makes us more alert.

Evaluation

- These systems evolved many millions of years ago and are common to all mammals. They evolved to cope with physical stressors, such as escaping predators or avoiding other dangerous situations. Unfortunately, in humans they are also activated by stressors that do not involve a physical response. If you lie in bed at 3 a.m. worrying about exams or paying the rent, or a relationship going wrong, these stressors can be as effective at activating the physiological stress response as spotting a leopard across the clearing. There is no obvious physical response to such non-physical stressors, unfortunately, such as running away. So we have a body prepared for physical action, but no physical action.
- It is thought that the high circulating levels of free fatty acids can then contribute to blocking of the arteries (atherosclerosis), while high blood pressure can lead to strokes and heart attacks. Corticosteroids also suppress the immune system; so long-term stress can leave the body vulnerable to a range of infections and illnesses.
- Many studies have shown a link between stress and illness. In a series of studies, Kiecolt-Glaser (e.g. 1984, 1987) has shown that people under long-term stress have significantly reduced immune function compared to control conditions. These include carers for patients with Alzheimer's disease and students taking important examinations.
- Cohen *et al.* (1991) found that participants reporting high levels of stressful life events were significantly more likely to catch the common cold (an index of reduced immune function).

In all these studies, however, there were important individual differences, and this brings us to psychological aspects of stress.

Psychological aspects of stress

Personality and stress

Type A personality – characterized by impatience, competitiveness and irritability/hostility.

It has long been felt that personality variables affect our reactions to stress. It is a common experience that certain people seem more or less vulnerable to the negative effects of stress. In the 1960s and 70s Freedman and Rosenman (e.g. Rosenman *et al.*, 1976) described the Type A personality as one that was especially vulnerable to stress-induced heart disease. This personality type is characterized by impatience, competitiveness and irritability/hostility, i.e. high levels of arousal combined with negative emotions.

Hardy personality – copes with stress well and is characterized by commitment, control and challenge.

As opposed to psychological factors that make us more vulnerable to stress, some research has investigated factors that may protect us. Kobasa (1979) identified the hardy personality. This personality type is characterized by high levels of commitment, a need for control over one's life, and challenge (the sense that stressful situations are there to be overcome rather than endured). Cohen *et al.*'s (1991) study indicated that life stress increased susceptibility to the common cold; in later work using similar methods, his group also investigated protective factors. They found that a positive emotional style (defined as a vigorous approach to life combined with a sense of calm and happiness) actually helped protect against stress-induced illness.

Evidence and evaluation

■ Although some evidence supported the relationship between Type A behaviour and CHD, other studies (e.g. Gallacher *et al.*, 2003) have found no association between this personality type and stress-related heart disease.

■ It now seems that one particular component of the Type A pattern, irritability/hostility, is more important than any of the others. Recent studies (e.g. Chida & Steptoe, 2009) have found that high levels of anger and hostility are linked to a higher probability of heart disease. Stress may be an additional factor, but it is the basic personality variable, hostility, that is critical.

■ Cohen *et al.*'s (1991) finding might help to explain the inconsistent findings with the Type A personality. People with a positive emotional style are active and engaged but also positive and happy in what they are doing, and are therefore protected against the negative effects of stress.

■ Kobasa has shown how people with high levels of hardiness, measured using questionnaires, had lower levels of stress-induced illness and absenteeism from work than people with low levels of hardiness.

Control and stress

Our basic definition of stress associates it with a discrepancy between the demands being made on us and our available coping responses. A crucial element in this model is the sense of control (or lack of control) over the events of one's life. The role of control has been investigated, especially in relation to workplace stress. For instance, Marmot *et al.* (1997) have studied Whitehall civil servants over many years, looking at workplace variables such as workload ('demand') and control, i.e. the extent to which individuals could control their workload. They found higher levels of heart disease in lower civil service grades than in the higher grades. After controlling for variables such as lifestyle, diet, obesity and smoking, they concluded that the sense of control was the critical factor. The higher grades may have had higher levels of responsibility, but they also had higher levels of control over workplace decisions and this protected them against stress-induced illness.

Social aspects of stress

One of the most exciting aspects of modern research into stress has been the growing awareness of the importance of social factors in moderating the effects of stress. Kiecolt-Glaser and Cohen found that social isolation and lack of social support increased the negative effects of stress, while social support has been found to improve survival rates and adjustment to serious illnesses such as cancer (De Boer *et al.*, 1999; Butow *et al.*, 1999).

In a major review of the area, Uchino *et al.* (1996) concluded that there was a significant relationship between social support and lower levels of resting blood pressure, and between social support and better immune function. Both of these effects would help protect against the negative effects of stress.

Thorsteinsson *et al.* (1999) reviewed carefully controlled laboratory studies of cardiac (heart) reactivity to stressful situations, such as taking IQ tests under time pressure. They concluded that the presence of just one other person, or even a pet cat or dog (!) significantly reduces cardiac reactivity in these situations. Reduced reactivity to stressful situations would reduce the chances of stress-induced heart problems.

Social support is a complex area – for instance, is it better to have a wide circle of friends, or just a few close friends? A social network provides emotional and practical support, and we do not know which elements are most important in protecting against stress. But it is clear that we are social animals who rely heavily on social support. It has also been shown in other primates, such as chimpanzees, that isolation from their colony induces a state that looks very like severe depression, so our reliance on our social groups may have a long evolutionary history.

Coping with stress

- Evaluate strategies for coping with stress (for example, stress inoculation therapy, hardiness training, yoga and meditation).

It is important to note that while the research emphasis has been on stress-induced illness, stress also has psychological effects. These include increased levels of anxiety and depression, and so the aims of coping strategies are not simply to prevent illness, but to improve psychological adjustment.

Cognitive behavioural approaches

Cognitive behavioural therapies (CBT) have become increasingly popular in treating a range of psychological disorders. They are designed to alter the way people perceive and appraise the world around them, and also try to alter behaviour so that the client is better able to cope with the stressors that life throws at them. Stress inoculation therapy and hardiness training are two forms of CBT.

Stress inoculation therapy

Stress inoculation therapy (SIT) has three stages:
- Identify and analyse sources of stress, and whether previous coping attempts have succeeded or, more likely, failed.
- Skills acquisition and rehearsal, e.g. if examinations are a major source of stress, then training can be given in learning and revising effectively. Some people find social settings particularly stressful and they can be helped using social skills training.
- Application in the real world, with a continuous review of successful and unsuccessful coping.

Hardiness training

Hardiness training is based Kobasa's work on the hardy personality and, like SIT, has three stages:
- **Focusing** – accurate identification of stressful situations.
- **Reconstruction** – reliving stressful encounters; could things have turned out better, or worse?
- **Self-improvement** – especially taking on challenges that can be managed, e.g. someone stressed by social encounters might be encouraged to talk to at least one new person at work. Beginning at this low level slowly increases confidence and self-efficacy. This latter concept is an important element in many forms of therapy. It refers to the sense of being able to influence events in one's own life and is closely linked to the idea of control. In general, CBT methods aim to increase self-efficacy.

Evaluation of CBT approaches

- A feeling of stress depends on cognitive processes such as perception and appraisal of threats and coping resources. The advantage of CBT approaches is that they try to alter these cognitions (the source of stress), and so lead to a permanent shift in how the client perceives the world around them.

- Issues with the approaches are that they involve a number of intense sessions analysing stressful experiences and developing new coping skills. This requires insight and motivation on the part of the client and a willingness to engage in behavioural changes, which can be difficult and stressful in itself.
- Clients have to invest money and time in the process, and in general we can say that although potentially highly effective, CBT approaches do not suit all people.

Physical exercise

Many of the negative effects of stress are caused by the high levels of physiological arousal it produces, which are maladaptive when most of our stressors now are psychological rather than physical. Burning up excess free fatty acids and sugars in physical exercise would therefore seem a sensible means of reducing the negative effects of stress.

Although exercise has been shown to reduce resting heart rate (Jones & Bright, 2001), it has been difficult to identify other clear physiological stress-related benefits. What has been established, however, is that regular exercise can be a key factor in maintaining a positive mood state and high levels of self-efficacy.

Note that earlier we outlined Cohen *et al.*'s work on positive emotional state and resistance to stress-induced illness. If regular physical exercise improves mood then it may indirectly help us to cope with everyday stress.

Regular exercise is time-consuming, and, if you use a gym, expensive. It can also lead to sprains and, in rare cases, serious heart problems up to and including fatal heart attacks. In general, however, it is an accessible and practical method of maintaining fitness, improving mood and increasing self-efficacy, all of which can contribute to resilience in the face of stressors.

Yoga, meditation and muscle relaxation

These related techniques are highly effective at reducing levels of physiological arousal, and in fact CBT techniques usually involve some training in relaxation for use in situations of extreme stress. Thirty minutes of meditation or progressive muscle relaxation will significantly lower heart rate and blood pressure. The problem is that these can rapidly rise again when you return to everyday life, with no long-term benefits.

The key is to make them part of a general attitude or approach to life, which includes a less stressed, calmer view of existence. In this respect yoga and meditation have advantages, in that they include a spiritual element that can carry over into your general lifestyle. Of course, you have to subscribe to this particular view of the world, but if you can attain a more philosophical approach to everyday life then it undoubtedly becomes less stressful.

Also note that although these techniques sound simple they need to be learnt in a disciplined fashion and applied systematically in the long-term. They are not short cuts to a stress-free life, and do not suit everybody.

> ### Link to the biological level of analysis
>
> Long-term (chronic) stress can lead to high blood pressure and risk of stroke and heart attack. Drugs such as beta-blockers and ACE inhibitors (angiotensin-converting-enzyme inhibitors) directly target the cardiovascular system and effectively reduce blood pressure. Benzodiazepines (BZs, such as Librium and Valium) have been among the most prescribed drugs over the last 40 years. They have a general antianxiety effect, producing lower arousal in stressful situations. Although drugs do not target the causes of stress and may have problems of side effects and addiction, they can be life savers.

SECTION SUMMARY
- The transactional model of stress argues that stress results from a gap between demands and ability to cope.
- Self-report measures of stress include the SRRS and Perceived Stress Scale.
- Selye's GAS conceptualized the stress response in three stages: alarm, resistance and exhaustion.
- Two arousal pathways are involved in stress: the HPA and SAM. They energize the body to deal with stressors. This response is unhelpful for many modern stressors.
- There are links between stress and illness. Stress influences the functioning of the immune system and is linked with heart disease.
- Type A personalities are more vulnerable to the negative effects of stress especially those with high levels of negative emotions. Hardy personalities and people who approach life with positive emotional styles generally cope better.
- Social support can provide a buffer against the negative effects of stress.
- Cognitive behavioural approaches to stress tackle the ways in which people perceive and appraise stressors.
- Physical exercise can be helpful in limiting the physical damage caused by stress.

Obesity and substance abuse

LEARNING OUTCOME
- Discuss factors related to overeating and the development of obesity.

Explanations of obesity

Obesity – an eating disorder whereby excess body fat accumulates to the extent of having a negative effect on health and well-being.

Obesity is an eating disorder of epidemic proportions in many cultures, with reported levels currently around 35 per cent in the USA. Only by gaining an understanding of the factors underlying the disorder will it be possible to formulate effective prevention strategies and treatments.

The search for biological factors related to obesity has focused on the role of brain structures and hormones, whereas psychological explanations based on the psychodynamic approach emphasize the importance of early childhood experiences, anxiety and unconscious conflicts in eating behaviour.

(*You can find more explanations within the Abnormal psychology chapter, page 92.*)

Biological factors in obesity

Neurological factors

Neurological factors are investigated by studying animals and faulty functioning brain structures and neurological mechanisms of obese individuals. The hypothalamus is the brain structure identified as playing the central role in the regulation of eating. Therefore neurological explanations focus on the idea that faulty functioning of the hypothalamus is associated with the development of obesity. Attention has concentrated on the workings of the ventromedial hypothalamus (VMH), which in normally functioning people acts as the satiety centre, informing individuals when they're full so that eating can cease.

Research has also focused on specific mechanisms. For example, the action of leptin, a hormone produced by fat cells in the stomach in proportion to the amount of body fat, on the proopiomelanocortin (POMC) and neuropeptide Y (NPY) neurones, is seen as especially important. The amount of leptin influences these neurones, which regulate appetite.

Evidence and evaluation

- Reeves and Plum (1969) conducted a post-mortem on an obese female, finding her VMH had been destroyed, suggesting the hypothalamus is associated with the development of obesity.
- Friedman (2005) reports obese people do produce leptin, but its ability to suppress the neuron POMC is blocked, so their appetite stays high and they gain weight up to a point thought to be genetically determined, demonstrating the role of neurological factors in combination with genetics.
- It was hoped leptin injections would prove an effective treatment for obesity, but these only work for a few people, casting doubt on the importance of leptin's role.
- Much research into leptin was done on mice and so the results may not be generalizable to humans.
- Stice *et al.* (2008) found obese people have a poorly functioning dorsal striatum, which leads to lessened dopamine-signalling in the brain, causing them to overeat. This demonstrates the role of the neurotransmitter dopamine in determining obesity.
- The evidence linking dopamine to obesity tends to be correlational and so it is not clear if dopamine is a cause or an effect of being obese.

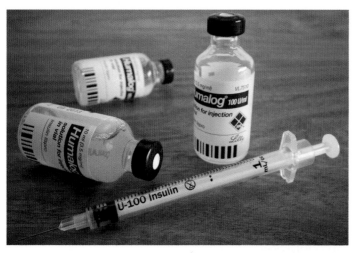

Figure 6.4 Insulin is one of several hormones that are associated with the development of obesity.

Hormones and obesity

Several hormones are associated with the development of obesity. Aside from leptin and its relationship to the NPY and POMC neurones, three hormones in particular have attracted research interest:

- **Insulin** – a hormone associated with the storage and usage of energy, insulin has attracted attention due to the link between insulin resistance and obesity. There is a link here to the genetic explanation, as insulin resistance occurs mainly due to genetic factors.
- **Cortisol** – is a glucocorticoid hormone exerting a strong metabolic effect. Individuals with high cortisol levels overeat, leading to weight increase and eventual obesity.
- **Ghrelin** – a growth hormone found in the stomach that is associated with slowing down metabolism and decreasing the body's ability to burn fat.

Evidence and evaluation

- Kahn and Flier (2000) found individuals with insulin resistance who eat large amounts of junk food, which has a high glycaemic value, become obese. This indicates insulin is involved in the development of obesity. Insulin isn't regarded as a direct cause of obesity, nor is its influence on obesity fully understood.
- Epel *et al.* (2001) found overeating of sweet foods occurred in females with high cortisol levels, suggesting cortisol is linked to the causality of obesity. Although cortisol is linked to obesity, it's not known whether this hormone is a cause or an effect of obesity.
- Yildiz *et al.* (2004) found ghrelin levels increase during the day in thinner people, suggesting there may be a flaw in the circadian system of obese individuals. Sun *et al.* (2006) report that ghrelin antagonists, drugs designed to combat obesity, may actually be effective against Type 2 diabetes rather than obesity, casting doubt on ghrelin being a causative agent for obesity.

▪ Critical thinking

Neurological and hormonal factors relate to the biological level of analysis, as both see obesity as rooted in the physiology of the body. It is best not to assess these factors in isolation from each other, however, but, along with other biological influences such as genetic and evolutionary ones, as having a collective effect on the establishment of obesity, for example the mediating effect of leptin on POMC and NPY neurones.

Psychological factors in obesity

The psychodynamic explanation of behaviour emanates from the work of Freud, seeing adult problem behaviours as due to unresolved conflicts that occurred during childhood development through the psychosexual stages.

The psychodynamic explanation is a psychological one, which sees obesity arising from unresolved conflicts, like emotional deprivation or overindulgence, during the oral stage where libido is focused on the mouth. An adult personality characterized by oral gratification develops as a result of unresolved conflicts during the oral stage, manifesting itself with overeating. Obesity may also be linked to other factors, such as depression or low self-esteem, with these factors explicable by psychodynamic means.

The psychodynamic explanation can be tested by seeing if psychotherapy reveals underlying common childhood based traumas and if psychodynamic therapies help to alleviate the condition.

Key study

Sleep eating and the dynamics of morbid obesity, weight loss and regain of weight (Felliti, 2001)

Felliti (2001) carried out an assessment of five cases of sleep eating in morbidly obese participants with a history of up-and-down weight fluctuations. A case study method was used. Five participants treated for morbid obesity and sleep eating self-reported on their condition.

- **Case 1** – 25-year-old female nurse weighing 410 lbs. Dieted to 132 lbs a year later. Returned to 400 lbs faster than she had lost the weight, generally as a result of sleep eating. She was sexually molested from the age of five.
- **Case 2** – 47-year-old female probation officer who was sexually molested by her father. Raped at age 20. At 27 weighed 140 lbs and married the first of four husbands. Her weight then fluctuated widely with marriage and divorce cycles.
- **Case 3** – 55-year-old housewife, molested by family members and neighbours as a child. Became obese during a traumatic marriage. Had episodes of losing and regaining 150 lbs of weight in short periods. Was unaware of her sleep eating.
- **Case 4** – 57-year-old morbidly obese female who had been lean as a child. Continually molested from age 10. Gained 150 lbs through sleep eating.
- **Case 5** – 31-year-old from a troubled family. Became obese in high school. Highly promiscuous from an early age and heavy drug taker. Became celibate and lost 200 lbs. Became promiscuous again, started sleep eating and put on 100 lbs.

Felliti's study shows how there is a relationship between childhood abuse/sexual behaviour, sleep eating and obesity, which can be understood by interpreting such behaviour as an unconscious protective device and anxiety reducer, with eating being seen as a de-stressor and obesity reducing sexual attractiveness.

This explanation may only be true for a few people, as the vast majority of obese people have not suffered such abuse and don't indulge in sleep eating.

Obesity has grown to epidemic proportions, but there's no evidence of a parallel rise in unresolved childhood conflicts, casting doubt on the explanation.

Cases of depression, etc., that are linked to obesity may actually be an effect of obesity rather than a cause.

■ Critical thinking

Although Felliti's study supports the psychodynamic approach as an explanation of obesity, other explanations should also be considered. For example, case study 1 had a mother over 400 lbs and siblings of similar weight, suggesting a genetic component.

Prevention strategies and treatments for obesity

LEARNING OUTCOME

■ Discuss prevention strategies and treatments for overeating and obesity.

(Treatments for overeating and obesity can also be found within the Abnormal psychology chapter, page 92.)

Link to the sociocultural level of analysis

The accessibility and affordability of healthy foods links to the sociocultural level of analysis, as in Western cultures lower socio-economic sub-cultural groupings have only limited access to such food stuffs and could not afford them if they did.

The best way to address obesity is through prevention strategies based on public health interventions and environmental changes. The key sources to prevention are health promotion approaches, legislation and public health policy, increasing opportunities for physical activity, and general health approaches.

Health promotion approaches

This approach is focused on promoting healthy foods and reducing the promotion of unhealthy foods within the media and supermarkets. Linked to this is the provision of role models who promote healthy eating and living.

■ Jeffery (2001) reviewed health education programmes in the USA, finding that these approaches have not been effective, with obesity levels increasing dramatically over the last 15 years. This suggests that legislation, for example changing the price structures of food, may be necessary if the problem is to be addressed.

■ An argument against the use of health education campaigns and the provision of leisure activities as a means of addressing obesity is the high financial costs associated with them. The financial costs of obesity in terms of medical care, reduced work efficiency, higher absenteeism rates, lower psychosocial functioning, etc., are much higher, however. Therefore in terms of a cost–benefit analysis, the financial costs of prevention strategies and public health interventions are easily justifiable.

Legislation and public health policy

This approach focuses on using the tax system to make healthy foods accessible and affordable to all (often such foods are not affordable or accessible to lower socio-economic sub-cultural groupings), and limiting unhealthy foods, such as high calorie and processed foods, through the imposition of a 'fat tax'. Controlling food quality in school and work environments is a key aspect of this.

■ It is estimated that a 20 per cent tax on sugary drinks would cut obesity in the USA by 3.5 per cent and a 17.5 per cent tax on unhealthy foods in Britain could lead to 2,700 fewer deaths per year from heart disease. Some countries have attempted to address obesity with legally enforced food price structures. In 2011 Denmark introduced a tax on food items containing over 2.3 per cent saturated fat (though this was abandoned in

2012, due to the impact on Danish jobs). Hungary also has a junk food tax, and France has a tax on sugary drinks. It is argued, however, that in order to work, such initiatives should be accompanied by subsidies for fruit and vegetables, with additional taxes placed on salt, sugar and refined carbohydrates.

■ Harsher forms of intervention against obesity have been suggested. Westminster Council in London, UK (2013) has proposed cutting benefit payments to obese residents unless they attend fitness classes, the idea being to reward those who take responsibility for their own health. Opponents argue that this would not address the underlying psychological reasons for many people being obese, and therefore could worsen the condition in many individuals.

Increasing opportunities for physical activity

This approach is focused on increasing opportunities for people to participate in physical activity and promoting the reduction of sedentary activities, such as TV watching and playing computer games.

■ DiPietro (1999) studied the relationship between regular exercise and obesity, finding that habitual physical activity played a greater role in stabilizing weight loss and preventing further weight gain, than it did in promoting actual weight loss. This implies that the promotion of physical exercise is more useful as a relapse prevention and maintenance of weight loss strategy.

General health approaches

This approach is focused on improving sleep patterns (inadequate and poor quality sleep are positively correlated with increased vulnerability to obesity) and reducing stress levels (heightened stress levels are also associated with increased vulnerability to obesity, especially through 'comfort eating' where people use food to deal with emotional stress rather than satisfying hunger).

■ Daubenmier and Epel (2011) studied the relationship between stress and obesity, finding that female participants receiving nine weekly sessions of training in stress reduction techniques and mindful eating techniques (recognizing bodily sensations associated with eating) reported greater reductions in deep abdominal fat than those not receiving training in stress reduction. As deep abdominal fat is associated with an elevated risk of developing heart disease and Type 2 diabetes, this suggests that stress reduction and mindful eating techniques are a cost-effective way of addressing obesity.

■ Knutson (2011) found that short and poor quality sleep is linked to obesity, as it impacts on appetite regulation, glucose metabolism and blood pressure. Signals from the brain controlling regulation of appetite were affected by sleep restriction, with inadequate sleep affecting secretion of the signal hormones ghrelin (which increases appetite to indicate when the body is sated). This led to increased food intake without the compensating energy expenditure. This therefore suggests that the establishment of better sleep patterns would be an effective means of addressing obesity, though the reasons for maladaptive sleep patterns (such as heightened stress levels) would first need to be addressed.

Practical applications

A major problem with strategies and therapies to address obesity is that of regaining weight after initial weight losses. This emphasises the need for relapse prevention training and/ or post-treatment contact directed at maintenance of weight loss through healthy living practices.

SECTION SUMMARY
- Obesity is a growing problem across the world.
- There is some evidence linking obesity to faulty functioning of the ventromedial hypothalamus and the dorsal striatum brain areas.
- Obesity is also linked with hormones, including leptin, grehlin, cortisol and insulin.
- Although hormone changes are linked with obesity, cause and effect is not clear.
- The psychodynamic explanation sees obesity as arising from unresolved conflicts, such as emotional deprivation in the oral stage.
- There is some case study support for this claim, but the rapid increase in obesity means it is unlikely to be explained entirely by abuse or deprivation.
- Health promotion and public health legislation are two key measures in the prevention of obesity.
- Legislative measures have been more effective than health promotion in many European countries.
- General measures to improve health, including the reduction of stress, have been effective in reducing obesity.

Substance abuse

LEARNING OUTCOME
- Explain factors related to the development of substance abuse or addictive behaviour.

What is substance abuse?

Substance abuse refers to a specific pattern of usage of a psychoactive substance that acts on brain chemistry. Two common psychoactive substances are nicotine and alcohol:

- **Nicotine** is found in tobacco, which is generally smoked but can also be taken orally (chewed) or nasally. Nicotine produces immediate effects, including raised heart rate, increased attention/reaction time and suppressed appetite. Nicotine is highly addictive.
- **Alcohol** acts as a stimulant at low doses leading to relaxed and uninhibited behaviour. At higher doses, however, it is a central nervous system depressant, producing impairments in movement and cognitive functions and having a sedative effect.

The *Diagnostic and Statistical Manual of Mental Disorders* of the American Psychiatric Association (DSM-IV) does not use the term addiction but refers to 'substance dependence'. In order for a diagnosis of substance dependence to be made, an individual should show three or more of the following symptoms within a 12-month period:

Table 6.2 Diagnostic criteria for a diagnosis of substance dependence (source: American Psychiatric Association, 2000)

BIOLOGICAL	BEHAVIOURAL	SOCIAL
Tolerance – over time, progressively larger amounts are needed to achieve the same effect.	Tolerance leads to increasing amounts of the substance being used.	Considerable time spent obtaining, using or recovering from use of the substance.
Withdrawal symptoms – unpleasant physiological and emotional responses when the substance is not used.	Withdrawal symptoms lead to unsuccessful attempts to cut down.	Social, occupational or recreational activities are given up (e.g. being too hungover to turn up for work).
Continuation of use despite recognition that it causes physical or psychological problems.		

These symptoms can be illustrated in relation to alcohol use. For many people, alcohol consumption remains under personal control and is unproblematic. However, some people increase their consumption in response to tolerance and develop dependency, however.

An addictive behaviour refers to a repetitive habit that increases the risk of personal and social problems. Addictive behaviours share many of the above symptoms of substance dependency. Pathological gambling is characterized by tolerance and the need to gamble with larger amounts of money, loss of control, along with repeated attempts to cut back, and withdrawal symptoms such as restlessness and irritability (American Psychiatric Association, 2000).

Biological factors in substance abuse

Psychoactive drugs – act on brain chemistry.

Psychoactive substances alter the functioning of neurotransmitters and neural pathways in the brain. As you read in Chapter 1 (*see page 5*), communication in the brain and central nervous system takes place through specialized nerve cells called neurons. Communication is electrical within neurons via action potentials, and chemical between neurons via neurotransmitters. An action potential in one neuron triggers the release of neurotransmitters, which seep across the synaptic cleft. Some of the neurotransmitters bind to specialized receptors on the post-synaptic neuron, with the remainder being metabolized by enzymes and excreted, or taken up by transporters and re-absorbed back into the pre-synaptic neuron. The most important group of neurotransmitters in relation to mood states and substance abuse is the monoamines: dopamine, serotonin and noradrenaline. Psychoactive drugs can affect any of the stages of neurotransmission.

Monoamines – a group of neurotransmitters strongly associated with motivational processes.

Cocaine works rapidly to block the re-uptake of dopamine, making much more available at the synapse. This forms the basis of the characteristic euphoric 'high' experienced by cocaine users. An effect of preventing re-uptake is that the synapse cannot synthesize more dopamine sufficiently quickly, however, which leads to a depletion. This is the physiological basis of the 'crash' or dysphoria that follows cocaine use (Toates, 2007).

Reward pathway – a neural pathway that is activated by dopamine and implicated in many addictive behaviours.

The mesolimbic dopamine system

The mesolimbic dopamine pathway (commonly referred to as the reward pathway) is a nerve pathway activated by neurotransmitters, notably dopamine. The pathway begins in the Ventral Tegmental Area (VTA) and continues through the nucleus accumbens in the limbic system, ending in the prefrontal cortex (Green, 1995). Under normal conditions neurons are spontaneously active, releasing a small amount of dopamine into the synaptic cleft in response to pleasurable activities. Some illegal drugs release between two and ten times the normal amounts of dopamine, making them highly enjoyable (Di Chiara & Imperato, 1988) and producing a greatly 'amplified' message. A useful analogy of this effect would be the difference between someone whispering in your ear or shouting into a microphone.

Alcohol and nicotine increase dopamine levels in the reward pathway (Altman *et al.*, 1996). When drugs are smoked or injected, the effect occurs almost immediately and they last longer than those produced by natural rewards, such as eating and sex. The reward pathway can also be activated during other addictive activities, such as gambling (Moss & Dyer, 2010).

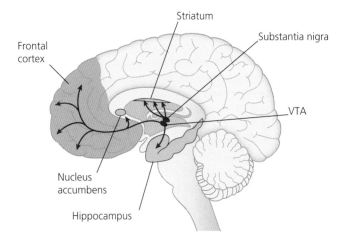

Figure 6.5 Drugs of abuse target the brain's pleasure centre.

Neuroadaptation

Many brain and bodily functions, such as body temperature, operate on a homeostatic principle, fluctuating within small amounts. When psychoactive substances are used, these disrupt the functioning of the brain, which automatically tries to correct this and restore homeostasis. When dopamine levels are increased by a psychoactive drug, the brain attempts to restore the balance by reducing the normal production of dopamine or by reducing the number of receptors that can receive dopamine. If a drug (e.g. nicotine) is used frequently, the brain adapts to be in balance when the drug is present. If the drug is discontinued (i.e. the smoker goes without a cigarette or the alcoholic without a drink), the adaptation is no longer needed and is experienced as withdrawal symptoms. These are extremely unpleasant and are relieved immediately by taking the substance.

Genes and addiction: the evidence

Addictions tend to run in families but it is difficult to tease out the relative contribution of genetics (nature) from upbringing (nurture) as most children share genes and environment with their biological parents. The study of pairs of monozygotic (MZ) and dizygotic (DZ) twins offers one possibility. MZ twins are genetically identical whereas DZ twins share 50 per cent of their genes and are no more alike than any pair of siblings. If genes play a role in addictive behaviours then MZ twins should resemble each other more closely in substance use than DZ twins.

The Minnesota Twin Study (McGue *et al.*, 1992) began with the aim of looking at a range of behaviours and psychological traits in relation to heredity. The researchers interviewed a large sample of MZ and DZ male twins about their alcohol use. The resultant data was used to calculate a concordance rate (CR): the extent to which a pair of twins shared the same level of alcohol use. The research team found that the CR in identical (MZ) twins was 77 per cent and in DZ twins 54 per cent, indicating that MZ twins appeared to be much more similar in their level of drinking. The difference in concordance rates implies that heredity has an influence on drinking behaviour.

There have been various attempts to identify the specific genes that play a role in addiction, although understanding of how these contribute to behaviour is still at a relatively early stage. Most of these genes influence dopamine and/or the reward pathway in some way. One line of interest has focused on the association between sensation/novelty-seeking and substance abuse. There is a significant relationship between some types of substance abuse and a gene known as DRD4 which is also associated with novelty-seeking behaviour. This gene is found within samples of heroin users and smokers with nicotine dependence, but non-significant results are yielded from samples of alcohol abusers (Lusher *et al.*, 2001).

RASGRF-2 is a gene that appears to regulate how rewarding alcohol is. Studies with laboratory mice have indicated that those bred with a particular version of the gene are more likely to seek out alcohol. The Imagen study is a multi-centre European research project investigating mental health and risk-taking behaviour in teenagers. The researchers are interested in the relative roles played by biological factors (e.g. brain activity patterns and genetic characteristics) and cognitive factors in risk-taking behaviours and mental health. Two-thousand 14-year-old children, their parents and research teams from England, France, Ireland and Germany are involved in this ongoing project. The researchers are particularly interested to see if variations of gene RASGRF-2 might play a role in responses to alcohol in teenagers.

Research methods include self-report questionnaires, behavioural assessment and interviews. Biological measures have included blood sampling for genetic analyses and neuroimaging of the brain. Initial investigations have shown that teenage boys with a particular variation of the RASGRF-2 gene drink more often than boys who do not have the gene variation. Brain scans carried out on the boys have also shown that those who carry the gene variation are more likely to show increased activity in the 'reward pathway'. These findings imply that an individual's genetic makeup is connected to brain activity and the sort of thrill-seeking behaviour that can lead to drug or alcohol addiction.

Practical applications

The Imagen study implies that gene variations might be used to predict whether an individual is likely to become a heavy drinker, and it may be possible to offer genetic tests at some point in the future to predict which people are more at risk of alcohol abuse. These findings may also lead to the development of new drugs to block the 'reward effect' some people get from drinking.

In relation to nicotine, Lerman *et al.* (1999) identified a gene called SLC6A3-9, which is sometimes referred to as the dopamine transporter gene (DAT). SLC6A3-9 appears to reduce dopamine transmission, meaning that smoking doesn't produce as much of a 'buzz'. Lerman found that DAT appeared to provide a protective effect against nicotine addiction, making those with the gene less likely to take up smoking. Carriers of the gene who started smoking were likely to have taken up the behaviour late in life. In support, Sabol *et al.* (1999) identified that smokers who carried the DAT gene found it easier to give up than smokers who do not have the gene. Replications by Vandenberg *et al.* (2002), however, on the role of the DAT gene in smoking, failed to support Lerman and Sabot's findings. Another gene of interest is DRD2 (known as the D2 dopamine receptor gene). In a study by Erblich *et al.* (2005), smokers were exposed to smoking cues such as an ashtray or a glass of wine, and asked to indicate the strength of their cravings. Smokers carrying the DRD2 (dopamine receptor gene) reported stronger cravings than non-carriers.

Psychological factors in substance abuse: reward and reinforcement

Psychoactive substances are used because they produce pleasurable effects and are highly rewarding. Behaviourist psychologist B.F. Skinner (1938) demonstrated how animals in a tightly controlled environment called a Skinner box would repeat behaviours that produced positive outcomes (e.g. the delivery of a food pellet). Skinner termed this idea 'positive reinforcement'. Skinner's work explains why experiences with nicotine and alcohol are likely to be repeated:

- Nicotine produces enjoyable physiological responses such as increased heart rate, reaction time and attention (often thought of as a 'buzz').

- Alcohol in low doses produces a relaxed state with reduced inhibitions. This is especially rewarding for people who are anxious in social situations.

- Smoking and drinking can also lead to psychological rewards such as acceptance by peer group and perceived status in young people.

These are all examples of positive reinforcement. Skinner also noted how animals would repeat behaviours that terminated unpleasant environmental stimuli, such as loud noises. This is the idea of negative reinforcement. As we have noted above, nicotine is highly addictive and regular smokers experience unpleasant withdrawal symptoms when they go without cigarettes, including

Figure 6.6 Small amounts of alcohol help to lower inhibitions in people who are anxious in social situations.

headaches, tremors, anxiety and general irritability. Similarly, dependence on alcohol leads to highly unpleasant withdrawal symptoms, including over-activity of the central nervous system. This is characterized by nausea, vomiting, tremors of the hands and, in some cases, hallucinations. These unpleasant symptoms are examples of negative reinforcement that are removed by the administration of nicotine/alcohol – further reinforcing the habit.

Sociocultural factors in substance abuse

The sociocultural level of analysis focuses on the importance of social and cultural norms in the use of alcohol and tobacco. Social norms provide clear rules about the use of cigarettes and alcohol, for example which drinks or cigarette brands are appropriate for men and women. In post-war Britain, 84 per cent of men smoked (Action on Smoking and Health), demonstrating how smoking was 'normal' for men. The social climate in the late twentieth century became less tolerant of smoking and legislation was introduced in many European countries banning smoking in public places and workplaces. Legislation of this nature has produced impressive results in reducing smoking rates, which we will consider later.

The extent to which alcohol is tolerated, regulated or banned completely (prohibition) varies in different places and times. In the USA, the manufacture and sale of alcohol was prohibited from 1920 to 1933, and during this time drinking was driven underground to 'speakeasies'. Most countries set a minimum age for the purchase and consumption of cigarettes and alcohol (for example, 21 in the USA) in acknowledgement of their addictive properties.

Bandura's social learning theory (SLT) argues that behaviours can be learnt through observation and imitation of role models. According to this approach, exposure to role models who smoke or drink plays an important role in experimentation with cigarettes and alcohol. Research has demonstrated the important influence of peers, parents and celebrities in the initiation of smoking.

Evidence and evaluation

■ Keyes *et al.* (2012) demonstrated how social norms influence prevalence of drinking and attitudes to alcohol. Using data from 32 national surveys of American high school students between 1976 and 2007, with a total of almost 1 million participants, Keyes investigated whether adolescents in time periods characterized by restrictive social norms were less likely to drink compared to those growing up in more favourable eras. Participants were asked to report on the frequency of their drinking over the previous year, along with any incidences of binge drinking (defined as five or more drinks in one sitting). Students who grew up in cohorts when social norms were broadly unfavourable to alcohol were less likely to drink than those who matured in cohorts in more permissive social periods.

■ Children have an increased risk of starting smoking if their friends and/or siblings smoke, with friends being most influential. Bricker *et al.* (2006) examined the relative influences of peers and parents on teenage smoking, using a large sample of 4,744 adolescents. They paid particular attention to key smoking transitions: trying cigarettes, becoming a regular smoker and a daily smoker. Peer influence played the most important role in the initiation of smoking, and for most teenagers first experiments with cigarettes took place amongst their peers. Having friends who smoked was a stronger predictor that a teenager would start smoking than having one or two smoking parents. The transition to daily smoking was more likely to be made if one or both parents smoked, demonstrating how smoking at home is more likely to be accepted by parents who are smokers.

■ Waylen *et al.* (2011) examined the link between exposure to popular films released between 2001 and 2005 (*Spider-Man*, *Bridget Jones's Diary* and *The Matrix*) and smoking in young people. Waylen found that adolescents who saw the most films depicting smoking were significantly more likely to have tried cigarettes than those exposed to fewer smoking role models in films. Even when the impact of parental smoking was removed, teenagers exposed to smoking models were still 32 per cent more likely to have tried cigarettes.

■ These studies rely on correlational evidence, which needs to be interpreted with caution: adolescents may encourage their friends to smoke/drink, or young people may select friends with similar habits. Cruz *et al.* (2012) suggest that both of these play a role.

Reducing addictive behaviour

LEARNING OUTCOME
■ Examine prevention strategies and treatments for substance abuse and addictive behaviour.

Preventing smoking

The most effective way to prevent addiction to nicotine is to dissuade young people from starting to smoke. The Framework Convention Alliance (FCA) is an international organization that aims to tackle the harm caused by tobacco. A recent agreement by the FCA calls for the following measures to be taken internationally to dissuade young people from starting smoking and to convince existing smokers to quit:

■ Comprehensive banning of tobacco advertising, promotion and sponsorship.
■ Providing education about the harmful nature of nicotine, including health warnings and graphic images on cigarette packets.
■ Banning the use of misleading terms on cigarette packets, such as 'light' or 'low-tar'.
■ Removing brand loyalty through the use of plain packaging for cigarettes.

The World Health Organization argues that the most effective way of reducing smoking is to use hard-hitting anti-tobacco adverts along with graphic images on cigarette packets. For maximum effectiveness, warnings should be provided in the local language and images should cover at least half of the front and back of the packet (WHO, 2012). Many Western countries now use legislation in the form of workplace smoking bans, along with bans on smoking in public places. These measures protect non-smokers from secondary smoke and can also reduce smoking in existing smokers.

Evidence and evaluation

■ Studies carried out after the implementation of package warnings in Brazil, Canada, Singapore and Thailand have consistently shown that pictorial warnings significantly increase awareness of the harm caused by cigarettes.
■ Reducing brand loyalty can also help to remove the appeal of smoking. In a naturalistic study in the UK, normal smoking habits were monitored in a large sample of smokers for two weeks, then the usual brand of cigarettes was transferred to plain brown packs for a further two weeks. The researchers found that the use of plain packaging increased negative perceptions about the brand and about smoking in general. It also led to avoidant behaviour such as hiding or covering the pack, smoking less around others, and thinking about quitting. Interviews with a sub-sample of participants found that almost half reported that the use of plain packs had increased avoidant behaviour or reduced consumption or led to thoughts about quitting (Moodie *et al.*, 2011). The use

of plain packaging was adopted in Australia in 2011 despite strong opposition from the tobacco industry.

■ Fichtenberg and Glantz (2002) carried out a review of 26 research studies examining the effects of smoke-free workplaces in the USA, Australia, Canada and Germany, prior to mandatory workplace bans. Researchers measured the daily cigarette consumption per smoker and smoking prevalence (percentage of the sample population who smoked). Smoke-free workplaces led to reductions of around three cigarettes smoked per day, and also reduced the prevalence of smoking, suggesting smoke-free workplaces provide motivation to quit.

■ Jones (2011) suggest that the introduction of smoking bans in Scotland and England has reduced the level of cigarette consumption in specific groups, including heavy male smokers, moderate and heavy female smokers and young people, but had had no impact on overall smoking prevalence (i.e. the number of smokers).

Figure 6.7 Although smoking bans have reduced cigarette smoking in specific groups, there has been little impact in reducing the number of smokers.

Cross-cultural focus

The above anti-smoking measures are largely implemented by affluent Western countries. Currently, around 10 per cent of the world's population are protected by comprehensive smoke-free laws (WHO, 2012). Just under half of countries, representing about 42 per cent of the world's population, use anti-tobacco adverts and graphic images on packets. None of these are low-income countries where smoking rates are the highest. Fewer than 20 countries, representing about 6 per cent of the world's population, have comprehensive national bans on tobacco advertising, promotion and sponsorship. The World Health Organization estimates that a comprehensive advertising ban could decrease tobacco consumption by about 7 per cent in Western countries, with low income countries experiencing a decrease of up to 16 per cent (WHO, 2012).

Treating nicotine dependency

Agonist drugs
– increase the action of neurotransmitters, whereas antagonists (blockers) reduce the action of neurotransmitters, for example by occupying receptors on the post-synaptic neuron.

Nicotine is a highly addictive substance and around 80 per cent of current smokers have tried to give up at least once. The most common biological treatment is nicotine replacement therapy (NRT) in which nicotine substitutes (e.g. patches, chewing gum, electronic cigarettes) are used as replacements, making this an agonist approach. Patches provide a slow release of nicotine that combats the unpleasant withdrawal symptoms and the cravings that characterize the addiction. Peak concentrations in the brain are generally lower than through cigarettes. The process is planned, with decreasing levels of nicotine provided in a phased process of withdrawal. In the UK, the majority of people who contact the National Health Service about quitting smoking receive NRT, and around half are still non-smokers at four weeks. Many smokers claim that they miss the action associated with smoking. Electronic cigarettes allow the administration of nicotine with none of the harmful toxins in tobacco. It remains to be seen how effective this approach will be in comparison with nicotine patches. Healthcare services supporting cessation are available in only 19 countries, however, representing just 14 per cent of the world's population, and there is no cessation assistance in 28 per cent of low-income countries (WHO, 2012).

While nicotine is clearly a biological addiction, many smokers miss the habits and rituals associated with smoking, which makes behavioural approaches to cessation useful as well. Relapse is often related to exposure to smoking cues (after a meal or when drinking alcohol). Two ways of preventing relapse are:

- **Avoiding cues**.
- **Building resistance to cues** through cue exposure therapy.

The latter approach is similar to systematic desensitization, aiming to teach alternative responses to smoking cues and thus extinguishing the link between the cues and smoking. Ex-smokers are encouraged to discuss the 'danger zones' that could lead to relapse and to develop coping strategies to deal with them.

Lando (1977) put forward an integrated model that combines insights from classical and operant conditioning. The process of quitting takes place in stages:

- A rapid smoking session lasting 25 minutes in which smokers are encouraged to inhale every 5 seconds (much more frequently than normal). Rapid smoking floods the synapses with huge amounts of nicotine, which leads to nausea rather than the usual pleasure.
- A one-week period when the normal smoking rate is doubled. The rationale behind this stage is to replace the pleasant feelings associated with smoking with nausea characterized by too much nicotine.
- This is followed by rapid and abrupt withdrawal. The ex-smoker is encouraged to identify problems and to develop strategies to combat these. Operant conditioning is used to provide positive reinforcement for successful abstinence (e.g. spending the money saved on a treat) and to punish lapses (donating money to cancer charities after each lapse). This approach has been seen to be highly successful, with a 76 per cent abstinence rate at 6 months.

SECTION SUMMARY

- Substance abuse is characterized by tolerance and withdrawal symptoms.
- Psychoactive substances increase the amount of dopamine in the reward pathway.
- Neuroadaptation occurs as the body tries to restore homeostasis.
- Genetic factors play a role in addictions. Several genes have been identified at this stage.
- Psychoactive substances provide positive reinforcement. Withdrawal symptoms are highly unpleasant and an example of negative reinforcement.
- Sociocultural factors, including social norms and role models, play an important role in the initiation of smoking and alcohol use.
- Key approaches to prevention include graphic adverts and plain packaging that reduces brand loyalty. Workplace smoking bans also reduce consumption.
- The most common treatment is nicotine replacement therapy. This needs to be combined with cue exposure for maximum effectiveness.

Health promotion

LEARNING OUTCOME

- Examine models and theories of health promotion (for example, health belief model, stages of change model).

Health promotion action aims to enable people to increase their control over and improve their health, and ultimately to lead to improved population and individual health outcomes (WHO, 1986). Health promotion refers to a wide range of activities undertaken by governments, health bodies and charities with the general aim of improving health and reducing 'risky' behaviours. Strategies may be targeted either at specific groups (for example, gay men or pregnant women) or at the population as a whole. Current programmes in many Westernized countries are focused on:

■ Reducing rates of obesity through exercise and healthy eating.
■ Reducing smoking and other drug use.
■ Reducing rates of contraction of HIV/Aids through changes to sexual behaviours.

In this section of the chapter we will begin by examining two influential models of health promotion: the **stages of change model** and the **health belief model** (HBM). The stages of change model focuses on how change occurs, conceptualizing this as a staged process. In contrast, the HBM focuses on identifying the variables that predict if and when behaviour change will take place (i.e. why change occurs), focusing on the role played by cognitive factors in health behaviours. We will then go on to consider the challenges and difficulties associated with measuring the outcomes of health promotion strategies.

The stages of change model (DiClemente and Prochoska, 1982)

The stages of change model is also known as the trans-theoretical model. The model describes the process of making health-related changes, arguing that this takes place in five stages:

■ **Pre-contemplation** – this stage occurs before the individual begins to think about their health-related behaviour.
■ **Contemplation** – the individual has thought about changing their behaviour, and intends to do so at some point in the future, for example giving up smoking, losing weight or reducing alcohol intake in the New Year.
■ **Preparation** – this stage involves making active plans, for example arranging to attend a smoking cessation support group or joining a gym.
■ **Action** – putting the plans into action.
■ **Maintenance** – the individual has now changed their behaviour but effort is still needed not to 'slip back' to previous habits.

The stages are not linear but are seen as dynamic, with some people moving backwards and forwards between contemplation, preparation and action. A smoker may make plans to quit and put this into action, but may relapse and return to the contemplation stage. This is sometimes referred to as the 'revolving door phenomenon'.

Key study

DiClemente *et al.* (1991)

DiClemente *et al.* (1991) studied a large sample of 1,466 smokers who had enrolled on smoking cessation programmes in Texas and Rhode Island, USA. Most were female, long-term smokers who consumed an average of around 30 cigarettes a day. The research team assessed the stage of each participant according to the stages of change model. At the start of the study, 166 were in the pre-contemplation stage, 794 in the contemplation and 506 in the preparation stages. The participants were followed up 1 and 6 months later and asked to complete a series of measures, including:

■ The Fagerstrom tolerance questionnaire, which measures tolerance to nicotine.
■ A self-efficacy scale measuring how confident they felt about quitting.
■ A perceived stress scale.
■ The smoking decisional balance scale (Velicer *et al.*, 1985), which measures the perceived pros and cons of smoking.

The research team found that participants in the three stages differed significantly in their scores on the scales. Those who were in the preparation stage at the start of the study smoked less, had higher self-efficacy scores and felt more confident they would quit than those in the pre-contemplation stage. They also rated the advantages of smoking as less important and the disadvantages as more important. This study suggests that the stages of change model possesses concurrent validity.

Evidence and evaluation

- The stages of change model has been praised for treating behaviour change as an ongoing process rather than an event. The model has been applied to many kinds of behaviour change, including smoking and alcohol use, exercise and health screening. The model provides a useful framework for health practitioners to tailor support and interventions for those wishing to change their behaviour. For instance, the support provided for a smoker in the contemplation stage would be different to a smoker in the preparation stage with clear plans to quit (Ogden, 2007).
- Cropley *et al.* (2003) found that people who were contemplating starting an exercise programme could identity more disadvantages (cons) than advantages (pros) when compared to a group who had started a programme and were classed as maintainers.
- While many smokers go through the process of preparing to quit as the model suggests, about half of all attempts to quit are made without planning. West (2006) carried out a large-scale survey of smokers who had tried to kick the habit, with some succeeding ($n=996$) and others being less successful ($n=918$). West found that around half of the decisions were made on the spur of the moment, without planning. Contrary to the stages of change model, these attempts to quit lasted on average about six months, making them just as successful as planned attempts (West & Shoal, 2006). West (2006) argues that the model over-emphasizes the importance of conscious decision-making in behaviour change.
- A major limitation of the stages of change model is its descriptive nature. It provides little explanation of why someone might move stages from contemplation to action. Some studies (e.g. Armitage & Arden, 2008) have indicated that there are particular difficulties in explaining the transition from preparation (thinking) to action (doing), and revisers suggest that the model could be simplified to two phases: a motivational phase that ends in the formation of a behavioural intent to change, and a volitional phase in which motivation is translated into action.
- The issue of motivation is tackled more satisfactorily by the health belief model, which argues that cognitions play an important role in driving health-related changes.

The health belief model (Becker & Rosenstock, 1984)

The health belief model (HBM) considers the underlying motivations (i.e. the 'whys') of behaviour change, with a particular focus on cognitive factors. We will begin by considering the original version of the model using an example: an overweight and sedentary man in his forties has been advised by his doctor to lose weight in order to reduce his risk of heart disease. It is recommended he do this through a combination of increasing activity and reducing calorie intake.

The HBM proposes that two types of health belief (or appraisal) influence whether or not our hypothetical patient complies with medical advice and changes his behaviour:

- **Evaluation of the threat** in relation to perceived susceptibility (how likely is a heart attack to happen?) and perceived severity (how bad would this be?). If susceptibility and severity are perceived as high, this will provide more impetus to change than if the threat is perceived as low.
- **Cost–benefit analysis of the change.** What would be the difficulties associated with making the change? What advantages would there be? In the above example, difficulties could include time taken up by exercise in a busy working life.

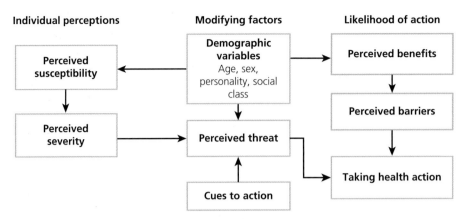

Figure 6.8 The health belief model (Becker & Rosenstock, 1984)

The original model has been extended to include other concepts:

- Bandura's idea of self-efficacy (Bandura, 1977), which refers to the confidence a person has in their ability to pursue a behaviour.
- The importance of environmental cues (e.g. media campaigns) in alerting people to health threats.
- A measure of health motivation (Becker *et al.*, 1977).

Key study

Abraham *et al.* (1992)

The HBM was tested extensively in the 1980s and 90s when a major health campaign focused on reducing the risk of HIV/Aids through safe sex practices. Abraham *et al.* (1992) assessed how the four variables in the HBM (susceptibility, severity, costs and benefits) influenced the health intentions of more than 350 sexually active Scottish teenagers. The study was carried out in and around Dundee, which had a high rate of HIV infection at the time. The researchers were partially interested in how well the HBM predicted agreement with health education campaigns aimed at encouraging safe sex practices.

Postal questionnaires were used to assess:

- Perceived threat of HIV (including the perceived likelihood of personally contracting the illness and the perceived severity of HIV).
- Intentions to carry and use condoms in future sexual encounters.
- Impact of environmental cues (such as memory of the 'Don't Die of Ignorance' leaflet).

Results indicated that the majority of teenagers agreed with 'safe sex' messages and reported an intention to carry condoms if they thought they might have sex with a new partner. They also agreed with the need to ask potential partners about their sexual history. Perceived barriers to condom use (for example, awkwardness of bringing up the subject, beliefs about reduction of pleasure) were also found to be important predictors of intentions. Health beliefs were moderately but not strongly associated with behaviour.

Evidence and evaluation

- The HBM acknowledges the importance of cognitive factors in health behaviour, combining these with 'social, economic and environmental factors' (NICE, 2007, p.3).
- Many of the studies undertaken with regard to the HBM are health behaviour studies or survey research focused on smoking, drug and alcohol use in college students.

- Examples of research into the HBM include Minugh *et al.* (1998), who used the HBM to study the relationship between health beliefs and alcohol consumption, and Hingson *et al.* (1990), who examined beliefs about Aids, use of alcohol and drugs, and unprotected sex in adolescents.
- The HBM has also been shown to predict attendance at health screening of various kinds (e.g. cervical and breast cancer screening). Murray and McMillan (1993) demonstrated how self-efficacy and barriers appear to be the most powerful predictors of screening attendance in a sample of more than 1,500 women in Ireland.
- The National Institute for Health and Clinical Excellence (NICE, 2007) argues that the HBM has a relatively weak predictive power in relation to many areas of health-related behaviours. One reason for this is poor definition of key variables. HBM researchers have employed a variety of measures in operationalizing perceived vulnerability and severity – which makes it difficult to compare findings of different studies.
- Yarbrough and Braden (2001) conducted a review of the health belief model in relation to predicting breast cancer screening behaviours and concluded that the application of the model was inconsistent. At best it 'explained 47 per cent of the observed variance in screening behaviour when socio-economic status was included. Otherwise predictive power was low, ranging from 15 per cent to 27 per cent' (NICE, 2007). Some critics have gone so far as to argue that the HBM is a list of variables and not a theory with clearly specified relationships between its core components.

Measuring the effectiveness of health promotion strategies

LEARNING OUTCOME
- Discuss the effectiveness of health promotion strategies (for example, measurement of outcomes, cultural blindness, and cognitive dissonance).

Evidence-based health promotion – involves integration of research evidence into the planning and implementation of health promotion strategies.

In most countries, the general climate is one of cost-cutting along with a need to demonstrate clear health gains from health promotion strategies. Health promotion programmes need to demonstrate that they are effective (i.e. that they work) and are also efficient (i.e. that they are effective in relation to costs). The demand is for evidence-based practice in all areas, including health promotion.

What to measure and how to measure it?

Establishing what to assess, and when and how to assess it, is an important part of planning health promotion campaigns. Health promotion strategies can be targeted at specific groups of people or at settings such as workplaces. Many programmes focus on increasing knowledge and awareness of risks. Effective strategies lead to improvements, such as a healthier lifestyle, decreased disability and increased life expectancy. These changes are referred to as **outcomes**. However, there may be a considerable time lag between a health education programme and behaviour change – which makes it difficult to directly attribute longer-term health outcomes to a specific health promotion programme. For this reason, researchers prefer to focus on more immediate changes in individuals. These changes are called **impacts**. Impacts for individuals could include improved health knowledge, skills and motivation, and changes to behaviour. In relation to settings, impacts could include reductions in workplace health risks and improvements to the physical environment to protect health.

An example of a clearly measureable impact could be, 'An increase in knowledge and awareness about risk and protective factors involved in HIV transmission in 70 per cent of the target population of young gay men'.

Both quantitative and qualitative methods can be used in impact evaluation:

■ **Qualitative methods** include in-depth interviews and focus groups.
  • **Focus groups** consist of semi-structured discussions with 8–12 participants, led by a facilitator who follows an outline and manages group dynamics. Proceedings are typically recorded. Focus groups provide in-depth information, and are relatively inexpensive to implement.
  • **In-depth interviews** can be carried out on the telephone or face-to-face. They can be used to investigate sensitive issues with a small number of people as they provide a more confidential environment than focus groups.
■ **Quantitative methods** include using surveys to measure attitudes or knowledge before and after the intervention. These are more suitable for larger populations as data can be collected relatively quickly. They are more effective in measuring health knowledge than behavioural intentions.

Outcomes research in health promotion

Randomized controlled trials – the comparison of groups who have been randomly allocated to programme or non-programme conditions.

In order to establish the impact of a health promotion programme, information about relevant changes in populations, individuals or their environments needs to be collected in a way that allows such changes to be attributed to the programme (i.e. cause and effect should be established). The standard method of establishing the effectiveness of any treatment or programme involves comparing one group of people who participate in the programme with another group who don't participate (the control group). It is important that the two groups are comparable on all other factors that may influence the outcome. The best way to ensure this is to use random allocation to groups (i.e. participation and non-participation). This design is called a randomized controlled trial (RCT) and is widely used in assessing effectiveness of therapeutic interventions.

However, RCTs are not feasible for many health promotion programmes. It would be unethical to randomly allocate people to groups in an HIV prevention programme or to have a control group of any kind at all. Random allocation to groups may also be impractical. An alternative approach where no control group is possible is the use of a pre-programme measurement to provide a baseline against which the post-programme results can be compared. Pre-programme measurements using quantitative methods have been used extensively (*see Table 6.3*).

Pre-programme measurements – measurement-of-health measure as a baseline before an intervention.

Table 6.3 Pre-programme measures used in health promotion campaigns (source: UK Health Development Agency, 1997)

FOCUS OF CAMPAIGN	MEASURE	OUTCOME	TIME PERIOD
Alcohol awareness	Knowledge of units in popular drinks.	Up 300 per cent.	1989–94
HIV awareness	Belief that condoms protect against HIV.	Increase from 66 per cent to 95 per cent.	1986–97
Use of folic acid in pregnancy	Sales of folic acid supplements and prescription rates (behaviour).	Up 50 per cent.	Eight-month period.
Vaccination against meningitis	Awareness of the Hib vaccine.	Increase from 5 per cent to 89 per cent.	1992–93

The absence of an appropriate control group or pre-programme measurement means that rival explanations for any changes cannot be ruled out and this needs to be acknowledged when interpreting the evaluation data.

SECTION SUMMARY

- The stages of change model sees the process of making health-related changes as one of stages.
- This model is largely descriptive and does not explain why people move from contemplation to action.
- The health belief model focuses on the importance of beliefs and cognitions in motivation to change.
- This approach predicts attendance at screening but has been criticized for its lack of operationalization.
- Health promotion programmes need to be cost effective and efficient.
- Impact evaluation is used to assess changes after a health promotion programme.
- Randomized controlled trials are relatively rare for ethical reasons. Instead, pre-programme measurements are commonly used to provide a baseline for comparison.

7 Psychology of human relationships

Introduction

In this section of the course we are going to consider what social psychology can tell us about relationships. Relationships come in many different forms, from long-term relationships with family members and friends, to short-term encounters. Some are characterized by mutual attraction and liking, whereas others involve feelings of antipathy or dislike, which may escalate into conflict. We are social animals, and we depend on others for our well-being so it is not surprising that conflict can threaten individual survival and the survival of social groups.

We will begin by examining the topic of social responsibility. Every day we are confronted with situations in which others require help. Appeals can come from people we know, from charity collectors or in response to natural disasters such as the Pacific Tsunami in 2004. What factors influence how we respond to these requests, offering help on some occasions but not on others?

In the second section of the chapter we will consider what psychologists have discovered about close relationships between partners. We will examine why we are attracted to some people more than others and the important roles played by communication in the regulation and breakdown of close relationships. We will also examine how relationships are organized and regulated within different cultures.

Some relationships are characterized by mutual dislike or conflict. The final section of the chapter will consider why some people behave violently towards others and how violence can be reduced. Acts of violence take place on different scales, occurring between individuals and between ethnic or religious groups, sometimes accounting for thousands of deaths. The last section of the chapter will consider the long- and short-term impacts of exposure to violence on our lives. The last 20 years have seen the rapid development of digital media and today most people have access to viewing violence through films, 24-hour news channels and computer games.

Throughout this chapter, we will examine how insights from social psychology can help us to tackle social problems. By understanding the complexities of relationships, we can consider how to improve communication, promote socially responsible behaviour and reduce violence between individuals and groups. The chapter will cover the following general learning aims:

LEARNING OUTCOMES
- To what extent do biological, cognitive and sociocultural factors influence human relationships?
- Evaluate psychological research (that is, theories and/or studies) relevant to the study of human relationships.

Social responsibility

Imagine the following scenario: You are watching the television in your flat late one night when you hear shouting outside. You look out of the window and see a man and woman apparently having an argument. Would you do anything?

In 1964, a young woman named Kitty Genovese was raped and murdered in a parking lot in Queens, New York by a man named Winston Moseley. Although 38 people in a nearby apartment block later reported hearing the incident, no one offered help to the victim. The murder of Kitty Genovese sparked an interest in the factors that lead people to help others who are in need and the factors that influence them to stand by (the origin of the term 'bystanderism'). In this section of the chapter, we are going to consider how psychology can help us to understand both of these kinds of responses to an emergency.

Altruism and pro-social behaviour

LEARNING OUTCOMES
■ Explain the difference between altruism and pro-social behaviour.
■ Contrast two theories explaining altruism in humans.

Pro-social behaviour – actions that help another person.

Altruism – actions aimed at helping another person that involve cost to the helper with no obvious reward.

Every day, people engage in behaviours to help other people, such as giving blood, running a race in aid of charity or volunteering to help younger children with reading or maths. All of these are examples of **pro-social behaviour**. Pro-social behaviour is the term given to any action that helps another individual regardless of the motive behind it. The term **altruism** also refers to behaviours that are aimed at helping another person, but for an action to be classed as altruistic it should involve some cost to the altruist (for example, in time, risk or money) and should not be motivated by anticipated reward (Barrett *et al.*, 2002). This issue of motivation is extremely difficult to establish as many altruistic actions make the helper feel good about themself and therefore offer some reward.

Two theories that explain altruism using different levels of analysis are Hamilton's kin selection theory, which takes an evolutionary perspective, and Batson's empathy-altruism hypothesis.

Hamilton's kin selection theory (1964)

For many years, altruism presented a paradox to evolutionary psychologists. Evolutionary theory is based on the premise that behaviours that lead to an increased chance of survival or reproduction will be passed onto offspring via genes. Carrying out costly or dangerous acts to help others appears to contradict evolutionary principles, which emphasize competition and survival of the fittest. Biological psychologists have pointed to the universal existence of altruism in human societies, however, implying a genetic basis to altruism (Workman & Reader, 2004).

Hamilton's kin selection theory explains altruistic acts directed towards those who are biologically related (kin) and applies equally to human and non-human animals. According to Hamilton, acting altruistically towards kin makes sense as our biological relatives share some of our genes. If we carried out an altruistic act that saved the life of a sibling, any offspring they produce would carry a small number of our genes, thus the act could increase our own reproductive success. This approach is based on the concept of the selfish gene put forward by Dawkins (1976). Genes compete for their place on the human genome (hence they are selfish) and any action that protects or sustains the individual's genes increases their chance of reproductive success.

Kin selection theory distinguishes two kinds of fitness:

■ Direct fitness involves passing on our genes to our own offspring (children).
■ Indirect fitness (also known as inclusive fitness) involves aiding the reproductive success of relatives who share some of our genes.

Hamilton's theory provides a clear explanation of why a father might donate a kidney to save the life of his child or why someone might rescue their brother or sister from a burning car. Siblings and offspring share 50 per cent of our genes, so actions that benefit them make evolutionary sense.

Kin selection theory makes a number of predictions about altruistic behaviour:

- We should be more likely to act altruistically to people who are related than non-relatives.
- We should act more altruistically to those who are more closely related.
- When people are equally related, such as siblings and offspring, we should act more altruistically to those with a greater capacity for reproductive success (for example, those who are younger).

Link to the biological level of analysis

Hamilton's kin selection theory rests on the assumption that altruism exists today because it was advantageous to our ancestors. Those who acted altruistically towards kin would have greater reproductive success than those who did not act altruistically. Over time, most members of the species would show the advantageous behaviour. A key aspect of the biological approach is that patterns of behaviour are coded for by genes and passed onto offspring. This level of analysis takes a functional approach to looking at why altruistic behaviour may be in the gene pool.

Evaluation of kin selection theory

Hamilton's kin selection theory has been supported by observations of kin altruism in many cultures. Hames (1987, 1988) observed how South American horticultural societies would offer help only to relatives in the form of labour and many studies have demonstrated how help is often given with childcare between related individuals (e.g. sisters). Smith *et al.* (1987) analysed over 1,000 wills in Canada, to consider who was more likely to inherit money. They found that close relatives were more likely to be left money than more distant relatives and when relatives were equally related (e.g. siblings and offspring), younger family members with higher reproductive value were more likely to be favoured, supporting Hamilton's claims.

However, observational studies do not indicate cause and effect. Experimental studies on kin selection have been few and far between. Madsen *et al.* (2007) carried out an ingenious experiment in which participants were paid to hold a demanding skiing posture for as long as they could with the amount of money paid directly related to the length of time the pose was held. Each day, participants were asked to decide to whom the money should be paid (self, parent, sibling, friend) before they attempted the exercise. They found that the length of time and thus amount of money was directly related to the degree of relatedness: the closer the recipient was related to them, the longer the demanding pose was held, providing experimental support for Hamilton's claims.

Hamilton's kin selection theory is limited in scope as it does not attempt to explain altruistic behaviour between non-related individuals or strangers. There are many examples of heroic acts occurring between non-related individuals, however, implying that there are other reasons for altruism than reproductive success. Cross-cultural studies which we will examine later demonstrate the important role played by socialization in altruistic behaviour.

Empathy-altruism theory: Daniel Batson

Kin selection theory sees altruistic behaviour as selfishness in disguise, designed to further our own genetic interest. American psychologist Daniel Batson has spent over 30 years trying to establish if genuine altruism exists. Starting from a point of disbelief, Batson has become convinced that it does, although he acknowledges that it is pretty rare.

According to Batson (1987) seeing someone in need of help can lead to two kinds of emotions:

- **Personal distress** – feelings of alarm, anxiety or fear, which are uncomfortable.
- **Empathic concern** – feelings of sympathy for the person who is in distress.

Both of these emotions could potentially lead to helping but for different motives. When we experience personal distress, helping the person in need is focused on reducing our own unpleasant feelings such as guilt or anxiety. This kind of helping would be classed as egoistic (selfish) as it is focused on our feelings rather than the other person. In contrast, when we experience empathic concern, Batson argues that helping is focused on reducing the distress of the sufferer and is therefore purely altruistic.

Where does empathy come from? Batson argued that empathy involves putting yourself into another person's shoes, imagining how they feel and thinking about how you would feel in similar circumstances. Thus, empathy is based on perspective-taking, which leads to empathic concern.

Evidence for Batson's theory

Altruism poses methodological challenges for psychologists. It is hard to establish which type of helping – egoistic or altruistic – is taking place as we cannot observe someone's intentions directly. If we ask people why they are helping, they will almost always produce a socially desirable answer even when there is an underlying motive. Finally, many helping behaviours benefit both the helper and the helpee (Batson, 2010).

Batson has carried out a series of ingenious experiments in which he has attempted to manipulate empathy and assess the effects on altruistic behaviour. In these experiments, female students are placed in a position where they can offer to swap with a young woman who is afraid of having painful electric shocks and receive the shocks in her place (the dependent variable). Batson has manipulated two independent variables, to assess how they influence helping behaviour:

- Level of empathy is manipulated by telling some of the participants they are similar to the victim (high empathy) and the others that they are different to the victim (low empathy).
- Ease of escape from the situation is manipulated, with some participants being able leave after two shocks (easy escape) and the others being made to watch ten shocks (difficult escape).

Batson refers to this experimental model as the '**escape x empathy**' paradigm and he has carried out more than 20 experiments using this method. These have supported his claims, demonstrating that those in high empathy conditions are likely to offer help even when they can reduce their own distress by escaping. In contrast, those in low empathy conditions will offer help when escape is difficult as a way of reducing their own distress. However, when escape is easy, many prefer to simply get out of the situation (Batson *et al.*, 1990).

■ Critical thinking

Such experimental manipulations have been criticized for a lack of ecological validity, notably the difficulty in creating genuine empathy by telling someone they are similar or different to a stranger. These experiments have also been criticized for the ethical implications, notably deception and stress, which are involved.

However, Batson's theory draws strong evidence from developmental psychology. Many studies have shown that as children develop the ability to empathize with others, they become more altruistic. Dunn *et al.* (1981) demonstrated how very young children aged between 2 and 4 years old will offer comfort to new siblings when they are crying. Empathy is an important part of Nancy Eisenberg's theory of pro-social reasoning, which argues that pro-social behaviour develops hand-in-hand with empathy (Eisenberg and Mussen, 1989).

Figure 7.1 The beginnings of empathy?

Contrasting these explanations

Both theories are well accepted as explanations of altruistic behaviour and both have generated a range of testable predictions. Attempts to test Batson's empathy theory have mainly been carried out in laboratory settings to allow manipulation of variables and these experiments have sometimes been rather contrived and lacking in validity as a consequence. In contrast, a large amount of observational studies have supported kin selection theory across many different cultures and other species of animals.

Kin selection theory is limited in range as it only relates to altruistic acts towards related individuals. However, the biological approach has been extended to explain help to non-relatives through the idea of reciprocal altruism – a form of helping that is based on the idea of payback, effectively 'you scratch my back and I will scratch yours'. Evolutionary approaches also overlook individual differences in altruistic behaviour, assuming that the genetic basis of kin altruism is universal. In contrast, Batson's theory can be applied equally to relatives and strangers. It can explain why some people are more altruistic than others, as they possess higher levels of empathy.

Both theories have generated discussion and debate of a philosophical nature centred on whether or not real altruism exists. Kin selection theory would argue that it does not and all helping is selfishness is disguise. Batson's empathy-altruism approach stands out as virtually the only explanation that sees human helping in a positive rather than selfish light. Can these theories be reconciled? De Waal draws attention to the existence of basic altruism in the form of response to another's pain across a range of animal species. He argues that perception of another person's emotional state automatically activates shared representations causing a matching emotional state in the observer. This approach sees empathy as an automatic, biological response, bringing the two approaches together (De Waal, 2008).

Cross-cultural differences in pro-social behaviour

LEARNING OUTCOME
■ Using one or more research studies, explain cross-cultural differences in pro-social behaviour.

Hamilton's kin selection theory (1964) argues that altruistic behaviour has genetic origins as it brought advantages in the past. This approach implies that altruism should occur universally across all cultures. Reactions to natural disasters, such as the 2004 Pacific Tsunami, show that people across the world are capable of generosity and compassion for others when tragedy strikes. However, many studies have demonstrated cultural differences in the extent and type of pro-social behaviour. Whiting and Whiting (1975) carried out a cross-cultural analysis that compared the amount of helping behaviour shown by children from six countries. The researchers found the highest rate of helping in Kenya where 100 per cent of the children in the sample demonstrated pro-social behaviour. The lowest rate of helping was found in the USA where only 8 per cent of children demonstrated helping behaviour. Whiting and Whiting's cross-cultural study indicated that pro-social behaviour was generally higher in collectivist than in individualistic cultures.

Nadler (1979, 1986) carried out a series of experiments examining pro-social behaviour in Israel. Israel is interesting to cross-cultural psychologists, as some children are raised in kibbutzim, communal farms that strongly promote collectivist values, whereas others are raised in traditional family environments, providing a naturally occurring independent variable. In 1979, Nadler compared the amount of pro-social behaviour shown by 67 children raised in a kibbutz with 61 who lived in Tel Aviv in traditional families. The children were asked to donate some or all of a reward they had earned in favour of poor children. Nadler also measured their attitudes towards helping using the **Attitudes of Social Responsibility Scale**. Children raised in kibbutzim had higher scores on the Social Responsibility Scale and were more generous in their donations than those brought up in Tel Aviv, demonstrating the importance of socialization in pro-social behaviour.

Yablo and Field (2007) compared 62 Thai and 56 US college students using various measures of altruism and found that Thais showed a greater tendency to offer altruistic interpretations of situations and to report that they would personally help in such situations. These findings suggest a relationship between religious values and pro-social behaviour.

Link to the sociocultural level of analysis

Individualistic and collectivist cultures adopt different models of the self, which may underpin differences in altruism. The collectivist view of self is interconnected with others and the social group is seen as more important than the individual.

The higher rates of pro-social behaviour seen in collectivist cultures relate to a combination of factors including:

- The different models of the self – individualistic cultures see the self as independent and emphasize the importance of individual achievement. This can lead to competition rather than cooperation between people. In contrast, the collectivist view of the interdependent self emphasizes the importance of the group and of shared goals over individual success and achievement.
- The important role played by religious beliefs and practices in promoting pro-social behaviours – Yablo's studies demonstrate the link between religion and pro-social behaviour. Buddhist culture, as practised in Thailand, emphasizes the importance of pro-social behaviours and Thais score higher on measures of altruism than Americans.
- Socialization processes including modelling – children who grow up in collectivist cultures and communities, notably the kibbutz studied by Nadler, have ample opportunity to observe pro-social and cooperative behaviours in the adults around them. Chapter 3, the Sociocultural level of analysis, introduced you to Bandura's social learning theory, which demonstrates how behaviours are learnt via observation and modelling. Other experiments have demonstrated how exposure to pro-social models leads to increased helping in young children.

Bystander behaviour – the behaviour of witnesses who do not intervene or offer help but 'stand by'.

Pluralistic ignorance – takes place when bystanders take their cue from others who are doing nothing.

Diffusion of responsibility – occurs when a crowd of people witness an event and the responsibility for helping is spread out between them.

Evaluation apprehension – occurs when bystanders fail to help as they are anxious about being judged.

Factors influencing bystanderism

LEARNING OUTCOME
■ Examine factors influencing bystanderism.

So far, we have considered explanations of why people may act altruistically towards others, sometimes putting their own lives at risk. There have been many documented examples where witnesses to an emergency have done little or nothing to help, however. The tragic case of Kitty Genovese (*see page 201*) led two American psychologists, John Darley and Bibb Latané, to investigate the concept of the 'unresponsive bystander' and to establish the factors that play a role in **bystander behaviour**.

Number of witnesses

Latané and Darley (1970) examined the Kitty Genovese case and argued that, counter to common sense, the large number of potential helpers played an important role in the ultimate lack of help. They proposed three explanations for why more witnesses might lead to less helping:

■ **Pluralistic ignorance** or 'no one else is doing anything' – refers to the interpretation of a situation as an emergency. Emergencies can be highly ambiguous: the man and woman arguing could be a drunken couple, actors in a reality show or strangers. In ambiguous situations, it is sensible to see what other people are doing. If they are not reacting then this could lead witnesses to label a situation as a non-emergency.
■ **Diffusion of responsibility** or 'someone else will do something' – when there are several witnesses to an emergency, the responsibility is shared (or diffused) between them, so each witness feels less responsibility to help.
■ **Evaluation apprehension** or the fear of being judged by others when offering help – this is referred to as **audience inhibition** by Latané and Nida (1981).

These explanations predicted that bystander behaviour would be more likely to occur when there were more rather than fewer witnesses or when the situation was ambiguous as opposed to a clear emergency. The late 1960s saw a range of ingenious experiments to test these predictions. In one, participants filled in a questionnaire alone or with two other people (confederates of the experimenter) and the room began to fill with smoke from an air vent. Participants who were alone acted rapidly and alerted the researcher to the smoke but those paired with inactive confederates ignored the fire, demonstrating pluralistic ignorance in action (Darley & Latané, 1968).

Key study

Darley and Latané (1968)

Darley and Latané (1968) carried out a laboratory experiment in which students were asked to take part in an intercom discussion on 'the stresses of college life'. Use of the intercom meant that participants were able to hear but unable to see the others in the 'group', which allowed Darley and Latané to manipulate the independent variable – the number of witnesses to the emergency. There were three conditions:

■ **Condition 1** – the participant believed they were taking part in a discussion with one other person.
■ **Condition 2** – the participant believed they were in a group of three people.
■ **Condition 3** – the participant believed they were in a group of six people.

Halfway through the intercom discussion, a confederate revealed health problems involving stress-related seizures and a taperecorded seizure was played over the intercom. The researchers measured two dependent variables: whether or not help was offered and how long it took for the genuine participant to alert the researcher to the emergency.

All of the participants in condition 1 responded in an average time of 52 seconds, taking rapid responsibility for the emergency. In contrast, only 62 per cent of participants in condition 3 responded and help was much slower to be offered (mean 166 seconds). This experiment demonstrates how diffusion of responsibility can occur when there are several witnesses to an event.

■ Critical thinking

Darley and Latané's experiment provides an ingenious way of examining the effects of group size on helping in a controlled setting. However, the situation is highly unusual and there are few examples of real-life emergencies that can be heard but not seen. The participants were aware they were taking part in an experiment and may have become suspicious of the scenario. These factors make it difficult to generalize the findings of this experiment to real-life events.

Type of emergency

The nature of the incident plays an important role in determining whether or not help is given. Situations that are ambiguous are less likely to lead to helping as witnesses may label them as non-emergencies. In contrast, clear emergencies often produce help even when there is considerable personal danger involved. One remarkable example is that of Wesley Autrey, who saved the life of a man who fell onto the New York Subway during a seizure. Autrey jumped onto the track and lay on top of the man to prevent him falling under a passing train. Piliavin *et al.*'s (1969) field experiment explored helping in a clear emergency.

Piliavin *et al.* (1969)

Piliavin, Rodin and Piliavin took their study of bystander behaviour into the field, making use of the New York underground system. Working in a team of four, one researcher played the role of a partially sighted or drunken passenger (indicated by a white cane or bottle of alcohol), who collapsed on a short train journey and remained unconscious on the train carriage floor. Piliavin *et al.* also varied the race of the victim, making four different conditions:

- White partially sighted
- Black partially sighted
- White drunk
- Black drunk.

If no help was given within 70 seconds, another member of the research team was primed to intervene and offer help to 'the victim'. In total 104 trials took place.

In this clear emergency, there was no diffusion of responsibility. Regardless of the number of witnesses in the carriage, the cane victim, whether black or white, was helped spontaneously and rapidly by a member of the public before the model had a chance to act. The drunken victim was also helped spontaneously on 19 out of 38 trials, although this took longer, suggesting that witnesses were appraising the situation in terms of personal risk. Piliavin *et al.*'s experiment implies that suggesting diffusion of responsibility may only operate when events are ambiguous rather than in the case of clear emergencies.

■ Critical thinking

Darley and Latané (1968) and Piliavin *et al.* (1969) both performed research into bystander behaviour, one using a laboratory experiment and the other a field experiment. Compare these two approaches in relation to their ethical implications and ecological validity. Which do you think provides the better test of bystander behaviour?

Other studies have indicated that more witnesses generally lead to an increased chance of help in serious emergencies – a finding that is consistent with common sense. Harari *et al.* (1985) used a simulated sex attack in a dark car park and found that witnesses were more likely to intervene when two people were present (85 per cent) compared to when there was a single witness (65 per cent). This is easy to explain: the clear risk in the situation deters single witnesses from involvement but there is strength in numbers.

Figure 7.2

Cognitive appraisals

The results of these and other experiments were used to construct a model of bystander behaviour by Darley and Latané (1970). The five-stage model focused on how bystanders make sense of possible emergency situations. According to this approach, witnesses make a series of rapid judgements before deciding whether or not to offer help in a potential

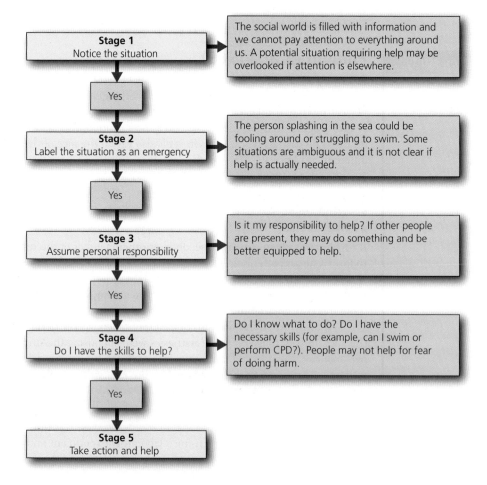

Figure 7.3 The five-stage model (Darley & Latané, 1970)

emergency. At each of these stages, a positive response (yes) moves the witness on to the next stage, ultimately leading to help being offered. A negative response at any decision point will lead to the witness deciding not to offer help.

The five-stage model assumes that people are largely rational and focuses on how they process social information. Helping results from a series of rational decisions, rather than instincts (kin selection) or emotions such as empathy (Batson). The model provides clear reasons why people may not help, and has been supported by a range of experiments that have demonstrated evidence for these claims.

Cognitive models emphasize the importance of the situation – such as number of witnesses and kind of emergency. In doing so, they largely overlook the idea that helping may be related to factors such as personality characteristics or group membership. An experiment carried out by Levine *et al.* (2005) demonstrated how existing group membership can exert an influence on helping and bystander behaviour. Levine *et al.* set up a situation in which a confederate posed as a football fan who was injured and requiring help after a game. The researchers examined the effect of different football shirts including the in-group shirt (same as fans), the rival team's shirt and an unbranded sports shirt. The confederate was more likely to be helped when he wore the in-group shirt than in either of the other conditions. This demonstrates the importance of shared identity between witness and victim – and is consistent with the predictions made by Tajfel's social identity theory. It also demonstrates how victim characteristics play an important role in bystander behaviour.

Link to the cognitive level of analysis

Research on bystander behaviour focuses largely on cognitive factors – how witnesses make sense of emergencies and how they process information. Helping is seen as a largely rational process and emotional responses are overlooked.

SECTION SUMMARY
- Altruism is voluntary behaviour that involves a cost to the helper.
- Kin selection theory argues that altruism has a biological base.
- The empathy-altruism hypothesis sees empathy as crucial to altruism.
- Altruism tends to be higher in collectivist cultures and is related to the interconnected self, religious values and pro-social models.
- Bystanderism is more common when there are more witnesses or when an event is ambiguous. Helping is more likely in clear emergencies.
- Cognitive models emphasize the importance of rational decision-making in bystander behaviour and helping.

Interpersonal relationships

This section of the chapter focuses on insights into close relationships. We will begin by examining how relationships start before going on to consider what social psychology can tell us about communication and the factors that lead some couples to split up. The study of long-term relationships poses many challenges for social psychologists. Experimental methods have little application in this area and were roundly criticized in the 1970s and 80s for providing 'snapshots' of relationships that overlooked their complexity and said little about how they change and develop over time. Longitudinal research, returning to study the same couples over long periods of time, is essential in order to identify the factors that may relate to happiness and relationship survival. In each of these sections, different levels of analysis can be used to illustrate how complex relationships can be understood using different frameworks.

Interpersonal attraction

LEARNING OUTCOME
■ Examine biological, psychological and social origins of attraction.

Biological origins of attraction

A wealth of metaphors is used in everyday language to describe strong attraction, for example when we talk about the idea of 'chemistry' between two people or meeting someone and just 'clicking'. Psychological research has demonstrated how attraction is influenced by biological, psychological and social factors. An important principle of the biological approach is that many of today's behaviours are rooted in the past and influenced by characteristics inherited from our early ancestors. Behaviours that increased the chance of survival or reproductive success for our ancestors millions of years ago continue to be reflected today.

For males, reproductive success is increased by choosing mates who are fertile and capable of producing offspring. As fertility is strongly linked to youth in females, males should be attracted to females who show signs of youth. This prediction is well supported by analyses of personal column adverts, which show that many males seek females who are several years younger than them (Pawlowski & Dunbar, 2001). Cunningham (1986) found that men were most attracted to women with large eyes, small noses and small chins, features commonly seen in young children. Fertility is also demonstrated by the typical 'hour glass' shape with large breasts and a slim waist, which demonstrate that a female is past the age of puberty, but is not pregnant. Across all cultures, a waist–hip ratio (WHR) of around 0.7 is seen as ideal for females – regardless of whether curvier or slimmer bodies are preferred (Singh, 1993). Dixson (2011) used eye-tracking techniques to measure the precise amount of time men spent looking at different areas of a woman on a photo. These photos had been digitally altered to vary the WHR (0.7 or 0.9) and breast size (small, medium or large). The majority of men in the sample began by looking at breasts and waist, rather than face, lower body or legs. They also looked more often and for longer at the breasts, irrespective of the WHR of the images. These studies indicate how men may be tuned in to respond to physical shortcuts to assess fertility.

In the hunter-gatherer era, reproductive success for women involved ensuring the survival of the relatively small number of offspring produced. The chance of survival was increased considerably by the presence of a male who would provide food and protection for the family unit. This would suggest that attraction for women would be based on features that indicate strength and masculinity. A study by Johnston *et al.* (2001) found that women preferred 'rugged' men with masculine features including a strong jaw, ridged eyebrows and small eyes. The features that signify attractiveness in men's face are those associated with maturity and social dominance. Female preferences for these types of features may have evolved as older men generally possessed more resources, which aided the survival of offspring. Masculine features are associated with higher levels of the male hormone testosterone and a preference for masculine facial features may have been linked with a mate who was good at defending resources. However, highly masculine men may be a double blessing: Waynforth (2001) found that women judged very attractive men as more likely to cheat than moderately attractive men. Other studies have indicated that female preference for male faces is linked to the menstrual cycle. Gangestad *et al.* (2007) found that women preferred highly masculine faces when they were fertile or considering a short-term mate but more feminine faces (i.e. pretty boys) were preferred at other times in the cycle.

Some features such as symmetrical faces (Bruce & Young, 1998) and long legs (Pawlowski and Sorokowski, 2008) are seen as attractive in both sexes. A preference for these features may have been naturally selected as they led to reproductive success. Long legs indicate good nutrition in childhood and symmetrical faces are thought to signify 'good' genes, which provide a strong resistance to illness.

Other biological factors include genes and hormones. The major histocompatability genes (MHG) play a key role in immune system functioning and assessment of genetic similarity takes place using olfactory cues (smell). Studies have indicated that women tend to prefer the odour of potential partners with MHC genes that are strongly dissimilar to themselves (Santos *et al.*, 2005) or moderately dissimilar (Jacob *et al.*, 2002). This makes sense as any resultant offspring of these encounters would be likely to have strong immune systems. It is unsurprising that use of the contraceptive pill disrupts this process, making women less sensitive to olfactory cues. Studies with males have not found consistent results.

Oxcytocin is a hormone that plays a key role in attraction and relationship formation. Oxytocin is released during labour and breast feeding and is known to play an important role in mother–child bonding. Oxytocin is also a neurotransmitter that acts on the limbic system, the centre of the brain that controls emotions. Much of the work on oxytocin has taken place using prairie voles – an unusual species that form exclusive pair bonds and remain faithful to each other for life. Some studies have found that oxytocin increases with orgasm in both men and women, increasing attachment and bonding. Other studies have suggested it may be involved in sexual arousal. Schneidermann *et al.* (2012) assessed the role played by oxytocin in the early stages of romantic love. They compared plasma levels of oxytocin in 120 new lovers (60 couples) with those in 43 unattached singles. Oxytocin was significantly higher in the lovers than the singles, suggesting that this hormone may play an important role at the first stages of romantic attachment. This implies that parental and romantic attachments may well be underpinned by some of the same biological mechanisms. Recently attention has turned to the importance of oxytocin in many other aspects of relationships, leading Zak (2011) to refer to it as 'social glue'. Claims are being made for the powers of oxytocin in fostering trust between strangers and increasing levels of empathy and altruism.

Psychological origins of attraction

While many people would like a very attractive partner, the truly gorgeous are few and far between and research studies indicate that most of us look for a partner who roughly matches us in attractiveness. This idea, generally referred to as the 'matching hypothesis' was put forward by Murstein (1972). Murstein argued that while we might desire the most physically attractive partner, we know that we are unlikely to get or keep them, so we look for someone similar to us to reduce the risk of rejection. Murstein (1972) asked participants to rate photos of 99 dating couples without knowing who was paired up with whom. He found that members of a couple were rated as broadly similar in attractiveness. Similar findings were obtained by Silverman (1971) who observed couples in bars and restaurants and found them to be roughly matched in levels of physical attractiveness. Some studies have found that the 'matching' concept can also be applied to pairs of school friends (McKillip & Riedel, 1983).

Once two people start getting to know each other, similarity of interests, attitudes and values become important. Byrne (1971) suggested that greater similarity of attitudes between two people was associated with greater liking, which was known as 'the law of attraction'. However, Byrne's research methods lacked validity and critics pointed out that in real life, we rarely have that much information about people's attitudes or values when we are getting to know them. Despite this, it is widely agreed that similarity of attitudes and interests plays an important role in attraction. Shared views about the world make communication easier and shared interests make it easy and rewarding to spend time together. Someone who shares our views, for example about music or politics, can validate us holding those views. We also believe that similar people are more likely to like and accept us. Differences in attitudes can certainly lead us to dislike people (Singh & Ho, 2000).

The attraction-similarity hypothesis (Morry 2005, 2007) predicts that attraction between two people leads to them perceiving themselves as similar – even when actual similarity may be relatively minor. Studies have demonstrated how this applies in both romantic couples and pairs of friends. Selfhout *et al.* (2009) studied attraction and the formation of friendships when students start university. A sample of almost 400 Dutch students aged between 18 and 19 completed personality questionnaires, which rated them using the 'Big Five' Personality Scale. Selfhout *et al.* observed who went on to become friends with whom. They found that genuine similarity between two people was not that significant, but that perceived similarity correlated strongly with higher liking. If a student saw herself as being like another person, she was likely to like them and be attracted to them – even if the actual personality profiles showed them to be pretty different.

Social origins of attraction

For attraction to occur between two people there has to be some form of contact between them. Contact can be face to face or take place in a virtual environment such as a chat room or social networking site. Until fairly recently, most people met potential partners and friends at school, college or work. Bossard (1932) demonstrated the strength of this effect when he found that more than half of 5,000 couples applying for marriage licences in Philadelphia, USA lived a couple of minutes' walk from each other. Over the last 20 years, physical proximity has become much less important, as developments in transport and in communication technologies such as texting and internet use mean that it is possible to develop a relationship at a much greater distance, with little or no face-to-face contact.

However, while we can meet and interact with a much wider pool of people in the social world of the twenty-first century, social factors continue to exert a strong influence on who is deemed appropriate as a possible partner. Many of us socialize with those who are similar in key ways – of the same age, drawn from the same ethnic group and with a similar level of education – and it is unsurprising that we are most likely to become friends with and form close relationships with people drawn from this demographically similar 'pool'. Kandel (1978) found that teenage pairs of close friends were similar in ethnic background, religion and economic background of parents. Hill *et al.* (1976) found that dating couples and pairs of friends were similar in ethnic group, social class and religion. Liu *et al.* (1995) asked American students from Asian, African, Latino and white ethnic backgrounds about their preferences for partners. All chose their own ethnic group as most desirable, even though other ethnic groups were sometimes ranked as more physically attractive. When asked about the reason for this, the most common answer related to the impact on the social network: partners from the same ethnic background were more likely to be welcomed by their family and friends.

Commentary: How do these features interact?

The above discussion has shown how each of the factors – biological, psychological and social – exerts an influence on attraction at different levels. Social factors exert a subtle influence, sorting people on the basis of demographic variables such as education and class. The filter model put forward by Kerckhoff and Davis (1962) refers to this process of social sorting as the **field of availables** being narrowed down into the **field of desirables**. In recent years, technological changes have lessened the impact of contact and proximity, making these less important in the development of relationships. The internet allows us to mingle with a much more varied group of people and technologies enable us to keep in contact with those who live far away. Despite this, there are still pressures to choose a partner from our own ethnic group (Liu *et al.*, 1995).

Biological factors also play a key role in attraction and we have seen how attractive physical qualities may signal fertility and the potential for reproductive success. However, very desirable people are few and far between and most people choose to settle for a partner who is of a similar level of attractiveness to themselves, showing the interaction between biological and psychological factors. Other biological factors such as genes and hormones influence our reactions to others at a much less conscious level. Marazziti (2005) argues that we are only just beginning to understand the importance of biological factors in attraction.

The role of communication in maintaining relationships

LEARNING OUTCOME
■ Discuss the role of communication in maintaining relationships.

Once a relationship has become established, it needs to be maintained. Common goals of maintenance involve ensuring the relationship remains sufficiently satisfying for both partners and repairing things when they go wrong. Communication is a vital aspect of relationship maintenance. Litzinger and Gordon argue that 'communication … is consistently and significantly related to couples' satisfaction' (2005, p.410).

An important aspect of communication relates to how a couple deals with conflict. Research suggests that it is not the presence of conflict that is significant but how partners deal with it. Tran and Simpson (2009) argue that 'the fate of any relationship – whether happy or haunted – depends on how partners think, feel and behave in difficult situations'. Rusbult and Zembrodt (1983) identified four kinds of strategies that were used when relationships run into difficulties. These included two active strategies, which involve taking action of some sort, and two passive strategies, which involve inaction. They further divided these into constructive and destructive strategies for the relationship. This typology provides four different ways of dealing with conflict.

Table 7.1   Dealing with conflict – Rusbult and Zembrodt (1983)

	ACTIVE	**PASSIVE**
Constructive	**Voice** involves expressing dissatisfaction and talking about the problem. This is an active, constructive strategy that aims to tackle the dissatisfaction.	**Loyalty** involves waiting for the relationship to improve. It demonstrates a level of commitment to stay in the relationship but does not tackle the problems.
Destructive	**Exit** involves ending the relationship. This strategy can be constructive for the 'leaver' but is destructive for the relationship.	**Neglect** involves ignoring the problem or refusing to discuss it. This is often interpreted as a lack of interest and is ultimately destructive for the relationship.

Research by Rusbult *et al.* (1991) has shown that there are broad sex differences in the use of these strategies. Women are more likely to respond to relationship problems actively by wanting to talk about them (voice) whereas men are more likely to respond passively. These differences can lead women to label men as 'not caring' and men to view women as 'nagging'. As Smith and Mackie note, these differences provide a 'rich soil for the seeds of misunderstanding' (2000, p.456).

John Gottman has devised a method for studying communication in couples, utilizing a range of different techniques including micro-observation in a specially constructed 'Lovelab' in America. This type of detailed observational research is providing valuable insights into how couples communicate and how different patterns relate to relationship satisfaction.

Key study

Gottman and Levenson (1983, 2002)

In 1983, Gottman and Levenson began an observational 'Lovelab' study with 85 American couples. In each observation, the couple was asked to arrive at the Lovelab having been apart for about 8 hours. They took part in three 15-minute conversations, which were filmed through hidden cameras. The conversations focused on the events of the day, something good in the relationship and a current area of conflict decided on by the couple. Each conversation was recorded and transcribed (written out) and the interactions were then coded by observers working independently. Each couple was studied again in 1987 and then observed once a year until 1997. The couple returned for a final observation in 2002, by which time 21 of the original 85 had divorced.

Gottman and Levenson were able to look back at the recordings and transcripts and compare the communication patterns shown by couples who stayed together with those who had divorced. Gottman found that **happy couples** provided, on average, five positive pieces of communication for every negative and fitted into one of three 'types':

- **Validating couples** discussed their differences openly and cooperatively. They showed positive feelings for each other and respected each other's opinions.
- **Conflict-avoiding couples** tried to avoid open conflict and preferred to focus on their similarities.
- **Volatile couples** were similar to validates as they addressed differences openly. They tended to compete rather than cooperate, however, and often attempted to persuade their partners towards their own viewpoint.

In contrast, **unhappy couples** were characterized by a much higher ratio of negative to positive communications. They showed four specific kinds of communication that Gottman and Levenson referred to as 'The Four Horsemen of the Apocalypse':

- **Criticism** – verbally attacking their partner.
- **Defensiveness** – claiming their behaviour was acceptable or justifying it.
- **Contempt** – showing scorn for their partner.
- **Stonewalling** – refusing to acknowledge or discuss problems in the relationship.

■ Critical thinking

The study of communication in close relationships poses many challenges for social psychologists. The process of studying communication can be obtrusive and natural patterns of communication may alter in response to demand characteristics and social desirability. In addition, close relationships are highly personal areas of our lives and many people do not wish to share them in order to further research on communication. Those who are willing to take part in lengthy studies may not be representative of the rest of the population.

Gottman has used these findings to develop the **two factor model** of relationship breakdown, which predicts when rather than why couples will split up. Divorce or break-ups are most likely to occur at two points in long-term relationships:

- **After around seven years** – couples who show high levels of anger towards their partner with arguments escalating negatively are most likely to end their relationships after about seven years. This pattern is referred to by Gottman as 'Unregulated volatile positive and negative affect'.
- **The mid-life of the relationship when children are leaving home** – couples who show boredom and apathy, with little interest or affection for each other are likely to divorce later on in the marriage, often when they are in their mid-forties. This pattern is referred to a 'neutral affective style'.

Gottman's findings have been supported by Lavner and Bradbury (2012) who studied 136 couples who reported high levels of happiness in the first four years of marriage. They compared couples who went on to divorce by the ten-year follow up with the couples who stayed married and found that the divorcing couples had shown more negative communication as newlyweds compared with the couples who did not divorce.

Kurdek*

Some studies have suggested that gay couples may be better at dealing with conflict than heterosexual partners. Kurdek (2004) carried out a longitudinal study in which he compared the communication patterns and ways of resolving conflict in a sample of 53 lesbian and 80 gay male cohabiting couples, with 80 cohabiting heterosexual couples. Krudek found that gay male couples used fewer 'demand/withdrawal' communication patterns than heterosexual couples and gay couples in general showed more positive communication styles than heterosexual couples. Kurdek's findings imply that gay couples may be better at resolving conflict than heterosexual partners as they do not descend into a gendered pattern of female demands and male withdrawal.

Can better communication patterns be developed?

Rusbult *et al.*'s work (1991) has important implications for relationship counselling: helping to interpret and use different communication patterns may well help couples to work through conflicts more positively. Studies have supported this claim. Hahlweg *et al.* (1998) trained 55 German couples in effective communication and problem-solving using a six-session programme while a control group of 17 matched couples received no training. Three years later the group who had received training was significantly less likely to have divorced than the control group; they also reported higher levels of relationship satisfaction. Similarly, Markman *et al.* (1993) found that sexual satisfaction improved when couples took part in a communication skills programme even though it included minimal focus on the couple's sex life. This demonstrates the importance of communication for other areas of marital happiness.

Practical applications

Studies of communication have powerful applications for psychologists who work with couples in relationship counselling. Interventions can focus on increasing the ratio of positive to negative interactions to improve relationships.

Culture and relationships

LEARNING OUTCOME
■ Explain the role that culture plays in the formation and maintenance of relationships.

Most of the research studies we have covered so far have been carried out in the Western, economically developed world, mainly in North America and Europe. In Western societies, relationships are based on the principle of personal choice and can be ended by separation or divorce if they are unsatisfactory. Relationships in individualistic cultures have been characterized as voluntary, temporary and individualistic (Moghaddam *et al.*, 1993). In contrast, in collectivist cultures, relationships are seen as unions between families, who play a much larger role in partner choice, often using systems of arranged marriages. Once formed, it may be very difficult to end an arranged marriage as this would bring shame on both families. Relationships in collectivist cultures are categorized as obligatory and permanent, and as alliances between families rather than two individuals (Moghaddam *et al.*, 1993).

Arranged marriages are the most common form of marital arrangement across the globe and are used in many cultures because of their advantages over love marriages (Goodwin, 1999). Arranged marriages enable economic links to be made between families and allow family elders to protect the family reputation and to exert control over younger family members. Arranged marriages are also stable and long-lasting whereas marriages based on attraction and love often 'fizzle out'.

Gupta and Singh (1982) compared 50 professional married couples living around Jaipur City, India. Twenty-five couples had married for love and the other 25 had arranged marriages. The couples were carefully matched for educational level and family background and had been married for between one and ten years at the time of the study. Gupta and Singh asked each member of the couple to complete two scales, on how much they loved their partner and how much they liked their partner. They found that couples who had married for love had – unsurprisingly – much higher love scores than those with arranged marriages for the first five years of the marriage. Love decreased over time for both men and women in love marriages, however, but increased in arranged marriages. After five years, both men and women in arranged marriages loved their partners more than those who had originally married for love. A similar pattern was shown for liking: scores were high at the beginning of love marriages but decreased dramatically after about two years, especially for men. In arranged marriages, liking started at a low level and increased in a similar way to love. Gupta and Singh's study demonstrates the claim that love marriages start hot and grow cold, whereas arranged marriages start cold and grow hot.

Figure 7.4

Arranged marriages are based on the idea that young people are unlikely to make a good choice of lifetime partner for themselves. Potential partners are identified by family members or professional matchmakers who consult with the parents about their preferences. These may include family background, education, prospects and profession as well as personal qualities such as appearance. The matchmaker identifies candidates who meet these criteria and presents them to the family of the bride or groom for approval. There is considerable variation in how these processes take place (Qureshi, 1991):

- **Traditional arranged marriages** – are planned entirely by parents, often with very little discussion. These are often viewed as forced marriages by the Western media.
- **Delegation marriages** – take place when children (more often males) explain the type of partner they are looking for to parents who then employ a matchmaker to find suitable candidates.
- **Joint venture** – parents and children are active in the mate selection process.

Arranged marriages are common in South Asia, notably Pakistan, India and Bangladesh, and in Middle Eastern and African countries. They are commonly practised by Hindus, Sikhs and Muslims. Traditional arranged marriages are more common in rural areas and in families with lower levels of education. Families with higher levels of education and those living in urban areas are most likely to have changed their practices to delegation or joint venture (Zaida & Shuraydi, 2002).

Arranged marriages also take place in Western societies. Second and third generation migrants grow up surrounded by Western culture, which views choice of marriage partner as desirable and essential for happiness, while their parents often continue to view arranged marriages as preferable. Ghuman (1994) studied British and Canadian Sikhs, Hindus and Muslims and found that arranged marriages were common but that there were considerable variations between the three groups. Sikh and Hindu families had modified their practice from traditional arranged marriages to varying degrees of delegation, with most young couples playing some part in the decision-making process. Goodwin *et al.* (1997) studied 70 Gujerati Hindu couples living in Leicester, UK and found that fewer than 10 per cent had traditional marriages, with most having a large element of choice involved. Muslim families were more likely to continue the practice of traditional arranged marriages and, unsurprisingly, young Muslims were the most likely to rebel out of all three religious groups (Ghuman, 1994). These studies demonstrate how Western ideas are gradually modifying traditional arranged marriages into more Westernized forms.

Commentary on the role of culture

Goodwin (1999) identifies a number of important challenges in cross-cultural research into relationships. The foremost of these is establishing how cultural systems, with their own ideas and beliefs, are internalized as the social norms that influence how people behave in their relationships. A second issue relates to social change. Over the last 20 years, many parts of the world, including Eastern Europe and East Asia, have undergone dramatic economic and political changes that have altered how people live their lives. These changes are often referred to as **modernization and Westernization**. Modernization refers to developments in health and education, whereas Westernization refers to the adoption of Western, individualistic beliefs such as the importance of the pursuit of happiness. These processes are leading to the merging of cultures, along with new cultural forms. One result is that many of the traditional cultural differences in relationships are being challenged by rapid social transitions. It also demonstrates how research findings may lack temporal validity in a rapidly changing world (Goodwin, 2006).

Breakdown of relationships

LEARNING OUTCOME
■ Analyse why relationships may change or end.

In Western cultures, just under half of marriages currently end in divorce and every day many short-term relationships breakdown and end. Some of these endings will be mutual decisions but many will be instigated by one partner. There are practical differences in the ending of short- and long-term relationships relating to the degree of interdependence between the couple and the extent of the barrier forces that keep them together, even when they may want to leave. These include potential impact on children, moral disapproval (the feeling that you ought to stay in the relationship) and the disruption to social networks with family and friends.

Dissimilarity is an important factor in the breakdown of short-term relationships. Hill *et al.* (1976) carried out a two-year study of 231 heterosexual student couples living around Boston, USA. During the study, 45 per cent of the couples split up, with the majority of the break-ups being instigated by one partner. Hill *et al.* found that couples who separated were more likely to be dissimilar in educational level, intelligence and physical attractiveness whereas those who stayed together were more likely to be 'matched' on these attributes. Hill *et al.* also carried out a series of interviews with the students in their sample who had split up. They found that those who were dissatisfied with the relationship took advantage of breaks in the college year, such as the end of term, to bring the relationship to a relatively painless end.

Baxter (1986) asked 157 students who had just split up with a partner to write a story about the reasons for the split and then compared the reasons given by men and women for ending the relationship. Both sexes agreed that having little in common was important, as was the desire for greater freedom. However, women were more likely to end a relationship due to of a lack of intimacy or support, whereas men were more concerned with the loss of excitement and 'magic' in the relationship.

Duck (1992) identified two types of reasons why long-term relationships end

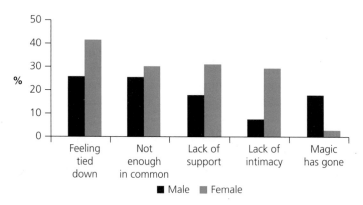

Figure 7.5 Reasons given for ending relationships (Baxter, 1986)

as 'precipitating factors' and 'predisposing factors'. Precipitating factors are external events that put pressure on the relationship and that often cannot be predicted. These could include work commitments that lead one member of the couple to work away or redundancy that puts severe stress on the relationship. Personal change for one member of the couple such as illness or disability may also lead to relationship breakdown. As we have seen earlier, it is not simply the events but how the couple communicate and deal with difficulties which emerge.

Predisposing factors are aspects of the individuals involved that make the relationship inherently unstable. An important predisposing factor is age: the younger two people are when they meet, move in together or marry, the greater the chance that their relationship will end (Mott & Moore, 1979). Having children at a young age is also linked with later divorce (McLanahan & Bumpass, 1988). Karney and Bradbury (1995) examined nearly 200 variables to establish which pre-disposing factors were linked with relationship breakdown. The most important factors to emerge were an unhappy childhood, anxiety or instability in one or both of the partners, and negative behaviours such as gambling or drinking. Terling-Watt (2001) studied 5,888 married people, following them up after five years to see who had divorced. She found that an important factor for both men and women was the childhood attachment/relationship with their own parents. Parental divorce and a poor relationship with the mother were most significant for women, and for men a poor or problematic relationship with their father was significant. These factors often led to loneliness and a lack of companionship in the relationship.

Duck's four-stage model of relationship breakdown

Steve Duck has argued that relationship breakdown can be seen as a staged process. In each of these stages, the focus of the couple changes and the move to the next stage happens when a threshold is reached – effectively something moves the process of splitting up forward.

- **Phase 1** – in the **intrapsychic phase**, the start of the break-up process is when one or both members of couple becomes seriously dissatisfied with some aspect of the relationship. In the intrapsychic phase, this unhappiness is generally kept inside. The focus is on the partner's inadequate behaviour in the relationship. Many people may exist in this 'phase' for a long period, unhappy but unwilling to move forward and press for changes in the relationship, especially if they have invested a great deal. If the dissatisfaction builds up to such a point that the individual can't stand it anymore, this will be the threshold that triggers the next phase.
- **Phase 2** – in the **dyadic phase**, once unhappiness has been expressed, the issue is out in the open air. The couple may discuss the problems, defend their own behaviour or engage in constructive 'relationship' talks about changes or seek help in the form of couples counselling. However, if the dissatisfaction cannot be resolved, one or both partners may reach the next threshold, '*I'd be justified in leaving*', where they feel that ending the relationship might be better than carrying on.
- **Phase 3** – in the **social phase**, the relationship problems become public as the couple tell friends and family about the problems and the possibility of splitting up. Family and friends may offer support to help the couple stay together, or they may take sides or advise them to split up. The break-up is becoming more likely. The final threshold, '*I mean it*', is reached when one partner takes the decision to instigate the end of the relationship.
- **Phase 4** – the **grave dressing** phase involves getting over the relationship. Both partners try to get their version of events over to friends and family so that they can emerge with some credibility. These versions are usually 'face saving', with the aim of showing other people that the break-up was justifiable.

Commentary on relationship breakdown

Statistical studies such as Karney and Bradbury's provide us with facts about *which* relationships end, but provide little explanation as to *why* these factors are important – the 'story' behind the facts. While younger people are statistically more likely to split up, this could be for a range of different reasons. It may be that people who are more impulsive marry at a young age and it is this factor that leads to later breakdown. Alternatively it could be younger partners are more likely to change and mature as they grow older, leading to them growing apart. Relationship breakdown is an experience that differs widely between individuals. Human experience is difficult to capture using quantitative methods and some social psychologists have begun to use qualitative methods, preferred by the sociocultural level of analysis, to consider how people experience and justify relationship splits.

Duck's model provides us with a useful framework to conceptualize the rather messy ending of relationships. It is consistent with the cognitive-social perspective as it focuses predominantly on cognitive activity – what the two people in the relationship think. The model applies specifically to relationships that have involved some degree of commitment. It is unlikely that a very short-term or superficial relationship would pass through these stages: in fact, a short-term relationship may be ended abruptly with little discussion or negotiation, sometimes by a change of Facebook 'status' or a text message.

Duck's model also considers how friends, family and the wider social network may become involved in relationship breakdown in the 'social' phase. Since its original inception, Duck has commented on the use of phase models to conceptualize relationship breakdown. He argues that models have conceptualized break-ups as existing separately from other aspects of human lives and been seen largely in a social vacuum.

SECTION SUMMARY

- Biological, social and psychological factors are important in attraction.
- Biological factors, such as genes and hormones, influence attraction below the level of conscious awareness.
- Communication is important in relationship success and survival.
- Happy and unhappy couples show different patterns of communication.
- Arranged marriages are common in many cultures and can be traditional, delegation or joint venture.
- Some studies show arranged marriages to be happy and long-lasting.
- Barrier forces make it difficult to end long-term relationships.
- Marriage at an early age and insecure childhood attachments are both predictors of marital breakdown.

Aggression – involves behaviours that are carried out with the deliberate intent to cause harm.

Violence – involves physical victimization of another person.

Violence

While the terms aggression and violence are used interchangeably in daily life, they have different meanings. **Aggression** refers to behaviours that are carried out with the deliberate intent to cause harm. This includes verbal aggression, such as spreading malicious rumours or damage to property. **Violence** is a specific kind of aggression that involves the physical victimization of another person. The Violence Prevention Alliance (2010) defines violence as 'the intentional use of force or power, threatened or actual, against another person that leads to or has a high likelihood of causing injury, death, psychological harm, poor development, or deprivation.'

Violence is not a new phenomenon, even though it may take new forms today. In the hunter-gatherer era, violent acts and threats would have been used to defend precious resources and to protect offspring, and evolutionary psychologists believe that conflict and warfare have been a 'part of human social life for as long as history can tell us' (Barrett *et al.*, 2002, p.260). However, while most people have the capacity to act violently under certain circumstances, the vast majority of people do not carry out violent acts. Groups such as the Amish, who practise a lifestyle of non-aggression, demonstrate the important role played by cultural factors in the use of violence. This section of the chapter will examine how sociocultural factors, including exposure to violent media, may influence violent behaviour before moving to consider strategies for reducing violence.

The problem of violence

Interpersonal violence (IV) is a huge problem worldwide. Violent acts take many different forms and vary in relation to:

- The type of act (e.g. physical, sexual violence).
- The target of the violent act (partner, stranger, child).
- The severity of the consequences (injury, death).

Violence also takes place between groups such as rival gangs. Large scale conflicts between ethnic and religious groups have accounted for most of the deaths due to violence over human history. Wartime rape is a pervasive problem of armed conflict. Some armed groups rape women then brand them like cattle, leaving lasting scars that can be seen by family and community members (Casanas, 2010). Violence directed towards women takes many forms including 'domestic' (partner) violence, rape, forced marriages and so called 'honour killings'. The USA has the highest murder rate of any industrialized country and this is most notable for young men aged between 15 and 30. Domestic violence is the leading cause of injury among women of reproductive age in the USA, and around 25 per cent of murders involve husbands killing their wives.

Social and cultural norms

LEARNING OUTCOME
- Evaluate sociocultural explanations of the origins of violence.

Link to the sociocultural level of analysis

Link to Principle 1 (*see page 66*): The social and cultural environment influences individual behaviour.

Sociocultural explanations of violence are based on the principles of the sociocultural level of analysis, which takes the view that individual behaviour is influenced by **social and cultural norms**. Cultural norms dictate the legal practices and judgements related to violence. In some parts of the world, the concept of 'crime of passion' is used to refer to violence that takes place when infidelity is uncovered. Many legal systems allow more lenient sentences to crimes of passion and legal practices related to honour crime often excuse perpetrators from punishment. The importance of cultural norms can also be seen in relation to the use of violence (hitting, spanking, and smacking) to punish children. In many cultures, parents have historically had the right to decide how and when to discipline their children and the right to use physical punishment if they wish. There have been several international attempts to ban the physical punishment of children and by 2010, 29 countries around the world – 22 of them in Europe – had made physical punishment of children illegal (Global Initiative to end all Corporal Punishment of Children, 2012). This is an emotive issue and many people hold strong opinions about whether or not children should be smacked and who has the right to decide (government, parents or schools).

Social norms are also influential. One reason why domestic violence and abuse of children is so common is the **norm of family privacy**. Studies of bystander effects have shown how witnesses are reluctant to intervene in an apparent violent argument when they believe the incident involves a couple rather than unrelated individuals. Shotland and Straw (1976) conducted an experiment in which a man attacked a woman in the presence of a bystander. Intervention occurred much more frequently when participants were led to believe that the couple were strangers (65 per cent) than when they were married (19 per cent). Shotland and Straw (1976) concluded that intervention depended on whether the violence was seen as a 'domestic' dispute or not. When asked why they had failed to intervene, participants in the 'married' condition justified their inaction by saying that the argument was a private matter or none of their business. The strong norm of family privacy also contributes to high rates of violence towards young children as this can also go unseen.

The American Psychological Association (2001) identifies a number of sociocultural factors that contribute to the high murder rates in the USA. American culture glorifies violence in films and American heroes are often lawless individuals. The American constitution gives its citizens the right to bear and use firearms in response to threats towards property or family and the easy availability of firearms in the USA goes some way to explaining the high murder rates. The **'culture of honour'**, which was discussed in Chapter 3, helps to explain why rural American states, such as Carolina, have three times the murder rate of densely populated areas such as Massachusetts. Other factors include poverty, socioeconomic inequality and prejudice/discrimination between different groups.

Evaluation of sociocultural explanations

Sociocultural explanations focus on the social environment and the norms that regulate behaviour. In doing so, they strongly emphasize the importance of socialization and nurture. Most people in America do not act aggressively, however, despite the wide availability of firearms. In focusing heavily on social forces, sociocultural explanations overlook the importance of individual biology and predispositions. Studies have demonstrated that biological factors also influence aggressive and violent behaviour. Adrian Raine, working in the USA, has found that there are clear differences, detectable by PET scans, between those convicted of violent and non-violent crimes. Raine *et al.* (1998) compared the brain activity of two groups of murderers – those who killed in a fit of rage (termed 'affective' murderers) and 'predatory' killers who planned the murder – with normal volunteers. Raine found anomalies in the scans of affective murderers, but not in those of predators. In a second study, Raine's team carried out MRI scans of 21 men with anti-social personality disorders who had committed violent crimes. Compared with normal volunteers, the men had shrunken prefrontal cortices that were reduced by up to 14 per cent in volume. These studies imply that some individuals may be more susceptible to behaving violently and may have less ability to control their aggressive impulses.

Other studies have indicated that nature and nurture interact together in relation to violence. Caspi *et al.* (2002) studied 442 boys born in Dunedin, New Zealand in 1972, following them from birth to adulthood. Of these boys, 154 had been maltreated in the first ten years, experiencing sexual abuse, beatings or rejection by mother or foster parents. Caspi's team found that a gene responsible for the levels of production of the enzyme monoamine oxidize A (MAO-A) was important. Children who had a high level of the enzyme were unlikely to develop anti-social problems even if they were maltreated, neglected or abused. In contrast, children with a low level of the enzyme were much more sensitive to environmental insults and those who suffered violence in childhood were likely to commit violent acts. These findings show how genes can moderate children's sensitivity to difficult environments and help to explain why not all victims of maltreatment grow up to victimize others.

Link to the biological level of analysis

The study by Caspi *et al.* (2002) demonstrates the complex interaction between environment and individual biology in explaining violence.

Sociocultural explanations of violence between groups

Much of the violence in the USA takes place between rival street gangs who see violence as an acceptable or desirable way of increasing the status of their own group. Gangs tend to be overwhelmingly male and almost 90 per cent of gang members are from ethnic minority groups, notably African American or Hispanic, although recent evidence

Figure 7.6 Realistic conflict theory and social identity theory are two theories of gang violence

suggests that white gangs, linked to right-wing political groups (e.g. skinhead and neo-Nazi) may be on the increase. Youths are motivated to join gangs for a sense of connection, belonging and identity. Gangs provide members with strong friendship links and with status, excitement and the opportunity to acquire resources. There may also be gains to self-esteem from group membership, depending on the group's perceived status and rank. Gang violence often results from provocation and members tend to be very sensitive to 'disrespect' and possible slights (American Psychological Association, 2011).

Two theories that provide explanations of conflict between groups are realistic conflict theory (Sherif) and social identity theory (Tajfel). These theories share the view that the desire to connect with others and to belong to a social group is an important factor and both agree that prejudice is at the root of conflict between groups.

Violence between groups occurs as an attempt to gain economic or political control over regions or when there is competition for scarce or coveted resources. Sherif's **realistic conflict theory (RCT)** argues that:

- Hostility and aggression arise when groups compete for resources that only one group can attain. This is referred to as 'negative goal interdependence'.
- Simple contact between two groups is insufficient to reduce negative attitudes, prejudice and conflict.
- Conflict between groups can be reduced or minimized by the establishment of superordinate goals, which require united, cooperative action – a state of 'positive goal interdependence'.

> **Link to the sociocultural level of analysis**
>
> Link to Principle 2 (*see page 67*): We want connectedness with, and a sense of belonging with, others.

Key study

Sherif *et al.* (1961)

Sherif derived his theory from a series of experiments known as the 'Robbers Cave' studies, named after an American summer camp in Oklahoma. Twenty-two white, middle class 11-year-old boys attending an American summer camp were divided into two groups living in separate cabins. For the first week of the camp, the boys were unaware of the other group's existence. They were encouraged to develop a strong group identity and adopt a team name – the Eagles and the Rattlers. In the second week of the camp ('friction'), the two groups were introduced to each other and took part in a tournament with competitions and prizes awarded. Each team showed strong hostility towards members of the other group, in the form of name calling and booing the opposing side. Individual fights between group members broke out. The level of conflict was demonstrated when one team burned the other's flag and raids took place on the opposing team cabins.

In the third stage of the experiment, Sherif instigated a stage of cooperation in which both teams of boys were required to work together in order to achieve mutual goals, the recovery of a 'broken down' truck and restoration of the camp's water supply, which had been cut off. The process of cooperation and working together reduced animosity and conflict between the group members.

Tajfel's **social identity theory** also presents an explanation of intergroup hostility and conflict. In contrast to realistic conflict theory, SIT argues that conflict arises purely from group membership and competition for resources is not needed. Tajfel *et al.*'s minimal groups experiments demonstrated how young boys would form strong attachments to their own 'in-group' and favour them over members of an out-group when allocating rewards. This tendency was so strongly marked that boys would allocate their own group fewer rewards in order to maximize the difference between the two groups. Discrimination and favouritism occurred, even though the distinction between the two groups was purely arbitrary (minimal).

SIT argues that we gain our sense of social identity and self-esteem through membership of social groups. While ethnic and religious groups can co-exist alongside each other, in many places there are hierarchies with some groups having greater access to power and resources than others. SIT argues that our self-esteem is strongly linked to the status of our group. If our group is looked down on or has less access to important resources, personal esteem will be low. The desire to increase social status and self-esteem can be achieved by a number of strategies including social mobility (moving to a higher status group) and social creativity (improving the status of our own group). When these options are unavailable in strongly stratified societies (for example, the Apartheid system in South Africa), conflict between groups is likely to occur.

Commentary on explanations of group violence

RCT and SIT provide valuable explanations of how and why violence occurs between different ethnic groups and rival gangs. Realistic conflict theory sees competition for resources as the basis for intergroup conflict and argues that conflicts can be reduced by the establishment of superordinate (shared) goals that de-emphasize group membership and require opposing groups to work together. This approach took place during the Northern Ireland Peace Process, in which the establishment of a power-sharing assembly became a joint goal for religious groups living in Northern Ireland.

In contrast, Tajfel's SIT argues that conflict between groups can occur in the absence of competition, purely as a result of group membership. Tajfel's minimal groups experiments demonstrated how teenage boys showed strong preferences for in-group members and prejudice against out-group members and it is not difficult to see how prejudice can turn into hostility between rival gangs. The most influential strategy to reduce prejudice and violence is known as the **contact hypothesis**, which is based on the idea that face-to-face contact between groups should challenge and remove prejudices. However, while contact between groups can reduce prejudice and conflict, it can also fuel them – a situation known as the paradox of contact (Allport, 1954).

Exposure to violence

LEARNING OUTCOME
■ Discuss the effects of short-term and long-term exposure to violence.

In Chapter 3, you were introduced to the experiments carried out by Bandura *et al.* (1963) (*see pages 76–7*). These showed how young children who were exposed to a role model acting aggressively towards a Bobo doll copied the actions of the model and behaved aggressively towards the doll when given the opportunity. Social learning theory (SLT) argues that:

■ Behaviours can be learnt through observation and imitation of role models.
■ Behaviour is more likely to be imitated when models are seen to be rewarded for their behaviour (**vicarious reinforcement**).
■ Role models who are similar (for example, in age and sex) exert the most powerful influences on children.

(*You can recap the principles of SLT by looking back at page 77.*)

The implication of SLT is that exposure to violence can lead to the imitation of violent actions. However, there has been lengthy debate regarding the ability to generalize Bandura's findings to real-life settings in which violence is watched. Many critics have drawn attention to the artificial nature of the laboratory setting, the deliberate use of cues to lead the children to act violently (such as placing the doll and mallet alongside each other), and the artificial stimuli used, which bore little resemblance to the kinds of programmes children would watch on television (Giles, 2004). The possible link between media violence and aggression has been debated extensively over the last 50 years and we can't cover all of this output here. However, this section of the chapter will give you a flavour of the different methods that have been used to study exposure to violence, as well as the conclusions that can be drawn about the short- and long-term effects of exposure to violence.

Physiological effects: arousal and desensitization

The immediate effect of exposure to violence is **physiological arousal**. Acts of violence – whether on screen or in real life – create an immediate bodily response mediated by the stress systems of the body. These include increased heart and breathing rates and skin conductivity (a measure known as the galvanic skin response or GSR). The effect is relatively easy to demonstrate experimentally in laboratory conditions, by showing violent films to participants. Physiological arousal also occurs with violent computer games. Tafalla (2007) has shown how the music that accompanies games like *Doom* can play an important part in increasing heart rate.

With regular exposure to violence in films or computer games, the stress response diminishes and the watcher/player no longer experiences the same strong feelings of excitement. This process is based on the behavioural principle of habituation and is referred to as **desensitization** (effectively becoming less sensitive to a stimulus). Carnagey *et al.*(2007) allocated participants to play a violent or a non-violent game for 20 minutes, then showed them a film of real-life violence. Those who had played the violent game showed desensitized responses to the film, including lower heart rates and galvanic skin response. Similarly, Bartholow *et al.* (2006) compared the extent of brain responses (using a neurological measure of the 'event potential') of people who regularly played violent games with those who didn't and found reduced brain responses to violence in regular gamers.

Cognitive effects: disinhibition and cognitive priming

Exposure to violent media may influence aggressive behaviour through cognitive mechanisms, notably disinhibition and cognitive priming. Disinhibition refers to the idea that watching violence enables watchers to shed their natural inhibitions towards acting aggressively and therefore normalizes aggressive responses, making violence appear a legitimate response to situations. As noted in Chapter 3, memories are stored in the long-term memory in the form of representations called schemas and scripts. Cognitive **priming** occurs when we encounter a situation similar to one we have witnessed in a film, and the aggressive schema is triggered by cues, making violent behaviour more likely to occur (Huesmann, 1986). Cognitive priming has been demonstrated in a range of research studies. For instance, Anderson *et al.* (2003b) asked participants to listen to songs, some with aggressive lyrics and others by the same artists with neutral lyrics. When asked to carry out a word completion test later, those who had listened to the aggressive songs were more likely to produce aggressive solutions (e.g. completing h*t as hit rather than hot) than those who had listened to the neutral lyrics.

Priming – exposure to aggressive behaviour makes aggressive behaviour more likely.

Violent behaviour

Exposure to violent media produces short- and long-term effects on users, but the issue of possible effects on behaviour continues to be hotly debated. Exposure to violent media is reported to have played a role in cases of extreme violence, such as the Columbine High School massacre, the abduction and murder of James Bulger in Merseyside, UK and the 2011 shooting in the Netherlands by Tristan van der Vlis in a shopping mall. In these atrocities, some of the actions bore strong resemblance to scenes from films and from computer games such as *Call of Duty: Modern Warfare 2*. However, examples do not constitute psychological evidence and in all of these cases, others factors played an important role.

Correlational studies have indicated a relationship between watching violent television in childhood and later adult aggression. Huesmann *et al.* (2003) carried out a longitudinal study with a sample of just under 500 US children aged between five and eight. The children were asked about their favourite TV programmes and characters. All participants who agreed to continue in the study were followed up in their early 20s and two measures of violent behaviour were obtained. Firstly the researchers interviewed someone who knew the participant well, and secondly they examined official records of criminal convictions. Huesmann *et al.* found that viewing violent television in childhood was positively correlated with both measures of adult aggression 15 years later. Males who had watched large amounts of violent television in boyhood had a three times greater rate of criminal convictions than males classed as low viewers of violence in boyhood.

A correlational study by Johnson *et al.* (2002) assessed the link between television viewing and aggressive behaviour over a 17-year period using a large sample of 707 people. The researchers found a significant association between the amount of time spent watching television during adolescence and early adulthood and the likelihood of subsequent violent acts, including assault and robbery. Anderson and Bushman (2001) argue that Johnson's study is important as it contradicts the commonly held view that TV violence only affects children. Secondly, the relatively large sample size (707 families) and time span (17 years) allows a meaningful test of the effects of television exposure on severe aggressive behaviour.

Natural experiments have taken advantage of the introduction of TV to geographically remote communities to examine if rates of violence change. Williams (1986) studied the impact of television on children's behaviour in a remote town in British Columbia. Williams used playground observers to record the aggressive acts that they saw in second grade children and found that the number of acts of pushing and taunting doubled after the introduction of television. However, contradictory findings were reported by Charlton *et al.* (2002) when they examined the impact of the introduction of television to the small Atlantic island of St Helena. Forty-seven young children aged between three and four were studied before TV was introducing in 1995 and for three years after its introduction. Charlton *et al.* found no overall increase in aggressive behaviour in the children. One explanation for this related to the social context. St Helena is a small, tight-knit community where people know each other well and there are few opportunities to behave aggressively without surveillance. However, Charlton established that children who had been rated by teachers as more aggressive before the introduction of television, tended to watch more aggressive TV, notably cartoons. Similar to Caspi's study, this demonstrates how pre-dispositions may shape different kinds of environments.

Theory of knowledge

While experimentation is the preferred method in the natural sciences, the human sciences make extensive use of correlation, largely for ethical reasons. It would be unacceptable to expose young children deliberately to violence to assess its possible effects on behaviour, but it is more acceptable to measure levels of exposure. However, it is impossible to conclude that watching violence causes aggression (i.e. a causal relationship between two variables) in correlational research. An alternative explanation is that more aggressive children may choose to watch violent programmes. There is some support for this claim from Bandura *et al.*'s (1963) study and from Charlton's natural experiment on St Helena, as both indicated that children rated as more aggressive tended to prefer violent programmes.

Strategies for reducing violence

LEARNING OUTCOME
■ Discuss the relative effectiveness of two strategies for reducing violence.

Kazdin (2011) conceptualizes violence as a 'wicked problem' for psychologists and policy makers. By this he means that there is no single agreement of the problem of violence. What is seen as acceptable in one culture (for example, honour killings) may be abhorrent to another. In addition, violence is a complex issue that does not have a single cause (such as exposure to violence in the media) but is likely to occur when a set of factors (biological disposition, poverty and abuse) co-exist and influence each other. Violence is embedded in other social problems, such as poverty, prejudice and discrimination. Together this makes it increasingly apparent that there is no single or simple solution that will eliminate violence.

Strategies for reducing violence can be divided into those that aim to prevent violence taking place, such as anti-bullying education programmes, and those that aim to alter the behaviour of those individuals who have a track record of violence, such as the anger management programmes used in many prisons.

Anti-bullying interventions

Bullying is an age-old problem, although today it can take new cyber forms. Bullying can have serious consequences, for those who are bullied and for the wider community. An analysis of 37 high school shootings found that many of the perpetrators had felt bullied, excluded or threatened by other students before taking their drastic actions. Estimates of the prevalence of bullying vary but rates are currently thought to be somewhere around one in five students.

One widely used programme offered in Norway's state schools is based on research by Olweus (1993, 2001) and is known as the 'Olweus Bullying Prevention Programme'. This programme has been identified as one of 11 'blueprint' or model programmes for reducing bullying by the American Psychological Association and is now used in American and British schools (APA, 2004). The programme aims to create a school environment that reduces opportunities for bullying and simultaneously removes the rewards available for bullies. The ideal anti-bullying school environment is characterized by:

■ warmth, interest and involvement from adults
■ clear limits on what constitutes unacceptable behaviour
■ consistent application of non-physical sanctions (i.e. punishments) for unacceptable behaviour and violation of rules
■ authoritative adults who act as positive role models.

A number of large-scale evaluations of the programme over the last 20 years have produced some positive results, including substantial reductions – typically in the 30–50 percent range – in the frequency with which students report being bullied and bullying others. Other benefits include reductions in other kinds of anti-social behaviours such as truancy, vandalism and theft, along with improvements in the 'social climate' of the class, such as improved order and discipline, more positive social relationships, and a more positive attitude towards schoolwork and school.

Anger management programmes

The most popular strategy for reducing violence at the individual level has been anger management. This method is based on the **cognitive behavioural approach** and takes the assumption that information processing biases are at the base of many aggressive and violent reactions. Anger management has been used in school settings and is widely used in prisons and secure settings. It offers a 'structured but flexible and individually tailored approach' to working clinically with violent offenders (Walker & Bright, 2009).

Feindler and colleagues (Feindler & Guttman, 1994; Feindler & Scalley, 1998) have developed various anger management programmes in the USA that aim to prevent the extreme kinds of violence seen in American high school shootings. Anger management programmes aim to reduce the intensity and frequency of anger expression and to develop alternative, non-aggressive responses to difficult situations. A meta-analysis carried out by Beck and Fernandez (1998) examined 46 studies considering the effectiveness of anger management programmes. About half of the studies in their analysis used schoolchildren, students or 'normal' volunteers with little history of violence. They found evidence to suggest that anger management is an effective intervention for school children.

However, there is mixed evidence that anger management is useful with violent offenders. Some studies show positive outcomes (for example, Beck & Fernandez, 1998), but others show little or no benefit. Walker and Bright examined the effectiveness of a CBT programme, Skills Training for Aggression Control (STAC) with adult male prisoners in the UK. Violent offenders who took part in the programme were compared with a matched control group who were placed on a waiting list for anger management. The findings provided little support for the effectiveness of STAC and Walker and Bright argue that caution is recommended before implementing anger management programmes with violent offenders. Others have pointed to the difficulties of using anger management as a group treatment (Sharry & Owens, 2000), and to the drop-out rates (Siddle *et al.*, 2003).

Some critics have disputed the assumption that anger is the cause of violence. For example, there are no differences in the levels of anger felt by men and women, but dramatic differences in violence (Archer, 2004), and many critics have pointed out that there is no clear relationship between anger and violence. Walker and Bright argue that anger management may not only be ineffective for violent offenders, but also irrelevant and they warn that 'Designing a single treatment for violence would be like giving analgesia as the sole treatment for chest pain – it may be a suitable treatment for some, but ineffective or inappropriate for others.'

SECTION SUMMARY

- ■ Sociocultural explanations of violence focus on social and cultural norms.
- ■ Intergroup conflict arises from competition for resources and from prejudice and discrimination.
- ■ The interplay of sociocultural factors with individual predispositions is important in understanding violence.
- ■ Exposure to violent media produces physiological and cognitive effects including arousal, cognitive priming and disinhibition.
- ■ Longer term exposure leads to emotional desensitization to violence.
- ■ Correlational studies show a link between viewing violence in childhood and later adult violence. Some experimental studies have also shown this effect.
- ■ Anger management programmes have shown success with schoolchildren but appear less effective with violent offenders.

Sport psychology

Introduction

Sport psychology is the scientific study of human behaviour in sport and exercise. It involves an assessment of how mental processes affect sporting performance, as well as the psychological and physical effects of participation in sport and exercise.

Emotion and motivation

LEARNING OUTCOME
- Evaluate psychological research (that is, theories and/or studies) relevant to the study of sport psychology.
- Evaluate theories of motivation in sport.

Several theories explain how performance and attainment in sport are affected by emotional and motivational factors. These theories can be evaluated in terms of their degree of research support and their practical applications.

> **Link to the cognitive level of analysis**
> Explanations of motivation in sport have cognitive components. **Cognitive-evaluation theory** sees the perception of motivational reasons for involvement in sport as linked to actual participation, while **AGT** sees motivation as linked to the perception of what success means to an individual. **Self-efficacy** has a cognitive component in seeing the cognitive processing of several factors as important to self-appraisal and self-persuasion.

Cognitive-evaluation theory (CET)

Cognitive-evaluation theory – an explanation of how external factors affect intrinsic motivation.

Intrinsic motivation – the incentive that comes from the joy of participating in an activity.

Extrinsic motivation – the incentive that comes from external factors, such as performing for money.

According to the **cognitive-evaluation theory**, **intrinsic motivation** is where participation itself is motivating, due to the sense of joy it brings, while **extrinsic motivation** is where participation occurs due to being externally rewarded, e.g. participating for the money. Research shows that an increase in extrinsic motivation (e.g. through rewards, threats or evaluation) lowers autonomy (independence) and choice and reduces intrinsic motivation, as the behaviour becomes controlled by the extrinsic rewards. In other words, being externally rewarded for participation reduces the internal joy that such participation brings. The exception is extrinsic rewards that give information about the quality of performance, as they are not controlling behaviour. In other words, extrinsic rewards in the form of information that strengthens the perception of competence improve intrinsic motivation.

Figure 8.1 Playing for a sense of inner joy involves intrinsic motivation, while playing to win a trophy involves extrinsic motivation.

For example, a man is plagued by boys kicking a ball against his house. Instead of rebuking them, he says he loves it so much that he will pay them to continue, which they do. This continues until the man tells them that he is short of funds and can pay only half the usual amount. Angrily, the boys refuse and disappear, never to return.

The ball-kicking had been motivated intrinsically through the sense of joy it brought. When the activity became extrinsically linked to payment and the payments ceased, however, the boys stopped as there was no intrinsic motivation.

Research

- Ryan (1979) found that college scholarship gridiron players had less intrinsic motivation than non-scholarship players, as the sports scholarships controlled their behaviour. Without the sports scholarship they wouldn't be at college. This supports the idea that extrinsic motivation that controls behaviour decreases intrinsic motivation. Female athletes on scholarships, however, had more intrinsic motivation than those not on scholarships, possibly because as scholarships were new and rare among females, they were perceived as providing positive evaluations about sporting ability. This supports the notion that extrinsic rewards that increase the perception of competence improve intrinsic motivation.
- Deci (1971) took an activity intrinsically motivating (completing puzzles) and paid participants to do it. When the extrinsic rewards stopped, less effort was directed at the task and participants reported it to be less enjoyable, supporting the idea of extrinsic rewards exerting control over the activity and decreasing intrinsic motivation. When Deci repeated the study, however, but with verbal praise as the extrinsic reward rather than money, task performance improved when the extrinsic rewards stopped, as intrinsic motivation was increased by the social approval that the verbal praise brought. This suggests that extrinsic rewards that don't reduce autonomy (freedom of choice to perform a task) can increase intrinsic motivation.

Evaluation

- CET explains that individuals who participate for intrinsic reasons experience harmonious passion, where participation brings feelings of joy, as the activity forms a core part of those individuals' identity, while those who participate for extrinsic reasons experience obsessive passion, where participation comes from an externally controlled need to complete the activity.
- A problem in assessing the validity of CET is that, unlike extrinsic rewards, it is difficult to objectively define and measure intrinsic rewards.

Theory of knowledge

A common problem when studying psychological phenomena, as with CET, is that of defining phenomena in an objectively measureable way. Often such definitions do not exist or may be so artificial as to have little relevance to real life.

Practical applications

Extrinsic rewards should not be used to encourage participation in already enjoyable activities. Coaches should put winning in perspective and emphasize intrinsic rewards, like fitness and improvement, rather than tie activities to extrinsic rewards.

Achievement goal theory – an explanation of the reasons for pursuing success in sport.

Achievement goal theory (AGT)

Achievement goal theory argues that comprehending motivation involves understanding what success means to individuals, with success being dependent on whether they believe different types of goals have been reached. Individuals therefore give meaning to behaviour through the goals they're trying to achieve.

AGT sees two main types of motivation, dependent on how individuals perceive achievement goals (success):

1. **Task-oriented goals** – indicators of success based on mastery of challenges and skills and self-improvement, e.g. better placement of a free kick than previously.
2. **Ego-oriented goals** – indicators of success based on performing better than others, e.g. beating an opponent at tennis.

Individuals can score differently or similarly on both types of motivation.

Research

- Ntoumanis (2001) found that task-orientation predicted motivational variables with high self-determination, where individuals had strong inner-motivation (for intrinsic reasons) to perform activities, while ego-orientation predicted motivational variables with low self-determination, where motivation was extrinsically based. This suggests a link between achievement goal theory and cognitive-evaluation theory.
- Weiss and Ferrer-Caja (2002) performed a meta-analysis to find that children with task-oriented goals who wish to learn new skills show persistence in doing so, while those with ego-oriented goals had less persistence and thus higher drop-out rates. This supports the predictions of AGT.
- Roberts (2001) found that athletes with task-oriented goals see success as due to effort, while those with ego-oriented goals see success as due to ability, which explains why task-oriented athletes persist more and have lower drop-out rates than ego-oriented athletes.

Evaluation

- AGT needs to include the situational factor of 'motivational climate', which regulates the relationship between goal-orientation and performance, as influenced by a coach's attitude and behaviour. A mastery climate occurs when coaches stress effort and skill development, with mistakes used as feedback and an aid to learning, while an ego-oriented climate occurs when athletes are compared with each other and mistakes are criticized and punished.
- The focus by AGT on task and ego-oriented goals has led to the neglect of other possible sporting goal orientations, like affiliative needs, concerning the desire to form social and emotional bonds with others.
- Harwood (2002) points out that goal orientations are not universal to all situations but instead are context-based, e.g. having different goal orientations in training and competition. Roberts (2001) argues goal orientations change during a game, e.g. an athlete begins with the ego-orientation of winning, but when they realize this isn't possible they change to a task-orientation of practising new skills.

Practical applications

AGT suggests a practical application in that coaches and PE teachers should encourage task-oriented motivation more, as it's linked with higher persistence with sport and lower drop-out rates, which could improve the fitness levels of society. Hardy *et al.* (1996) stress, though, that an element of ego-orientation is needed for elite sporting success.

Self-efficacy theory
– an explanation of
how an individual's
perception of their
ability affects their
capability to attain
goals.

Self-efficacy theory

Self-efficacy theory concerns the degree to which individuals believe they can perform tasks successfully to obtain particular outcomes, like scoring a penalty to ensure victory. Self-efficacy involves self-appraisal and self-persuasion, gained through cognitive processing of:

1. **Perceptions of past performances** – perceptions of successful past performances enhances self-efficacy, with the influence of past performance dependent on the perceived difficulty of tasks, the effort expended, the amount of guidance given and the perception of whether abilities are natural or learnt.
2. **Social comparison with others** – self-efficacy rises if performance is seen as successful in comparison to others.
3. **Self-modelling** – enhancement of self-efficacy comes from focusing on the positive parts of performance and using this as a model for future performance.
4. **Persuasion of others** – self-efficacy is increased through feedback, praise, etc., of others, dependent on their status and credibility.
5. **Physiological arousal** – self-efficacy is affected by physiological information, such as degree of arousal and self-doubt.
6. **Emotional states** – experiencing positive emotions during performance increases self-efficacy.
7. **Imaginal experiences** – self-efficacy is increased through imagining executing skills successfully.

Research

■ Bandura (1997) found that perceptions of past performances was the richest form of efficacy information, as it gave detail concerning an individual's mastery of necessary skills. This implies that certain components of self-efficacy are more important than others.
■ Miller (1993) found a negative correlation between high self-efficacy in swimmers and motivational levels when they were given unchallenging goals, supporting the idea that perceived success on difficult tasks, performed without assistance, results in greater levels of self-efficacy.

■ George *et al.* (1992) found that the less experience athletes had of a competitive situation, the more they looked to others to judge their own capabilities, which demonstrates the value of social comparison in determining self-efficacy levels and suggests that social comparison is more influential in certain circumstances.
■ Singleton and Feltz (1999) found that hockey players who used self-modelling videotapes for several weeks produced greater shooting accuracy and heightened self-efficacy for competition performance, illustrating the role of self-modelling in raising efficacy levels.

Figure 8.2 Ice hockey players who viewed self-modelling video tapes had greater shooting accuracy and heightened self-efficacy for competition performance.

Theory of knowledge

Research can never 'prove' theories to be true (although can show them to be false), as there's always the possibility that chance factors have caused the differences in findings between research conditions. This is why results only ever 'suggest' facts to be so.

Evaluation

- Self-efficacy levels also influence thought patterns concerning such things as goal intentions, fears and causal attributions (an individual's perceptions of why they succeed or fail), as well as emotional reactions like pride, joy, etc., and such thought patterns influence motivational levels themselves. This demonstrates an indirect effect of self-efficacy on motivation.
- The outcome of self-efficacy is not only a determination of an individual's motivational levels, but additionally an effect on the types and difficulties of challenges undertaken, how much effort will be expended and the degree of perseverance when difficulties arise.

Practical applications

A practical application of self-efficacy theory is that athletes should be encouraged to focus on successes more than failures, as successes provide more encouragement and enhancement of self-efficacy, which lead to greater performances.

> **Link to the cognitive level of analysis**
>
> Goal setting links to the cognitive level of analysis in seeing target-setting as linked to the perception of motivation and confidence.

> **Goal setting** – creating specific standards of task proficiency to attain, usually within a set time period.

Goal setting in sport

LEARNING OUTCOME
- Using research studies, explain the role of goal setting in the motivation of individuals.

Goal setting involves creating targets involving specific standards of task proficiency, usually to be attained within a given time period. Goal setting thus becomes strongly tied to motivational, commitment and confidence levels and creates focus, stopping athletes from becoming confused and anxious.

Ultimate (final) goals are referred to as **long-term** or **product-oriented goals**, which are reached by achieving a series of **short-term** or **process-oriented goals** that lead up to the long-term goal. Achieving short-term goals doesn't ensure long-term goal success; it merely increases the chances of doing so.

Goals should be **objective** (measureable), and difficult but attainable, so that athletes are truly stretched.

Goals need to be **realistic** to create motivation, and must actually be achieved in order to increase motivation. **Unrealistic** goals lead to feelings of failure, frustration, anxiety, loss of motivational and confidence levels, and ultimately high drop-out rates.

Goals also need to be **specific** so that they are objective, allowing an assessment of whether they have been reached. 'Winning' and 'doing well' aren't specific goals, while 'scoring an average of 30 points a game' is a specific goal.

Goals should be pre-determined so they can be specifically trained for. They shouldn't be over-specific but should be more **open-ended** (possessing an upper and lower limit), so as not to inhibit excellent performances.

Athletes should be included in the goal-setting process to create ownership of goals and stronger efforts to reach them, while the interaction and interest of others in goal setting, like coaches, is motivating in itself.

Figure 8.3 The Sydney Swans (formerly the South Melbourne Swans) victory in the 2012 Australian rules Grand Final is an example of a long-term/product-oriented goal, whereas their victories in the individual games leading up to the Grand Final are examples of short-term/process-oriented goals.

Early short-term goals should be easy to ensure achievement and thus increased confidence, commitment and motivation to reach the next goal. Subsequent goals become harder, leading to systematically increased efforts towards the long-term goal.

Through goal setting, athletes engage in systematic target-setting. This eventually becomes **internalized** and **automatic**, allowing the production of self-directed sporting behaviours.

Research

- Locke (1990) reviewed 110 studies, finding that in 90 per cent of studies, specific, difficult but attainable, open-ended goals led to better performances than easy, over-specific or non-specific goals, because they allowed the better formation of training schedules, as well as increasing motivation and persistence levels. This supports the idea that open-ended goals do not restrict excellent performances, and that goals that stretch performers lead to better performances than easy-to-achieve ones.
- O'Block and Evans (1984) devised interval goal setting (IGS) to determine short- and long-term goals, although it works best with immediate short-term goals. IGS creates realistic goals by using past performances and has four steps: re-engagement (from the previous interval goal), activation, practice, trial and measurement. IGS is calculated as follows, with an example given from a 5,000 m runner:
  A Average of last five events (14 minutes 00 seconds)
  B Best performance of last five events (13 minutes 45 seconds)
  C Difference between average and best performance (A − B) (15 seconds)
  D Lower boundary of the interval (13 minutes 45 seconds)
  E Interval mid-point (D − C) (13 minutes 30 seconds)
  F Interval upper point (E − C) (13 minutes 15 seconds)

  E is realistic, while F allows for exceptional performances. Any performances outside the interval goal are failures, but are used to calculate the next interval goal. The benefit of IGS is that it allows variability in performance to be seen as successful, while being constantly updated to reflect current levels of capability. IGS also allows sportspeople to predict future performances by objectively evaluating the past and relating it to the present.
- Swartz and Wayne (1979) reported that top marathon runners use predetermined set goals, because the process of setting such goals helps modify mental expectancies. This suggests that setting prior goals mentally guides athletes in their physical preparation towards achieving targets.
- Creel (1980) designed a form of goal setting for gridiron footballers that placed short-term goals in a sequential order leading up to a long-term goal. Goal objectives were divided into three aspects of a game: attacking, defending and kicking. Each aspect was then sub-divided into specific, targeted goals. For example, for attacking:
  1. maintaining a 4 yards per play average
  2. averaging three touchdowns per game
  3. permitting no interceptions
  4. scoring on all goal line situations.

  Creel found that attaining these goals didn't guarantee long-term goal success, but did enhance the chances of doing so, emphasizing how setting measureable short-term goals is an effective strategy in reaching ultimate long-term goals.

Key study

Stout (1999)

Stout (1999) examined goal setting strategies and locus of control beliefs among 219 competitive swimmers aged 18–24 who swam around 20 hours per week. An internal locus of control refers to those who see performance as within their own control, such as through personal levels of skill and effort, while those with an external locus of control

Key study

see performance as determined by factors outside their control, like the degree of luck or the quality of the opposition. Using questionnaires Stout found that most swimmers had an internal locus of control, which suggests they set more difficult goals (which they tend to achieve), as they exert greater levels of effort and persistence than non-sporting persons and leisure swimmers. Locke and Latham (1985) supported this view, as they found that athletes reduce effort and persistence when they perceive performance as controlled by external forces.

Figure 8.4 Females use goal setting more frequently and more effectively than males.

Evaluation

- Long-term goals are often too far distant in time to maintain attention and interest. Combining short-term and long-term goals is therefore the optimal way of maximizing performance over extended time periods. Tennenbaum *et al.* (1991) supported this by finding that combining short- and long-term goals led to better performances than did short- or long-term goals on their own.

- Short-term goals are a richer source of motivation than long-term goals, as they provide immediate feedback and incentives about performance. Short-term goals also allow ultimate, long-term goals to be constantly updated, so that they remain constructive and attainable.

- A methodological problem is that very little research involves athletes in real-life settings (i.e. competitive and training arenas), with most research involving artificial laboratory settings and non-sporting/recreational samples. This suggests that findings may not be applicable to athletes, who possess different levels of motivation and cognitive mind sets.

- Little research has been done to examine possible differences in goal setting between different sports, such as individual sports like athletics and team sports like cricket.

Practical applications

A practical application of research is that coaches should provide reinforcement in the form of positive feedback about performance when short-term goals are reached, because as well as being informative and instructive, it is also highly motivating, increasing the chances that future, more difficult short-term goals (and ultimately the long-term goal) will be reached, through increased commitment, belief and persistence.

Link to the biological level of analysis

Explanations of arousal and anxiety relate to the biological level of analysis, as arousal and anxiety have physiological components, the levels of which determine the quality of performance.

Link to the sociocultural level of analysis

Gender differences exist within goal setting, with Weinberg *et al.* (1993) finding that females use goal-setting more frequently and more effectively than males. This may be because females tend to utilize short-term goals more than males, providing clearer pathways to long-term targets.

Arousal and anxiety

LEARNING OUTCOME

- Discuss theories relating arousal and anxiety to performance.

Sport involves high levels of arousal and anxiety. Athletes can have talent, fitness, excellent training facilities, etc., but if they cannot cope with the arousal and anxiety associated with competition and turn it to their advantage, they will not achieve and reach their goals. Sport psychologists have developed several theories explaining the effects of anxiety and arousal on performance.

Drive theory (Hull, 1943)

Performance = habit (skill level) x drive (level of arousal)

Drive theory – the belief that as arousal increases, so does the level of performance.

The **drive theory** sees a linear relationship between arousal and performance, whereby performance is low at low levels of arousal, after which increases in arousal lead to heightened performance. The theory also explains that the more learnt a skill is, the more likely it is that high arousal produces good performances.

Hull proposed the existence of a bond between a stimulus and a response, with this bond created due to a drive that creates motivation. In other words the demands of a task, like scoring a penalty, create a motivation (drive) to do this successfully. Once accomplished, the drive is reduced and this is reinforcing (rewarding). As the successful execution of the task is rewarding, the athlete continues; the drive is further reduced and learning takes place. Eventually a 'habit' of successful performance is produced.

Drive theory proposes, therefore, that arousal increases to meet the perceived demands of a task. The more difficult a task, the higher the arousal. Performance reflects the dominant habit (the most usual behaviour). If a skill isn't learnt, the dominant performance habit is to produce errors, resulting in poor performance. If a skill is learnt, the dominant performance habit is execution of the correct technique, resulting in good performance. Even better performances will occur with increased arousal.

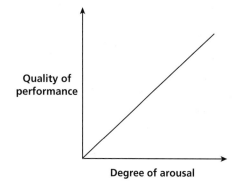

Figure 8.5 Drive theory

Research

- Hull (1943) counted the number of mistakes rats made running through a maze to locate a reward of food, finding that arousal aided the speed of learning on simple tasks where there was already a strong habit strength, while on complex tasks where there were weak stimulus–response bonds, high arousal interfered with learning. This suggests that high arousal activates incorrect stimulus–response bonds (habits) that compete with the correct responses, in line with drive theory.
- Spence and Spence (1966) reported that in unskilled performers, anxiety led to the activation of incorrect responses (mistakes), which thus resulted in a poor performance, giving support to drive theory.

Evaluation

- There is a wealth of research evidence supporting other theories, like the inverted 'U' hypothesis, thus lowering support for drive theory.
- A problem with drive theory is that by increasing drive (arousal), performers resort to previously learnt skills, because these are dominant. But these may be incorrect. Also, even highly skilled athletes 'choke' in highly arousing circumstances, which the theory can't explain.
- Hull based drive theory around the concept of homeostasis, the idea that the body actively works to maintain a state of balance. There was no evidence that this was true of the relationship between arousal and performance, however.

Inverted 'U' hypothesis – the belief that as arousal increases, the level of performance increases up to an optimal point, after which further arousal leads to a downturn in performance.

■ Drive theory is based on behaviourism, where human behaviour is seen as resulting from classical and operant conditioning, a theory whereby humans learn to associate certain stimuli with specific responses through repetition. Behaviourism fails to include the role of cognitive (mental) and emotional factors, however, which motivate much behaviour.

Inverted 'U' hypothesis (Yerkes & Dodson, 1906)

'Get psyched up, not psyched out.'

According to the **inverted 'U' hypothesis**, athletes perform poorly with low levels of arousal, because they are not 'psyched up'. Levels of both physiological arousal and psychological arousal are too low. With moderate levels of arousal, performance is **optimal** (best), while subsequent heightening of arousal leads to anxiety and a reduction in the quality of performance; the athlete has become 'psyched out'.

This explains why individual differences in optimal arousal levels exist. Simple tasks tolerate greater arousal levels before performance declines. A task may also be simple for one athlete but complex to another, due to inherent skill or experience levels and this also affects optimal arousal levels on specific tasks.

Fine motor tasks (requiring precision movements, e.g. pistol shooting) have less margin for error than gross motor tasks (involving the large muscle groups, e.g. weight-lifting), thus gross motor tasks tolerate greater levels of arousal before the optimal level is passed and performance declines.

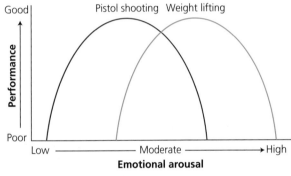

Figure 8.6 Optimal arousal levels for different sport tasks

Onexdine (1970) matched sports skills with different levels of optimal arousal:

Table 8.1

OPTIMAL AROUSAL	SPORT
Level 5	Weight-lifting
Level 4	Judo
Level 3	Basketball
Level 2	Tennis
Level 1	Pistol shooting

Optimal arousal levels are lower with sports requiring information processing, e.g. golf-putting, while tasks requiring little information processing are not as heavily affected by higher arousal levels, e.g. squat thrusts.

Research

■ Yerkes and Dodson (1908) found that heightening arousal levels by increasing the intensity of electric shocks given to the feet created a curvilinear (inverted 'U') effect, whereby in a simple visual discrimination task, performance improved up to moderate arousal, after which increased arousal led to a gradual decline in performance. Optimal performance occurred at a lower level of arousal with more complex tasks. These findings support the inverted 'U' hypothesis.

■ Martens and Landers (1970) subjected high school males, rated as either low, medium or high in anxiety, to tasks involving three levels of psychological stress, finding results that also supported the hypothesis.

- Shawn and Landers (2003) gave 104 college students a simple reaction time task to perform while riding a stationary bicycle at between 20 and 90 per cent of heart rate capability, finding optimal performance was between 60 and 70 per cent of heart rate capability, supporting the inverted 'U' hypothesis.

Evaluation

- The hypothesis explains, as drive theory cannot, why skilled performers sometimes get nervous and perform poorly.
- A criticism of the theory is that it uses the terms 'arousal' and 'anxiety' as interchangeable, which they are not. Arousal refers to bodily activation, while anxiety is an emotional state characterized by negative feelings.
- The theory cannot explain why, when the optimal point is reached, further increases in arousal lead to a catastrophic rather than gradual decline in performance.

Practical applications

The theory suggests a practical application in that optimal arousal levels for different skills and performers can be identified and relaxation/motivational strategies used to adjust arousal levels to the optimal amount for a good performance.

Reversal theory

Reversal theory
– the idea that individuals switch between different motivational styles, rather than having a fixed motivational style.

Reversal theory explains how exhibiting changeable and inconsistent behaviour reflects a switch between different motivational states. The theory demonstrates how behaviour alternates within short time periods, for example the roar of spectators produces positive arousal one moment, but reverses to a negative state the next moment. This reflects a change in meta motivational state, which affects performance differently.

The theory perceives four domains, or pairs of alternative motivational states, known as metamotivational states:

1. **Means-ends states**, alternating between **telic** (serious) and **paratelic** (playful) states.
2. **Rule states**, alternating between **conformist** (operates within rules and expectations) and **negativist** (rebellious) states.
3. **Transaction states**, alternating between **mastery** (motivated by power and control) and **sympathy** (motivated by care and compassion) states.
4. **Relationship states**, alternating between **autic** (motivated by self-interest) and **alloic** (motivated by the interest of others) states.

Metamotivational states interact to bring about behaviour, with individuals **dominant** in certain motivational states, so that someone who is negativist-dominant can be in a conformist state, but revert back to their rebellious self with ease.

Reversal theory links motivational state to emotion, whereby if the needs of a state an individual is in are met, then positive emotions occur, while if the needs aren't met, negative emotions result.

Research

- Kerr (1991) used the Telic Dominance Scale to find that individuals participating in risky sports, such as parachuting, were paratelically dominant in having a high need for stimulation, supporting the view of reversal theory that risk sports participants are arousal seekers.
- Kerr (1994) applied reversal theory to hooliganism, finding that much hooligan behaviour was of a paratelic, playful nature motivated by the pursuit of excitement and the symbolism of confrontation between different hooligan groups and the police. Reversal theory therefore explains why hooligans take risks in the pursuit of violence

and why measures to combat hooliganism are generally ineffective, as they do not address the motivational needs of hooligans.

■ Cindy and Lindner (2005) used the Participation Motivation Inventory, a 30-item questionnaire, to study motivational reasons for sports participation, finding evidence to support the existence of metamotivational states underpinning sports behaviour, in line with reversal theory. The study also found that task and ego motivational orientations of goal achievement theory were linked to specific motivational orientations of reversal theory, suggesting the two theories are linked together through motivational constructs.

> **Link to the cognitive level of analysis**
>
> Reversal theory has a cognitive component in athletes switching between perceived states of metamotivation, pairs of alternate motivational states.

Evaluation

■ Psychometric tests that measure motivational states, like the Telic Dominance Scale, don't just assess dominance (in which states an individual is more dominant over time), but also assess the reversals themselves (how motivational states change in specific situations).

■ Reversal theory provides an alternative theoretical framework to more traditional motivational theories, e.g. drive theory. This framework is more suitable to the multi-motivational nature of sport and offers a practical application through the monitoring and manipulation of arousal levels during performance.

SECTION SUMMARY

■ Several explanations of motivation exist, each with strengths and weaknesses.
■ Goal setting is tied to motivational, commitment and confidence levels and works best when a series of short-term goals lead up to an ultimate long-term goal.
■ Several theories explain how arousal and anxiety relate to performance, each with strengths and weaknesses, though reversal theory probably best explains the multi-motivational nature of sport.

Skill development and performance

LEARNING OUTCOME

■ Evaluate techniques for skill development used in sport.

Heightened performance in sport often reflects skill development, with several theories for such development having been put forward and assessed by sports psychologists in terms of their efficiency and effectiveness of explanation.

Repetition

> **Link to the biological level of analysis**
>
> Repetition has a biological component in the idea of motor skills being physically located within the brain as motor reflexes.

> **Repetition –** the repeating of fundamental physical skills in order for them to become automatic.

Physical development consists of physical fitness and motor skill development; **repetition**, through constant practising of a skill, imprints motor skills within the brain as motor reflexes.

When performing a skill the brain relays signals to the motor units (individual nerves and muscle fibres) at exact intervals to oversee the contraction of the required muscles; repetition affects the formation of these signals.

Simple skills develop first so that more complex skills for specific sports movements may be acquired later.

Research

- Simon and Chase (1973) reported that much variation in performance among chess players was due to differences in practice time, a view supported by Ericsson *et al.* (1993) that increases in performance in any domain are the result of adaptations to task constraints through repetitive practice. This implies that skill proficiency is directly related to the amount of repetition performed during training, though Ericsson *et al.* (1993) further argued for repetition based on **deliberate practice**, involving both physical effort and cognitive processing, to fully enhance skill development.

- Schmidt and Wrisberg (1991) reported that it takes 300–500 repetitions to learn a new motor pattern (skill) and 3,000–5,000 repetitions to erase and correct a bad motor practice. This suggests that constant repetition is an effective means of skill development and also illustrates the durability of motor patterns once they have been learnt.

- Farrow (2008) reported that swimmers found practice variability (performing a skill in different ways) more effective in learning a skill than simply repeating the same skill, as swimmers had to constantly adapt their technique to achieve consistent performance objectives. Practice variability involves more active cognitive processing than the passive processing of repetition, which suggests that practice variability engages athletes more fully in the skill-acquisition process and thus the resulting learning is stronger and more permanent.

Figure 8.7 Much variation in performance between chess players is due to differences in time spent practising.

Evaluation

- One problem in assessing the effectiveness of repetition on skill development is whether changes in performance are permanent or are merely temporary improvements that disappear quickly.
- Repetition, through its passive, unthinking nature, restricts the cognitive processing necessary for the development of many motor skills, hampering skill development.

Mental imagery

Mental imagery – visualizing the successful execution of physical skills.

Link to the cognitive level of analysis

Mental imagery has a cognitive component, in seeing performance as enhanced by the mental rehearsal of skills, especially in elite athletes.

Imagery enhances performance by mental rehearsal of skills. This is rooted in cognitive psychology, where thoughts and cognitions are seen to underpin behaviour, with **mental imagery** reinforcing learnt movements and establishing movement coordination and sequencing of sports skills.

Imagery works best as preparation for competition, especially for elite athletes, i.e. those with required levels of ability. Self-report methods measure the effects of imagery, like the Sports Imagery Questionnaire, which assesses the motivational and cognitive functions of imagery.

There are five main categories of imagery:

1. **Motivational-specific** (MS) – imagining successful performance to boost motivation and effort during training.
2. **Motivational general-mastery** (MG-M) – imagining coping in difficult circumstances in order to develop expectations of success.
3. **Motivational general-arousal** (MG-A) – imagining being relaxed during performance in order to mediate physiological arousal.
4. **Cognitive specific** (CS) – imagining performance of specific skills, e.g. tennis serve, to aid mastery of such skills.
5. **Cognitive general** (CG) – imagining strategies necessary for successful performance, e.g. serve and volley strategy at tennis.

Research

- Jacobsen (1930) reported that when individuals imagine movements, muscular activity is produced. This effect is greatest in those with experience of producing such movements, suggesting imagery has a physical effect and works best for elite performers.
- Hall *et al.* (1998) found that imagery was used by athletes for motivational purposes, like imagining emotion-arousing situations, and for cognitive purposes, like imagining the cognitive skills necessary for successful performance. This implies imagery has separate functions and that novice athletes should use cognitive imagery most, as they are concerned with skill development, while experienced athletes should use motivational imagery more, as their prime concern is with winning.
- Biddle (1985) argues that in learning situations, combining mental imagery with physical practice enhances skill acquisition, while in competition situations, mental imagery before and during competition enhances the level and consistency of performance, illustrating how imagery is used for different purposes.

Evaluation

- The fact that imagery works better for some, e.g. elite performers, illustrates that there are individual differences in the effectiveness of this technique.
- To develop practical applications, there is a need to determine what types of imagery are best for particular sporting situations.

Attention control

Link to the cognitive level of analysis

This explanation is based within cognitive psychology, as it sees the kind and intensity of attentional focus (concentration) used when learning skills as being related to the quality of performance.

Attention control/ concentration training – the focusing of awareness on relevant cues in order to maximize performance.

The degree and type of **attentional focus** (concentration) developed during execution of skilled motor movements affects performance. Attention can be focused **inwardly**, e.g. on the angle of the bat during a cricket stroke, or **externally**, e.g. on spectators in the crowd, with the effects of such attention dependent on skill level. For experts, focusing attention inwardly on movement execution results in worsened performance, while for less skilled performers focusing attention externally degrades performance, as it directs concentration away from skill execution.

Shifting attentional focus is associated with 'choking', e.g. missing a penalty shot. High-pressure situations prompt expert performers to shift concentration inwards to focus on skill execution, which hinders performance, as movements formerly controlled by efficient automatic motor programmes (motor memory) now become controlled by explicit (conscious), error-prone attentional processes.

High anxiety is seen as responsible for shifting attentional focus, whereby goal-directed attentional focus becomes impaired and stimulus-driven attentional focus increases.

Research

- Gray (2004) found that expert baseball batters produced fewer hits in pressure situations (when offered money to perform well) and focused more on the step-by-step components of skill execution than in non-pressure situations. Beilock and Gray (2007) explained these effects as due to regression to a lower skill level associated with an earlier stage of skill-acquisition, supporting the idea that 'choking' relates to focusing attention inwards during performance.
- Wilson *et al.* (2009) found that when experienced footballers were anxious, they had less accuracy when taking penalties, with shots becoming centralized and within the goalkeeper's reach. This suggests that anxiety impairs performance by switching attention to a more stimulus-driven attentional control system, for example by the goalkeeper becoming perceived as more 'threatening'.
- Beilock *et al.* (2002) found that experienced golfers and footballers performed best under **dual-task** conditions, where attention was distracted away from focusing on skill-execution, while novices performed best in **skill-focused** conditions, with focus on step-by-step skill execution. This supports the idea that different types of attentional focus affect different types of athletes in dissimilar ways.

Evaluation

- There are difficulties in creating methodologies to objectively assess attentional focus. Recent innovations include **gaze recognition systems**, which measure (using frame-by-frame film analysis) the direction and length of attentional focus.

Practical applications

Identifying attentional problems during skill execution has a practical application in that coaches can construct remedy strategies, like training experienced athletes not to over-concentrate on a skill during its execution.

■ Critical thinking

Where several explanations exist, as with techniques for skill development, students often feel they have to work out which are the 'correct' and 'incorrect' strategies. A better strategy is to assess each explanation in terms of its strengths and weaknesses.

The effect of coaches on individual and team behaviour

LEARNING OUTCOME
■ To what extent does the role of coaches affect individual or team behaviour in sport?

Coaches perform many functions with individual athletes and teams, with a coach's effectiveness depending on the type of relationship existing between them and their athletes, though the type of sporting situation, the goals set, etc., also exerts an influence.

Many sports have **coaching accreditation** schemes, where coaches become qualified to different levels to show their worthiness. Such schemes teach physical and skill development and psychological preparation of athletes.

Most coaches are assessed in terms of meeting targets shared by all those involved, e.g. team members, administrators, etc., and for many sports this is seen as producing winning athletes and teams. Lyle (2002) proposes that coaching effectiveness should be assessed by:

- Evaluation of specific coaching performances.
- Evaluation of coaching effectiveness over time and across circumstances.
- Evaluation of competence and expertise.

Many coaches are considered successful in certain circumstances, such as producing winners or teams that avoid relegation, but not in all circumstances, because certain coaching styles suit different individuals and situations best.

There are two major coaching styles:

- **controlling** style, where coaches behave in a dictatorial, authoritarian way ('*do as I say*'), imposing set ways of thinking and behaviour
- **autonomous** (democratic) style, where athletes participate in decision-making and personal growth is stressed.

Margeau and Vallerand (2003) argue that an autonomous style is best, as it creates self-determined (intrinsic) forms of motivation, leading to greater effort, persistence, self-esteem and superior performances. They see the autonomous style as superior, as it contributes to the satisfaction of psychological needs, like autonomy (independence), competence (the degree to which individuals feel able to meet their goals) and relatedness (the extent to which individuals feel connected to others). They recommend seven coaching behaviours to promote autonomy:

1. Provide choice within reason.
2. Give justifications (reasons) for tasks to be performed.
3. Show respect for others' feelings and viewpoints.
4. Give athletes independence and input into strategies for solving problems.
5. Give competence feedback that leads to positive behaviour changes.
6. Avoid coaching behaviours that control athletes.
7. Avoid coercion (forcing people to behave in a certain way) and bullying.

Controlling coaching styles create an external locus of control (where athletes see outcomes as controlled by factors outside their control) and blocking of psychological needs, impairing performance. In certain situations, however, controlling coaching styles can be effective. For example, being indifferent and threatening to athletes can create interpersonal rivalries leading to increased team cohesion and enhanced performances.

A combination of autonomous and controlling coaching styles can be achieved, e.g. using conditional regard as a disciplinary strategy, for instance, only valuing individuals when they attain certain standards (controlling style), but explaining/justifying the reasons for adopting this strategy (autonomous style).

Research

- D'Arripe-Longueville *et al.* (1998) assessed the coaching culture within the French women's judo team, considered the best in the world. A controlling, autocratic style was found, which promoted interpersonal rivalry between squad members. Coaches provoked members verbally, displayed favouritism/indifference (interest or lack of interest in certain individuals) and direct conflict in the form of threats. This produced a successful team characterized by high team cohesion and exceptional individual performances. This suggests that an autocratic coaching style is effective within certain situations.
- Mallett (2005) assessed the coaching culture within the successful Australian athletics sprinting squad, finding an athlete-centred, democratic coaching style, where personal growth through care and interest in individual athletes was shown, along with a cooperative approach to learning and a focus on technical excellence under stress. Athletes had a choice of training venues and regimes, regular team meetings were held where decisions/aims, etc., were discussed and explained, and personal responsibility

for skill development was encouraged. This illustrates, when compared with D'Arripe *et al.*'s study, that different coaching styles suit different types of situations and that the autonomous style can also be effective.

- Baker *et al.* (2000) assessed the relationship between coaching style and anxiety levels in 228 athletes from 15 different sports, finding controlling coaching styles created poor interpersonal relationships between athletes and coaches that were associated with heightened anxiety and ultimately poor performances and high drop-out levels. This illustrates the potentially negative effects of controlling coaching styles.
- Howe (1984) investigated the preferred coaching styles of 160 elite athletes at the World Student Games, finding more males preferred controlling coaching styles than females, suggesting a gender difference in preferred coaching style. Athletes competing in team sports also preferred more controlling coaching styles than athletes in individual sports, which additionally suggests a difference in preferred coaching styles between types of sports. Also, Howe found elite athletes preferred more autonomous coaching styles than less able 'club' athletes, which suggests that performance at superior levels relates to the tendency of autonomous coaching styles to satisfy athletes' psychological needs.

Evaluation

- Objectively measuring the effectiveness of coaches, beyond assessment of their win–loss record, is difficult. For example, the exact contribution of coaches to performance is hard to assess, particularly what they have contributed to each individual's performance within a team setting, also determining where the threshold is between coaches being effective and ineffective.
- The use of controlling coaching styles can be perceived as lacking trust in the athletes, leading to feelings of distrust and resentment towards coaches, which ultimately leads to a breakdown in the coach–athlete relationship. Additionally, controlling coaching styles can lead to over-training, injury and burnout (*see Burnout, page 255*), as the athlete's perspective is not considered.
- Jones *et al.* (1993) argue that effective coaches possess an admirable win–loss record, but additionally are 'politically successful', gaining the approval of stakeholders, e.g. the athletes themselves, team owners, administrators, supporters, etc. This illustrates the complex and even contradictory needs and goals that coaches must address to be considered successful.

Link to the sociocultural level of analysis

Team cohesion has a sociocultural element, with teams being seen as subcultural groupings in possession of separate identities and behavioural norms.

Team cohesion – the extent to which being together assists members of a group in pursuing mutual goals and objectives.

Relationships between team cohesion and performance

LEARNING OUTCOMES
- Explain relationships between team cohesion and performance.
- Describe aids and barriers to team cohesion.

Successful teams have **cohesiveness** (togetherness) and are not simply a collection of individual efforts. **Team cohesion** can be a cause of and an effect of group closeness, and it works in two ways:

1. The total sum of forces binding a group together.
2. Resistance by a group to disruptive forces.

Early research examined the role of individuals within a group; more recent research has concentrated on studying the team as a whole.

Cohesion is difficult to study, as it is hard to isolate, with five methods commonly used to assess the nature of cohesion and its effects:

1. Measure degree of interpersonal attraction between team members.
2. Measure each individual's desire to remain within the group.

3. Measure the level of closeness and identification felt by group members.
4. Measure the attractiveness of the group to individuals.
5. A combination of 1 to 4.

These five methods were incorporated into Martens's (1972) **Sports Cohesiveness Questionnaire**, which has seven measures occurring in three categories:

- **Attraction** – concerns individual-to-individual relationships between team members.
- **Enjoyment/belonging** – concerns individual-to-group relationships.
- **Teamwork/closeness** – concerns how the group works as a unit.

In sports with a high need for cooperation between players, interactional skills are important and it may be necessary to select less able players if they 'fit' the team more. The development of cohesion, though, is dependent on several factors (including group size, costs incurred in joining the team, leadership style, team maturity and success level of the team), with the two best ways of assessing the development of team cohesion being to look at the motivational reasons for joining a group and the stages of group formation.

Cohesion is measured using the **Group Evaluation Questionnaire**, with cohesion consisting of individuals' level of attraction to a group, and social and task cohesions. Eighteen questions assess:

- group integration – task
- group integration – social
- individual attraction to group – task
- individual attraction to group – social.

Effects of team cohesion on performance

Cohesion brings stability, which increases the chances of success as other factors, such as skill levels, can be developed. Better performances lead to greater cohesion and even better performances, making a team more attractive to its members. However, cohesion does not guarantee success, and it is instead often better performances that lead to heightened cohesion.

Carron (1982) pointed out the distinction between:

- **Task cohesion** – how well a team operates as a unit.
- **Social cohesion** – how well members like each other and identify with the team.

Successful performances rely more on task cohesion, though the relation between cohesion and performance is also dependent on the type of group structure (kind of team) involved. Group structure can either be:

- **Co-active** – relating to sports where members perform the same task at different times and do not require others to be successful for them to be successful, e.g. batting at cricket.
- **Interactive** – relating to sports involving a high degree of work effort, not just the sum of individual efforts, e.g. hockey.

Interactive teams are more successful when high cohesion is perceived by team members. For such teams high cohesion is more important than individuals' skill levels.

Co-active teams can be successful when low cohesion is perceived by team members, as conflicts and rivalries become a spur to success, driving individuals to greater performances. The West German men's rowing eight at the 1968 Olympics loathed each other so much they didn't talk to one another. They won gold.

Generally, the more players are interdependent on each other and the more team performance depends on coordinated action, the greater the role for cohesion.

Cohesion can adversely affect performance, as in small groups high cohesion hinders players from expressing their individuality. High team cohesion may also lead to players performing to the same standard, minimizing healthy competition within the team, especially in training. In this case coaches should introduce conflict within the team to heighten motivation.

Research

- Muller and Copper (1994) performed a meta-analysis of 66 cohesion–performance relationships from 49 studies, finding that the relationship between cohesion and performance was due to task commitment rather than interpersonal attraction or group pride, suggesting task (not social) cohesion is important for performance.
- Carron *et al.* (2002) performed a meta-analysis of 46 studies, finding no difference in the relationship between task cohesion and performance between co-active and interactive sports teams. In both types of sports high task cohesion was related to good performances, suggesting that high task cohesion is beneficial to all teams and going against the idea that low task cohesion is necessary for co-active teams to perform well. It may be low social cohesion driving co-active teams to greater performances, not task cohesion.
- Rovio *et al.* (2009) found that high cohesion in an ice hockey team led to impaired performances, due to pressures for individual players to perform similarly and conform to group norms, illustrating how high cohesion can have adverse effects on performance.

Key study

Matheson *et al.* (1997)

Matheson *et al.* (1997) assessed 56 participants from two co-active teams (swimming and gymnastics) and two interactive teams (lacrosse and basketball) on levels of cohesion, using the Group Evaluation Questionnaire. Measurements were taken pre-season, after winning, and after losing. It was found that interactive teams scored higher on task cohesion than co-active teams for winning performances, supporting the idea that high task cohesion is more important with interactive team sports.

Evaluation

- Escovar (1974) argued that interpersonal attraction is not part of team cohesion, as it does not explain cohesion in response to adversity, e.g. in response to the threat of relegation, and it does not explain improvements in teamwork.
- The effects of cohesion on performance are difficult to assess, as sports differ from one another and require different levels of team cohesion.
- Some sports are a mixture of interactive and co-active group structures (e.g. tug-of-war) and it's difficult to assess what role cohesion plays. Individual sports appear neither interactive nor co-active (e.g. mountain running) and cohesion plays no part, unless team events are included within the competition.
- Muller and Copper's influential meta-analysis (1993) included non-sporting groups, like business and military groupings. Indeed, only eight of the 66 studies were sports-specific, suggesting the results may not be applicable to sports teams.

Aids and barriers to team cohesion

Cohesive teams are more successful, possessing greater group identity and staying together longer, allowing development of successful skills and strategies, as well as pulling together more persistently in the face of adversity (e.g. during a losing streak). Therefore establishing and maintaining cohesion is desirable, with several aids and barriers to this process. Removal of such barriers is an aid to increased cohesion by itself.

Social loafing

Ringelmann (1913) found the greater the size of a group, the less effort was put in by individual members. If one person is pulling on a rope they will put in 100 per cent effort, if two people are pulling they will put in 93% average individual effort, while eight people will put in just 49% individual effort.

Some reasons for social loafing concern cohesion. For example, **diffusion of responsibility**, where decreased effort occurs due to the lack of identifiability of individual efforts. This barrier to cohesive performance can be addressed by setting members identifiable individual roles, like monitoring individual performances (number of tackles/passes made, saves-to-shots ratio by goalkeepers, etc.) and giving individual feedback to reinforce good practice. Latané (1980) argued that if individual performers are more identifiable, the group situation provides a social incentive, through team cohesion, to perform better. The establishment of set individual roles also addresses the problem of team cohesion hindering performance due to a loss of individuality within the team and the loss of healthy competition between team members.

Coaches should identify individual behaviours important to group success and increase their identifiability, so that players do not become submerged within the team.

Cliques

Cliques (sub-groups) increase cohesion by embracing diversity (individuality) within a team, but **toxic cliques** lower cohesion by being disruptive and counter-productive to the aims and functions of a team. They exhibit exclusionary behaviours and foster resentment and distrust, leading to destructive in-fighting. Favouritism by coaches can produce toxic cliques. Early intervention and democratic coaching styles help prevent the establishment of toxic cliques.

Recruits

Cohesive teams have low turnover rates, but new additions will occur in all teams. To maintain cohesion and prevent toxic cliques, recruits should be made aware of group norms and given chances to adhere to them, as well as being given individual roles and included in social interactions and the formation and pursuit of team goals.

Group roles

Cohesive groups have individual roles for members. Team cohesion suffers when **role-conflict** occurs by individuals perceiving a lack of ability, motivation or understanding to fulfil their role. Role conflict leads to decreased cohesion and psychological burnout, characterized by apathy, ineffectiveness and emotional exhaustion. Cohesion should be maintained by setting clear, compatible and achievable individual roles.

- **Inter-role conflict** – occurs when individuals have incompatible roles, e.g. player–coach.
- **Person–role conflict** – occurs when a role requires behaviour individuals aren't motivated to do.
- **Intra-role conflict** – occurs when there are contradictory demands within the same role, e.g. scoring goals while maintaining a key defensive role.

Team environment

Team environments increase cohesion by:

- **Togetherness** – putting team members repeatedly into situations that require close physical proximity.
- **Distinctiveness** – creating a distinctive identity that sets the team apart from other teams.

Team processes

Processes that occur within a team can aid cohesion by:

- **Sacrifices** – members making sacrifices for the group, e.g. playing through pain.
- **Goal setting** – team goals being set collectively by members.
- **Cooperation** – creating opportunities for cooperation between players in training and competition.

Link to the sociocultural level of analysis

Cliques have a sociocultural element, as they consist of small sub-cultural groupings (cliques) within larger sub-cultural groupings (teams), and exert a negative effect on team cohesion.

Additional barriers

- **Breakdown in communication** – effective channels of communication should be maintained between management and players, and between players. The use of democratic coaching styles offering opportunities for regular meetings and honest debate can help, as well as communication training for team members.
- **Clashes of personalities** – disruptive clashes can be avoided by setting individuals clear, non-overlapping roles that complement rather than frustrate each other.
- **Focus on outcome goals** – over-focusing on overall, long-term goals, e.g. winning promotion, lowers motivation and reduces cohesion. The focus should be on **process** (short-term) goals that provide daily successes, achieved by collective effort. Cohesion is additionally attained by increasing a team's shared belief that outcome goals can be reached.

Research

- Ingham (1974) asked blindfolded participants to pull on a rope in the belief that other people were also pulling. As the perceived size of the group increased, individual effort decreased, in line with Ringelmann's idea of social loafing. Ingham backed up his findings using Olympic rowing times to show that coxed fours were only 13 per cent faster than coxed pairs, and coxed eights only 23 per cent faster than coxed pairs.
- Gross (1982) found that players who received feedback about individual performances outperformed those who didn't, illustrating how the negative effects of social loafing can be deterred.
- Bass (1980) found that disruptive cliques form due to poor communication and unclear goals, illustrating the need for a democratic coaching style that fosters good communication channels, and the formation of clear goals and the pathway to their realization.
- Gardner *et al.* (1996) found coaches could promote cohesion by providing two-way communication channels, social support, positive feedback and avoiding autocratic leadership, illustrating how democratic coaching styles best aid the development of cohesion.
- Sullivan and Feltz (2006) found from a study of 681 athletes that a key factor in team cohesion was team distinctiveness, with males demonstrating this more, supporting the idea of distinctiveness being positively correlated with cohesion and suggesting a gender difference in this area.

■ Critical thinking

It is a useful strategy to consider if results show a gender difference, as with Sullivan and Feltz's (2006) study, because this aids the understanding of behaviour and provides reasons why males and females are affected differently.

Evaluation

- Other factors contribute to social loafing as well as cohesion, such as loss of control, distraction of the group, etc., therefore the effect is not fully attributable to a lack of cohesion.
- Cohesion is measured through **sociograms**, diagrammatic techniques that display interpersonal preferences between team members. They can highlight and isolate less-preferred members, however, though a more positive practical application is using sociograms to identify and break up toxic cliques and form strategies to incorporate 'outsiders' into a cohesive whole.

■ Cohesiveness is not a static state. Systematic adjustments in team dynamics are required to address constant situational fluctuations, like changes in team personnel, alterations in team goals, etc.

SECTION SUMMARY
■ Several methods of skill improvement exist, with each more applicable to certain types of skills and athletes.
■ Coaches perform many functions, with their effectiveness dependent on their relationship with their athletes and the autonomous coaching style being generally preferred.
■ Cohesion brings stability to a team, increasing the chances of success, with task cohesion generally seen as more important than social cohesion.
■ Several barriers to cohesion exist, with the removal of such barriers being an aid to increased cohesion.

Link to the biological level of analysis

Stress and injury have biological components in their physiological effects on the body; stress through effects on bodily systems, like the immune system, and injury through damage to the body.

Stress-based model – the perception of injury risk as being related to stress levels.

Problems in sports
Stress and chronic injury

LEARNING OUTCOME
■ Discuss athlete response to stress and chronic injury.
■ To what extent do biological, cognitive and sociocultural factors influence behaviour in sport?

Link to the cognitive level of analysis

Models of reactions to stress and injury have cognitive elements. The **stress-based model** involves cognitive factors of personality and perceived coping resources as determining risk of injury, while **grief reaction response** involves the cognitive stages of distress, denial and determined coping as determining recovery from injury. The **cognitive appraisal model** sees mental assessment of harm/loss, threat and challenge as determining responses to and recovery from injury.

Sport involves stress and periodic injury. It is estimated athletes spend 20 per cent of their time injured or recovering from injury. Sports psychologists have developed several theories to explain this process.

Figure 8.8 Sportspeople spend on average about 20 per cent of their time recovering from injury.

Stress-based model

The **stress-based model** perceives high levels of stress, from within and outside sport, as increasing the likelihood of injury. Andersen and Williams (1988) proposed a dynamic, multicomponent life stress–injury model that saw a mixture of personality factors (e.g. competitive trait anxiety, hardiness, locus of control) as well as coping resource variables (e.g. social support systems and coping skills) as affecting the stress–injury relationship. Athletes with a history of stressors, personality factors that worsen the stress response and few coping resources, are more likely to perceive situations as stressful and to display greater physiological activation (bodily responses) and disruption to cognitive processing. It is this chronic response to stress that causes heightened injury risks.

Research

- Petrie (1992) found that with low social support, female college gymnasts were most vulnerable to stress-related injuries, with stress accounting for 12–22 per cent of injury variance, while Smith *et al.* (1990) found that athletes low in social support and coping skills were more likely to develop time-loss injuries. This supports the idea of social support levels being related to injury risk and provides support for Andersen and Williams's explanation of multiple factors combining to produce an athlete's given risk level to stress.

Key study

Bum (1998)

Bum (1998) assessed 320 Australian athletes, finding that injured athletes had higher levels of stress than healthy athletes, with the highest levels of stress associated with severe injuries and the lower levels with minor injuries. Twenty PE students were assessed on visual attention tasks, with those in stress conditions more likely to make attentional errors. These findings support Andersen and Williams's (1988) proposal that stress has both physiological and cognitive effects.

Evaluation

- By identifying attentional problems during skill execution, coaches can construct remedy strategies, such as not over-concentrating on skills during their execution.

Practical applications

The explanation suggests a practical application in that periodic monitoring should occur, using established psychological inventories, to assess stress levels, coupled with stress reduction strategies to lower dangerous stress levels and thus reduce the risk of injury.

Link to the sociocultural level of analysis

The model does not account for gender differences. As females tend to have better social support systems, it would be expected that male athletes would have greater injury risks under stress. It is also not clear if stress affects contact and non-contact sportspeople differently.

Grief reaction response

The **grief reaction response model** sees athletes responding to injury similarly to people responding to terminal illness, going through several emotional stages. The cycle of injury focuses on distress, denial and determined coping:

- **Distress** emphasizes the emotional disruption of injuries, with feelings of shock, anger, anxiety, depression, guilt, humiliation, preoccupation and helplessness.
- **Denial** emphasizes the sense of disbelief and refusal to accept the severity of injury, with athletes commonly expecting a quick return to fitness. Denial ranges from mild to severe and varies over time and circumstances. Denial additionally interferes with the rehabilitation progress.
- **Determined coping** emphasizes the acceptance of the severity of injury and how this affects short- and long-term goals. It is characterized by the purposeful application of coping resources to facilitate recovery. Determined coping depends on the ability to move from an emotionally reactive mind set (denial, distress) to a less emotional, decision-making mind set.

Grief reaction response model – the perception of dealing with a chronic injury as similar to the process of facing a terminal illness.

In initial stages distress and denial dominate, but eventually a move to determined coping occurs as recovery starts. Shifts in emotional response between denial, distress and determined coping may occur at any time, e.g. a shift from determined coping to distress when recovery is interrupted by injury recurrence.

Research

- Mainwaring *et al.* (2001) found that injured dancers reacted with negative consequence, e.g. denying the severity of an injury and thus causing more serious damage and distress, with more positive reactions occurring as injuries healed. This supports the grief reaction response model of injured athletes moving between states of distress, denial and determined coping.
- Greenberg (2001) reported that injured female athletes' reactions to injury were characterized by perceptions of the consequence of injury rather than physical injury itself. Such perceptions focused on potential losses of fitness, self-esteem and status and it was these perceptions that caused feelings of distress and denial, supporting the grief reaction response explanation of reactions to injury.

Evaluation

- The model doesn't consider the mediating effects of personality, level of knowledge about injuries, social support and coping strategies, on athletes' emotional responses to injury. Also, emotional impact may vary with different types and causes of injury, e.g. overuse versus traumatic incident.
- The model emphasizes that intense, negative emotional reactions are a natural part of the cycle of recovery from injury and that understanding this helps athletes to move to more positive emotional states of determined coping.

Cognitive appraisal

> **Cognitive appraisal model** – the perception that mental assessments control emotional responses to injury.

Cognitive appraisals are seen as determining the emotional responses to injury, which influence the behavioural responses, such as adhering to a recovery programme. The coping process that follows involves engaging in a cognitive appraisal of the injury, followed by consciously selecting a coping strategy to deal with it.

Cognitive appraisal consists of an individual's assessment of what is at stake for them, and whether the environment is stressful to their well-being. Personal factors (perceived intensity, controllability, etc.) and situational factors (source of the stress, feedback from the environment, etc.) jointly affect an individual's appraisal of injury. Appraisal can be **primary**, where an individual assesses what is at stake, or **secondary**, where they assess what can be done.

Cognitive appraisals consist of:

- **Harm/loss** – damage that has already happened, e.g. loss of confidence.
- **Threat** – potential loss or harm, e.g. loss of ability.
- **Challenge** – anticipation of beneficial outcomes, e.g. having the capabilities to recover.

In sport it's the way in which athletes perceive injuries that influences perceived stress intensity, which in turn influences coping responses. The effectiveness of coping is dependent on the 'goodness of fit' between coping strategies and the appraisal of a situation.

Research

- Daly *et al.* (1995) assessed recreational and competitive athletes undergoing recovery from knee surgery following injury and found that, in line with cognitive appraisal theory, cognitive appraisal was related to level of emotional disturbance, with this having a behavioural knock-on effect in determining level of adherence to recovery programmes, e.g. attending clinic appointments.

- Anshel *et al.* (2001) assessed 151 Israeli athletes' cognitive appraisals of harm/loss, threat and challenge in reaction to the acute stressors of sporting competitions, finding that appraisals influenced subsequent use of coping strategies (avoidance, approach), supporting the model.

Evaluation

- The cognitive appraisal explanation of psychological adjustment to injury provides a viable conceptualization of how athletes cope with injury that is widely supported by research.
- The cognitive appraisal model is superior to the grief response reaction model, as it accounts for individual differences in response to injury by reference to the form of cognitive appraisal used.

Drug use in sport

LEARNING OUTCOME
- Examine reasons for using drugs in sport.

Link to the sociocultural level of analysis

Reasons for drug use relate to the sociocultural level of analysis, as certain cultures, like East Germany, introduced state-sanctioned doping programmes to promote heightened international standing through excellence in sport.

Performance-enhancing drugs – substances abused by athletes to improve results.

The use of **performance-enhancing drugs** is not new. Roman and Greek athletes used herbs in ancient times, while professional long-distance walkers took opium and nitroglycerine in the late 1800s and Tom Hicks (USA) received two strychnine injections during his run to Olympic marathon victory in 1904. Amphetamines became popular after World War II, before the abuse of anabolic steroids in the 1960s. The International Olympic Committee banned drug use in 1967, but it continues with different drugs popular with different sports, such as EPO boosting stamina in cyclists and diuretics helping jockeys to lose weight.

Drug taking is cheating, with penalties for those who get caught, therefore the perceived benefits of taking drugs have to be substantial for athletes to take them. But the rewards for success in sport are so great and the boundaries between winners and losers so small, that many are willing to take drugs to gain a winning advantage. Some athletes have been given drugs, often from an early age, without their knowledge, as part of state organized drug abuse, like the doping programme operated by East Germany to promote nationalism and heightened international standing.

Drug taking occurs among leisure-oriented athletes, like the taking of anabolic steroids by body builders in pursuit of heightened body image, raised self-esteem and the regard of others. Young athletes have resorted to drug abuse to gain selection onto university sport scholarships.

Some justify drug taking, like the view in cycling that drugs merely replace substances lost from the body through exertion, rather like taking vitamin supplements. Others see drug use as necessary, due to the high physical demands that sport place on athletes, and the belief that top-level performances are not possible without doping. There are sports where drug taking became so endemic that clean athletes felt they had to take drugs in order to not be disadvantaged. Some argue that from an ethical point of view, doping is no different to wearing high-tech swimsuits or eating energy gels.

The reasons for banning drug use centre on its health risks and the gaining of an unfair advantage.

Theory of knowledge

Investigating drug taking in sport is problematic, as there are ethical concerns over the potential harm to participants, both in terms of the possibility of making drug taking attractive and of revealing the identities of those who have doped.

Anabolic steroids

Anabolic steroids are synthetic versions of testosterone, the male sex hormone, with athletes abusing them due to their ability to increase muscle mass, bone density and physical strength. Steroids travel to androgen receptors within cells, stimulating hormone receptors to release the genetic messenger mRNA, which signals an individual's DNA to construct specific proteins. These travel around the body, stimulating growth. Steroids allow harder training with accelerated muscle recovery, gaining benefits way beyond normal. Steroid abuse first appeared in weight-lifting, then spread to other sports where size mattered, like shot-putting. Data show that between the Olympic Games of 1956 and 1972, the average weight of shot-putters increased by 14 per cent compared to 7.6 per cent among steeplechasers, which suggests popular use of steroids by shot-putters during this period.

Erythropoietin (EPO)

Erythropoietin (EPO) is a protein hormone produced by the kidneys. EPO binds with receptors in the bone marrow to stimulate the production of erythrocytes (red blood cells). It is favoured by endurance athletes, as it increases the oxygen-carrying properties of the blood, allowing boosting of aerobic capacity over prolonged periods. Abuse was rife, as testing for EPO is notoriously tricky, with cycling using a haematocrit level of above 50 per cent to bar cyclists from competition – not as proof of drug abuse, but for health reasons.

Research

- Kadi *et al.* (1999) reported that muscle biopsies from weight-lifters showed that the number of muscle fibres and average muscle size in the trapezius was significantly greater among users of anabolic steroids than non-users, illustrating the ability of steroids to build muscle mass for power-based sports.
- Weismann *et al.* (2012) reported that in addition to the physical boost EPO gives endurance athletes, there is an additional 'brain boost', elevating motivation to perform at a higher level. Mice that were genetically modified so that their brains engineered EPO, performed as well on exercise tests as mice injected with EPO, but did not have the physical blood changes associated with EPO use. This suggests the reason for taking EPO may be its motivation-enhancing properties, as well as physical benefits.
- Michels-Lucht (2011) assessed 74 male body builders, finding that steroid use was associated with high levels of self-esteem. This implies that usage is tied to producing positive self-regard and is therefore more attractive to those with low self-esteem.
- Green *et al.* (2001) used questionnaires to assess the drug-taking habits of male and female American college athletes from 30 sports and 991 colleges, finding that most student-athletes used mainly recreational drugs, like marijuana (28.4 per cent of respondents), rather than performance-enhancing ones, like anabolic steroids (1.1 per cent of respondents). This suggests drug use by athletes is also for relaxation and stress-relief purposes, owing to the high demands of being involved in competitive sport.

Evaluation

- Do steroids enhance performance? Scientific research is difficult, due to the illicit nature of steroid use in sport, and it may be that a large part of steroids' success is merely a placebo effect (performance improves, as there is an expectation of improvement), albeit one that comes with enhanced health risks (*see The effects of drug taking in sport, page 253*).

- If the effects of drugs could be tailored to be purely motivational, then the ethical question arises as to whether taking substances that work cognitively, but not physically, should be classed as drug abuse.
- An additional reason for drug use becoming popular in sport from the 1960s was the liberal attitude towards drug taking. People increasingly took drugs to heighten pleasure and alleviate health problems, therefore drug taking to boost physical performance was merely a logical extension of this phenomenon.

Link to the biological level of analysis

Drug taking has a biological element, as performance-enhancing drugs produce physiological effects on the body, both enhancing to performance and destructive to health through their side effects.

The effects of drug taking in sport

LEARNING OUTCOME
- Discuss the effects of drug use in sport.

Athletes take drugs to boost performance, with different types of drugs popular with different sports; there are severe health risks associated with drugs, however, with many deaths attributable to their misuse. Athletes continue to take them, illustrating the risks they are prepared to take to succeed.

There are six major classes of doping agent identified and banned by the International Olympic Committee (*see Table 8.2*), and an extra four drug classes subject to restrictions (*see Table 8.3*).

Table 8.2   Doping agents banned by the International Olympic Committee

DOPING AGENTS	EFFECTS	SIDE EFFECTS
Stimulants (e.g. cocaine, caffeine)	Mask fatigue and release adrenalin, improve alertness, competitiveness and aggression.	Anxiety, erratic heart rate, tremors, headaches and insomnia.
Narcotic analgesics (e.g. opiates)	Mask pain and induce euphoria.	Respiratory depression (trouble breathing), addiction and overdose.
Anabolic steroids	Improve muscle bulk, power (especially in power events), aggression and competitiveness. Allow athletes to train harder without becoming fatigued (*see also Drug use in sport, page 251*).	Mania, changes in libido (sex drive), acne, tumours, alterations in sexual features, e.g. testicular atrophy.
Beta-blockers	Decrease heart rate and reduce muscle tremor.	Heart damage, muscle fatigue, depression, anorexia, impotence and reduced exercise tolerance.
Diuretics	Promote rapid weight loss and mask banned substances.	Electrolyte depletion, dehydration, cramps and heart damage.
Peptide hormones and analogues	Increase lean body weight and accelerate bone growth.	Gigantism, cartilage damage and impotence in males.

Table 8.3   Doping agents subject to restriction

DOPING AGENTS	EFFECTS	SIDE EFFECTS
Alcohol, marijuana and sedatives	Improve relaxation and boost confidence.	Decreased reaction time, poor coordination, loss of balance and major organ damage.
Local anaesthetics and sedatives	Mask pain and produce euphoria.	Water retention, damage to immune system and osteoporosis.

Detecting drugs involves many techniques, the main problem being the production of new drugs and masking agents that cannot be tested for. The short life span of some drugs makes detection difficult (EPO is apparent in urine for just a few days, but gives a benefit lasting four weeks), with often random testing being the only way to catch dopers, but seven time Tour de France winner Lance Armstrong passed over 500 random drugs tests and it was only the hearsay of others that finally got him to admit to doping. Even when drug cheats are caught, national associations often hide such results. American multiple Olympic gold medallist Carl Lewis failed three drugs tests prior to the 1988 Olympics, but the USA Olympic committee turned a blind eye to this.

East Germany

For East Germany, it was win at any cost. They did win, but the full cost of state-organized doping (damaged fertility, freakish sex changes, and life-threatening physical and psychological damage) only later became clear. Hundreds of trainers, medics, etc., were involved in the doping of thousands of athletes, some as young as ten years of age, with the country obsessed with proving the supremacy of their political system. Unsuspecting athletes were told drugs were vitamins; males developed breasts and lost their libido, while women grew facial hair, acquired deep voices and suffered gynaecological complaints and infertility. Shot-put champion Heidi Krieger was turned physically into a man as a result of drug taking and is now known as Andreas. She was senior European champion by 1986, then her career fell apart due to drug-related damage, depression and suicidal tendencies.

Figure 8.9 Catherine Menschner was a top East German swimmer, but her life was ruined by anabolic steroids that she didn't even realize she was taking.

All Olympic sports (except yachting) involving East Germans were corrupted by drug use. By 1975 over 2,000 athletes were receiving drugs, with the pay-off being supremacy on the world sporting stage. By 1998, however, 12 East German male athletes had had breasts removed, with more treated for or dying from liver, lung and kidney cancers. Catherine Menschner won her first swimming race aged six and was sent to a sports academy where she was given drugs daily. At age 11 she could do 100 press-ups and weight-lift 65 lbs. Her career was ended at 14 through spinal injury and she subsequently suffered from infections in her oversized lungs. As an adult she was told she shouldn't lift anything above 250 g. She also suffered drugs-related miscarriages and depression. Her story is not uncommon; many children's lives were sacrificed so that a few could rise to the top.

Research

- Choi *et al.* (2004) monitored strength athletes over several months, finding that those using anabolic steroids developed increased levels of aggression compared to non-users. 'Stacking' (multiple drug use) was associated with the highest levels of aggression, one user admitting to attempted murder, illustrating the serious side effects of drug usage.
- Franke and Berendonk (1997) reported that documents from the East German government showed the extent of state-sponsored doping, with top ranking academics and doctors involved in the testing and distribution of drugs to several thousand athletes (including children), and the production of techniques to evade detection, with huge sums of money dedicated to the programme. The programme continued despite knowledge of serious side effects, demonstrating the lengths the state would go to gain international sporting stature.

- Pfitzinger (2011) reported on the sudden deaths of 18 Dutch and Belgian cyclists between 1987 and 1990, when EPO appeared in Europe. EPO causes blood-clots that lead to heart attacks, especially when asleep, illustrating the risks associated with EPO. The seriousness of the problem was supported by Megret (2011), finding evidence of EPO usage among 29 per cent of 154 cyclists tested, suggesting its usage is widespread.

The risk of death by heart attack while asleep is so acute in EPO abusers that many cyclists have heart monitor alarms to wake them up when their resting heart rate falls below critical levels. They then cycle on a stationary bike for 20 minutes to elevate their heart rate, before returning to bed. In the words of one top cyclist, 'By day I live to ride, but at night I ride to live'.

Evaluation

- Due to the extent of doping within cycling, many traditional backers of cycling teams have withdrawn sponsorship, not wishing to be associated with such corruption, illustrating the damage done by doping to the status of the sport.
- Aside from the damage to individuals through drug abuse, there is the damage done to the ability of sport to promote functional and desirable behaviours, especially when increasingly sedentary lifestyles are contributing to epidemic levels of obesity and diabetes, creating a huge need for participation in sport.
- Until effective methods of detection are created and uniform sanctions (including life bans) applied, doping will continue. It would be better for sport (and thus indirectly for society) if the associated prizes of sport (wealth, status, etc.) were not so high and if rampant nationalism was removed from the sporting arena, as the doping they inspire has caused such damage to what should be a shining example of how individuals should conduct themselves in the pursuit of excellence.

Burnout

LEARNING OUTCOME
■ Compare models of causes and prevention of burnout.

Link to the biological level of analysis

Burnout has a biological element, as it involves negative physiological effects, like insomnia and reduced immune system functioning.

Link to the cognitive level of analysis

Explanations of burnout have cognitive elements to them; the **cognitive-affective appraisal model** through mental assessment of the demands of a situation, the **negative training stress model** through perception of imbalances between training demands and coping abilities, and the **investment model** through perceived motivational reasons for sports participation.

Most sports require dedication, sacrifice and effort, but overcook the process and burnout results. Burnout is characterized by physical and emotional tiredness, a reduced sense of achievement and sport devaluation. Those with burnout exhibit chronic stress levels and motivational changes. Sports psychologists have offered several explanations for the phenomena, with a view to constructing effective prevention strategies.

Cognitive-affective stress model

Smith (1986) saw the causes of burnout occurring in two categories:

1. **Environmental factors** – features of an athlete's environment that contribute to burnout, e.g. through **physical** factors (over-training, injury, etc.), **logistical** factors (time constraints, organizational problems, etc.) and **social-interpersonal** factors (problems with others).
2. **Personal factors** – characteristics of the athlete that contribute to burnout, e.g. high expectations, lack of assertiveness, perfectionism, etc.

Environmental and personal factors do not automatically cause burnout, according to the **cognitive-affective stress model**; it is a result of the cognitive appraisal (mental assessment) of the athlete's ability to meet the demands of a situation, with burnout occurring if the perceived demands outweigh the perceived coping resources.

The model has four stages:

1. **Situational demands** – athletes perceive heightened stressors, for example, high training volume/intensity or high expectations for success.
2. **Cognitive appraisal** – athletes assess the situation to see whether they have the necessary resources to meet the demands of the situation.
3. **Physiological responses** – if cognitive appraisal suggests that situational demands outstrip resources, bodily reactions occur, such as muscular tension, tiredness and insomnia.
4. **Behavioural responses** – athletes react to the burnout, for example by experiencing de-motivation, lessened performance, substance abuse, etc.

Research

- Vealey *et al.* (1992) administered the Maslach Burnout Inventory to 381 high school and 467 college coaches, finding that trait anxiety was the strongest predictor of burnout, with several cognitive perceptions also predictive of burnout. This provides a degree of support for the idea that burnout is related to cognitive appraisal.
- Kelly and Gill (1993) investigated burnout in 214 college basketball coaches, finding that cognitive appraisal of stress factors was associated with burnout, supporting the cognitive-evaluation model.
- Anshel *et al.* (2001) reported a relationship between cognitive appraisals of situational stressors and subsequent use of coping strategies in 251 Israeli athletes, supporting the cognitive appraisal model. A gender difference was apparent, with females experiencing more threat, but less harm and challenge appraisals than males.

Evaluation

- Coakley (1992) believed that stress is a symptom of burnout, not a cause. He argued that an athlete's sense of identity is focused solely on success in sport, so that experiencing injury, lack of success, etc., leads to burnout, as such athletes have little sense of control due to coaches dictating all their behaviour, therefore they cannot perceive alternative means of coping with the stressors.

Figure 8.10 The negative training stress model sees burnout as occurring due to overtraining and inadequate rest.

Negative training
stress model – an
explanation of
athletic burnout
that centres on an
imbalance between
training demands
and coping abilities.

Negative training stress model

The **negative training stress model** sees burnout as occurring due to over-training and inadequate rest. When training volume is too high, intense and persistent, staleness results, followed by burnout. Over-loading can be an effective training method if adequate rest is taken, so it is the physical demands of training and the lack of rest that combine to cause burnout. The model basically sees positive and negative adaptations to training, with burnout a negative adaptation, due to lack of coping resources.

■ Critical thinking

An effective way to evaluate a theory is to assess its potential for practical applications. Good theories should be practically applicable. Therefore a good theory of burnout would be one that suggested ways of addressing the problem.

Research

- Kellman *et al.* (1997) assessed 41 German junior national rowing team athletes during preparation for the 1995 World Championships. Burnout scores positively correlated with over-training, demonstrating support for the negative training stress model.
- Hassmen (1998) reported that athletes who haven't recovered 72 hours after training have over-trained, and that such a break from training is detrimental to fitness for most elite athletes. A **total quality recovery** (TQR) process is recommended to measure the training process to prevent burnout. By using a TQR scale (created around an athlete's perception of recovery and active measures that aid recovery), structured around the scale for **ratings of perceived exertion** (RPE), the recovery process can be monitored and assessed against the breakdown (training) process (TQR versus RPE). In this way adaptations to stressful training remain positive and benefit fitness rather than leading to burnout.

Evaluation

- A problem with explaining burnout is that it's difficult to see what exactly is being explained, as it isn't easy to define. Maslach and Jackson (1984) see it as '*a psychological syndrome of emotional exhaustion, depersonalization and reduced sense of performance accomplishment, occurring among individuals who work with people in some capacity*', but this describes the phenomena in terms of its characteristics, rather than stating what it is.
- The negative training stress model helped provide the impetus and theoretical basis behind a lot of psychosocial injury research. Thus the model has contributed to the understanding of burnout and the creation of effective strategies to deal with it.

Investment model
– the perception
of athletic burnout
as due to such
high investment
of resources that
participation in
a sport occurs
more because an
individual feels
they have to than
because they
want to.

Investment model

The **investment model** sees athletes who participate in sport for intrinsic motivational reasons, such as a sense of empowerment, are less likely to experience burnout than those who feel trapped into participating, with little perception of control over their behaviour. Therefore, burnout results from perceived imbalances between the costs and benefits of sports participation. The model has five determinants of burnout:

1. rewards
2. costs
3. satisfaction
4. investment in sport
5. alternatives to sport.

It is the evaluation of these determinants that decides whether participation is due to enjoyment or entrapment.

Research

- Schmidt and Stein (1991) reported that athletes are more likely to experience burnout if participation is based on entrapment. That is, high costs and low rewards are perceived, alongside a feeling that they've invested too much to quit and that there are no realistic alternatives to pursue, thus supporting the investment model.
- Raedeke (2010) surveyed 141 swimming coaches on levels of commitment and feelings of exhaustion, finding that coaches with characteristics of entrapment showed greater increases in exhaustion. This supports the investment model's central idea that participation in sport that relates more to entrapment than pleasure increases the risk of burnout.
- Gustafsson *et al.* (2007) interviewed ten Swedish elite athletes who quit sport due to burnout, finding that feelings of entrapment related to burnout, providing support for the investment model. However, other contributing factors were also identified, including lack of recovery time, perfectionist tendencies, high-expectations, etc., which points towards a multi-dimensional explanation of burnout incorporating elements of several models.

Evaluation

- The model differentiates dropout from burnout. Those prone to burnout perceive an increase in their investment in their sport and a decrease in alternatives to sport, while those prone to dropout perceive a decrease in investment and an increase in alternatives to sport.
- The model is useful in that it specifies conditions necessary for burnout-prevention. Athletes and sports practitioners (such as coaches, teachers, etc.) need to ensure that sport is played for intrinsic motivational reasons and not let perceptions of entrapment dominate or have the scope to develop.

Table 8.4 Strategies to prevent burnout

PREVENTION STRATEGY	DESCRIPTION
Schedule breaks	Have regular rest periods built into a training schedule.
Autonomy	Develop an athlete's sense of personal control.
Coping skills	Teach communication and stress management techniques.
Variety	Create some unpredictability in training to prevent staleness.
Control outcomes	Set realistic, achievable targets so that an athlete experiences success.

SECTION SUMMARY

- Several explanations of how athletes respond to injury exist, each having strengths and weaknesses, with the cognitive appraisal model being best supported by the research.
- Different performance-enhancing drugs are used within different sports to try and gain a winning advantage, although other factors exert an influence too.
- Although drugs bring performance benefits, they incur serious side effects too.
- Several models of burnout have been developed, each with strengths and weaknesses, with the investment model best for suggesting strategies to prevent burnout.

Qualitative methods

Theory and practice in qualitative research

LEARNING OUTCOME
■ Distinguish between qualitative and quantitative data.

Qualitative methods deal with the ways in which researchers interpret the words, ideas and actions of their participants. These interpretations are subjective: individual researchers may be listening to the same words or observing the same behaviours from participants, but are likely to perceive them in different ways. Researchers' perceptions are recorded and comprise the data that will be used in describing, discussing and presenting the findings of their investigations.

This differs significantly from the approach used in quantitative research, where researchers have a positivist approach to their investigations. The quantitative approach will mean that a deductive perspective is taken, which is frequently expressed in the experimental hypothesis that has been formulated for the experiment. The wording of the hypothesis is usually derived from reading and understanding relevant theories and previous studies related to the phenomenon under investigation. Objectivity is required and records of participants' words and behaviours will often be in a quantifiable form. A quantitative approach is not usually related to any emotional feelings that people may have at the time of the research, but is more likely to be interested in obtaining a quantifiable measure of participants' actions or their responses to specific questions. The objective approach also does not need to take account of the feelings that quantitative researchers may have as they collect their data.

Quantitative research data is expressed primarily in numbers, which are often the results of measures or scores gathered as the research progresses, to test whether a dependent variable in an experiment is likely to have been affected by manipulation of the independent variable. These data are often subjected to statistical tests to determine whether the results can be accepted or rejected at an appropriate level of significance. In experienced hands these tests are comparatively straightforward to administer, and since the software and computers employed for calculation are powerful, the results are obtained speedily.

If you have already been involved in conducting one or more psychology experiments, you will be aware that in preparing to conduct an experiment it is important to select a sample of people who have offered to become participants for your research. Choosing a sample needs care since there are several ways of selecting your participants from the sample.

Random sampling – a sampling method where each individual from the parent population has an equal chance of being selected for the sample.

The sampling method most frequently mentioned in quantitative research is known as random sampling, so called because a random manner of sampling is used to identify the participants who will be selected. In many psychology experiments the number of participants will be relatively small, and in schools will typically be between 20 and 30 people. Using a random number generator could be as simple as putting into a hat all the names of the volunteers, each on a separate piece of paper, and then drawing out the 20 or 30 names required. Alternatively, a computer-operated random number generator could be used for this purpose. Random selection is preferred to ensure that no bias occurs on the part of the experimenters in choosing certain participants for their experiment. Each volunteer has an equal chance of being selected.

Qualitative methods do not require that a random selection of participants be used. Instead, purposive sampling may be used, in which individuals from the relevant population each possess the same characteristic that is under investigation. The sample is usually relatively small in number, often in single figures. The data that researchers collect is mainly in the form of words, although this data could well be supplemented by video or sound recordings, for instance. In combination or singly, these types of data are likely to be much richer in the information that they are able to convey to the researchers than are the numbers or scores available to quantitative researchers. By analysing the words or actions used by their participants, researchers are able to interpret how they construct their world, how new meanings are expressed as new experiences are felt, or new phenomena observed. The new thinking about the world becomes absorbed by people; it becomes part of their constructed world.

Strengths and limitations of qualitative research

LEARNING OUTCOME
■ Explain strengths and limitations of a qualitative approach to research.

Good qualitative research should encourage the reader to empathize with the emotions that are expressed by the participant since this remains an effective way by which to understand how specific thinking and subsequent actions occur. This understanding is vital when the researcher attempts to categorize the ideas and actions expressed by the participant, to explain why and how certain responses are made, e.g. 'I thought what he said to my girlfriend was an insult to her, so I hit him.' If this thinking and the action that follows it are seen to be the result of previous and similar interchanges between two young men, then remedial action to reduce this violent behaviour may be more effective.

The choice of a specific method to provide rich data will depend on the researcher. In this case it may be that a semi-structured interview will produce sufficient data to reveal what has happened to provoke such an extreme reaction. If the researcher believes that greater insight is needed then it may be that a case study of the social interactions of the participant needs to be conducted, for example, looking at whether the parents of the young man used hitting as a means to discipline him when he was growing up.

The very process of qualitative research can reveal a number of hitherto unsuspected behaviours that need further understanding in order to resolve present behaviour patterns. This real-life approach has ecological validity, which is so often lacking in laboratory-based investigations. The latter approach enables a more scientific approach to be used but it cannot replicate what goes on in real life, and as such, the results from such work cannot be validated.

Qualitative researchers do not bring a deductive approach to their investigations in the way that quantitative researchers are likely to do. Qualitative research depends on an inductive approach, by which researchers 'draw out' meanings from the explanations given by participants. The expressions, words and body language that participants use are what provides the data from which analyses are made by the researchers. This approach can and does lead to new theories being developed, which can be applied to subsequent problems that may arise. Rich data is produced using qualitative methods, because sensitive problems may be investigated as the rapport and trust between participant and researcher are developed over a period of weeks or months.

There are downsides to producing such a mass of data. Analyzing the data takes both time and finance; researchers need to plan carefully and realistically to take these important elements into account. Qualitative research will inevitably cost more than quantitative research, but its findings can also be more revealing. Where several national governments have previously relied almost entirely on quantitative research, several are

Deductive approach – used primarily in quantitative research, where a hypothesis is subsequently tested by using the experimental method. Rarely used in qualitative research but may be employed occasionally, for example as part of the process of inductive content analysis.

Inductive approach – the term used for inductive content analysis in which interpretations of interviewees' answers, the data, are drawn out from the words used.

now spending considerable sums on investigating the emotional aspects of policies they are about to implement or have recently implemented.

Since qualitative research frequently involves small numbers of participants, the claim is often made that generalizations from such a limited base should not be accepted. Counter-arguments to this claim will be examined later in this chapter.

It is in the nature of qualitative research that researchers give subjective meanings to the words and actions of participants. As with all of us, researchers will be biased in the ways that they interpret both words and actions. For the sake of transparency offered to readers of the research, qualitative investigators, in particular, have generally adopted a policy that they should show reflexivity in their research articles. This means that a short explanation of their own biases or emotional predisposition towards certain relevant aspects in the research should be offered near the beginning of their written article. This disclosure should go some way to alerting readers that the author is aware of the dangers that such biases may bring and wishes to draw attention to this point.

Generalizability

LEARNING OUTCOME
■ To what extent can findings be generalized from qualitative studies?

Generalizability – the claim, often contested, by which the findings of an investigation can be transferred to people or situations other than those in the original investigation.

Generalizability according to Silverman (2010, p.434) refers to, 'the extent to which a finding in one setting can be applied more generally'.

This definition may appear innocuous enough, but qualitative researchers have found that a wish to generalize their work is both difficult and frustrating. Many researchers suggest because of the small number of participants involved in qualitative research that generalizing from one setting to another is not valid and should not happen. Others, such as Alasuutari (1995, pp.156–57), suggest that the word 'generalization' should be replaced with the word 'extrapolation'. If this suggestion was adopted it would help us to tackle issues that are raised in discussions on generalization. Willig (2001), in her chapter on case studies, quotes Stake (1994, p.245):

'Whereas the single or a few cases are poor representation of a population of cases and poor grounds for advancing grand generalization … case studies are of value in refining theory and suggesting complexities for further investigation, as well as helping to establish the limits of generalizability.'

Both of these suggestions appear to be rather negative reactions to using generalization. The approach taken by Silverman (2010, p.140) is considerably more positive. He suggests different answers in order to obtain generalizability, including:

■ Combining qualitative research with quantitative measures of populations.
■ Purposive sampling guided by time and resources.
■ Using an analytic model that assumes generalizability in the existence of any case.

Silverman (2010) suggests that researchers with a single case study should use Hammersley's (1992) approach. This is to take the one case and compare it to salient points taken from a larger number of relevant cases. The task is to establish how representative the single case is of the population of the larger number of cases. This idea is supported and strengthened by Perakyla (2004, p.296):

'The comparative approach directly tackles the question of generalizability by demonstrating the similarities and differences across a number of settings.'

Generalization from a single case or a very small number of cases has a long history in medical research. Jenner in 1798 noted that milk maids, who worked on farms and had the task of milking cows, did not usually suffer from cowpox. His experiments vaccinating volunteer patients with very small doses of cowpox revealed that the farm workers' exposure to small samples of the disease had conferred at least some degree of immunity on them. In researching the prevention of specific illnesses, medical researchers carry out studies on very small samples and compare their diagnoses with a larger number of patients who already have the disease. This type of thinking and application has helped the development of other parallel methods used in qualitative research.

There are occasions when researchers have access to extremely small numbers of participants, or a single example of an event. The question then arises of whether any of the findings produced in such limited circumstances can be applied in other cases. Perakyla (2004, p.297) cites his own work focused on Aids counselling in a London hospital:

'…the practices that I analysed are very likely to be generalizable. There is no reason to think that they could not be made possible by any competent member of (at least any Western) society. In this sense the study produced generalizable results. The results … were generalizable as descriptions of what any counsellor or other professional, with his or her clients, can do, given that he or she has the same array of interactional competencies as the Aids counselling sessions have.'

Alasuutari (1995, p.155) used an hourglass metaphor to illustrate a similar point. In an earlier study, Alasuutari investigated how increased urbanization in Finland in the 1970s affected the behaviour of males who regularly frequented their local pubs. In a follow-up study, he narrowed the focus to concentrate on men whose drinking was heavier and who were in many cases divorced. Alasuutari used his findings to justify his claim that:

'Ethnographic research of this kind is not so much generalization as extrapolation … the results are related to broader entities.'

The hourglass metaphor indicates that although the qualitative researcher may start with a very small number of participants, by searching for further cases that are contrary or parallel to the original sample, there will be an increase in the number of salient features, such as divorce or heavier drinking, that will also need to be considered. All the cases will eventually end up in the bottom of the hourglass.

Figure 9.1 Alasuutari's hourglass metaphor shows how qualitative research can become generalizable.

Ethical considerations

LEARNING OUTCOME
■ Discuss ethical considerations in qualitative research.

Ethical considerations – the rules and moral principles that guide the conduct of researchers in investigations.

Ethical considerations should permeate all aspects of qualitative research, including:

- the research question itself
- the methods employed in the research
- the selection and care of participants before, during and after their involvement in the research
- the care of researchers
- the ways in which findings are arrived at
- the dissemination of findings to other researchers and the public.

There are occasions in which insufficient attention is given to ethical matters in social research; this can lead to a distrust of not only the specific study under consideration but also other research studies, as these can be contaminated by the opprobrium caused by the first case.

The research question needs to be clear and concise and to be understood by each participant and each researcher. In no way should the research process demean or harm participants. If, despite precautions, any aspect of harm does occur during the research, the reasons for this should be thoroughly investigated and remedial action taken where appropriate. Psychological research could well look at, and possibly adopt, ways in which the best medical research takes responsibility for errors that occur in the course of its studies. This aspect of research is significant, as the differences between medical and psychological research can become blurred. Both disciplines, for example, may deal with diagnoses and remedial action taken for certain mental conditions. The researchers themselves may be physically assaulted in specific types of research, for example where clients with behavioural abnormalities may lose self-control at the questions they are being asked. In some studies the safety of researchers needs to be considered as a priority, in addition to the safety of the client.

Once the findings of research are known it is important that experienced people are informed, possibly in the form of an ethics committee. The task of such a body is not only to take responsibility for commissioning research, but also to consider the potential effects of publishing the findings. Governments are known to prohibit or at least delay publication of findings if it is decided that this action is not in the public interest. For example, drug experts may be commissioned to research the effects of making a specific drug liable to a higher or lower punishment by law. Their eventual finding may be that it will make little difference to the rate of drug-taking if the law is amended. The judgement of the expert committee may well be ignored by the government if the recommended action would be likely to cause a decrease in government popularity among the public at the time of an impending general election.

Qualitative researchers are sometimes asked to become involved in work related to sensitive areas of human behaviour, such as religious practices, sexual behaviours, domestic violence, cultural practices, personal health, or criminal activity. While each of each of these behaviours is interesting, it is appropriate in a publication based on the International Baccalaureate that consideration should be given to issues that can arise when researchers and participants come from different cultures.

Silverman (2010) published an illuminating case that illustrates this issue with the work of one of his students – Queenie Eng. She conducted her PhD research with Chinese participants who lived in the UK who suffered from diabetes. The Western tradition for participants involved in research is that they sign consent forms, but in the traditions of the Chinese a 'gentlemen's agreement' – conveyed by an oral agreement between researcher and participant – is sufficient. No signature on official forms is involved. It became apparent that placing their signature on an official-looking document, such as the consent form, meant that participants perceived themselves as dealing with officialdom and that repercussions could ensue. Many of them refused to sign the consent form. Eng eventually resolved the impasse by giving a choice to each participant as to whether they signed the consent form before or after their interview.

Some participants also mistakenly thought that they would learn something about the nature of their illness directly from the researchers and felt cheated when no such information was offered. Despite a clear explanation being offered in the focus group discussion at the start of the research, the misunderstanding continued. This may have been because some of the gatekeepers who were originally engaged in explanatory sessions deliberately avoided using the word 'research', because they argued that the word could have negative connotations for the participants. Some of the participants remained adamant they had been led to believe that their participation in the research was in

Gatekeeper – an individual who is responsible for denying or allowing access to data that is important to the research process.

exchange for receiving information about diabetes. Their righteous anger was directed personally against Queenie Eng. The issue was eventually resolved by a resourceful in-group participant, who also acted as a medical interpreter for the Chinese Community Centre. She argued that, in line with Confucian ethics, the participants had a duty towards the younger members of the community and that the findings obtained by the research could have a beneficial effect for future young people who might otherwise suffer from diabetes. The participant group agreed with the points made.

There are many sub-cultures within the same country and some of these may well need extreme sensitivity in the ways that they become part of a research process. The author of this chapter has been engaged in several qualitative research studies, including one that involved teaching a small number of 16–18-year-olds who had birth defects as the result of their mothers being advised to take the drug thalidomide in order to alleviate severe morning sickness. The effects of the drug were that some children were born with vestigial limbs. This condition meant that some of the study participants were forced to use their feet and toes as substitute hands and fingers, and many had developed remarkable skills in this respect. In small numbers they joined an 'A' level psychology class in a mainstream school for about five hours a week. Any difficulties they had or progress they displayed was sensitively discussed with their specialized staff in the hospital school in which they had full-time residence. The students were informed that they were being observed but not in an obtrusive manner, and that any useful findings derived from the study would be employed for future classes that included students with similar medical conditions. (*See Observations on page 274.*)

In all examples of qualitative research it is essential that every participant is informed of the nature of anonymity and confidentiality, and that strict measures be taken to implement these crucial aspects of research. This is to ensure that a responsible attitude is taken by the research team and that participants are fully aware of such precautions. Interestingly, there may be some occasions when participants not only do not want anonymity but positively seek self-publicity for their part in the research – they may even refuse to participate if this publicity cannot be guaranteed. In cases such as this the researcher should point out clearly that research protocol requires that ethical responsibility to the participants must be maintained in all cases. If the potential participants do not change their minds then, regrettably, they should not be included in the research study.

The sampling method used to select participants for qualitative research can also raise ethical issues. Purposive sampling can lead to researchers focusing on one salient feature within a group, and ignoring others that could have as much, or more, effect on behaviour. Snowball sampling can lead to an increasingly biased sample. (*See Sampling techniques, below, for more detail.*)

Sampling techniques

LEARNING OUTCOME
■ Discuss sampling techniques appropriate to qualitative research.

Purposive sampling is widely used by qualitative researchers and requires that the researcher ensures that the salient aspects of the research question are present in the population of cases under consideration. Thus the initial selection of cases will take care and effort but is a necessary part of the research process.

It can often be the case that participants who possess the salient aspects required are difficult to find in the general population. It can then be beneficial to the research process to use a snowball method, where one desirable participant is located and is willing to identify other potential and willing participants. Each new participant is often able to

Purposive sampling – a sampling method often used by qualitative researchers, where participants are selected because they possess characteristics that are central to the research question.

Snowball sampling – sampling strategy in which the first participant names a second participant; he or she then nominates a subsequent participant, and the process of naming continues. Used in qualitative research when target participants are difficult to locate.

identify others in this way. This might occur, for example, where highly intelligent people are needed, or people who have suffered from certain medical conditions, or individuals who are extremely able in a certain aspect of sport.

An alternative sampling method is known as convenience sampling, where people who are close at hand and are willing to act as participants are recruited for research purposes. This often occurs when schoolchildren are used as participants, but in this case it is very important that a strict adherence to ethical guidelines is implemented. (*See Ethical considerations on page 262.*)

Bias

Where purposive sampling is employed and participants are selected on the basis of their salient features it is likely that an element of bias can occur. For example, an investigation may be focused on groups of young men who have been selected purposively for assertive behaviour that has been noted to permeate their general response to mundane problems in their working lives. The researchers might wish to claim generalization from the findings of their study that depends on the assertive characteristics that they have noted. What they may not have noticed is that all the young men are very fit. In large part their continued assertiveness depends on this fitness; they are only able to continue with this energy-sapping assertive element of their behaviour over long periods of time if they remain physically fit. In such circumstances it may be that fitness is the major variable that contributes to assertive behaviour, and that generalization claims have been biased and invalidated.

Bias may also occur in snowball sampling where there is a continual reliance on people who know each other and who are likely to share similar emotions and attitudes

towards the types of experiences they have all had. A biased sample could then occur that may invalidate findings of research. The relatively few participants who are identified in this manner are likely to know each other and empathize with the emotional attitudes displayed by people in their group, meaning that issues of confidentiality are threatened, even though deliberate collusion does not happen. Similar criticisms may be made when samples are based on purposive samples, where small numbers are usually involved, and where individuals have been chosen because they share specific characteristics or experiences.

Figure 9.2 Samples for qualitative research tend to be much smaller than for quantitative research.

Convenience sampling
Convenience sampling – a sampling technique based on the comparative ease of recruiting volunteers as participants. Often used with students at school or in higher education institutions.

Bias – a process that distorts the data or findings of a research investigation, which subsequently makes the research invalid.

Audience effect – the ways in which participants may change their normal behaviour when researchers are present, especially when overt observation occurs.

Participant expectation and researcher bias

Participant expectation occurs when people know they are being observed and have been told of the reasons for the investigation. The investigation is **overt**. In these conditions people start to act in the way that they think the observer expects of them; this phenomenon is called the audience effect. People change from their normal behaviour and make the findings decidedly less valid. If researchers decide to use **covert observation**, then the people being observed continue in their normal way. Those researchers who use covert observation may, however, be justifiably accused of using unethical methods.

Where covert observation is used, the researcher should try to obtain **retrospective consent** for the study, although there may be some reluctance on the part of those under observation to agree to a consent form. Two steps may be taken to help lessen such objections. The first is to explain clearly what was intended by the investigation, and why a covert approach was necessary; the second point is to assure the participants that in order to retain their anonymity and confidentiality, all raw data, including recordings by audio or videotapes, will be destroyed once the study has been published.

In some circumstances, covert investigation is insufficient by itself to reveal the nature of activity that needs to be observed. For example, a researcher's observations and understanding of the interactive processes of individuals who are in a gang can only gain real insights by becoming a member of that group. The observer does not reveal his or her identity but covertly observes and records how group members interact with each other. The researcher may be within the group for many months, meaning the growing acceptance of his or her presence may allow for rather more confidences to be shared. Becoming accepted as a group member means that intimate communication between individuals allows the researcher to collect far richer material for investigation than that permitted by other methods. This is more likely to happen when the researcher already possesses several of the attributes typical of the group – by sharing a similar appearance, speaking, thinking and acting as a group member. Merriam *et al.* (2001), for example, suggest that:

'The more one is like the participants in terms of culture, gender, race, socio-economic class and so on, the more it is assumed that access will be granted, meanings shared and validity of findings assured.'

Membership of the group can last for several months and may be very expensive, but in some instances it can also be dangerous for the researcher. The researcher has to contend with a difficult situation where a professional distance should be maintained and the development of close friendships should be avoided. Long-term membership of a group can lead to the situation where the researcher 'goes native'; he or she starts to absorb subconsciously the concepts of the group, to accept their decisions and adopt their norms. Hall (2000) suggests that the covert researcher has to walk a fine line, whereby the researcher is 'at home' within the group but not to the extent that individual cover is blown.

Flick (2009) observes that although triangulation of observation (*see page 268*) using different observers is a useful technique to employ when observing in a public place, there are greater difficulties for women compared to men. Flick claims that the possibilities for access are more restricted for women. On the other hand, women's perceptions of both dangers and restrictions are more sensitive than those of men, and this enables women to observe in a different way to men. Women are more sensitive to the nuanced behaviour of small movements or appearance, such as small changes of facial colouring, enlargement of pupils, changes in muscle tone or subtle differences in voice production, and selection of clothing for various social occasions. These mixed abilities displayed by the two genders tend to promote the choice of mixed-gender teams when researchers are selected to carry out observational studies.

Participant expectations and researcher bias can each have devastating effects on findings of investigations where either or both of these conditions are present. Researchers have to be on constant guard to avoid the effects of these two undesirable contaminants on their interpretations of the actions they record. It is made difficult for some people because biases that have been internalized by an individual researcher may no longer be recognized as such by that researcher.

Alasuutari (2007) contributed a thought-provoking chapter on this topic in Seale *et al.*'s (2007) jointly edited text, *Qualitative Research Practice*. The point made in Alasuutari's chapter, 'The globalization of qualitative research', is that, contrary to the implications of the chapter title, most publications in qualitative research are written in the English language and published in the USA. This leads some critics to claim that thinking in this discipline must therefore be centred on Anglo-American-developed theories. Alasuutari, who is Director of the Research Institute for Social Sciences at the University of Tampere, Finland, makes a counterargument: many social scientists emigrated to the USA in the years following the end of the Second World War, knowing that their work stood a better chance of publication if it was written in English, the internationally accepted language for science, and published in the USA. They took with them theories they had developed from research of their own cultures, theories that had been nurtured in their various homelands. Several groups of social scientists created their ideas of social studies independently from each other. These ideas were gradually integrated within the American culture and were contagious in various ways that they soon became incorporated into theories from different disciplines in the social science.

The biases formulated by critics of the Anglo-American publishers are seen to be superficial when the incipient foreign theories were developed in and became part of the American culture. These publishers also encourage a reciprocation of ideas that has been given further impetus by ongoing developments in email and websites and the huge facilities that enable knowledge to be stored and efficiently accessed.

The importance of credibility in qualitative research

LEARNING OUTCOME
■ Explain the importance of credibility in qualitative research.

According to Gray (2009), credibility in the social sciences is:

'…seen by some supporters of qualitative approaches as more important than validity or reliability. It is established through building confidence in the accuracy of data gathering and interpretation.'

Credibility – ways of confirming the truthfulness, accuracy and transparency of data and interpretations used in research.

The gathering of data in the social sciences can be difficult and very time-consuming. It demands practice and even in the hands of experienced researchers, it can take considerable dedication and energy. In specific circumstances it may also involve great patience and sensitivity and the capability to empathize with the participant without biasing his or her responses. Interviews and observation research, in their various forms, rely for their credibility on the accuracy of the data collected. For this reason, it is often recommended that two researchers should be recruited to gather data, and that prior to the investigation they should be trained in an explicit manner so that their method of retrieving data is similar. Researcher triangulation (*see page 268*) adds to the credibility of the data.

Credibility can be enhanced with interviews when, following the collection of raw data and its initial interpretation, the interviewee can be asked to listen to what responses have been made to specific questions, and to inform the research team whether their interpretations of the responses are correct.

Triangulation can be applied to the researchers as they seek agreement with other interviewers on the most correct interpretation of responses when participants are difficult to contact. This team approach is also useful while data is analysed, especially when interviews are subjected to inductive content analysis and subsequently placed in appropriate levels of abstraction. The team leader must exert authority to ensure that no single member is too biased, or too assertive, so that others are swayed by the opinions expressed.

In a similar way, the observations made by the team benefit from a team consensus. Integrity is needed to allow for each member of the team to express his or her interpretation and approach to analysis. No-one should be ridiculed for expressing a view that is different from the majority, although all should accept a democratic approach can be taken when disagreements arise. Credibility in data collection and analysis is a team effort.

Triangulation

LEARNING OUTCOME
■ Explain the effect of triangulation on the credibility/trustworthiness of qualitative research.

Triangulation –
using different
combinations
of methods that
may include
data, methods,
researchers,
theories.
Triangulation
is used to claim
greater validity for
the findings of a
study.

Where doubt exists about the methods employed in a study, it is thought desirable by many researchers to increase the trustworthiness of the data by using one or more forms of triangulation. The most common form employed is data triangulation, which allows findings derived from the different methods of research to be compared. Similar findings from different methods should indicate that greater trust can be placed in the findings. As Flick (2009, p.445) argues:

'...triangulation should produce knowledge on different levels, which means they go beyond the knowledge made possible by one approach and thus contribute to promoting quality in research.'

There are many different types of triangulation; among the most commonly used are **method triangulation** and **researcher triangulation**. Method triangulation uses different methods within one study, for example qualitative and quantitative. Its aim is to limit the effects of bias and to increase the trustworthiness of the methods used. Researcher triangulation employs more than one researcher in gathering and analysing the data, including subjective interpretations of participant responses to qualitative approaches. The team effort involved in analysis will reduce the bias offered by a single individual member. Greene *et al.* (1989, pp.255–74) confirm:

'Many studies make use of triangulation because the application of multiple methods ensures that the inherent bias of one measure is counterbalanced by the strength of the other. Hence, using multiple methods, the results converge or corroborate one another, strengthening the validity of findings.'

There are criticisms of triangulation. The use of different methods could add considerably to the time and costs of research; while on other occasions the findings resulting from various approaches are so different that resolving them may not be considered feasible in the time allocated for the research. The comparatively restrictive answers that can be elicited from participants in semi-structured interviews could be different from those obtained in the freer form of a conversation interview, for instance. The respondent could have different perceptions since the former approach constrains their answers compared to the free form of thinking encouraged by the latter. As Krahn *et al.* (1995, p.208) suggest:

'Obtained responses then address related but different issues and are not easily blended to form a single, well integrated interpretation.'

Bryman (2007) claims that some individuals could be guilty of bias towards a specific method and hence sway the findings towards that particular approach. Most scathing of all is the evaluation made by Giddings (2006, p.198), who comments that the mixed methods advocated by proponents of triangulation are 'nothing more than positivism dressed up in drag'. Gray remarks, in a rather more formal criticism, that the mixed methods approach:

'...finds itself located within the thinking of positivism because it rarely reflects a constructionist or subjective view of the world. Thinking is planned in advance; designs are set in place and protocols followed. Qualitative methodological designs that focus on meaning, symbolism and the power of words are marginalized.'

Reflexivity

Reflexivity –
acknowledgement
by researchers
of the extent to
which their own
biases are likely to
impact on their
interpretation of
experiences related
by participants.

Gray (2009) suggests that reflexivity is the voice of the researcher and is used to illuminate the relationship that is built up between the researcher and the object of the study. The term is mainly used by qualitative researchers as they collect interview data (Ryan & Golden, 2006). The researcher cannot be regarded merely as a neutral observer, since he or she is actively involved in the construction of knowledge while acting within the research context itself. Qualitative researchers have perceptions of the actions and words that they see and hear; when they interpret this data they cannot avoid writing about the constructs that they make. They use the cumulation of their past experiences in their present day selves to help in the interpretation of their data.

Mauthner and Doucet (2003, pp.413–31) assert that in many research accounts, the researcher '...is rendered invisible as are the interpersonal, social and institutional contexts.' They further suggest that the ways in which computer-assisted qualitative data analysis is enabled has '...given an air of scientific objectivity to what remains a fundamentally subjective and interpretive process.'

As researchers, psychologists necessarily bring their own private prejudices to focus on the data presented to them. If they are able to reveal their biases to the readers of their studies then this offers a transparency that enables a greater trust to be placed in their research. According to Gray (2009), the personal beliefs and attitudes of researchers tend to shape the research. There is also the distinct possibility, however, that the research process also affects the beliefs and attitudes of the researchers themselves. Dupuis (1999) suggests that the researcher is '...firmly within the dynamic of the research process in a continuous, intentional and systematic self-introspection.'

Mauthner and Doucet (2003) state their opinion that, while reflexivity continues to increase in importance, there is little research literature that shows how it can be achieved. But some newer approaches could be usefully adopted for this purpose, such as:

'*...designing research that involves multiple investigators. This can encourage dialogue and the critical interchanges of ideas – pushing researchers to make transparent their epistemological positions and personally held beliefs.*'

Dupuis (1999) further encourages the use of reflexivity by proposing that:

'*...[in] reporting research perspectives, values and beliefs in any research report, researchers are recommended that this is done pre and post data collection so that changes in personal feelings can be made explicit.*'

SECTION SUMMARY
■ Rather than the positivist, deductive methods used in quantitative research, qualitative research is more inductive. Rich data is collected and then themes and theories are drawn out.
■ Qualitative research produces rich data that can reveal more than can be revealed by narrowly focusing on one hypothesis, and it is more ecologically valid than quantitative research.
■ Qualitative research does have disadvantages: issues of time, money and resources needed to analyse large amounts of data; issues of generalizability and researcher bias.
■ Generalizing from qualitative research is difficult, but by looking at how closely the subject of research represents other similar cases it is possible to assess generalizability.

- It is imperative to consider ethics in qualitative research, especially as it often involves sensitive subjects.
- Qualitative research rarely uses random sampling, instead purposive or snowball sampling are often favoured.
- Participant expectation can become an issue in qualitative research when participants are informed of the purpose of the research. Not informing them has ethical ramifications, however.
- Each researcher will have their own prejudices and expectations and this can bias how they interpret the data they collect. This can be mitigated by researcher triangulation and reflexivity.
- Credibility is important, and can be strengthened by researcher triangulation, reflexivity and the proper training of researchers.
- Data triangulation involves collecting several different types of data and looking at whether they support each other. Researcher triangulation involves having multiple researchers look at the same data to ensure their interpretation is consistent. Triangulation is important to ensure credibility of research.
- Reflexivity is the ability of researchers to recognize that they interpret their findings through the prism of their own expectations, prejudice and biases, rather than purporting to be neutral observers.

Interviews

LEARNING OUTCOMES
- Evaluate semi-structured, focus group and narrative interviews.
- Discuss considerations involved before, during and after an interview.

Although there are many types of interviews, this section of the chapter will focus on semi-structured, focus groups and narrative interviews, as selected in the International Baccalaureate syllabus for Paper 3. Interviews provide researchers using qualitative methods with their main means of obtaining data. For each of the three types of interviews mentioned, the same ethical precautions associated with other forms of investigation should be put into place. These include informed consent and anonymity.

Semi-structured interviews

The most commonly used method is the semi-structured interview. As its name suggests, this type of interview is characterized by an over-arching structure of open and/or closed questions that need to be asked by the researcher, but he or she is given a certain degree of flexibility in the wording of the questions and the order in which they are asked. This freedom of action is decided by the researcher, who takes into account the reactions of the participant in establishing a mutual rapport just before the interview proper.

The interview is essentially a dialogue that involves turn-taking between the interviewer and the interviewee. It is often the case that the interviewer may need to give encouragement to interviewees to develop their responses in order to ensure clarity of meaning. The turn-taking element of the interview can promote a conversational quality to the process that should result in richer data.

In semi-structured interviews the list of questions is prepared in advance of the interview, and additional questions may need to be asked as a result of responses that are given. More probing may be needed to order to expand on a rather brief response earlier in the interview.

Because of the conversational nature of some interviews it is appropriate that the turn-taking, which is characteristic of this mode of interview, leads to an interaction in which either the interviewer or the interviewee can lead. This mode of interaction, where

Figure 9.3 The semi-structured interview is the most commonly used interview technique.

equality is apparent, is likely to result in an increase in the richness of data.

Although it is usual for such interviews to be face-to-face, they are also suitable for telephone interviews, or where communication is devised though the use of computerized links. Any recording of the interviews, whether by sound or images, and their future access or publication, will need to be agreed with participants, as will the use of such media by legitimate third parties.

For most semi-structured interviews it is probably better, with the agreement of the participant, that an audio recording is made rather than a visual recording. A video camera or similar device needs to be used with a visual recording, and these devices can distract some participants and cause many of them to act in an artificial manner. Whichever method of recording is used, participants should be given an opportunity to listen to the audio recording or see the visual recording and to make amendments to the recordings where they think it is necessary.

It is essential that researchers thoroughly check their recording devices prior to the start of an interview. This advice particularly applies to any batteries that may be used. If these fail during the course of an interview and no replacement is available, then the effect on the research process can be catastrophic.

It is likely that as electronic and computer-linked communication becomes faster and more sophisticated that ethical problems will arise that will need to be resolved on an *ad hoc* basis. Difficulties are also likely to occur that will need new legislation to prevent further intrusion on the rights that individuals have to protect their own privacy and security.

Although visual recording brings benefits in the way of illustrating body language, this benefit is outweighed by the distraction mentioned. In order for researchers to analyse the data, the words from the recording need to be transcribed and printed to hard copy. It is during this process that the notions of traditional and postmodern transcription are used. The former process is used when the researchers have decided that the focus of their analyses should be solely on words; when a decision has been made for a postmodern approach to be taken, then the transcription needs to be annotated with brief references also to meaningful sounds other than words. This might include sighs, laughter, sounds of annoyance or anger, humming, clapping, sounds of frustration or impatience.

It is important that researchers realize that interviews take up considerable time and money, not only in the time taken to collect data but also in data transcription costs, the complex analyses involved, consultation with colleagues and travel costs.

Debriefing
– informing participants at the conclusion of an investigation of the precise nature of the research and the reasons for its implementation.

At the end of the interview each participant should be thanked and then debriefed. The last term means that the participant is reminded that the recorded interview will be anonymous and kept confidential, and the recording will be destroyed once the study has been published. Researchers have become more aware of their continued responsibility to interviewees, even after the interviews have been completed. They need to enquire about the feelings of the interviewee immediately following the interview, and to try to ensure that he or she has not suffered any adverse emotions as a result of the interview. If the interviewee remarks on any such upset the matter should be mentioned immediately to the team leader.

Focus group interviews

This type of interview normally involves one interviewer and a group of up to about six interviewees (Willig, 2001). Willig rightly claims that if more interviewees are included in a focus group there will be a danger that some individuals will be left out of the discussion.

Focus groups may be regarded as an alternative to the semi-structured interview since it represents a group interview where ensuing discussion provides data for later analysis.

There are occasions when more than one researcher should be involved, and this is particularly germane to focus groups where different ethnic or cultural groups participate. Differences in presentation of self, the use of language or differences in perception can intrude on the rich data that would otherwise be produced by the focus group. One researcher should act as a moderator and use a light touch to steer the group to the prearranged focus of discussion. Another researcher should take notes of what is said while research assistants could be engaged to help interpret what is said by individual members of the group. The first task of the moderator is to ask each individual to introduce themselves to the group and then to provide the topic for discussion. From then on the moderator has a role to encourage discussion on previous statements and claims made by fellow members of the group, and to persuade them to develop interesting comments. Rich data is expected to be generated from focus groups and it may well be that new constructs are developed by individuals or sub-groups as they adjust their ideas about relevant and central issues.

Gray (2009) claims that researchers need to make themselves aware of the problems that can occur with multicultural interviews. He also mentions Vazquez-Montilla *et al.* (2000) in their advice for culturally responsive interviewing that is aware of multi-ethnic cultural perspectives; they also suggest that their concept of triple A (AAA) practices be adopted: authenticity, affinity and accuracy. Montilla *et al.* (2000, p.4) found that in their investigations of Hispanic families in Florida that the past Hispanic experiences of the team were fundamental to its establishment of authenticity in the study and that the researchers felt able to 'validate their ethnic match and cultural backgrounds'.

Willig (2001, p.29) suggests that focus groups can be:

- **Homogenous**, where participants share key features, or **heterogenous**, where participants are different.
- **Pre-existing** groups, such as a group of friends or work colleagues.
- **Concerned**, where participants have a stake in the subject matter, or **naïve**, where participants do not have any particular commitment in relation to the subject matter.

It is not necessarily the case that focus groups are the best type of interview even though they are likely to produce rich data. There are many topics where semi-structured interviews are better, especially where a good rapport is evident throughout an interview, based on discussion of very sensitive issues, for example on financial, sexual or moral problems that need to be treated in strict confidence.

> **Culturally responsive interviewing** – sensitivity in conducting and reporting on the research process and its findings that acknowledges cultural differences that may be present.

Narrative interviews

As Gray (2009, p.171) claims, narrative interviews and their resultant analyses are:

'...a chronologically told story, with a focus on how the various elements of the story are sequenced. Key elements in narratives include scripts, predictive frames that people use to interpret events and stories that expand on scripts, adding evaluative elements that reveal the narrator's viewpoints.'

There is a tendency for narrative interviews to be used, particularly for sensitive studies where experiences may feel more safely stated in story form due to deep emotional feelings. The story form may allow for a certain degree of abstraction by the interviewee, as though the subject of the story is not necessarily the participant him- or herself but a more objectivized person. This tendency also allows for incorporation of ethical, sexual, moral or cultural issues in the story that may not otherwise be expressed. Bennett (2005) suggests that during the twentieth century there was increasing recognition by the public to regard everyday events as dynamic, pluralistic and contested.

These developments were associated with a diminution of the functions of social class, ethnic background and occupation. There was also an important contribution from the media in changing social identity to incorporate alternative forms of consumption and leisure, such as films and music or the pursuit of fitness and sporting activities. Importantly there was the rise of feminist studies and the increasing expectation for women to enter higher education, to the point where currently the number of women in higher education in the UK, for example, exceeds that of men.

Narrative interviews have been used extensively in feminist studies and have successfully revealed, through biographical narratives, how women have had to confront difficult problems in a male-dominated world. Gender is regarded as constructed with the help of the media such as films, television, novels and also through various aspects of academic study including psychology, anthropology and sociology (Cranny-Francis *et al.*, 2003). This construct has encouraged women to use a more assertive approach in their conversations and in their writing. It has given rise to an increased recruitment of women in several professions, including teaching, medicine, many of the caring professions and politics. More women than men are now employed as teachers and also as doctors, but many feminists and others would rightfully claim that there is still some way to go to ensure equality between men and women in several walks of life.

Inductive content analysis

LEARNING OUTCOME
■ Explain how researchers use inductive content analysis (thematic analysis) on interview transcripts.

Content analysis developed from several different approaches, including a quantitative one. At the end of the nineteenth century, the discovery of gold and other valuable minerals on the West Coast of the USA and Canada caused consternation within the financial industry, which was located mainly on the eastern side of the continent. The stock-market dealers needed to know what new discoveries of valuable deposits had been made, how much of this substance was likely to be recovered and how much it was worth. This information was treated as highly confidential by newspapers until it was ready for release as a scoop by a specific paper. Other competing newspapers quickly followed with the news in their own publications.

For the stock-market dealers it was necessary to discover how many times mention was made in the East Coast papers of any new mineral discovery. The more frequently mention was made, the greater the chance that the information was true. The counting of each statement related to the find was a quantitative form of content analysis that is still followed in many commercial enterprises today.

Qualitative inductive content analysis finds its data in a different format, by identifying relevant phrases used in written transcripts based on interviews. The researcher formulates the research question, conducts the interview and once the transcript is available, makes a very thorough search for any phrases that could be interpreted as germane to answering the research question. A second member of the research team is often employed to confirm that the original analysis identified all relevant material, and this might be followed by a third and fourth analysis.

The critical inductive process is then introduced in an effort to draw out, or induce, the meaning of the phrases that have been identified. This rather contentious task can be made slightly easier by grouping similar phrases together, even where these come from different parts of the interview. The interpretation of the meaning of words and phrases is cognitively demanding. Where two or three people have this same task there can be very different interpretations of what the interviewee meant when they used a certain phrase. Even where one person works alone on the transcript it is possible for self-doubt

Inductive content analysis – usually applied after semi-structured interviews. Allows researchers to draw out meanings of statements made by interviewees and to construct an analysis based on interpretation of the statements.

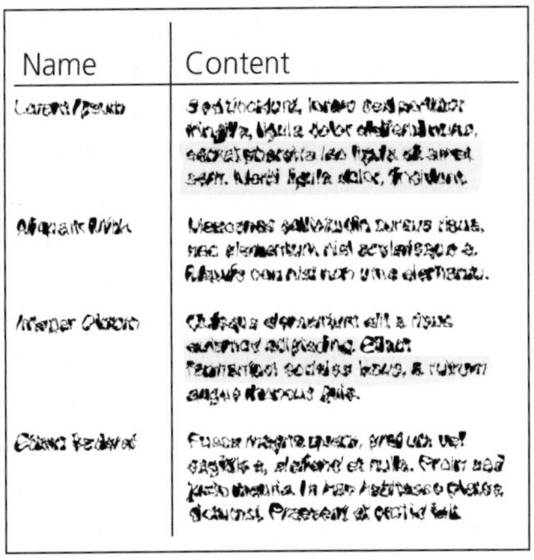

Figure 9.4 Inductive content analysis looks for themes in interview transcripts.

to insinuate itself as different interpretations present themselves.

When agreement about the interpretations has been agreed, the phrases are coded into agreed themes or categories, and subsequently placed into higher level themes. There are usually three levels; each succeeding level is given a higher level of abstraction of the interpretations. The interpretations are again checked with the original interview transcript to certify that agreement is consistent. If the interviewee is available, he or she will be consulted to ensure that the meaning inferred by the researchers is what the interviewee intended.

A discussion is then produced and this uses the framework provided by the inductive content analysis. The framework also acts as a chronological guide for the sequence of events revealed by each interviewee, but cumulative effects of each inductive interpretation remain the constant on which overall findings are based. The method described above is not fixed in stone, but instead is a dynamic process and subject to improvement, as many qualitative methods also change in the light of experience and application.

SECTION SUMMARY

- Semi-structured interviews involve a researcher asking a participant a set of questions, but with the flexibility to deviate from the set questions should they feel the need to.
- Focus group interviews involve researchers talking to a group of about five to eight participants.
- Narrative interviews are where the participant is encouraged to talk about an experience in the form of a story; this is particularly useful when dealing with sensitive topics.
- Several issues need to be considered when organizing an interview, including: how the interview should be recorded and the effect this might have on the participants' behaviour; whether transcription should focus only on words spoken (traditional) or include other meaningful sounds and actions (post-modern); ethical issues such as debriefing at the end of the interview.
- Inductive content analysis aims to draw out meaning from interview transcripts. Word and phrases from the transcript are interpreted by the researcher (or researchers) and grouped into themes and categories.

Observations

LEARNING OUTCOME

- Evaluate participant, non-participant, naturalistic, overt and covert observations.

Observation, as it is used in psychology, incorporates received sensations from each of the senses – sight, sound, smell, touch and taste. As humans we tend to give priority to visual stimuli, but the smell of burning electrics, paper or cooking will quickly alert people to the potential danger of fire and the safety of themselves and others in the locality. When a person looks at the same object or event from the same position, they will perceive it in different ways from others. Their perceptions are likely to be based on different scripts or constructs, depending on their past learning and experiences.

Researchers themselves are also prone to interpret what they observe in different ways from other researchers. As Gray (2009) suggests, each of us is governed by our own set of emotions and prejudices, where we select what we observe to fit in with our own **schemas**, yet ignore phenomena within the same field of vision, sound or other sense in order to focus on what we know from past experience. A further danger also exists that when we, as researchers, become involved with a group of participants, we may be lured into affecting their perceptions and thence influence succeeding events. This could well happen when studying people in their natural environments, for example in playing sport. Our primary task might be to act as observer, but our enthusiasm for playing in a match may lead us to score a goal, commit a foul, or cause an accidental injury to an opponent. Each of these events, among others, could lead to an unwanted influence on the game that we originally only intended to observe.

Participant observation

The example given above of an observer joining a sports team is an illustration of participant observation, where the researcher joins a group and behaves as a member of that group. This approach to observation is very close to ethnography. In the case of team games, such as football, hockey, netball or rugby, the researcher not only joins in the game as one of the team but also participates in the social life centred on the team players, particularly after matches. Researchers need not necessarily become players, but could

become volunteers to help with food, drinks, and possibly with first aid, physiotherapy or coaching. Notes should be taken and themes identified for further analysis or discussion.

Participant observers in the examples mentioned above are associated with overt observation; the team or group members know of their presence. This knowledge can make the researcher an outsider to the group and the desired level of rapport may not be attained. Other attributes may also prevent close ties, including gender, ethnic group, age difference or social class. The closer the researcher is to the group members on relevant variables such as these, the greater the success will be in merging with the group. As with other methods of qualitative research,

Figure 9.5 Participant observation involves the researcher becoming a member of the group.

there are matters of bias and subjectivity to take into account, but these should not be insurmountable. Researchers should ensure that they use reflexivity to inform readers of their report of their predilection towards potential bias, and to indicate how such bias may have arisen.

Non-participant observation

This type of observation is less common in the qualitative research associated with psychology, but has its advantages. In participant observation, participants may be biased in their behaviour if they are made aware of researchers in their midst. It is possible for non-participant observers to regard the participants from a distance or to be engaged in another task not associated with what the participants are engaged in. The presence of the researchers may be overt or covert. In covert observation the participants are unaware that they being observed. This means that their behaviour is natural (or valid) and not biased by a known presence of observers. The validity of non-participant observation is increased by its tendency to be used in natural settings.

Gray (2009, p.405) is adamant that researchers should take notes in the form of an aide-mémoire that will inform them as they come to write comprehensive **field notes** concerning their observational study. Field notes become the preliminary stage of analysis as they are written. At a later stage it will become possible to add any personal feelings experienced during observations. Gray illustrates his meaning with observations of a till service in a busy staff canteen:

'*Description:*

'*There was a smell of fried food mixed with disinfectant. Young white male (about 20 years of age), medium height and build, wearing staff canteen smock, short, neat brown hair. Right ear pierced.*

'*The till worker looked up at the customer as she approached the till, but then looked away. He adjusted the till roll, and opened and closed the cash till twice. He made eye contact with the customer when she arrived at the till, and smoothed his hand through his hair. I felt that this was an unhygienic thing to do. I felt a sudden rush of antagonism towards him that I then tried to repress.*'

Berg (2006) proposes that researchers should visit the environment where people will be observed and try to establish a rapport with its inhabitants. It is advisable to inform them about the nature of the research and to reassure people on matters of confidentiality. In many organizations it is likely that sub-groups will have developed that may have developed antagonistic behaviour towards other groups. In such cases there may well be attempts for a particular group to persuade the researcher to join them in order to strengthen their position in the internal conflict with other groups.

Preparation for participant observation is time-consuming and might require considerable diplomacy to deal with internal friction that has established itself over many years. It may not be a popular exercise with all workers, who could show hostility towards outside observers.

Naturalistic observation

Naturalistic observation takes place in the normal environment of the workplace, home, hospital, or within everyday settings where people meet and interact with each other. These observations are characterized by having high ecological validity. As with other forms of observation, the naturalistic approach may incorporate a covert or overt approach. If the former is used there will be an ethical concern since those being observed have not given their consent and may rightly object to their actions being observed. Some researchers may argue there is no other way that certain behaviours or verbal interactions can be investigated without risking non-valid findings as a result of participants reacting in a biased manner towards the presence of researchers.

An advantage of naturalistic observation is that the method can be used with similar participants but in different environments. This means that it becomes possible to investigate how groups could behave in simulated exercises involving extreme conditions, say of a threatened fire or flood, or in the presence of a catastrophic accident. The observations and their analyses make a valuable contribution to training groups to react effectively in the face of such eventualities.

Ecological validity – a descriptor of an investigation conducted that reflects normal conditions of the entity or process under investigation. Unlike quantitative research, qualitative research is not used in laboratory conditions. Instead it is conducted in the real world environment.

Overt observation – a method of observing in which the participants are made aware of the reasons they are being observed.

Overt and covert observation

Covert observation
– an observation
technique in which
the people who
are being observed
are unaware of the
observation process.

Overt observation occurs when participants are aware that they are being observed, while in the case of covert observation they are unaware of being observed.

In the former case there is usually little that is contentious in ethical terms and participants are likely to give their informed consent providing that they think that the study is worthwhile. As has been mentioned, however, there is sometimes a temptation for some researchers to become too focused on their task and to inadvertently bias their perceptions of the events they are observing.

For covert observation the major ethical concern is based on the lack of knowledge on the part of participants. This method often conflicts with guidance given by the ethics committees of professional bodies, institutes of higher education or examination boards. To some individuals it is reprehensible to give permission for research projects that involve deliberate deception. This view is countered by other individuals in the research community who argue strongly that covert methods are sometimes the only possible way of gaining information that, for example, increases the safety of a community.

Setting up and conducting observations

LEARNING OUTCOME
■ Discuss considerations involved in setting up and carrying out an observation.

Ethical issues –
behaviour that
affects participants
and researchers
in a negative
way, particularly
where participants
perceive that
they have been
demeaned. Ethical
issues may also
include religious,
racial, sexual or
ageist slurs.

Once the researchers have agreed to use observation as their method for investigation, a further decision has to be made as to which approach – from observational, non-observational, naturalistic, overt or covert – will be used. It is clearly possible to triangulate the methods selected, and to use more than one method to research the same phenomena, but there are usually conditions of time and cost that inhibit use of additional methods.

In all studies that include observation, the ethical issues involved should be given major consideration. Where a covert approach is taken, the research proposal should include reference to whether there should be a retrospective consent obtained, as occurred in the case of the Chinese participants who had diabetes (*see pages 263–4*). The method and timing of destroying raw data should be decided on in order to guard against any lack of security subsequent to the study.

The sampling method will also need to be discussed, including the steps that should be taken if insufficient numbers of participants are recruited at the original attempt. Even where purposive sampling is chosen, there should be consideration of how the concept of 'purpose' may need to be broadened should the required number of participants fail to materialize at the first attempt.

In the collection of raw data there should be detailed discussion with the team to ensure training in what should be recorded and how it should be recorded. The researchers themselves should be selected on an agreed number of criteria, particularly where sensitive issues such as gender, ethnicity or age are likely to affect the richness of data that is gathered. This element will be particularly important in the case of participant observation.

If covert participation is needed, there needs to be a means devised to ensure the safety of researchers against potential dangers from whichever group they are required to join. Realistic discussion is needed with researchers who may find themselves on the frontline of dangerous behaviour.

As has been noted, when researchers stay for a considerable time in the field, they tend to adopt the norms of the group which they have joined. While this may be advantageous in strengthening their disguise, it does not bode well for a valid report. Planning needs to be implemented to prevent this from causing a problem. Reflexivity may help to increase the validity of reporting.

Analysing data from observational research

LEARNING OUTCOME
■ Discuss how researchers analyse data obtained in observational research.

Field notes written during the observational process, or as soon after as possible, are the main source of raw data. If this data is sufficiently full and effectively recorded, it will provide an adequate framework on which to base an inductive content analysis. It is also most helpful for later recall if the researcher is able to take descriptive notes of the environment in which the observations occur. This puts the observations into context, especially when senses in addition to the visual sense are used. The senses of smell and hearing can be very evocative and aid in the recall of visual observation. Think back to the staff canteen till worker mentioned earlier and the lingering '…smell of fried food mixed with disinfectant.' This redolent phrase will, for some people, be even more memorable than its associated visual setting.

Identifying raw data phrases that are relevant to the research question begins the first stage of inductive content analysis. As these phrases are categorized into lower- and higher-level themes, the perceptions used by researchers are examples of induction. Answers to each of these questions gradually accumulate into a schema of the environment and actions under observation.

There are alternative forms of analysis that are used when a report has to be written for a specific audience. It is possible to include photographs, diagrams and video to illustrate how schema can be developed and these may well include apt quotations as raw data. From data analysis there can be further development of theory that helps to inform the investigative work of future researchers. The written reports that emanate from observation research still continue to cause controversy among different groups of qualitative researchers. Those with a positivistic approach support the notion that their research is authentic since it is ethologically valid and based on reality. This view is rejected by those who favour a post-modern approach to the research, who hold to the view that any perception that is identified is just one among a host of alternative interpretations.

SECTION SUMMARY
■ Participant observation is when the researcher joins the group under investigation as a member of that group.
■ Non-participant observation occurs when the researcher observes a group from a distance rather than being a part of it.
■ In overt observation the participants are made aware they are under observation; this is ethically preferable but can influence the behaviour of the participants. In covert observations the participants don't know they're being observed; although this is ethically questionable, some argue it is the only way to research certain topics.
■ Several issues need to be considered when organizing an observation, including: sampling method; ethical issues (particularly in relation to covert observations); researcher triangulation; protection of the researcher from harm; characteristics of the researchers and how these will affect their ability to relate to the group.
■ Researchers should take field notes during their observation or very soon afterwards; the notes should be as full as possible. Inductive content analysis can then be used to find themes in the research.

Case studies

LEARNING OUTCOME
■ Evaluate the use of case studies in research.

Case studies – a research method that focuses on a single person or group. Its findings are considered to be limited by the constraints placed on this method in terms of finance, time, and number of participants.

Yin (2003, p.13) defines a case study as 'an empirical enquiry that investigates a contemporary phenomenon within its real-life context, especially when the boundaries between phenomenon and context are not clearly evident.' Researchers involved in case studies are frequently asked to discover the nature of the relationship between a specific phenomenon and the context in which it appears. Case studies usually focus on a single individual or institution. For example, a school may change its status from a single sex school to one that teaches both males and females. After four or five years it could investigate its examination results against those of similar schools and find that its own results are just above average. While this may be reasonably satisfying news, the governing body of the school and senior staff may wish to accelerate this measure of modest success.

The school could introduce a case study approach that would collect data on each of the variables that may contribute to academic success, such as numbers of males and female students, their objective academic attainments on entering the school, the elements of the school curriculum, the quality and numbers of staff, the financial state of the school, the external examination boards used by the school, and the academic and commercial destinations of students on leaving the school. These are only a few of the variables that would need to be considered by those organizing the case study, but they would need to be reduced in number or to become more narrowly focused to ensure that the case study was worthwhile.

Using case studies

LEARNING OUTCOME
■ Explain how a case study could be used to investigate a problem in an organization or group.

When using case studies, a theoretical approach needs to be developed in order to ensure that the data collection and its analysis are relevant to the aims of the case study, and that initially at least the approach should be deductive rather than inductive. Case studies require not only a great deal of time, effort and finance, they also require a flexible approach, where high level skills are needed. For an example of a situation where a case study could be used to solve a problem in an organization, let's consider again a school. A school wants to introduce an expensive and reliable software system to deal with both its administrative and academic functions. This is a vital decision that will affect the smooth running of the school for many years ahead.

Much consultation will be sought from other schools that have developed their own systems, through application of the case study approach. This will require an analytical investigation of the needs of the school, and the likely division of the school into subsections that will undertake their own case studies of the specialized needs of, for example, different subject areas of the curriculum or various areas of administration or curriculum support.

Generalizing case study findings

LEARNING OUTCOME
■ Discuss the extent to which findings can be generalized from a single case study.

Care should be taken when generalizing from one case study (*see Generalizability on page 261*). It is likely that there will be similarities between a case study and other similar cases, however, and that information learnt in an individual case study could be applied to successive cases, even where the individual case study has its own set of specific circumstances.

For an example of generalizing from a case study, let's look again at the case of a school. A modern languages department wants to find out what the impact of introducing laptops for students would be on the quality of work. To test this, they decide that students studying Spanish as a foreign language should do all written work using a laptop computer; this would include notes, essays and exercises in grammar. The teacher would then assess the quality of the students' work. The first time that this was put into practice it was found that students' work was improved on average by a whole grade or more.

The question then arose: could this single study be generalized to other subject areas? The answer did not show resounding agreement. In the Spanish example, only in those students who were able to 'think' in the language they were studying did the big increase in grades occur. For many students, their feedback mentioned that they had to translate the language they were using back into their own home language, and these students didn't experience such a distinct improvement in performance. In addition, some students were able to think in Spanish, but not so easily in French and even less so when using German. The findings of the original study could be generalized, but with the proviso that the student could think in the new language.

Sometimes, as in the case described above, the findings from a single case study can be generalized, particularly where the conditions are similar to those in the original study. It will also come as no surprise that practically every new theory starts with a single case study; it is by the repetition of similar studies that provide similar findings that more robust confirmation of the original case can be generalized.

SECTION SUMMARY
■ Case studies usually involve an in-depth study of one individual or institution. They aim to produce rich research to allow a deep understanding of the salient issues affecting the individual/institution.
■ Case studies can be a useful method of investigating a problem in an organization or group, by considering a variety of variables and developing a deep understanding of the group. This approach requires time, money and flexibility.
■ Generalizing from one case study can be problematic, but it is likely a case study will share similarities with other similar situations and the information learned from one case study could be applied to successive cases.

10 Simple experimental study

Introduction

The purpose of the internal assessment is for students to get some hands-on experience of what it is to be a 'proper' psychologist by conducting some actual research themselves. Not only should this activity be enjoyable and motivating in itself, but it will also demonstrate to students how psychology works, especially in helping to understand the essential role that research plays in the subject. Students should also gain a familiarity with how research is used to evaluate psychological theories and explanations, allowing such explanations and theories to be either validated (accepted) or falsified (rejected).

SL/HL requirements
SL students

■ SL students plan, undertake and write up a replication of a simple experimental study.
■ The report is worth 25 per cent of overall marks.

HL students

■ HL students plan, undertake and write up either a replication or a modification of a simple experimental study.
■ The report is worth 20 per cent of overall marks.
■ More extensive background research related to the experimental study is required than at SL.
■ Operationalized experimental and null hypotheses are required.
■ Inferential statistical analysis of results is required.

There are some differences in:

1. The format of how SL and HL reports must be written up.
2. The criteria used to assess SL and HL reports.

These differences in requirements are detailed later in this chapter. The final report will be internally assessed by a teacher and then externally moderated by the IB.

Points to consider

■ Students should seek advice from their teachers on what experiment to choose, what practical and ethical issues need to be considered and how their work will be assessed.
■ Students can work in groups of up to four students. Each group must collect their own data, though this may be pooled with data from other groups. Different students or groups can use the same research aim (SL) or the same hypotheses (HL), but each write up must be the work of an individual student.
■ Students' work must be completely their own with no **plagiarism** occurring (presenting the work of another as your own). Referencing others' work (such as by describing previous relevant research) is allowable, as long as sources are credited.
■ Ethical considerations must be adhered to in planning, carrying out and writing up the report (this will be covered in greater detail later on).
■ All work must be authenticated by a teacher as not containing any malpractice (such as plagiarism, unethical conduct, etc.).

- Advice can be gained from teachers, after a first draft of the report has been written, on how to improve it. The next version, though, is the final one and further alterations cannot occur.
- The same piece of work cannot be used for the internal assessment as for the extended essay.
- Adapting materials that have been used in previous research is permissible, but software packages that remove the necessity for students to plan, design, conduct or write up reports should not be used.

Choosing an experiment

The experiment students choose to do must comply with SL/HL requirements (*see page 281*) and should be something that interests students and that will not be too complex to perform. Before preparing any materials, let alone attempting to carry out the study, students should think about what practical requirements will be involved and what ethical considerations need to be taken into account. It would be a good idea at this point to also consider what the **aim, hypotheses** and **variables** of the study will be. The experimental method requires the study to have an **independent variable** (IV) that is manipulated by the researcher(s). For this reason IVs that are based on pre-existing features of participants aren't permissible, for example, gender, age, cultural background, etc. As it is to be a simple experimental study, only one IV should be manipulated. As **correlational studies, quasi-experiments** and **natural experiments** don't require manipulation of an IV, such studies won't be permissible for students to conduct. This means that students are limited to carrying out either a **laboratory** or a **field** experiment (*see Experiments, below*). Similarly, only one **dependent variable** (DV) should be measured (the DV is where the data from the study will originate).

Experiments
Laboratory experiments

Laboratory experiments involve researchers controlling as many variables as possible, i.e. there's control over 'who, what, when, where and how'. This is usually done in a laboratory using standardized procedures, but can be conducted anywhere provided it's a controlled environment. Participants are randomly allocated to experimental groups.

Advantages

- ✔ **High degree of control** – experimenters control all the variables. For example, the IV and DV are very precisely operationalized (defined) and measured. This leads to greater accuracy and objectivity.
- ✔ Replication – other researchers can repeat the experiment to check results.
- ✔ **Cause and effect** – as long as all other variables are controlled, the effect (the change in the value of the DV) can be assumed to be caused solely by the manipulation of the IV.
- ✔ **Accurate measurements** – the laboratory facilitates the use of sophisticated technological equipment, which permits accurate measurements to be made.

Weaknesses

- ✗ **Investigator bias** – experimenters' expectations about a study can affect results and participants may be influenced by these expectations (*see page 288*).
- ✗ **Low** external validity – high degrees of control can make experimental situations artificial and unlike real life, and therefore it can be difficult to generalize results to other settings. Laboratory settings can be strange and intimidating places and people may not act in a way representative of their normal behaviour.

Experimental method – a research method using random assignment of participants and the manipulation of variables to determine cause and effect.

Laboratory experiment – an experiment conducted in a controlled environment, allowing the establishment of causality.

Replication – repetition of research to confirm results.

External validity – the extent to which the findings of a study can be generalized beyond the confines of the research setting.

✗ **Demand characteristics** – sometimes participants try to guess the purpose of experiments and act accordingly. In contrast, the 'screw you' effect is where participants guess the purpose of an experiment and act in a deliberately contradictory way (*see page 288*).

Figure 10.1 Laboratory settings can be strange and intimidating places. People may not act normally, making generalization of behaviour difficult.

Field experiments

Field experiments are performed in the 'real world' rather than the laboratory. The IV is manipulated by the experimenter and as many other variables as possible are controlled.

Advantages

✔ **High ecological validity** – due to the 'real world' environment, or naturally occurring environment, results relate to everyday behaviour and can be generalized to other settings.

✔ **No demand characteristics** – often participants are unaware of the experiment, and so there are no demand characteristics.

Weaknesses

✗ **Less control** – it's more difficult to control extraneous variables, either 'in the field' or in naturally occurring situations.

✗ **Replication** – it's difficult to precisely replicate field or natural experiments since the conditions are never exactly the same again.

✗ **Sample bias** – since participants aren't randomly allocated to groups, there may be sample bias.

Ethical guidelines

High-quality research involves good ethical practice and ethical implications must be fully considered before research is conducted. How ethical considerations will be dealt with should be included within each student's initial proposal and be provided to a teacher for scrutiny and approval.

■ **Informed consent** – whenever possible, investigators should inform participants of the objectives and aims of investigations. Parental consent should be obtained in the case of children under 16 years of age. Additionally consent should be obtained from children old enough to understand a study and from teachers if research is conducted within a school setting. Informed consent cannot be gained from adults not in a fit state of mind to respond freely and independently (for instance, as a result of drugs, alcohol or mental infirmity).

■ **Avoidance of deception** – the withholding of information or the misleading of participants is unacceptable if participants are likely to object or show unease once debriefed. Intentional deception of the participants over the purpose and general nature of investigations should be avoided wherever possible. Participants shouldn't deliberately be misled without scientific or medical justification, though sometimes deception is unavoidable. There are a number of possible ways to deal with the problem of deception:

1. **Presumptive consent** – this is gained from people of a similar background to participants in a study. If they state they'd have been willing to participate, then it's deemed that the actual participants would too.

2. **Prior general consent** – this involves participants agreeing to being deceived without knowing how they will be deceived. As participants know they will be deceived, this can affect their behaviour.

Field experiment – an experiment conducted in a naturalistic environment where the researchers manipulate the independent variable.

Ethical considerations – the rules and moral principles that govern the conduct of researchers in investigations.

3. **Retrospective consent** – this involves asking participants for consent after they have participated in a study. However, they may not consent and yet have already taken part.

If deception is used, participants must be told immediately afterwards and given the chance to withhold their data from the study. Before conducting such a study, the investigator has a special responsibility to: determine that alternatives that avoid deception aren't available; ensure participants are provided with sufficient information at the earliest stage; consult appropriately on the possible effects of withholding information or deliberate deception.

- **Adequate briefing/debriefing** – all relevant details of a study should be explained to participants before and afterwards. A debrief is important if deception has been used. Participants should leave the study in no worse state than when they started it. Debriefing doesn't provide justification for any unethical aspects of the procedure.
- **Protection of participants** – investigators have a responsibility to protect participants from physical and mental harm during the investigation. Risk of harm must be no greater than in ordinary life.
- **Right to withdraw** – participants are made aware that they can leave a study at any time, regardless of whether payment or inducement has been offered. This is difficult to implement during observations. Participants should also be aware they can withdraw their data at any point in the future.
- **Confidentiality** – participants' data is confidential and shouldn't be disclosed to anyone, unless agreed in advance. Numbers should be used instead of names in any subsequent published articles. Confidentiality is easily confused with anonymity. Confidentiality means data can be traced back to names, whereas anonymous data cannot, as the researchers collect no names. Confidential data collection is preferable in cases where participants might be followed up later.
- **Giving advice** – during research, investigators may obtain evidence of psychological or physical problems of which a participant is, apparently, unaware. The investigators have a responsibility to inform the participant if they believe that by not doing so the participant's future well-being may be endangered.
- **Colleagues** – investigators share responsibility for the ethical treatment of participants with collaborators, assistants, students and employees. A psychologist who believes another investigator may be conducting research that isn't in accordance with ethical principles should encourage that investigator to re-think what they are doing.
- **Non-human animals** – should not be used in experimental studies.

Before research is conducted, investigators must seek expert guidance (for example, from teachers), consult likely participants for their views, establish a cost–benefit analysis of short-term and long-term consequences (with research only proceeding if the benefits are assessed as outweighing potential costs), and assume responsibility for the research. If, during the research process, it becomes clear there are negative consequences resulting from the research, it should be stopped and every effort made to correct for the negative consequences. Any researcher having ethical concerns about a fellow student should discuss concerns with them in the first instance, and if their concerns are not allayed, consult a teacher.

Theory of knowledge

Psychology uses the scientific method of rigorous testing performed under controlled conditions to discover 'truths' about the human condition. However, psychologists have a moral obligation to always put the safeguarding of their participants' mental and physical health, as well as their dignity, first. If ethical considerations are not met, the reputation of psychology becomes tarnished and people will be reluctant to offer themselves up as participants in experiments. Without such willing participants psychology could not exist.

Consideration also needs to be given to what type of data your study will generate. SL students are only required to use and interpret **descriptive statistics**, but HL students are required to apply an appropriate **inferential statistical test** to their data. Ensure in advance that data generated will meet these requirements. (*See Levels of data measurement, page 297, and Choosing the appropriate statistical test, page 300.*)

The overriding concern should be that the investigation will be feasible in terms of the available resources and that students will be able to prepare, carry out and write up the investigation in the timeframe dictated by the teacher. If students are going to be working in a group, it's a good idea that each person has designated roles in terms of what they're going to be doing, for example who will be providing what materials, etc. It's also a good idea to draw up a schedule that includes all tasks to be performed and in what timeframe these should be achieved.

Key study

Sheldrake (1998)

For the purposes of explaining what will be necessary for the internal assessment to be carried out, reference will be made to Sheldrake's (1998) laboratory experiment into whether or not people have the seemingly psychic ability to detect unseen stares.

Sheldrake (1994), from earlier work by Titchener (1898), who reported the phenomenon whereby people feel a tingling sensation on their neck when being stared at, proposed the 'Alice Through the Looking-Glass' theory of perception, where perception is seen as a two-way process involving a movement of light into the body and an outward projection from the body of mental images. He therefore saw the mind as being able to reach out and 'touch' the things we look at, so that people should be able to detect being stared at by an unseen person, due to the physical strains and pressures of the tendons, skin, muscles and joints being exerted by the person doing the staring. This led him to design and conduct a study whereby participants underwent 20 trials each, using more or less equal amounts of control (not being stared at) and experimental (being stared at) trials. Each trial lasted about ten seconds and the order of control and experimental trials was presented as random sequences, with the experimenter who was present during the conducting of the study unaware of the content of these sequences. The findings were subjected to statistical analysis and a significant difference was found beyond chance factors that led Sheldrake to conclude that the ability to detect unseen stares is a real phenomenon that gives support to his theory of perception.

Sheldrake's claims have, however, been very controversial and have led to claims and counter-claims about the validity of his findings, mostly centring on his methodology (how he conducted his studies).

For more information on Sheldrake's work visit: http://sheldrake.org or http://theskeptic .org.uk/magazine/onlinearticles/498-sheldrake-p3-staring

■ Critical thinking

Sheldrake's research into unseen stares is classed as a part of parapsychology, the study of extraordinary phenomena, and this branch of psychology highlights the important point that science must always study phenomena with an open mind and be ready to accept results that are contradictory to one's own beliefs. Pre-judgements about the impossibility of phenomena are as inappropriate in science as being biased in favour of such abilities existing.

Forming the aim

Aim – a precise statement of why a study is taking place.

An **aim** is a precise statement of why a study is taking place. It should include what is being studied and what the study is trying to achieve. For example, the aim in Sheldrake's (1998) study was 'to investigate whether people have the ability to detect an unseen person staring at them'.

Constructing the hypotheses (HL only)

Hypotheses – precise, testable research predictions.

Dependent variable – the factor measured by researchers in an investigation.

Independent variable – the factor manipulated by researchers in an investigation.

A hypothesis is more precise than an aim and predicts what's expected to happen. **Hypotheses** are testable statements. An experiment will have two types of hypothesis – the experimental hypothesis and the null hypothesis.

Experimental hypothesis – this predicts that differences in the **dependent variable** (DV), the variable being measured, will be beyond the boundaries of chance, as a result of manipulation of the **independent variable** (IV), the variable being manipulated.

Differences in the DV resulting from manipulation of the IV are known as significant differences.

There are two types of experimental hypotheses:

- **Directional ('one-tailed') hypothesis** – this predicts the direction of the results, e.g. 'participants will be significantly more able to detect whether an unseen person is staring at them'.
- **Non-directional ('two-tailed')** – this predicts there will be a difference, but doesn't predict the direction of the results, e.g. 'there will be a significant difference between the number of times participants can and cannot detect an unseen person staring at them'.

Directional hypotheses are used when previous research evidence suggests results will go in one particular direction, or when replicating a previous study that also used a directional hypothesis.

Null hypothesis – this is the 'hypothesis of no differences'. It predicts that the IV won't affect the DV. Any differences in results will be due to chance factors, not the manipulation of the IV, and therefore will not be significant, e.g. 'there will be no significant difference between the number of times participants can and cannot detect an unseen person staring at them'.

Rather than trying to prove the experimental hypothesis, the experimenter is attempting to refute the null hypothesis. In doing so, one of the two hypotheses will be supported by the findings and will thus be accepted, with the other one being rejected.

Theory of knowledge

Although psychology uses the experimental method common to the natural sciences, there always remains the problem that the investigation of psychological phenomena is not merely confined to physically observable and measurable factors. For example, Sheldrake's belief that some people may have a psychic ability to detect unseen stares does not completely lend itself to a form of investigation that focuses solely on objective criteria.

Establishing and controlling variables

LEARNING OUTCOMES
- State operational definitions of variables.
- Describe potential confounding variables.
- Explain the controls needed for an experiment (for example, maturation, contamination, placebo effect).

Experiments require the manipulation and control of variables in order to establish causality (cause-and-effect relationships). Variables are any features of an experiment that can vary.

The experimenter manipulates an independent variable (IV) to see its effect on the dependent variable (DV). The IV is the variable that's altered by the experimenter to see its effect on the DV. The DV is the measured result of the experiment. Any change in the DV occurs as a result of the manipulation of the IV. For example, whether an unseen person is staring at someone (IV) could be manipulated to see whether the unseen stares were detected or not (the DV).

Extraneous variables are any other variables that may affect the DV. Controls are used to prevent extraneous variables spoiling the results. If extraneous variables aren't carefully controlled, they can confound (confuse) results. When extraneous variables do vary from one condition to another, then changes in the level of the DV may be due to the manipulation of the IV or they may instead be due to the presence of the extraneous variables. For example, if some participants performed under a higher temperature than others, their performance might be due to the temperature rather than the manipulated IV. When this happens, these are called **confounding variables**. The presence of confounding variables can minimize the value of results.

In Sheldrake's study, if participants received feedback (by being told if each individual decision as to whether they were being stared at or not was correct or wrong), this feedback could form an extraneous variable of them being able to learn the supposedly random sequence of whether they were being stared at or not. This would mean that the researchers couldn't be sure whether a participant's performance was due to the extraneous variable or to the effect of the manipulated IV on the DV. Results would be confounded and worthless. This could easily be controlled, though, by participants not being given such feedback.

A **pilot study** is a small-scale 'practice' investigation, where researchers check all aspects of their research and changes to the design, method, analysis, etc., can be made. It is always advisable to conduct a pilot study before embarking on the main study, as it means that the chances of extraneous variables confounding the results are reduced. Participants may be able to suggest appropriate changes, for example, participants may admit they guessed the purpose of the study and acted accordingly (demand characteristics). Pilot studies improve the quality of research, help avoid unnecessary work, and save time and effort.

The term 'operationalization' means being able to define variables simply and easily in order to manipulate them (IV) and measure them (DV). An operationalized IV should be stated in such a way that clearly identifies it without any confusion or vagueness as to what it is, while an operationalized DV should be stated in a clear, measureable way. For instance, in Sheldrake's study, the IV is clearly operationalized as being whether an unseen person is staring at someone or not, while the DV is clearly operationalized as the number of times participants can or cannot detect unseen stares.

IVs and DVs need to be 'operationalized' accurately and objectively to maintain the integrity of research studies. Without accurate operationalization, results aren't reliable or valid, and cannot be replicated and checked.

Extraneous variables – variables other than the IV within a research setting that can affect the DV.

Confounding variables – uncontrolled variables other than the IV within a research setting that affect the DV and thus 'confuse' the results.

Pilot studies – small-scale, practice investigations.

Operationalization – the process of defining variables into measureable factors.

Participant and researcher expectations and other forms of bias

LEARNING OUTCOME

■ Explain effects of participant and researcher expectations and bias (including demand characteristics, expectancy effects, observer bias, Hawthorne effect).

As participants in experiments are generally aware they are being scrutinized, this can create participant expectations. Researchers also bring their own expectations into the research arena, with such expectations influencing behaviour and thus confounding results.

There are several features of research studies that enable participants to guess what a study is about and what's expected of them. Such demand characteristics can involve participants:

■ Guessing the purpose of research and trying to please the researcher by giving the 'right' results.
■ Guessing the purpose of the research and trying to annoy the researcher by giving the wrong results; this is called the 'screw you' effect.
■ Acting unnaturally out of nervousness or fear of evaluation.
■ Acting unnaturally due to social desirability bias (responding in a way that society would expect).

In Sheldrake's study, participants may answer 'yes' or 'no' in response to being asked whether an unseen person is staring at them, not because they believe their answers are true, but because they are nervous at being tested or because they wish to give the answer they think is required.

Observer bias can also occur, where researchers have a cognitive bias that makes them unconsciously influence participants' responses. For instance, in Sheldrake's study the researcher could unconsciously suggest to a participant whether they should be saying 'yes' or 'no' in response to being asked if an unseen person was staring at them (see *The interesting case of Kluger Hans, page 289*).

The Hawthorne effect concerns the tendency for participants to alter their true behaviour merely because they know they're the focus of attention. Knowing that they're being studied can therefore act as an alternative IV and thus become a confounding variable.

Investigator effects occur where researchers inadvertently influence the results of their research. This can occur in several ways:

■ Certain physical characteristics of investigators may influence results, including age, ethnicity, etc. For example, male participants may be unwilling to admit sexist views to female researchers.
■ Less obvious personal characteristics of investigators, like accent, tone of voice, etc., can influence results. Participants may pick up on this and not act normally.
■ Investigators may be accidentally biased in their interpretation of data and 'see what they want to see'. In Sheldrake's study the researcher could interpret non-committal answers such as 'maybe he's staring', as a correct answer, thus increasing the chances of 'proving' their hypothesis.

The interesting case of Kluger Hans

Kluger Hans (Clever Hans in English) was a horse who had apparently been taught mathematics by his owner Wilhelm Von Osten and could perform simple arithmetic tasks, such as adding, subtracting, dividing and multiplying, by tapping out the correct answer with his hooves. There was no deliberate deception involved; Von Osten truly believed his horse had the ability to perform these sums. A panel of 13 experts headed by psychologist Carl Stumpf investigated Von Osten's claims and concluded in 1904 that the horse was genuine and no trickery was involved. Kluger Hans became front page news around the world, but further evaluation by Oskar Pfungst in 1907 found that Kluger Hans only answered correctly if his questioner knew the answer to the question being asked and if he could see his questioner. Eventually Pfungst realized the horse would stop tapping his hoof when he reached the right answer due to unconscious facial cues and changes in posture from the questioner.

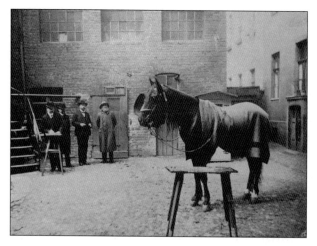

Figure 10.2   Many experts were convinced that Kluger Hans was a horse who truly had a knowledge of mathematics.

Kluger Hans's behaviour is a good example of observer bias, where an investigator's cognitive bias allows them to unconsciously influence participants' behaviour, often resulting in gaining the findings the researcher expects or desires to occur. Only by using a double-blind technique can this problem be counteracted. If Kluger Hans's questioner didn't know the answer to the written question he was holding up for the horse to read, or if the horse couldn't see his questioner, he couldn't demonstrate his seemingly intelligent behaviour.

Techniques for limiting the effects of expectation and bias

Single-blind procedure – a procedure whereby the participants are not aware of the research aims or which condition of the IV they are performing under.

LEARNING OUTCOME
■ Explain the use of single- and double-blind techniques.

A technique that reduces demand characteristics is the single-blind procedure. This is where participants have no idea which condition of a study they're in. In drug trials, they wouldn't know whether they're being given a real drug or a placebo (an ineffective sugar pill).

A technique that reduces investigator effects is the double-blind procedure. This is where neither participants nor investigators know which condition participants are in.

Double-blind
procedure – a
procedure whereby
neither the
researcher nor
the participants
is aware of which
condition of the IV
the participant is
performing under.

Standardized
procedure – a set of
research steps that
are all the same for
all participants.

Repeated
measures design
– experimental
design where each
participant performs
under all conditions
of an experiment.

They are both 'blind' to this knowledge. This prevents investigators from inadvertently giving participants clues as to which condition they're in and therefore reduces demand characteristics, though there is an investigator in overall charge aware of the allocation of participants to conditions. For example, in Sheldrake's study the researcher, as well as the participants, would be unaware of the randomized sequences of whether an unseen person was staring at them or not. Another researcher, who was not present during testing, would have produced the random sequences.

Standardized procedures involve all participants receiving identical instructions and following the same procedural steps throughout the experiment. This acts as a form of experimental control and helps to reduce investigator effects, such as researchers asking leading questions to elicit desired responses from participants. Standardized procedures also help to improve internal reliability (*see page 294*).

Experimental designs

LEARNING OUTCOME
■ Discuss the strengths and limitations of experimental designs.

There are three main types of experimental design.

Repeated measures design (RMD)
Each participant is tested in both (or indeed more) conditions of the experiment.

Sheldrake's unseen stares study uses a repeated measures design, as participants perform under both conditions of the IV:

1. When an unseen person is staring at them.
2. When an unseen person isn't staring at them.

Advantages

✔ **Group differences** – as the same people are measured in both conditions, there are no **participant variables** (differences between individuals) between the conditions.
✔ **More data/fewer participants** – as each participant produces two scores, twice as much data is produced as from an independent measures design (IMD). Therefore half as many participants are needed as with an IMD to get the same amount of data.

Weaknesses

✗ **Order effects** – with RMD, participants participate in both conditions and the order in which they participate in these conditions can have an effect on the results. Participants may perform *worse* in the second condition due to fatigue or boredom (**negative order effect**) or perform *better* due to practice or learning (**positive order effect**). **Counterbalancing** can control this, where half the participants do Condition A followed by Condition B, and the other half do Condition B and then Condition A. This counterbalancing procedure is known as 'ABBA', for obvious reasons.
✗ **Lost participants** – if a participant drops out of the study, data is 'lost' from both conditions.
✗ **Guess aim of study** – by participating in both conditions, it's more likely participants may guess the purpose of the study. This makes demand characteristics more common.

Independent groups design (IGD)

Different participants are used in each of the conditions; therefore each group of participants is independent of the other. Participants are usually **randomly allocated** to each condition to balance out differences.

Advantages

✔ **Order effects** – as different participants take part in each condition there are no order effects.

✔ **Demand characteristics** – participants take part in one condition each, therefore there's less chance of them guessing the purpose of the study.

✔ **Time saved** – both sets of participants can be tested at the same time, saving time and effort.

Weaknesses

✗ **More participants** – with participants each taking part in just one condition and thus only producing one piece of data each, twice as many participants are needed as for an RMD.

✗ **Group differences** – differences in results between the two conditions may be due to participant variables (individual differences) rather than manipulations of the IV. This is minimized by random allocation of participants to each condition.

Matched pairs design (MPD)

This is a special kind of RMD. Different, but similar, participants are used in each of the conditions. Participants are matched on characteristics important for a particular study, e.g. age. Identical (monozygotic) twins are often used, as they form perfect matched pairs, sharing identical genetic characteristics.

Advantages

✔ **Order effects** – as different participants take part in each condition there are no order effects.

✔ **Demand characteristics** – participants take part in one condition each, therefore there's less chance of them guessing the purpose of the study.

✔ **Time saved** – both sets of participants can be tested at the same time, saving time and effort.

✔ **Group differences** – participant variables are more closely matched between conditions than in an IGD.

Weaknesses

✗ **More participants** – with participants each taking part in only one condition, twice as many participants as needed as for an RMD.

✗ **Matching is difficult** – it's impossible to match all variables between participants. The one variable missed might be vitally important. Also, even two closely matched individuals will have different levels of motivation, fatigue, etc., at any given moment in time.

✗ **Time consuming** – it's a lengthy process to match participants. This can become almost a research study in itself.

■ **Critical thinking**

There is no 'best' type of experimental design and each should be considered in terms of its strengths and weaknesses. Repeated measures is often most favoured, as its strengths generally outweigh its weaknesses, especially as it is usually possible to counterbalance order effects, which is its main weakness. There are, however, situations where independent groups or matched pairs designs are best to use, but as with repeated measures, there will always be drawbacks to consider.

Sampling procedures

LEARNING OUTCOMES
■ Discuss sampling techniques appropriate to quantitative research.
■ Explain the concept of representative sampling.
■ Discuss how participants are allocated to experimental and control groups.

Sampling – the selection of participants to represent a wider population.

Experiments involve using **samples** drawn from larger **populations**. Sampling is essential to avoid studying entire populations. A sample should be **representative** of the population from which it's drawn, possessing the same characteristics as that population (i.e. represent the different types of people within that population). The term **target population** is used, as this is the group of people whom researchers **target** or generalize their results to. In general, the larger the sample, the better it is, but the more time consuming it is, too. Psychologists use several sampling techniques to try and obtain unbiased samples:

Random sampling

Random sampling is where every member of a population has an equal chance of being selected. The easiest way to do this is place all names from the target population in a hat and draw out the required sample number. Computer programs can also generate random lists. This results in a sample selected in an unbiased fashion. However, it can still result in a biased sample. Selection was unbiased, but the resulting sample is biased.

Evaluation

✔ The sample is selected in an unbiased fashion.
✗ It's sometimes difficult to get full details of a target population to select a sample, plus not all members may be available or wish to take part, making any sample **unrepresentative**.
✗ There is no guarantee of a sample being representative, for example, if ten boys' and ten girls' names were placed in a hat, there is a possibility the first ten names drawn from the hat could all be boys' names.

Opportunity sampling

Opportunity sampling involves selecting participants who are available and willing to take part. This could simply involve asking anybody who's passing. Sears (1986) found 75 per cent of university research studies use undergraduates as participants simply for the sake of convenience.

Evaluation

✔ Samples are fairly easy and quick to assemble.
✗ Samples may be biased, as only certain types of people will be available to participate. This causes problems in generalizing findings to larger populations.

Self-selected sampling

Self-selected sampling involves people volunteering to participate. They select themselves as participants, often by replying to adverts.

Evaluation

✔ An easy and practical method, as participants select themselves.
✘ Samples are likely to be biased, as volunteers are generally more motivated and thus perform differently than randomly selected participants. Bauman (1973) found different results on reported sexual knowledge, attitudes and behaviour of undergraduate students dependent on whether they were willing or non-willing volunteers.
✘ Volunteers are generally keen to please and thus may be more prone to demand characteristics.

Systematic sampling

Systematic sampling involves selecting every one out of so many people, e.g. every fifth person.

Evaluation

✔ Selection is unbiased.
✔ The selection process is not time-consuming.
✘ Selection is not truly random (unless the frequency of selection and first person selected occur via a random method).

Stratified sample

Stratified sampling involves selecting groups of participants in proportion to the frequency with which they occur in a target population. The different **strata** (types of people within a population) are identified and individuals from those strata are selected randomly.

Evaluation

✔ Stratified sampling produces the most truly representative samples.
✘ Stratified sampling can be complicated and time-consuming to carry out.

■ Critical thinking

It is important when conducting research to create representative samples, ones that occur without bias in selection. The best way to accomplish this is to use random sampling. This isn't as easy as it sounds, however, as humans are very poor at making random choices. If you ask ten people to randomly select a number between 1 and 10, each of the ten numbers should, theoretically, be chosen once, but certain numbers will be favoured more than others. The use of non-representative samples can seriously confound results, which is why unbiased methods of selection, such as names drawn from a hat, should always be used wherever possible.

Participants can be allocated to testing groups by **random allocation**, where assignment to experimental and control groups occurs by unbiased, random selection. As overall random samples are difficult to achieve, due to not all members of a target population being available or willing to participate, true random selection only really occurs in this fashion.

Participants can also be assigned to testing groups as **matched pairs** (*see Matched pairs design, page 291*).

Evaluation of research
Reliability and validity

LEARNING OUTCOMES
- Discuss conditions that increase a study's reliability.
- Discuss the concepts of internal and external validity.

Reliability – the extent to which an experiment produces consistent results, both within the research setting (internal reliability) and over time (external reliability).

Researchers try to produce results that are reliable and valid. If results are **reliable**, they're **consistent**. If Sheldrake's study was repeated using the same method, design and measurements, the same results should be obtained and the results would be said to be reliable.

- **Internal reliability** – refers to whether a test is consistent **within itself**. For example, a set of scales should measure the same weight between 50 and 100 grams as between 150 and 200 grams.
- **External reliability** – refers to whether a test measures consistently **over time**. A participant should produce the same score for detecting unseen stares at different times if their ability to do so has remained constant. This is called the **test–retest method**. Making sure a **standardized procedure** is used and a full account of an experiment's methodology is detailed in the practical report ensures the study can be **replicated** in order to check the reliability of the results. Baker (2000) replicated Sheldrake's study and failed to find that participants could significantly detect unseen stares. However, Sheldrake (2000) pointed out that Baker did not replicate his study, because he used a very different methodology, therefore Baker did not show Sheldrake's findings to be unreliable.
- **Inter-rater reliability** – refers to the degree to which different raters give consistent estimates or scores of the same object or phenomenon. If different raters agree then they have inter-observer reliability, but if they disagree then they don't have inter-rater reliability. Efforts should also be made before a study is conducted to ensure that raters agree on how ratings will be made and that their ratings of the same object/phenomenon are consistent. Videoing events can also assist this process.

If results are unreliable, they cannot be trusted. However, results can be reliable, but not be accurate. For example, if you do the sum 1+1 several times and each time calculate the answer as 3, then your result is reliable (consistent), but not **valid** (accurate). Sometimes measuring instruments may be reliably (consistently) producing inaccurate results.

To be valid, results must accurately measure what they're supposed to measure.

Validity – the extent to which results accurately measure what they claim to measure, due to the manipulation of the IV (internal validity) and the ability of the findings to be generalized beyond the research setting (external validity).

- **Internal validity** – concerns the degree to which an observed effect, such as being able to detect unseen stares, is due to the manipulation of the IV, rather than other confounding variables, such as being given constant feedback on whether attempts to detect unseen stares are correct or wrong. Internal validity can be improved by minimization of investigator effects, reduction of demand characteristics, the use of standardized instructions and the use of random samples. These factors ensure that a study is highly controlled, leaving no doubts that observed effects are due to the methodology.
- **External validity** – refers to whether results are valid beyond the experimental setting and can be generalized to the wider population or to different settings or different time eras. For example, Sheldrake's study was conducted in the USA; the results may therefore not be generalizable to people of other cultures. It's often difficult to test whether studies have external validity, as it only becomes clear when research findings are found to either apply or not apply to different situations. Field experiments are regarded as high in external validity, because results can be generalized to other real-life settings.

■ **Critical thinking**

Researchers generally have expectations (and even preferences) about how research will turn out, but this can create a serious bias that acts to confound results. Sheldrake reports that when believers in the ability to detect unseen stares replicate his study, they tend to find the ability is real, while when sceptics perform the research they generally don't find evidence to support its existence. They cannot both be right. Only by conducting completely bias-free research can truly effective research ever be performed.

Analysis and interpretation of quantitative data: application of descriptive statistics

Measures of central tendency – descriptive statistics that give information about 'typical' scores for a set of data.

LEARNING OUTCOMES
■ Apply descriptive statistics to analyse data.
■ Distinguish between levels of measurement (including nominal, ordinal, interval, ratio).

It will be necessary to apply appropriate measures of central tendency and measures of dispersion to data generated from the experimental study. Measures of central tendency are used to summarize large amounts of data into typical midpoint values or averages. There are three averages: the **median**, the **mean** and the **mode**.

The median

Measures of dispersion – descriptive statistics that give information about the 'spread' of scores within a set of data.

This is the central score in a list of rank-ordered scores. With an odd number of scores, the median is the middle number. With an even number of scores, the median is the mid-point between the two middle scores and therefore may not be one of the original scores.

The advantages of the median are:

✔ It's not affected by extreme 'freak' scores.
✔ It's usually easier to calculate than the mean.
✔ The median can be used with **ordinal** data (ranks), unlike the mean.

The weaknesses are:

✘ It's not as sensitive as the mean, because all the scores aren't used in the calculation.
✘ It can be unrepresentative in a small set of data. For example:
    1, 1, 2, 3, 4, 5, 6, 7, 8 – the median is 4
    2, 3, 4, 6, 8, 9, 12, 13 – the median is 7.

The mean

This is where all scores are added up and divided by the total number of scores. It's the mid-point of the combined values.

The advantages of the mean are:

✔ It's the most accurate measure of central tendency as it uses the interval level of measurement, where the units of measurement are of equal size, e.g. seconds in time.
✔ It uses all the data in its calculation.

The weaknesses are:

✘ It's less useful if some scores are **skewed**, i.e. if there are some large or small scores.
✘ The mean score may not to be one of the actual scores in the set of data.

The mode

This is the most common, or 'popular', number in a set of scores.

The advantages of the mode are:

✔ It's less prone to distortion by extreme values.

✔ It sometimes makes more sense than the other measures of central tendency, for example, the average number of children in a British family is better described as 2 (mode) rather than 2.4 children (mean).

The weaknesses are:

✘ There can be more than one mode in a set of data, e.g.:
2, 3, 6, 7, 7, 7, 9, 15, 16, 16, 16, 20 – modes are 7 and 16.

✘ It doesn't take into account exact distances between values.

✘ It doesn't use all the scores.

Measures of dispersion

Measures of dispersion are measures of the **variability** or spread of scores. They include the **range**, **interquartile range** and **standard deviation**.

The range

This is calculated by subtracting the lowest value from the highest value in a set of scores.

The advantages of the range:

✔ It's fairly easy and quick to work out.

✔ It takes full account of extreme values.

The weaknesses are:

✘ It can be distorted by extreme 'freak' values and doesn't show whether data are clustered or spread evenly around the mean.

✘ For example, the range of the two sets of data below is the same, despite the data being very different:
2, 3, 4, 5, 5, 6, 7, 8, 9, 21
2, 5, 8, 9, 10, 12, 13, 15, 16, 18, 21

Interquartile range

This shows the spread of the middle 50 per cent of a set of scores. For example, the following set of data contains 16 scores:
4, 5, 6, 6, 7, 8, 8, 9, 11, 11, 14, 15, 17, 18, 18, 19

Four scores are in the first 25 per cent, four scores in the last 25 per cent and eight scores in the middle 50 per cent. The middle eight scores begin with 7 and end with 15. The upper limit of the interquartile range lies between 15 and 17 and is calculated as the mean of these two values, i.e. 16. The lower limit of the interquartile range lies between 6 and 7, with the mean being 6.5. The interquartile range is the difference between the upper and lower limits, i.e. between 16 and 6.5, and therefore is 9.5.

The advantages of the interquartile range are:

✔ It's fairly easy to calculate.

✔ It's not affected by extreme scores.

The weaknesses are:

✘ It doesn't take into account extreme scores.

✘ It's inaccurate if there are large intervals between the scores.

Standard deviation

This is a measure of the spread or variability of a set of scores from the mean. The larger the standard deviation, the larger the spread of scores.

Calculate standard deviation by the following steps:

- Add all the scores together and divide by the number of scores to calculate the mean.
- Subtract the mean from each individual score.
- Square each of these scores.
- Add all the squared scores together.
- Divide the sum of the squares by the number of scores minus 1. This is the **variance**.
- Use a calculator to work out the square root of the variance. This is the **standard deviation**.

The advantages of standard deviation:

- ✔ It's a more sensitive dispersion measure than the range since all scores are used in its calculation.

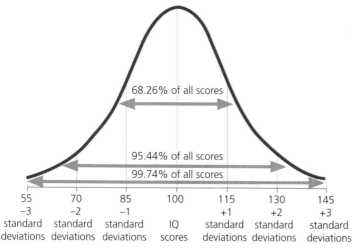

- ✔ It allows for the interpretation of individual scores; thus in Figure 10.3, anybody with an IQ of 121 is in the top 5 per cent of the population, between +2 and +3 standard deviations of the mean.

The weaknesses are:

- ✗ It's more complicated to calculate.
- ✗ It's less meaningful if data aren't normally distributed.

It will also be necessary to assess what level of measurement has been attained by the data generated. This is especially important for HL students, who will need this information to help decide which statistical test to apply to their data (*see page 300*).

Figure 10.3 Standard deviation: IQ scores

Theory of knowledge

Experiments generate numerical data that is made sense of by statistical analysis, such as descriptive statistics (like measures of central tendency and dispersion), as well as inferential statistical tests. Through this scientifically approved process hypotheses are accepted or rejected, but is it ever really possible to take the emotional phenomenon of human experience and reduce it down to mere numbers? Does human experience always go beyond such simplistic analysis?

Levels of data measurement

There are three basic levels of measurement: nominal, ordinal and interval/ratio.

- **Nominal data** – the simplest level of measurement, nominal data involves counting frequency data. For example, how many days of the week were rainy/sunny? Do people like broccoli (yes/no)? Tally charts are used to record this type of basic data.
- **Ordinal data** – involves ranking data into order, with each value being greater/larger/better than another. Rating scales are often used, for example the finishing

places in an athletics race, 1st, 2nd, 3rd, 4th, etc. It's known which athletes are better than others, but the distances between individual athletes may be different. The distance between 1st and 2nd may be shorter than between 2nd and 3rd; or one person's subjective rating of the number 7 may be very different from another's rating of 7. Ordinal data is more informative than nominal data, but not as informative as interval/ratio data.

Figure 10.4 The finishing places in a race, 1st, 2nd, 3rd, 4th and so on, provide an example of ordinal level data.

- **Interval/ratio data** – the most accurate form of measurement as it uses equal measurement intervals, for example one second in time is the same length as any other second in time. Standardized measurement units like time, weight, temperature and distance are interval/ratio measures. The same statistical tests are chosen regardless of whether the data is interval or ratio, therefore they're classified together. Interval data has an arbitrary zero point, whereas ratio data has an absolute zero point. For example, a temperature of 0° doesn't mean there's no temperature (interval data), whereas someone with zero money in their bank account would have no money (ratio data).

Analysis and interpretation of quantitative data: application of graphing techniques

LEARNING OUTCOME
- Apply appropriate graphing techniques to represent data.

Graphs – easily understandable pictorial representations of data.

Graphs allow data to be represented in a visually meaningful way, providing an easily understandable alternative viewpoint to a purely numerical presentation of data. Graphs therefore should not be overly complex and should allow viewers to 'eyeball' patterns within a set of data, aiding their comprehension.

Bar charts

These show data in the form of categories that the researcher wishes to compare, e.g. males and females. Categories are placed on the x-axis (the horizontal axis). The columns of bar charts should be the same width and separated by spaces. The use of spaces illustrates that the variable on the x-axis isn't continuous. Data are 'discrete', like the mean score of several groups. It can also involve percentages, totals, ratios, etc.

A bar chart can display two values together, for example, if the male and female groups were divided into two further groups: under and over 20 years of age (*see* Figure 10.5).

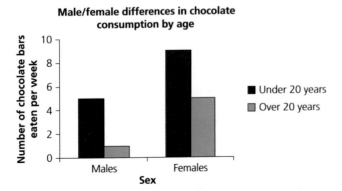

Figure 10.5 A bar chart can display two values together.

Histograms

Students often confuse histograms and bar charts. The main difference is histograms are used for continuous data, e.g. test scores like the example in Figure 10.6. These continuous scores or values should ascend along the x-axis. The frequency of these values is shown on the y-axis (the vertical axis). There are no spaces between the bars since the data are continuous. The column width for each value on the x-axis should be the same for each equal category interval. Thus the area of each column is proportional to the number of cases it represents throughout the histogram.

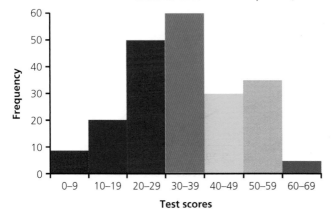

Figure 10.6 Example of a histogram

Frequency polygon (line graph)

This is similar to a histogram in that the data on the x-axes are continuous. A frequency polygon is produced by drawing a line from the mid-point top of each bar in a histogram. The advantage of a frequency polygon is two or more frequency distributions can be displayed on the same graph for comparison (*see Figure 10.7*).

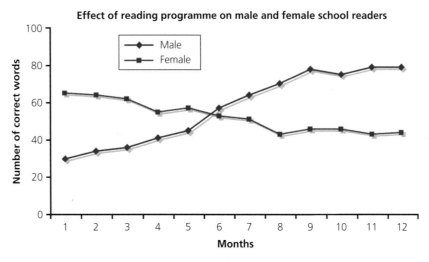

Figure 10.7 Example of a frequency polygon

General points to consider with the presentation of graphs

- All graphs and charts must be fully labelled with appropriate titles, and the x- and y-axes labelled accurately.
- Graphs and charts look best if the y-axis height is three-quarters of the x-axis width.
- Only one graph or chart is used to illustrate a set of data.
- An appropriate scale should be used on the axes. Don't be misled by using inappropriate scales – something political parties often do to present biased data.
- Raw data shouldn't be presented; instead a chart or graph summarizes the data. Each individual score is also not presented, as the raw data table will already show this.

Here is an example of how using inappropriate scales on graphs can mislead people. The two figures in Figure 10.8 overleaf display the same data about the aggression rates of children attending different amounts of daycare. If you wanted to suggest that daycare is harmful in terms of increased aggressiveness in children, you would be tempted to use the figure on the right, the steeper curve of which seems to indicate stronger evidence for your belief. It doesn't. Both graphs display exactly the same data.

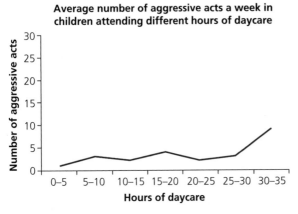

Figure 10.8   Using inappropriate scales to mislead

Analysis and interpretation of quantitative data: application of statistical tests (HL students only)

LEARNING OUTCOME
■ Apply an appropriately chosen statistical test in order to determine the level of significance of data.

Quantitative data – data that occurs in a numerical form.

Quantitative data requires analysis by a statistical test. To select an appropriate statistical test it is necessary to know what level of measurement has been used (*see below*), and whether the research utilizes a repeated measures design (including matched pairs) or an independent measures design (*see Experimental designs, page 290*).

Statistical tests – mathematical means of analysing data.

Once these criteria have been established, the appropriate statistical test can be selected (*see Table 10.1*).

Choosing the appropriate statistical test

Table 10.1   Choosing the appropriate statistical test

LEVEL OF MEASUREMENT	TYPE OF RESEARCH DESIGN	
	INDEPENDENT (UNRELATED)	**REPEATED (RELATED)**
Nominal data	Chi-square	Sign test
Ordinal data	Mann-Whitney U test	Wilcoxon (matched pairs)
Interval data	Independent t test	Related t test

The use of inferential analysis

Inferential tests show how likely it is that patterns observed in sets of data occur by chance and whether it's possible to infer (deduce) the same patterns exist in the general population. There are six main tests that use can be used.

■ **Chi-squared** – used when a difference is predicted to occur between two sets of data, the data is of at least nominal level and an independent groups design has been used.

- **Sign test** – used when a difference is predicted to occur between two sets of data, the data is of at least nominal level and a repeated measures or matched pairs design has been used.
- **Mann-Whitney U test** – used when a difference is predicted to occur between two sets of data, the data is of at least ordinal level and an independent groups design has been used.
- **Wilcoxon signed-matched ranks** – used when a difference is predicted to occur between two sets of data, the data is of at least ordinal level and a repeated measures or matched pairs design has been used.
- **Independent t test** – used when a difference is predicted to occur between two sets of data, the data is of interval/ratio level and an independent groups design has been used.
- **Related t test** – used when a difference is predicted to occur between two sets of data, the data is of interval/ratio level and a repeated measures or matched pairs design has been used.

The data generated from Sheldrake's study could be argued to be of at least ordinal level, as it would be possible to rank participants in their degree of accuracy in assessing whether they were being stared at by an unseen person. (The degree of certainty participants feel for each individual estimate of being stared at or not by an unseen person would not necessarily be equal, therefore data is not of interval/ratio level.) As the study utilizes a repeated measures design, a Wilcoxon test could be used, though a sign test would be satisfactory too.

Making sense of statistical analysis

Statistical analysis produces an **observed** value, which is compared to a **critical** value in order to determine if the observed value is significant (beyond the boundaries of chance). Critical value tables need to be referenced, taking into consideration such information as whether a hypothesis is directional or non-directional (one-tailed or two-tailed), the number of participants or participant pairs (N) used, and what level of significance, e.g. 5 per cent, is being used.

- The Mann-Whitney, sign and Wilcoxon tests require observed values to be **equal to or less** than the critical value to be accepted as significant, allowing the null hypothesis to be rejected.
- The Chi-squared, independent t and related t tests require an observed value to be **equal to or greater** than the critical value to be accepted as **significant**, allowing the null hypothesis to be rejected.

Significance levels – statistical criteria that determine if observed differences are beyond the boundaries of chance.

Probability – the likelihood of observed differences being determined by chance factors.

Significance levels

Psychological research generally looks for differences or relationships between sets of data. Of prime importance, however, is whether such differences and relationships are significant ones, i.e. beyond the boundaries of chance.

If a coin is tossed 100 times, then by the law of averages there should be 50 heads and 50 tails. However, it might be 52 heads and 48 tails, meaning there's a difference between the two sets of data, but is it beyond the boundaries of chance? Probably not, but how is the cut-off point determined for the difference between the two sets of data being significant or insignificant? Fifty-five heads to 45 tails? Sixty to 40? This is where the idea of probability comes in.

Probability is denoted by the symbol p and concerns the degree of certainty that an observed difference or relationship between two sets of data is a real difference/relationship rather than having occurred by chance factors. It's never 100 per cent certain that such differences and relationships are real ones, i.e. beyond the boundaries of chance; this is why it's impossible to prove something beyond all doubt. So an accepted cut-off

Figure 10.9 How many heads would be statistically significant?

point is needed and in psychology, and in science generally, a significance (probability) level of $p \leq 0.05$ is used. This means there's a 5 per cent possibility that an observed difference or relationship between two sets of data isn't a real one, but instead that it occurred by chance factors. This is deemed to be an acceptable level of error.

On certain occasions a stricter, more stringent level of significance may be needed, e.g. if testing out untried drugs or in new research areas. Then a significance level of $p \leq 0.01$ might be used, meaning there's a 99 per cent certainty an observed difference/relationship is a real one, but there's still a 1 per cent chance it occurred due to chance factors. An even stricter level of $p \leq 0.001$ would mean there's a 99.9 per cent certainty of a real difference/relationship, but even so there's still a 0.1 per cent chance it occurred by chance.

Type 1 and type 2 errors

A type 1 error occurs when a difference/relationship is accepted as a real one, i.e. beyond the boundaries of chance, and this is wrong because the significance level has been set too high (for example, 5 per cent). This means the null hypothesis would be wrongly rejected. For example, if a pregnancy test revealed a woman to be pregnant and she wasn't. With a 5 per cent significance level this means, on average, for every 100 significant differences/relationships found, 5 of them will have been wrongly accepted.

A type 2 error occurs when a difference/relationship is accepted as being insignificant, i.e. not a real difference/relationship, and this is wrong because the significance level has been set too low (for example, 1 per cent). This means that the null hypothesis would be wrongly accepted. For example, a pregnancy test reveals a woman not to be pregnant when she is.

Stricter significance levels mean then there's less chance of making a type 1 error, but more chance of making a type 2 error, and vice versa. One way to reduce the chance of making these errors is to increase the sample size.

A 5 per cent significance level is the accepted level, as it strikes a balance between making type 1 and type 2 errors.

Reference can be made to specialist books of statistical analysis, which explain how to carry out appropriate analysis in a step-by-step fashion. Such information is also easily accessible via the internet.

Theory of knowledge

Levels of significance are used in psychology to determine whether hypotheses can be accepted or rejected, that is to say whether observed differences are beyond chance factors and are 'real' differences due to a manipulated independent variable. However, although significance levels allow theories and hypotheses to be disproved, they can never be used to absolutely prove them beyond all doubt. With a significance level of $p \leq 0.0001$ there would indeed be a 99.99 per cent certainty that a significant difference was a real difference, but that still means there would be a very slight possibility that it was due to chance factors. That possibility can never be completely removed, however strict a level of significance is used.

Writing up the report

Once a practical has been designed, approved, carried out and made sense of through analysis, comes the task of writing up the practical report. There is a set convention as to how such reports are written, with the overriding principle that it is written up in such a way to permit replication by others wanting to check the reliability of results.

It is usual to write up research in continuous prose, in the past tense, avoid slang terms/colloquialisms and have a clear, unambiguous writing style.

The basic requirements of a report are to communicate:

■ what was done
■ why it was done
■ what was found
■ what it means.

There is no single best way to set out a report, but the general format for sections is as follows:

■ title
■ abstract
■ introduction
■ method
■ results
■ discussion
■ references
■ appendices.

There are some differences in requirements between SL and HL students as to what must be included in each section.

Title page

■ Title (SL/HL).
■ Student name and number (SL/HL).
■ Subject and level (SL/HL).
■ Day, month and year of submission (SL/HL).
■ Number of words (SL/HL).

Abstract

■ Statement of aim (SL only) and hypotheses (HL only).
■ Summary of methods (SL/HL).
■ Summary of results (SL/HL).
■ Conclusion (SL/HL).

Introduction

■ Aim of the study (SL/HL).
■ Identification and explanation of the study being replicated (SL only).
■ Literature review (analysis of relevant background studies and theories) (HL only).
■ Operationalized experimental hypothesis (HL only).
■ Operationalized null hypothesis (HL only).

Method

Design

- Type and justification of experimental design (SL/HL).
- Controls, ethical considerations, including informed consent, identification of independent and dependent variables (SL/HL).

Participants

- Characteristics of sample (SL/HL).
- Sampling technique (SL/HL).
- Allocation of participants to conditions (SL/HL).
- Target population (HL only).

Materials

- List of materials used (SL/HL).
- Reference to copies in appendices (SL/HL).

Procedures

- Described in sufficient detail to allow full replication (SL/HL).

Results

- Statement of the measure(s) of central tendency (as appropriate) (SL/HL).
- Statement of the measure of dispersion (as appropriate) (SL/HL).
- Justification of the choice of descriptive statistic (SL/HL).
- Appropriate use of fully explained graphs and tables (may be computer-generated) (SL/HL).
- Reporting of inferential statistics and justification for their use (calculations in appendix) (HL only).
- Statement of statistical significance (HL only).

Discussion

- Interpretation of descriptive statistics (SL/HL).
- Interpretation of inferential statistics (HL only).
- Comparison of findings to the study being replicated (SL only).
- Comparison of findings to studies and theories reviewed in the introduction (HL only).
- Identification of limitations of the student's research (SL/HL).
- Suggestions for modification to address limitations of the student's research (SL/HL).
- Conclusion (SL/HL).

References

- Work cited within the report listed in a standard format (SL/HL).

Appendices

- Raw data and calculations (SL/HL).
- Supplementary information (SL/HL).
- One copy of instrument(s) used (SL/HL).
- Copy of standardized instructions and debriefing notes (SL/HL).
- Copy of blank informed consent form (participant and/or parent) (SL/HL).

Words

- Word total – not including supplementary information such as abstract, title page, references, section headings, citations as quotations, graphs, charts and appendices – 1,000–1,500 (SL), 1,500–2,000 (HL).
- Marks – 20 (SL), 28 (HL).

Assessment criteria

The IB has **assessment criteria** against which practical reports will be judged, initially done internally by a teacher and later on externally by a moderator appointed by the board. Therefore each section of the report should be written in a way that attempts to maximize attainment of the marks available for each assessment criteria. There are some differences in requirements between SL and HL students. SL students are assessed against **seven** criteria, while HL students are assessed against **nine** criteria.

Standard level (SL)

Criterion A

Introduction (2 marks)

- The replicated study is clearly identified and relevant details explained.
- The aim of the student's study is clearly stated.

Criterion B

Method: Design (2 marks)

- The IV and DV are accurately identified and operationalized.
- The experimental design is appropriate to the aim and its use is appropriately justified.
- A clear indication and documentation of how ethical guidelines were followed is given.

Criterion C

Method: Participants (2 marks)

- Relevant characteristics of the participants are identified.
- The sample was selected using an appropriate method and this method is explained.

Criterion D

Method: Procedure (2 marks)

- The procedural information is relevant and clearly described, so that the study would be easily replicable.
- Details of how ethical guidelines were applied are included.
- Necessary materials are included and referenced in the appendices.

Criterion E

Results (4 marks)

- Accurate results are clearly stated, which reflect the aims of the research.
- Appropriate descriptive statistics (one measure of central tendency and one measure of dispersion) have been applied to the data and their use explained.
- Graph is accurate, clear and directly relevant to the aim of the study.
- Results are presented in both words and tabular form.

Criterion F

Discussion (6 marks)

- Discussion of results is well-developed (for example, differences in the results of the calculations of central tendency and/or dispersion are explained).
- The findings of the student's study are discussed with reference to the study being replicated.
- Limitations of the design and procedure are stated, are highly relevant and have been rigorously analysed.
- Modifications are suggested and ideas for future research given.
- The conclusion is appropriate.

Criterion G

Presentation (2 marks)

- The report is within the word limit of 1,000–1,500 word.
- The report is complete and in the required format.
- The reference for the replicated study is cited using a standard method of listing references.
- Appendices are labelled appropriately and referenced within the body of the report.
- The abstract is clearly written and includes a summary overview of the student's study, including the results.

Higher level (HL)

Criterion A

Introduction (5 marks)

- Background theories and/or studies are adequately explained and highly relevant to the hypotheses.
- The aim of the study is clearly stated.
- Experimental and null hypotheses are appropriately stated and operationalized.
- The prediction made in the experimental hypothesis is justified by the background theories and/or studies.

Criterion B

Method: Design (2 marks)

- The IV and DV are accurately identified and operationalized.
- The experimental design is appropriate to the aim and its use is appropriately justified.
- A clear indication and documentation of how ethical guidelines were followed is given.

Criterion C

Method: Participants (2 marks)

- Relevant characteristics of the participants are identified.
- The sample was selected using an appropriate method and this method is explained.
- The target population is identified and is appropriate.

Criterion D

Method: Procedure (2 marks)

- The procedural information is relevant and clearly described, so that the study would be easily replicable.

- Details of how ethical guidelines were applied are included.
- Necessary materials are included and referenced in the appendices.

Criterion E

Results: Descriptive (2 marks)

- Accurate results are clearly stated and reflect the hypotheses of the research.
- Appropriate descriptive statistics (one measure of central tendency and one measure of dispersion) have been applied to the data and their use explained.
- Graph is accurate, clear and directly relevant to the aim of the study.
- Results are presented in both words and tabular form.

Criterion F

Results: Inferential (3 marks)

- An appropriate inferential statistical test has been chosen and explicitly justified.
- Results of the inferential test are accurately stated.
- The null hypothesis has been appropriately accepted or rejected according to the results of the statistical test.
- A statement of statistical significance is given that is appropriate and clear.

Criterion G

Discussion (8 marks)

- The discussion of results is well developed and complete (for example, descriptive and inferential statistics are discussed).
- The findings of the student's study are discussed with reference to relevant background theories and/or studies.
- Limitations of the design and procedure are given, are relevant and have been rigorously analysed.
- Modifications have been suggested and ideas for future research stated.
- The conclusion is appropriate.

Criterion H

Citation of sources (2 marks)

- All in-text citations and references are provided.
- A standard citation method has been used consistently throughout the body of the report and in the references section.

Criterion I

Report format (2 marks)

- The report is within the word limit of 1,500–2,000 words.
- The report is complete and in the required format.
- Appendices are labelled appropriately and are referenced in the body of the report.
- The abstract is clearly written and includes a summary overview of the student's study, including the results.

11 Extended essay

Introduction

The extended essay for the International Baccalaureate Diploma Programme involves students in consistently working on their chosen research question. The rewards for this work are several. Not only does success in achieving a pass grade in the Extended Essay contribute to success in the Diploma, the knowledge and understanding that comes with writing an in-depth essay implies that the individual author of the essay is likely to become a relative expert who is able to defend the essay's findings against informed criticism. This demonstrable skill can often impress university admission tutors or potential employers. The ability to argue a case is paramount in practically all walks of working life. It is also the essence of democratic life when crucial decisions continually need to be made in the face of finely balanced judgements.

The International Baccalaureate publishes an extended essay Guide to help candidates and supervisors in their preparation for the essay. This excellent publication should be required reading for those about to embark on the essay. Its philosophy is made clear in the IB learner profile that is to be found immediately before the contents page. Among other desired qualities the profile indicates that IB learners should strive to be inquirers who:

'develop their natural curiosity. They acquire the skills necessary to conduct inquiry and research and show independence in learning. They actively enjoy learning and this love of learning will be sustained throughout their lives.'

Right from the start of Guide and continued throughout its pages there is an expectation that IB learners incorporate an understanding of different cultures that includes respect for, though not necessarily agreement with, the different views reflected in those cultures.

Nature of the extended essay

Students who embark on the Diploma programme will become aware that this is a broadly based series of academic subjects from which a range of six are chosen from the six groups of subjects presented. The subject areas are illustrated as the Diploma programme hexagon, the core of which contains the extended essay, theory of knowledge and a section devoted to creativity, action and service. Psychology is a Group 3 subject where it is located with other social sciences.

Students are normally advised to write their extended essay on a topic selected from one of their chosen subjects for the IB Diploma. It is possible to write an extended essay on a topic related to a different subject from those being studied by the student. Whilst this option certainly exists, the extra work involved can make for academic difficulties for students who initially choose this course of action. In those schools that do not offer psychology as a Diploma subject it is advised that the student does not offer a psychology research question for an extended essay, unless there is someone on the staff who is willing to offer expert supervision in the subject.

The IB requires that schools appoint an appropriately qualified supervisor for each student taking an extended essay. The supervisor is to be a member of the teaching staff at the same school that the student attends. An important early cooperative task between student and supervisor is to choose a research question or topic for investigation. This choice is crucial and will be examined in some depth later in this chapter. The IB recommends that approximately 40 hours of work are given by the student to complete the extended essay. This duration should include typing time on the part of the student. When the essay is completed the supervisor is advised to arrange a brief interview or *viva voce* with the student to review the essay.

The essay is intended to be based on the independent choice of the student, although the supervisor may well offer points of consideration from an early stage of thinking about the precise nature of the research question. The essay is to be not more than 4,000 words long and should be presented in a formal academic style.

The aims of the essay include opportunities for students to engage in independent research on an appropriate psychological topic that can reasonably be accomplished within the 40-hour timeframe suggested by the IB Guide. Within this timeframe students are expected to develop their research and communication skills, in addition to skills of creative and critical thinking.

In helping to achieve these aims, the Guide indicates that schools are required to:

'Provide supervisors and students with general and subject-specific information and guidelines for the extended essay contained in the IB Guide.'

Schools are also required to provide supervisors with recent subject reports that are based on the comments of extended essay assessors who have assessed the quality of essays that have been submitted in recent sessions.

These requirements should be necessary preparatory steps to enable both students and their supervisors to undertake the work on extended essays to maximum effect. While the majority of candidates achieve these aims, there are occasional instances where students seem to be unaware of what is expected from them in their extended essays, or they fail to implement the guidance that the IB Guide provides. This can result in disappointment and possibly an expensive and time-consuming further attempt to re-take the examination.

In order to avoid such an event it is essential that students thoroughly familiarize themselves with the assessment criteria for extended essays and read previous essays in psychology. Both the Guide and previous essays can be obtained from the International Baccalaureate based in Cardiff.

Researching and writing the extended essay

Choosing a subject, topic and research question

Choosing an appropriate research question is key to the student's work that follows. In order to do this the student should select a topic area in psychology that is characterized by three main elements. It should:

- Be of importance to the student so that the recommended 40 hours spent on researching the question sustains interest throughout, despite occasional difficulties that may arise.
- Be in an area of psychology where there is some element of controversy.
- Have sufficient published and accessible academic studies about the topic area to enable the student to become thoroughly immersed in the arguments involved.

Each of these three elements contributes to the other two. For example, the existence of controversy means that the student will discover different and possibly contradictory

Step 1
Choose an appropriate Diploma Programme subject for your essay.

Step 2
Choose your topic.

Step 3
Formulate your research question.

Step 4
Plan your investigation and writing your essay. Think about:
- How you will gather material
- What system of referencing you will use
- Setting yourself deadlines (consult with your teacher on this).

Step 5
Plan a structure for your essay, think about your main headings. You might find that you amend the structure as you progress with your research, but it is helpful to have a sense of direction.

Step 6
Do some preparatory reading.
Now is the time to think about whether you will be able to find the material you need to tackle your research question. If you have concerns at this stage talk it over with your teacher.

Step 7
Carry out the investigation.
Structure material in a logical way and tie in with the structure of your essay.

Figure 11.1 Flowchart of the seven steps of the research project

views on the question and that these views are firmly held by academic researchers of high repute.

Psychology has many appropriate topics, such as:
- the debate about human intelligence
- factors that can be learnt from observation of and experimentation on non-human animals and the extent to which such findings can be applied to humans
- cultural differences and how these can best be reconciled
- what benefits can accrue if specific findings from medical research were to be applied to a wider population.

Plan the investigation

Access to academic studies is increasingly available by electronic means, particularly the impressive range of studies provided on the internet. Students need to be very aware that some of the information available by this means comes from non-academic sources and may be suspect. As a preliminary guide it is useful to note that the information has the name of a university or similar institute of higher education attached to it. Throughout the research process students should take careful note of the details associated with the research they are likely to use. This material is intended to form the basis for the system of academic referencing that will be used.

Plan a structure

The final submitted work should contain the following elements:
- title page
- abstract
- contents page
- introduction
- main section, to include development, methods and findings
- conclusion
- references and bibliography
- appendices.

The main task is writing the main section and as the student gathers new material, there should be a growing awareness of how this may be made into a structured essay. The structure depends on how the student wishes to present a particular case. The aim is to present an argument that the reader will be able to follow at the first time of reading. For this reason there should be a flow to the argument where various sides of the argument are presented, not as a series of disconnected points. It should presented as a debate in which claims and counter claims follow along a coherent path until a conclusion is reached. A certain degree of planning is involved in this exercise but students need also to realize that the initial structure may need to be changed as more information is discovered.

There will be times when the student realizes that it will be difficult or impossible to gather sufficient evidence to proceed with the original question selected. In this situation a meeting should be arranged with the student's supervisor and following consideration of the circumstances, the best course of action may be to abandon the original question and change to an alternative. If this is the decision then it is better to implement it as soon as possible in order to maximize available time on the new question.

Equally important is the need to recognize a point where the structure needs to be altered as the growing body of research discovered throws some doubt on the original thinking of the student. This is quite a common occurrence in writing an extended essay, and its implementation can show signs of increasing competence on the part of the student. The actual process of research is shown to have a desirable effect on the thinking of the student and forms an integral part of the learning process.

Assessment criteria

Having written about the research question, it is appropriate here to indicate the criteria that examiners use to assess the extended essay. When students submit their essay as complete and hand it to their supervisor, they are required to complete the front of the extended essay cover. This will require the student's signature against a formal declaration that includes the sentence:

'The extended essay I am submitting is my own work (apart from guidance allowed by the International Baccalaureate).'

On the back of this same cover sheet are listed the various criteria and the maximum marks allocated to each criterion:

Table 11.1

CRITERION	MAXIMUM MARK
A – research question	2
B – introduction	2
C – investigation	4
D – knowledge and understanding	4
E – reasoned argument	4
F – analysis and evaluation	4
G – use of subject language	4
H – conclusion	2
I – formal presentation	4
J – abstract	2
K – holistic judgement	4
Total mark	**36**

The reason for the student to sign on the front of the cover sheet is to ensure that the writing that is contained in the essay is that of the person whose name and candidate examination number occurs at the top of this cover sheet. The candidate's signature is a requirement of the International Baccalaureate (IB). Failure to comply with this request means that a grade may not be issued for this aspect of the assessment. Compliance implies that the written work contained in the essay is that of the candidate and that no plagiarizing has been included. This means that no work is copied from another source unless it is clearly indicated as a citation from that source.

Research question

This criterion assesses how the purpose of the essay is specified. It is not always expressed as a question. It should be tightly focused and you should be able to address it within the recommended time parameters.

Many of the research questions offered for extended essays are registered as 'psychology'. Both students and their supervisors need to be certain that the research question is psychological. Regrettably there have been some essays registered as psychology that would have been better registered under an alternative subject. Other essays fall outside any subject offered by the IB for the Diploma programme and these necessarily have to be rejected.

The importance of the research question has been mentioned earlier, but little was indicated about the wording of the question. The IB does not insist on the essay title being expressed as a question *per se*. The question may be written as a statement that is then treated as a question as long as it is focused and subsequently subjected to a thoughtful and constructed argument. The majority of psychology essays do have a question in their title. This may be because students are more likely to refrain from long descriptive passages in their essays rather than reminding themselves that it should be an argument that is required of them.

This critical approach is helped by the quality of research that the student discovers and its relevance to the question that has been devised. On no account should questions be too ambitious or be well beyond the level of understanding of the student. Some students in the past have presented three-part questions that had little hope of being satisfactorily answered within the limited time span available to a candidate. It would be far better and fairer to the student if a realistic question was attempted that was within the limitations imposed on IB candidates.

The question should be clear, precise and well-focused. Both student and supervisor should reassure themselves that the student has access to research material related to the question. This may be available on internet sources, within school, college or public libraries, and sometimes with the help of a nearby higher education institute such as a university or equivalent.

The psychology section of the extended essay Guide indicates that experiments, surveys, case studies or interviews conducted by the student do not form part of the extended essay. These methods are covered in other parts of the IB psychology course. Their inclusion in an extended essay will not be awarded credit and could well result in the candidate receiving a lower mark than their efforts would otherwise deserve. It would be extremely helpful if supervisors were able to guide their psychology students away from such pursuits and towards more rewarding forms of relevant research.

It is sometimes difficult for examiners to understand what the research question is. This occurs when the cover sheet has one wording of the question, the title page has another and the introduction has yet another form of the question. It is far better that the research question should maintain consistency and integrity regardless of its repetition. Reference to this point should be helpful to those students who sometimes are lured away from their main task to pursue a fascinating side issue of little or no relevance to the title question. Such distractions can cause disaster to essays that previously have been on course, but later tended to be diverted by enticing and exciting novel ideas that had no place in a response to their research question. This may be a hard lesson for students to learn in their first foray into an independent long essay, but it is also an indication of the academic discipline that is so necessary at this and later stages of work.

Abstract

The abstract should state the research question, how it was investigated and the conclusions of your essay.

This rather difficult section appears as the first side of continuous writing to be seen by the reader and certainly needs its own form of discipline to be imposed on its writing.

The abstract should not be written until the whole essay has otherwise been completed.

The reason for having the above text in bold is that several students appear to think that the abstract should convey to the reader what they intend to do in their research. Their writing uses the future tense. Instead, the abstract should be written in the past tense in order to put the writing into context, and to indicate what findings or conclusions have been made. These findings may include those that can throw new light on the research question, or indications of what may need to be done in order to resolve the research question or to make progress in resolving it. This information is not likely to present itself at an early stage of the research but rather as a result of hard and prolonged application on the part of the researcher.

There is a prime need for the student to use a succinct form of expression in writing the abstract. Placing the research question into context requires a brief summary of the present position of research and thinking on this issue. This should be followed by a clear indication of how the student obtained his or her personal views on this research and finally the findings that followed the ensuing argument.

As the abstract is composed by the student there should be a reflection on how the argument they are focusing on was developed, what the discoveries were that led to progress, what the difficulties were that had to be resolved or left before the next stages in the argument. In psychology there are many examples of areas where there has been progress and controversy that would be suitable for the extended essay. For example:

- What evolutionary developments were beneficial for human intelligence?
- How does learning occur in babies and young children?
- What are the benefits and detrimental effects of using drugs in human medicine?
- What problems occur with the worldwide increase of an ageing population?

It is the process of research that is the tool that leads to discovery. If the findings are seen as all too obvious from the outset of the research, the student should consider whether the research is worth doing, and should consult the supervisor at the earliest stage to obtain a further opinion on what decision should be made in these circumstances.

The extended essay Guide for the IB's Diploma indicates that three elements need to be clearly shown in the abstract. They are:

- the research question under investigation
- the scope of the investigation
- the conclusion(s) of the extended essay.

The abstract should not exceed 300 words, and should be typed on one side of a sheet of paper that is then placed directly after the title page of the essay.

Introduction

Your introduction should make clear how your research question fits in to the existing body of knowledge and why it is significant and worth researching.

Although it is not necessary to name this section as an introduction, it should reflect the characteristics that are mentioned below.

This section should indicate how the research question has arisen and how the question had sufficient interest that it could sustain long-term debate and develop interesting arguments. The question should be put into the context of the current level of knowledge and understanding and research evidence. It is this aspect that informs the student, not only at this point of the essay but in those sections that follow.

At an early stage of the introduction the research question needs to be restated. This will remind both reader and writer of the nature of the essay. The student should also explain why the research question is important, but lengthy descriptive passages should be avoided since they tend to become superficial. The author's personal experiences and opinions should also be avoided in a formal essay of this nature.

Also in preparation for future sections, the student should begin to become aware of arguments that pervade many developments in psychological research. Many of these will demonstrate a healthy and vibrant debate that is characteristic of developing theory, including the necessary skills of analysis and evaluation.

Investigation

This assessment criterion will be assessed on how well students planned their investigation and whether they consulted an appropriate range of sources. Remember that the essay is not an experiment, case study or correlation and that conducting one of these will receive no marks.

Psychology contains a wide range of topics, many of which fascinate members of the general public. In response to this interest, in recent years many 'pop' psychology books have been published, intended for general readership. However, these publications don't undergo the same rigorous peer review process as, for example, journal articles and therefore they should not be cited in a formal academic essay. For similar reasons material available on the internet that cannot be verified as coming from an academically approved source should also not be used in the essay. In contrast, it is clear that the internet does contain a massive quantity of detailed information that certainly is relevant and verifiable as emanating from a recognized higher education institution, and which has usually been subjected to peer approval.

While the internet is regarded as a key source of information and is likely to become increasingly important, there are still several sources that are available as hard copies in bookshops or libraries, or several other forms of media. Many researchers still prefer hard copy resources as the prime media for their own specific means of accessing research. For most researchers a combination of several resources is currently used, although continual development of electronic systems and associated software is certain to involve further developments in this form of media. As a student of psychology, it may well have occurred to you that this very issue is one that causes controversy among psychologists and that it has potential for a research project in its own right.

The investigation is the first assessment criterion that carries a higher mark tariff. It provides the first in-depth section of the essay where students have an opportunity to display an indication of reaching some of the characteristics regarded as desirable for an IB learner to develop. These are indicated by the IB, which states that students are:

'to a large extent, responsible for their own independent learning, through which they acquire and communicate in-depth knowledge and understanding.'

The investigation should show evidence of forward-planning on the part of the student and the extent to which appropriate sources have been researched. A reasonable range of resources should have been considered and from this, a selection of material should be garnered. The range itself should be imaginative and may well reflect an element of risk as to its appropriateness. It is a task of the student to justify how the material to be included in the essay justifies its presence. If it cannot be justified fairly succinctly it should be rejected even though the decision may be difficult to make.

The student should consider the investigation material in some detail in order to ensure that it is relevant and capable of contributing to a thought-provoking argument in the sections that follow.

Knowledge and understanding of the topic studied

To achieve top marks for this criterion the student's essay should show a good understanding of the topic area and, where appropriate, show knowledge of how the student's investigation is situated in the wider academic context.

The term 'context' is very important in this chapter. For example, the IB indicates that essays should be put into an 'academic context' and the extended essay Guide indicates that this latter term refers to the current state of the field of study under investigation. The IB fully recognizes that its learners are at a pre-university stage of education and that the investigation can be regarded as sufficient to 'relate the investigation to the principal lines of investigation in the relevant field…'

Each of the assessment criteria covered in this chapter is sequential. Each relies on information from the previous section to build up a sequence to the development of the argument that ensues.

In this section students are expected to demonstrate a firm grasp of the topic that is the focus of research. Reading about the topic and the notes that are made will provide a framework for this sector. It is imperative that throughout the writing process that the topic continues to be addressed. The full depth and breadth of the burgeoning argument will almost certainly not have emerged at this stage but its genesis should become discernible. There may well be a greater need to exercise self-discipline since it is not uncommon for some students to become so excited by their discoveries that they forget to make a full note of where quotations or ideas are taken from. There is a need for students to maintain a continual track of each and every source of information. This advice is ignored at the student's peril. It is a long, protracted and frustrating business to retrace one's academic steps in order to find elusive nuggets of lost information that were originally discovered by the hard work involved in research.

This section's subheading includes the term 'understanding'. While descriptions of knowledge are relatively straightforward, the associative level of understanding is a more cognitively demanding exercise. It is advisable that most elements of knowledge should be accompanied by an indication of understanding. This should not be expressed in a formulaic manner, but in a way in which knowledge and understanding are offered so that they naturally bond together, for example:

'Early studies of sleep tended to adopt a holistic approach and included topics such as dreams and their association with rapid eye movement. The functions of individual brain cells had not yet had a sufficient number of research studies devoted to them, nor had the technology for such research been fully developed.'

Reasoned argument

You should present ideas clearly and in a logical, coherent fashion. Your essay should also be presented as a reasoned and convincing argument.

It is here that early research work on selecting a suitable research question to engender a sustained argument begins to pay dividends. Assessment criteria clearly indicate that:

'where the research question does not lend itself to a systematic investigation in the subject in which the essay is registered, the maximum level that can be awarded for this criterion is 2.'

In other words the maximum award for this section is now effectively halved. The same reduction of score is used for this section where:

'There is some attempt to present ideas in a logical and coherent manner, and to develop a reasonable argument in relation to the research question, but this is only partially successful.'

The presentation of material should come from notes and references made in the previous sections, but these notes need to be marshalled in such a way that they demonstrate both a logical and a coherent form.

A **logical** approach could be to follow the way in which progress concerning the whole or partial resolution to a psychological problem occurred as a result of sustained research. While research is ongoing it tends to indicate that there are still matters to be resolved and hence arguments develop as to what has been discovered and what remains to be done. Scientific and medical research can be particularly expensive to conduct. The ways in which research is conducted or its findings are applied tend to impact on the very nature of research itself. A lack of sufficient research funds or difficulty in recruiting a representative sample of participants mean that the research is unable to proceed even though its potential findings may have been valuable.

Coherence is apparent in the ways that the logical approach that has been adopted is able to show links between successive stages of development. This is where one step leads to another. It is often the case that the next step can only be taken if the problem that arose with the previous step can be resolved. For example, understanding of some of the crucial mechanisms that account for transmission of inherited characteristics in humans was delayed until the mysteries on DNA and the human genome had been researched and their findings explained.

Argument should come from the conflict or exchange of ideas that arises as research proceeds. Scientific thinking is in general still a result of collaborative effort in which a community of scientists maintains an idealistic approach to their work. Their research is published in journals that are often publicly available, although some of this information is limited by the cost of such research. Expensive fees can be charged before access to journals or other resource material is granted. The source of material for argument should be identified and quoted. It is the task of the student to develop reasoned and convincing arguments that are related to the research question, but whenever assertions are made on either side of the argument, they should be supported by relevant evidence from your reading and notes. Without conflicting points being made there can be little chance of developing an argument. Bear in mind that points made by counterarguments may eventually be incorporated in findings that emerge.

Students should not be entirely biased towards one side of the argument. There should be recognition that alternatives need to be considered fairly and that sometimes decisions are made between alternatives that are based on very fine judgements. It should also be remembered that counterarguments may well be the very source of irritation that throws new light on a seemingly intransient position adopted by proponents of that argument. Their very deviancy from a proposal becomes a necessary aspect of the resolution. These arguments exist in psychology in matters related to education, welfare or clinical judgements, among many other specialist areas.

Application of analytical and evaluative skills appropriate to psychology

Your essay must show you have effective and sophisticated analytical and evaluative skills.

The heading for this section clearly states that the analytical and evaluative skills are appropriate to psychology. Material that is offered that is not considered by examiners to be psychological will not receive credit. The way to avoid an essay becoming subject to such criticism is to ensure that reading and note taking come from academically approved sources and can be cited as such. These same sources of information form the backbone of critical awareness that is the key to this section.

Material that is very descriptive in nature has no place in this section. Examiners are looking for writing that is highly perceptive in identifying the strengths and limitations of the points that are positive or negative in relation to the argument being pursued.

Analysis and evaluation frequently overlap. Students should have exercised analytical skills as they assembled contributions from their research work that was either for or against their argument. Further analytical skill would have been required to select studies that showed a relevant cohesiveness in their approach to the research question. Were the selected studies actually following a similar approach, or did each study contain a subtle difference in the methodology employed?

Evaluation needs to examine both the method and the findings claimed by the studies used in analysis. Questions should be raised and answers provided from the studies presented. Is the research question itself biased? Were the researchers aware of the dangers inherent in not asking themselves about their own ignorance in such matters? Were they reflexive in considering their own potential biases?

These are not insignificant questions. The past history of psychological research indicates glaring examples of studies that show ignorance of sensitivities that needed more attention. In the earlier half of the last century the vast majority of university and higher education institutions had overwhelmingly male students. As a result most experiments that were conducted used male participants within a limited age range. Yet the findings that were published from this work did not draw attention to these limitations.

In a similar way, many psychologists from Western countries still conduct their experiments on volunteers, usually students from their own culture. Some may be unaware of the natural reticence of students from many Asian countries whose own cultures impose restraints on people from volunteering for new research studies, even a reluctance to be interviewed about attitudes towards certain phenomena. Their culture is one where loyalty is towards their extended family or their workplace. Western societies, in contrast, encourage the individual and freedom of personal choice as the imperatives for life.

Whenever assertions are made in aid of a specific point, study or theory, students should discuss their assertions by citing relevant studies that offer valid interpretations of the point. Assertions should not be made without such discussion. These considerations should be used to link the threads of the argument so that a natural flow of ideas occurs.

Use of language appropriate to the subject

> You must communicate your argument using clear and accurate language. You should also use terminology related to your field of study proficiently.

Students will know that three different levels of analysis are used in the core of the written examination for Paper 1. These are the biological level, the cognitive level and the sociocultural levels of analysis. For Paper 2 there are five options – abnormal, developmental and health psychology, the psychology of human relationships and sport psychology. Each of these levels or options represents a particular approach to discussions in psychology, and each has developed its own terminology in order express thoughts that are associated with that subject area. For example, the option related to sport psychology tends to use a specialist vocabulary that includes terms such as arousal theory, self-efficacy theory, mental imagery, causes and prevention of burnout or barriers to team-cohesion.

Students who do not study this option may react in a bemused fashion to these unfamiliar terms, but understanding of these words should be well known by sport psychology specialists. For example, self-efficacy is to do with the self-confidence that an individual player has in his or her ability to play at an acceptable standard. This belief is not fixed but fluctuates according to how the player regards the quality of their playing of the sport at a given time.

Players are generally good at realizing their level of performance; it is not uncommon for a cricketer, for example, to realize when self-efficacy is beginning to wane and that retirement from the sport needs to be seriously considered if team mates are not to consider him or her as a liability to the team's chances of winning. Where specialist terms are introduced students should provide a clear and precise definition of the term straight after it is first used.

Conclusion

Your conclusion must clearly relate to your research question and the evidence presented in your essay.

It is a good practice with this section to provide a subheading. Where students fail to do this it is often difficult for the examiner to determine where a conclusion starts or indeed whether there is an actual conclusion. A subheading should at least prevent such doubt. The conclusion should be a direct response to the research question and it needs to be expressed concisely.

No new material should be included in the conclusion. If it is it will be ignored by examiners. The conclusion relies on the information that has already been discussed, including the argument itself and the knowledge and understanding that is linked to the argument. There should still be a flow to this section with its various points smoothly and concisely linked together.

Formal presentation

This criterion will assess how far your essay follows a standard format in terms of appearance, layout, structure and formal elements (including title page, table of contents, page numbers, illustrative material, references, citations, bibliography and appendices).

The various aspects needed to fulfil this criterion require particular attention to detail. As its name suggests, presentation is to do with the way that information appears on the page and should follow the precise details required by academic psychology research that appears in journals. There should be a title page, an indication of the number of words used in the essay (this number should not include words in the abstract, acknowledgements, contents page, any maps, diagrams or tables, references, footnotes or endnotes, bibliography or appendices), a table of contents that is informative to the reader, and page numbers.

Importantly there should be a reference section and/or a bibliography. The type of reference system used in this section is not chosen by the IB. References should follow an approved academic style but these styles may vary from one discipline to another and also from one country to another. What is common to nearly all documentation styles is presentation of authors' surnames in alphabetical order. The IB requires internet references should include:

'the title of the extract used, the website address, the date it was accessed and if possible the author's name and initials. The more important a particular point is to the essay, the more the quality of its source needs to be evaluated.'

Tables or graphs, where they are used, should have clear titles and their source and date of origin must be acknowledged as part of the graphical presentation. Students are not required to conduct their own original quantitative research in the form of experiments, case studies, surveys or interviews as part of their extended essays, and these will not be awarded credit if they are presented. An opportunity to assess this type of work is given elsewhere in the psychology assessment.

Holistic judgement

This criterion assesses the factors that make an essay stand out from the average. This includes intellectual initiative, depth of understanding and insight.

Qualities that are rewarded under this criterion include the following:

- **Intellectual initiative** – this is shown by the choice of topic and the way in which the research question deals with controversies generated by a broad range of sources; credit is also awarded for research investigation that is innovative yet effective in the context of the research question.

- **Insight and depth of understanding** – this is likely to be shown by a dedicated approach in maximizing the depth of discussion that is revealed by diligent research, and by the use of reflexivity to ensure a well informed and balanced argument that consistently addresses the research question.

- **Originality and creativity** – these will be apparent by clear evidence of personal engagement by the student, backed up by effective research and reasoning.

The explanations offered above form the main materials that examiners will use to determine credit for this criterion of holistic judgement. It would be a useful exercise for both candidate and supervisor to check the essay at agreed time intervals in order to confirm that most, or possibly all, of the attributes mentioned are being reflected in the essay during its construction.

Glossary

Abnormality – a psychological or behavioural state leading to impairment of interpersonal functioning and/or distress to others.

Accommodation – altering or updating a schema in the light of experience.

Achievement goal theory – an explanation of the reasons for pursuing success in sport.

Action potentials – brief bursts of electrical activity. Usually generated at synapses on dendrites, action potentials travel down the neuron and along the axon to axon terminals. At the synapse they may be transmitted to the next neuron, or they may be lost. Action potentials are 'all or none', and always have the same electrical characteristics. All information in the nervous system is carried in the form of patterns of action potentials.

Adolescence – the transitional stage between puberty and adulthood (i.e. legal age of majority).

Affective disorders – mood disturbances that affect thoughts, behaviours and emotions.

Affordances – the quality of objects that permit actions to be carried out on them.

Aggression – involves behaviours that are carried out with the deliberate intent to cause harm.

Agonist drugs – increase the action of neurotransmitters whereas antagonists (blockers) reduce the action of neurotransmitters, for example by occupying receptors on the post synaptic neuron.

Aim – a precise statement of why a study is taking place.

Altruism – voluntary actions aimed at helping another person that involve some cost to the helper.

Anonymity – participants in an investigation are assured that their names will not be disclosed to any other persons.

Anterograde amnesia – the inability to learn new facts and information, contrasted with retrograde amnesia, the inability to recall previously learned material. Classic cases have been caused by temporal lobe damage and by Korsakoff's syndrome (chronic alcoholism).

Anxiety disorders – abnormal conditions characterized by extreme worry, fear and nervousness.

Asperger's syndrome – a mild form of autism, and one of the 'autism spectrum disorders'.

Assimilation – applying a schema to new objects.

Attachments – emotional ties between two people.

Attention control/concentration training – the focusing of awareness on relevant cues in order to maximize performance.

Attributions – explanations about the cause of behaviour.

Audience effect – the ways in which participants may change their normal behaviour when researchers are present, especially when overt observation occurs.

Autism – a developmental disorder found mainly in males, with impairments in social communication, language and behavioural flexibility. Baron-Cohen argues that autism may represent an extreme version of the 'male pattern' brain, with an important role for prenatal testosterone.

Axon – part of the neuron, a long process emerging from the cell body. The axon usually has many branches that end at synapses close to neighbouring neurons.

Axon terminal – the part of the axon branch just before the synapse between the axon and the following neuron. The axon terminal contains packets (vesicles) of neurotransmitters that are released into the synapse when action potentials arrive at the axon terminal.

Behavioural therapies – treatments of abnormality that modify maladaptive behaviour by substituting new responses.

Bias – a process that distorts the data or findings of a research investigation, which subsequently makes the research invalid.

Biological approach – a model of abnormality that perceives mental disorders as illnesses with physical causes.

Biomedical approaches – physiological treatments of abnormality based on the biological model.

Bottom-up (direct) processing – perception that arises directly from sensory input without further cognitive processing.

Bystander behaviour – the behaviour of witnesses who do not intervene or offer help but 'stand by'.

Case studies – a research method that involves study and testing of an individual person or a small group of people. Its findings are considered to be limited by the constraints placed on this method in terms of finance, time, and number of participants.

Cell membrane – the outer covering of all cells, including neurons. With neurons, the cell membrane has a highly complex layered structure that allows it to transmit electrical impulses.

Cognitive appraisal model – the perception that mental assessments control emotional responses to injury.

Cognitive approach – a model of abnormality that perceives mental disorders as due to negative thoughts and illogical beliefs.

Cognitive behavioural therapy – treatment of abnormality that modifies thought patterns to alter behavioural and emotional states.

Cognitive psychology – the study of mental processes.

Cognitive-affective stress model – an explanation of the nature, causes and consequences of athletic burnout that incorporates situational, cognitive and behavioural components.

Cognitive-evaluation theory – an explanation of how external factors affect intrinsic motivation.

Compliance – agreeing to direct requests.

Conformity – changing attitudes or behaviour in response to pressure from a group. Also known as majority influence.

Confounding variables – uncontrolled variables other than the IV within a research setting that affect the DV and thus 'confuse' the results.

Convenience sampling – a sampling technique based on the comparative ease of recruiting volunteers as participants. Often

used with students at school or in higher education institutions.

Covert observation – an observation technique in which the people who are being observed are unaware of the observation process.

Credibility – ways of confirming the truthfulness, accuracy and transparency of data and interpretations used in research.

Cultural norms – rules which regulate behaviour within a particular culture.

Cultural relativism – definitions of what is regarded as normal functioning vary from culture to culture and have equal validity.

Culturally responsive interviewing – sensitivity in conducting and reporting on the research process and its findings that acknowledges cultural differences that may be present.

Culture – refers to the shared habits of a community.

Debriefing – informing participants at the conclusion of an investigation of the precise nature of the research and the reasons for its implementation.

Deductive approach – used primarily in quantitative research, where a hypothesis is subsequently tested by using the experimental method. Rarely used in qualitative research but may be employed occasionally, for example as part of the process of inductive content analysis.

Demand characteristics – a research effect where participants form impressions of the research purpose and unconsciously alter their behaviour accordingly.

Dendrites – a part of the neuron. Dendrites are short processes that usually receive synaptic

connections from the axon branches of other neurons; so nerve impulses (action potentials) are usually generated on dendrites.

Dependent variable – the factor measured by researchers in an investigation.

Depression – a mood disorder characterized by feelings of despondency and hopelessness.

Developmental disorder – disorders such as autism and dyslexia that can be identified in the developing child, and appear to be subtle problems in the normal development of the brain and brain function.

Deviation from ideal mental health – failure to meet the criteria for perfect psychological well-being.

Deviation from social norms – behaviour that violates accepted social rules.

Diagnosis – the identification of the nature and cause of a disorder.

Diffusion of responsibility – occurs when a crowd of people witness an event and the responsibility for helping is spread out between them.

Dispositional attributions – see behaviour as originating from inside the person (i.e. traits).

Double-blind procedure – a procedure whereby neither the researcher nor the participants is aware of which condition of the IV the participant is performing under.

Drive theory – the belief that as arousal increases, so does the level of performance.

Drug therapy – treatment of mental disorders with medicines.

DSM-IV – a diagnostic classification system produced and used in the USA.

Eclectic treatments – the use of multiple therapies in the treatment of mental disorders.

Ecological validity – a descriptor of an investigation conducted that reflects normal conditions of the entity or process under investigation. Unlike quantitative research, qualitative research is not used in laboratory conditions. Instead it is conducted in the real world environment.

ECT – treatment of mental disorders by application of electrical voltage to the brain.

Emic analysis – assumes that behaviours are culture-specific and research findings cannot be assumed to apply to other cultures.

Emotion – a state of mind determined by one's mood.

Endogenous depression – depression that is linked to internal biochemical and hormonal influences.

Episodic memory – a category of long-term memory, episodic memory is memory for events in our own lives. These require conscious recollection, and are often dramatically affected in cases of retrograde amnesia.

Ethical considerations – the rules and moral principles that govern the conduct of researchers in investigations.

Ethical issues – behaviour that affects participants and researchers in a negative way, particularly where participants perceive that they have been demeaned. Ethical issues may also include religious, racial, sexual or ageist slurs.

Etic analysis – assumes that findings from research in one culture can be applied universally to other cultures.

Etiology – the causes or origins of a disorder.

Evaluation apprehension – occurs when bystanders fail to help as they are anxious about being judged.

Evidence-based health promotion – involves the integration of research evidence into the planning and implementation of health promotion strategies (Wiggers & Sanson-Fisher, 1998).

Exogenous depression – depression that is linked to external stressful experiences.

Experimental method – a research method using random assignment of participants and the manipulation of variables to determine cause and effect.

Extended essay – the extended essay is an independent, in-depth study of a topic from one of the approved IB Diploma subjects, usually, but not always, from one that the student is studying. It must be no longer than 4,000 words. Students must obtain a pass for their extended essay to obtain their Diploma.

External validity – the extent to which the findings of a study can be generalized beyond the confines of the research setting.

Extraneous variables – variables other than the IV within a research setting that can affect the DV.

Extrinsic motivation – the incentive that comes from external factors, such as performing for money.

Eyewitness testimony (EWT) – the recall of observers of events previously experienced.

Face recognition – the means by which faces are processed and made sense of.

Failure to function adequately – an inability to cope with day-to-day living.

Field experiment – an experiment conducted in a naturalistic

environment where the researchers manipulate the independent variable.

Focus groups – a research method, similar to a group interview, in which usually five to eight people discuss a single issue of concern to them that has been chosen by the researcher.

Foot in the door (FITD) technique – a compliance technique based on gaining agreement to a small request followed by a large request.

Functional magnetic resonance imaging (fMRI) – a form of brain scanning involving alterations in magnetization between oxygen-poor and oxygen-rich blood flow.

Fundamental attribution error (FAE) – the tendency to attribute other people's behaviour to dispositional causes.

Gatekeeper – an individual who is responsible for denying or allowing access to data that is important to the research process.

Gender – behaviours that are appropriate for men and women (i.e. masculine and feminine).

Generalizability – the claim, often contested, by which the findings of an investigation can be transferred to people or situations other than those in the original investigation.

Goal setting – creating specific standards of task proficiency to attain, usually within a set time period.

Graphs – easily understandable pictorial representations of data.

Grief reaction response model – the perception of dealing with a chronic injury as similar to the process of facing a terminal illness.

Group approaches – forms of therapy where a collection

of patients meets regularly to interact with each other and a therapist.

Groupthink – the tendency for groups to make poor decisions driven by the need for a united front and conformity.

Hardy personality – copes with stress well and is characterized by commitment, control and challenge.

Hawthorne effect – the tendency of participants to change their behaviour because they know they're being observed.

Higher mental functions – complex reasoning skills.

Horizon ratios – invariant sensory information concerning the position of objects in relation to the horizon.

Hormones – chemical messengers released from glands. They travel in the bloodstream and affect the activity of other glands and structures in the body. They can also directly affect brain activity.

Hypotheses – precise, testable research predictions.

ICD-10 – a diagnostic classification system produced by the World Health Organization and used in Great Britain.

Identity – a consistent and reliable sense of who we are.

Idiographic approach – concentration on the uniqueness of each individual.

Independent groups design – experimental design where each participant performs one condition of an experiment.

Independent variable – the factor manipulated by researchers in an investigation.

Individual approaches – forms of psychological therapy in which a client is treated on a one-to-one basis with a therapist.

Inductive approach – the term used for inductive content analysis in which interpretations of interviewees' answers, the data, are drawn out from the words used.

Inductive content analysis – usually applied after semi-structured interviews. Allows researchers to draw out meanings of statements made by interviewees and to construct an analysis based on interpretation of the statements.

Informed consent – prior to taking part in an investigation, researchers should ensure that participants understand what the study involves, including how the findings may be used, and provide assurances of anonymity. When informed consent is impossible, e.g. with children or brain-damaged participants, there are alternative routes to consent, e.g. gaining consent from the family or other responsible adults.

Intrinsic motivation – the incentive that comes from the joy of participating in an activity.

Inverted 'U' hypothesis – the belief that as arousal increases, the level of performance increases up to an optimal point, after which further arousal leads to a downturn in performance.

Investigator bias – the effects researchers' expectations can have on participants, causing them to behave in non-genuine ways.

Investigator effects – features of a researcher that influence participants' responses.

Investment model – the perception of athletic burnout as due to such high investment of resources that participation in a sport occurs more because an individual feels they have to than because they want to.

Laboratory experiment – an experiment conducted in a controlled environment, allowing the establishment of causality.

Low-ball – a compliance technique based on getting agreement to an attractive deal, which is then made less attractive.

Magnetic resonance imaging (MRI) – a form of brain scanning involving magnetic fields and pulses of radio wave energy.

Matched pairs design – experimental design where participants are in similar pairs, with one performing in each condition.

Measures of central tendency – descriptive statistics that give information about 'typical' scores for a set of data.

Measures of dispersion – descriptive statistics that give information about the 'spread' of scores within a set of data.

Memory – the retention of experience.

Mental imagery – visualizing the successful execution of physical skills.

Mental representations – theoretical internal structures of cognitive processes.

Minority influence – occurs when an individual or small group 'converts' the larger group to their view.

Misleading information/questions – information or questions that suggest a desired answer.

Monoamines – a group of neurotransmitters strongly associated with motivational processes.

Multistore model of memory – Atkinson and Shiffrin produced this early model of the stages of memory formation, storage and retrieval. It served to stimulate much research, and was supported in part by some classic case studies, such as HM. It has now been superseded by more complex models that include, for instance, different types of long-term memory.

Narrative interviews – an interview technique where the researcher encourages interviewees to relate their life experiences in a story form.

Negative training stress model – an explanation of athletic burnout that centres on an imbalance between training demands and coping abilities.

Neural plasticity – the ability of the nervous system, especially the brain, to adapt to the environment. Plasticity is most obvious in the infant brain, which can adapt to brain damage and to enriched environments by growing more neurons. Recently, spatial memory in humans has been shown to lead to growth in the hippocampus, another example of neural plasticity.

Neurogenesis – the growth of new neurons. Had been thought to end in humans when the brain matures at about 20 years of age, but recent research suggests neurogenesis is the basis for some forms of memory in adults.

Neuroimaging – the production of images of the brain by non-invasive scanning methods.

Neuron – the basic unit cell of the nervous system. Neurons are specialized to transmit electrical impulses (or 'action potentials') along their length. It is estimated that the brain alone may contain in the order of 100 billion neurons.

Neurotransmitters – neurochemicals such as dopamine, serotonin and acetylcholine that are stored in axon terminals and released into the synapse when action potentials arrive at the axon terminal. They combine with postsynaptic receptors and this combination allows action potentials to be generated in the postsynaptic neuron.

Neurotypical – term now used for 'normal' control participants when compared with brain-damaged patients or participants with developmental disorders such as autism.

Nomothetic approach – establishing broad generalizations that apply to large groups of individuals.

Nucleus – all cells, including neurons, contain a nucleus. Within the nucleus we find the chromosomes, the genetic material. Besides transmitting genetic information from one generation to the next, chromosomes in the nucleus also control the biochemical activities of the living cell.

Obesity – an eating disorder whereby excess body fat accumulates to the extent of having a negative effect upon health and well-being.

Observer bias – an investigator effect whereby a researcher's cognitive bias unconsciously influences participants' behaviour.

Obsessive-compulsive disorder – an anxiety disorder characterized by persistent, recurrent unpleasant thoughts and repetitive, ritualistic behaviours.

Operationalization – the process of defining variables into measureable factors.

Optic flow patterns – unambiguous sources of information that directly inform perception.

Optical array – the structure of patterned light received by the eyes.

Overt observation – a method of observing in which the participants are made aware of the reasons they are being observed.

Oxytocin – a hormone released from the pituitary gland, which plays important roles in reproductive and maternal behaviour, e.g. lactation. Recent research has also shown a role for oxytocin in early bonding between mother and child and in adult pair-bonding.

Perception – the interpretation of sensory data.

Perceptual defence – the process by which stimuli are not perceived or are distorted due to their threatening or offensive nature.

Performance-enhancing drugs – substances abused by athletes to improve results.

Pilot studies – small-scale, practice investigations.

Pluralistic ignorance – takes place when bystanders take their cue from others who are doing nothing.

Positron emission tomography (PET) – a form of brain scanning involving the tracking of radiation within the brain.

Post-event information – misleading information added to an incident after it has occurred.

Pre-programme measurements – measurement-of-health measure as a baseline before an intervention.

Priming – exposure to aggressive behaviour makes aggressive behaviour more likely.

Probability – the likelihood of observed differences being determined by chance factors.

Procedural memory – category of long-term memory that involves sensory-motor skills such as word processing, riding a bike, and playing the piano. These skills are not affected even by brain damage that produces severe retrograde amnesia for episodic memories.

Pro-social behaviour – actions that help another person.

Prosopagnosia – a visual agnosia where objects can be described, but not recognized.

Psychoactive drugs – act on brain chemistry.

Psychological moratorium – a socially approved postponement of decisions.

Psychosurgery – treatment of abnormality by irreversible destruction of brain tissue.

Purposive sampling – a sampling method often used by qualitative researchers, where participants are selected because they possess characteristics that are central to the research question.

Quantitative data – data that occurs in a numerical form.

Random sampling – a sampling method where each individual from the parent population has an equal chance of being selected for the sample.

Randomized controlled trials – the comparison of groups who have been randomly allocated to programme or non-programme conditions.

Reflexivity – acknowledgement by researchers of the extent to which their own biases are likely to impact on their interpretation of experiences related by participants.

Reliability – the extent to which an experiment produces consistent results, both within the research setting (internal reliability) and over time (external reliability). Also the extent of consistency of diagnosis of psychological disorders.

Repeated measures design – experimental design where each participant performs under all conditions of an experiment.

Repetition – the repeating of fundamental physical skills in order for them to become automatic.

Replication – repetition of research to confirm results.

Resilience – the ability to cope positively with negative events and to bounce back.

Retrograde amnesia – the inability to recall previously learnt material, contrasted with anterograde amnesia, the inability to learn new facts and information.

Reversal theory – the idea that individuals switch between different motivational styles, rather than having a fixed motivational style.

Reward pathway – a neural pathway that is activated by dopamine and implicated in many addictive behaviours.

Risky shift – the tendency for groups to make a decision that is more extreme (riskier) than any of the individual members' views.

Role diffusion – drifting without making a commitment to the future.

Sampling – the selection of participants to represent a wider population.

Scaffolding – providing help to a child to achieve a task in their ZPD and gradually removing it as the child becomes competent.

Schemas – simple ideas built up from experience; mental structures or packages of knowledge.

Scripts – complex memories about how to behave in social situations.

Self-efficacy theory – an explanation of how an individual's perception of their ability affects their capability to attain goals.

Self-serving bias – tendency to use internal attributions for our successes but external attributions for our failures.

Semantic memory – category of long-term memory that deals with facts and information about the world, e.g. the capital of Turkey or the name of the Prime Minister. In general this is less affected by brain damage than episodic memory, although some cases of amnesia clearly show a semantic memory deficit.

Sex – the biological state of being male or female.

Significance levels – statistical criteria that determine if observed differences are beyond the boundaries of chance.

Single-blind procedure – a procedure whereby the participants are not aware of the research aims or which condition of the IV they are performing under.

Situational attributions – see behaviour as originating from situational forces.

Snowball sampling – sampling strategy in which the first participant names a second participant; he or she then nominates a subsequent participant, and the process of naming continues. Used in qualitative research when target participants are difficult to locate.

Social cognition – making sense of the social environment and other people's behaviour.

Social learning theory – claims that behaviours are learned through observation of role models and imitation of their behaviour.

Sociocultural approach – a model of abnormality that perceives mental disorders as determined by social and cultural environments.

Standardized procedure – a set of research steps that are all the same for all participants.

Statistical tests – mathematical means of analysing data.

Stereotypes – generalizations about social groups.

Stress based model – the perception of injury risk as being related to stress levels.

Stressor – something that requires an individual to make some sort of adjustment.

Synapse – the small gap, measured in thousandths of a millimetre, between axon terminals and the dendrites of the following neuron. Release of neurotransmitters, such as dopamine and serotonin, from the axon terminal allows some action potentials to cross the synapse. The synapse is essential to information processing in the nervous system.

Team cohesion – the extent to which being together assists members of a group in pursuing mutual goals and objectives.

Temporal lobectomy – operation used for temporal lobe epilepsy where the tip of the lobe is surgically removed. This tip includes the amygdala and part of the hippocampus. The patient HM had a bilateral temporal lobectomy that led to profound anterograde amnesia.

Testosterone – a hormone released from the testes in males but also found in females. Important in male sexual characteristics and behaviour, testosterone released early in embryonic development directly affects the brain. Baron-Cohen suggests that this produces the 'male pattern' brain.

Texture gradient – surface patterns that provide sensory information about objects.

Top-down (indirect) processing – perception that involves cognitive processing that goes beyond mere sensory input.

Triangulation – using different combinations of methods that may include data, methods, researchers, theories. Triangulation is used to claim greater validity for the findings of a study.

Type A personality – characterized by impatience, competitiveness and irritability/hostility.

Validity – the extent to which results accurately measure what they claim to measure, due to the manipulation of the IV (internal validity) and the ability of the findings to be generalized beyond the research setting (external validity). Also the accuracy of diagnosis of psychological disorders.

Vesicles – small storage packets found in the presynaptic axon terminal, which contain neurotransmitters such as dopamine and serotonin. When action potentials arrive at the axon terminal they cause vesicles to travel to the cell membrane, rupture, and release their contents into the synaptic gap.

Violence – involves physical victimization of another person.

Visual agnosia – a condition involving an inability to make sense of or use familiar stimuli.

Visual illusions – visually perceived images that differ from objective reality.

Zone of proximal development (ZPD) – the range of mental abilities that children can achieve with the help of others.

References

Abed, R. and Pauw, K. (1998) An evolutionary hypothesis for obsessive-compulsive disorder: a psychological immune system? *Behavioural Neurology*, 11(4), 245–50.

Abelson, R. (1974) A patient by another name. Clinical group difference in labelling bias. *Journal of Consulting and Clinical Psychology*, 42, 4–9.

Abraham, C., Sheeran, P., Spears, R. and Abrams, D. (1992) Health beliefs and promotion of HIV-preventive intentions among teenagers: a Scottish perspective. *Health Psychology*, 11(6), 363–70.

Abramson, L.Y., Seligman, M.E.P. and Teasdale, J.D. (1978) Learned helplessness in humans: critique and reformulation. *Journal of Abnormal Psychology*, 87(1), 49–74.

Action on Smoking and Health (ASH). http://ash.org.uk/files/documents/ASH_106.pdf (accessed 19 March 2013).

Adachi, Y. (2005) Behavior therapy for obesity. *Japan Medical Association Journal*, 48(11), 539–44.

Agras, W. (1989) *Eating Disorders: Management of Obesity, Bulimia and Anorexia Nervosa*. Ann Arbor, MI: Pergamon Press.

Ainsworth, M.D. and Bell, S.M. (1970) Attachment, exploration and separation: illustrated by the behavior of one-year-olds in a strange situation. *Child Development*, 41(1), 49–67.

Akelaitis, A.J. (1944) A study of gnosis, praxis and language following section of the corpus callosum and anterior commissure. *Journal of Neurosurgery*, 1, 94–102.

Alasuutari, P. (1995) *Researching Culture: Qualitative Method and Cultural Studies* (155). London: Sage.

Alasuutari, P. (2007) *Laadullinen tutkimus [Qualitative Research]*. Vastapaino: Tampere.

Allport, G.W. (1954) *The Nature of Prejudice*. Reading, MA: Addison-Wesley.

Allport, G. and Pettigrew, T. (1957) Cultural influence on the perception of movement. *Journal of Social and Abnormal Psychology*, 55(1), 104–13.

Altman, J., Everritt, R.J., Glautier, S., Markou, A., Nutt, D., Oretti, R., Phillips, G.D and Robbins, T.W. (1996) The biological, social and clinical bases of drug addiction: commentary and debate. *Psychopharmacology*, 125, 285–345.

American Psychiatric Association (1987) *The Diagnostic and Statistical Manual of Mental Disorders*, 3rd edition, revised. Washington DC: American Psychiatric Association.

American Psychiatric Association (2000) *The Diagnostic and Statistical Manual of Mental Disorders*, 4th edition, text revision. Washington DC: American Psychiatric Association.

American Psychological Association (2001) Report of the American Psychological Association Commission on Violence and Youth, Vol. I. Washington, DC: American Psychological Association.

American Psychological Association (2002) *Ethical Principles of Psychologists and Code of Conduct*. Washington, DC: American Psychological Association.

American Psychological Association (2004) School bullying is nothing new, but psychologists identify new ways to prevent it. http://www.apa.org/research/action/bullying.aspx (accessed 21 March 2013).

American Psychological Association (2010) Staying connected: a guide for parents on raising an adolescent daughter. http://www.apa.org/pubs/info/brochures/girls.aspx?item=6 (accessed 21 March 2013).

American Psychological Association (2011) Report of the American Psychological Association Commission on Violence and Youth, Vol. I. Washington, DC: American Psychological Association.

American Psychological Association (2012) Big kids. http://www.apa.org/monitor/2012/12/cover-obesity.aspx (accessed 21 March 2013).

Anastasi, J. and Rhodes, M. (2006) Evidence for own-age bias in face recognition. *North American Journal of Psychology*, 8(2), 237–53.

Andersen, M. and Williams, J. (1988) A model of athletic stress and injury: prediction and prevention. *Journal of Sport and Exercise Physiology*, 10(3), 294–306.

Anderson, C.A., Berkowitz, L., Donnerstein, E., Huesmann, L.R., Johnson, J.D., Linz, D., *et al.* (2003a) The influence of media violence on youth. *Psychological Science in the Public Interest*, 4, 81–110.

Anderson, C.A. and Bushman, B.J. (2001) Effects of violent video games on aggressive behavior, aggressive cognition, aggressive affect, physiological arousal, and prosocial behavior: a meta-analytic review of the scientific literature. *Psychological Science*, 12(5), 353–59.

Anderson, R., Buckwalter, K. and Buchanan, R. (2003b) Validity and reliability of the Minimum Data Set Depression Rating Scale (MDSDRS) for older adults in nursing homes. *Age and Ageing*, 32(4), 435–38.

Anderson, R. and Pichert, J. (1978) Instantiation of general terms. *Journal of Verbal Learning and Verbal Behaviour*, 15, 6667–79.

Anshel, M., Jamieson J. and Raviv, S. (2001) Coping with acute stress among male and female Israeli athletes. *International Journal of Sport Psychology*, 32, 271–89.

Antunes, P. and Fleck, M. (2009) Clinical outcomes and quality of life in patients submitted to electroconvulsive therapy. *Journal of ECT*, 25(3), 182–85.

Archer, J. (2004) Sex differences in aggression in real-world settings: a meta-analytic review. *Review of General Psychology*, 8, 291–332.

Archer, J. and Lloyd, B.B. (1982) *Sex and Gender*. Harmondsworth: Penguin.

Armitage, C.J. and Arden, M.A. (2008) How useful are the stages of change for targeting interventions? Randomized test of a brief intervention to reduce smoking. Health Psychology, 27(6), 789–98.

Armitage C.J. and Conner, M. (2000) Social cognition models and health behaviour: a structured review. *Psychology and Health*, 15(2), 173–89.

Artigas, L., Jarero, I., Mauer, M., López Cano, T. and Alcalá, N. (2000) EMDR and traumatic stress after natural disasters: integrative treatment protocol and the butterfly hug. Poster presented at the EMDRIA Conference, Toronto, Canada.

Asch, S.E. (1951) Effects of group pressure upon the modification and distortion of judgements. In H. Guetzkow (ed.), *Groups, Leadership and Men*. Pittsburgh, PA: Carnegie Press.

Atkinson, R.C. and Shiffrin, R.M. (1968) Human memory: a proposed system and its control processes. In K.W. Spence and J.T. Spence, *The Psychology of Learning and Motivation, Volume 2* (89–195). New York: Academic Press.

Auyeung, B., Baron-Cohen, S., Ashwin, E., Knickmeyer, R., Taylor, K. and Hackett, G. (2009) Fetal testosterone and autistic traits. *British Journal of Psychology*, 100, 1–22.

Baer, L. (1991) Behaviour therapy for obsessive-compulsive disorder. *Archives of General Psychiatry*, 48, 730–38.

Baker, J., Cotes, J. and Hawes, R. (2000) The relationship between coaching behaviours and sports anxiety in athletes. *Journal of Science and Medicine in Sport*, 3(2), 110–19.

Baker, R. (2000) Can we tell when someone is staring at us from behind? *Skeptical Inquirer*, March/April, 34–40.

Balcetis, E. and Dunning, D. (2006) See what you want to see. Motivational influences on visual perception. *Journal of Personality and Social Psychology*, 91(4), 612–25.

Bandura, A. (1973) *Aggression: A Social Learning Analysis*. Englewood Cliffs, NJ: Prentice-Hall.

Bandura, A. (1977) *Social Learning Theory*. Englewood Cliffs, NJ: Prentice-Hall.

Bandura, A. (1997) *Self-efficacy: The Exercise of Control*. New York: Freeman.

Bandura, A., Ross, D. and Ross, S.A. (1963) Imitation of film – mediated aggressive models. *Journal of Abnormal and Social Psychology*, 63, 3–11.

Banyard, P. (1996) *Applying Psychology to Health*. London: Hodder & Stoughton.

Barker, E.T. and Bornstein, M.H. (2010) Global self-esteem, appearance satisfaction and self-reported dieting in early adolescence. *Journal of Early Adolescence*, 30(2), 205–24.

Barrett, L., Dunbar, R. and Lycett, J. (2002) *Human Evolutionary Psychology*. Basingstoke: Palgrave Macmillan.

Barrett, P. and Healey, L. (2002) Do parent and child behaviours differentiate families whose children have obsessive-compulsive disorder from other clinic and non-clinic families? *Journal of Clinical Psychiatry*, 43(5), 597–607.

Bartholow, B.D., Bushman, B.J. and Sestir, M.A. (2006) Chronic violent video game exposure and desensitization to violence; behavioural and event-related potential data. *Journal of Experimental Social Psychology*, 42(4), 532–39.

Bartlett, F. (1932) *Remembering: A Study in Experimental and Social Psychology*. Cambridge: Cambridge University Press.

Bass, B. (1980) *Bass & Stodgill's Handbook of Leadership: Theory, Research and Managerial Applications*. New York: Free Press.

Batson, C.D. (1987) Prosocial motivation: is it ever truly altruistic? In L. Berkowitz (ed.), *Advances in Experimental Social Psychology* (20, 65–122). New York: Academic Press.

Batson, C.D. (2010) Empathy-induced altruistic motivation. In M. Mikulincer and P.R. Shaver (eds), *Prosocial Motives, Emotions, and Behavior: The Better Angels of Our Nature*. Washington, DC: American Psychological Association.

Batson, C.D., Batson, J.G., Slingsby, J.K., Harrell, K.L., Peekna, H.M. and Todd, R.M. (1990) Empathic joy and the empathy-altruism hypothesis. *Journal of Personality and Social Psychology*, 61(3), 413–26.

Bauman, K. (1973) Premarital sexual attitudes of unmarried university students: 1968 v 1972. *Archives of Sexual Behaviour*, 5(1), 29–37.

Baxter, L. (1986) Gender differences in the heterosexual relationship rules embedded in break-up accounts. *Journal of Social and Personal Relationships*, 3(3), 289–306.

Beck, A. (1963) Thinking and depression: idiosyncratic content and cognitive distortions. *Archives of General Psychiatry*, 9, 324–33.

Beck, A. (1967) *Depression: Clinical, Experimental, and Theoretical Aspects*. New York: Harper and Row.

Beck, A. (1987) *Cognitive Therapy of Depression*. New York: Guilford Press.

Beck, R. and Fernandez, E. (1998) Cognitive-behavioral therapy in the treatment of anger: a meta-analysis. *Cognitive Therapy and Research*, 22(1), 63–74.

Becker, A., Burwell, R.A., Herzog, D.B., Hamburg, P. and Gilman, S.E. (2002) Eating behaviours and attitudes following prolonged exposure to television among ethnic Fijian girls. *British Journal of Psychiatry*, 180, 509–14.

Becker, M.H., Maiman, L.A., Kirscht, J.P., Haefner, D.P. and Drachman, R.H. (1977) The health belief model and prediction of dietary compliance: a field experiment. *Journal of Health and Social Behavior*, 18, 348–66.

Becker, M.H. and Rosenstock, I.M. (1984) Compliance with medical advice. In J. Ogden (2005), *Health Psychology*. Maidenhead: Open University Press.

Beilock, S., Carr, T., MacMahon, C. and Starkes, J. (2002) When paying attention becomes counterproductive: impact of divided versus skill-focused attention on novice and experienced performance of sensorimotor skills. *Journal of Experimental Psychology: Applied*, 8, 6–16.

Beilock, S. and Gray, R. (2007) Why do athletes 'choke' under pressure? In G. Tenenbaum and B. Eklund (eds), *Handbook of Sport Psychology*, 3rd edition (425–44). Hoboken, NJ: John Wiley & Sons.

Bekerian, D. and Bowers, J. (1983) Eyewitness testimony: were we misled? *Journal of Experimental Psychology: Learning, Memory and Cognition*, 9(1), 139–45.

Bem, S. (1974) The measurement of psychological androgyny. *Journal of Consulting and Clinical Psychology*, 42, 155–62.

Bennett, A. (2005) *Culture and Everyday Life*. London: Sage.

Benton, D. and Roberts, G. (1988) Vitamin and mineral supplementation improves the intelligence of a sample of school children. *The Lancet*, 1(8578), 140–43.

Berg, B.L. (2006) *Qualitative Research Methods for the Social Sciences*, 6th edition. Needham Heights, MA: Allyn and Bacon.

Berman, R. (2004) The risk to the American fast food industry of obesity litigation. *Cornell Hospitality Quarterly*, 48(2), 201–14.

Beroqvist, E. (1999) US Department of Health and Human Services, Volume 269.

Biddle, S. (1985) Mental preparation, mental practice and strength tasks: a need for clarification. *Journal of Sports Sciences*, 3, 67–74.

Bierut, L., Heath, A., Bucholz, K., Dinwiddie, S., Madden, P., Statham, D., Dunne, M. and Martin, N. (1999) Major depressive disorder in a community-based twin sample: are there genetic and environmental contributions for men and women? *Archives of General Psychiatry*, 56, 557–63.

Bitterman, M. and Kniffin, C. (1953) Manifest anxiety and perceptual defence. *Journal of Abnormal and Social Psychology*, 48(2), 248–52.

Bond, R. and Smith, P.B. (1996) Culture and conformity: a meta-analysis of studies using Asch's (1952b, 1956) line judgment task. *Psychological Bulletin*, 119(1), 111–37.

Borland, R. (1990) Slip-ups and relapse in attempts to quit smoking. *Addictive Behaviors*, 15(3), 235–45.

Bossard, J. (1932) Residential propinquity as a factor in marriage selection. Cited in M. Eysenck (2001), *Psychology for A2 Level*. Lewes: Psychology Press.

Boury, M., Treadwell, T. and Kumar, V. (2001) Integrating psychodrama cognitive therapy: an exploratory study. *International Journal of Action Methods*, 54, 13–28.

Bower, T.G.R. and Wishart, J.G. (1972) The effects of motor skill on object permanence. *Cognition*, 1, 28–35.

Bowlby, J. (1953; 2nd edition 1965) *Child Care and the Growth of Love*. Harmondsworth: Penguin.

Bowlby, J. (1969) *Attachment and Loss. Vol. 1: Attachment.* Harmondsworth: Penguin.

Brasel, S., Zimbardo, P. and Slavich, G. (2006) A blind man's eye: perceptual defence mechanisms and aschematic visual information. *Advances in Consumer Research*, 33, 305.

Bray, G., Neilsen, S. and Popkin, B. (2004) Consumption of high fructose corn syrup in beverages may play a role in the epidemic of obesity. *American Journal of Clinical Nutrition*, 79, 537–43.

Bregin, P. (1997) *Brain Disabling Treatments in Psychiatry*. New York: Springer.

Bricker, J.B., Peterson, A.V., Andersen, M.R., Rajan, K.B, Leroux, B.G. and Sarason, I.G. (2006) Childhood friends who smoke: do they influence adolescents to make smoking transitions? *Addictive Behaviors*, 31(5), 889–900.

Bricker, J.B., Rajan, K.B., Zalewski, M., Andersen, M.R., Ramey, M. and Peterson, A.V. (2009) Psychological and social risk factors in adolescent smoking transitions: a population-based longitudinal study. *Health Psychology*, 28(4), 439–47.

Brimacombe, C., Quinton, N., Nance, N. and Garrioch, L. (1997) Is age irrelevant? Perceptions of young and old eyewitnesses. *Law and Human Behaviour*, 21, 619–34.

British Psychological Society (2009) *Ethical Principles.* Leicester: British Psychological Society.

Brochet, F. and Dubourdieu, D. (2001) Wine descriptive language supports cognitive specificity of chemical senses. *Brain Language*, 77, 187–96.

Bruce, V. and Young A. (1986) Understanding face recognition. *British Journal of Psychology*, 77(3), 305–27.

Bruce, V. and Young, A. (1998) *In the Eye of the Beholder: The Science of Face Perception*. New York: Oxford University Press.

Brunsdon, R., Coltheart, M., Nickels, L. and Joy, P. (2006) Developmental prosopagnosia: a case analysis and treatment study. *Cognitive Neuropsychology*, 23, 822–40.

Bryman, A. (2007) *Quantity and Quality in Social Research*. London: Taylor and Francis.

Buchanan, K., Anand, P., Joffe, H. and Thomas, K. (2007) Perceiving and understanding the social world. In D. Miell, A. Phoenix and K. Thomas (eds), *Mapping Psychology, Volume 2*. Milton Keynes: Open University Press.

Bum, D. (1998) Stress, attention and sports injury. http://vuir. vu.edu.au/15445/ (accessed 1 March 2013).

Burkhauser, R. and Cawley, J. (2007) The value of more accurate measures of fatness and obesity in social science research. *Journal of Health Economics*, 27(2), 519–29.

Buss, D.M. (1989) Sex differences in human mate preferences: evolutionary hypotheses tested in 37 cultures. *Behavioural & Brian Sciences*, 12, 1–49.

Bussey, K. and Bandura A. (1984) Influence of gender constancy and social power on sex-linked modelling. *Journal of Personality and Social Psychology*, 47, 1292–1302.

Butow, P.N., Coates, A.S. and Dunn, S.M. (1999) Psychosocial predictors of survival in metastatic melanoma. *Journal of Clinical Oncology*, 17(7), 2256.

Byrne, D. (1971) *The Attraction Paradigm*. New York: Academic Press.

Campbell, A. (2008) Attachment, aggression and affiliation: the role of oxytocin in female social behaviour. *Biological Psychology*, 77(1), 1–10.

Campbell, A., Shirley, L. and Candy, J. (2004) A longitudinal study of gender-related cognition and behaviour. *Developmental Science*, 7(1), 1–9.

Campbell, A., Shirley, L., Heywood, C. and Crook, C. (2000) Infants' visual preference for sex congruent babies, children, toys and activities: a longitudinal study. *British Journal of Psychology*, 18, 479–98.

Campos, J., Haith, M. and Tucker, P. (1972) Infants' sensitivity to subject contours. Habituation and recovery of visual response in the alert human being. *Journal of Experimental Child Development*, 13, 339–49.

Carnagey, N.L., Anderson, C.A. and Bushman, B.J. (2007) The effect of video game violence on physiological sensitization to real-life violence. *Journal of Experimental Social Psychology*, 43, 489–96.

Carron, A.V. (1982) Cohesiveness in sports groups: interpretations and considerations. *Journal of Sports Psychology*, 4, 123–83.

Carron, A., Bray, S. and Eys, M. (2002) Team cohesion and team success in sport. *Journal of Sports Sciences*, 20(2), 119–26.

Casanas, G. (2010) UN: wartime rape no more inevitable, acceptable than mass murder. In A.E. Kazdin (2011), Conceptualizing the challenge of reducing interpersonal violence. *Psychology of Violence*, 1(3), 166–87.

Caspi, A., McClay, J., Moffitt, T.E., Mill, J., Martin, J., Craig, I., Poulton, R. and Taylor, A. (2002) Role of genotype in the cycle of violence in maltreated children. *Science*, 297(5582), 851–54.

Caspi, A., Sugden, K. and Moffitt, T. (2005) Influence of life stress on depression: moderation by a polymorphism in the 5-HTT gene. *Science*, 301, 386–89.

Centers for Disease Control and Prevention (2010) *Overweight and Obesity*. NCHS Data Brief 82.

Chang, S. and Hynie, M. (2011) Effects of life stress, social support, and cultural norms on parenting styles among mainland Chinese, European Canadian, and Chinese Canadian immigrant mothers. *Journal of Cross-Cultural Psychology*, 42(6), 944–62.

Chao-Cheng, L., Yu-Chuan, L., Ya-Mei, B., Mei-Chun, H., Shih-Jen, T., Chia-Hsuan, W., Wen-Chen, O.-Y. and Chia-Yih, L. (2002) Test-retest reliability of internet-based self-assessment program for depression. *Proceedings of the AMIA Symposium*, 1083.

Charlton, T., Gunter, B. and Hannan, A. (2002) *Broadcast Television Effects in a Remote Community*. Mahwah, NJ: Lawrence Erlbaum Associates.

Chen, T., Lan, T., Yang, C. and Yuang, K. (2006) Postpartum mood disorders may be related to a decreased insulin level after delivery. *Medical Hypotheses*, 66(4), 820–23.

Chepko-Sade, B., Reitz, K. and Sade, D. (1989) Sociometrics of Macaca mulatta IV. Network analysis of social structure of a pre-fission group. *Social Networks*, 11, 293–314.

Chida, Y. and Steptoe, A. (2009) Cortisol awakening response and psychosocial factors: a systematic review and meta-analysis. *Biological Psychology*, 80(3), 265–78.

Choi, P., Parrott, A. and Cowan, D. (2004) High-dose anabolic steroids in strength athletes: effects upon hostility and aggression. *Human Psychopharmacology*, 5, 349–56.

Christensen, R., Kristensen, P., Bartels, E., Bliddal, H. and Astrup, H. (2007) Efficacy and safety of the weight loss drug Rimonabant: a meta-analysis of randomized trials. *The Lancet*, 370(9600), 1706–13.

Christianson, S. and Hubinette, B. (1993) Hands up! A study of witnesses' emotional reactions and memories associated with bank robberies. *Applied Cognitive Psychology*, 7(5), 365–79.

Chua, A. (2011) *Battle Hymn of the Tiger Mother*. London: Bloomsbury.

Cialdini, B., Guadagno, R.E., Asher, T. and Demaine, L.J. (2001) When saying yes leads to saying no: preference for consistency and the reverse foot in the door effect. *Personality and Social Psychology Bulletin*, 27(7), 859–67.

Cindy, H. and Lindner, K. (2005) Motivational orientations in youth sport participation: using goal achievement theory and reversal theory. *Personality and Individual Differences*, 38(3), 605–18.

Claridge, G. and Davis, C. (2003) *Personality and Psychological Disorders*. London: Arnold.

Clark, D. (1992) The assessment of unwanted intrusive thoughts: a review and critique of the literature. *Behaviour Research and Therapy*, 33(8), 967–76.

Clark, R.D. III (1998) Minority influence: the role of the rate of majority defection and persuasive arguments. *European Journal of Social Psychology*, 28, 787–96.

Clark, R.D. III (1999) The effect of majority defectors and number of persuasive minority arguments on minority influence. *Representative Research in Social Psychology*, 23, 15–21.

Clark, R.D. and Hatfield, E. (1989) Gender differences in receptivity to sexual offers. *Journal of Psychology and Human Sexuality*, 2(1), 39–55.

Coakley, J. (1992) Burnout among adolescent athletes: a personal failure or social problem? *Sociology of Sport Journal*, 9(3), 271–85.

Cochrane, R. (1977) Mental illness in immigrants to England and Wales: an analysis of mental hospital admissions. *Journal of Social Psychiatry*, 12, 25–35.

Cohen, A.B., Li, Y., Johnson, K., Williams, M.J., Knowles, E.D. and Chen, Z. (2011) Fundamental(ist) attribution error: Protestants are dispositionally focused. Journal of Personality and Social Psychology, 102(2), 281–90.

Cohen, G. and Faulkner, D. (1989) Age differences in source forgetting: effects on reality monitoring and on eyewitness testimony. *Psychology and Aging*, 4, 10–17.

Cohen, S., Kamarck, T. and Mermelstein, R. (1983) A global measure of perceived stress. *Journal of Health and Social Behavior*, 24, 385–96.

Cohen, S., Tyrell, D.A. and Smith, A.P. (1991) Psychological stress and susceptibility to the common cold. *New England Journal of Medicine*, 325, 606–12.

Cole, E.M. and Wertsch, J.V. (1996) Beyond the individual social antinomy in discussions of Piaget and Vygotsky. In M.K. Damianova and B.G. Sullivan (2011), Rereading Vygotsky's theses on types of internalization and verbal mediation, *Review of General Psychology*, 15(4), 344–50.

Coleman, J. and Hendry, L. (1990) *The Nature of Adolescence*, 2nd edition. London: Routledge.

Cordioli, A. (2008) A randomized clinical trial of cognitive-behavioural group therapy and sertraline in the treatment of obsessive-compulsive behaviour. *Journal of Clinical Psychology*, 67(7), 1133–39.

Cousins, S.D. (1989) Culture and self-perception in Japan and the United States. *Journal of Personality and Social Psychology*, 56(1), 124–31.

Cox, M. (1992) Children's drawings of the human figure. *Child Development*, 67(6), 2743–62.

Cranny-Francis, A., Waring, W., Stavropoulos, P. and Kirkby, J. (2003) *Gender Studies: Terms and Debates*. Basingstoke: Palgrave Macmillan.

Creel, M. (1980) Short-term goals in sequential order leading up to a long-term goal. In J. Silva and R. Weinberg (eds) *Psychological Foundations of Sport*. Champaign, IL: Human Kinetics.

Creem-Regehr, S., Willemsen, P., Gooch, A. and Thompson, W. (2003) The influence of restricted viewing conditions on egocentric distance perception: implications for real and virtual environments. *Perception*, 34(2), 191–204.

Cropley, M., Ayers, S. and Nokes, L. (2003) People don't exercise because they can't think of reasons to exercise: an examination of causal reasoning within the trans-theoretical model. *Psychology, Health and Medicine*, 8(4), 409–14.

Cruz, J.E., Emery, R.E. and Turkheimer, E. (2012) Peer network drinking predicts increased alcohol use from adolescence to early adulthood after controlling for genetic and shared environmental selection. *Developmental Psychology*, 48(5), 1390–1402.

Cserjesi, R., Molnar, D., Luminet, O., Lenard, L. (2007) Is there any relationship between obesity and mental flexibility in children? *Appetite*, 49, 675–78.

Cunningham, M.R. (1986) Measuring the physical in physical attractiveness: quasi-experiments on the socio-biology of female facial beauty. *Journal of Personality and Social Psychology*, 50(5), 925–35.

D'Arripe-Longueville, F., Fournier, J. and Dubois, A. (1998) The perceived effectiveness of interactions between expert French judo coaches and elite female athletes. *Sport Psychologist*, 12, 317–32.

Dailey, M. and Cottrell, G. (1999) Organization of face and object recognition in modular neural networks. *Neural Networks*, 12, 1053–73.

Daly, J., Brewer, B.W., Van Raalte, J.L., Petitpas, A.J., and Sklar, J.H. (1995) Cognitive appraisal, emotional adjustment and adherence to rehab following knee surgery. *Journal of Sport Rehabilitation*, 4, 23–30.

Damianova, M.K. and Sullivan, G.B. (2011) Rereading Vygotsky's theses on types of internalization and verbal mediation. *Review of General Psychology*, 15(4), 344–50.

Daniel, B. and Wassell, S. (2002) *Adolescence: Assessing and Promoting Resilience in Vulnerable Children 3*. London: Jessica Kingsley.

Darley, J.M. and Gross, P.H. (1983) A hypothesis confirming bias in labelling effects. *Journal of Personality and Social Psychology*, 44, 20–33.

Darley, J.M. and Latane, B. (1968) Bystander intervention in emergencies: diffusion of responsibility. *Journal of Personality and Social Psychology*, 8, 377–83.

Darwin, C. (1859) *The Origin of Species by Means of Natural Selection*. London: John Murray.

Das, A., Olfson, M., McCurtis, H. and Weissman, M. (2006) Depression in African Americans: breaking barriers to detection and treatment. Journal of Family Practice, 55(1), 30–39.

Dasen, P.R. (1994) Culture and cognitive development from a Piagetian perspective. In W.J. Lonner and R.S. Malpass (eds), *Psychology and Culture*. Boston: Allyn & Bacon.

Daubenmier, J. and Epel, E. (2011) Mindfulness intervention for stress eating to reduce cortisol and abdominal fat among overweight and obese women: an exploratory randomized controlled study. *Journal of Obesity*, 2011, article ID 651936.

Davison, G. and Neale, J. (1994) *Abnormal Psychology*. New York: Wiley.

Dawkins, R. (1976) *The Selfish Gene*. New York: Oxford University Press.

Day, J., Ternouth, A. and Collier, D.A. (2009) Eating disorders and obesity: two sides of the same coin? *Epidemiologia e Psichiatria Sociale*, 18(02), 96–100.

De Boer, M.F., Ryckman, R.M., Pruyn, J.F.A. and Van den Borne, H.W. (1999) Psychosocial correlates of cancer relapse and survival: a literature review. *Patient Education and Counseling*, 37(3), 215–30.

De Craen, A., Roos, P., De Vries, A. and Kleijnen, J. (1996) Effect of colour of drugs: systematic review of perceived effect of drugs and of their effectiveness. *British Medical Journal*, 313(7072), 1624–26.

De Jong-Meyer, R. and Hautzinger, M. (1996) Results of two multicenter treatment studies among patients with endogenous and nonendogenous depression: conclusions and prospects. *Zeitschrift fuer Linische Psychologie*, 25(2), 155–60.

De Mathis, M., Diniz, J., Hounie, A., Shavitt, R., Fossaluza, V., Ferrao, Y., Leckman, J., De Braganca Pereira, C., Do Rosario, M. and Miguel, E. (2011) Trajectory in obsessive-compulsive disorder comorbidities. http://www.researchgate.net/publication/230760566_de_Mathis_MA_et_al._Trajectory_in_obsessive-compulsive_disorder_comorbidities (accessed 14 March 2013).

De Waal, F. (2008) Putting the altruism back into altruism: the evolution of empathy. *Annual Review of Psychology*, 59, 279–300.

Deacon, B. and Abramovitz, J. (2004) The Yale-Brown Obsessive Compulsive Scale: factor analysis, construct validity, and suggestions for refinement. *Journal of Anxiety Disorders*, 19, 573–85.

Deci, E. (1971) Effects of externally mediated rewards on intrinsic motivation. *Journal of Personality and Social Psychology*, 18, 105–15.

Deffenbacher, K. (1983) The influence of arousal on reliability of testimony. In Lloyd-Bostock, S. and B. Clifford (eds), *Evaluating Witness Evidence* (235–51). Chichester: Wiley.

Deffenbacher, K. (2004) A meta-analytic review of the effects of high stress on eyewitness testimony. *Law and Human Behaviour*, 28(6), 687–706.

Delvenne, J., Seron, X., Coyette, F. and Rossion, B. (2003) Evidence for perceptual deficits in associative visual (prosop) agnosia: a single case study. *Neuropsychologica*, 42, 597–612.

Dement, W. and Kleitman, N. (1957) The relation of eye movements during sleep to dream activity: an objective method for the study of dreaming. *Journal of Experimental Psychology*, 53(5), 339–46.

Department of Health (2001) A systematic review of controlled trials of the effectiveness and cost-effectiveness of brief psychological treatments for depression. *Health Technology Assessment*, 5(35), 1–6.

Der, G. Batty, G.D. and Deary, I.J. (2006) Effect of breast feeding on intelligence in children: prospective study, sibling pairs analysis, and meta-analysis. *British Medical Journal*, 333(7575), 945.

Deregowski, J. (1972) Pictorial perception and culture. *Scientific American*, 227, 82–88.

Deutsch, M. and Gerard, H.B. (1955) A study of normative and informational social influences upon individual judgement. *Journal of Abnormal and Social Psychology*, 51, 629–36.

Devlin Committee Report (1976) *Report of the Committee on Evidence of Identification in Criminal Cases*. 1976 Cmnd 338 134/135, 42.

Di Chiara, G. and Imperato, A. (1988) Drugs abused by humans preferentially increase synaptic dopamine concentrations in the mesolimbic system of freely moving rats. *Proceedings of the National Academy of Sciences of the USA*, 85, 5274–78.

Di Nardo, P. and Barlow, D. (1987) Anxiety disorders interview schedule – revised (ADIS-R). Albany, NY: Phobias and Anxiety Disorders Clinic, State University of New York.

DiClemente, C.C. and Prochoska, J.O. (1982) Self change and therapy change of smoking behaviour: a comparison of processes of change in cessation and maintenance. In J. Ogden (2005), Health Psychology. Maidenhead: Open University Press.

DiClemente, C., Prochaska, J.O. and Fairhurst, S.K. (1991) The process of smoking cessation: an analysis of precontemplation, contemplation, and preparation stages of change. *Journal of Consulting and Clinical Psychology*, 59(2), 295–304.

DiPietro, L. (1999) Physical activity in the prevention of obesity: current evidence and research issues. *Medicine and Science in Sports and Exercise*, 31(11), 542–46.

Dixson, B.J., Grimshaw, G.M., Linklater, W.L. and Dixson, A.F. (2011) Eye-tracking of men's preferences for waist-to-hip ratio and breast size of women. *Archives of Sexual Behaviour*, 40(1), 43–50.

Dolin, D.J. and Booth-Butterfield, S. (1995) Foot in the door and cancer prevention. *Health Communication*, 7(1), 55–66.

Donaldson, M. (1978) *Children's Minds*. London: Fontana.

Duck, S. (1992) *Human Relationships*, 2nd edition. London: Sage.

Dunn, J., Kendrick, C. and Macnamee, R. (1981) The reaction of first-born children to the birth of a sibling: mothers' reports. *Journal of Child Psychology and Psychiatry*, 22, 1–18.

Dunphy, D.C. (1963) The social structure of urban adolescent peer groups. *Sociometry*, 26, 230–56.

Dupuis, S.L. (1999) Naked truths: towards a reflexive methodology in leisure research. *Leisure Sciences*, 21(1), 43–64.

Dutton, D. and Aron, A. (1974) Some evidence for heightened sexual attraction under conditions of high anxiety. *Journal of Personality and Social Psychology*, 30, 510–17.

Egan, S.E. and Perry, D.G. (2001) Gender identity: a multidimensional analysis with implications for psychosocial adjustment. *Developmental Psychology*, 37(4), 451–63.

Eisenberg, N. and Mussen, P.H. (1989) *The Roots of Prosocial Behaviour in Children*. Cambridge: Cambridge University Press.

Elardo, R., Bradley, R. and Caldwell, B.M. (1975) The relation of infants' home environments to mental test performance from six to thirty-six months: a longitudinal analysis. *Child Development*, 46, 71–76.

Elias, M., Elias, J. and Elias, P. (1990) Biological health influences on behaviour. In J. Birren and J. Schaie (eds), *Handbook of the Psychology of Aging* (79–102). San Diego, CA: Academic Press.

Elias, M., Elias, P., Sullivan, L., Wolf, P. and D'Agostino, R. (2003) Lower cognitive function in the presence of obesity and hypertension: the Framington heart study. *International Journal of Obesity*, 27, 260–68.

Engel, G.L. (1977) The need for a new medical model: a challenge of biomedicine. In J. Ogden (2005), *Health Psychology*. Maidenhead: Open University Press.

Engel, G.L. (1980) The clinical application of the biopsychosocial model. In J. Ogden (2005), *Health Psychology*. Maidenhead: Open University Press.

Ensor, R., Hart, M., Jacobs, L. and Hughes, C. (2011) Gender differences in children's problem behaviours in competitive play with friends. *British Journal of Developmental Psychology*, 29, 176–87.

Epel, E., Lapidus, R., McEwen, B. and Brownell, K. (2001) Stress may add bite to appetite in women: a laboratory study of stress-induced cortisol and eating behaviour *Psychoneuroendocrinology*, 26, 37–49.

Erblich, J., Lerman, C., Self, D.W., Diaz, G.A. and Bovbjerg, D.H. (2005) Effects of dopamine D2 receptor (DRD2) and transporter (SLC6A3) polymorphisms on smoking cue-induced cigarette craving among African-American smokers. *Molecular Psychiatry*, 10(4), 407–14.

Ericsson, K., Krampe, R. and Tesch-Romer, C. (1993) The role of deliberate practice in the acquisition of expert performance. *Psychological Review*, 100, 363–406.

Erikson, E. (1968) *Identity, Youth and Crisis*. New York: W.W. Norton and Co.

Escovar, L. (1974) The cohesion of groups: alternative solutions. Paper presented at the Canadian Sociology and Anthropology Association, Toronto.

Ewing Lee, E.A. and Troop-Gordon, W. (2011) Peer socialization of masculinity and femininity: differential effects of overt and relational forms of peer victimization. *British Journal of Developmental Psychology*, 29, 197–213.

Eysenck, M.W. and Keane, M.T. (1990) *Cognitive Psychology: A Student's Handbook*, 4th edition. New York: Lawrence Erlbaum Associates.

Fagot, B.I., Leinbach, M.D. and O'Boyle, C. (1992) Gender labelling, gender stereotyping, and parenting behaviors. *Developmental Psychology*, 28, 225–30.

Farrow, D. (2008) Challenging traditional practice approaches to skill development. *American Swimming Magazine*, 6, 6–8.

Faust, M.S. (1983) Alternative constructions of adolescent growth. In J. Brooks-Gunn and A.C. Petersen (eds), *Girls at Puberty: Biological and Psychosocial Perspectives* (105–25). New York: Plenum.

Feeney, J.A. and Noller, P. (1992) Attachment style and romantic love: relationship dissolution. *Australian Journal of Psychology*, 44, 69–74.

Feindler, E. and Guttman, J. (1994) Cognitive-behavioural anger control training for groups of adolescents. In C.W. LeCroy (ed.), *Handbook of Child and Adolescent Treatment Manuals* (170–99). New York: Lexington Books.

Feindler, E. and Scalley, M. (1998) Adolescent anger management groups for violence reduction. In K. Stoiber and T.R. Kratochwill, *Handbook of Group Intervention for Children and Families*. Needham Heights, MA: Allyn and Bacon.

Feldman, R., Weller, A., Zagoory-Sharon, O. and Levine, A. (2007) Evidence for a neuroendocrinological foundation of human affiliation plasma oxytocin levels across pregnancy and the postpartum period predict mother–infant bonding. *Psychological Science*, 18(11), 965–70.

Felliti, V. (2001) Sleep eating and the dynamics of morbid obesity, weight loss and regain of weight in 5 patients. *Permanente Journal*, 5(2), 31–34.

Fernandez, I., Gallinari, E. and Lorenzetti, A. (2004) A school-based intervention for children who witnessed the Pirelli building airplane crash in Milan, Italy. *Journal of Brief Therapy*, 2, 129–36.

Fichtenberg, C.M. and Glantz, S.A. (2002) Effect of smoke-free workplaces on smoking behaviour: systematic review. *British Medical Journal*, 27, 325(7357), 188.

Fiske, A.P., Kityama, S., Markus, H.R. and Nisbett, R.E. (1998) The cultural matrix of social psychology. In M.A. Hogg and G.M. Vaughan (2005), *Social Psychology*. Harlow: Pearson Education.

Flament, M., Rapoport, J., Berg, C., Sceery, W., Kilts, C., Mellström, B. and Linnoila, M. (1985) Clomipramine treatment of childhood obsessive-compulsive disorder: a double-blind controlled study. *Archives of General Psychiatry*, 42(10), 977–83.

Flannaghan, T., Sutcliff, L., Rother, L. and Lincoln, N. (1997) Evaluation of cognitive-behavioural treatment for depression after stroke: a pilot study. *Clinical Rehabilitation*, 11, 114–22.

Fleiter, J.J., Lennon, A.J. and Watson, B. (2010) How do other people influence your driving speed? Exploring the 'who' and 'how' of social influences on speeding from a qualitative perspective. *Transportation Research. Part F: Traffic Psychology and Behaviour*, 13(1), 49–62.

Flick, U. (2009) *An Introduction to Qualitative Research*, 4th edition. London: Sage.

Flynn, J.R. (1994) IQ gains over time. In R.J. Sternberg (ed.), *Encyclopedia of Human Intelligence* (617–23). New York: Macmillan.

Foa, E., Kozak, M., Salkovskis, P., Coles, M., Amir, N. (1998) The validation of a new obsessive–compulsive disorder scale: The Obsessive–Compulsive Inventory. *Psychological Assessment*, 10(3), 206–14.

Fontenelle, L., Mendlowicz, M., Marques, C. and Versiani, M. (2004) Trans-cultural aspects of obsessive-compulsive disorder: a description of a Brazilian sample and a systematic review of international clinical studies. *Journal of Psychiatric Research*, 38(4), 403–11.

Foster, R., Libkuman, T., Schooler, J. and Loftus, E. (1994) Consequentiality and eyewitness person identification. *Applied Cognitive Psychology*, 18(2), 107–21.

Franke, W. and Berendonk, B. (1997) Hormonal doping and androgenization of athletes: a secret program of the German Democratic Republic government. *Clinical Chemistry*, 43(7), 1262–79.

Frayling, T., Timpson, N., Weedon, M. and Zeggini, E. (2007) A common variant in the FTO gene is associated with body mass index and predisposes to childhood and adult obesity. *Science*, 316(5826), 889–94.

Freedman, J.L. and Fraser, S.C. (1966) Compliance without pressure: the effect of guilt. In M.A. Hogg and G.M. Vaughan (2005), *Social Psychology*. Harlow: Pearson Education.

Freeman, J., Garcia, A., Coyne, L., Ale, C., Przeworski, A., Himle, M., *et al.* (2008) Early childhood OCD: preliminary findings from a family-based cognitive-behavioural approach. *Journal of the American Academy of Child and Adolescent Psychiatry*, 47(5), 593–602.

Frichtel, M. and Lecuyer, R. (2006) The use of perspective as a depth cue with a 2D display in 4- and 5-month-old infants. *Infant Behaviour and Development*, 30, 409–21.

Friedman, J. (1994) Scientists link obesity to 'thrifty gene' of our ancestors. http://www.questia.com/library/1P2-1748488/scientists-link-obesity-to-thrifty-gene-of-our-ancestors (accessed 14 March 2013).

Friedman, J. (2005) Acute leptin deficiency, leptin resistance and the physiologic response to leptin withdrawal. *Proceedings of the National Academy of Sciences of the USA*, 102(7), 2537–42.

Fruzzetti, A.E., Tolland, K., Teller, S.A. and Loftus, E.F. (1992) Memory and eyewitness testimony. In M.M. Gruneberg and P.E. Morris (eds), *Aspects of Memory: The Practical Aspects* (18–50). London: Academic Press.

Furukawa, T., Geddes, J., Carney, S., Davies, C., Kupfer, D., Frank, E. and Goodwin, G. (2003) Relapse prevention with antidepressant drug treatment in depressive disorders: a systematic review. *The Lancet*, 361, 653–61.

Gallacher, J.E., Sweetnam, P.M., Yarnell, J.W., Elwood, P.C. and Stansfeld, S.A. (2003) Is Type A behavior really a trigger for coronary heart disease events? *Psychosomatic Medicine*, 65(3), 339–46.

Gangestad, S.W., Garver-Apgar, C.E., Simpson, J.A. and Cousins, A.J. (2007) Changes in women's mate preferences across the ovulatory cycle. *Journal of Personality and Social Psychology*, 92(1), 151–63.

Gardner, D., Shields, D. and Bredemeier, B. (1996) The relationship between perceived coaching behaviours and team cohesion among baseball and softball players. *Sport Psychologist*, 10, 367–81.

Gauld, A. and Stephenson, G. (1967) Some experiments relating to Bartlett's theory of remembering. *British Journal of Psychology*, 58, 39–50.

Gauthier, I., Skudlarski, P., Gore, J. and Anderson, A. (2000) Does visual subordinate-level categorization engage the functionally defined fusiform gyrus face area? *Cognitive Neuropsychology*, 17, 143–63.

Gaver, W. (1996) Situating action II: affordances for interaction: the social is material for design. *Ecological Psychology*, 8(2), 111–29.

Gay, J. and Cole, M. (1967) *The New Mathematics and an Old Culture: A Study of Learning Among the Kpelle of Liberia*. New York: Rhinehart SC Winston.

Geller, D., Doyle, R., Shaw, D., Mullin, B., Coffey, B., Petty, C., Vivas, F. and Biederman, J. (2006) A quick and reliable screening measure for OCD in youth: reliability and validity of the obsessive-compulsive scale of the Child Behavior Checklist. *Comprehensive Psychology*, 47(3), 234–40.

George, T., Feltz, D. and Chase, M. (1992) The effects of model similarity on self-efficacy and muscular endurance: a second look. *Journal of Sport and Exercise Psychology*, 14, 237–48.

Geschwind, N. and Galaburda, A.M. (1985) Cerebral lateralization: biological mechanisms, associations, and pathology: I. A hypothesis and a program for research. *Archives of Neurology*, 42(5), 428.

Ghuman, P.A.S. (1994) Canadian or Indo Canadian? A study of South Asian adolescents. In R. Goodwin (1999), *Personal Relationships Across Cultures*. London: Routledge.

Gibson, E. and Walk, R. (1960) The visual cliff. *Scientific American*, 202, 64–71.

Gibson, J. (1950) *The Perception of the Visual World*. Boston, MA: Houghton Mifflin.

Giddings, L.S. (2006) Mixed methods research: positivism dressed in drag? *Journal of Research in Nursing*, 11, 195–203.

Giles, D. (2004) *Media Psychology.* Hove: Psychology Press.

Ginet, M. and Verkampt, F. (2007) The cognitive interview: is its benefit affected by the level of witness emotion? *Memory*, 15(4), 450–64.

Global Initiative to End All Corporal Punishment of Children (GITEACPOC) (2012) States with full abolition. http://www.endcorporalpunishment.org/pages/progress/prohib_states.html (accessed 14 March 2013).

Godden, D. and Baddeley, A. (1975) Context dependent memory in two natural environments: on land and water. *British Journal of Psychology*, 66(3), 325–31.

Godfrey, K.M., Sheppard, A., Gluckman, P.D., Lillycrop, K.A., Burdge, G.C., McLean, C., *et al.* (2011) Epigenetic gene promoter methylation at birth is associated with child's later adiposity. *Diabetes*, 60(5), 1528–34.

Golan, M., Weizman, A., Apter, A. and Fainaru, M. (1998) Parents as the exclusive agents of change in the treatment of childhood obesity. *American Journal of Clinical Nutrition*, 67(6), 1130–35.

Goodman, J. (2003) Paternal postpartum depression, its relationship to maternal postpartum depression, and implications for family health. *Journal of Advanced Nursing*, 45(1), 26–35.

Goodwin, R. (1999) *Personal Relationships Across Cultures.* London: Routledge.

Goodwin, R. (2006) Age and social support perception in Eastern Europe: social change and support in four rapidly changing countries. *British Journal of Social Psychology*, 45(4), 799–815.

Goodwin, R., Adatia, K., Sinhal, H., Cramer, D. and Ellis, P. (1997) Social support and marital wellbeing in an Asian community. In R. Goodwin (1999), *Personal Relationships Across Cultures.* London: Routledge.

Gordon, K., Friedman, M., Miller, I. and Gaertner, L. (2005) Marital attributions as moderators of the marital discord–depression link. *Journal of Social and Clinical Psychology*, 24, 876–93.

Goswami, U. (1998) *Cognition in Children*. Hove: Psychology Press.

Gothelf, D., Presburger, G., Zohar, A., Burg, M., Nahmani, A., Frydman, M., *et al.* (2004) Obsessive-compulsive disorder in patients with velocardiofacial (22q11 deletion) syndrome. *American Journal of Medical Genetics*, 126B(1), 99–105.

Gottfried, A. and Gottfried, A. (1984) *Home Environment and Early Cognitive Development.* Orlando, FL: Academic Press.

Gottman, J. (2002) A two-factor model for predicting when a couple will divorce: exploratory analyses using 14-year longitudinal data, *Family Processes*, 41, 83–96.

Gottman, J.M. and Levenson, R.W (1992) Marital processes predictive of later dissolution: behaviour, physiology and health. *Journal of Personality and Social Psychology*, 63, 221–23.

Gray, D.E. (2009) *Doing Research in the Real World*, 2nd edition. London: Sage.

Gray, R. (2004) Attending to the execution of a complex sensorimotor skill: expertise differences, chokings and slumps. *Journal of Experimental Psychology: Applied*, 10, 42–54.

Green, G., Uryasz, F., Todd, P. and Bray, C. (2001) NCAA study of substance abuse and abuse habits of college-student athletes. *Clinical Journal of Sports Medicine*, 11, 51–56.

Green, S. (1995) *Principles of Biopsychology*. Hove: Psychology Press.

Greenberg, B., Rauch, S. and Haber, S. (2008) Invasive circuitry-based neurotherapeutics: stereotactic ablation and deep brain stimulation for OCD. *Neuropsychopharmacology*, 35(1), 317–36.

Greenberg, D. (2001) Psychology and the injured female athlete. In Swedan, N. (ed.), *Women's Sports Medicine and Rehabilitation* (330–40). Philadelphia, PA: distributed by Lippincott Williams & Wilkins.

Greenberg, D. and Witztum, E. (1994) The influence of cultural factors on obsessive-compulsive disorder: religious symptoms in a religious society. *Israel Journal of Psychiatry and Related Sciences*, 31(3), 211–20.

Greene, J.C., Caracelli, V.J. and Graham, W.E. (1989) Toward a conceptual framework for mixed method evaluation designs, *Educational Evaluation and Policy Analysis*, 11(3), 255–74.

Greenfield, P.M. and Lave, J. (1982) Cognitive aspects of informal education. In K. Durkin, *Developmental Social Psychology.* Oxford: Blackwell.

Gregory, R. (1970) *The Intelligent Eye.* London: Weidenfeld and Nicolson.

Grootheest, D., Cath, D., Beekman, A. and Boomsma, D. (2005) Twin studies on obsessive-compulsive disorder: a review. *Twin Research and Human Genetics*, 8(5), 450–58.

Gross, A. (1982) Athletic skill and social status in children. *Journal of Social and Clinical Psychology*, 2(1), 89–96.

Gunnar, M.R., Fisher, P.A. and the Early Experience, Stress and Prevention Network (2006) Bringing basic research on early experience and stress neurobiology to bear on preventive interventions for neglected and maltreated children. *Developmental Psychopathology*, 18(3), 651–77.

Gupta, U. and Singh, P. (1982) An exploratory study of love and liking and type of marriages. *Indian Journal of Applied Psychology*, 19(2), 92–97.

Gustafsson, H., Hassmen., P, Kentta, G. and Johansson, M. (2007) A qualitative analysis of burnout in elite Swedish athletes. *Psychology of Sport and Exercise*, 9(6), 800–16.

Hahlweg, K., Markman, H.J., Thurmaier, F., Engl, J. and Eckert, V. (1998) Prevention of marital distress: results of a German prospective longitudinal study. *Journal of Family Psychology*, 12(4), 543–56.

Hall, C., Mack, D., Pavio, A. and Hausenblas, H. (1998) Imagery use by athletes: development of the Sport Imagery Questionnaire. *International Journal of Sport Psychology*, 29, 73–89.

Hall, T. (2000) At home with the young homeless. *International Journal of Social Research Methodology*, 3, 121–33.

Hames, R. (1987) Garden labor exchange among the Ye'kwana. *Ethology and Sociobiology*, 8(4), 259–84.

Hames, R. (1988) The allocation of parental care among the Yek'wana. In L. Barrett, R. Dunbar and J. Lycett (2002) *Human Evolutionary Psychology*. Basingstoke: Palgrave Macmillan.

Hamilton, C.E. (1994) Continuity and discontinuity of attachment from infancy through adolescence. In T. Cooper and I. Roth (eds) (2007), *Challenging Psychological Issues*. Milton Keynes: Open University Press.

Hamilton, W.D. (1964) The genetic evolution of social behaviour. *Journal of Theoretical Biology*, 37, 1–52.

Hammersley, M. (1992) *What's Wrong with Ethnography? Methodological Explorations.* New York: Routledge.

Harari, H., Harari, O. and White, R. (1985) The reaction to rape by American male bystanders. *Journal of Social Psychology*, 125(5), 653–58.

Hardy, G. and Legge, D. (1968) Cross-modal induction of changes in sensory thresholds. *Quarterly Journal of Experimental Psychology*, 20(1), 20–29.

Hardy, L., Jones J. and Gould, D. (1996) *Understanding Psychological Preparation for Sport: Theory and Practice of Elite Performers.* Chichester and New York: Wiley.

Harlow, H.F. and Harlow, M.K. (1962) Social deprivation in monkeys. *Scientific American*, 207, 136–46.

Hart, P. (1998) Preventing groupthink revisited: evaluating and reforming groups in government. *Organisational Behaviour and Human Decision Processes*, 73, 2–3.

Harwood, C. (2002) Assessing achievement goals in sport: caveats for consultants and a case for contextualization. *Journal of Applied Sports Psychology*, 14, 106–19.

Hassmen, P. (1998) Overtraining and recovery: a conceptual model. *Sports Medicine*, 26(1), 1–16.

Hauptmann, J., Lucas, C. and Boldrin, M. (2000) Orlistat in the long-term treatment of obesity in primary care settings. *Archives of Family Medicine*, 9, 160–67.

Hay, D.F., Nash, A., Caplan, M., Swartzentruber, J., Ishikawa, F. and Vespo, J.E. (2011) The emergence of gender differences in physical aggression in the context of conflict between young peers. *British Journal of Developmental Psychology*, 29, 158–75.

Hay, D.F., Pawlby, S., Waters, C.S., Perra, O. and Sharp, D. (2010) Mothers' antenatal depression and their children's antisocial outcomes. *Child Development*, 81(1), 149–65.

Hazan, C. and Shaver, P. (1987) Romantic love conceptualized as an attachment process. *Journal of Personality and Social Psychology*, 52(3), 511–24.

Health Development Agency (1997) *The Effectiveness of Health Education Authority Programmes.* London: Health Education Authority.

Heider, F. (1958) *The Psychology of Interpersonal Relations.* New York: Wiley.

Hemond, C.C., Kanwisher, N.G. and de Beeck, H.P.O. (2007) A preference for contralateral stimuli in human object – and face – selective cortex. *PLoS One*, 2(6), e574.

Hersen, M., Bellack, A., Himmelhoch, J. and Thase, M. (1984) Effects of social skills training, amitriptyline and psychotherapy in unipolar depressed women. *Behaviour Therapy*, 15(1), 21–40.

Hill, C.T., Rubin, Z. and Peplau, L.A. (1976) Breakups before marriage: the end of 103 affairs. *Journal of Social Issues*, 32(1) 147–68.

Hines, M. and Kaufmann, F.F. (1994) Androgen and the development of human sex-typical behavior: rough-and-tumble play and sex of preferred playmates in children with congenital adrenal hyperplasia (CAH). *Child Development*, 65, 1042–53.

Hingson, R.W., Strunin, L., Berlin, B.M. and Heeren, T. (1990) Beliefs about AIDS, use of alcohol and drugs, and unprotected sex among Massachusetts adolescents. *American Journal of Public Health*, 80(3), 295–99.

Hirschfield, R. (1999) Efficacy of SSRIs and newer antidepressants in severe depression: comparison with TCAs. *Journal of Clinical Psychiatry*, 60(5), 326–35.

Hodges, J. and Tizard, B. (1989) Social and family relationships of ex-institutional adolescents. *Journal of Child Psychology and Psychiatry*, 30, 77–97.

Hofstede, G. (1980) *Culture's Consequences: International Differences in Work-Related Values.* Beverly Hills, CA: Sage.

Hofstede, G. (2001) *Culture's Consequences: Comparing Values, Behaviors, Institutions, and Organizations Across Nations*, 2nd edition. Thousand Oaks, CA: Sage.

Hogg, M.A. and Turner, J.C. (1987) Intergroup behaviour, self-stereotyping and the salience of social categories. *British Journal of Psychology*, 26, 325–40.

Hogg, M.A. and Vaughan, G.M. (2002) *Social Psychology*, 3rd edition. Harlow: Pearson Prentice Hall.

Hogg, M.A. and Vaughan, G.M. (2005) *Social Psychology*, 4th edition. Harlow: Pearson Prentice Hall.

Holland, A.J., Hall, A., Murray, R., Russell, G.F. and Crisp, A.H. (1984) Anorexia nervosa: a study of 34 twin pairs and one set of triplets. *British Journal of Psychiatry*, 145, 414–19.

Holme, A., MacArthur, C. and Lancashire, R. (2009) The effects of breastfeeding on cognitive and neurological development of children at 9 years. *Child: Care, Health and Development*, 36(4), 583–90.

Hong, E., Ko, H., Cho, Y., Kim, H., Ma, Z., Yu, T., *et al.* (2009) Interleukin-10 prevents diet-induced insulin resistance by attenuating microphage and cytokine response in skeletal muscle. *Diabetes*, 58, 2525–35.

Horwath, E. and Weissman, M. (2000) The epidemiology and cross-national presentation of obsessive-compulsive disorder. *Psychiatric Clinics of North America*, 23(3), 493–507.

Houghton, S., Curran, J. and Ekers, D. (2008) Behavioural activation in the treatment of depression. *Mental Health Practice*, 14(7), 18–23.

Houston, S. (2010) Building resilience in a children's home: results from an action research projects. *Child and Family Social Work*, 15, 357–68.

Howe, B. (1984) The coaching preferences of elite athletes competing at Universiade '83. *Canadian Journal of Applied Sports Sciences*, 9(4), 201–08.

Hu, B. (2003) Television watching and other sedentary behaviours in relation to risk of obesity and type 2 diabetes mellitus in women. *Journal of the American Medical Association*, 289(14), 1785–91.

Hudson, W. (1960) Pictorial depth perception in sub-cultural groups in Africa. *Journal of Social Psychology*, 52, 183–208.

Huesmann, L.R. (1986) Psychological processes promoting the relation between exposure to violent media and aggressive behavior by the viewer. *Journal of Social Issues*, 42, 125–40.

Huesmann, L.R. (2010) Nailing the coffin shut on doubts that violent video games stimulate aggression: comment on Anderson *et al.* (2010). *Psychological Bulletin*, 136(2), 179–81.

Huesmann, L.R., Moise, J., Podolski, C.P. and Eron, L.D. (2003) Longitudinal relations between childhood exposure to media violence and adult aggression and violence: 1977–1992. *Developmental Psychology*, 39, 201–21.

Hughes, M. (1975) *Egocentrism in Preschool Children*. Unpublished doctoral dissertation. Edinburgh University.

Hull, C.L. (1943) *Principles of Behaviour*. New York: Appleton, Century Crofts.

Humphreys G. and Riddoch, M. (1987) *To See, But Not to See: A Case Study of Visual Agnosia*. Hillsdale, New York: Lawrence Erlbaum.

Imagen Consortium, a European research project on risk-taking behaviour in teenagers. http://www.imagen-europe.com/en/consortium.php (accessed 17 March 2013).

Ingham, A. (1974) The Ringelmann effect: studies of group size and group performance. *Journal of Experimental Social Psychology*, 10, 371–84.

IBO (2011) *Extended Essay Guide*. The Hague, Netherlands: International Baccalaureate Organisation.

Jacob, S., McClintock, M.K., Zelano, B. and Ober, C. (2002) Paternally inherited HLA alleles are associated with women's choice of male odor. *Nature Genetics*, 30, 175–79.

Jacobs, J.R. (2009) Re-examining the long-term effects of experiencing parental death in childhood on adult psychopathology. *Journal of Nervous and Mental Disease*, 197(1), 24–27.

Jacobsen, E. (1930) Electrical measurements of neuromuscular states during mental activities. I. Imagination of movement involving skeletal muscles. *American Journal of Physiology*, 91, 547–608.

Jahoda, M. (1958) *Current Concepts of Positive Mental Health*. New York: Basic Books.

James, W. (1894) and Lange, C. (1885). In W. Cannon (1927), The James–Lange theory of emotions: a critical examination and an alternative theory. *American Journal of Psychology*, 39(1/4), 106–24.

Janis, I.L. (1972) *Victims of Groupthink: A Psychology Study of Foreign-policy Decisions and Fiascos*. Boston: Houghton Mifflin.

Jeffery, R. (2001) Environmental influences on eating and physical activity. *Annual Review of Public Health*, 22, 329–35.

Jeffery, R., Baxter, J., McGuire, M. and Linde, J. (2006) Are fast food restaurants an environmental risk factor for obesity? *International Journal of Behavioural Nutrition and Physical Activity*, 3, 2.

Jenner, E. (1798) *An Inquiry into the Causes and Effects of the Variolae Vaccinae: A Disease Discovered in Some of the Western Counties of England, Particularly Gloucestershire, and Known by the Name of the Cow Pox*. London: Sampson Low.

Johnson, J.G., Cohen, P., Smailes, E.M., Kasen, S. and Brook, J.S. (2002) Television viewing and aggressive behavior during adolescence and adulthood. *Science*, 295(5564), 2468–71.

Johnston V.S., Hagel, R., Franklin, M., Fink, B. and Grammer, K. (2001) Male facial attractiveness – evidence for hormone-mediated adaptive design. *Evolution and Human Behavior*, 22, 251–67.

Jones, A. (2011) A model of the impact of smoking bans on smoking with evidence from bans in England and Scotland. ECRS Conference paper. http://www.esrc.ac.uk/my-esrc/grants/RES-060-25-0045/outputs/read/b51f37c0-8488-48ba-8fe0-047eef8459c6 (accessed 19 March 2013).

Jones, B., Wells, L., Peters, R. and Johnson, D. (1993) *Guide to Effective Coaching: Principles and Practice*, 3rd edition. Boston: WCB McGraw-Hill.

Jones, E.E. and Davis, K.E. (1965) From acts to dispositions: the attribution process in person perception. In D. Miell, A. Phoenix and K. Thomas (eds), *Mapping Psychology, Volume 2*. Milton Keynes: Open University Press.

Jones, E.E. and Harris, V.A. (1967) The attribution of attitudes. *Journal of Experimental Social Psychology*, 3(1), 1–24.

Jones, F. and Bright, J. (2001) *Stress – Myth, Theory and Research*. Harlow: Pearson Education.

Jonsson, J. and Hougaard, E. (2009) Group cognitive-behavioural therapy for obsessive-compulsive disorder: a systematic review and meta-analysis. *Acta Psychiatrica Scandanavica*, 119, 98–106.

Jurges, H. (2008) Self-assessed health, reference levels and mortality. *Applied Economics*, 40(5), 569–82.

Kadi, F., Ericsson, A., Holmner, S., Butler-Browne, G. and Thornell, L.-E. (1999) Cellular adaptation of the trapezius muscle in strength-trained athletes. *Histochemistry and Cell Biology*, 111, 189–95.

Kagitcibasi, C. and Berry, J. (1989) Cross-cultural psychology: current research and trends. *Annual Review of Psychology*, 40, 493–531.

Kahn, B. and Flier, J. (2000) Obesity and insulin resistance. *Journal of Clinical Investigation*, 106(4), 473–81.

Kandel, D.B. (1978) Similarity in real-life adolescent friendship pairs. *Journal of Personality and Social Psychology*, 36, 306–12.

Kanner, A.D., Coyne, J.C., Schaefer, C. and Lazarus, R.S. (1981) Comparison of two modes of stress measurement: daily hassles and uplifts versus major life events. *Journal of Behavioural Measurement*, 4, 1–39.

Kanwisher, N., McDermott, J. and Chun, M. (1997) The fusiform face area: a module in human extrastriate cortex specialized for face recognition. *Journal of Neuroscience*, 17, 4302–11.

Karney, B.R. and Bradbury, T.N. (1995) Assessing longitudinal change in marriage: an introduction to the analysis of growth curves. *Journal of Marriage and the Family*, 57, 1091–108.

Kazdin, A.E. (2011) Conceptualizing the challenge of reducing interpersonal violence. *Psychology of Violence*, 1(3), 166–87.

Keating, D. (1979) Adolescent thinking. In J. Adelson (ed.), *Handbook of Adolescent Psychology*. New York: Wiley.

Kelley, H.H. (1967) Attribution theory in social psychology. In K. Buchanan, P. Anand and H. Joffe (2002), Perceiving and understanding the social world. In D. Miell, A. Phoenix and K. Thomas (eds), *Mapping Psychology* (57–109). Milton Keynes: Open University Press.

Kellman, M., Altenberg, D., Lormes, W. and Steinacker, J. (1997) Assessing stress and recovery in elite rowers during preparation for the World Championships in rowing. *Sport Psychologist*, 15, 151–67.

Kelly, B. and Gill, D. (1993) An examination of personal/situational variables, stress appraisal and burnout in collegiate teacher-coaches. *Research Quarterly for Exercise and Sport*, 64, 94–102.

Kelly, O. (2011) When should my family be integrated into my OCD treatment? http://ocd.about.com/od/treatment/f/When-Should-My-Family-Be-Integrated-Into-My-Ocd-Treatment.htm (accessed 19 March 2013).

Kendler, S., Kendler, M., Gatz, M., Gardner, C. and Pederson, N. (2006) A Swedish national twin study of lifetime major depression. *American Journal of Psychiatry*, 163(1), 109–14.

Kerckhoff, A.C. and Davis, K.E. (1962) Value consensus and need complementarity in mate selection. *American Sociological Review*, 27, 295–303.

Kerr, J. (1991) Arousal-seeking in risk sport participants. *Personality and Individual Differences*, 12, 613–16.

Kerr, J. (1994) *Understanding Soccer Hooliganism*. Maidenhead: Open University Press.

Keyes, K.M., Schulenberg, J.E., O'Malley, P.M., Johnston, L.D., Backman, J.G., Li, G. and Hasin, D. (2012) Birth cohort effects on adolescent alcohol use: the influence of social norms from 1976 to 2007. *Archives of General Psychiatry*, 69(12), 1304–13.

Kiecolt-Glaser, J.K., Garner, W., Speicher, C., Penn, G.M., Holliday, J. and Glaser, R. (1984) Psychosocial modifiers of immunocompetence in medical students. *Psychosomatic Medicine*, 46(1), 7–14.

Kiecolt-Glaser, J.K., Glaser, R., Shuttleworth, E.C., Dyer, C.S., Ogrocki, P. and Speicher, C.E. (1987) Chronic stress and immunity in family caregivers of Alzheimer's disease victims. *Psychosomatic Medicine*, 49(5), 523–35.

Kirsch, I., B.J. Deacon, T.B. Huedo-Medina, A. Scoboria, T.J. Moore and B.T. Johnson (2008) Initial severity and antidepressant benefits: a meta-analysis of data submitted to the Food and Drug Administration. *PLoS Medicine*, 5(2), 45.

Klein, M. (1926) *The Psychological Principles of Early Analysis, The Writings of Melanie Klein, Volume 1*. London: Hogarth Press.

Klimek, V., Stockmeier, C., Overholser, J., Meltzer, H., Kalka, S., Dilley, G. and Ordway, G. (1997) Reduced levels of norepinephrine transporters in the locus coeruleus in major depression. *Journal of Neuroscience*, 17(21), 8451–58.

Knutson, K. (2011) Association between sleep duration and body size differs among three Hispanic groups. *American Journal of Human Biology*, 23(1), 138–41.

Kobasa, S. (1981) Stressful life events, personality, and health: an inquiry into hardiness. *Journal of Personality and Social Psychology*, 37, 1–11.

Kohlberg, L. (1966) A cognitive-developmental analysis of children's sex role concepts and attitudes. In E.E. Maccoby (ed.), *The Development of Sex Differences*. Stanford, CA: Stanford University Press.

Kozulin, A. (2004) Vygotsky's theory in the classroom: introduction. *European Journal of Psychology of Education*, XIX(I), 3–7.

Krackow, E. and Lynne, S. (2003) Is there touch in the game of twister? The effects of innocuous touch and suggestive questions on children's eyewitness memory. *Law and Human Behaviour*, 27, 589–604.

Krahn, G.L., Holn, M.F. and Kime, C. (1995) Incorporating qualitative approaches into clinical child psychology research. *Journal of Clinical Child Psychology*, 24(2), 204–13.

Kroger, J., Martinussen, M. and Marcia, J.E. (2010) Identity status change during adolescence and young adulthood: a meta-analysis. *Journal of Adolescence*, 33(5), 683–98.

Kung, W. (2000) Marital adjustment as a predictor of outcome in individual treatment of depression. *Psychotherapy Research*, 10(3), 267–78.

Kuntz, B. and Lampert, T. (2010) Socioeconomic factors and obesity. *Deutsches Arzteblatt International*, 107(30), 517–22.

Kurdek, L.A. (1992) Relationship stability and relationship satisfaction in cohabiting gay and lesbian couples: a prospective longitudinal test of the contextual and interdependence models. *Journal of Social and Personal Relationships*, 9(1), 125–42.

La Fromboise, T. and Rowe, W. (1983) Skill training for bi-cultural competence: rationale and application. *Journal of Counselling Psychology*, 30(4), 589–95.

Lando, H.A. (1977) Successful treatment of smokers with a broad spectrum, behavioural approach. In J. Ogden (2005), *Health Psychology*. Maidenhead: Open University Press.

Latane, B. (1980) Many hands make light work: the causes and consequences of social loafing. *Journal of Personality and Social Psychology*, 37(6), 822–32.

Latane, B. and Darley, J. (1970) *The Unresponsive Bystander: Why Doesn't He Help?* New York: Appleton-Century-Crofts.

Latane, B. and Nida, S. (1981) Ten years of research on group size and helping. *Psychological Bulletin*, 89(2), 308–24.

Lau, R.R. and Russell, D. (1980) Attributions in the sports pages. *Journal of Personality and Social Psychology*, 39, 29–38.

Lavner, J.A. and Bradbury, T.N. (2012) Why do even satisfied newlyweds eventually go on to divorce? *Journal of Family Psychology*, 26(1), 1–10.

Lazarus, R. (1982) Thoughts on the relations between emotion and cognition. *American Psychologist*, 37(9), 1019–24.

Lazarus, R. and McCleary, R. (1951) Autonomic discrimination without awareness: a study of subception. *Psychological Review*, 58(2), 113–22.

Leckman, J. and Chittenden, E. (1990) Gilles de la Tourette's syndrome and some forms of obsessive-compulsive disorder may share a common genetic diathesis. *L'encephale*, XVI, 321–23.

Leeper, R. (1935) A study of the neglected portion of the field of learning: the development of sensory organization. *Journal of Genetic Psychology*, 46, 41–75.

Leman, P.J. and Tenenbaum, H.R. (2011) Practising gender: children's relationships and the development of gendered behaviour and beliefs. *British Journal of Developmental Psychology*, 29, 153–57.

Lemmens, G., Eisler, I., Buysse, A., Heene, E. and Demyttenaere, K. (2009) The effects on mood of adjunctive single family group therapy in the treatment of hospitalized patients with major depression. *Psychotherapy and Psychosomatics*, 78, 98–105.

Lenane, M., Swedo, S., Leonard, H., Pauls, D., Sceery, W. and Rapoport, J. (1990) Psychiatric disorders in first degree relatives of children and adolescents with obsessive-compulsive disorder. *Journal of the American Academy of Child and Adolescent Psychiatry*, 29(3), 407–12.

Lerman, C., Audrain, J., Main, D., Boyd, N., Caporaso, N., Bowman, E., Lockshin, B. and Shields, P. (1999) Evidence suggesting the role of specific genetic factors in cigarette smoking. *Health Psychology*, 18(1), 14–20.

Levine, M., Prosser, A., Evans, D. and Reicher, S. (2005) Identity and emergency intervention: how social group membership and inclusiveness of group boundaries shapes helping behaviour. *Personality and Social Psychology Bulletin*, 31, 443–53.

Levy, M.B. and Davis, K.E. (1988) Lovestyles and attachment styles compared: their relations to each other and to various relationship characteristics. *Journal of Social and Personal Relationships*, 5(4), 439–71.

Lindsay, M., Crino, R. and Andrews, G. (1997) Controlled trial of exposure and response prevention in obsessive-compulsive disorder. *British Journal of Psychiatry*, 171, 135–39.

Linssen, H. and Hagendoorn, L. (1994) Social and geographical factors in the explanation of the content of European nationality stereotypes. *British Journal of Social Psychology*, 33(2), 165–82.

Litzinger, S. and Gordon, K. (2005) Exploring relationships among communication, sexual satisfaction, and marital satisfaction. *Journal of Sex* and *Marital Therapy*, 31, 409–24.

Liu, H., Jin, J., Tang, J., Sun, W., Jia, H., Yang, X., *et al.* (2008) Preclinical study: Chronic deep brain stimulation in the rat nucleus accumbens and its effect on morphine reinforcement. *Addiction Biology*, 13(1), 40–46.

Liu, J.H., Campbell, S.M. and Condie, H. (1995) Ethnocentrism in dating preferences for an American sample: the in-group bias in social context. In M.A. Hogg and G.M. Vaughan (2005), *Social Psychology*, 4th edition. Harlow: Pearson Prentice Hall.

Locke, E. and Latham, G. (1990) *A theory of goal setting and task performance*. Englewood Cliffs, New Jersey, USA: Prentice Hall Inc.

Locke, E. and Latham, G. (1985) The application of goal setting to sports. *Journal of Sport Psychology*, 7, 205–22.

Loftus, E. (1975) Leading questions and the eyewitness report. *Cognitive Psychology*, 7(4), 560–72.

Loftus, E., Loftus, G. and Messo, J. (1987) Some facts about weapons focus. *Law and Human Behaviour*, 11, 55–62.

Loftus, E. and Palmer, J. (1974) Reconstruction of automobile destruction: an example of the interaction between language and memory. *Journal of Verbal Learning and Verbal Behaviour*, 13(5), 585–89.

Loftus, E. and Pickrell, J. (2003) False memories in childhood. http://unisci.com/stories/20012/0613011.htm (accessed 14 March 2013).

Logothetis, N. and Pauls, J. (1995) Shape representation in the inferior temporal cortex of monkeys. *Current Biology*, 5, 552–63.

Lomax, C., Oldfield, V. and Salkovskis, P. (2009) Clinical and treatment comparisons between adults with early- and late-onset obsessive-compulsive disorder. *Behaviour Research and Therapy*, 47(2), 99–104.

Lonsdale, A.J. and North, A.C. (2009) Musical taste and in-group favouritism. *Group Processes & Intergroup Relations*, 12(3), 319–27.

Lorant, V., Deliege, D., Eaton, W., Robert, A., Philippot, A. and Annseau, M. (2003) Socioeconomic inequalities in depression: a meta-analysis. *American Journal of Epdemiology*, 157(2), 98–112.

Lorenz, K.Z. (1935) The companion in the bird's world. *Auk*, 54, 245–73.

Lowe, M. and Timko, C. (2004) What a difference a diet makes: towards an understanding of differences between restrained dieters and restrained non-dieters. *Eating Behaviours*, 5, 199–208.

Lusher, J.M., Chandler, C. and Ball, D. (2001) Dopamine D4 receptor gene (DRD4) is associated with novelty seeking (NS) and substance abuse: the saga continues. *Molecular Psychiatry*, 6, 497–99.

Luthar, S.S. (2000) The construct of resilience: a critical evaluation and guidelines for future work. *Child Development*, 71(3), 543–62. http://www.ncbi.nlm.nih.gov/pmc/articles/PMC1885202/ (accessed 15 March 2013).

Luthar, S.S., Cicchetti, D. and Becker, B. (2003) The construct of resilience: a critical evaluation and guidelines for future work. *Child Development*, 71(3), 543–62.

Lyle, J. (2002) Sports coaching concepts: a framework for coaches' behavior. New York: Routledge.

Lytton, H. and Romney, D.M. (1991) Parents' differential socialisation of boys and girls: a meta-analysis. *Psychological Bulletin*, 109, 267–92.

Maccoby, E.E. (1980) *Social Development: Psychological Growth and the Parent–Child Relationship*. San Diego, CA: Harcourt Brace Jovanovich.

Madsen, E.A., Tunney, R.J., Fieldman, G., Plotkin, H.C., Dunbar, R.I.M., Richardson, J. and McFarland, D. (2007) Kinship and altruism: a cross-cultural experimental study. *British Journal of Psychology*, 98(2), 339–59.

Maggard, M., Shugarman, L., Suttorp, M., Maglione, M., Sugerman, H.J., Livingston, E.H., *et al.* (2005) Meta-analysis: surgical treatment of obesity. *Annals of Internal Medicine*, 142, 547–59.

Maguire, E.A., Woollett, K. and Spiers, H.J. (2006) London taxi drivers and bus drivers: a structural MRI and neuropsychological analysis. *Hippocampus*, 16(12), 1091–1101.

Main, M. and Hesse, E. (1990) Parents' unresolved traumatic experiences are related to infant disorganized attachment status: is frightened and/or frightening parental behaviour the linking mechanism? In M.T. Greenberg, D. Cicchetti and E.M. Cummings (eds), *Attachment in the Preschool Years*. Chicago: University of Chicago Press.

Main, M. and Solomon, J. (1990) Procedures for identifying infants as disorganised/disoriented during the Ainsworth Strange Situation. In M.T. Greenberg, D. Cicchetti and E.M. Cummings (eds) (1993) Attachment in the Preschool Years: Theory, Research, and Intervention. Chicago: University of Chicago Press.

Mainwaring, L., Krasnow, D. and Kerr, G. (2001) And the dance goes on: psychological impact of injury. *Journal of Dance Medicine and Science*, 5(4), 105–15.

Mallett, C. (2005) *Self-determination Theory: A Case Study of Evidence-based Coaching*. Champaign, IL: Human Kinetics.

Mallet, L., Polosan, M., Jaafari, N., Baup, N., Welter, M.-L., Fontaine, D., *et al.* (2008) Subthalamic nucleus stimulation in severe obsessive-compulsive disorder. *New England Journal of Medicine*, 359(8), 33–48.

Mann, J., Malone, K. and Sweeney, J. (1996) Attempted suicide characteristics and cerebrospinal fluid amine metabolites in depressed inpatients. *Neuropsychopharmacology*, 15, 576.

Marazziti, D. (2005) The neurobiology of love. *Current Psychiatry Reviews*, 1(3), 331–35.

Marcia, J.E. (1966) Development and validation of ego-identity status. *Journal of Personality and Social Psychology*, 3. 551–58.

Marcia, J.E. (1980) Identity in adolescence. In D. Miell, A. Phoenix and K. Thomas (eds), *Mapping Psychology*. Milton Keynes: Open University Press.

Margeau, G.A. and Vallerand, R.J. (2003) The coach–athlete relationship: a motivational model. Journal of Sport Sciences, 21, 883–904.

Markman, H.J., Renick, M.J., Floyd, F.J., Stanley, S.M. and Clements, M. (1993) Preventing marital distress through communication and conflict management training: a 4-and 5-year follow up. *Journal of Consulting and Clinical Psychology*, 61, 10–11.

Markus, H. and Kitayama, S. (1991) Culture and the self: implications for cognition, emotion, and motivation. *Psychological Review*, 98, 224–53.

Marmot, M.G., Bosma, H., Hemingway, H., Brunner, E. and Stansfeld, S. (1997) Contribution of job control and other risk factors to social variations in coronary heart disease incidence. *The Lancet*, 350(9073), 235–39.

Martens, R. (1972) *Sports Cohesiveness Questionnaire*. Champaign, IL: University of Illinois.

Martens, R. and Landers, D. (1970) Motor performance under stress: a test of the inverted U hypothesis. *Journal of Personality and Social Psychology*, 16(1), 29–37.

Martin, C.L. and Halverson, C.F. (1981) A schematic processing model of sex typing and stereotyping in children. *Child Development*, 52, 1119–34.

Maslach, C. (1979) Negative emotional biasing of unexplained arousal. *Journal of Personality and Social Psychology*, 37, 953–69.

Maslach, C. and Jackson, S. (1984) Burnout in organizational settings. *Applied Social Psychology Annual*, 5, 133–53.

Masten, A.S. (2001) Ordinary magic: resilience processes in development. *American Psychologist*, 56, 227–38.

Mather, G. and West, S. (1993) Recognition of animal locomotion from dynamic point-light displays. *Perception*, 22, 759.

Matheson, H., Mathes, S. and Murray, M. (1997) The effect of winning and losing on female interactive and co-active team cohesion. *Journal of Sport Behaviour*, 20, 284–99.

Mauthner, N.S. and Doucet, A. (2003) Reflexive accounts and accounts of reflexivity in qualitative data analysis. *Sociology*, 32(4) 733–45.

McCauley, C. (1989) Group dynamics in Janis's theory of groupthink: backward and forward. *Organisational Behaviour and Human Decision Processes*, 73(2–3), 142–62.

McDermut, W., Miller, I. and Brown, R. (2001) The efficacy of group psychotherapy for depression: a meta-analysis and review of the empirical research. *Clinical Psychology: Science and Practice*, 8(1), 98–116.

McGinnies, E. (1949) Emotionality and perceptual defence. *Psychological Review*, 56(5), 244–51.

McGue, M., Lykken, D.T., Bouchard, T.J. Jr and Tellegen, A. (1992) Heritability of interests. *Journal of Applied Psychology*, 78(4), 649–61.

McIntosh, C.N. and Fischer, D.G. (2000) Beck's cognitive triad: one versus three factors. *Canadian Journal of Behavioural Science*, 32(3), 153–57.

McKillip, J. and Riedel, S.L. (1983) External validity of matching on physical attractiveness for same and opposite sex couples. *Journal of Applied Social Psychology*, 13, 328–37.

McLanahan, S.S. and Bumpass, L. (1988) Intergenerational consequences of family disruption. *American Journal of Sociology*, 94, 130–52.

McMahon, F., Weinstein, S.P., Rowe E., Ernst, K.R., Johnson, F., Fujioka, K. and the Sibutramine in Hypertensives Clinical Study Group (2002) Sibutramine is safe and effective for weight loss in obese patients whose hypertension is well controlled with angiotensin-converting enzyme inhibitors. Journal of Human Hypertension, 16, 5–11.

Mead, M. (1928/1961) *Coming of Age in Samoa*. New York: Morrow.

Mead, M. (1930/1961) *Growing Up in New Guinea*. New York: Morrow.

Meeus, W., van de Schoot, R., Keijsers, L., and Branje, S., (2012) Identity statuses as developmental trajectories: a five-wave longitudinal study in early-to-middle and middle-to-late adolescents. *Journal of Youth and Adolescence*, 41(8), 1008–21.

Meeuwesen, L., van den Brink-Muinen, A. and Hofstede, G. (2009) Can dimensions of national culture predict cross-national differences in medical communication? *Patient Education and Counseling*, 75(1), 58–66.

Megret, A. (2011) French federation doctor wants tighter corticoid checks. *Cycling News*, 26 October 2012.

Merriam, S.B., Johnson-Bailey, J., Ming-Yeh, L., Youngwha, K., Gabo, N. and Mazanah, M. (2001) Power and positionality: negotiating the insider/outsider status within and across cultures. *International Journal of Lifelong Education*, 20(5), 405–16.

Mezulis, A.H., Abramson, L.Y., Hyde, J.S. and Hankin, B.L. (2004) Is there a universal positivity bias in attributions? A meta-analytic review of individual, developmental, and cultural differences in the self-serving attributional bias. *Psychological Bulletin*, 130(5), 711–47.

Michels-Lucht, F. (2011) Steroid use in free time bodybuilders. Psychotherapie, Psychosomatik, Medizinische Psychologie, 61(12), 512–17.

Miller, E. and Morley, S. (1986) *Investigating Abnormal Behaviour*. London: Weidenfeld & Nicolson/Lawrence Erlbaum.

Miller, J.G. (1984) Culture and the development of everyday social explanation. In D. Miell, A. Phoenix and K. Thomas (eds), *Mapping Psychology, Volume 2*. Milton Keynes: Open University Press.

Miller, M. (1993) Efficacy and performance in competitive swimmers of different skill levels. *International Journal of Sports Psychology*, 24, 284–96.

Milner, B., Corkin, S., and Teuber, H.L. (1968) Further analysis of the hippocampal amnesic syndrome: 14-year follow-up study of HM. *Neuropsychologia*, 6(3), 215–34.

Mindell, J.A., Sadeh, A., Weigand, B., How, T. and Goh, D. (2010) Cross-cultural differences in infant and toddler sleep. *Sleep Medicine*, 11(3), 274–80.

Minugh, P.A., Rice, C. and Young, L. (1998) Gender, health beliefs, health behaviors, and alcohol consumption. *American Journal of Drug and Alcohol Abuse*, 24(3), 483–97.

Moca, G., Freshma, A., Blender, J., Ravina, B. (2007) The Montreal cognitive assessment. *Movement Disorders*, 23 (7), 1043–46.

Moghaddam, K.M., Taylor, D.M. and Wright, S.C. (1993) *Social Psychology in Cross Cultural Perspective*. New York: W.H. Freeman.

Money, J. and Erhardt, A. (1972) *Man and Woman: Boy and Girl*. Baltimore: Johns Hopkins University Press.

Moodie, C., MacKintosh, A.M., Hastings, G. and Ford, A. (2011) Young adult smokers' perceptions of plain packaging: a pilot naturalistic study. *Tobacco Control*, 20(5), 367–73.

Morry, M. (2005) Relationship satisfaction as a predictor of similarity ratings: a test of the attraction-similarity hypothesis. *Journal of Social and Personal Relationships*, 22(4), 561–84.

Morry, M. (2007) The attraction-similarity hypothesis among cross-sex friends: relationship satisfaction, perceived similarities, and self-serving perceptions. *Journal of Social and Personal Relationships*, 24(1), 117–38.

Moscovici, S., Lage, E. and Naffrechoux, M. (1969) Influence of a consistent minority on the responses of a majority in a colour-perception task. *Sociometry*, 32, 365–80.

Moss, A. and Dyer, K. (2010) *Psychology of Addictive Behaviour*. Basingstoke: Palgrave MacMillan.

Mott, F.L. and Moore, S.F. (1979) The causes of marital disruption among young American women: an interdisciplinary perspective. *Journal of Marriage and the Family*, 43, 335–65.

Muller, B. and Copper, C. (1993) The relationship between group cohesiveness and performance: an integration. *Psychological Bulletin*, 115, 210–27.

Murray, M. and McMillan, C. (1993) Health beliefs, locus of control, emotional control and women's cancer screening behaviour. *British Journal of Clinical Psychology*, 32, 87–100.

Murstein, B.I. (1972) Physical attractiveness and marital choice. In R.D. Gross (1993), *Psychology: The Science of Mind and Behaviour*, 3rd edition. Bath: Hodder & Stoughton.

Musani, S., Erickson, S. and Allison, D. (2008) Obesity – still highly heritable after all these years. *American Society for Clinical Nutrition*, 87(2), 275–76.

Nadler, A. (1986) Help-seeking as a cultural phenomenon: differences between city and kibbutz dwellers. *Journal of Personality and Social Psychology*, 51, 976–82.

Nadler, A., Romek, E. and Shapira-Friedman, A. (1979) Giving in the kibbutz: prosocial behaviour of city and kibbutz children as affected by social responsibility and social pressure. *Journal of Cross-cultural Psychology*, 10(1), 57–72.

National Health and Nutrition Survey (2010) Obesity and extreme obesity rates decline among low-income preschool children. *Journal of the American Medical Association*, 308(24), 2563–65.

National Institute for Clinical Excellence (2007) A review of the use of the Health Belief Model (HBM), the Theory of Reasoned Action (TRA), the Theory of Planned Behaviour (TPB) and the Trans-Theoretical Model (TTM) to study and predict health-related behaviour change. http://www.nice.org.uk/nicemedia/live/11868/44524/44524.pdf (accessed 15 March 2013).

Neisser, U. (1967) *Cognitive Psychology*. New York: Appleton-Century Crofts.

Neisser, U. (1996) Intelligence: knowns and unknowns. *American Psychologist*, 51(2), 77–101.

Newman, T. (2002) *Promoting Resilience: A Review of Effective Strategies for Child Care Services – Summary*. Barkingside: Barnardos. http://www.barnardos.org.uk/resources/research-publications/documents/RESILSUM.PDF (accessed 18 March 2013).

Neziroglu, F., Yayura-Tobias, J., Walz, J., McKay, D. (2000) The effect of fluvoxamine and behaviour therapy on children and adolescents with obsessive-compulsive disorder. *Journal of Adolescent Psychopharmacology*, 10(4), 295–306.

Nisbett, R.E. and Cohen, D. (1996) *Culture of Honor: The Psychology of Violence in the South*. Boulder, CO: Westview Press.

Nobles, W. (1976) Black people in white insanity: an issue for black community mental health. *Journal of Afro-American Issues*, 4(1), 21–27.

Nolen-Hoeksema, S. and Girgus, J.S. (1994) The emergence of gender difference in depression during adolescence. *Psychological Bulletin*, 115, 424–23.

Noppa, H. and Bengtsson, C. (1980) Obesity in relation to socio-economic status. A population study of women in Goteborg, Sweden. *Journal of Epidemiology and Community Health*, 34, 139–42.

Novin, S., Rieffe, C., Banerjee, R., Miers, A. and Cheung, J. (2011) Anger response styles in Chinese and Dutch children: a socio-cultural perspective on anger regulation. *British Journal of Developmental Psychology*, 29, 806–22.

Ntoumanis, N. (2001) A self-determination approach to the understanding of motivation in physical education. *British Journal of Educational Psychology*, 71, 225–42.

Nunes Carraher, T. (1991) Mathematics in the street and in schools. In P. Light, S. Sheldon and M. Woodhead, *Learning to Think*. London: Routledge.

O'Block, F. and Evans, F. (1984) Goal setting as a motivational technique. In J. Silva and R. Weinberg (eds), *Psychological Foundations of Sport*. Champaign, IL: Human Kinetics.

O'Hara, M. and Phillips, L. (1991) Prospective study of post-partum depression: 4½-year follow-up of women and children. *Journal of Abnormal Psychology*, 100, 151–55.

O'Kearney, R., Anstey, K., Von Sanden, C. and Hunt, A. (2006) *Behaviour and Cognitive-Behavioural Therapy for Obsessive-Compulsive Disorder in Children and Adolescents: A Review*. Chichester: The Cochrane Library, John Wiley & Sons.

O'Rourke, P., Shaw, K., Del Mar, C. and Kenardy, J. (2008) Psychological interventions for overweight or obesity. *Cochrane Database of Systematic Reviews*, 18(2), CD003817.

Oddy, W.H., Li, J., Whitehouse, A.J., Zubrick, S.R. and Malacova, E. (2004/2011) Breastfeeding duration and academic achievement at 10 years. *Pediatrics*, 127, 137–45.

Ogden, J. (2007) *Health Psychology*, 4th edition. Maidenhead: Open University Press.

Olweus, D. (1993) *Bullying at School: What We Know and What We Can Do*. New York: Blackwell.

Olweus, D. (2001) *Olweus' Core Program Against Bullying and Antisocial Behavior: A Teacher Handbook*. Bergen, Norway: author.

Onexdine, J. (1970) Emotional arousal and motor performance. *Quest*, 13, 23–30.

Ottawa Charter for Health Promotion (1986). In *Health Promotion*, Volume 1 (iii–v). Geneva, Switzerland: World Health Organization.

Paguin, B., Bouchard, S., Payeur, R., Allard, M., Rivard, V. and Fournier, T. (2008) Psychotherapy on symptoms of depression and attrition: a meta-analysis. *Clinical Psychology*, 15(3), 243–53.

Parkin, A.J. (1996) *Explorations in Cognitive Neuropsychology.* Oxford: Blackwell.

Pawlowski, B. and Dunbar, R.I.M. (2001) Human mate choice decisions. In L. Barrett, R. Dunbar and J. Lycett (2002), *Human Evolutionary Psychology*. Basingstoke: Palgrave Macmillan.

Pawlowski, B. and Sorokowski, P. (2008) Adaptive preferences for leg length in a potential partner. *Evolution and Human Behaviour*, 29(2), 89–91.

Pediatric OCD Treatment Study (POTS) Team (2004) Cognitive-behavior therapy, sertraline, and their combination for children and adolescents with obsessive-compulsive disorder: the Pediatric OCD Treatment Study randomized controlled trial. *Journal of the American Medical Association*, 292(16), 1969–76.

Penland, E., Masten, W., Zelhart, P., Fournet, G. and Callahan, T. (2000) Possible selves, depression and coping skills in university students. *Personality and Individual Differences*, 29(5), 963–69.

Perakyla, A. (2004) Reliability and validity in research based upon transcripts. In D. Silverman (ed.), *Qualitative Research: Theory, Method and Practice*, 2nd edition (296–97). London: Sage.

Perrin, S. and Spencer, C.P. (1981) Independence or conformity in the Asch experiment as a reflection of cultural and situational factors. *British Journal of Social Psychology*, 20(3), 205–09.

Pesonen, A.K. and Räikkönen, K. (2012) The lifespan consequences of early life stress. *Physiology & Behavior*, 106(5), 722–27.

Peters, D. (1988) Eyewitness memory in a natural setting. In M. Gruneberg, P. Morris and N. Sykes (eds), *Practical Aspects of Memory: Current Research and Issues. Volume 1: Memory in Everyday Life* (89–94). Chichester: Wiley.

Peterson, C. and Seligman, M.E.P. (1984) Attributional style and depressive symptoms amongst children. *Journal of Abnormal Psychology*, 93(2), 235–38.

Peterson, T. (2006) Enhancing the efficacy of antidepressants with psychotherapy. *Journal of Psychopharmacology*, 20(3), 19–28.

Petrie, T. (1992) Psychological antecedents of athletic injury: the effects of life stress and social support on female collegiate gymnasts. *Behavioural Medicine*, 18, 127–38.

Pettigrew, T., *et al.* (1978) How cultural set affects perception. In T. Malin (1994), *Cognitive Processes*. Basingstoke: Palgrave MacMillan.

Pfitzinger, P. (2011) EPO illegal, effective and deadly. http://www.pfitzinger.com/labreports/epo.shtml (accessed 14 March 2013).

Pfungst, O. (1911) *Clever Hans (The Horse of Mr von Osten): A Contribution to Experimental Animal and Human Psychology* (trans. Rahn, C.). New York: Henry Holt. (Originally published in German, 1907.)

Phelps, E., Ling, S. and Carrasco, M. (2006) Emotion facilitates perception and potentiates the perceptual benefits of attention. *Psychological Science*, 17(4), 292–99.

Phoenix, A. (2007) Identities and diversity. In D. Miell, A. Phoenix and K. Thomas (eds), *Mapping Psychology*. Milton Keynes: Open University Press.

Piaget, J. (1963) *The Origins of Intelligence in Children*. New York: Norton.

Piaget, J. and Inhelder, B.A. (1967) *The Psychology of the Child*. London: Routledge and Kegan Paul.

Piccinelli, M., Pini, S., Bellatuono, C. and Wilkinson, G. (1995) Efficacy of drug treatment in obsessive-compulsive disorder. A meta-analytic review. *British Journal of Psychiatry*, 166, 424–43.

Piliavin, I., Rodin, J. and Piliavin, J. (1969) Good Samaritanism: an underground phenomenon? *Journal of Personality and Social Psychology*, 13(4), 289–99.

Plowden Committee (1967) *Children and their Primary Schools*. London: HMSO.

Polimeni, J. (2005) Could obsessive-compulsive disorder have originated as a group-selected adaptive trait in traditional societies? *Medical Hypotheses*, 64(5), 655–64.

Pollack, R. and Silva, S. (1967) Magnitude of the Müller-Lyer illusion in children as a function of the pigmentation of the fundus oculi. *Psychonomic Science*, 8, 83–84.

Poole, D. and Lindsay, D. (2001) Reducing child witnesses' false reports of information from parents. *Journal of Experimental Child Psychology*, 81, 117–40.

Poppe, E. and Linssen, H. (1999) In-group favouritism and the reflection of realistic dimensions of difference between national states in Central and Eastern European nationality stereotypes. *British Journal of Social Psychology*, 38(1), 85–102.

Pornpitakpan, C.F. and June, N.P. (2001) The effect of cultural differences, source expertise and argument strength on persuasion: an experiment with Canadians and Thais. *Journal of International Consumer Marketing*, 13(1), 77–101.

Postman, L. and Bruner, J. (1947) Emotional selectivity in perception and reaction. *Journal of Personality*, 16(1), 69–77.

Poulin-Dubois, D., Serbin, L.A., Eichstedt, J.A., Sen, M.G. and Beissel, C.F. (2002) Men don't put on make-up: toddlers' knowledge of the gender stereotyping of household activities. *Social Development*, 11(2) 166–81.

Prapavessis, H. (1997) Sacrifice, cohesion and conformity to norms in sports team. *Group Dynamics: Theory, Research and Practice*, 1(3), 231–40.

Pratt, M.W., Green, D., MacVicar, J. and Bountrogianni, M. (1992) The mathematical parent: parental scaffolding, parent style and learning outcomes in long-division mathematics homework. *Journal of Applied Developmental Psychology*, 13(1), 17–34.

Qureshi, R.B. (1991) Marriage strategies among Muslims from South Asia. In A. Zaida and M. Shuraydi (2002) Perceptions of arranged marriages by young Pakistani Muslim women living in a western society. *Journal of Comparative Family Studies*, 33(4), 495.

Raedeke, T. (2010) Coach commitment and burnout: a one-year follow-up. *Journal of Applied Sport Psychology*, 16(4), 333–49.

Raine, A., Meloy, J.R., Bihrle, S., Stoddard, J., Lacasse, L. and Buchsbaum, M.S. (1998) Reduced prefrontal and increased subcortical brain functioning assessed using positron emission tomography in predatory and affective murderers. *Behavioral Sciences & the Law*, 16(3), 319–32.

Reeves, A. and Plum, F. (1969) Hyperphagia, rage and dementia accompanying a ventro-medial hypothalamic neoplasm. *Archives of Neurology*, 20, 616–24.

Richter, E., Davis, K., Hamsani, C., Hutchinson, D., Dovstrovsky, J. and Lozano, A. (2004) Cingulotomy for psychiatric disease: microelectrode guidance, a callosal reference system for documenting lesion location, and clinical results. *Neurosurgery*, 54(3), 622–30.

Ridley, M. (1999) *Genome*. London: 4th Estate.

Ringelmann, M. (1913) Research on animate sources of power: the work of man. *Annales de l'Institut National Agronomique*, 2e Série, 12, 1–40.

Rivers, W. (1901) *Reports of the Cambridge Anthropological Expedition to Torres Straits, Vol. II*. Cambridge: Cambridge University Press.

Rizzolati, G. and Sinigaglia, C. (2008) *Mirrors in the Brain: How Our Minds Share Actions and Emotions*. Oxford: Oxford University Press.

Roberts, C. (1978) Psychological treatment of obesity with phentermine resin as an adjunct. *American Journal of Psychiatry*, 135(8), 936–39.

Roberts, G. (2001) Understanding the dynamics of motivation in physical activity: the influence of achievement goals on motivational process. In G. Roberts (ed.), *Advances in Sport and Exercise* (1–50). Champaign, IL: Human Kinetics.

Roberts, K. and Lamb, M. (1999) Children's responses when adults distort details during investigative interviews. *Legal and Criminological Psychology*, 4, 23–32.

Romero-Corral, A., Somers, V., Sierra-Johnson, J., Thomas, R., Collazo-Clavell, M., Korinek, J., *et al.* (2008) Accuracy of body mass index in diagnosing obesity in the adult general population. *International Journal of Obesity*, 32, 959–66.

Roosen, M., Safer, D., Adler, S., Cebolla, A. and Van Strien, T. (2012) Group dialectical behavior therapy adapted for obese emotional eaters; a pilot study. *Nutrición Hospitalaria*, 27(4), 1141–47.

Rosenhan, D. (1973) On being sane in insane places. *Science*, 179(4070), 250–58.

Rosenhan, D. and Seligman, M. (1989) *Abnormal Psychology*, 2nd edition. New York: W.W. Norton.

Rosenman, R.H., Brand, R.J., Sholtz, R.I. and Friedman, M. (1976) Multivariate prediction of coronary heart disease during 8.5-year follow-up in the Western Collaborative Group Study. *The American Journal of Cardiology*, 37(6), 903.

Rosenzweig, M.R., Krech, D., Bennett, E.L. and Diamond, M.C. (1962) Effects of environmental complexity and training on brain chemistry and anatomy: a replication and extension. *Journal of Comparative Physiological Psychology*, 55, 429–37.

Ross, L.D. (1977) The intuitive psychologist and his shortcomings: distortions in the attribution process. In D. Langdridge, S.W. Taylor and K. Mahendran (2012), *Critical Readings in Social Psychology*. Milton Keynes: Open University Press.

Rothman, R. (2009) Treatment of obesity with 'combination' pharmacotherapy. *American Journal of Therapy*, 17, 596–603.

Rovio, E., Eskola, J., Kozub, S., Duda, J. and Lintunen, T. (2009) Can high group cohesion be harmful? A case study of a junior ice-hockey team. *Small Group Research*, 40(4), 421–35.

Rowe, M., Chamala, S., Beckstead, W. and McClellan, D. (2007) Evolutionary selective pressure on three mitochondrial SNPs is consistent with their influence on metabolic efficiency in Pima Indians. *International Journal of Bioinformatics Research and Applications*, 3(4), 504–22.

Rusbult, C.E., Verette, J., Whitney, G.A., Slovik, L.F. and Lipkus, I. (1991) Accommodation processes in close relationships: theory and preliminary empirical evidence. *Journal of Personality and Social Psychology*, 60, 553–78.

Rusbult, C. and Zembrodt, I.M. (1983) Responses to dissatisfaction in romantic involvements: a multi-dimensional scaling analysis. *Journal of Experimental Social Psychology*, 19, 274–93.

Rutter, M. (2009) Resilience concepts and findings: implications for family therapy. *Journal of Family Therapy*, 21, 119–44.

Rutter, M. Colvert, E., Kreppner, J., Beckett, C., Castle, J., Groothues, C., Hawkins, A., O'Conner, T., Stevens, S. and Sonuga-Barke, E. (2007) Early adolescent outcomes for institutionally deprived and non-deprived adoptees. I: Disinhibited Attachment. *Journal of Child Psychology and Psychiatry*, 48(1), 17–30.

Rutter, M., Quinton, D. and Hill, J. (1999) Adult outcome of institution-reared children: males and females compared. In T. Cooper and I. Roth (eds) (2007), *Challenging Psychological Issues*. Milton Keynes: Open University Press.

Ryan, E. (1979) Attribution, intrinsic motivation and athletics: a replication and extension. In L. Gedvilas and M. Kneer (eds), *Proceedings of the National College of Physical Education Association for Men/National Association for Physical Education for Women, National Conference*. Chicago: Office of Publications Services, University of Illinois at Chicago Circle.

Ryan, L. and Golden, A. (2006) 'Tick the box please': a reflexive approach to doing quantitative social research. *Sociology*, 40(6), 1191–200.

Saad, G. (2006) Sex differences in OCD symptomatology: an evolutionary perspective. *Medical Hypotheses*, 67(6), 1455–59.

Sabol, S.Z., Nelson, M.L., Fisher, C., Gunzerath, L., Brody, C.L., Hu, S., *et al.* (1999) A genetic association for cigarette smoking behaviour. *Health Psychology*, 18(1), 7–13.

Sackeim, H., Haskett, R. and Mulsant, B. (2001) Continuation pharmacotherapy in the prevention of relapse following electroconvulsive therapy: a randomized controlled trial. Journal of the American Medical Association, 285, 1299–307.

Sackheim, H. (1989) Treatment-resistant depression: therapeutic approaches. *Medscape Psychiatry and Mental Health Journal*, 1(2).

Sacks, O. (1985) *The Man Who Mistook His Wife for a Hat*. London: Gerald Duckworth & Co.

Saisto, T., Salmela-Aro, K., Nurmi, J. and Halmesmaki, E. (2001) Psychosocial indicators of disappointment with delivery and puerperal depression. *Acta Obstetricia et Gynecologica Scandinavica*, 80, 39–45.

Sameroff, A.J. and Seifer, R. (1993) Stability of intelligence from preschool to adolescence: the influence of social and family risk factors. *Child Development*, 64, 80–97.

Samuels, J., Shugart, Y., Grados, M., Willour, V.L., Bienvenu, O., Greenberg, B., *et al.* (2007) Significant linkage to hoarding on chromosome 14 in families with obsessive-compulsive disorder: results from the OCD collaborative genetics study. *American Journal of Psychiatry*, 164(3), 493–99.

Sanchez-Villegas, A., Schlatter, J., Ortuno, F., Lahortiga, F., Pla, J., Benito, S. and Martinez-Gonzalez, M. (2008) Validity of a self-reported diagnosis of depression among participants in a cohort study using the Structured Clinical Interview for DSM-IV (SCID-I). *BMC Psychiatry*, 8, 43.

Santos, P.S.C., Schinemann, J.A., Gabardo, J. and Bicalho, M.D. (2005) New evidence that the MHC influences odor perception in humans: a study with 58 southern Brazilian students. *Hormones and Behavior*, 47, 384–88.

Sato, T., Uehara, T., Sakado, K., Sato, S., Nishioka, K. and Kasahara, K. (1996) The test-retest reliability of the inventory to diagnose depression, lifetime version. *Psychopathology*, 29, 154–58.

Schachter, S. and Singer, J. (1962) Cognitive, social and physiological determinants of emotional state. *Psychological Review*, 69, 379–99.

Schaffer, H.R. and Emerson, P.F. (1964) The development of social attachments in infancy. *Monographs of the Society for Research in Child Development*, 29(3), 1–70.

Schank, R. and Abelson, R. (1977) *Scripts, Plans, Goals, and Understanding: An Enquiry into Human Knowledge Structure*. Hillsdale, New York: Lawrence Erlbaum.

Schmidt, G. and Stein, G. (1991) Sport commitment: a model integrating enjoyment, dropout and burnout. *Journal of Sport and Exercise Psychology*, 13(3), 254–65.

Schmidt, R. and Wrisberg, C. (1991) *Motor Learning and Performance*. Champaign, IL: Human Kinetics.

Schneider, H., Friedrich, N., Klotsche, J., Pieper, L., Nauck, M., John, U., *et al.* (2010) The predictive value of different measures of obesity for incident cardiovascular events and mortality. *Journal of Clinical Endocrinology & Metabolism*, 95(4), 1777–85.

Schneiderman, I., Zagoory-Sharon, O., Leckman, J.F. and Feldman, R. (2012) Oxytocin during the initial stages of romantic attachment: relations to couples' interactive reciprocity. *Psychoneuroendocrinology*, 37(8), 1277–85.

Schoenthaler, S.J., Bier, I.D., Young, K., Nichols, D. and Jansenns, S. (2000) The effect of vitamin-mineral supplementation on the intelligence of American schoolchildren: a randomized, double-blind placebo-controlled trial. *Journal of Alternative and Complementary Medicine*, 6(1), 19–29.

Schwartz, R.P., Hamre, R., Dietz, W.H., Wasserman, R.C., Slora, E.J., Myers, E.F., et al. (2007) Office-based motivational interviewing to prevent childhood obesity. Journal of the American Medical Association: Pediatrics, 161(5), 495–501.

Schwartz, S.J. (2002) Convergent validity in objective measures of identity status: implications for the identity status theory. *Adolescence*, 37(147), 609.

Schwarzwald, J., Bizman, A. and Raz, M. (1983) The foot in the door paradigm: effects of second request size on donation probability and donor generosity. *Personality and Social Psychology Bulletin*, 9(3), 443–50.

Scoville, W.B., Dunsmore, R.H., Liberson, W.T., Henry, C.E. and Pepe, A. (1953) Observations on medical temporal lobotomy and in the treatment of psychotic states. *Research Publications – Association for Research in Nervous and Mental Disease*, 31, 347–69.

Seale, C., Gobo, G., Gubrium, J. and Silverman, D. (eds) (2007) *Qualitative Research Practice*. London: Sage.

Sears, D. (1986) College sophomores in the library: influences of a narrow data base on social psychology's view of human nature. *Journal of Personality and Social Behaviour*, 51, 515–30.

Segal, Z., Teasdale, J., Williams, J. and Gemar, M. (2002) The mindfulness-based cognitive therapy adherence scale: inter-rater reliability adherence to protocol and treatment distinctiveness. *Clinical Psychology and Psychotherapy*, 9, 131–38.

Segall, M., Campbell, D.T., Herskovits, M.J. (1966) *The influence of culture on visual perception*. Indianapolis, IN: Bobbs-Merrill.

Segall, M., Campbell, D. and Herskovits, M. (1963) Cultural differences in the perception of geometrical illusions. *Science*, 139, 769–71.

Selfhout, M., Denissen, J., Branje, S. and Meeus, W. (2009) In the eye of the beholder: perceived, actual and peer rated similarity in personality, communication and friendship intensity during the acquaintance process. *Journal of Personality and Social Psychology*, 96(6), 1152–65.

Seligman, M. (1974) *The Psychology of Depression: Contemporary Theory and Research*. Oxford: John Wiley & Sons.

Seligman, M.E.P. and Csikszentmihalyi, M. (2000) Positive psychology: an introduction. *American Psychologist*, 55, 5–14.

Seltzer, C., Stoudt, H., Bell, B. and Mayer, J. (1970) Reliability of relative body weight as a criterion for obesity. *American Journal of Epidemiology*, 92, 339–50.

Selye, H. (1950) Stress and the general adaptation syndrome. *British Medical Journal*, 1(4667), 1383–92.

Sergent, J. (1992) Functional neuroanatomy of face and object processing. A positron emission tomography study. *Brain*, 115, 15–36.

Shackleford, T.K. (2005) An evolutionary psychological perspective on cultures of honor. *Evolutionary Psychology*, 3, 381–91.

Shapiro, F. (2001) *Eye Movement Desensitization and Reprocessing (EMDR): Basic Principles, Protocols, and Procedures*. New York: Guilford Press.

Shapiro, F. (2006) Efficacy of the eye movement desensitization procedure in the treatment of traumatic memories. *Journal of Traumatic Stress*, 2(2), 199–223.

Sharry, J. and Owens, C. (2000) 'The rules of engagement': a case study of a group with 'angry' adolescents. *Clinical Child Psychology and Psychiatry*, 5, 53–62.

Shawn, M. and Landers, D. (2003) Arousal, anxiety and performance: a re-examination of the inverted U hypothesis. *Research Quarterly for Exercise and Sport*, 74(4), 436–44.

Sheldrake, R. (1994) *Seven Experiments that Could Change the World*. London: 4th Estate.

Sheldrake, R. (1998) The sense of being stared at: experiments in schools. *Journal of the Society for Psychical Research*, 62, 311–23.

Sheldrake, R. (2000) The 'sense of being stared at' does not depend on known sensory clues. Biology Forum, 93, 209–24.

Sherif, M., Harvey, O., White, B.J., Hood, W. and Sherif, C. (1961) *Intergroup Conflict and Co-operation: The Robber's Cave Experiment*. Norman, OK: University of Oklahoma Institute of Intergroup Relations.

Shotland, R.L. and Straw, M.K. (1976) Bystander response to an assault: when a man attacks a woman. *Journal of Personality and Social Psychology*, 34, 990–99.

Siddle, R., Jones, F. and Awenat, F. (2003) Group cognitive-behaviour therapy for anger: a pilot study. *Behavioural and Cognitive Psychotherapy*, 31, 69–83.

Silverman, D. (2010) *Doing Qualitative Research*, 3rd edition. London: Sage.

Silverman, I. (1971) Physical attractiveness. *Sexual Behaviour*, 22–25 September.

Simon, H. and Chase, W. (1973) The mind's eye in chess. In W. Chase (ed.), *Visual Performance Processing* (215–81). New York: Academic Press.

Singh, D. (1993) Adaptive significance of female physical attractiveness: role of waist-to-hip ratio. In L. Barrett, R. Dunbar and J. Lycett (2002), *Human Evolutionary Psychology*. Basingstoke: Palgrave Macmillan.

Singh, R. and Ho, S.Y. (2000) Attitudes and attraction: a new test of the attraction, repulsion and similarity-dissimilarity asymmetry hypotheses. *British Journal of Social Psychology*, 39 (2), 197–211.

Singh-Manoux, A., Czernichow, S., Elbaz, A., Dugravot, A., Sabia, S., Hagger-Johnson, G., Kaffashian, S., Zins, M., Brunner, E.J., Nabi, H. and Kivimäki, M. (2012) Obesity phenotypes in midlife and cognition in early old age: the Whitehall II cohort study. *Neurology*, 79(8), 755–62.

Singleton, D. and Feltz, D. (1999) *The Effect of Self-modelling on Shooting Performance and Self-efficacy Among Intercollegiate Hockey Players*. Unpublished manuscript. Michigan State University.

Skeels, H. and Dye, H.B. (1939) A study of the effects of differential stimulation on mentally retarded children. *Proceedings and Addresses of the American Association on Mental Deficiency*, 44, 114–36.

Skinner, B.F. (1938) *The Behaviour of Organisms: An Experimental Analysis*. Cambridge, MA: B.F. Skinner Foundation.

Skodak, M. and Skeels, H. (1949) A final follow up of 100 adopted children. *Journal of Genetic Psychology*, 75, 85–125.

Sloan, S., Stewart, M. and Dunne, L. (2010) The effect of breast-feeding and stimulation in the home on cognitive development in one-year-old infants. *Child Care in Practice*, 16(2) 101–10.

Smith, E. and Mackie, D. (2000) *Social Psychology*. Hove: Psychology Press.

Smith, M., Kish, B. and Crawford, C. (1987) Inheritance of wealth as human kin investment. In L. Barrett, R. Dunbar and J. Lycett (2002), *Human Evolutionary Psychology*. Basingstoke: Palgrave Macmillan.

Smith, R. (1986) Towards a cognitive-affective model of athletic burnout. *Journal of Sport Psychology*, 8(1), 36–50.

Smith, R., Smoll, F. and Ptacek, J. (1990) Conjunctive moderator variables in vulnerability and resiliency research: life stress, social support and coping skills, and adolescent sport injuries. *Journal of Personality and Social Psychology*, 58(2), 360–70.

Solley, C. and Haigh, G. (1948) How children perceive Santa Claus. *Psychology*, 27, 203–08.

Sorensen, A. and Stunkard, T. (1994) Overview of the adoption studies. In C. Bouchard (ed.), *The Genetics of Obesity* (49–61). Boca Raton, FL: CRC press.

Speisman, J., Lazarus, R., Mordkoff, A. and Davison, L. (1964) Experimental reduction of stress based on ego-defence theory. *Journal of Abnormal and Social Psychology*, 68(4), 367–80.

Spence, K. and Spence, J. (1966) The motivational components of manifest anxiety. In C. Spielberger (ed.), *Anxiety and Behaviour*. New York: Academic Press.

Sperry, R.W. (1968) Hemisphere deconnection and unity in conscious awareness. *American Psychologist*, 23, 723–33.

Stake, R.E. (1994) Case studies. In N.K. Denzin and Y.S. Lincoln (eds), *Handbook of Qualitative Research*. Thousand Oaks, CA: Sage.

Stewart, V. (1973) Tests of the carpentered world hypothesis by race and environment in America and Zambia. *International Journal of Psychology*, 8(2), 83–94.

Stice, E., Spoor, S., Bohon, C. and Small, D. (2008) Relation between obesity and blunted striatal response to food is moderated by TaqIA A1 allele. *Science*, 322(5900), 449–52.

Stout, J.T. (1999) *Goal-setting Strategies, Locus of Control Beliefs, and Personality Characteristics of NCAA Division IA Swimmers*. Unpublished thesis. University of North Texas. http://digital.library.unt.edu/ark:/67531/metadc2236/ (accessed 14 March 2013).

Stumpf, C. (1911) Mr Von Osten's method of instruction. In Pfungst, O. (1911) *Clever Hans (The Horse of Mr von Osten): A Contribution to Experimental Animal and Human Psychology* (trans. Rahn, C.). New York: Henry Holt. (Originally published in German, 1907.)

Sue, S., Zane, N. and Young, K. (1994) Research on psychotherapy with culturally diverse populations. In A. Bergen and S. Garfield (eds), *Handbook of Psychotherapy and Behaviour*, 4th edition (783–817). New York: Wiley.

Sullivan, P. and Feltz, D. (2006) Applying social psychology to sports teams. In F. Schneider, J. Gruman and L. Coutts (eds), *Applied Social Psychology: Understanding and Addressing Social Problems* (129–49). Thousand Oaks, CA: Sage.

Sun, Y., Asnicar, M., Saha, P., Chan, L. and Smith, R. (2006) Ablation of ghrelin improves the diabetic, but not obese, phenotype of ob/ob mice. *Cell Metabolism*, 3(5), 379–86.

Swaab, D.F. and Fliers, E.A. (1985) A sexually dimorphic nucleus in the human brain. *Science*, 228, 1112–15.

Swartz, D. and Wayne, R. (1979) How to mentally prepare for better performances. *Runners' World*, 14, 90–91.

Sweeting, H. and West, P. (2002) Gender differences in weight-related concerns in early to late adolescence. *Journal of Epidemiological Community Health*, 56, 700–01.

Synder, M. and Uranowitz, S. (1978) Reconstructing the past: some cognitive consequences of person perception. *Journal of Personality and Social Psychology*, 39, 941–50.

Szasz, T. (1962) *Law, Liberty and* Psychiatry. Syracuse, NY: Syracuse University Press.

Tafalla, R.J. (2007) Gender differences in cardiovascular reactivity and game performance related to sensory modality in violent video game play. *Journal of Applied Social Psychology*, 37(9), 2008–23.

Tajfel, H., Billig, M., Bundy, R.P. and Flament, C. (1971) Social categorisation and intergroup behaviour. *European Journal of Social Psychology*, 1, 149–77.

Takamura, M. (1996) Prosopagnosia: a look at the laterality and specificity issues using evidence from neuropsychology and neuropsychiatry. *The Harvard Brain*, spring, 9–13.

Tal-Or, N. and Papirman, Y. (2007) The fundamntal attribution error in attributing fictional figures' characteristics to the actors. *Media Psychology*, 9(2), 331–45.

Taylor, S., Koch, W., Woody, S. and McLean, P. (1995) Anxiety, sensitivity and depression: how are they related. *Journal of Abnormal Psychology*, 105(3), 474–79.

Telch, C. and Agras, W. (2000) Dialectical behavioural therapy for binge eating disorder. *Journal of Consulting and Clinical Psychology*, 69(6), 1061–65.

Tennenbaum, S., Mathieu, J., Salas, E. and Cannon-Bowers, J. (1991) Meeting trainees' expectations: the influence of training fulfilment on the development of commitment, self-efficacy and motivation. *Journal of Applied Psychology*, 76(6), 759–69.

Terling-Watt, T. (2001) Explaining divorce: an examination of the relationships between marital characteristics and divorce. *Journal of Divorce*, 35(3–4), 125–45.

Thorsteinsson, E.B., James, J.E., Douglas, M.E. and Omodei, M.M. (1999) Effects of social support on cardiovascular and cortisol reactivity during passive and active behavioral challenge. *Journal of Psychiatry, Psychology and Mental Health*, 3(1), 1–12.

Titchener, E. (1898) A psychological laboratory. *Mind*, 7, 311–31.

Tizard, B. and Hodges, J. (1978) The effect of early institutional rearing on the development of eight-year-old children. Journal of Child Psychology and Psychiatry, 19(2), 99–118.

Toates, F. (2007) Biological psychology. In D. Miell, A. Phoenix and K. Thomas (eds) *Mapping Psychology, Volume 1*. Milton Keynes: Open University Press.

Totsika, V. and Sylva, K. (2004) The home observation for measurement of the environment. *Revisited Child and Adolescent Mental Health*, 9(1), 25–35.

Tran, S. and Simpson, J.A. (2009) Pro-relationship maintenance behaviours: the joint roles of attachment and commitment. *Journal of Personality and Social Psychology*, 97(4): 685–98.

Tranel, T. and Damasio, A. (1985) Knowledge without awareness: an autonomic index of facial recognition by prosopagnosics. *Science*, 228(4706), 1453–54.

Triandis, H.C. (1980) Values, attitudes and interpersonal behaviour. In R.D. Gross (1996) *Themes, Issues and Debates in Psychology*. London: Hodder & Stoughton.

Triandis, H. (1990) Theoretical concepts that are applicable to the analysis of ethnocentrism. In R.W. Brislin (ed.), *Applied Cross-cultural Psychology*. Newbury Park, CA: Sage.

Triplett, N. (1898) The dynamogenic factors in pace making and competition. *American Journal of Psychology*, 9, 507–33.

Trivers, R. (1972) *Parental Investment and Sexual Selection*. Cambridge, MA: Aldine Publishing Company, Harvard University.

Turnbull, C. (1961) Some observations regarding the experiences and behaviour of the BaMbuti pygmies. *American Journal of Psychology*, 74(2), 304–08.

Turner, J.C. and Brown, R. (1978) Social status, cognitive alternatives, and intergroup relations. In H. Tajfel (ed.), *Differentiation between Social Groups*. London: Academic Press.

Tyas, S.L. and Pederson, L.L. (1998) Psychosocial factors related to adolescent smoking: a critical review of the literature. *Tobacco Control*, 7(4), 409–20.

Uchino, B.N., Cacioppo, J.T. and Kiecolt-Glaser, J.K. (1996) The relationship between social support and physiological processes: a review with emphasis on underlying mechanisms and implications for health. *Psychological Bulletin*, 119(3), 488–531.

Udry, J.R. (2000) Biological limits of gender construction. *American Sociological Review*, 65, 453–57.

Valsiner, J. and Rosa, A. (2007) *The Cambridge Handbook of Sociocultural Psychology*. New York: Cambridge University Press.

Van Balkom, A. (1998) Cognitive and behavioural therapies alone versus in combination with fluvoxamine in the treatment of obsessive-compulsive disorder. *Journal of Nervous and Mental Disorders*, 186, 492–99.

Van Ijzendoorn, M.H. and Kroonenberg, P.M. (1988) Cross-cultural patterns of attachment: a meta-analysis of the Strange Situation. *Child Development*, 59, 147–56.

Van Wagenen, W.P. and Herren, R.Y. (1940) Surgical division of commissural pathways in the corpus callosum: relation to spread of an epileptic attack. *Archives of Neurology and Psychiatry*, 44, 740–59.

Van Weel-Baumgarten, E. (2000) The validity of the diagnosis of depression in general practice: is using criteria for diagnosis as a routine the answer? *British Journal of General Practice*, 50(453), 284–87.

Vandenberg, D.J., Bennett, C.J., Grant, M.D., Strasser, A.A., O'Connor, R., Stauffer, R.L., *et al.* (2002) Smoking status and the human dopamine transporter variable number of tandem repeats (VNTR) polymorphism: failure to replicate and finding that never-smokers may be different. *Nicotine & Tobacco Research*, 4(3), 333–40.

Vazquez-Montilla, E., Reyes-Blanes, M.E., Hyun, E. and Brovelli, E. (2000) Practices for culturally responsive interviews and research with Hispanic families. *Multicultural Perspective*, 2(3), 3–7.

Vealey, R., Udry, E., Zimmerman, V. and Soliday, J. (1992) Interpersonal and situational predictors of coaching burnout. *Journal of Sport and Exercise Psychology*, 14, 40–58.

Velicer, W.F., DiClemente, C.C., Prochaska, J.O. and Brandenburg, N. (1985) Decisional balance measure for assessing and predicting smoking status. *Journal of Personality and Social Psychology*, 48(5), 1279.

Violence Prevention Alliance (2010) Definition and typology of violence. http://www.who.int/violenceprevention/approach/definition/en/ (accessed 14 March 2013).

Vogel, P. and Vogel, E. (1992) Therapist manual for exposure treatment of obsessive-compulsives. *Psychotherapy: Theory, Research, Practice, and Training*, 29, 368–75.

Vygotskii [Vygotsky], L.S. (1984) Problemy detskoi (vozrastnoi psikhologii). In V.K. Zaretskii (2009), The zone of proximal development: what Vygotsky did not have time to write. *Journal of Russian and East European Psychology*, 47(6), 70–93.

Walker, J.S. and Bright, J.A. (2009) Cognitive therapy for violence: reaching the parts that anger management doesn't reach. *Journal of Forensic Psychiatry & Psychology*, 20(2), 174–201.

Wardle, J., Carnell, S., Haworth, C. and Plomin, R. (2008) Evidence for a strong genetic influence on childhood adiposity despite the force of the obesogenic environment. *American Journal of Clinical Nutrition*, 87, 398–404.

Warren, W. (1984) Perceiving affordances: visual guidance of stair climbing. *Journal of Experimental Psychology: Human Perception and Performance*, 10(5), 683–703.

Waylen, A.E., Leary, S.D., Ness, A.R., Tanski, S.E. and Sargent, J.D. (2011) Cross-sectional association between smoking depictions in films and adolescent tobacco use nested in a British cohort study. *Thorax*, 66(10), 856–61.

Waynforth, D. (2001) Mate choice trade-offs and women's preference for physically attractive men. *Human Nature*, 12(3), 207–19.

Waza, K., Graham, A., Zyzanski, S. and Inoue, K. (1999) Comparison of symptoms in Japanese and American depressed primary care patients. *Family Practice*, 16(5), 528–33.

Weinberg, R., Burton, D., Yukelson, D. and Weigand, D. (1993) Goal-setting in competitive sport: an exploratory investigation of practices of collegiate athletes. *Sport Psychologist*, 7, 275–89.

Weismann, G., Kariko, K., Muramatsu, H. and Keller, J. (2012) Increased erythropoiesis in mice injected with submicrogram quantities of pseudouridine-containing mRNA encoding erythropoietin molecular therapy. http://www.nature.com/mt/journal/vaop/ncurrent/full/mt20127a.html (accessed 1 March 2013).

Weiss, M. and Ferrer-Caja, E. (2002) Motivational orientations and sport behaviour. In T. Hom (ed.), *Advances in Sport Psychology*, 2nd edition (101–70). Champaign, IL: Human Kinetics.

Wender, P., Seymour, S., Kety, M., Rosenthal, D., Schulsinger, F., Ortmann, J. and Lunde, I. (1986) Psychiatric disorders in the biological and adoptive families of adopted individuals with affective disorders. *Archives of General Psychiatry*, 43(10), 923–29.

West, D., DeLillo, V., Bursac, Z., Gore, S. and Greene, P. (2007) Motivational interviewing improves weight loss in women with type 2 diabetes. *Diabetes Care*, 30(5), 1081–87.

West, R. (2006) *Theory of Addiction*. Oxford: Blackwell.

West, R. and Shoal, T. (2006) 'Catastrophic' pathways to smoking cessation: findings from national survey. *British Medical Journal*, 332(7539), 458–60.

Westminster Council in London, GB (2013) Obese people should have benefits cut if they do not exercise, argues proposal for Westminster Council. http://www.huffingtonpost.co.uk/2013/01/03/obese-benefits-cut-westminster_n_2400708.html (accessed 19 March 2013).

Whitfield, G. and Williams, C. (2003) The evidence base for cognitive-behavioural therapy in depression: delivery in busy clinical settings. *Advances in Psychiatric Treatment*, 9, 21–30.

Whiting, B.B. and Edwards, C. (1973) A cross-cultural analysis of sex differences in the behavior of children aged 3 to 11. *Journal of Social Psychology*, 91, 171–88.

Whiting, B.B. and Edwards, C.P. (1988) *Children of Different Worlds: The Formation of Social Behavior.* Cambridge, MA: Harvard University Press.

Whiting, B. and Whiting, J. (1975) *Children of Six Cultures: A Psychocultural Analysis.* Cambridge, MA: Harvard University Press.

Wiggers, J. and Sanson-Fisher, R. (1998) Evidence-based health promotion. In R. Scott and R. Weston (eds), *Evaluating Health Promotion*. Cheltenham: Stanley Thornes.

Williams, J.M. and Currie, C. (2000) Self-esteem and physical development in jearly adolescence. *Journal of Early Adolescence*, 20(2), 129–49.

Williams, T.M. (1986) The impact of television: a natural experiment in three communities. http://world.std.com/~jlr/comment/tv_impact.htm (accessed 14 March 2013).

Willig, C. (2001) *Introducing Qualitative Research in Psychology.* Buckingham: Open University Press.

Wilson, B.A. and Wearing, D. (1995) Prisoner of consciousness: a state of just awakening following herpes simplex encephalitis. In R. Campbell and M.A. Conway (eds), *Broken Memories: Case Studies in Memory Impairment* (14–30). Oxford: Blackwell Publishers Ltd.

Wilson, M., Wood, G. and Vine, S. (2009) Anxiety, attentional control, and performance impairment in penalty kicks. *Journal of Sport and Exercise Psychology*, 31, 761–75.

Wilson, S.A., Tinker, R.H., Hofmann, A., Becker, L. and Kleiner, K. (2000) A field study of EMDR with Kosovar-Albanian refugee children using a group treatment protocol. Paper presented at the annual meeting of the International Society for the Study of Traumatic Stress, San Antonio, TX.

Wing, R. (2002) Behavioural weight control. In T. Wadden and A. Stunkard (eds), *Handbook of Obesity Treatment*. New York: Guilford Press.

Winter, D.A. (1999) Psychological problems: alternative perspectives on their explanation and treatment. In D. Messer and F. Jones (eds), *Psychology and Social Care*. London: Jessica Kingsley.

Wood, C., Littleton, K. and Oates, J. (2002) Lifespan development. In T. Cooper and I. Roth (eds) (2007) *Challenging Psychological Issues*. Milton Keynes: Open University Press.

Wood, D. and Middleton, D. (1975) A study of assisted problem solving. *British Journal of Psychology*, 66, 181–91.

Woollett, K. and Maguire, E.A. (2011) Acquiring 'the Knowledge' of London's layout drives structural brain changes. *Current Biology*, 21(24), 2109–14.

Workman, L. and Reader, W. (2004) *Evolutionary Psychology.* Cambridge: Cambridge University Press.

World Health Organization (2011) Cross-national epidemiology of DSM-IV major depressive episode. *BMC Medicine*, 9(1), 90.

World Health Organization (2012) Tobacco Free Initiative. http://www.who.int/tobacco/en/ (accessed 15 March 2013).

Wright, A. and Holiday, R. (2007) Enhancing the recall of young, young-old and old-old adults with the cognitive interview and a modified version of the cognitive interview. *Applied Cognitive Psychology*, 21, 19–43.

Xia, L. (2012) Chinese citizens sent to mental hospitals to quiet dissent. *USA Today*, 29 December 2011.

Yablo, P.D. and Field, N.P. (2007) The role of culture in altruism: Thailand and the United States. *Psychologia: An International Journal of Psychology in the Orient*, 50(3), 236–51.

Yarbrough, S.S. and Braden, C.J. (2001) Utility of health belief model as a guide for explaining or predicting breast cancer screening behaviours. *Journal of Advanced Nursing*, 33(5), 677–88.

Yerkes, R. and Dodson, J. (1908) The relation of strength of stimulus to rapidity of habit formation. *Journal of Comparative Neurology and Psychology*, 18(5), 459–82.

Yildiz, B., Suchard, M., Wong, M.-L., McCann, S. and Licinio, J. (2004) Alterations in the dynamics of circulating ghrelin, adiponectin and leptin in human obesity. *Proceedings of the National Academy of Sciences*, 101(28), 10434–39.

Yin, R.K. (2003) *Case Study Research: Design and Methods*, 3rd edition. Thousand Oaks, CA: Sage.

Young, W.C. (1964) Hormones and sexual behaviour. *Science*, 143, 212–18.

Yuille, J. and Cutshall, L. (1986) A case study of eyewitness testimony of a crime. *Journal of Applied Psychology*, 71(2), 291–301.

Zaghrout-Hodali, M., Alissa, F. and Dodgson, P. (2008) Building resilience and dismantling fear: EMDR group protocol with children in an area of ongoing trauma. *Journal of EMDR Practice and Research*, 2(2), 105–13.

Zaida, A. and Shuraydi, M. (2002) Perceptions of arranged marriages by young Pakistani Muslim women living in a western society. *Journal of Comparative Family Studies*, 33(4), 495.

Zajonc, R. (1984) On the primacy of effect. *American Psychologist*, 39(2), 117–23.

Zak, P. (2011) Oxytocin: could the 'trust hormone' rebond our troubled world? http://www.guardian.co.uk/science/2011/aug/21/oxytocin-zak-neuroscience-trust-hormone (accessed 14 March 2013).

Zeelenberg, R. and Bocanegra, B. (2010) Auditory emotional cues enhance visual perception. *Cognition*, 115(1), 202–06.

Zhou, Z., Zhen, J., Karpowich, N., Goetz, R., Law, C., Reith, M. and Wang, D.-N. (2005) LeuT-Desipramine structure reveals how antidepressants block neurotransmitter reuptake. *Science*, 317(5843), 1390–93.

Zimmerman, P., Becker-Stoll, F., Grossman, K., Scheurer-Englisch, H., and Wartner, U. (2000) Longitudinal attachment development from infancy through adolescence. *Psychologie in Erziehung und Unterricht*, 47(2), 99–117.

Zubenko, G. (2002) Genetic linkage of region containing the CREB1 gene to depressive disorders in women from families with recurrent, early onset, major depression. *American Journal of Medical Genetics*, 14(8), 980–87.

Index